N.W. ROWELL: ONTARIO NATIONALIST

MARGARET PRANG

N.W. Rowell:
Ontario nationalist

UNIVERSITY OF TORONTO PRESS

Toronto and Buffalo

© University of Toronto Press 1975
Toronto and Buffalo
Printed in Canada

Library of Congress Cataloging in Publication Data

Prang, M. E.
  N. W. Rowell, Ontario nationalist
  Includes bibliographical references and index
  1. Rowell, Newton Wesley, 1867–1941
  Law   340'.092'4 [B]   73–89843
  ISBN 0-8020-5300-9

Contents

Acknowledgments

Over the years in which I have been interested in the subject of this book I have incurred many debts. Professors A.R.M. Lower and F.H. Underhill stimulated my interest in the relationship between Methodism and liberalism, and Professor D.G. Creighton provided sympathetic and critical direction of a thesis on aspects of Rowell's political career.

For their understanding and patient interest in an enterprise they would have liked to see completed much sooner, I wish to express my gratitude to N.W. Rowell's daughter, Mrs H.R. Jackman, and to Mr Jackman, of Toronto. In addition to giving me unrestricted use of the substantial collection of family letters and diaries in their possession, without which it would have been impossible to write a biography, they were always willing to answer requests for information while refraining from any attempt to influence my interpretation of events or persons. It was my good fortune to talk with the late Mrs Rowell over a period of several years and to form a first-hand impression of the qualities which assured her an important place in this book. I profited also from discussions with Mr Frederick N.A. Rowell of Vancouver, Mr H.E. Langford and Mr Peter Wright of Toronto, and Mr R.M. Fowler of Montreal. Lady Lynn Bagnall, who, as Miss Madge Edgar, was N.W. Rowell's secretary in the twenties, provided valuable impressions of his habits of work, while the late Rev. Dr R.P. Bowles was a helpful source of information concerning his religious and educational interests.

My thanks are due to Mr Henry Borden and Professor Craig Brown for permission to quote from the diaries of Sir Robert Borden, and to the executors of the estate of Sir Edmund Walker for allowing me to consult the Walker papers. Most of my other obligations are indicated in the footnotes; not the least of them is to the staff of the Public Archives of Canada.

I am grateful to Dean Emeritus F.H. Soward of the University of British Columbia for his critical scrutiny of matters both of fact and interpretation in the manuscript, to my colleagues Margaret Ormsby and Charles Humphries, and my friends Craig Brown and Ramsay Cook for their willingness to discuss the work at various stages and for their careful criticisms.

It is a pleasure to record that I am among the many Canadian historians who have benefited from the interest and encouragement of Francess Halpenny, formerly managing editor of the University of Toronto Press and now dean of the Faculty of Library Science at the University of Toronto. To the executive editor of the Press, M. Jean Houston, and to Larry MacDonald of the Editorial Department, my thanks for their informed and patient assistance.

The University of British Columbia gave me a year's leave of absence to work on the book and a grant from its research fund to aid in preparing the manuscript for publication. The book has been published with the assistance of a grant from the Social Science Research Council of Canada, using funds provided by the Canada Council, and a grant from the Andrew W. Mellon Foundation to the University of Toronto Press.

MP

PART ONE

1
Methodists and reformers

Joseph Rowell's decision in 1842 to leave 'The Breakings' near Carlisle, Cumberlandshire, was not easily made. The small farm in the valley formed by the Black and White Lyne Rivers furnished a modest living for himself and his wife, Mary, and for his aging parents, and he was able to add to his income by shoemaking. At the age of thirty-four he was highly respected in the district, especially by his fellow Wesleyans, among whom he had served as a lay preacher ever since his conversion to Methodism from the Church of England when he was twenty. Unfortunately, none of these assets could ensure anything but a doubtful future for his growing family. On the land or in the factories of the expanding industrial towns his children faced a life of hard toil and slender reward. Emigration to North America seemed to provide the only escape, as it did for so many inhabitants of the disappearing small farms of the north of England.

An older brother, John, had already visited Canada West and returned with a favourable account of the progress of friends recently settled there. Thus encouraged, their own small savings augmented by borrowing from friends in the Wesleyan congregation in the neighbouring town of Brampton, Joseph and Mary Rowell began their preparations for the journey to Canada. With their several children, and in the company of two other families whom they knew well, they sailed from Liverpool on 7 July 1842. The 1200-ton *Leander* was vastly superior in size and amenities to the sailing vessels which carried most British immigrants to North America in the first half of the nineteenth century. Thanks to the relatively good living conditions there was little sickness and only one death during the trip, but for all that the eight-week voyage to New York had its difficulties in becalmings, water shortages, and storms. Joseph Rowell 'often thought we would all be lost but the lord delivered us and Brought us safe to Land.'[1] A lesser trial was the conduct of the Irish immigrants who accounted for most of the ship's 265 passengers. Their 'very bad order,' the fighting which broke out among them 'every Sunday but one,' and their 'dancing [and] playing on the flute and the teamberean' distressed the quieter English travellers.[2]

The Rowells and their friends could ill afford to linger over the sights of New York. Within two hours of clearing customs they were on their way up the Hudson River by steamboat. The heavy traffic of barges and boats on the river, the good crops, the abundant food, the public buildings and solid brick houses of the state capital at Albany, all offered encouraging testimony to the prosperity of the descendants of earlier settlers in America. The party stopped at Albany for a few days at the home of a friend from Brampton while the men did farm work to replenish their finances a little, and then moved on by passenger tow-boat through the Erie and Oswego Canals and thence by steamboat across Lake Ontario to Toronto.

Joseph Rowell had no difficulty in securing day labour with a local builder and he soon had his family settled in a room on King Street, rented for two dollars a month. The new arrivals were well pleased with Toronto, not least because of their frequent encounters in the street or at church with friends and neighbours from home. But it was never Rowell's intention to stay in the city, and when he received a message from a friend that a mutual acquaintance near London needed assistance on his farm he decided to take the job. Once again the family was on the move, this time a hundred miles by wagon along the Dundas Road to London township. After helping to bring in the harvest and having found a steady demand for his services as a shoemaker, Joseph Rowell concluded, after less than two months in Canada, that he liked 'America as well as I Expected for ther is two Chances for one for a man getting along heer to what there is at home for Living is verrey Chep heer.'[3]

The next year when he purchased a farm on the fourteenth concession of London township near Arva (then known as St John's), about six miles from London, Joseph Rowell was establishing himself in a part of Canada West that had moved beyond the roughest of pioneer days. Farm life was still hard, but the fruits of one's labour were reasonably certain. As a local preacher Rowell quickly made many friends among the Methodists in the district, and with the support of his new acquaintances and some old friends from England he soon took the lead in organizing one of the first temperance societies in the county. After fifteen years at Arva, when their children were grown, Mary Rowell died. Two years later, in 1860, Joseph Rowell married Nancy Green, the eldest daughter of Edward and Mary Green, whose family of ten helped to swell the Methodist congregation at Arva. Nancy Green was twenty years younger than her fifty-year-old husband and bore him three daughters and two sons. The fourth child, and second son, born on 1 November 1867, was baptised with the names of the founder of Methodism and of one of his most illustrious successors, Robert Newton, a Wesleyan preacher popular in the north of England in the two decades before Joseph Rowell's emigration to Canada.

When Newton Wesley Rowell was a few months old his grandfather, Edward Wilkins Green of nearby Pine Grove Farm, died. Their grandfather's death had important consequences in the lives of the young Rowells for their widowed grandmother now invited their father to take over the running of Pine Grove Farm. When Joseph and Nancy Rowell agreed to move to the farm on 'the Proof Line' their children were brought into a closer relationship with some deeply rooted Canadian traditions than they would otherwise have enjoyed. Edward Wilkins Green came to Canada in 1818 with his father, a Quaker surveyor from County Down in the north of Ireland, and purchased a partially cleared farm in London Township in 1824. Within a decade Pine Grove Farm was famous in the western section of the province for its progressive agricultural methods, and visitors from miles around came to see its fine fruits and grains.[4] By the time of Edward Green's death the resources of the district had been well exploited and Pine Grove Farm had lost its agricultural pre-eminence, but it still had other attractions. It was a comfortable home and boasted a library impressive by the standards of Middlesex County. Most valuable of all, perhaps, was the reputation of the senior member of the household, Mrs Green, as an intelligent and lively conversationalist on a wide variety of topics.[5] The animated discussions of religion and politics in which she often engaged with visitors to the farm and with other members of the family were an education for her grandchildren.

Mary Green had vivid memories of politics in Upper Canada. Her father, Henry Coyne, was an Irish immigrant whose inn on the Talbot Road south of London was a rallying point for agitation against the autocratic methods of the 'Lake Erie baron,' Colonel Thomas Talbot. Her mother, Ann Gardiner Coyne, also came of a family of early Reformers and was herself an expert in dealing with the. 'old Colonel,' while her uncle, Thomas Gardiner, was a vigorous opponent of Colonel Talbot in the London District Council.[6] Although they belonged to the British Wesleyans, the Greens and the Gardiners, like all Upper Canadian Methodists, had to struggle for freedom from the social disabilities imposed by the dominantly Anglican ruling group in its self-interested zeal to save the colony from the republican influences infiltrating the colony through the many Methodists whose origins were in the United States. Mary Green's own wedding ceremony had been performed by a Church of England clergyman because the Methodist preachers of the day were denied the legal right to solemnize marriages. When she moved from the Talbot settlement as a bride to Arva in 1824 there was already a growing Reform movement in London township. By the summer of 1837, when the more radical Reformers had become rather vociferous, London township was the scene of several political scuffles as Tory and Orange elements in the neighbourhood tried to break up meetings of the Reformers.[7] Although the London area was a Reform stronghold, the failure of the Duncombe uprising of December 1837, which was to have been a major action in the greater Mackenzie rebellion planned for that year, was proof that the majority were reformers, not revolutionaries.

Newton Rowell's great-grandfather, Henry Coyne, was typical of Middlesex Reformers. He resisted constituted authority by every peaceful means, but when rebellion broke out he provided supplies to the volunteer troops raised to restore order.[8] The naturally conservative sentiments of most British Wesleyans were correctly expressed by Egerton Ryerson's break with William Lyon Mackenzie; the moderate reformism of Robert Baldwin was legitimate protest, but rebellion was unthinkable. The Coynes and the Greens could rejoice when Baldwin's patience and theirs was rewarded by the granting of responsible government. They observed disapprovingly the upheavals of 1849 over the Rebellion Losses Bill when there was fighting in the streets of London; the Tories burned Francis Hincks and Louis Lafontaine in effigy, and the Reformers retaliated with similar treatment of Sir Allan MacNab. A few months later the Queen's faithful subjects in Middlesex County were chagrined when a Tory gang cut down the decorative arches erected on the outskirts of London in honour of the visit of the governor general, Lord Elgin, whose signature of the Rebellion Losses Bill had put the final seal on responsible government. But, in the end, moderation carried the day and the Queen's representative and the majority of the local population all agreed that London put on a magnificent reception.

Thus, Newton Rowell's boyhood imagination was shaped by the moderate Reformers' version of the Upper Canadian past and by the social traditions and economic necessities of a community dynamic enough to have produced, in the decade of his own birth, the initial impetus for the creation of a new nation 'from sea to sea.'

In the village school at Arva, Newton Rowell was an enthusiastic and competent student, notably in English composition. When he was eleven an essay on 'The Horse,' an early display of thoroughness in searching out facts, won him the highest marks in his class. In the Christmas examinations the following year he won a prize for general proficiency, a copy of *Robinson Crusoe*.

The Rowells were bound together by deep but undemonstrative affection and a family spirit that prompted each member to show an active interest in the welfare and progress of all the others. As was natural in a devout Methodist family much of life was centred in the church and its good works. Of perennial interest was the cause of temperance. Joseph Rowell travelled throughout the countryside preaching and lecturing on temperance and was given major credit for the overwhelming majority accorded the endorsement of the Canada Temperance Act of 1878 in Middlesex County.[9] The Sunday School picnics, strawberry festivals, fall suppers, and Christmas concerts organized by the congregation were enjoyed by both children and adults. Attendance at church and class meeting occupied much of every Sunday for all ages. The mid-week prayer meeting, the special services conducted by visiting evangelists, and regular family prayers offered further opportunities for the conversion and sanctification essential to the spiritual growth of Methodists. If they needed any, the Rowells had a solemn reminder of the importance of attendance on the means of grace for their welfare in both this world and the next in the piety of the oldest daughter, Emma, whose death in the spring of 1880 at the age of nineteen ended a long battle against tuberculosis.

Pine Grove Farm provided a comfortable but far from idle life and every member of the household had regular chores. Like the other children, Newton was proficient at milking cows and gardening. At the age of eleven he was proudly driving to town on Saturdays with apples, vegetables, and mutton for sale in the London market and was registered as a member of the London Agricultural Association. He soon embarked on an enterprise of his own – poultry raising – and began to exhibit at fairs in neighbouring towns. He specialized in Pekin ducks, with Toulouse geese as a second line, and shipped to customers in the western section of the province. Business flourished after one of his Pekin drakes took first prize at the London Fair in 1882 and he began to advertise his quality products in the farm press.[10]

Unfortunately, this enterprise could not produce the cash surplus which might have covered the expense of a formal high school education. When he was fifteen Newton went to live with his grandmother, who had retired from Pine Grove and taken up residence on Craig Street in London, then a city of about twenty thousand. A scholarship of forty dollars admitted him early in 1883 to a six-month business course at the London Commercial College and prepared him for general clerical work in the flourishing wholesale dry goods and millinery business of his uncle, John Green, with whom his elder brother, Edward, was already employed. With the sale of Pine Grove Farm, Newton's parents and his two sisters, Sarah ('Sazie'), who was five years his senior, and Mary, two years his junior, joined the boys in London and the family moved into a cottage next door to grandmother Green.

Newton and Edward had been attending Queen's Avenue Methodist Church but the family now became pillars of the congregation in the new and nearer London South Church on Askin Street. The new congregation, composed mainly of working people, had a more socially varied membership than the established and well-to-do Queen's Avenue, and there was challenge and interest in helping to build up its life. Sazie's marriage to Gordon Wright of Columbus, Ohio, was the first in the family and the first in the new church.

Newton Rowell found little enjoyment in his three years' labour on parcels and ledgers. He was bothered by the feeling that he owed his job to his uncle's favour, although it appeared that his brother was being advanced in the firm on merit and that John Green hoped his nephews would eventually take over the business. Alternative careers all presented financial hurdles, and in any case he was not yet sure how he wanted to earn his living. His consultations with visiting phrenologists, so popular at the time, were not helpful. Even when he had his head 'bumped' by Dr Fowler, whose advice was sought on the strength of his reputation as 'the greatest one living,' a disconcerting range of possibilities was suggested.[11] Many of the friends and relatives who observed his effectiveness as a class leader in the London South Church assumed that he was headed for the Methodist ministry. Newton Rowell's own assessment of his endowments and interests settled that question easily. He never doubted that he would serve his church, but opportunities for service were as great for Methodist laymen as for parsons. If he were ever able to pursue his growing ambition to enter public life they might even be greater.

Whatever his occupation he wanted more education. The Home Reading Course of the Chautauqua Literary and Scientific Circles was planned for young people in just his circumstances. With Edward and Mary and several friends he helped to organize the London South Chautauqua Group and began the home study program in the autumn of 1884. The prescribed readings and assignments were discussed at the regular meetings of the local group. The first year's work ranged from outlines of Greek history, Christian Evidences, and English history to American literature, plant biology, and Canadian history. During the two succeeding winters the course of study ran through elementary chemistry, Latin, studies in political economy, Roman history, the Reformation, and Browning's poetry, to readings of Horace Bushnell's *The Character of Jesus*, Lyman Abbott's *A Study in Human Nature*, and Macaulay's *Warren Hastings*.[12] Conscientiously followed, the Chautauqua program was a fair substitute for a formal high school education, and in some respects, perhaps, better.

The lectures sponsored by the London Mechanics Institute, in which his uncle, Thomas Green, a successful building contractor, was a moving spirit, provided other eagerly accepted opportunities for self-improvement. In later years Newton Rowell also remembered with gratitude the valuable training he received in his first years in London from his grandmother Green. He was required to report to her every Sunday on the sermons of the day with texts, headings, arguments, and conclusions set out in orderly fashion, a useful exercise in sifting out points quickly. Although now in her seventies, Mary Green's mind was as alert as ever. She was still a faithful reader of the *Christian Guardian*, but, as always, her interests ranged beyond that far from narrow journal. In the pages of the Toronto *Globe* and the London *Advertiser* she usually turned first to the foreign news, and especially to the triumphs of the hero of Liberals everywhere in the Empire, Prime Minister Gladstone, whose advocacy of Irish Home Rule had her strongest sympathy. In her gallery of political worthies Ontario's Liberal premier and self-styled 'Christian statesman,' Oliver Mowat, occupied a prominent place. That being so, it was almost axiomatic that she mistrusted John A. Macdonald and all his works.[13] Her death in 1886 by no means ended the lively discussions in the Rowell household but the loss was felt by every member of the family.

By the fall of 1886 Newton Rowell had determined to become a lawyer. He took six months off from his work to complete his private study for the high school matriculation examinations and wrote them successfully. This concentrated effort impaired his health and moved a sympathetic aunt, Emma Green, to send him on a two-week Great Lakes cruise to Duluth, Minnesota. On the longest journey he had yet taken Rowell was duly impressed by the grandeur of the shores of Lake Superior and the starkness of Duluth's barren setting. From the YMCA he explored Duluth and observed an 'almost incredible number of saloons ... on one street thirteen of them with but two stores between.'[14]

His health restored by the trip, he was able to begin his study of law. Attendance at Osgoode Hall in Toronto was financially out of the question, and he therefore entered the profession by the route commonly taken at the time, joining a London law office, Fraser and Fraser, as a student. With the practical training there and his own study he hoped to be ready to take the examinations of the Law Society of Upper Canada in three years' time. The granting of his request that he be given the office boy's job in the law firm, in addition to his other duties, brought in a welcome two dollars a month extra. Partly to make room for Sazie, her husband, Gordon, and their small son, Ward, who had come back from Ohio in an impecunious state, the house on Craig Street was sold and everyone moved into a larger home at 133 Elmwood Avenue, an arrangement which continued for several years while Gordon advanced in the Green millinery business.

That winter Rowell finished the Chautauqua correspondence courses. In the summer, with Edward and some other members of the London South Circle, he went to Lake Chautauqua in upper New York State for the graduation exercises and part of the summer school. The Chautauqua movement had not yet taken to the road and the big tent to become the educational show business that carried it into thousands of cities and towns across the continent after the turn of the century. In its second decade it still expressed the aims of its founder and continuing president, the Methodist Episcopal clergyman, Dr John H. Vincent, whose combined program of liberal education and religious knowledge was designed to raise the general level of Sunday School teaching among North American Protestants. His exposition of this familiar purpose to the two thousand men and women who received their certificates in the Chautauqua amphitheatre before an audience of another six thousand on a warm August evening evoked enthusiasm in Newton Rowell but most of the lectures delivered in the Hall of Philosophy were disappointing.[15]

For Rowell, by far the outstanding attraction at Chautauqua was the series of lectures on Christian ethics given by Professor Andrew Martin Fairbairn, who had just become the first principal of Mansfield College, the Congregational theological college in Oxford. Dr Fairbairn was pre-eminent among the British Free Church theologians who were endeavouring to lead Nonconformist theology into the main stream of European philosophy and historical criticism. Lord Acton once told Fairbairn's friend, James Bryce, that he doubted if there was anyone in Oxford whose learning equalled Fairbairn's.[16] At the same time Fairbairn was without peer with popular audiences, and was highly successful at Chautauqua on several occasions. Rowell judged him 'not very eloquent if you take any impetuous flow of language as eloquence'; to some he was dry, but his theology was 'very deep' and clearly presented, and Rowell would have been happy to listen much longer.[17]

During the winter of 1889 he read the course for Methodist lay preachers, which depended heavily on Wesley's journals and sermon notes. To Newton's regret his father, for sixty years a lay preacher, was not among the congregation which heard his trial sermon, for Joseph Rowell had died some months earlier in his eightieth year. The friends and relatives in London South Church who did hear his forty-minute sermon received it well. 'You could have heard a pin drop during almost any part,' the preacher reported to his brother, now a buyer in the millinery firm and in England on business. A week later the official board of the church voted unanimously to approve the designation of Newton Rowell as a lay preacher.[18]

In the meetings of the Baconian Club Rowell also enhanced his ability to command an audience. As the club's presiding officer in 1889 he was in charge of the fortnightly Saturday evening meetings of the forty members, mostly Liberals, either studying law or recently called to the bar, who read papers to one another on literary, scientific, and non-partisan political topics. Clubs and church activities were enjoyed to the full but most of his evenings were spent over his law books. In the spring of 1889 he had passed the intermediate examinations of the Law Society at the head of a class of fifty with a scholarship of one hundred dollars. His heart was now set on winning the gold medal in the final examinations the next spring.

In the summer of 1890, Fraser and Fraser proposed to send the firm's senior student to Manitoba and the Northwest Territories to collect debts on behalf of a client, the London Branch of Molson's Bank, which was endeavouring to recover the debts of two bankrupt London farm-implement distributors. Many western farmers had been unable to meet their payments on farm machinery because crop and market conditions had been uncertain in the eighties and their incomes much less than anticipated, while others had refused to pay for machines they claimed were faulty.

Through their representatives in Winnipeg, Fraser and Fraser had been handling these accounts for several years, and now it was decided to send a man through the west to clean up the remaining 'hard core' cases. The job required enough knowledge of agriculture to assess the prospects of the debtors, sufficient persuasive powers to extract the maximum from them, and, when necessary, the judgment to decide the effect of threatening to take them to court. Rowell found the offer both disturbing and exciting. Acceptance would mean the postponement of his final examinations and probably some loss of income. The work itself would add nothing essential to his training as a lawyer, but the locale of the assignment was irresistible. He decided to see the west.

In anticipation it was easy to think of Manitoba as an extension of home – so many families and young men from Middlesex County were among the thousands of Ontarians who had settled there in the preceding decade. And events in the Territories, with their political repercussions in eastern Canada, had dominated the politics of recent years. As an eighteen-year-old, Rowell had watched the men of the 7th Fusiliers of London march along Dundas Street and off to the prairies in the spring of 1885 to assist in quelling the rebellion of Louis Riel's Métis. Three months later these avengers of the murdered Orangeman, Thomas Scott, a former London resident, returned victorious to the fanfare of the local citizenry. Never to be forgotten either was the great rally organized by the Young Liberals of London in December 1886, when the leading Quebec Liberal in the House of Commons, Wilfrid Laurier, courageously defended his opposition to the hanging of Riel and explained his differences with the twenty-three Liberal members of Parliament from Ontario who voted with Sir John A. Macdonald's Conservative government in support of the execution. In the club rooms of the Young Liberals on Dundas Street where Rowell was an occasional visitor the issues raised by Riel's career had been hotly debated over many months, until at length much of the heat was transferred to discussions of the equally contentious Jesuit Estates Act passed by the Quebec Legislature in 1889. The London District Meeting of the Methodist Church had been in the forefront of Protestant bodies across the province in demanding the disallowance of the Act, as another of 'the aggressions of the hierarchy of the Roman Catholic Church,' a measure working 'to the serious detriment of ... civil and religious liberty.'[19] Now, on the western plains, fresh debates of the old issues, debates that would determine the character of the expanding nation, had already begun.

The fourteen-hundred-mile journey to Winnipeg by Great Lakes' steamer to Port Arthur and then by the CPR offered welcome hours for reading the cheap editions of the books Rowell had purchased for the trip. By the time he arrived he had enjoyed Thackeray's *Henry Esmond*, had begun *The Pilgrim's Progress* and Ruskin's *Sesame and Lilies*, and was about to start on Henry Drummond's recently published *Natural Law in the Spiritual World*.[20] He often abandoned his reading for talk with other passengers, and the rugged country of the Laurentian Shield and the vivid colours of his first prairie sunset were dramatic enough to warrant description in the first of a series of articles he had promised to the London *Advertiser*.[21]

In Winnipeg Rowell quickly became a willing captive of the optimism and easy friendliness of Winnipeggers who had recently been reserved easterners, but soon modified his initial enthusiasm for Manitoba's rich, black loam after encountering it 'thick and sticky like glue' while driving in a buckboard cart near Birtle after a heavy rain.[22] He was rarely lonely in Winnipeg where there was a host of former residents of London and Middlesex County to visit. He enjoyed their hospitality and reported on the state of their health, houses, and businesses in his regular Sunday letters to those at home. On his first Sunday in Winnipeg, Rowell went to morning service at Grace Church where the prosperous congregation and fine church testified to the progress of Methodism in the city. For the duration of his six weeks' stay he attended the large Bible class conducted in the church by one of Winnipeg's leading lawyers and citizens, J.M. Aikins, and there made some new friends among men in business and the professions. A family friend, Rev. Albert Crews, was the pastor of another Methodist congregation in the city and Rowell was a frequent and welcome visitor in the Crews home, and, on one occasion, in the pulpit. When he moved on westward to Brandon there were fewer friends and on his first Sunday there he suffered from a bout of homesickness. By the time he had attended church and the Hon. J.W. Sifton's Bible class, and had received a pressing invitation from the superintendent of the Sunday School to attend a meeting of the Epworth League the following night, he was more cheerful.

Two weeks spent in Brandon when cold, wet weather was raising acute anxiety about the crop provided an unforgettable demonstration that wheat was king in Manitoba. A visit to one of the most successful farmers in the Brandon district, a Middlesex County man, illustrated the extent of the threatened disaster. He had come west five years earlier with two thousand dollars and

> this year has 1800 acres of wheat & 400 acres of oats with an estimated yield of over 30 bushels of wheat per acre and 60 of oats ... This is farming for you ... He has one field 640 acres, a mile square, all one magnificent crop of wheat. Natural scenery is grand but where will you see a ... grander sight than to look upon such fields as these of waving golden grain and one might truthfully say (if he could forget the rain and frost) truly this is a goodly land, a land flowing with milk & honey; God has given them a bountiful harvest. Has he sent the rain & frost?[23]

No answer to this theological question could be expected from the recently established Dominion Experimental Farm at Brandon but Rowell was cheered by what he learned there about the new and hardier strains of wheat and small fruits being developed at the farm,[24] an institution whose services to the prairies invited some small comparison to the more informal contribution of Pine Grove Farm to Middlesex County two generations earlier.

He knew not a soul in any town between Brandon and Banff. The prospect of the six weeks it would take to make his calls north and south of the eight-hundred-mile stretch of the railway made him feel somewhat forlorn. His sense of being alone in a strange land was increased by the realization that the newly settled people of the Territories had a less than firm hold on the essentials of Christian civilization: 'The people out west here are not overburdened with religion. A gentleman at the breakfast table this morning wanted to know if I was going driving today. I told him no. He replied there was not much to see unless I went chicken or duck shooting. I told him that it had not been my custom to do this kind of work on Sunday. He admitted I was right but said that out west they got into a different way of living. This gentleman was as decent a fellow as you would care to meet and most obliging, but such is life.'[25]

In Moosomin, a town of four hundred inhabitants, which served as his base of operations for two weeks, the Methodists, with their attractive brick church, the finest Rowell had seen since leaving Winnipeg, were doing their best to maintain standards of Sabbath observance, but owing to the claims of another preaching point on their minister they had no morning service. One Sunday Rowell therefore went to the 'English church ... They are very High church in this Diocese and as far as I am concerned are welcome to it. I came away very well satisfied with Methodism. The minister was a young fellow of about 25 years of age & he read us a nice little Essay (you buy them about 25¢ per 1000) on ''Son thy sins are forgiven thee''. He never once looked at the congregation but alternately from the book to the ceiling, twice he lost his place ... and had to go back, but it did not appear to disturb him in the least.' It was a relief to get back that afternoon to the familiar warmth of the Methodist Sunday School where he accepted the superintendent's invitation to expound the lesson, and to the evening service where a Methodist preacher of 'strong physique' delivered his well prepared message in a voice 'loud enough for thousands to hear.'[26]

One of Rowell's journeys by horse and buggy, on which he usually acted as his own driver, took him to Cannington Manor, forty miles south of Moosomin, where a group of well-to-do Englishmen had been engaged for the past eight years in an attempt to transplant the homes, parish church, fox hunting, and cricket of an English country town to the Canadian prairie. The son of western Ontario Grits was unimpressed, especially by the immigrants' reluctance 'to associate with plebeian Canadians.' But he did not forget that there were better types of Englishmen in the west, 'men who recognize that in this country all are equal before the law, and that a crest or a coat of arms must give way to intellect and ability, and ancestral title must bow to true and noble character.'[27]

Everywhere in the Territories Rowell heard tales of the recent Riel troubles and listened to accounts of the continuing political struggle and attacks on the Dominion's reluctance to concede self-government. During his two weeks in Regina, the capital of the Territories, the controversy between Ottawa, represented by the lieutenant governor, Joseph Royal, and the local Legislative Assembly over their respective powers was in a state of deadlock. On the strength of his assignment from the London *Advertiser* Rowell secured an interview with Royal. The French Canadian lieutenant governor impressed him as intelligent and conscientious, not a man who could be guilty of 'debauching the territories' through maladministration of the liquor laws, as many Liberals, Protestant church courts, and temperance societies in the east charged. And yet Royal was a Conservative who had publicly defended Dominion government policies that had led to rebellion; he could not be granted total approval. Rowell saw the pattern of events in the Northwest as a repetition of the earlier controversy over responsible government in Upper Canada, the Dominion government playing the role in which the Colonial Office had once been cast, with Royal caught in the middle just as the colonial governors had been. He had no doubt that the early concession of self-government was the only solution to the impasse, and he applauded F.W.G. Haultain and the 'Noble Thirteen' whose current obstructionist tactics were designed to bring the governor's council and the total revenue of the Territories under the control of the elected assembly. His observation of the politicians of the Territories, most of whom were Ontario men, assured him beyond doubt that once the battle against colonial rule by Ottawa was won, local leadership would be quite adequate to the problems it would face.[28]

Beyond the delay in settling the political future of the Territories Rowell could see only one cloud on the western horizon – the power of the CPR. In the expanding wheat acreage and the growing communities of the southern prairies he recognized the material benefits bestowed by the railway. Yet with true Grit suspicion of corporations, and especially of one conceived in scandal and corruption and now maturing in continuing alliance with the Conservative party, he feared that the railway was establishing a stranglehold over the western economy. The recent abolition of the CPR's formal monopoly over railway building might inhibit this somewhat, but the company was bound to exercise an economic influence in the west that would bear constant scrutiny.[29]

His train ticket was only to Regina, but he found it hard to put aside the thought of going through to Vancouver and home through the United States. When they were consulted, Fraser and Fraser agreed to give him additional time from the office and even forwarded the names of a few clients in British Columbia to provide extra income to help pay for the extended trip. Thus, to his great excitement, he stood at a window in the Alberta Hotel in Calgary gazing westward at the white peaks of the Rockies and feeling 'something like Moses on the mountain viewing the promised land, with this difference that I may perchance enter and see while he was denied.'[30]

After two days beside the towering giants of Banff, he continued by CPR over the Great Divide, on through Craigellachie where, a little more than five years before, the last spike had been driven in the railway, past the developing ranching and lumbering of the North Thompson Valley, then along the steep walls of the Fraser canyon and at length into that great river's broad, green delta to the sea. Vancouver, in the fifth year of its incorporation, was the fastest growing city in Canada, and despite the setback of the catastrophic fire of 1887 boasted a population of ten thousand; 'a pushing city', Rowell observed, 'where everything is new and fresh ... one of the cities of the future.'[31] He was captivated for life by the British Columbians' sense of the unlimited prospects of their province.

In Vancouver he was among friends again. He stayed for two weeks in the home of his half-sister, Lizzie, the wife of Thomas Godfrey, who had recently established a hardware business in the city. The Godfrey household was a large one and he enjoyed being with a family again. But it was most annoying to be laid up for much of his visit by the doctor's order to keep a poultice on the large boil that had appeared on his leg – the consequence, he thought, of an excess of apple pie eaten on the way across the prairies. Despite this restriction he managed to hear some excellent sermons, attend the Chinese Methodist Mission when the minister 'administered the sacrament to some twenty communicants ... an interesting sight,' visit several family friends in Vancouver and New Westminster, and purchase his Christmas presents, most of them small and unfamiliar imports from the Orient.[32]

After brief visits to friends in Victoria and cousins in Seattle and Tacoma he reached Portland to catch the ss *Oregon* for a rough two-day voyage to San Francisco. Like all visitors he was greatly impressed by the beauty of San Francisco, but the city had its weak points. 'Sunday ... is not what we would call Sunday. It is the big excursion day & cheap trips run in all directions. The theatres and places of amusement make it a high day and every saloon is in full blast.' His interest in seeing the Mormon country was intense enough to make him accept the unpleasantness of travelling on Christmas Day in order to work in a stop at Salt Lake City. From there he headed north east towards Winnipeg. Finding himself in Grand Forks, North Dakota, on a Sunday evening between trains he attended the Presbyterian Church, where the minister was a former Methodist from London. When a student for the ministry he had been known among the Rowells as the one 'who always prayed about the cherubim & seraphim,' as Newton reminded his brother with amusement. Now he had a large church with 'pipe organ, good choir & a swell looking congregation ... He is quite a sport. Keeps a large kennel & was one of the judges last fall in Manitoba at the "field trials," dog races ... He preached not a bad sermon on "Ideals" but said nothing that would seriously trouble men's consciences.'[33]

After enjoying New Year's with his Winnipeg friends, he had two weeks of further work involving several stops at places as far as three hundred miles west of Winnipeg. In the midst of a prairie winter, he had had more than enough of travelling and he got through his calls with dispatch.[34] Moreover, he was anxious to get home for his sister Mary's twenty-first birthday. Much to everyone's delight he was able to make the birthday party a family reunion as well.

Looking back, he felt it had all been very much worthwhile. Contrary to his fear that he would be out-of-pocket on the trip, he had actually made money. Fraser and Fraser had generously allowed him every cent of his travelling expenses and his full salary of fifty dollars per month even for the five weeks in British Columbia and the United States when he was on leave from the firm. Professionally, matters were less satisfactory. The law books he had carried across the continent and back had remained unopened, and he had 'thrown over three months' in his examinations. But still he had no great regret.[35] There was more than adequate compensation in his memory of fields of golden grain and of the new cities of the prairies, in his vision of Canada's future as a Pacific nation, and in his awareness of the opportunities and the difficulties of building a Christian and Canadian society west of the Great Lakes.

An Upper Canadian was becoming a Canadian.

2
The young Toronto lawyer

Ontario's growing provincial capital provided greater opportunities in his profession than the small city of London, and Rowell decided to make his career there. Toronto was also the centre of political and religious activities of increasing interest to him. Accepting the offer of two former Londoners, Tom Reid and Ed Owens, to become their senior law student at the top salary of six dollars a week, he did what he could in the brief time remaining to prepare for his law examinations. The results were disappointing, for he stood only fifth in a group of forty who wrote the provincial bar examinations. He took some comfort from the realization that the gold medalist was a university man who, like the others with higher standings, had done nothing but study for six months before.[1] More satisfying, a few months later, were the solicitors' examinations in which he won the silver medal of the Law Society of Upper Canada for the second highest standing. Upon his call to the bar in the autumn of 1891 he entered the newly opened Toronto office of the London firm headed by I.F. Hellmuth, one of the most distinguished lawyers in the province. Hellmuth, Ivey, and Thomas had their offices in the new Traders Bank chambers at the corner of Yonge and Colborne streets, in the heart of the city's business district and within pleasant walking distance of the law courts in Osgoode Hall and of Mrs Dick's boarding house at 275 Jarvis Street where Rowell was comfortably and gratefully settled. His salary of fifty dollars a month was augmented by whatever he earned out of 'agency' by handling work in the city for several London solicitors. Altogether, he could look forward to an income of about nine hundred dollars in the coming year.[2]

In the last decade of the nineteenth century, Toronto was quietly prosperous and had doubled her population in ten years to 180,000. In the Romanesque solidity of the slowly rising city hall, in the new University of Toronto library, the Union Station, and the battlements of the armouries on University Avenue, and in the red sandstone mass of the legislative buildings the city reflected its pride as a provincial capital and its confidence in the future. Torontonians of the 1890s also saw the promise of loftier things to be in Robert Simpson's new department store at Queen and Yonge, just across the street from the older and still expanding Eaton's. Further south on Yonge Street stood the new headquarters of the Board of Trade, the first building in Toronto to possess a steel skeleton, and a symbol of the aspirations of the business community toward the future commercial domination of the nation.

Immediate and practical signs of progress were the advent of electric street cars in 1892 and the laying of the first long stretch of asphalt on Jarvis Street where wealthy citizens maintained fancy carriages and large houses in ornate late Victorian style. The Christian conscience of the carriage trade furnished some of the leadership, and most of the money, for the fight against Sunday street cars, a controversial feature of Toronto life during the nineties. For all these advances, much of Toronto was still reminiscent of 'muddy York.' Sidewalks, where they existed, were built of wood and most of the streets were lighted by gas. Settlement had not yet crept up 'the hill,' but weekend strollers enjoyed walking to the top of Avenue Road to see 'Benvenuto,' the imposing new residence of S.H. Janes. From his grey limestone chateau with its red glazed tile roof Janes looked out over the residential area at the foot of the hill known as the Annex, the site of the successful real estate promotion that supported the opulence of 'Benvenuto.' A walk along Bloor Street to the open fields near Bathurst Street took hundreds of interested sightseers past the new mansion of the distiller and financier, George Gooderham, at the corner of St George and Bloor streets. The combination of carved stone, red brick, and green copper roofing in the massive proportions of the Gooderham residence was Toronto's most notable example of the current Romanesque style adapted to home building, but there were many others on a smaller scale in the neighbourhood.

The unspectacular but steady business growth of Toronto in the early nineties provided abundant work for good lawyers. Rowell's first cases were in property and corporation law, such as those in which he acted for Molsons' Bank and the Ontario Loan and Deposit Company. The legal fraternity of Toronto at the time displayed a brilliance probably unexcelled in any other period of its history. It was an education for a young man to begin the practice of law in the world of Samuel and W.H. Blake, the several Oslers, Christopher Robinson, A.B. Aylesworth, Charles Moss, D'Alton McCarthy, E.F.B. Johnston, and Zebulon A. Lash. In one of his first courtroom cases, in the autumn of 1892, Rowell found his recent training pitted against the skill and long experience of one of the most eminent members of the Canadian bar, then at the height of his career, B.B. Osler.

Conacher v. *the City of Toronto* involved issues of public policy which prompted the presiding judge, Mr Justice Rose, to describe it in the Court of Common Pleas as one of the most important cases ever to come before him. The central question raised by the case was the extent of the responsibility of Ontario municipalities for the health of local residents. This issue was being hotly debated in the Toronto press, and among the public generally, because of the more than one hundred deaths from typhoid in the city during 1892. Most of these deaths were commonly attributed to leakages in the city's water system and to the deficiencies of the municipal sewage disposal, and there was a vociferous popular demand for safer water and sewage services. Rowell's client, Conacher, lived in a house built on a scow at the foot of Spadina Avenue near a municipal sewer emptying into Toronto Bay. In the spring of 1892 three of Conacher's children died, not of typhoid but of diphtheria. Conacher instituted legal proceedings against the city, charging that the death of his children was a direct result of the city's negligence in maintaining faulty sewers.

In gathering the copious medical evidence on which he rested most of his case Rowell displayed the thoroughness in the investigation of highly specialized matters which characterized all his legal work. His argument hinged on two key points: he must prove that the city sewer was the source of the germs that brought death and suffering to the Conacher family, and he must establish that the city was responsible for providing more efficient sewage disposal. A court reporter found Rowell's initial presentation unusually strong and his delivery memorable. A senior barrister observed that Osler would 'have trouble to break him down.' Osler himself introduced his argument by congratulating Rowell on 'his able address' and 'his manner of eliciting expert advice,' but asserted that his impressive medical evidence was general rather than specific and established no necessary connection between the city's sewer and the Conacher deaths. In any case, there could be no municipal responsibility for the control of disease, since that would place an intolerable burden on the taxpayers of the growing city. Finally, Osler commended to the court the view of 'a writer who said that pestilence, war, and famine are necessary to carry off the weak and allow the strong to live; it is a wise provision of nature and a serious matter to consider.'

Mr Justice Rose declared his wish 'to join with Mr Osler in congratulating the young learned counsel. It is a pleasure to do so when there is an exhibition of ability joined with becoming modesty; they are not always joined together.' The jury found in favour of Conacher, the court awarded him damages of fourteen hundred dollars, and the principle of municipal responsibility for public health seemed to have been advanced. Certainly the case could do nothing but good for the career of a twenty-six-year-old lawyer. To Rowell's regret the favourable verdict was set aside and the action dismissed when the city appealed the case to the Divisional Court. He did not appear in the hearing before the superior court, since he had by then left the Hellmuth firm to become the junior partner in Kerr, Bull, and Rowell, and the case was taken by another lawyer. Despite the final verdict in the case he could take some satisfaction in the court's declaration that the city was in error in dumping sewage into public waters even although there was no proof that this action had caused the deaths in question.[3]

Just before his move to Toronto Rowell had cast his first vote in a federal election. The prime minister, Sir John A. Macdonald, declaring 'A British subject I was born, a British subject I will die,' had charged that Canada's very existence as a nation was threatened by the Liberal policy of unrestricted reciprocity with the United States. Newton Rowell intended to remain a British subject too, and a Liberal as well. He cast his vote for Charles S. Hyman and against Sir John Carling who had held London for the Conservatives ever since Confederation, with the exception of the years of Alexander Mackenzie's ministry. Hyman appeared to win, although his election was later declared void, but in the nation as a whole the Liberals lost by a narrow margin and once again had to live on hopes deferred.

The winter election campaign had killed Sir John A. Macdonald as well as unrestricted reciprocity. Now, Rowell told his brother, 'the whole talk' in the city, not least in the churches on that first Sunday in June, was of 'the greatest Canadian that has so far lived, or words to that effect.' He thought much of it excessive, including the fifteen-minute eulogy he heard from the pulpit of Sherbourne Street Methodist Church. He could not endorse Rev. Dr Ezra Stafford's assertion that Macdonald's 'faults were only the faults of other great statesmen, Walpole, Pitt, etc., & that posterity would overlook these trifles ... There is too much gush to suit me. I don't go quite so far as Tom Reid when he remarked yesterday, "they are making a terrible fuss over the death of that old reprobate", but it makes me tired to hear preachers talking of his faults & failings as if, at the worst, they were but errors of judgment, and all committed because of his supreme love for Canada & therefore not only not censurable but even praiseworthy.'[4] Thereafter, he followed with little surprise and much disgust the news from Ottawa of the McGreevy-Langevin scandals in the Department of Public Works and the Conservative squabbles over the succession to Macdonald.

When Newton Rowell first joined the Toronto Young Liberals in the autumn of 1891 the members were debating Canadian independence from Britain. The resolution under discussion decried the state of the economy, the continuing loss of population to the United States, and the corruption in Ottawa; much of the trouble was due to 'the fact that our public men and civil servants are taught loyalty to a country 3,000 miles away with which we have nothing in common but language and literature.' The cure for Canada's 'deplorable state' lay in 'a strong spirit of nationality, which can only be generated by the independence of the Dominion.'

Rowell spoke against the motion and in support of an amendment, which carried by a slim majority, favouring the retention of colonial status for the present and the pursuit of freer trade relations with the United States. Among the other debaters were three young men who were to remain his friends to the end: W.E. Rundle, a junior official of the Freehold Loan and Savings Company, J.J. Warren, about to receive his call to the bar, and Joseph E. Atkinson, fresh from his first term in the parliamentary press gallery as Ottawa correspondent for the *Globe*.[5] Another active member and new friend was John S. Willison, a past president of the club and now, at the age of thirty-five, editor of the *Globe*.

A strong spirit of nationality was much in evidence when Rowell attended the 'Canadian Literature Evening' organized by the Toronto Young Liberals early in 1892. The crowd assembled in the art gallery of the Ontario Society of Artists included several senior patrons of Canadian letters: G. Mercer Adam, the publisher who had done so much to encourage Canadian writers, Ontario's minister of Education, G.W. Ross, co-author of a life of Alexander Mackenzie just sent to press, and Rev. Dr E.H. Dewart, editor of the *Christian Guardian*. The evening's program gave Dr Dewart a partial answer to his much quoted plea for a distinctly Canadian literature, written twenty-seven years earlier in the introduction to his anthology of Canadian verse, the first such collection published. The authors who presented readings from their own works represented the first flowering of Canadian literature that had marked the decade of the 1880s and included Agnes Machar ('Fidelis'), one of the most prolific and admired of the established Canadian authors, Mrs J.F. Harrison, the 'Seranus' of the literary periodicals, the poets Wilfred Campbell and Duncan Campbell Scott, the young Montreal lawyer and writer, W.D. Lighthall, and Pauline Johnson, whose first public reading that night of the melodramatic 'A Cry from an Indian Wife' began her long career as a recitalist throughout North America and Britain. It was a memorable occasion; Canada was acquiring one of the marks of a nation – an indigenous and worthy literature.[6]

In the spring of 1892, Rowell moved out of the sometimes academic debating of the Young Liberals into the arena of active politics. His participation in two provincial by-elections did little to change the picture in dominantly Tory Toronto, but it proved him to be thoughtful and effective on the political platform. Admittedly defending the record of Sir Oliver Mowat's government was not a particularly difficult task, for there was no doubt that economic growth, freedom from public debt, and progress on many fronts had marked the twenty years of Liberal power in the province. Mowat had come to seem almost as permanent a star in the firmament as Ontario itself.

When W.D. Gregory, one of the leaders of the currently active commercial union movement, invited a few senior Toronto Liberals and a number of younger men to his home to meet the leader of the federal Liberal party, Wilfrid Laurier, he included Rowell. Among the other guests were John Willison, Robert Jaffray, publisher of the *Globe*, Andrew Pattullo, member of the legislature for North Oxford, and Goldwin Smith, the grey eminence of the commercial unionists. For Rowell, as for most of the Young Liberals, it was their first personal meeting with Laurier.[7] Whatever was said that night about commercial union with the United States, nothing made Rowell question his allegiance to the Liberal party.

Rowell's election by the Toronto Young Liberals as an alternate non-voting delegate to the national Liberal Convention, held in Ottawa in June 1893, enabled him to take a minor part in the first national political convention in the country's history. He accepted with alacrity the invitation to speak in support of the convention resolution condemning the current federal franchise on the grounds that it allowed political manipulation and corrupt practices, and was slow and expensive to revise. If the subject was satisfying, so too was the thought that at twenty-five he was one of the youngest members of the convention and therefore able to 'voice the sentiment of the young men not only of Ontario but of the Dominion ...' Those young men, Rowell declared, were revolted by Tory gerrymandering and revision of voters' lists by the government's own appointees, practices which were 'a disgrace in the eyes of every Briton ... The Old Flag ... has been dragged down to wrap around the corruption and dishonesty of a corrupt and dishonest administration.' Only the Liberals could restore true British principles to the practice of government in Canada.[8]

That the conference was very much Ontario's was symbolized in Sir Oliver Mowat's role as chairman and given concrete embodiment in the resolution favouring the maintenance of the British connection, and in the turning away from unrestricted reciprocity to advocacy of a reciprocity treaty based on moderate protection. At the same time, Laurier comforted English Canadian delegates by reaffirming that his political principles were 'entirely derived from the great English Liberal school ... the school of Fox in the last century, and of Gladstone in this.' Welcome to Rowell, as to many delegates from every province, was the adoption of a resolution pledging a Liberal government to hold a Dominion plebiscite to 'clearly ascertain ... the mind of the people ... on the question of prohibition.'[9]

Choosing a church congregation in Toronto was a serious matter, and Rowell took his time about it. He was not overly impressed by the quality of Toronto preaching, and especially distressed to hear Dr Stafford at Sherbourne Street Church 'preaching good works as a means of salvation.' Shortly after his arrival in Toronto he began to work at the Fred Victor Mission, an enterprise of Metropolitan Church, financed chiefly by the Massey family, for welfare and evangelistic work in the poorest area of the city between King Street and the water front. Initially he was doubtful that he could do much good there. For the men and boys among whom he laboured, telling the truth seemed to be 'a lost art & to lie ... as natural as to breathe ... Worst of all, or almost so, as far as Mission work is concerned, nearly all are Roman Catholics and they come just so long as they enjoy it & have what they consider a good time.'[10] This discouraging prospect did not prevent him from becoming assistant superintendent of the Sunday School at the mission, a position he held for several years. He joined Metropolitan Church, 'the cathedral of Canadian Methodism,' whose Gothic tower was a landmark in downtown Toronto. In the three decades since the building of the church, the congregation, like most urban Methodist congregations in Ontario, had reflected the changing social position of Methodists. Earlier, it had included few professional men and almost none of wealth, but now many leading figures in Metropolitan were doctors, lawyers, and captains of industry. Chester D. Massey and W.E.H. Massey, farm-implement manufacturers, Edward Gurney, manufacturer of stoves, T.G. Mason, maker of high-grade pianos, W.P. Gundy, financier, Dr J.J. Maclaren, a learned member of the Toronto bar, George Kerr and B.E. Bull, established lawyers who shortly invited Rowell to become the junior partner in their law firm, were all active members of the Metropolitan congregation.

Within a year of his arrival in the city, Rowell was elected a lay delegate of the congregation to the Toronto Conference of the Methodist church, the youngest man ever to sit in that assembly. He was in great demand as a lay preacher and broke another record when, in the illness of the pastor, he occupied the Metropolitan pulpit, the first local preacher to do so. 'Had a very good time' was his usual comment on his experiences in the pulpit. But there was a limit to how much of this kind of enjoyment he could allow himself. Between his religious and political interests he was receiving by the autumn of 1893 an impossible number of invitations to speak – an average of one a day. But the law was his first commitment, and he rejected nearly all of them.[11]

The speaking engagements he did accept were often in connection with the Epworth League, the Methodist young people's organization he had discovered at Chautauqua and had introduced to young Methodists in London. He helped to organize the first annual provincial convention of Epworth Leagues, an event which brought over four hundred young Methodists to Metropolitan Church for three days.[12] The success of the League was further evidenced by the registration at the first annual meeting of the Methodist Young Peoples' Union of Toronto, when the eight hundred delegates listened to Rowell's exposition of the literary work of young people's societies;[13] he was shortly elected president of the union of groups within the Toronto Conference. At the General Conference of the church, where he was once again the youngest man in the assembly, he was the leader of a group of clergy and laymen who argued successfully for the recognition of the Epworth League, a denominational movement, as the official young people's organization of the Methodist Church in Canada, instead of the non-denominational Christian Endeavour Society, which had also been introduced from the United States and was strongest among Presbyterians. Rowell was firmly convinced of the superiority of a young people's movement with a distinctly Canadian orientation and directly under the control of Canadian Methodists, compared with the Christian Endeavour Society whose programs were prepared in the United States.[14] Thus, the yearly 'Reading Courses,' the core of Epworth League activities, in whose planning and early development Rowell had a large share,[15] had a distinctly Canadian flavour and became an important part of the informal education of many young Canadians in the years down to the first world war. They dealt not only with Christian doctrine and the history and principles of Methodism, with scientific discovery and the lives of world statesmen, but also with the growth of the Empire, with Canadian explorers, missionaries, and pioneers, and with Canadian literature.

Although the Epworth League served general educational purposes, the church saw it primarily as a new form of evangelism, replacing evangelistic methods like the old-fashioned revival meetings that had served a less sophisticated society. As Rowell explained the new circumstances, Canadian Methodists had passed the stage when it was deemed 'necessary for a child born in a Christian home to have the same experience of salvation as a hardened sinner.' No one would deny that 'saving a drunkard or a profligate is a work of grace, but one tenth of the effort ... put forth on that man's soul might keep some young person in the church ... to ... exercise in the world a much greater influence than the profligate.'[16] The Methodist reading courses were an expression of the belief that 'education into faith' was possible and young people from Methodist homes could be kept within the church if they were adequately instructed and nurtured.

One of the most interesting features of Rowell's first General Conference was the report of the first Committee on Sociological Questions. Officially, Canadian Methodists were agreed that drinking, gambling, dancing, most forms of theatrical entertainment, and Sunday street cars, were social evils. A few were interested in factory legislation, but on the whole they had been concerned primarily with individual sin and salvation rather than with building the Kingdom of God on earth. While the institutional downtown church, such as the Fred Victor Mission, was in form a new approach to old social sins in an urban setting foreign to the traditions of nineteenth-century Canadian Protestantism, it was essentially conservative and rested on no fundamental criticism of society. Good individuals would create a good society, or at least save themselves from a sinful world. Now, the Committee on Sociological Questions invited Canadian Methodists to look at social issues in a broader perspective. The delegates to the General Conference assented to the declaration of the committee that 'as a church our sympathies are with the struggling masses everywhere, and we stand ready to aid to the utmost in ameliorating their condition ... We consider it ... the duty of all Christians ... to watch the social movements of the day and to make all proper efforts to secure the most satisfactory economic conditions through appropriate legislation.' There was no reference to any specific legislation. To the suggestion that 'new social theories and movements' might merit the support of individuals was added the assertion that 'as a church we hesitate to commit ourselves to any of them, as they are in a tentative stage and must be measured by their results.'[17] Canadian Methodists would not officially pioneer in testing the socialist doctrines to which some of their British counterparts were being drawn, nor were they notably eager to espouse the 'social gospel' tenets currently expounded in the United States by Washington Gladden and Walter Rauschenbusch.

Whatever new directions Methodism might take, there were still old causes to be served. Rowell worked vigorously for a 'yes' vote in Toronto in the provincial plebiscite on prohibition on 1 January 1894 and to ensure the re-election of Mayor R.J. Fleming, prohibitionist, Methodist, Liberal, and railway worker. Mayor Fleming was defeated, but by a majority of over 2,500 votes Toronto approved 'the immediate prohibition by law of the importation, manufacture and sale of intoxicating liquors as a beverage.' In the province as a whole prohibition had a majority among both urban and rural male voters, and the thirteen thousand women who possessed the municipal franchise.

The carrying of the plebiscite could not guarantee the early establishment of a dry Ontario. The old question of the relative responsibility of provincial and federal governments for liquor legislation was once again before the courts, a situation consoling to most of the politicians since it enlarged the opportunities for procrastination on a politically dangerous issue. Premier Mowat assured a delegation of prohibitionists that if the Judicial Committee of the Privy Council decreed that it was within provincial power to pass a prohibitory liquor law, he would introduce such a bill in the Legislature in the session immediately following the judgment. Not a few critics suggested that Mowat was only too glad to call a provincial election before the court decision was handed down.

Thus the most contentious issue of the provincial general election of 1894 was not temperance, but 'popery.' Denouncing Mowat's 'alliance' with the Roman Catholic bishops, his acceptance of separate schools as established by the BNA Act, and his tolerance of French-language schools, the recently organized Protestant Protective Association made itself a political force of some account. The PPA program for Ontario included the abolition of separate schools and the exclusion of Roman Catholics from both public service and private employment. Although there was no formal understanding between the PPA and the Conservatives, a number of prominent Conservatives, including the party leader W.R. Meredith, were on record as favouring the abolition of separate schools and to that extent they shared the same platform. At the local level numerous agreements were entered into by the PPA and the Conservatives, and in several ridings having a PPA candidate no Conservative was nominated. In effect the PPA was an arm of the Conservative party.[18] Another new element on the political scene was the Patrons of Industry, an agrarian movement spawned by the farmers' fears of loss of political influence in the face of the rapid growth of the urban sector of Ontario society.

In a contest in which the Liberals were under attack for being pro-Catholic the party had important work for a leading Protestant layman, and Rowell gave several addresses in the southwestern part of the province, where the PPA was strongest, and in Toronto. Lauding Mowat as the great unifier of races and creeds, and in a questionable interpretation of the constitutional facts of life, as the defender of the established and total separation of church and state, Rowell urged resistance to the Tory effort to widen the religious divisions in the province as a grave disservice not only to Ontario but to the whole country.[19] The Liberals were also aided by the support of several prominent Protestant leaders of independent politics, notably Principal G.M. Grant of Queen's. For days before the election the *Globe* carried Mowat's picture with Grant's declaration underneath: 'Ontario cannot afford to dismiss Sir Oliver Mowat.' Ontario heeded the advice and Mowat came once more to power on the backs of the Catholic bishops, the Presbyterian General Assembly, the solid Grits of rural Ontario, an expectant body of earnest prohibitionists, and the old faithfuls among the liquor interests. But the result was far from a triumph. When the collection of PPA representatives, agrarian Patrons of Industry, and Independents had sorted themselves out in the Legislature the Mowat government's majority was a shaky one.

The 'no popery' cry had failed to bring down the Liberals, and never again would sectarian warfare be so bitter in a provincial election in Ontario. At the same time it was evident that the alliance of forces which Mowat had effectively manipulated for so long was changing. So far there was little sign of new thought or fresh policies that might give the Liberal party a firmer mandate to govern the province.

An expanding law practice and his political and religious activities provided a good deal of the informal sociability and good talk that Rowell always enjoyed. He frequently took advantage of the standing welcome awaiting him in the Church Street home of two other members of the Metropolitan congregation, G.H. Parkes and his wife, where he could always count on a cup of tea and a good chat. Often he took a meal with former London friends now studying or working in Toronto, or met Will (Hamar) Greenwood, a student at the university, for an evening's discussion of the state of the world. Always stimulating were the gatherings at the home of Dr W.H. Withrow, the learned and versatile editor of the *Canadian Methodist Magazine*.

Among an increasing number of social events, there were dinners which frequently seemed to have been arranged to permit a meeting between the hostess's daughter or niece and a young lawyer of character and excellent prospects. Rowell paid only the normal courtesy to these young ladies, as to all the others he met, usually in Epworth League and other church activities. He did, however, make the occasional visit to the home of Rev. A.L. Langford, his former pastor in London and now the minister of the Methodist church in Brampton, just outside of Toronto. Although Newton Rowell was always glad to see any member of the Langford family, it was the presence of Nellie that made the trip really worthwhile. Seven years his junior, she had been a member of his Sunday School class in London. Her enrolment in the fall of 1893 at Victoria College, just moved from Cobourg to its new site in Queen's Park, was a boon to him. Fortunately, the home of Nellie's older brother and Rowell's friend, Arthur Langford, recently married and appointed to lecture in Greek at Victoria, provided a frequent meeting place.

The sudden death from typhoid of his brother Edward, aged twenty-seven, meant increased financial and personal responsibilities for Newton in caring for his mother and for his sister Mary, who was closely attached to her brothers, partly because her older sister Sazie's dominant personality had inhibited the development of her own self-confidence. Newton always did his best to nourish Mary's feeling of independence and encouraged her to make a career for herself. In the autumn of 1893 he was affluent enough to send her to the Methodist Ladies College at Whitby to complete her high school matriculation, and subsequently to Victoria College to study modern languages.

Although he spent little on himself, he was always immaculately dressed. The purchase of an expensive otter cap, wholesale, to be paid for in legal services, was a noteworthy event justified by the severe cold and only incidentally by what it added to 'the personal appearance of your humble servant.' After less than three years in Toronto, and at the beginning of the new year, 1894, he could review his own and his family's lot with satisfaction. 'The past year has been to us all rich in blessing, blessing beyond what we could have in our most hopeful moments hoped for, and if any should have hearts filled with gratitude to the Giver of all good gifts we should.' His advancement in his profession and the intimations he received that he had effectively influenced others in the Christian life renewed his sober sense of responsibility. 'If God has placed it within my power to influence others ... how careful I should be that my influence should always be helpful and ennobling ... I am resolved by God's help that it shall be such.'[20]

'This is the place of all places, the City of all cities ... I am now at Hyde Park watching the nabobs driving past in their carriages in the fashionable centre for the Elite to display their Eliteness ...' He had been in London five days and was enjoying his first holiday in England even more than he had expected. His arrival in Liverpool had been followed by sightseeing among the Roman ruins at Chester, a pilgrimage to a shrine of Liberalism – Gladstone's home at Hawarden Castle – a short stop in Birmingham, and a visit to Shakespeare's grave in Stratford. Reading the announcement in the papers of a Liberal rally under the auspices of the London Liberal and Radical Union, he changed his plans for a leisurely trip to London, in order to be present for the occasion.[21]

The resignation of the fifteen-month-old Liberal administration of Lord Rosebery and the advent of the Conservatives to power under Lord Salisbury had coincided with Rowell's arrival in England. He was familiar with the broad outlines of current British politics, for the *Globe* had kept its readers well informed of the House of Lords' rejection of the Second Irish Home Rule Bill, Gladstone's retirement, and the confusion and drift which had thereupon beset an unhappy Liberal party. Now he 'was delighted beyond measure' to join ten thousand cheering London Liberals in the Albert Hall, listening to Lord Rosebery and three other ex-Liberal ministers – Lord Tweedmouth, Sir Henry Campbell-Bannerman, and H.H. Asquith. The oratory was of a high order. Rowell judged all the speeches 'magnificent' but was most impressed with Rosebery, a preference that some English Methodists would have found difficult to share, so strongly did certain elements in Nonconformity disapprove of 'the racing prime minister' whose horses had twice won the Derby. Rowell warmed to Rosebery's proud reaffirmation of his membership in the school of 'Liberal Imperialists,' standing for the maintenance of the Empire, the emigration of surplus population, suppression of the slave trade, the development of commerce, and the promotion of missionary enterprise. The most immediate and pressing reform for which the Liberal party must fight, Rosebery declared, was the ending of the 'medieval control' exercised by the House of Lords.[22] To all this Rowell gave willing assent, but what pleased him most was 'the demonstration of approval which greeted the announcement of Lord Rosebery that the Liberal party would continue to fight the whiskey ring.'[23]

A Sunday in London in the golden age of the popular preacher was an embarrassment of riches. In the morning he heard the Bishop of Ripon, Dr William Carpenter, 'The Queen's favorite preacher, said to be the ablest Anglican preacher in England.' That afternoon in Westminster Abbey Archdeacon Frederick William Farrar, whose *Life of Christ* had been for twenty-five years one of the most widely read religious books in the language, preached a sermon on missions. At home Rowell might refer to an Anglican Church as 'the English Church,' but Westminster Abbey was something else, the heart of all British Christianity. 'What a church, what a subject, what a preacher. It was magnificent, & his arraignment of the liquor traffic as a foe of missions was most vigorous. The central thought was England's greatness, her wealth, her commerce, her language, her civilization, the nation of the future, & all these great gifts given her by Heaven that she might distribute & be the means of the world's salvation ... It was a stirring appeal in the great national church that England as a nation might be missionary.' After that it was something of an anti-climax to attend the Congregationalist City Temple in the evening to hear one of the best known Free Church preachers. The colloquial, unconventional, and somewhat histrionic Dr Joseph Parker 'was good but not so good' as Rowell expected. 'Yet what a feast in one day.'

After a visit to the law courts he took in the usual tourist attractions, heard the Edward Strauss Orchestra of Vienna in the Great Hall of the Imperial Institute in Kensington, and in Covent Garden listened to the Royal Italian Opera with the brilliant coloratura, Melba, singing the role of Micaela in 'Carmen.' He had rarely been to the theatre before, but an adaptation of Tennyson's 'King Arthur' with Ellen Terry and Sir Henry Irving, who had contributed greatly to the dissipation of English Methodist abhorrence of the theatre, was safe and enjoyable fare for a colonial Methodist abroad.[24]

One object of Rowell's holiday trip was the improvement of his general health, because the concentrated work of establishing himself in his profession had been hard on him. Two weeks of walking and climbing near Lucerne was beneficial, and in Germany he continued his program of out-door activity, but also found time to investigate the German system of social insurance. To have restored his health and had a first exciting look at England and the continent, all for three hundred dollars, was an excellent investment.

The first week of January 1896 brought an unprecedented cabinet crisis in Ottawa. In the wake of the announcement in the speech from the throne that the government would introduce legislation to restore separate schools in Manitoba, seven cabinet ministers bolted, and Prime Minister Sir Mackenzie Bowell made several unsuccesful attempts to resign. Although peace was restored before long, the bankruptcy of Conservative leadership had been demonstrated for all to see.

Through the early weeks of 1896 English-speaking Protestant Liberals, none more than those in Toronto, were plagued by their own crisis. The Manitoba school issue was just as full of peril for the Liberals as it was for the Conservatives. Wrongly handled, it might rob them of office despite the manifest weakness of the Tory party. From the outset Laurier had used the relative freedom of opposition to avoid taking a position on the issue. Always he had called for further investigation while the government was drawn by the inescapable demands of office ever more deeply toward a policy. When that policy turned out to be the remedial bill to restore the separate schools the burden of decision finally rested on Laurier. Initially, Laurier did not see how he could oppose it without losing Quebec. A number of prominent Ontario Liberals, including Mowat, G.W. Ross, and the

Globe's Board of Directors were at first prepared to go along with Laurier in supporting the measure. The editor of the *Globe* refused to agree. John Willison was a spokesman for the many Ontario Liberals who would not support the remedial bill, and who were almost certainly numerous enough to deprive the party of victory at the polls if they were alienated. Assured by Israel Tarte that he and Laurier together could handle Quebec, Laurier took the plunge and announced a policy that Ontario Protestants would accept. 'In the name of the constitution' and 'in the name of peace and harmony' he opposed the remedial legislation in favour of the compromise and reconciliation that he promised to effect. The Liberals continued to oppose with every possible obstruction through days and nights of debate until the life of Parliament ran out and the school question was before the people in a general election.

In his several addresses during the campaign, Rowell spoke little of the school issue, beyond praising the statesmanship of Laurier's policy of reconciliation. Rather, it was the failure of the National Policy and the need to amend the tariff that formed much of his appeal, notably in the manufacturing cities of Berlin and Hamilton. The issue above all, he argued in every speech, was the question of honour and integrity in public life. Before ten thousand voters at an open air meeting in Dundurn Park in Hamilton, where he shared the platform with G.W. Ross, Rowell concluded a peroration against corruption in high places with the declaration that if the Liberals in office proved no better than the party of McGreevy and Langevin 'it would be the duty of the people to turn them out, and keep turning them out until honest government was secured.'[25]

To Laurier's comfortable, although less than overwhelming, victory at the polls in 1896, Ontario contributed substantially, sending almost half her members to sit on the government benches. Despite the outspoken opposition of the bishops to his school policy, Laurier had captured forty-nine of Quebec's sixty-five seats, in a triumph which suggested to many Ontario Protestants that perhaps Quebec was not as 'priest ridden' as they had supposed, and that it was safe after all to support a party led by a French Canadian. Ontario voters could soon find many reasons for liking their first taste of Laurier Liberalism. There were few who did not follow with pride the newspaper accounts of the prime minister's reception at Queen Victoria's Diamond Jubilee celebrations in London in June 1897 although some, like the recipient of the honour, had doubts about whether it was seemly for him to have become 'Sir Wilfrid.' But there was no doubt, as Laurier rode at the head of the colonial premiers in the Jubilee procession and later sat at the right hand of the colonial secretary, Joseph Chamberlain, at the Colonial Conference, that Canada was receiving unprecedented attention. In Ontario, especially, it was all highly satisfying: at one and the same time Canada's growing position in the world was recognized and she gained further stature still from the grandeur of the Empire. For the present, English-Canadian nationalism and imperial sentiment were happily mingled.

Moreover, the new preferential tariff that gave Britain a privileged position in the Canadian market was sentimentally and commercially agreeable. That Canada's rapidly increasing sales to Britain were due to the new tariff could not be proved, but the Liberal claim of direct connection was highly plausible.

The settlement achieved in the Manitoba school controversy was also generally accepted in Ontario. A few Orange die-hards protested that the severely limited provisions for religious instruction and the use of the French language in Manitoba schools were still too much, but the majority of Protestants were content with the Laurier-Greenway agreement. The view that what Manitoba was now to have was a far cry from a full separate school system was confirmed by the resistance of the Roman Catholic bishops to the settlement. Now Ontarians could reasonably feel that an Anglo-Saxon society was firmly established in Manitoba.

True to an earlier promise, Laurier's new cabinet included Sir Oliver Mowat as minister of justice. Ontario Liberals rightly sensed that Mowat's retirement from the premiership marked the end of an era. Speaking on behalf of the younger Liberals of the province at a testimonial dinner in recognition of Mowat's twenty-four years in office, Rowell lauded the retiring premier for his never failing respect for the constitution, his belief in the permanency of the British Empire, his broad toleration of all classes and creeds, and his firm faith in the reality of the Christian religion and high ideals; it was a political code to which Ontario must continue to adhere.[26] In the next decade, amid the collapse of Mowat Liberalism, that code was to face severe tests.

One indication that Oliver Mowat's Ontario was changing – for the worse, in Rowell's view – came with the loss of the fight against Sunday street cars. In the spring of 1897 the voters of the municipality of Toronto decided in favour of Sunday cars by a majority of 321. Shortly thereafter, Rowell and J.J. Maclaren appeared before a county court judge on behalf of a group of citizens petitioning for a scrutiny or recount of the vote. The Sabbatarians believed that the corrupt practices of their opponents had determined the result. If the plebiscite could be declared invalid they were confident they could win a new contest. The judge confessed his great difficulty in sorting out the conflicting and lengthy arguments put to him by the lawyers on both sides as to whether the Municipal Act permitted a petition of the kind Rowell had presented to him, and decided that it did not.[27] Henceforth Torontonians could go to church and Sunday School by street car – or, more likely, to picnics in the parks.

Early in 1898 Ontario Liberals faced their first provincial contest without Sir Oliver Mowat at the helm. For the new premier and party leader, the Brantford lawyer, A.S. Hardy, the cares of office were a visible burden and even among staunch Liberals there was little optimism about his leadership. But the faithful rallied around him, and Rowell delivered addresses in several ridings. Under their new leader, J.P. Whitney, the Conservatives were trying to live down their anti-Catholic past,[28] while the Liberals laboured to prevent that decent burial by dragging out earlier Conservative policies and statements and by insinuating that perhaps the Opposition was now too pro-Catholic. This was a tactic that required skilful handling if it were not to backfire. In speaking for Dr Dewart, whose recent retirement as editor of the *Christian Guardian* had freed him to contest North Toronto, Rowell pointed out that in 1894 the Conservatives had had six planks on education in their platform, five of them related to separate schools; all five had been dropped from the present platform; what, then, he asked, was the Tory policy on separate schools?[29] In Kingston, where he addressed a meeting in support of one of the two Roman Catholic members of the cabinet, Hon. William Harty, there was no mention of separate schools. There, as in other centres, Rowell defended the policy of the Hardy and Mowat administrations on the selection and printing of school texts, a subject which was hotly discussed throughout the election. That policy had effected enormous economies by sharply reducing the number of pre-scribed texts, and had required all those in use in the schools to be written by Canadians and published in Canada. Previously, nearly all the texts were written by Americans and published south of the border.[30] The nationalistic tone of his discussion of the text-book issue brought frequent rounds of applause, and after one of these speeches, John Willison began his own address with a tribute to Rowell as 'a man destined beyond peradventure to hold a leading place in the affairs of this country in years to come.'[31]

The Liberal failure to present any imaginative platform or to give sufficient attention to party organization, coupled with Hardy's lacklustre leadership, brought the party close to disaster. The government's majority was cut from twenty-five to six, and before long there were charges of corruption in West Elgin in the general election and in the by-election which followed that resulted in the unseating first of a Conservative, then of a Liberal, and the eventual election of a Conservative. Investigation revealed corruption by the Liberal candidate's own admission, and two government employees were found guilty of manipulating votes in what G.W. Ross, who became premier in 1899 after Hardy's resignation, had to admit were 'gross irregularities.' It was the beginning of a painful process of disillusionment for many Liberals.

The provincial election was barely over before it was time to prepare for another battle. Reluctantly, but true to his promises, Laurier announced a Dominion plebiscite on the liquor question. Every Canadian voter was to be asked: 'Are you in favor of passing an Act prohibiting the importation, manufacture, or sale of spirits, wine, ale, cider, and all other alcoholic liquors for use as a beverage?'

By upbringing, religious inheritance, and personal conviction Rowell was a prohibitionist. By now he knew the arguments for his position inside out, but he prepared with enormous care for the 'opportunity never before afforded a whole country ... to blot out the curse of the liquor traffic.' If Canada could do that at the beginning of the twentieth century she could build a society of unprecedented happiness and prosperity.[32] The notes for his many speeches in the plebiscite campaign set out the full indictment against the liquor traffic: it menaced democratic government through its sinister influence on politicians and voters, and the whole of civilization through the dethronement of reason and the stifling of conscience; it wasted the economic resources of individuals and society; it encouraged crime and brought poverty, illness, and sometimes death to thousands; and it undid the good work of school and church in preserving the moral fabric of the community. As in many reformers of the day, Rowell's advocacy of prohibition reflected at one and the same time his desire to preserve the rural values of the past and his deep concern about the quality of life in a new urban society.[33]

Of the 44 per cent of the voters who went to the polls, 51.3 per cent chose the good life. Every province except Quebec showed a majority of voters in favour of prohibition, and in Ontario the majority was nearly 40,000 out of a total vote of about 270,000. Soon a deputation from the Dominion Alliance for the Total Suppression of the Liquor Traffic was waiting on Laurier to ask when the promised legislation would be introduced. Five months later Laurier gave his answer: although it was true that a majority of those voting had favoured prohibition, they comprised less than 23 per cent of the total electorate, and no good purpose would be served by the passing of a measure so little supported by the people.[34] The prohibitionists were bitterly disappointed, charging that the morality of the nation was being dictated by Quebec, and some of their leaders threatened to bring Laurier down at the next election. But where could a temperance Liberal go? The Conservatives showed no sign of willingness to espouse the cause. The question was prickly enough in every province, but no leader of a national party could be expected to face the especially strong feeling against prohibition in Quebec. The only hopeful avenue to temperance reform now lay in provincial legislation. And in Ontario progress towards sobriety was undoubtedly being made. Despite a growing population and the repeal of the Canada Temperance Act in every county where it had once been in effect, the number of saloon licences was thirteen thousand fewer in 1897 than twenty years earlier, while the number of persons arrested for drunkenness had declined by two-thirds in the same period.[35] To the temperance forces these facts were evidence that the province was ready for prohibition, but to others they proved that a sober Ontario could be achieved by less drastic means. The fight was by no means over.

As the old century drew to a close, Rowell's attention was not wholly devoted to the future of his country and province. The shape of his own personal future was becoming more interesting. Since her graduation from Victoria College, Nellie Langford had been teaching at the Methodist girls' school, Alma College in St Thomas, where his sister Mary was also on the staff as a teacher of French. Whenever he could manage it, he saw her during weekend visits to London or occasionally at her parents' home in Orangeville and later in Owen Sound. In the summer of 1900 he spent some time with Mary and Nellie holidaying in Quebec at Cap à l'Aigle. Then, while he went fishing in the Lake St Jean district, the young women took a boat trip up the Saguenay River to meet him for the return journey to Toronto. It was an exhilarating holiday, though his high spirits could be attributed only partially to the clear Laurentian air.

3
Liberalism in East York

With the approach of the federal election of 1900 the leaders of Toronto Liberalism, notably J.S. Willison, decided that it was time for N.W. Rowell to enter Parliament. The tall spare figure in the black suit, the neat black moustache, the serious but lively eyes, and the rather thin high-pitched voice that nevertheless commanded attention, were now as well known to Liberals as to the Methodist faithful. Rowell's grasp of public questions and his oratorical powers had won him a front place among the younger Liberals of Ontario.

On a late August afternoon Willison, accompanied by the president of the Toronto Reform Association, J.H. Mackenzie, called on Rowell to ask that he allow them to nominate him as the Liberal candidate in East York. Their proposal was no surprise; it had been made tentatively earlier in the summer and he had rejected it emphatically.[1] Now he was confronted with a formal invitation that required an early answer.

He still thought it was impossible to accept the nomination. He had business commitments stretching many months ahead and his physician warned him that he was already working to the limit of his strength. Moreover, he believed that a candidate should provide at least part of his own campaign expenses, something he could not manage at the moment. The most serious obstacle of all was that many voters might think his attitudes on moral questions 'decidedly narrow' and would feel that 'a candidate for political honours requires a certain flexibility which I know I do not possess.' No one need expect him to 'deviate a hair's breadth' from the stands he had already taken 'on all moral questions.' Willison assured him that he need not worry about money – it would be found – and was certain that Rowell could win the seat without sacrifice of his principles.[2]

There had rarely been a better time for an Ontario Liberal to enter federal politics. The general prosperity of the country and the youth and vigour of Laurier's government, now facing its first test at the polls, augured well for the Liberal forces. Since Laurier was almost certain to hold his own in Quebec any contribution to the maintenance of Liberal strength in Ontario would further the building of a strong national party with reliable support from both French- and English-speaking Canada. The political crisis precipitated by demands from Ontario that Canada participate in the Boer War had posed a severe threat to party unity, but there was reason to hope that Laurier's deft manœuvring had brought the party through the controversy without severe damage to Liberal prospects in Ontario.

However auspicious the omens for the Liberal party as a whole, Rowell needed an answer to a very specific question: Could any Liberal win a seat in the Toronto area, with its record of Conservative victories ever since Confederation? Of the six Toronto and York seats, only one was held by a Liberal; North York had been securely in the grasp of William Mulock for the past eighteen years. The only Toronto or York seat which the Liberals could hope to add was East York, and the question of how to bring it back into the Liberal fold had received a great deal of attention from Liberal strategists long before the election was called.[3] Although W.F. Maclean had won the seat with a good majority in 1892 in the by-election occasioned by Alexander Mackenzie's death, he had held it by only three votes in 1896. Liberal hopes of ousting Maclean were increased by his recent relations with his own party because he was fast establishing a reputation for independent opinion and slender regard for party loyalty. As owner and editor of the Toronto *World* he had lately carried on a campaign against the Conservative member of Parliament for Toronto Centre, E.F. Clarke, who was running for the mayoralty of Toronto. Currently, Maclean was publicly critical of J.P. Whitney's leadership of the Ontario Conservative party and many Conservatives were predicting that Maclean might not enjoy the total support of party officials in the forthcoming campaign. Yet, whatever his formal relations with his party, Maclean's personal popularity with his own constituents made him a formidable opponent.

While he was trying to reach a decision Rowell received a personal appeal from Laurier. Laurier's assessment of East York showed that Rowell 'would be by far the best candidate we could have there'; he recognized that he was 'asking a great sacrifice,' but added, 'I do not hesitate to do so both in the name of the party and in my own personal name.'[4] It was hard to refuse such a request, and yet Rowell hesitated. He had no desire to devote precious time and energy to the contest unless his chances of winning were good, and he still had doubts about his physical capacity to withstand the campaign and the life of a member of Parliament if elected. He was aware that not all East York Liberals were convinced that he would be the best candidate. A group of Catholic Liberals was promoting another nominee, Peter Ryan, and complained to Laurier that Postmaster General Mulock was trying to control the nomination on behalf of the party hierarchy in Ottawa and Toronto and to prevent Ryan's nomination. The Ryan supporters petitioned Laurier to secure a postponement of the nominating convention until the discord could be settled.[5] If this warring faction proved to be a large one the Liberals would probably fail to make the most of their opportunities in East York. There was a further source of apprehension. Prohibition was not an issue in this election but Rowell had reason to believe that the liquor interests would endeavour to prevent him from getting a start in public life. In the past the three brewers and the numerous saloon keepers in East York had thrown their support behind the Liberals. If they went over to the other side in a close race they might well determine the result. However, he had the assurances of the party strategists that these forces would not be set in motion against him.[6] Two days before the convention a deputation of thirty, representing every ward and including most of the Liberal stalwarts in the riding, waited on Rowell to assure him that his candidature would 'secure harmony among the different interests.' In the face of this display of unity he put aside his misgivings and agreed to stand.[7]

Rowell's lingering suspicion that Peter Ryan's supporters had not given up their resistance to 'the Mulock machine'[8] was confirmed at the nomination meeting. The proceedings had only commenced when men began springing to their feet in all corners of the hall to nominate candidates who were obviously not serious contenders; by the time these unwilling nominees had withdrawn, leaving only Ryan and Rowell, the impression of extensive opposition to Rowell had been created.

Peter Ryan was a colourful and popular figure in Toronto's commercial and political life. In the twenty-five years since his migration from Ireland, he had prospered in the wholesale dry goods business, as well as in lumbering and various industrial enterprises; he was one of Ontario's best Liberal orators and enjoyed the personal friendship of two former premiers, Sir Oliver Mowat and Arthur S. Hardy. A leader among the Irish Catholics of the province, Ryan always took ironic delight in setting out pitchers of cold water on a long table in front of his house on Grosvenor Street every 12 July to quench the thirst of weary Orangemen on parade.[9] That night his noisy and persistent friends were at a serious disadvantage: they were unable to prove that their man was available. Significantly, Ryan was not present to speak for himself and all attempts to find him and bring him to the meeting failed. With difficulty the chairman quelled the babel of conflicting statements about Ryan's willingness to run and took the vote. Rowell had a bare majority. The controversy was not yet ended. When the chairman issued the usual call to make the nomination unanimous, the Ryanites refused; they proposed, in accordance with the Reform Association's constitution, to demand meetings in every polling subdivision for a vote on the two names. Even the most adamant Ryan supporters were finally persuaded that Ryan himself would not approve this course, and they grudgingly made the choice unanimous. Rowell made a conventional acceptance speech and declared that he was sure he had no better friend than Peter Ryan.[10]

Once under way the campaign in East York excited unusual public interest. It was the only Toronto or York riding in which an electoral upset seemed possible, and the personalities of the two candidates added to the sharpness of the battle. Although both relatively young, 'Billie-Bug-Eyes' Maclean and Newton Wesley Rowell belonged to different worlds. The forty-four year old publisher of the *World* was far from being a Puritan; he was strongly opposed to prohibition, enjoyed a drink himself, and in the decade just ended had been one of the leading spirits in the successful fight for Sunday street cars in Toronto. He had further defied the rigid Sabbatarians by publishing the weekly *Sunday World*; the printing was done on Saturday night, but the hosts of righteousness could not prevent its being read on Sunday. The door of Maclean's office in the *World*'s premises near the corner of King and Yonge streets was always open to friends who dropped in for a little political gossip. On the platform he was boisterous and witty and was sure to give his audience a good time even if he did not destroy his opponents' arguments. If elections could be won solely on debating points there was no doubt that Rowell would have it all over Maclean. As it was, some experienced Liberals, while agreeing that Rowell could count on the solid Liberal vote especially in the rural sections of the riding, and that he might capture 'the church vote' where it was not irrevocably Conservative, still had their doubts about the appeal of his well-prepared, reasoned, and only occasionally humorous speeches to the all-important floating voters in the city polling divisions.[11]

One of Maclean's biggest political assets was his personal control of a city newspaper. The Liberals hoped this could be offset by the more than nominal support Rowell received from J.S. Willison and Stewart Lyon of the *Globe*, and from J.E. Atkinson, the new editor of the *Toronto Star*, who had just launched his crusade to prove that a paper deliberately appealing to industrial workers and 'the little people' generally could be both profitable and politically influential. The three editors addressed meetings on Rowell's behalf and did their best to convince their readers that the Liberal candidate in East York was an exceptionally able and sincere young man whose gifts the party and the nation should appropriate without delay. Atkinson's opposition to Maclean was not without difficulty, for the *World* had established itself as a vigorous exponent of a policy close to Atkinson's heart: the public ownership of utilities. However, Atkinson had decided that, by and large, the Liberals were the progressives and should have his support. It was especially agreeable to him to approve Rowell's advocacy of the Saturday half-holiday, his promise to reintroduce a bill legalizing the union label, and his determination to carry on the fight for the 'short line' from Collingwood to Toronto, a railway guaranteed to make Toronto the nation's greatest port, with consequent blessings for workers and employers alike.[12]

The East York campaign accurately reflected the battle in Ontario generally in its concentration on two main questions. Did credit for Canada's growing prosperity belong to the Conservative 'National Policy' or to Liberal administration and policies? Which party was the more reliable custodian of the imperial connection? Through their participation in the Boer War that question was now endowed with the most practical import for Canadians. Fittingly for a green aspirant to public office, Rowell launched his campaign with a presentation of his political creed as a preamble to his discussion of these more immediate issues. He thought it necessary to begin with an appeal to the historical record, since the Conservatives, notably Sir George Foster, were traversing the country claiming credit for all the constructive measures behind the modern Canada. To this Rowell replied that to say that any one party was responsible for everything good in national life was to misread history: the names 'Liberal' and 'Conservative' represented two distinct currents of thought in every civilized country. 'The word Conservative stands for things as they are; the maintenance of autocratic government where it exists ... The word Liberal or Reform ... stands for progress, for the rights of the individual, for enlarging the scope of human liberty, and for the removal, as far as possible, out of the pathway of every citizen, all obstacles that would hamper him in the attainment of his highest good.' Hence, it was not surprising that the system of democratic government enjoyed by Canadians was largely the creation of the Reformers: it was William Lyon Mackenzie of York County and Robert Baldwin, labouring against Conservative cries of disloyalty, who established in Canada the British principle that governors must be responsible to the governed; and it was Baldwin who led the fight for religious and educational equality and fashioned Ontario's municipal institutions in spite of Conservative hostility. Rowell saved his greatest scorn for the Conservatives' contention that they were the sole architects of Confederation. On the contrary, it was the Liberal W.H. Merritt who introduced the first Confederation resolution in the Canadian Assembly and George Brown who presented a similar proposal to the Reform convention of 1859 and again to the Assembly of 1860, only to have the Conservatives laugh at it. As late as 1863, John A. Macdonald had opposed Brown's report advocating Confederation and only agreed to the idea when he realized that he could not rule the country under any other scheme. After Confederation, who fought for restriction of the governor general's powers, the secret ballot, Senate reform, and the removal of 'the Gerrymander Act?' Alexander Mackenzie and the Liberals. It was chiefly to the Liberals that Canadians owed their full possession of the liberties of British subjects.

Without doing violence to the truth, Rowell's treatment of Liberal history was a skilful attempt to counteract the heavy reliance of the Conservatives on appeals to their National Policy as the only significant Canadian political achievement. He was careful not to attack the validity of the policy itself. By stressing the *British* inspiration of Liberal achievements he might help to turn aside the perennial Conservative charge that the Liberals were still a continentalist party bent on dangerous overtures to the United States. It was especially desirable to make this emphasis in the face of opposition charges in Ontario that, under Laurier and a party lukewarm toward Britain, the country had done less than her duty in South Africa.

Was there some lesson for the present to be drawn from the Liberal past? To Rowell the answer was obvious: a party that had contributed so soundly to Canadian constitutional development was eminently fitted to preside over the resolution of the next great problem, that of formally recognizing Canada's increasing importance in the Empire. Already, Canadian involvement in the war in South Africa had strengthened Canadian national feeling and in practice had altered the imperial relation.[13] When he was preparing his speech Rowell wrote that the Canadian contribution to the Boer War 'must be a precedent,'[14] but in the end, probably in deference to Laurier's assertion that it need not be a precedent, he refrained from using the phrase. Nevertheless, Rowell's hearers could be in no doubt about his feeling on the subject. Ignoring the heart-searching among many English Canadians and the downright opposition of most French Canadians to the South African venture, he described a nation whose heart 'responded as the heart of one man to the appeal of our honoured leader, as in the parliament of Canada he prayed that with the mingling of the blood of English-speaking and French-speaking Canadians on the South African veldt ... would be buried forever all the racial jealousies and animosities which have disturbed this Canada of ours during the past century.' The sacrifice of Canadian lives had even broader implications: 'the Australian, the New Zealander, the Englishman, the Irishman, and the Scotchman ... died fighting for a common cause ... but they are not really dead. "That which thou sawest thou sawest not that body that shall be." And that body that shall be is the body of a united, consolidated empire ...' Unless all those owing allegiance to the British flag were brought together to 'act as a unit in all Imperial emergencies' England would lose her place as the first power in the world and 'the most potent force for the preservation of the world's peace will have passed away. We believe in Imperialism, not for conquest or aggression, but an Imperialism which means greater unity that there may be greater peace, greater progress, greater prosperity. The mission of the empire is not to kill but make alive, to quicken heart and intellect and conscience, in the accomplishment of her great work of civilization.'[15]

Rowell's opponent in East York was a devotee of imperial federation. Were the voters to conclude that Rowell was also committed to Joseph Chamberlain's schemes for formal imperial unity, to which Laurier had made clear his opposition?

Rowell did not mention Chamberlain or imperial federation and went no further than to suggest that the desired imperial unity could be achieved through a 'consultative council' or a body growing 'less directly from our present form of government.'[16] Thus, at the beginning of his campaign he had placed himself clearly in the 'imperialist' wing of his party.

Although Liberals spoke in a variety of tongues on imperial questions in the election of 1900, the discussion of economic policy was much simpler for them. The country's prosperity spoke for itself and provided a strong antidote to Conservative prophecies of the doom to which the economy was bound under Laurier's British preferential tariff. The farmers of East York scarcely needed Rowell's reminder that since 1896 the export of butter and bacon to Britain had increased five-fold and the export of flour nearly 600 per cent. Residents of Markham could see for themselves that, whereas the town's carpet factory went out of business under the National Policy, they now had a new shoe factory employing three times as many men. Scoffing at Maclean's prediction of 1897 that the Markham woollen mill would soon close in the face of competition from British goods, Rowell asserted that everybody in the district knew that it *was* closed under the Conservatives and had only reopened under the improved conditions since 1896. Rowell could also point out that in eighteen years of Conservative government the total value of Canadian trade had increased in value by only thirty-six million dollars compared to the increase of one hundred and forty million in the last four years alone; no city had profited more from this growth than Toronto where there were now 4,500 more industrial workers than four years earlier.[17] On other occasions when Premier G.W. Ross, and federal cabinet ministers – Hon. William Paterson, minister of customs, and Hon. Sydney Fisher, minister of agriculture – appeared in East York with Rowell, they had no difficulty in confirming this saga of prosperity with their own facts and figures.

The statistics were impressive and could not be denied. All that the Conservatives could do was to claim that the National Policy would bring even better results if the Liberals would stop tampering with it. Maclean joined with the rest of his party in demanding that the preferential tariff granted to Britain in 1897 be replaced by a mutual imperial preference, and in charging that 'the Crow's Nest Steal' agreement with the CPR was too big a price to pay for Liberal prosperity. More specifically, Maclean alleged that Rowell was the servant of 'the big interests' who were growing fat at the public's expense and cited his relation to the Nipigon Pulp, Paper and Manufacturing Company as proof.[18] Rowell readily acknowledged that he had acted for the Nipigon company in negotiations with the Ontario government, but he roundly denied the implication of graft on his part. The company had received only the normal twenty-one-year cutting rights and he could see no reason for shame in having helped to establish 'in a part of Ontario almost untrodden by the foot of man an industry that would employ two hundred men.'[19] The Crow's Nest agreement, far from making the Liberal party subservient to a big corporation as Maclean charged, was 'the best ever made by any government with any corporation.' The concessions wrested from the CPR would in the long run add to the public wealth more than enough to compensate for the government subsidy of $11,000 a mile for the Crow's Nest extension. Indeed, the CPR's acceptance of reduced freight rates on its lines west of Fort William as part of the agreement had put an additional $600,000 in the pockets of Manitoba farmers in the first year of its operation through increased shipments of grain and flour. Rowell later completed his exposition of the hollowness of the Conservative attack on the Crow's Nest agreement by quoting the favourable comment on it by the Conservative leader, Sir Charles Tupper, in the House of Commons; in fact, Tupper and Maclean had voted for the agreement in a House where there had been no opposing vote. Could there be more conclusive proof that the Conservatives were denouncing the agreement now solely for election purposes? The Tories wanted to persuade the Ontario working man that the Liberals had sold out to the CPR, when in truth they had exacted a highly advantageous bargain for the people of Canada.[20] Maclean had no rebuttal to the reminder that he had voted for the agreement. Rowell raised the question a number of times in the urban sections of the riding, believing that he had scored a point which should be driven home to the city voters who would win or lose the election for him.

As the campaign neared its climax an aspect of the imperial question assumed dominance over all other issues. Like many another Ontario Conservative, Maclean made increasing and deadly use of what had become known as 'the Tarte issue.' Israel Tarte, a cabinet minister and Laurier's most valued strategist and party manager in Quebec, had opposed the sending of Canadian troops to South Africa without direct parliamentary authorization. Subsequently, in the spring of 1900, as Canadian commissioner to the Paris Exposition, he had given several addresses extolling the 'Frenchness' of French Canadians and suggesting the future emergence of an independent Canada dominantly French in culture. In the resulting furore among English Canadians, the veteran Liberal, John Charlton, had said in extreme terms what many felt: that the time was coming when a British garrison would have to be stationed in Quebec to keep Canada a British country. Now, with a general election under way, the whole Tarte affair was acutely embarrassing to English-speaking Liberals.

Rowell could find no way of explaining or excusing Tarte's Paris utterances and tried to ignore them whenever possible. But Tarte himself could not be by-passed entirely. Hence Rowell directed attention to Tarte's exposé of the scandals in the previous Conservative administration and implied that this was really why the Conservatives hated him. Above all, Rowell tried to overcome the effect of the Tarte issue by playing up Laurier as the unchallenged leader of the party and the government, as the man who had put Canada on the map in British eyes and had dedicated his life to making Canada a great nation by uniting the two races in understanding and harmony. Laurier's honesty and consistency, Rowell declared, was in laudable contrast to the duplicity of Sir Charles Tupper who said in Quebec that Laurier was 'too English for him,' condemning Laurier for sending the contingent to South Africa, while in Ontario denouncing him for not sending it sooner. Since he had nothing to hide, Laurier had been able to say in Ontario exactly what he was saying in Quebec.[21]

In declaring November 5, two days before the election, a public holiday to honour the returning veterans of the South African war, the Liberal government no doubt hoped to achieve some political good in English-speaking Canada. The Conservatives, including their candidate in East York, also thought the occasion might be put to good use. On 5 November the *World* devoted the whole of its front page to Tarte, featuring excerpts from his speeches on the war and his Paris prophecies of a future French Canada. The headlines asked: 'Are we to be British or are we to be French? Is Canada for the French Canadians, led by Israel Tarte?' Naturally all the Toronto papers paid tribute to the returning heroes, but none reached the *World*'s emotional heights. Inside the paper, readers found a description of the parade witnessed by twelve thousand citizens: 'Toronto spoke in tones of thunder yesterday and Tarte and his minions are forever answered. Traitors, however high their rank, cannot mistake the significance of the demonstrations from Halifax to Toronto.' The editor of the *World* elaborated on the implications of all this for the election: 'Tarte will be the dominating influence in every polling booth in the land. Ask yourselves whether the country is safe with Mr Tarte as the controlling power in the Cabinet?' The *Star* countered with a display of Tarte's affirmation, 'I am a loyal subject,' and Tupper's declaration in Quebec that 'Laurier is too British for me.' On election day, one-line reminders scattered through the *World* warned that 'A vote for Rowell is a vote for Tarte.'[22]

As Rowell awaited the election returns with the other Toronto candidates and Liberal supporters in the offices of the *Globe* he was less confident than he had been through most of the campaign. Until the very end he had expected to win.[23] But now he feared that the Tarte cry had done considerable harm, and he had learned that at least some elements among the liquor interests were working against him. The early returns from the city polling divisions gave an accurate forecast of the result in the riding as a whole. He had lost to Maclean by 642 votes. The small majorities he had chalked up in Markham and Scarborough townships were more than offset by Maclean's showing in the urban sections of the riding. In a brief and not very spirited speech he attributed his defeat to the effective organization of the liquor interests and to the use of the cry that a vote for Rowell was a vote for French supremacy, a campaign disgraceful to those who conducted it. But Liberals could rejoice in Laurier's victory in the country as a whole and in the defeat of the two men most responsible for the racial and religious tone of the campaign in Ontario and Quebec, Sir Charles Tupper and Sir George Foster.[24]

On the morrow of the election the Liberal party could not blink the fact that although it had carried the nation it had lost some ground in Ontario. The Conservatives had won twelve additional seats in Ontario, leaving thirty-seven of the ninety-two Ontario ridings in the Liberal column. In a majority of constituencies the Conservative vote had increased significantly, including the six Toronto and York seats where representation remained unchanged and William Mulock was still the sole Liberal member from the district. On the other hand, the Liberals had swept Quebec, carrying all but seven seats. Laurier's success in his own province in 1896 had apparently been more than a flash in the pan, and he could be expected to pursue policies which would solidify his support in Quebec.

Willison had no doubt about the chief cause of the result in Ontario. 'We are discovering, as perhaps we ought to have discovered sooner, but the whole thing was carried on with extreme secrecy, that the province was filled with PPA lodges pledged to give no vote for a Catholic premier. Of course the Tarte cry was worked ... to its utmost. I am amazed to find how many Liberals were carried away by this shriek ... As you know I am not generally bitter in my politics, but as I learn what was done in this province I can reach no other conclusion than that the tactics of our opponents were simply infernal.'[25]

As Rowell settled down again into his legal work he continued to hear tales about the conduct of the campaign by his opponents in East York. It was now evident that 'the liquor party in Ontario practically centred on East York. They wanted to teach the Liberal party a lesson that they could not nominate a temperance candidate & hope to win. I don't suppose I got a dozen votes because of my temperance principles & I am sure that I lost hundreds.'[26] The temperance issue had been used with no lack of imagination. He learned that in the last few days of the campaign a story 'was circulated that when returning from a meeting at Eglinton I had been injured by the electric car & nearly killed & this story had not travelled far before it had added to it that it was thought I had been taking something (to drink). It is hard to please everybody, is it not?'[27]

The defeated candidate was more than satisfied with the excellent health he had enjoyed during the demanding days of the election contest. He was surprised at the way he had withstood even the last three weeks with meetings every night. Perhaps his doubts about whether he had the physical stamina for politics were unfounded. It was also reassuring to know that many of the city's prominent Liberals hoped he would run again. George A. Cox, who had been a senator since shortly after Laurier's first victory, told him that he 'must under no circumstances give up the idea of entering parliament in the near future, that simply I must be there. It may be the fates are driving me that way, but not for five years more at least. Senator Cox said a great deal more' that he would not repeat even to his favourite sister.[28]

For the present, his education had been advanced by a first hand experience of the power of the liquor interests and of the realities of race and religion in Canadian politics. Under the Laurier banner even a candidate with Rowell's impeccable Protestant and pro-British credentials was unacceptable in East York.

No one followed the East York contest more closely than Nellie Langford. When it was over she hastened to congratulate the loser on his 'non-support by the liquor men' and on having 'so nearly conquered by fair means.' She confessed to a certain limitation in her political commitment. 'I suppose if I were a real good party man, I should rejoice over the Liberal sweep but as I am only a candidate man I may be pardoned in feeling disappointed over particular results and proud of the contest rather than the result.'[29] The candidate wished that she were 'more of a party man' but he 'could scarcely be expected to wish [her] less of a candidate man. Most people are frail enough to prefer personal interest to general – as a class of the species "Liberal". Well, the fight is all over & I feel none the worse for it. The Quebec air carried me through. Strange what a tonic influence some air has.'[30]

Nellie Langford was by no means in rebellion against her upbringing in a Methodist parsonage, but she was more than ready to move out of the somewhat constricting life of small-town Methodism into the more interesting world to which her lively mind had been introduced at the university. Newton Rowell had a firm foot in both those worlds. She knew, too, that he was not as cold and aloof, as 'born solemn,' as more distant observers assumed. It was true that his quiet humour only rarely led to noisy hilarity, but he was often doubled up in silent laughter over some amusing episode. Through her friendship with Mary Rowell she was aware how often his warm affection for the members of his family was expressed in thoughtful and practical contributions to their welfare. In later years she often told him that it was the spirit in which he took the East York defeat that decided her in his favour. The magnitude of his good fortune in her decision he could not then fully comprehend, but he was happy in the knowledge that she shared his moral and religious ideals and could appreciate his interest in public affairs. Added to that, as everyone could see, Nell Langford was beautiful.

At New Year's they were engaged, an event that put them on terms of first name intimacy. The Langford family, now in Owen Sound, were scarcely surprised when Newton Rowell's weekend visit in their home culminated in the engagement announcement, and they took the news calmly. The successful suitor felt that 'perhaps they thought it was inevitable and were resigned to their fate ... Mr Langford was suffering from one of his headaches after the labors of the Sabbath & the watch night service & I think the shock must have cured him. He appeared much better afterwards.' His friends and prospective brothers-in-law, Arthur

Langford and Henry, crown attorney at Rat Portage, could not have given him a warmer welcome into the family, while his sister Mary was more excited than anyone else over the match between an idolized brother and a close friend.[31]

Henry Langford's sudden death that spring from pneumonia meant that the wedding would be a quiet one. At the end of June the ceremony took place in the First Methodist Church in Owen Sound with only the immediate relatives present and the bride's father and her brother Fred, a minister in Calgary, officiating. That afternoon the couple left on the CPR steamer for Port Arthur and Rat Portage, where Rowell was to take some cases for Henry Langford's firm and fulfil his duties as executor of the estate. A widow's home was a sombre setting for the first month of married life, but the newlyweds were glad to comfort Jennie Langford as best they could.

Early in August they began a more conventional honeymoon. Holidaying in the British Isles offered opportunities for much walking and some climbing and for visits to literary and religious shrines long familiar in imagination. In Dublin the haunts of Jonathan Swift and in Scotland those of John Knox and Sir Walter Scott were especially appreciated. Ten days in the Lake District with the two volumes of H.D. Rawnsley's recently published *Literary Associations of the English Lakes* as a guide were of absorbing interest, the highlight being Brantwood, the home of John Ruskin, for whom both travellers had the greatest admiration. On the way south there were several stops, notably at Wesley's birthplace, Epworth, 'which delighted Newton's heart,' and thence to their ultimate destination, the Third Ecumenical Methodist Conference in London.[32]

4
Shaping Canada's century

'Whether it be in the realms of peace, or on the field of war, whether it be in the Union of Methodist churches or in the front of the battle line at Paardeberg, Canada claims to be in the first place.' The delegates from around the world at the Third Ecumenical Methodist Conference listening to Rowell's report of conditions among their brethren in Canada could be pardoned for wondering whether the young Canadian was a crusader for Methodism or for Canadianism. He had no doubt that Canada would maintain her pre-eminent place. By the middle of the century, he predicted, Canada would have as many people as the present population of Great Britain (41 million) and by the end of the century as many as the present United States (75 million). The mission of Canadian Methodism, sprung from British and American parents, was to 'bind together the two great branches of the Anglo-Saxon race – one in religion, one in laws, one in language, one in hope, and one in Providential design and purpose for the world's evangelisation.'[1]

Rowell saw many strengths in the Canadian religious scene. Thanks largely to the Methodists, there was no state church in Canada: 'We have no Methodist chapels in Canada; they are all churches.' Theologically, Canadian Methodism was conservative, and essentially evangelical and practical. Forms and ceremonies meant little in Canada: 'Above the voice of the preacher who prescribes certain rules and says "He that keepeth these shall live, while he that keepeth them not shall die" is heard the voice of the prophet declaring, "What doth the Lord require of thee? But to do justly, and to love mercy, and to walk humbly with thy God?"' Nevertheless, there was at least one rule that Canadian Methodists kept: they were in the forefront of the temperance movement and boasted a clergy two thousand strong, all total abstainers.[2]

His earlier visits to England had given Rowell a first hand acquaintance with British Methodism, but the Ecumenical Conference offered an unequalled opportunity to meet its leaders. 'The Nonconformist conscience,' with its devotion to the maxim, 'What is morally wrong cannot be politically right' was at the peak of its influence. Nobody had done more to create that conscience than the independent and impassioned popular preacher, Hugh Price Hughes, still the most influential Methodist in Britain. Through his Welsh oratory and his accomplished editorship of *The Methodist Times*, Hughes had pressed the claims of 'Social Christianity' among his fellow Wesleyans and had led thousands of them to join with other Nonconformists in supporting Gladstonian Liberalism. 'The Nonconformist conscience' had demonstrated its power to create significant political issues out of Parnell's adultery, temperance, the control of prostitution, gambling and horseracing, and educational equality. After the turn of the century many Methodists felt that in concerning themselves with such issues they had gone as far as was necessary to respond to Hughes' summons, 'Let us not only save people's souls, but let us sanctify their circumstances,'[3] and they were complacent about the almost exclusively middle-class appeal of their denomination. But other Methodists were uneasily aware that for most of the working classes religion had little relevance to either their souls or their circumstances. That was the lesson Rev. J. Scott Lidgett had drawn from his Bermondsey Settlement, and it had led him to increasingly radical conclusions about the need for a reorganization of society of a magnitude that could only be achieved by the extensive intervention of the state. But his was still a minor voice, and at the Ecumenical Conference Lidgett was perhaps the only prominent Wesleyan minister with an articulate collectivist social theory.[4]

Rowell found the British debate about the proper expression of Methodist social concern in the kind of industrial society that was well established in Britain and developing in Canada intensely interesting, and he formed a number of enduring bonds with British Methodists who were active in Liberal politics. Arthur Henderson, an official of the Friendly Society of Iron Founders, and a member of the Newcastle city council, had not yet begun the parliamentary career that carried him to the front rank of the future Labour party. Walter Runciman had been defeated after one brief session in Parliament but was not to be long in returning to the House of Commons and a notable career there. At the peak of his political influence was Robert Perks, 'the member for Nonconformity,' founder and president of the Nonconformist Parliamentary Council, and one of the Empire's most successful railway builders and financiers, who was currently promoting the Georgian Bay Canal scheme in Ontario.

At the end of September they were back in Toronto, settling in their first home at 87

Crescent Road in Rosedale, the newest and most popular residential district for citizens of substantial means or good prospects. Now they looked forward to April and the birth of a child. Nell felt that if it were a boy he should bear a name from his father's family, as the first grandson of the Rowell name. But when a son arrived the baby's father thought otherwise. 'Feeling several inches taller' in his new dignity he informed the London relatives of his preference for 'William,' since he knew that 'nothing would please Nell more.' Her brother Will, a medical student at the University of Toronto, was fighting a long and losing battle against tuberculosis. Had he lived, Will Langford would have had a dual relationship to the child for he had been expected to marry Mary Rowell. Now all that could be done was to give 'dear Will' the joy of knowing 'that his name and memory would be kept ever before us'; the boy would be William Langford.[5]

Another advance in status came that year with Rowell's appointment as King's Counsel, a recognition of his growing stature as a corporation lawyer. A few months later he joined S. Casey Wood jr and his colleague of over a decade earlier, Tom Reid, in forming a new legal firm in which he was the senior partner. From the office in the Lawlor building at the corner of King and Yonge Streets he would walk home, often in the company of John Willison, who had recently left the *Globe* to become editor of the Toronto *News*, given new financial backing by J.W. Flavelle. Not infrequently in the early days of her marriage Nell fretted over a dinner growing cold while her husband stood at the corner of Bloor and Yonge settling affairs of state with Willison before proceeding home. In his two-volume biography of Laurier, just published, Willison had made the latest of his many contributions to the Liberal party, but now he was more and more disposed to sit lightly to party allegiance and had welcomed the invitation to edit the independent, sometimes Conservative, *News*. As a director of the *Globe* Rowell had participated in the naming of Willison's successor, Rev. Dr J.A. Macdonald, editor of the Presbyterian church paper, *The Westminster*, and a popular orator on subjects ranging from Burns to temperance. The publisher of the *Globe*, Robert Jaffray, and the directors believed that in Macdonald they had found a worthy upholder of the Liberal and evangelical traditions of their paper.

Over a period of many months just after Willison's departure from the *Globe*, Rowell often had occasion to discuss with him an activity that consumed much of Rowell's time. When the Ontario government decided to intervene to prevent the total collapse of the Clergue enterprises in northern Ontario, Premier G.W. Ross called on Rowell for assistance in determining the measures to be taken. It was an assignment offering large opportunities for service to the development of the province, and to two Liberal governments, and it was fully in keeping with views of the state's responsibility for economic life that Rowell found congenial. Through railway subsidies and guarantees of bonds, both the Laurier and Ross governments had a stake in the industrial empire of F.H. Clergue, whose energy and capacity as a promoter had started a variety of power, mining, and pulp and paper ventures that had grown in less than a decade to sustain ten thousand people in Sault Ste Marie and numerous shareholders elsewhere. Laurier entertained the hope that the Clergue industries would 'largely revolutionize the industrial world of Canada,'[6] although reservations about Clergue's business competence dictated refusal of government support on the scale Clergue had requested. Such reservations had proved to be well founded. Clergue's resignation from the management could do nothing to erase the errors in financing and overexpansion that had brought the Lake Superior Corporation and several of its subsidiaries to the edge of total disaster. The government of Ontario could not allow the Clergue enterprises to fail. Not only would the economy suffer from the loss of the productivity immediately involved, but the whole current mining boom in the northern part of the province might be jeopardized if prospective American investors lost confidence in enterprises in the province.

According to Willison, Rowell was 'the master mind which adjusted the relations between the Province and the company and solved the almost insuperable difficulties which were met at every step of the reorganization.'[7] The new Consolidated Lake Superior Corporation had on its Board of Directors three representatives of the Ontario government, including the president, C.D. Warren, and Rowell. Among their other duties, the government nominees were to ensure that the province's guarantee of $2 million of the bonds of the Algoma Central Railway, a subsidiary of the corporation, resulted in the early building of the railway necessary to extend timber operations north of Lake Superior and to develop the Helen Mine, already the largest iron ore producer in the province. For this work Rowell received no payment from the public treasury, although after his resignation from the Board of Directors on the defeat of the Ross government he was appointed solicitor for the Algoma Central and later did legal work for other subsidiaries of the Lake Superior Corporation.

In the meantime, Rowell had continued to play a minor part in provincial politics under increasingly discouraging conditions. He had grown tired of the perennial defence of government surpluses, with its strong appeal to the merely commercial instincts of the voters and its declining political effectiveness, and was giving a good deal of thought to the new ground that the party might occupy. Early in 1901 he had urged on Premier Ross the wisdom of the party's adopting a broad program of social reform that would appeal to the consciences of the electors. Advanced liquor legislation would be an important part of the new program and so would legislation for the Saturday half-holiday, further measures regulating conditions of factory labour, and proposals for the expansion of welfare and educational services in the province. Ross agreed that Rowell's line of argument was sound, but for the moment he saw no issue on which a rousing appeal to the electors could be made. The premier thought prohibition would not serve as a major issue, since the outcome of the challenge in the courts to the validity of Manitoba's prohibition law of 1900 had to be awaited to see whether the kind of legislation Ontario prohibitionists also wanted was within provincial powers, and 'even then we might have to pause lest we should be taking a leap in the dark.'[8]

Within a few months the Judicial Committee of the Privy Council threatened to provide a major issue when it declared Manitoba's prohibition law to be within the constitutional powers of the province. Proclaiming his faithfulness to earlier Liberal promises, Ross himself now introduced in the 1902 session of the Ontario Legislature a bill embodying provisions similar to those enacted in Manitoba. But the prohibition bill carried a rider; it would come into force only after approval in a referendum. Ross's lengthy defence of the use of a referendum within a system of British parliamentary government seemed irrelevant to the now furious prohibitionists, who contended that there had been more than enough expressions of public opinion on the subject. They had been betrayed, not by an anti-prohibitionist like Premier Rodmond P. Roblin of Manitoba who had also announced a referendum whose purposes were obvious, but by one of their own: Ross was a Past Most Worthy Patriarch of the Sons of Temperance of North America.

Within two weeks of Ross's introduction of the bill, the Dominion Alliance had organized in Toronto the largest prohibition rally ever held in Canada. The principal issue was the acceptance or rejection of the referendum, a procedure which the prohibitionists viewed as a trick since a referendum had never been mentioned in earlier government promises. Moreover, the conditions under which the referendum was to be held were stiff; to pass, it had to receive more than half of the number of votes cast in the coming provincial election, although the referendum was to be held on a different day than the election, when it would be harder to get the voters out to the polls. And what guarantee was there that the government would enforce the measure even if the referendum carried? Reluctantly, the executive of the Dominion Alliance recommended acceptance of the referendum and an all-out battle to carry it.

After the executive's policy had been sharply debated for some time, Rowell rose from his place on the platform to urge the delegates to keep their sights on the long-term interests of the temperance cause, rather than on the immediate effect they might have on the present government. He defended the premier's good faith; he had been assured by members of the cabinet that if 'the great mass of the people were in favour of the law the premier would accept the full and absolute responsibility for its enforcement.' But the government could only adopt a policy that had the support of the large public opinion that lay 'in between the liquor men and the prohibition workers. Legislation only for those in the vanguard of any great moral movement would not be supported or defended.' He thought the premier's bill imperfect and with other interested persons had already urged certain changes. Rowell now embodied these in an amendment to the resolution to support the referendum, urging the government to reduce substantially the vote needed to bring the law into force and to change the form of the referendum so that those who wished to see it defeated must come out and vote against it, rather than defeat it merely by staying away from the polls. His amendment was rejected by the convention, apparently because of the uncertainty of many delegates about its acceptability to the government.[9]

The next day Rowell was a member of a delegation from the convention which persuaded Premier Ross to postpone the referendum from the proposed date in October 1902 until December and to modify the requirement for passage to a majority of the votes cast, provided that majority equalled a majority of the votes polled in the provincial election of 1898.[10]

With the referendum postponed until the end of the year, the liquor question could not be a major issue in the general election held in the spring of 1902. 'Premier Ross Builds Up Ontario' was the Liberal theme, and Rowell's main contribution was made in several speeches on the development of northern Ontario, and, notably, as the chief defender of the government's timber policy. The Ross administration had adopted a policy of granting twenty-one-year timber cutting rights in northern Ontario under certain conditions. The Conservative opposition claimed that if timber lands were put up for sale at public auction the province would receive much larger revenues and political favouritism would be eliminated. Early in the campaign Rowell prepared a long, closely argued, and highly statistical refutation of the opposition's claims, reflecting his experience with the legal aspects of pulp concessions and his careful study of American timber laws. Reprinted over almost a full page of the *Globe*, it furnished valuable ammunition to many other Liberal speakers. Rowell contended that the timber policy being advocated by the Conservatives had been discarded half a century earlier for good reasons; if reinstituted now it would soon denude the province of timber and place vast timber resources in the hands of speculators, most of whom would be Americans. Under the conditions established by Liberal policy there was encouragement for the orderly development of timber resources, for settlement, for the growth of Canadian companies, and adequate care for long-term forest conservation. In the presentation of this complex issue Rowell had rendered an important service to his party.[11]

The party needed all the assistance it could get. The election produced a narrow Liberal victory. With only six more seats in the Legislature than the Conservatives, Premier Ross had reason to be thankful that his resort to the referendum on prohibition had removed from the election the question that might have wiped out his slight margin. But next the referendum itself, set for 2 December, had to be held. At one of the largest of the many prohibition rallies held in Toronto during the campaign, the premier urged a large affirmative vote on the question to be put in the referendum: 'Are you in favour of bringing into force the Liquor Act of 1902?' Following him, Rowell declared that all groups among the electorate could reasonably register a 'yes' vote. To prohibitionists the act was a step in the right direction, but the man who was not a prohibitionist could also support it, since he would still be permitted a drink in his own home. Against the contention that most hotels would go bankrupt if their bars were closed, Rowell urged that it was time for temperance people and travellers generally to make honest men of the hotel keepers by paying their own way and thus ending the need for such a subsidy.[12]

Nearly 200,000 Ontarians voted for the liquor act, but under the conditions of the referendum 213,723 favourable votes were needed. Although prohibition had more supporters than in the plebiscites of 1894 and 1898 and had carried by at least a simple majority in eighty-four of the ninety-seven constituencies, the referendum as a whole had not been carried. In all these plebiscites the vote for prohibition would have been overwhelming had women been able to vote, the Dominion Alliance claimed, and therefore it was clear that an impressive majority of adult citizens supported prohibition; although technically the referendum had not carried, the government could still feel justified in bringing the act into force.[13] But the Liberal majority had now been reduced to four seats and no one was surprised by the procrastination that characterized the government's treatment of the temperance issue during the next few months.

The Ross government had its hands full on several other fronts. The aftermath of the election of 1902 had been a series of charges of corruption against the government and several contested elections. A serious blow was dealt the Liberals by the defection of S.H. Blake, who publicly accused the Ross government of starting 'a carnival of corruption' that threatened to engulf the country.[14] On top of this, came 'the Gamey case,' in which the Conservative member of the Legislature for Manitoulin, R.R. Gamey, claimed to having received $5,000 from a Liberal organizer acting on behalf of the provincial secretary, J.R. Stratton, in return for an announcement of his support for the government in the recent election. A royal commission investigating the affair found no conclusive evidence of bribery,[15] but even the most faithful Liberals found it hard to believe that their party was without sin. To a generation of Ontario Liberals brought up in the belief that the party of Sir Oliver Mowat was 'the pure party,' the Gamey case marked the end of an era; one of the comforting moral distinctions in their universe had been obliterated, or at least severely blurred.

Within the next year there were eight protested elections, five in Liberal seats, and the resulting trials produced further unsavoury revelations of electoral corruption. The most spectacular was 'the case of the *Minnie M.*' It appeared to be proven beyond doubt that Liberal organizers, with the knowledge of the provincial secretary, had used the steamboat *Minnie M.*, owned by the government-subsidized Allied interests at Sault Ste Marie, to transport American personators to vote in the Michipicoten area.[16]

In an effort to clear the air and get off to a fresh start the party leaders called a provincial convention toward the end of 1904, the first such gathering since 1883. Defeated candidates in the last elections, both federal and provincial, were among the three thousand delegates, and Rowell attended in this capacity. On the first day he moved a resolution calling on the party to repudiate every form of political corruption, and to espouse legislation decreeing sterner punishment for violations of the election laws. Emphasizing that Liberals had always been against electoral abuses, as against anything that thwarted the will of the people, and that uprightness in public life was no new principle with the party, he added: 'I must confess this afternoon that it has in some respects a new application ... I say it with regret ... that there have been circumstances during the past few years which compel us as Liberals, in all honesty and sincerity, to apply some of that sincerity to the conduct of men professing to act in the interests of our own party.' Another Toronto delegate, A.T. Hunter, protested that Rowell's resolution was too general; he proposed that the convention demonstrate its convictions by adding a rider that would commit every Liberal candidate to refuse assistance from any outside organizers who had been judicially noted for corrupt practices. Along with Rowell's original motion, this rider was carried unanimously.[17]

It proved much easier for the convention to record its abhorrence of electoral corruption than to agree on a liquor policy. The prohibitionists, smarting under Ross's 'betrayal' of their cause, were determined to secure some firm commitment on the question. Another group, nervously aware that the government's small majority made an early election likely, had hoped to evade the issue altogether. When that proved impossible, a struggle developed between delegates who simply proposed to tighten the licence laws and the ardent prohibitionists who urged the immediate abolition of bars and liquor shops in every municipality or county that had given a majority for prohibition in the referendum of 1902. After hours of haggling a compromise resolution was presented to the convention, advocating the taking of a vote on the abolition of bars and shop licences at the municipal elections of 1 January 1906, a majority vote to be decisive in each case; it was further declared that no new licences should be granted in the unorganized districts of New Ontario and no new hotel sites should be sold by the government except on the understanding that no liquor was to be sold in the hotels. It was clause 3 that precipitated the angriest uproar from the floor, for it declared that in all municipalities that voted to abolish the bars and the shop licences, or either one, the vote should be final, with no provision for any future appeal to the electorate that might reverse the decision.[18] Several members of the Legislature declared that they would lose their seats and the party would be deprived of the opportunity to pass any legislation at all if this became party policy. In an attempt to save the intention of clause 3 from total defeat Rowell moved a compromise amendment which would allow a further appeal after five years to the voters in municipalities where licences had been discontinued by less than a two-thirds majority; elsewhere a vote for prohibition would be final. This still went too far for most members of the convention, and both Rowell's amendment and the original clause were voted down by large majorities.[19] With the deletion of this most disputed clause the earlier motion passed and the party was now committed to a policy of local option.

Premier Ross declared his satisfaction with the temperance plank in a party platform devoted mainly to generalizations about the economic development of the province and prepared to appeal to the people. Many of the leading spirits in the Dominion Alliance had concluded that the present Liberal party had no serious intention of adopting advanced legislation;[20] if they did not go so far as to work against the Ross government, at least they could not urge their followers to support it. Although Rowell found the temperance policy somewhat lacking in rigour he could accept it as a step in the right direction. More important in his eyes was the corruption issue; he believed the party had dealt with that firmly enough to merit his support in the election.[21] But his advocacy was less than enthusiastic and he took no active part in the campaign.

On 25 January 1905 James P. Whitney and his Conservative party won sixty-nine of the ninety-six seats in the Legislature. In contemplating their fall many Ontario Liberals were forced to agree with Dr S.D. Chown, the general secretary of the Methodist church: 'The agony is over. The Liberals of Ontario have vindicated their honor, and the Independents have once more shown their power. We join the *Globe* in saying that the victory of the Conservatives was not the defeat but the defence of the Liberal Party.'[22]

Rowell's other interests were in more flourishing condition than the fortunes of the provincial Liberal party. The law firm's steady growth was marked by the addition of two new partners, George Wilkie and Thomas Gibson, and soon the more spacious offices acquired in the Canada Life building at 46 King Street West were fully occupied. The establishment was large enough to organize its own athletics and, on Saturdays after the morning's work, the partners and the juniors in the office doffed their coats for a game of cricket on a nearby playing field. The four stenographers who watched the game and helped to consume the sandwiches and tea provided by a caterer engaged by the seniors were never convinced that the head of the firm really enjoyed himself, but he always played.

Expansion was the order of the day at home as well. A daughter, easily named Mary Coyne after her aunt, was born a few months before the family made the short move along Crescent Road to No. 134 where the new house built to their specifications was ready for occupancy. The fifteen-room, three-storey, brick house with many fireplaces and casement windows without being ornate presented an air of solid comfort. A second floor study overlooked a small gully, an offshoot of a Rosedale ravine, and its shelves were soon lined with the law books and works of history and biography which composed Rowell's growing library. Absence from the city at missionary committee meetings in Lindsay and business engagements in New York saved the head of the household from much of the confusion of the first days in the new house. Nell managed the succession of plumbers, carpenters, and painters who came and went from the unfinished house, shopped for new furnishings, and interviewed girls for the positions of cook and housemaid until all was in order.[23]

The pleasures and responsibilities of family life diminished the attractions of Sunday preaching engagements, and Rowell now took them only rarely. For a family man it was more congenial to serve as superintendent of the Sunday School at Metropolitan, a position which he accepted shortly after his marriage. This work, and his later election to the church's Board of Trustees, kept him closely involved in the activities of his own congregation. At the same time he was playing an increasingly prominent part in the wider life of the church.

In meeting for the first time west of the Great Lakes in Winnipeg in 1902 the Methodist General Conference symbolized its realization of the significance of the transformation of the prairies for the church and the nation. The assembly's consciousness of the west was evident throughout its deliberations, from the approval of plans for extending home mission work to the enthusiastic reception accorded the surprise proposal of the last day by the fraternal delegate from the Presbyterian church, Dr W.A. Patrick, principal of Manitoba College, that Methodists and Presbyterians should begin to work together for the organic unity which similarity of doctrine and excess of missionary opportunity made so imperative.

Like other Canadians, Methodists were aware that the spectacular prosperity of the whole country was due mainly to the large-scale immigration that had been gathering momentum for over five years. Fortunately, eastern Canada and the British Isles were contributing their thousands to the swelling westward movement, but they were unable to send enough people to fill up the prairies. The hordes of settlers from continental Europe and from the United States were also economic assets; unlike Canadians and Britons their arrival posed alarming questions about the future of western Canadian society.

No one presented the picture of the new west to the Conference more dramatically than Rowell. Just two years before, he told his fellow delegates, 'Ponoka' was merely a sign on a telegraph pole. Today it was a thriving town of five hundred souls. Since 1897 thousands of settlers had created Ponokas all across the prairies. Their coming was full of promise, but it brought danger as well. They 'have not been accustomed to living under free institutions ... and do not know what Anglo-Saxon civilization means ... it is our duty to assimilate these people, to give them a conception of our institutions, to furnish them with high ideals, to make of them good Canadian citizens. The schools will do much, but the church should do more, and if numbers are any criterion of responsibility, then the Methodist Church, more than any other in Canada, has the right to assume this responsibility.' He granted that settlers from the United States were a less acute problem than the Europeans, since they had known some experience of democratic government, and even if they were originally from Europe most of them now spoke English. However, they too might alter Canadian life profoundly; already they threatened the Winnipeg sabbath, and could scarcely be expected to do other than weaken British traditions on the prairies unless the existing institutions of the community made a determined effort to counteract their influence.[24] This call to the defence of Ontario's way of life was underlined, although rather obliquely, in the address of a Winnipeg Methodist, Hon. Clifford Sifton, minister of the interior in the Laurier government and architect of the vigorous immigration policy that was so drastically changing the country. Sifton warned the delegates that unless the Methodist church learned very quickly to meet the challenges presented in the west it would soon lose its position as the largest Protestant denomination in Canada.[25]

Few of the prospective prairie converts to Methodism were aware of the deliberations of church courts. Had they known of these plans for their future they might have been alarmed to learn that the Methodist Discipline was up for discussion again. As secretary of the Committee on the Discipline, Rowell reported, in the face of violent objection from the floor, that the committee had once again rejected a proposal to alter Rule 35 with its proscription of dancing, card-playing, theatre-going, and 'other diversions injurious to the spiritual life.'[26] In his observations on a number of proposals to amend the committee's recommendations, Rowell made it plain that he thought the present rule should stand. So, too, in his view should a ruling of the General Conference of 1894, which had declared a proposal to change the wording of certain sections of the Discipline to admit women to the church courts to be a constitutional amendment requiring a two-thirds majority. Rowell's motion declaring the Conference's belief that it was inexpedient to revise that decision was carried.[27]

There was much less discussion of the report from the Committee on Sociological Questions. The Conference approved unanimously its several recommendations, including one urging the Saturday half-holiday in industry, another supporting 'a living wage' for workmen, and yet another favouring control of public utilities by governments and looking to the future development of the country's natural resources by government. Since the meaning of 'control' and 'development' was left undefined, it was impossible to say precisely what role the delegates intended the state to play. Equally general was the approval given to systems of 'industrial partnership.' Less vague was the unanimous endorsation of compulsory arbitration, which was hailed as the only effective means of ending strikes. No voice was raised to question its efficacy as an instrument of social justice. For many members of the Conference the appointment of a full-time secretary for a new Board of Temperance and Moral Reform was more important than the adoption of the resolutions on industrial reform, while others saw the two steps as integral and related parts of a broad program for social advancement.[28]

No other lay delegate was on his feet more often during the meetings of the Conference than Rowell. When the standing committees were elected for the next four years his interest, especially in missions, was fully acknowledged in his appointment to the General Board of Missions, the other lay members being Chester D. Massey, Senator G.A. Cox, J.J. Maclaren, J.W. Flavelle, and J.M. Aikins. In due course, along with Massey, A.E. Ames, J.H. Gundy, E.R. Wood, and Holt Gurney, he was also appointed to the joint committee of Methodists, Presbyterians, and Congregationalists to begin consideration of church union. He was well established now as one of Methodism's lay statesmen, especially on problems concerning western Canada.

The west was also occupying a large place in the affairs of the federal Liberal party, and as the election of 1904 approached, Laurier did his best to focus attention on the broad outlines of the drama of western development, while avoiding specific commitments on the terms under which the long-promised new provinces were to be carved out of the North West Territories. In some quarters in Ontario, notably in Willison's office at the *News*, there was much anxiety about the character of the educational system to be established in the new prairie provinces, but Laurier's pre-election silence on the subject prevented the question from becoming an issue in the campaign. The spectacular industrial progress of Ontario under the Laurier regime was the dominant theme of Liberal speakers in the province. 'See Our Tall Chimneys Now' cried Liberal election posters in every city from Cornwall to Windsor and from Sault Ste Marie to Hamilton. From his place on the platform at Laurier's great Toronto rally, Rowell could almost believe that the crowd's enthusiasm for 'Laurier and a Larger Canada' was a forecast of unprecedented Liberal victories in the city. Subsequently, in several centres, he extolled Laurier's policies, none more eloquently than the government's agreement with the Grand Trunk Railway for the construction of a second transcontinental railway.[29]

Laurier's railway policy was under heavy attack from groups variously motivated and he had recently lost his minister of railways, A.G. Blair, over the latter's objection to an expansionist policy formulated and negotiated by the prime minister himself. Rowell's first-hand knowledge of the west and his optimistic assessment of its future made it easy to refute charges that a second railway was premature. Moreover, he had no dispotion to hold sacred the position of the CPR, and he had no aversion to government construction of the eastern sections of the transcontinental as provided for under the Grand Trunk agreement; he did have a decided objection to Mackenzie and Mann, the scheming railway promoters who planned to expand their own Canadian Northern Railway into a transcontinental line and who were behind a good deal of the resistance to Laurier's policy.

On election night, in a new departure in public relations, the *Globe* invited five thousand of its city subscribers to Massey Hall to watch the election returns as they were projected on a large screen. As the Liberal tally mounted and victory was hailed by successive Liberal politicians who graced the platform, Rowell responded to insistent demands from the crowd for a speech. He could only regret that five of the six Liberal candidates in the Toronto area were again going down to defeat, but he had not given up hope that Laurier would carry a majority of the Ontario seats. In the morning the completed returns showed otherwise, but the province had done fairly well by Laurier; in electing thirty-eight Liberals to forty-eight Conservatives the province had contributed significantly to the national Liberal majority of seventy-four, the largest so far obtained under Laurier's leadership. But the most solid block of Liberal support was still in Quebec.

As the first session of the new Parliament progressed, speculation about the education clauses in the 'autonomy bills' that would create the new western provinces revived. After six weeks there was no sign of a bill, but Toronto rumour had it that the one being drafted by the Roman Catholic minister of justice, Charles Fitzpatrick, would require the maintenance of separate schools. Rowell's apprehensions moved him to advise Laurier on the only acceptable course in a most delicate situation. He understood why it was politically impossible to rule out separate schools in the new provinces 'for all time to come'; at the same time, 'large and influential sections of the population' would object strenuously to legislation making separate schools mandatory. To Rowell, the way out of the dilemma was clear. Laurier must recognize 'the good Liberal doctrine of "provincial rights" and leave the new provinces free to deal with the question of education as they may deem best in the public interests.'[30]

Whatever influence his opinion might have had earlier, it could have no practical effect now. The very next day Laurier introduced the long awaited bills in the House of Commons, and the day after that he wrote to Rowell expressing confidence that his presentation of the considerations behind the government's school policy would be 'appreciated by the country ... and command your respect.'[31] Much to Rowell's regret, that was far from being the case. He was in painful and serious disagreement with the leader of his party. Laurier's proposals for Alberta and Saskatchewan appeared to re-establish and protect forever the system of separate schools instituted in the North West Territories under Dominion legislation of 1875. Since then, notably in a series of ordinances of the Territorial Legislature in 1892 and 1901, the original separate schools had been modified beyond recognition as parochial schools in any sense accepted by the Roman Catholic clergy. Indeed, Catholic parents could see so little that was distinctive in the separate schools beyond the option of a half-hour's religious instruction at the end of each day that they were increasingly reluctant to support them. In the whole of the Territories there had never been more than sixteen separate schools and now there were only eleven, despite the doubling of the total number of schools in the preceding four years. Left to the natural course of events, unbolstered by the intervention of the Dominion government, they were unlikely to play a significant part in the system of education in either province, and they might even disappear from the scene entirely.

Laurier had presented the contentious clause 16 of his bills to the Commons as an extension to new provinces of a principle that had made the original Confederation possible – the protection of the educational rights of minorities as they existed at the time of union. And he had gone further than he had ever publicly ventured before in justifying separate schools as possessing positive social and educational value.[32]

Confined to bed with a heavy cold that threatened pneumonia, Rowell did not immediately reply to Laurier. He had plenty of time to study again Pope's *Confederation Documents* and to follow the controversy in the Toronto press. There was little support for Laurier's bill anywhere in Ontario, except among Roman Catholics. The prime minister had a first class political crisis on his hands, as became abundantly clear with the resignation of the minister of the interior, Clifford Sifton. Sifton had discussed the Alberta and Saskatchewan bills with Laurier before they were drafted and had then gone off to the United States to seek relief from his arthritis believing that it had been agreed that the school clause would permit the continuation of separate schools only as they currently existed. Even that had been something of a concession on Sifton's part, and he would go no further. Now few Ontarians were reassured by Laurier's assertion that the differences between himself and Sifton were 'more of words than of substance.'[33] Sifton obviously thought otherwise.

Hoping to influence the revision of clause 16 that was reportedly under way, Rowell wrote to Laurier again at length. Like the prime minister he appealed to the spirit of Confederation, but he understood that spirit very differently. To Rowell it was evident that the basic principle concerning education to which the Fathers of

Confederation had been pledged was provincial autonomy, not the protection of minority rights. In order to bring about Confederation they had found it necessary to concede minority rights in the two Canadas. While the education clause in the British North America Act was 'somewhat broader' than clause 43 of the Quebec Resolutions, he could find neither there nor in the Confederation debates any 'ground for concluding that the real intention of leaving education to the provinces was materially modified. If the spirit as well as the letter of the British North America Act is to prevail, the new provinces whenever admitted to the union are entitled to come in with the full constitutional powers possessed by all the other provinces except the two Canadas.' No action taken by the Parliament of Canada in delegating certain powers to the territorial governments of past years could modify the rights the new provinces enjoyed at the moment of their creation and admission to the union.[34] That being so, there could be no justification for the declaration in the school clause that Alberta and Saskatchewan were to be treated as if they were already provinces. As for general considerations of present public policy, Rowell found the reasons for giving the provinces exclusive control over education just as forceful now as they had been in 1867. He entirely rejected Laurier's defence of separate schools as contributors to national development. 'While I think it is a matter for the people of the new provinces to settle themselves, yet if the Dominion is to deal with it ... my study of the conditions existing in the west at the present time would lead me to an entirely different conclusion from that at which you have evidently arrived.'[35]

As usual on questions concerning the west, there was more agitation among Ontarians than among the westerners themselves. Laurier was getting tired of Ontario, and the feeling showed in his next, somewhat acid, communication to Rowell. 'If the change in the language from the resolutions to the Act does not convey to you the certainty that the rule was laid down for all provinces coming in with a system of separate schools, nothing that I can do will change your mind, and therefore, I dismiss the subject altogether ... You will be surprised to hear that this legislation was introduced by Sir Alexander T. Galt for the protection of the minority in Quebec and all minorities similarly situated.' As for the merits of separate schools, 'I do not much care what views are held on this. I was brought up in a province where separate schools have existed for over sixty years, and perhaps my views have been tinged with this early association.'[36]

Galt's part in the educational provisions of 1867 was well known to Rowell and the reminder of it could not change his interpretation of the constitution. For Laurier's benefit he now produced a long commentary on the subtleties of the possible interpretations of the disputed resolution and of the subsequent section 93. None of them yielded any indication that the Dominion Parliament had 'the obligation to curtail the legislative powers of the new provinces in respect of education.'

Rowell could respect the opinion, held by a majority of both Catholics and Protestants, that religious instruction in the schools was necessary for the highest type of citizenship, although he did not share it; he would leave religious teaching entirely to the church and the home. That course was sound, not only religiously and educationally, but politically as well. The current controversy over education demonstrated all over again one of the first lessons of the Canadian experience. 'The views conscientiously held on this question by the different classes of our citizens are so radically different that the introduction of the question into Dominion politics ... will always produce the same unfortunate results as were produced prior to Confederation, and it is in large measure to get rid of these difficulties by relegating such matters to the provincial governments that Confederation was brought about ...' He feared that the present educational proposal would add more to the difficulties Laurier had always faced in Ontario than any other issue of the past decade.[37]

Two days later, on the second reading of the bill, Laurier presented an amended clause 16. Ontario was to have its way. The revised measure, drafted by Sifton, permitted the continuation of separate schools only in their present form. In place of the guarantee of proceeds from the sale of school lands for which the Roman Catholic minority had pleaded, there was only a general directive that in distributing public funds for education there should be no discrimination against any class of schools. This was less than the full recognition of provincial rights that Rowell had hoped for, but the bulk of the party was prepared to accept the compromise, and he would do the same.

A serious break in the party had been avoided, but the whole episode left seeds of doubt about the nature of Laurier Liberalism in the minds of many Ontario Liberals. In Rowell's good friend, John Willison, it did more than that. Believing that Laurier had forsaken 'his devotion to the federal principle and his resolute resistance to clerical interference in education,' Willison announced editorially that 'from this hour the historical Liberal party ceases to exist,' and the *News* continued its gradual movement toward the Conservative party.[38]

The school settlement found few friends among prominent Methodists; and Methodist Conferences across the country, not least the Toronto Conference, condemned it almost unanimously. In contrast, the General Assembly of the Presbyterian church declined by a large majority to discuss the question at all, while several Presbyterian ministers publicly approved the amended clause.[39]

As the dust was settling in the autonomy controversy, Rowell was out of the country. His failure to shake off his late winter cold was a sign of extreme fatigue, and his doctor had prescribed a long rest. The day after the unveiling of the amended education clause he and Nell left for New York to take ship for Naples and the beginning of three months of travel in the Middle East and the Mediterranean.

Finding themselves immersed in the sights and sounds of Moslem culture – four Sundays without a Christian service of any kind – visiting the bazaars of Cairo, the Pyramids, and the Sphinx, approaching the temples and tombs of Luxor on camel's back, were new and always fascinating experiences for both travellers. Despite much that was strange, the Easter season in the Holy Land brought them to places and Biblical associations familiar since childhood, as did shorter sojourns in Istanbul, Athens, and Rome. A thoroughly absorbing and relaxing holiday, it had the desired result.[40]

In the summer of 1906 Rowell visited western Canada again. He especially wanted to see the agricultural development in the Okanagan Valley, and departed from British Columbia the owner of some fruitland near Okanagan Centre and of thirty acres on the edge of the Coldstream Valley near Vernon that had originally been part of Lord Aberdeen's ranch. On the train east a promoter of an irrigation scheme in the Okanagan capitalized on his enthusiasm for the area and persuaded Rowell to invest a substantial sum of money in his venture. When the enterprise shortly faced bankruptcy he put more money into it, and his law partner, George Wilkie, and J.J. Warren also came to the rescue. Despite successive investments of further funds, the project never paid, although it did help to open up the country. In later years he sometimes observed jokingly that had he been warned by Nell's intuitive mistrust of the promoter of the scheme he would have been a very wealthy man.

With these impressions of the west fresh in his mind he attended the September meetings of the Methodist General Conference in Montreal. The ever-accelerating flow of immigrants to the prairies ensured that 'the problem of the west' would occupy an even larger place on the agenda of the Conference of 1906 than it had four years earlier. Since many Methodists were less than satisfied with the recent settlement of the 'autonomy issue' they were more than ever conscious of the heavy religious and cultural responsibilities that lay upon their church in shaping a Protestant future for the west. A major controversy developed in the Conference over the best means of carrying this burden, and for the special correspondents sent to Montreal to cover the meetings for the Toronto papers it soon surpassed all other subjects of debate in news value.

Since the last General Conference Rowell had been chairman of the Standing Committee on Missions, and he now had to give an account of its work. The committee had concluded that the whole organizational structure of Methodist missionary work must be changed radically if the demands of the mission fields at home and abroad were to be met. For many years there had been one general secretary for both home and foreign missions, plus several field secretaries for specific areas. Rowell's committee now proposed that this arrangement be abolished and that there be four general secretaries, two for each branch of missions. In his advocacy of the new plan, Rowell charged that 'routine has choked leadership; that the progress which is being made is due to the weight, mass, and innate zeal of Methodism rather than to the laying of farseeing plans, the quick adjustment of means to ends, the clear thinking which make zeal irresistible, and multiply the effects of energy.'[41] Rowell and the group of younger men, both clergy and laymen, who provided most of the support for the reorganization, soon realized that change could not be made easily. They had to contend with the Rev. Dr Alexander Sutherland, who had been general secretary of the Board of Missions for thirty-two of his seventy-two years and not unnaturally felt that his own administration was under attack. 'I have no complaint or regret at what has been accomplished in the past, however imperfect you may think it,' he told the Conference. 'Whatever the Missionary Society of the Methodist Church is to-day, by God's help I made it, and let no man rob me of my boasting.' As for the new scheme: 'There can be no efficiency with two heads ... anything with two heads is a monstrosity.'[42]

It was difficult to battle unreservedly against an elderly and respected churchman, but much was at stake and the reformers pressed on to rebut the arguments of Dr Sutherland and his supporters. Obviously enjoying the fight, the correspondent of the Toronto *World* wrote: 'Mr Rowell drew his rapier to-day and passed it again and again through the corpus. The general secretary got up, however, and made a vicious stab under the young advocate's fifth rib. J.W. Flavelle, LLD, then arose with a bishop's mace and bludgeoned the game old warrior in approved ecclesiastical fashion. He drew no blood but you could hear the dull thuds.'[43] Rowell and the heralds of the new order carried the day, and large plans were launched to raise the funds necessary to make the reorganization effective in action.

Much of the new zeal that appeared among North American Protestants in the decade before the first world war was expressed in the Laymen's Missionary Movement, organized in the United States in 1906. In the following year Rowell took a leading part in introducing the movement into Canada, where some of its American leaders, including John R. Mott and Robert E. Speer, were already well known. Rowell had early formed a high opinion of Speer's mixture of mysticism and practical good sense and this was the beginning of a friendship lasting many years. The appeal of the Laymen's Missionary Movement, with its motto, 'The Evangelization of the World in This Generation,' was many-sided. Its interdenominational character made it a manifestation of the Protestant co-operation he was already advocating in Canada. Perhaps even more appealing was the social context in which the movement saw its task, for its leaders' conception of evangelism was broader than 'plucking brands from the burning' for the next world; heaven was by no means ruled out, but the evangelization of mankind was to bring the dawn of social betterment and international peace for all men in this world.

But could such a program be financed? Clearly the Lord had prospered North American laymen beyond all others in Christian history. If enough of them responded to the mixture of social Darwinism, humanitariansim, national pride, and self-interest on which the movement rested, its financial resources would be formidable. Even if only a few of the very wealthiest laymen could find, in the offering of their millions for the evangelization of the world, a balm for guilty consciences acquired in the attainment of wealth, spiritual welfare at home and abroad would be well served. Any prosperous Canadian Methodists who felt such a need would be robbed of their comfort if they took seriously the statement of their own church's Committee on Sociological Questions in 1906. While commending those who gave 'for the higher things of civilization,' the committee (whose membership included none of the wealthiest business men present but several professors and preachers) declared that philanthrophy could not 'make restitution or reparation for wrongs perpetrated in the iniquitous acquisition of wealth. The blood of the oppressed toiler will continue to cry to heaven for justice, notwithstanding the high plaudits with which these gifts are greeted.'[44]

The international implications and the monetary responsibilities of an intensive foreign missions program were emphasized in an address Rowell gave before an audience in Parkdale Methodist Church in Toronto in the winter of 1907. How could the influence of Christian missions on the life of the nations where the gospel was preached be assessed? 'The least result, in one sense,' Rowell replied, 'is the number of converts added to the church. The larger and more important results are the great changes wrought in the whole social and intellectual life and character of the people.' Protestants had been slow to realize this truth: 'until recently the Roman Catholic Church alone possessed the imperial vision of the universal domination of our Lord and sought to make that vision real.' Protestants should forget their differences, as they were increasingly doing, and 'sympathetically and energetically co-operate in the establishment of this Empire.'[45]

With the whole world for a parish was there any area that had priority? In Rowell's view the most strategic mission field was in China, 'where more than one-fourth of the human race is awakening from the sleep of ages' and education, science, and the changing status of women had begun a social revolution weighted with consequence for all nations. 'That great English statesman who has given his life service to China,' Sir Robert Hart, inspector general of the Chinese customs service, had declared that '"China is today the greatest menace to the world's peace unless she is Christianized."' Since all the foreign mission work of Canadian Methodists was in China and Japan their influence could be decisive indeed.[46] He might have added that the recent agreement by the Methodist church in Canada to join with American Methodists and Baptists and British Quakers in the establishment of West China Union University in Chengtu province was an important advance in China, and one in which he and J.W. Flavelle, as founding members of the Board of Governors, were taking an active part.

If Canadian Christians honoured their obligations overseas it would cost them a great deal more than they were now spending on foreign missions, a fact which Rowell frequently tried to bring home to his audiences. His penchant for statistics produced some astonishing figures when applied to evangelism: In 1907 the Anglo-Saxon world as a whole was supporting 85 per cent of all Protestant missionary activity, with Great Britain bearing as much of the load as the United States and Canada together. Obviously this was an unfair division of labour; on the basis of one missionary for every 25,000 persons, North Americans ought to be responsible for the conversion of 500 million people, or 50 per cent of the total. Canada's share of this would be one-twelfth, or about 40 million, one-third of whom should be the care of Canadian Methodists. At the present rate of contribution all Canadian Protestants together were raising only about $600,000 a year for foreign missions – enough to evangelize only 7$^1/_2$ million in the near future. Clearly they would have to do better to meet their quota.[47]

The energy Rowell devoted to the cause of foreign missions in no way diminished his concern about western Canada, and he hoped that home missions too would benefit from the growth of the Laymen's Missionary Movement. In an address at Victoria University in the early autumn of 1908 he pointed out that 30 per cent of the immigrants now reaching the prairies were non–English-speaking, and that the dangers and wastage of overlapping among the Protestant churches in their work with these people as well as with British and American immigrants grew more obvious every year. Rowell warned his audience of clergy, faculty, and students, not to make the mistake of thinking that the immigrants to western Canada were like the New Englanders who came to America in search of freedom of worship; the present newcomers sought 'solely to improve their material conditions' and the church must ensure that 'they did not get bread alone ... If a man is to live in decency, comfort, and security, if old age is to be revered, infancy protected, womanhood honoured and human life held in due regard – if we are to establish and maintain those Christian institutions which are the crowning glory of our civilization, the way must be cleared, the foundations laid and the life of the community constantly inspired by the Gospel of Christ.'[48]

The role of the church in western Canada was the one given greatest emphasis a few weeks later when Rowell and three other Toronto businessmen visited several cities in the west to help organize local committees of the Laymen's Missionary Movement and to arouse interest in the National Congress of Laymen planned for the following year in Toronto. His companions were another Methodist, H.H. Fudger, president of the Robert Simpson Company, and two Baptists, S.J. Moore, president of a firm distributing business forms (later the Moore Corporation), and James Ryrie, head of one of Toronto's oldest and largest jewellery concerns; they were accompanied by Campbell White, the American executive secretary of the Laymen's Movement, and in the west were joined by W.H. Cushing, minister of public works in the Liberal government of Alberta. Rowell, as the chief orator of the group, enjoyed many favourable comments from the press, typified by a Calgary reporter's description of his address to a local businessmen's banquet: 'Seldom has this city ever heard so inspiring and thrilling an address.' Rowell's argument that religion was being left too much to women, children, and young people, carried a good deal of weight with the men, 'including many of very good standing in business who have not been known to be too interested in religion.'[49]

Rowell's increasing awareness of the social implications of religion and his interest in Christianity as a civilizing influence at home and abroad never, as in some men, became in the least a substitute for personal faith. Always there were family prayers before breakfast. Early in 1908 his son Edward Newton, born only seven months earlier, died suddenly of an undiagnosed illness. There was less cause for sorrow in Rowell's mother's death a month later at the age of eighty-one. Rather, that was an occasion for resolving again to follow her good example of faith in God and service to others, and for assurances to his sister Mary that, although her mother was gone, she was cherished by him and his family. Langford, now nearly six, took great pleasure in imagining how much his grandmother and his baby brother were enjoying one another's company in heaven. Although Newton Rowell did not share the child's interest in the precise character of family relationships on 'the other side,' he was no less convinced of their reality. Perhaps the loss of the baby helped to reinforce his determination to try to spend more time at home. Some weeks he saw little of the two children except on Sundays, which were always free of work. Sometimes he got home from the office on a Saturday afternoon in time to join the children in sleighriding down the hill beside the house or in walking through Rosedale, but these enjoyable occasions were all too rare. On Sunday evening there was usually hymn singing and marching with the children, followed by his vivid telling of a Bible story and a prayer.[50]

The work of his law firm could have consumed every waking hour. He was at the top of his profession, and there were always more cases available than he and his partners could handle. He continued to serve as solicitor for the Algoma Central Railway, and also acted for the Nipigon Pulp and Paper Company. For nearly two years much of his time was occupied as counsel for the town of Kenora in two cases brought against the town by the Keewatin Power Company and the Hudson's Bay Company. At issue were the expropriation procedures followed by Kenora and compensation for land on the banks of the Winnipeg River and on three islands in the river.[51] Rowell lost the case, but not before he had become learned in the geography of the Lake of the Woods district, the terms of surrender of the Hudson's Bay Company charter, and the interpretation of Mowat's 'Rivers and Streams' legislation of 1884.

Much earlier history was involved in determining the ownership of lands at Oka on the Island of Montreal, originally granted to the Sulpician Order in 1663, and in dispute over a period of many decades. In the latter half of the nineteenth century some of the Oka Indians were converted from Roman Catholicism to Methodism, and in 1907 when the Department of Indian Affairs referred the land dispute to the courts Rowell was appointed by the Dominion government to act for the Methodist Indians. With customary thoroughness he dispatched one of the firm's juniors, R.S. Fairty, to Paris to spend a month poring over the early documents concerning the land grants in the archives of the Conseil de Marine.[52] The interests of the Methodist and non-Methodist Indians were shortly combined and represented by a Montreal lawyer, and Rowell did not continue in the case, which the Indians eventually lost.

In a general practice like the one conducted by Rowell's firm there was no predicting the next area of involvement. Rowell's agreement to represent Chester B. Duryea of New York in a suit against the Edwardsburg Starch Company and its manager for breach of patents and secret processes introduced him in detail to the distinctions between glucose, maltose, and modified starch, and left his 'devil' feeling that both he and Rowell were well qualified as superintendents in a corn syrup plant, although they lost the case.[53]

Closely related to the thoroughness for which he was now famous was his capacity for becoming completely and happily absorbed in the case at hand, whatever the new fields of knowledge it might involve, and for presenting the relevant data fully and clearly. With his election in 1911 as a bencher of the Law Society of Upper Canada came the pleasure of recognition and honour from the leaders of his profession.

During the first decade of 'Canada's century' Newton Rowell had become established as one of Toronto's ablest corporation lawyers, a leader among Canadian Methodists, and a person of some influence in the Liberal party. In the course of his work he was closely associated with businessmen interested in the development of the resources of northern Ontario and western Canada in a period of unprecedented growth, an experience that encouraged in Rowell an almost unlimited enthusiasm for Canada's future greatness. But he was not an exponent of material progress for its own sake, nor an uncritical advocate of policies congenial to the business community.[54] He was apprehensive about the effects of industrialization on Canadian life and convinced that, given the right direction, Canada could avoid the concentration of wealth and the social evils bedevilling urban communities in older societies. That direction must in large measure be provided by the state. While much of his work was with companies financed by American capital and involved frequent trips to New York on legal business, his Methodist inheritance and imperial sentiment disposed him to look to British precedents for social legislation adaptable to Canadian needs. Although he sometimes spoke in 'social gospel' tones and as an officer of the Moral and Social Reform Council of Canada was committed to that body's broad program of social reform, he was not a leader in the social gospel movement and his social philosophy stopped far short of the Christian socialism of the radical social gospellers.[55]

Industrialization was not the only source of alarm in a changing Canada. Like his business associates and English Canadians generally, Rowell welcomed the large-scale immigration of these years because it was economically desirable. At the same time he was an eloquent spokesman for the fears aroused among Anglo-Saxon Protestants by the arrival of large numbers of 'new Canadians' from Europe. Paradoxically, the immigrants who were so essential to the economic expansion which would make Canada a great nation, able to assume a large share of the burden Providence had assigned to the Anglo-Saxon peoples in leading mankind into the paths of democracy and Christian civilization, also threatened that destiny. Like many Ontarians, Rowell possessed an 'Ontario nationalist' dream of western Canada in which the public schools and the Protestant churches would Canadianize and Christianize the European immigrants to create beyond the Great Lakes a 'new Ontario.' If that dream were unrealized Canadian society would be gravely altered for the worse and Canada's contribution to the world severely restricted.

In his concern for the character of Canadian society Rowell was within the firmly established tradition of Canadian Methodism, given new intensity by the challenges presented by current social and economic conditions.[56] In the social and religious imperialism of the vigorous missionary movement of the English-speaking world in the early twentieth century his Canadian nationalism found an even grander meaning beyond the seas where Canada's destiny became part of the larger purposes of God for the world.

Much was at stake in the shaping of Canada's century.

5
Higher criticism and Canada's destiny

At the end of February 1909, Rowell returned to Toronto after three weeks' absence on legal business in New York to find Toronto Methodism engaged in a theological feud so intense that prominent church members were attacking one another in the public press. He was immediately alarmed. The controversy would scarcely have a salutary effect on the forthcoming National Congress of the Laymen's Missionary Movement, now only a month away. Could the delegates and the world take that great gathering as seriously as they should if there was no agreement about what gospel was to be preached?

The row had been precipitated four days earlier when Dr Albert Carman, the general superintendent of the Methodist Church and chairman of the Board of Regents of Victoria College, wrote a letter to the *Globe* attacking the views of Rev. George Jackson, recently appointed professor of English Bible at Victoria, and objecting to the arrangement under which he had come to Canada from the British Wesleyan church. The general superintendent charged that in a recent address on 'Early Narratives in Genesis' to a group in the YMCA Jackson had claimed that 'a correct theory of the origin of the universe, the origin of the human race, and the origin of sin, is no part of the Christian faith.' That statement, said Carman, showed 'very superficial and attenuated thinking.' On the contrary, 'the record of sure and certain facts is not a myth, a fancy, a legend, no matter how gorgeous or how simple the rhetoric ... It is not an achievement to startle the uninstructed youth of the Young Men's Christian Association ... by attacking the historicity of Holy Writ on points absolutely unassailable, if we have any Christian faith at all, thus loosening moral bonds, debauching the public mind, and producing ten or a hundred doubters, when, as he boasts, he might forsooth effect the cure of one or two.' Referring to the arrangement under which Jackson had first come to Canada to become the minister of Sherbourne Street Church in Toronto as one that he trusted 'may never be repeated in our Methodism,' Carman said that Jackson was neither a minister nor a member of the Canadian Conference, and his expression of his questionable views was a violation of the hospitality extended to him.[1]

Jackson's reply to Carman had been published in the next day's *Globe*. After eighteen years in an honourable position in British Methodism, Jackson believed that he deserved better than to be 'treated as some poor clerical vagrant at the door of Canadian Methodism.' At the same time he stated briefly the view that the Bible must be understood as a revelation of spiritual truth and not as a textbook on history or science.[2] In the same paper Rowell read a letter accorded special prominence on the front page. It was from J.W. Flavelle, a member of the pulpit supply committee of Sherbourne Church. Flavelle accused the general superintendent of his church of 'holding up to contempt a gentle-spirited man ... in a manner from which a man in the ordinary walk of life, among those you term Godless people, would be protected by the instinct of good breeding, untempered by the grace of religious profession.' Members of all denominations were 'shocked and distressed,' said Flavelle, by 'the bitter spirit of the heresy hunter' evident throughout Carman's letter. 'There are many men who are not members of Christian churches who walk softly in the presence of the problems of sin and misery ... and there is an ever increasing body of men identified with every branch of the Christian Church who profoundly sympathize with them in their anxious enquiry as to how the teachings of the New Testament can be applied to these problems, and how the baneful effect of intolerant ecclesiasticism and churchly pretension can be minimized.'[3] The pulpit supply committee of Sherbourne Church had also come to Jackson's support with a public statement explaining the circumstances under which he had come to Canada, circumstances that Carman had fully understood and approved at the time, and expressing complete satisfaction with the service he had given at Sherbourne Street and to Canadian Methodism as a whole.[4]

Carman had then confronted both Jackson and Flavelle in a statement to the *Globe*, defending his action in every respect. 'I spoke ... for the Methodist Church from ocean to ocean and not merely for Toronto Methodism ... A firm believer in the integrity, sufficiency, and trustworthiness of Holy Scripture must in these days take his stand ... A plain declaration brings things into the light and that which maketh manifest is light.'[5] In the same issue of the *Globe*, Chester D. Massey declared Carman's attack to be 'as intolerant as an encyclical of a medieval Pope ... Mr Jackson ... has done more since he came to Toronto to elevate the standard of pulpit efficiency in Canadian Methodism than any other clergyman in the Dominion ... A crying need of the Methodist Church is more ripe scholarship in the pulpit, and more earnest study of the Bible such as we see in the work of the Rev. George

Jackson.' In Massey's observation of the religious scene 'those who are attacked as modern critics of the Bible bear more of the spirit of Christ than those who bitterly oppose them. Surely if anything can stand the searchlight of investigation through all the ages it is the Word of God. I am not afraid to trust my Bible in the hands of such men as Mr Jackson – humble, evangelical, Christ-like students of the Word.'

Without waiting to investigate recent events any further, Rowell decided to write to Carman. He had not yet read what Jackson had actually said, but for the moment that was not the point. If Carman had correctly quoted Jackson then Rowell regretted the public expression of such views. But whatever had been said he was convinced that Carman had attributed to Jackson a spirit entirely foreign to him; nothing could justify Carman's attack through the press. Rowell had come to know Jackson well in the past two summers when they occupied neighbouring summer cottages on Lake Simcoe and had always found him 'a most lovable, devout and reverent man' and an effective and sound preacher. If by any chance Jackson's views did 'contravene the standards of the Methodist Church,' he told Carman, then 'our Discipline provides all the machinery necessary to deal with the situation and it is under disciplinary conditions that the charge, if any, should be made.' Unfortunately, as Rowell could see only too plainly from his reading of the newspapers of the last few days, it was too late to confine the matter to the church courts. He could only plead with Carman to desist from further public strife. 'The agitation of the matter in the public press ... can only tend to provoke a theological controversy in our church from one end of the country to the other, and divert the thought and attention of the members of our church from the great missionary movement toward which we have been endeavouring to direct their attention.'[6]

Carman replied at once, professing sympathy with Rowell's alarm at the possible effect of the controversy on the Missionary Congress which was claiming so much of his energy; but 'it is no use Brother Rowell to labor to raise money for missions if these destructive critics are to be nursed in our bosom ... Mr Jackson stops for the present with eleven chapters but the others do not.' Contrary to Rowell's opinion, Jackson could not be dealt with in the courts of the Canadian Conference of the church, and therefore it was necessary to act outside the established channels to stop him and the men who supported his heresies.[7]

The tone of Carman's letter was scarcely encouraging, and Rowell knew the general superintendent well enough to realize that he was not a man likely to give up a stand once taken. Carman was accustomed to command. He had been the last bishop of the Methodist Episcopal church in Canada before the union of that body in 1884 with the Wesleyan Methodists and other smaller Methodist groups had made him general superintendent of the new and larger church. He remained in spirit a bishop of imperious temper, much admired for his administrative skill and Puritan self-discipline but little loved in the church for any manifestation of the gentler aspects of religion.[8] In the public mind, Carman was well established as a didactic defender of the faith. Although he had once taught physics at the Methodist academy, Albert College, in Belleville, his brush with science had done nothing to ease his passage to an appreciation of new Biblical theories. On a previous occasion, in 1891, he had been a prime mover in securing the departure from Victoria College of Dr G.C. Workman, whose denial that the messianic prophecies of the Old Testament had any direct reference to the Christ of the New Testament threatened orthodox views of prophecy. Subsequently, Dr Workman had been appointed to Wesleyan Theological College, Montreal, where he was soon under attack again. As a member of the church's Court of Appeal Rowell had supported the right of the Board of Governors of Wesleyan College to appoint a committee to consider Dr Workman's doctrinal position. That board, of which Dr Carman was a member, had then dismissed Dr Workman. An appeal by his supporters to the Court of Appeal during the winter of 1907 and another in 1908 for a review of his dismissal had both been rejected. During these proceedings Rowell was an apparently silent member of the Court of Appeal,[9] but their outcome, which was viewed as extremely regrettable by scholars like Chancellor Nathaniel Burwash and Professor R.P. Bowles of Victoria, whom Rowell knew and respected, may have informed his opinion that this new controversy over Jackson should go to the Court of Appeal directly. The Workman controversy had been confined mainly to theological and intellectual circles and had evoked little interest among the general church membership.[10] Dr Carman had made sure that such would not be the case with the Jackson controversy. There was no alternative but to be prepared for his next move.

Rowell began by finding out exactly what Jackson had said in the address that had so aroused Dr Carman. He was not expecting to be shocked. Jackson had asserted that multitudes had silently surrendered their Christian faith because it had been presented to them 'bound up with doctrines concerning man and the universe which they now know to be false.' In discussing the Biblical stories of the Creation, the Fall, the Flood, and the Tower of Babel, he had argued that new truth was to be found in these myths and legends through 'the science of literary and historical criticism which is one of God's best gifts to the intellectual life of our generation.' Rowell discovered that Carman had misquoted Jackson in charging him with having said that 'a correct theory of the origin of the universe ... of the human race ... and of sin, is no part of the Christian faith.' In fact, Jackson had said that 'a *precise* theory' was not essential,[11] a difference of considerable significance in Rowell's eyes.

There was nothing here to provoke a crisis of faith in Rowell. He had moved among the clergy and professors of theology at Victoria enough to understand the general influence on recent theology of the historical criticism of the German scholar Harnack and his continental and British followers. His friend R.P. Bowles had described to him a dramatic moment in his student days when Dr Burwash had begun his lectures on Isaiah by pushing aside his notebooks with the declaration: 'Gentlemen, I would be dishonest if I continued to lecture from these notes. We now have a new and better method of understanding this material.'[12] In the more than twenty years since then, a succession of theological students had been exposed to 'higher criticism' at the hands of Burwash and other Victoria professors. In himself Burwash embodied a reconciliation of science and religion, for he had taken his first degree in science at Yale and had been professor of natural history and geology at Victoria before joining the faculty of theology. Many Methodists had been sustained and even encouraged in their Biblical studies by the recognition that John Wesley himself had held no doctrine of a completely literal and infallible Bible and thought that human life had developed through a process of gradual change.

Knowing all this, Rowell was also aware that the new approach to the Bible had made its way slowly among the general church membership, sometimes because of outright resistance from the clergy, but more often because preachers were doubtful about the capacities of their congregations to absorb the new theology without disturbing consequences and therefore tried to avoid the issues raised by Biblical criticism. In response to the determination of a growing number of younger ministers who shared the conviction of their professors that the faith of Methodists could be conserved only if more laymen were acquainted with the best modern scholarship, the Ontario Conferences of the church had co-operated in the winter of 1905–6 in sponsoring 'District Institutes for the Extension of University Teaching in Biblical Literature and Church History.' Through these institutes many laymen had their first explicit and systematic encounters with unfamiliar approaches to the Bible. For some the experience brought a welcome intellectual freedom, but to others it occasioned only anguish of soul. Rowell's sister Sara was one whose attendance at courses given by Rev. Elmer Crummy (Old Testament), Rev. A.J. Irwin (New Testament), and Rev. Alfred Lavell (Church History) elicited protests against the church's sponsorship of 'false teachers.' So devastating was the influence of the institute held in London, Ontario, that some formerly prominent Methodists were now taking a lead in plans to build a Unitarian church. In common with hundreds of other confused church members, Sara Wright appealed to Dr Carman for guidance on the 'sadly perplexing question' of the authority of the Bible.[13] Confidence in Dr Carman's power to make tradition prevail was no doubt weak among the many Methodists who had read the popular novel published by his son Albert in 1900. Carman had failed with his own family. *The Preparation of Ryerson Embury* was a tale of a student in a college that sounded suspiciously like Victoria who had lost his early literalist religion and after much struggle had won through to a liberal Christianity that impelled him to give serious consideration to 'the industrial question' and to embark on a career as a labour lawyer.

Rowell's anxiety about the success of the Missionary Congress was only the most immediate cause of his active interest in the attack on Jackson. He had other reasons for concerning himself with it. As a member of the Board of Regents of Victoria he had some responsibility for the welfare of the college. Moreover, he had had a good deal to do with bringing Jackson to Canada. Before they met at the Ecumenical Conference in London in 1901, Rowell was acquainted by hearsay with Jackson's work. A Yorkshireman and a minister of the British Wesleyan church, Jackson was at that time the pastor of a flourishing Methodist congregation in Edinburgh. He had made a name for himself, especially among the better educated, as a scholarly and powerful preacher to whom Scots, even in the citadel of Presbyterianism, listened with approval. On learning that Jackson was to give a series of lectures in the United States in the summer of 1902 Rowell had arranged that he should come to Canada as well. Consequently, Jackson travelled from Montreal to Vancouver preaching in a number of the larger centres to congregations which included many recently migrated Scots who had known him in Edinburgh. He spent some time in Toronto where he was heard with appreciation by many of the leading Methodist laymen in the city and by the faculty of Victoria College.[14]

The rest of the story was known to Rowell too, but he rehearsed its complexities now in order to stand on firm ground with Carman. When Jackson first received an invitation to Victoria in 1905 he already knew enough about the religious climate in Toronto to realize that the controversy over fundamentalism and higher criticism was exciting much interest in church circles there. As a 'higher critic' he had enquired whether the position at Victoria would offer the same degree of intellectual freedom he enjoyed in Britain. To make sure that his position was understood he had forwarded a copy of an address on Biblical interpretation delivered two years earlier at Wesleyan University in Middletown, Connecticut. Chancellor Burwash had been entirely reassuring: 'As to intellectual freedom, some of us have fought that battle here, and I think the course is perfectly clear.'[15] The committee on academic appointments was unanimous in its invitation to Jackson to accept the position of professor of homiletics. After due consideration Jackson decided that he would prefer to preach rather than to teach others to preach, and he declined the invitation. Thereupon, the minister of Sherbourne Street Church, Rev. R.P. Bowles, was appointed to the position in the college. When Bowles suggested to the several members of the college Board of Regents who were active in Sherbourne Street Church, including H.H. Fudger, Senator G.A. Cox, and J.W. Flavelle, that they should secure Jackson for the Sherbourne pulpit they readily agreed, for they shared Bowles's belief that Jackson would bring strength to Canadian Methodism at a time when 'the intellectual and cultural life of the people had advanced beyond the prevailing type of preaching and a reaction was setting in.'[16]

Jackson had accepted the invitation to the Sherbourne Street pulpit for a three-year period and had taken up his duties there in the autumn of 1906. Technically, his position in the Methodist Church in Canada was a little unusual; he did not sever his formal connection with the British Methodist Conference because he wanted to retain his interest in its benevolent funds, since he would have no claim on the Canadian pension fund under his three-year temporary appointment. To keep the procedure in line with Canadian church practice another minister was appointed as superintendent of the church, but it was understood that he would be the assistant and Jackson the pastor. Of considerable importance now that Carman was attacking Jackson was the fact that this whole arrangement had been made with the full approval of the highest church officials, including Carman himself.[17]

From the beginning, Jackson had preached to large and appreciative congregations in Toronto, but he was embarrassed by the automatic assumption in many quarters that an established minister of the Methodist church in the mother country would naturally be a recruit for the battle against the new and heretical views of the Bible. Like other ministers he realized that in the average sermon it was unnecessary to explain precisely the exegetical theories on which the exposition of doctrine or moral teaching rested. It was possible to avoid attacking the problem head on, but he was worried lest silence be cowardice and wondered whether he should declare himself. Bowles advised him to wait awhile until he was better known to his congregation and the Methodist community generally. In the summer of 1907 Jackson had been goaded into action. A visiting lecturer at a Methodist Bible school held near Toronto had denounced the leading British Biblical archaeologist of the last half of the nineteenth century, George Adam Smith, as an atheist. This was too much for Jackson to take in silence. He wrote a letter to the *Globe* contending that Smith's discovery of similarities between the creation myths and other stories in the Old Testament and the myths of other cultures was an aid rather than a hindrance to understanding the Bible; he declared flatly that Smith was not an atheist. Jackson followed this up very shortly by addressing his Men's Bible Class on 'What is Higher Criticism?' The men of the Sherbourne Street congregation were keenly interested and at their request Jackson repeated his talk for the benefit of their wives and older children and during the following winter gave a series of lectures on problems in Old Testament scholarship to the men's class in the church. At least in Jackson's own congregation his teaching had proved acceptable.[18]

As Rowell reviewed these developments of the last few years he was puzzled about why Carman had gone back on his earlier approval of inviting Jackson to a position in the Canadian church. Was it because the general superintendent had failed to understand Jackson's theological position four years ago? Or was it that he was prepared to tolerate Jackson in a single pulpit, but considered him much more dangerous in the chair of English Bible at Victoria? In the latter capacity Jackson would be lecturing to the more than 40 per cent of the general student body who elected religious knowledge courses,[19] as well as to candidates for the ministry in the faculty of theology. Whatever lay behind Carman's attack it seemed clear that he was determined to prevent Jackson from taking up his appointment in the college in the coming fall term. The harm he might do in the process was increasingly painful for Rowell to contemplate.

A second and fuller letter to the general superintendent might help. Rowell thought possibly both the YMCA and Jackson were in error in giving the disputed lecture before a young men's group, 'but if all were to be anathematized for errors of judgment very few of us would stand much chance in this life or in the life to come.' However, that was the least important aspect of the matter. He believed that Carman had misinterpreted Jackson so seriously, in substituting the phrase 'correct theory' for 'precise theory,' that a public apology was required from Carman. It had been common knowledge for years that many respected Methodists did not adhere to the belief in the verbal inspiration of scripture which Carman seemed to require, and all Rowell's own reading and discussion with theologians confirmed his view that there was no specific theory of inspiration in the Methodist church. More serious than the content of the dispute was the method Carman had adopted in attacking Jackson.

> The right to a trial in the properly constituted Courts of the church is the right of every member of the Methodist Church, under the Discipline … For the General Superintendent or any officer of the church to prejudge any minister's case and to impair, if not destroy his usefulness, by any official pronouncement on his conduct, is … contrary to the spirit and Constitution of our Church. If … you hold to the other view … no man's character as a member of the Methodist Church is safe, and the guarantee in the Constitution of our Church of a fair trial by a man's peers, is a delusion.

But the lawyer and member of the Court of Appeal could see even broader implications in Carman's position. 'Nothing can be more paralyzing to the intellectual and spiritual life of our church than any effort to force the thought and convictions of the men of our church into some cast iron mould, particularly when it is a matter which beyond all doubt is a non-essential to the Christian faith and life.' Finally, he returned to the practical and 'disastrous consequences' that would ensue if Carman pursued his present course of action. If adequate funds for missions were not forthcoming or the union of the churches was delayed because of 'a barren theological controversy' the responsibility would lie largely at Carman's door.[20]

Carman's assurance to Rowell that he did not believe in verbal inspiration and that all would be well if Jackson would only say that he accepted '*the facts*' of the creation and fall was of little help.[21] The very next day Carman broke into print again in the *Globe*, but not with the public apology Rowell had recommended. Far from retracting any of his previous charges Carman elaborated on them: 'I saw a power in the church interfering with its pulpits and pastoral arrangements ... if one church could call in from abroad a man in no way responsible to us, another could do the same thing. Where then should we land?' As for doctrine, Carman charged that Jackson had claimed that all anyone needed to understand the Bible was common sense. For Carman common sense was not enough: 'I do not find a word about the Supernatural, or Miracles, or Revelation, and scarcely a breath about Inspiration ... With this marvellous rule of interpretation Gladstone's impregnable rock of Holy Scripture is levelled by a whiff of Huxley's breath ... What need of Bradlaughs and Ingersolls if they are out-Bradlaughed and out-Ingersolled by doubtful liveries within the precincts of the House of God?' Turning to critics of his methods, the seventy-six-year-old Carman boasted: 'They say the old man is dogmatic, given to high ecclesiasticism, and good material for a pontiff of the Middle Ages. So far as the pontiffs of the Middle Ages stood by the Word of God and the rights of their ministers I am with them. Dogmatic! and why not? I grew up in a dogmatic country, in a dogmatic age and among a dogmatic people. We demand facts and build our business and our religion on facts and not on theories.'[22]

Still lamenting the harm Carman was doing to missionary enthusiasm and exhorting the general superintendent to behave like 'the Apostle James, who by his wise and Christianlike decision preserved the peace of the early church,' Rowell decided to tackle him face to face. Within a few hours of the publication of Carman's second letter Rowell asked for an appointment.[23] When they met, Carman suggested that Jackson and he should each publish statements defining their positions so that the public would know exactly where they stood. Rowell rejected this proposal, believing that it would simply aggravate the dispute. Instead, he persuaded Carman that if any further public pronouncements were to be made they should be issued by the Board of Regents.[24] In the earnest hope that it would end the dispute, Rowell, Rev. R.P. Bowles, and H.H. Fudger prepared a draft statement which they discussed with Carman and Chancellor Burwash before its submission to the full Board of Regents.[25] On Sunday, Jackson, on Rowell's suggestion,[26] clarified his reference to common sense by explaining to his men's class, and thus to the press, that no amount of it could 'help a man to see the truth of Scripture if he is spiritually blind,' but that common sense would enable anyone to understand the origins of Biblical writings just as it would explain the origins of any historical literature.[27] The next morning Carman and Fudger went to Rowell's office where Carman expressed complete satisfaction with Jackson's explanation.[28]

The Board of Regents accepted in essence the statement prepared by Bowles, Rowell, and Fudger. Although it asserted that there were at least two views of the inspiration of the Bible and that both were compatible with traditional Methodist doctrine, the general tenor of the document, and especially the assertion that the Fall was 'not an historical event but a moral act, past and present,' favoured the higher critics. In dealing with the freedom of Victoria's professors the Board was more direct:

Inasmuch as honesty in the investigation of truth and perfect candor in its statement are essential parts of our religion, and especially imperative in our schools of theology, standing as they do side by side with the great institutions of learning in the country, so long as our theological professors maintain their personal vital relation to Christ and Holy Scripture, and adhere to the doctrinal standards of our own church, Victoria College recognizes that they must be left free to do their own work in order that ... they may conserve the faith of our church in the minds of those who in days to come shall minister in our pulpits. Our experience is that only as the young men of a great university have full confidence that their instructors give them honest convictions reached by perfectly candid and scientific methods, will they retain their faith in Christianity itself.[29]

All the members of the Board of Regents, not excepting its chairman, Dr Carman, or Rev. Dr J.S. Ross, who had urged Carman on in the whole affair, accepted this declaration of policy and it was subsequently signed by every professor of theology in the college. The Regents agreed that 'whatever had been written of a personal character calculated to wound the feelings of brethren or interfere with their work be withdrawn ...' If any further communications were made to the press they would be issued only by the Board through Rowell. The Regents sealed this happy amity by singing together 'Blest Be the Tie that Binds' and adjourned,[30] while the principal figures in the controversy tried to patch up their strained relations. Rowell lauded Carman's spirit, and Carman reciprocated with appreciation of what the church owed to 'yourself and Brother Fudger for your truly Christian view of the situation.' As for his own role, Carman added, 'as soon as duty pointed to peace my heart longed for it, especially in view of the great interests at stake; the rest was easy ... I may be rigid on fundamentals as I view them but I think I am somewhat of a Catholic in spirit.'[31] To J.W. Flavelle, Rowell's mediation of the dispute was the greatest of his many services to his church[32] and the end result a cause for thanksgiving 'for deliverance from great trouble.'[33] The secular press of Toronto, which, with the exception of the *World*, had favoured Jackson, now prepared for extensive coverage of the National Missionary Congress, due to begin in a week's time, and talk of discord gave way to praise of Christian unity.

'Canadian Army Enters Upon Greatest of All Crusades,' announced the *Globe* in its major headline over a full report of the opening session of the National Missionary Congress. Rowell as chairman welcomed some four thousand delegates from across Canada to a conference 'of commanding importance in the religious and national life of Canada ... No more representative and virile body of men has ever been gathered together in Canada.'[34] Massey Hall was 'plainly decorated with British and Canadian [sic] flags.' The wall behind the platform displayed a large map of the world superimposed with 'Thy Kingdom Come,' while banners hung from the galleries asked 'Will Canada evangelize her share of the world?' or admonished: 'Weekly as the Lord has prospered you – systematic, sensible, scriptural.' After opening prayers by the Anglican Bishop of Toronto, Rowell called on the lieutenant governor of Ontario, Sir John Gibson, to welcome the delegates. Messages for the success of the Congress were read from the British ambassador in Washington, James Bryce, and from religious leaders in Britain and the United States.[35] Rowell then introduced the key speaker of the Congress, Sir Andrew Fraser, who had spent many of his thirty-seven years in India as lieutenant governor of Bengal and was present at the Congress in a dual capacity as moderator of the Presbyterian church in India and a representative of the Laymen's Movement in Scotland. For Rowell, Fraser was the embodiment of the best Britain had given to the world: 'It has been given to Great Britain, more than to any other nation of ancient or modern times, to breed a class of men who, dwelling among the less advanced and progressive races of the world, have carried with them the principles of British Government, and have worked for the upbuilding of those less advanced and progressive nations; her great pro-consuls in various parts of the world – men like Cromer in Egypt and Milner in South Africa and Fraser in India.'[36] Sir Andrew's major addresses would come later in the Congress. The chief address of the opening evening was given by the chairman on 'Canada's Opportunity at Home and Abroad.'

Rowell's title sounded the nationalistic note that characterized the whole Congress. His opening words declared that this gathering of Canadians was the first *national* missionary congress since the first century. His message had already been preached across the country, and as always it was illustrated with the most up-to-date statistics. These now showed that, in 1907 alone, immigration into Canada averaged between 4 and 5 per cent of the existing population. 'The United States had a population of over 20,000,000 before the people of that country were called upon to receive and bring into touch with their American and Christian ideals' a proportionate number of newcomers. And this was only the beginning, since Canada still possessed an unsettled area 'at least half as large as the continent of Europe, which, so far as we know at present, should be the home of men.' With such future growth in prospect, who could 'foretell the tides of commerce which will sweep across our land? Who can foretell Canada's place in the world's politics, when, in the fullness of her strength, she stands by her mother in the councils of the empire, and through the empire makes her influence felt in the world?' Canada would play an important role in an area of which Canadians were now only dimly aware: just as geography had made the Mediterranean the great highway of the Middle Ages, so it had made the Pacific the artery of the coming century. 'During this century, on this ocean, must the world's drama largely be acted. Canada, with her face to the Pacific must in this drama play no inconspicuous part.' For Rowell his country's strategic position was no mere accident. Canada was one of the Christian and civilized nations to whom alone 'the All-Wise Father has ... unlocked the mysterious secrets and forces of the universe which have ... placed such power in the hands of man ...' If western science and education were to be 'instruments in the hands of ... Eastern peoples for their social and moral progress and uplift rather than instruments for their and our undoing it will only be as they come to know Him "in whom are hid all the treasures of wisdom and knowledge."' Within this providential ordering of history Canada was assigned a distinctive part, having already led the way in the nineteenth-century unions of churches that had unified Presbyterians on the one hand, and Methodists on the other, and having continued to do so in the current negotiations for a wider Protestant unity in Canada. The next step must be taken by 'the Christian men of Canada ... As the Roman was called to teach the world law, the Greek to teach the world art, the Hebrew to teach the world religion, so we in Canada, if true to our responsibilities, may be called to lead the world in the work of world-wide evangelization.'[37]

Before the end of the Congress a Dominion Council of the Laymen's Movement was formed and a 'National Missionary Policy' adopted, which pledged Canada's 900,000 Protestant church members to raise $1,300,000 annually for home missions and $3,200,000 for foreign missions, sums many times greater than they were then contributing. At the closing session Rowell was taken by surprise when the American secretary of the Laymen's Movement, Campbell White, proposed that 'the one man in this Dominion ... who is almost the walking embodiment' of the movement should leave his law practice to become its full-time secretary in Canada. Amid applause White added: 'I have heard Mr Rowell from one end of this country to the other say that this is the biggest business in the world; that this constitutes the higher politics. He has already made great sacrifices for the work. But I believe we need the illustration of men in business giving up subordinate business to go into the biggest business in the world.' Rowell had no difficulty in giving a brief and decisive answer: 'I have chosen my profession.' However, he did agree to continue as chairman of the Dominion Council,[38] and later accepted the chairmanship of the Methodist committee of the movement.

Rowell had not many weeks for undisturbed rejoicing in the success of the Missionary Congress. One of the two members of the Board of Regents who had supported Carman, Rev. Dr J.S. Ross of Hanover, presently published a pamphlet, 'A Review of Rev. George Jackson's Lecture on the Early Narratives of Genesis.'[39] Reluctantly, Rowell entered the fray once more. Ross denied Rowell's strongly worded accusation that he had violated both the letter and the spirit of the Board of Regents' agreement.[40] Ross, and others who thought like him, had never agreed to refrain from expressing their disapproval of Jackson's views. Their failure to speak out would only confirm the public in its impression that Jackson had been completely vindicated, an impression strengthened by the current refusal of the press, notably the *Globe* and the *Christian Guardian*, to open their columns to anti-Jackson views. Ross had had personal experience of the attitude of these papers, since both had refused to publish the material in his pamphlet. In any case, Jackson had already broken the agreement, Ross charged. He was 'so saturated with German Rationalism' that he had been unable to refrain from expounding his 'myth theories' once more in a series of lectures at Wesleyan University in Delaware, Ohio.[41] Rowell's version was quite different. Ross's pamphlet was in direct opposition to the agreement that newspaper publicity and 'public controversy dealing distinctly with Jackson's views' were to be avoided. On his side, Jackson had honoured the agreement to the letter. Everyone on the Board knew that Jackson was scheduled to lecture in Ohio and he was not expected to alter his views for that or any occasion.[42]

Carman now renewed his attack by supporting Ross's interpretation of the meaning of the agreement. Clearly the conservative forces were engaged in a last-ditch attempt to prevent Jackson from taking up his teaching duties in the fall. As the correspondence went on, Rowell wondered whether there were any limits to his antagonists' capacity for devious and illogical argument. His repeated rehearsal of the steps leading to the agreement and of the adherence of Carman and Ross to it had no effect whatever. They completely rejected the plain meaning of the agreement that there was room in the Methodist church for at least two views of Biblical inspiration, one of which was certainly Jackson's, and that all anyone had agreed to do was to withdraw the personal attacks that had been made.[43]

For about six weeks Carman and Ross were again silent. Then the general superintendent protested to Chancellor Burwash and the Regents about the views expressed by certain speakers at a recent ministerial conference at the college, adding the threat that it was unlikely that he would 'be a second time imposed upon in this matter.'[44] Pleading the pressure of his duties at the beginning of a new university term Burwash declined to discuss the question.[45] The refusal of the pro-Jackson forces to be drawn into further combat was disconcerting to Carman and Ross. But the publication in London that fall of Jackson's book, *Studies in the Old Testament*, provided an opening. When the *Globe* accorded the book a favourable review, Carman wrote a long letter attacking it, which the editors refused to print. Carman now joined Ross in pamphleteering, with the publication of *The Toronto Globe and the Higher Criticism*,[46] obviously an attempt to discredit the laymen who were supporting Jackson. No names were mentioned, but Carman decried the power often banefully wielded by men of wealth; there could be no doubt that his charge that the *Globe* was under undue pressure from one or more of its directors was aimed at Rowell. As before, none of the active participants in the earlier dispute rose to this fresh bait. With only one member of the Board of Regents, Mr Justice J.J. Maclaren, supporting them, Carman and Ross abandoned their attempt to influence that body directly. The majority of the clergy had been trained at Victoria, and most of them were therefore 'tainted' by false teaching. Their only hope was to rally lay opinion, and at this they laboured behind the scenes for the next several months.

Rowell's appointment as a delegate to the World Missionary Conference in Edinburgh in June 1910 prevented him from witnessing in person the next round of the fight with Carman and Ross, but from the *Globe* and from the letters of Burwash, Fudger, and Jackson he had a detailed picture of the unseemly squabbling of the Toronto Conference. It was all in distressing contrast to the spirit of the Edinburgh Conference, the most representative Protestant gathering ever held and one which laid firm foundations for the growth of the Protestant ecumenical movement.

It was a relief to Rowell to learn that a resolution urging the elimination from Methodist colleges of 'such teaching concerning the Holy Scriptures and the fallibility of Christ as is contained in Rev. George Jackson's book, "Studies in the Old Testament,"' had been defeated in the Toronto Conference. But the amendment proposed by Jackson's supporters had passed by a vote of only 130 to 116, and in a separate meeting of the lay delegates it had been agreed to send the original resolution to the General Conference in the fall. The conservatism of the laymen was also evident in the results of the election of lay delegates to the General Conference.[47] To his surprise, Rowell was the only pro-Jackson delegate elected from the Toronto Conference. Reviewing the results, he especially regretted the Conference's rejection of Fudger. But in Fudger's assessment the situation was not desperate. All the other Ontario Conferences had elected a majority of both clergy and laymen who could be counted on to support Victoria. That, and their own limitations, would prevent the Toronto laymen from doing much harm: 'They represent no debating strength and little personal influence and probably having secured the holiday trip to the coast may not be so extreme.'[48]

Rowell's interviews and correspondence with leading Methodist clergy and professors of theology in Britain added to his armoury, for it was unanimously agreed that there was no alternative but to fight the issue through to a finish before the General Conference which was soon to meet in Victoria, British Columbia. But as Jackson observed, it was 'something much worse than pathos to drop from the Edinburgh heights to the ... theological wrangles of Toronto.'[49]

Although Rowell had argued consistently that the merit of Jackson's views was 'a matter for Biblical scholars just the same as a question of law is a matter for lawyers,'[50] that attitude had never fully encompassed his involvement in the conflict. Over a period of nearly two years his library had looked increasingly like a theologian's as he gave himself a course in Biblical criticism through books usually suggested by Professor Bowles, who commended especially the works of the British scholar Marcus Dods.[51] As the General Conference drew near he was as well prepared for 'the Jackson case' as for any legal battle.

Had his will to defend the new theology needed fortifying, it would have been provided by a letter that awaited his arrival at the Empress Hotel in Victoria. Chester Massey, a member of the Board of Regents whose father had endowed the chair of English Bible at Victoria College, was well able to speak for the wealthy Methodists who had recently given substantial sums to the college or might do so in the future.

These men ... have succeeded because they have used up-to-date methods, and using a trade phrase, have adopted the 'latest tools and machinery.' Now they are not going to give liberally to a church whose institutions are not up-to-date, and who do not turn out up-to-date men, but to a church which looks about for the best men it can get ... wherever they can get them, and in short doing everything in a business-like manner to build up our institutions and these professors ... will not come with their mouths padlocked by any annual conference ... The Jackson controversy was dealt with by the Board of Reasons [sic] of Victoria College, and supposed to have been settled permanently.

Drawing out the precise implications of his words, Massey went on to assert that he and the other executors of his father's estate, who had provided the money for the men's residence now under construction at the college and for earlier buildings, would not make further gifts if 'the policy of the Church was to overthrow the action of the Board of Regents and drive Mr Jackson from his post.'[52]

Carman was still in fighting form. In his annual presidential address on the state of the church he recounted the past glories of Methodism with generous notice of his own share in them. But now the church was in decline, as evidenced by the fact that the growth in membership and in candidates for the ministry lagged behind the general increase in population. This weakness was due mainly to the excessive power of the wealthy in the church. Reminding his audience of 'the words of John Wesley ... that we are to beware lest we make rich men a necessity to us' Carman declared that 'rich men must be listened to like other men in the Church of God,' but not to the extent that had allowed some of them to make irregular arrangements for filling the pulpit of 'one of our wealthiest churches.' This same wealth disposed the church 'to sink into the lap of formalism and naturalism and of worldly comfort and ease. At such times ... novelties are preached for the well-proven doctrines of concerting grace and sanctifying power. The eye of the church is dimmed and her arm paralyzed.' Despite the obvious sickness of the church the report of the chancellor of Victoria College to the present General Conference contained a plea for new faculty appointments in 'philosophy, psychology and kindred subjects,' which could only strengthen the influence of 'German rationalism and Scottish idealism' and diminish the reliance of young Methodists on 'the indestructible foundations ... of revelation, inspiration, authority and miracle.'[53]

The general superintendent's address was not open to discussion, a convention helpful to Jackson's defenders, for they had worked out a strategy and had no wish to see the issue come before the whole Conference just yet. Rather, they brought it up in the Committee on Education. There, Rowell had a share in securing the adoption, after bitter struggle, of a proposal that henceforth any dispute about a theological professor's teaching should be dealt with by a tribunal of five other ministers. This recommendation, with a detailed outline of the procedure to be followed, then came before the whole Conference as a part of the committee's report. When the conservatives tried to move an amendment to the motion for the adoption of the report, an amendment censuring certain phrases Jackson had used in his book, Dr Carman himself, now as always the competent presiding officer, had to rule it out of order as not directly related to the report. The approval of the report was followed by the moving of the motion of censure, which was quickly countered by an amendment stating that the Conference had 'provided adequately for cases such as are referred to in the resolution.'[54]

At last the debate could begin. The movers of the motion of censure rehearsed the old charges against Jackson. Then Chancellor Burwash explained at length the policies pursued at Victoria and the importance of freedom of thought in the college. Rowell followed with his first public comment on the controversy. Clearly he had done his theological homework well. Moving through a demonstration that even the most conservative theologians declined to accept everything in the Bible as history or science but understood the function of myths in illustrating great truths, he came to the immediate issue. He had read Jackson's book three times and took no exception to it. Thus, while it had been charged that Jackson denied the perfection of Christ's knowledge, he could find in the book 'nothing more radical as to the limitations of Jesus' knowledge than the things I find in Wesley's notes on the New Testament.' As in the beginning his final plea was for the eschewing of conflict in the service of the practical: 'Brethren, let us go forth as men to preach that God is able and willing to save men from their sins, and let us cease this haggling about non-essentials.'[55]

With the approval by a vote of 125 to 84 of the amendment proposed by Jackson's friends the victory was won. No one came forward to invoke the use of the procedure just agreed upon against Jackson. He remained at Victoria for another three years before returning with some alacrity to the less turbulent atmosphere of British Methodism and a professorship in theology in Didsbury College, Manchester. At about the same time, in his eightieth year, Carman retired amid the growing opinion of many churchmen that he had more than outlived his usefulness as chief shepherd of Canadian Methodists.

R.P. Bowles perhaps understood Rowell's religious temper as well as any friend could. For him, Rowell's part in the Jackson controversy illustrated his essential quality as 'a practical mystic.'[56] It was also a commentary on John Wesley's famous entry in his Journal that the Methodists 'do not insist on your holding this or that opinion; but they think and let think.'[57] Since the faith of devout Methodists was based on personal experience and only confirmed by the Bible and the teaching of the church, it was relatively invulnerable to destruction by changing theories about the Bible. Thousands of Canadian Methodists reacted to the Jackson controversy in a spirit that owed a good deal to this liberal emphasis in the Methodist heritage. Typical of these was a country doctor in northern Ontario, Dr A.R. Dafoe, who deplored Carman's attack on 'a man honest enough to express his opinions – opinions that are held by all educated Methodists of the present day. If this matter occurred in a Roman Catholic Church, or an English Church it would be easy to understand it, but to have liberty of thought prevented in a Methodist church of all churches is most ridiculous.'[58]

That the Toronto laymen who found an effective spokesman in Rowell were open to the newer interpretation of the Bible was due not only to their Methodist traditions but also to certain features of their environment. The sum total of the business experience of A.E. Ames, J.W. Flavelle, Chester D. Massey, Senator G.A. Cox, and H.H. Fudger represented much of the force of the transcontinental outreach of Toronto's commercial empire in the two decades before the first world war. In the unprecedented expansion of the Canadian economy accompanying the settlement of the west they owed much of their success to their mastery of bold methods of business financing, to company mergers on a scale unprecedented in Canada, and to the increased efficiency furnished by the most modern methods of selling bonds, packing meat, harvesting wheat, building railways and mining coal, and organizing department stores. It was easier for them than for men of lesser talents and opportunities to believe that movements for the union of the churches and new techniques in Biblical criticism also meant progress. They could not deny the continuing popularity of old-style evangelists like the Canadian Methodist team, Crossley and Hunter, or the Americans, Torrey and Alexander, who had enthralled thousands of Torontonians for a whole month during the winter of 1906. Yet they observed many men in the business and professional world around them falling away from the churches and statistics informed them that the Methodist church was failing to keep up with the general increase in population. A partial answer might be found in the more intellectual fare that they themselves enjoyed from preachers like Jackson. Few of Jackson's prominent supporters in Sherbourne Church were men with much formal education, but they were well read and eager to add to their general knowledge. During his ministry at Sherbourne Street, Jackson conducted a reading circle in English classical and contemporary literature that met regularly in Fudger's home. Fudger himself read a good deal of philosophy and theology and at the time of the Jackson controversy was developing a distinctly liberal theological position, which held that Paul had largely misinterpreted Jesus by equating Jesus with God rather than seeing him as a unique manifestation of God's nature.[59]

With his Biblical scholarship and his skilful use of English literature Jackson combined a direct and essentially evangelical appeal that produced enough of the familiar emotional response to keep his preaching comfortably within the Methodist ethos for most of his hearers. For some of his Sherbourne congregation the fact that Jackson expressed little direct interest in social movements and was radical only in his Biblical theories may have offered a welcome escape from the alarming dimensions of 'the social gospel' that a few Methodist clergymen were beginning to find attractive. In the view of the Methodist élite Jackson represented the best of both old and new in religion, and it was to this influence that they wished to expose the younger generation in the lecture halls of Victoria and the Methodist churches of the Dominion.

The question whether Rev. George Jackson could properly occupy the chair of English Bible in Victoria College was discussed from one end of Canada to the other, and not among Methodists only; for it acted as a focus for the struggles of a generation of Canadian Protestants to reconcile evangelical Christianity with their growing awareness of scientific thought and the complexities of human history. While the Jackson case was shaking the Methodist church, S.H. Blake, champion of the evangelical wing of the Church of England and a staunch friend of the low church Wycliffe College, was attacking the University of Toronto for what Blake contended was a violation of the terms of university federation, which prohibited the teaching of theology in the government-supported University College. Blake charged that the Department of Oriental Languages was in fact teaching theology through courses in Biblical literature and languages.[60] Although Blake opened his attack on constitutional grounds, his pamphlets and addresses left no doubt that 'higher criticism' was the enemy, and he and Carman publicly supported one another. Like Carman, Blake lost his battle, for the special committee of the university senate appointed to investigate his charges ruled that the disputed courses were not courses in theology.[61]

It was the misfortune of the Protestant churches in Canada that they were called upon to face the full impact of natural science on religious faith at the very moment when they were trying to hold or win the thousands of settlers in the west. The acceptance of the new critical approach to the Bible was a less effective bulwark of faith than churchmen like Burwash and Bowles, Rowell and Fudger, believed. Even with greater intellectual resources and more personnel it is doubtful that Canadian Protestantism could have survivied its dual challenge in undiminished strength, for the drift to secularism continued throughout the Christian world and was given new impetus everywhere by world war. Many who did not lose their faith felt unsatisfied by the new liberalism of the established churches, and on the prairies especially they often found refuge in the familiar, comforting terminology and emotional warmth of 'the old-time-religion' of the fundamentalist sects such as the Pentecostals. That the west did not become the 'new Ontario' that Rowell and many eastern Protestants envisioned was due in part to the inadequacies of the established churches.[62]

PART TWO

6
A Liberal Moses

In the years following the defeat of the Ross government and the 'autonomy crisis,' Rowell appeared on political platforms only rarely. During the federal election campaign of 1908 he had spoken once in Winnipeg South on behalf of his friend, D.C. Cameron, the wealthy lumberman and manufacturer whom he had first known as mayor of Rat Portage. In the provincial election of the same year he had addressed one meeting in his home riding, North Toronto, in support of Rev. D.C. Hossack, a Presbyterian minister and lawyer who had publicly denounced corruption in the Ross government in 1905. This aloofness from election campaigns was no indication of a declining interest in politics, for he had continued to give a good deal of thought to both federal and provincial politics.

He attached some importance, as a considered statement of his political creed,[1] to an address given before the First Ward Liberal Association of Toronto in the winter of 1906 on 'Some Desirable Reforms.' The most essential reform was a change in the public attitude toward morality in public life, a change which could be encouraged by improved methods of detecting and punishing electoral misdemeanours, an end to the 'saw-off,' and the appointment of a public prosecutor to watch over electoral proceedings, as in Britain. He had high praise for the recent arguments advanced by the leader of the Conservative opposition in Ottawa, Robert Borden, for the appointment of a public prosecutor at the federal level, and argued for a permanent civil service with promotion on merit, a cause Borden had also espoused. Rowell believed that Canadian public life would also be enhanced by the passage of a law preventing any lawyer from receiving fees from an individual or corporation to promote any legislation before any elected assembly of which he was a member, and by prohibition of donations from corporations to political campaign funds. Beyond the purification of political morality, Rowell saw a second desirable objective for Canada: measures to ensure a more equitable distribution of wealth than existed in the United States. He had no detailed suggestions as to how this could be achieved; however, again borrowing from British example, he suggested that a start could be made if the federal government would sell annuities and small insurance policies to working men through the Post Office Department.[2]

Like many other active Protestants Rowell looked on the organization in 1907 of the Moral and Social Reform Council of Canada, representing all the major Protestant denominations, and supported by the Trades and Labor Congress, the Dominion Grange, and the Orange Lodge, as a step toward the elevation of Canadian life; shortly he became one of its vice-presidents. Even before the council's inauguration the bodies comprising it had some taste of success in helping to secure the passage of the Lord's Day Act. It was less effective in its opposition to professional betting on Canadian race tracks. When H.H. Miller, the Liberal member for South Grey, introduced in the House of Commons a private bill to prohibit race track gambling, A.B. Aylesworth, the minister of justice and Laurier's chief lieutenant from Ontario, made a lighthearted and sarcastic display of his detestation of 'the Puritan conscience,' of which he considered 'the Miller bill' a manifestation. Aylesworth suggested that possibly 'before the end of this parliament we shall have a proposition to make it a crime to play cards, or to dance, or to indulge in any other amusements which there are some in the community think constitute very nearly, if not quite, a sin.'[3]

Rowell found the tone of Aylesworth's remarks objectionable and protested to another Ontario cabinet minister, and a fellow Methodist, George P. Graham, whom he hailed as 'the real leader of Ontario Liberals in Dominion politics' rather than Aylesworth. Rowell reported 'on all sides the deepest resentment ... that in voicing his opposition he [Aylesworth] should have treated with contempt the conscientious conviction and the sentiments of the church-going people at least of this province, and, I believe, largely of all the provinces.' The government should not forget, Rowell warned, that 'the strength of the Liberal party throughout this country will be found in those classes who believe in the church and in religious institutions and who have strong views on moral issues, and who do not believe in legalized professional gambling.'[4] At the same time Rowell urged the editor of the Globe, who had supported the Miller bill from the outset, to keep up his editorial agitation until the original measure was approved.[5] The compromise legislation that Parliament eventually passed was no more pleasing to Rowell, the Globe, or the Moral and Social Reform Council than it was to the Canadian Hackney Association or the Ontario Horse Breeders; while permitting legalized bookmaking, it limited the racing season at any one track to two weeks each year.[6]

Only a week after his offensive remarks on the Miller bill, Aylesworth provoked attack from the same quarters on another count. As minister of justice he announced the release of two Toronto men, Skill and King, after they had served only two months of the one-year term to which they had been sentenced for selling obscene literature. Aylesworth declared that in his judgment the men were not guilty of the crime for which they had been condemned; some of the books, which included works by Petronius, Balzac, and Brantôme, might be considered indecent by some sections of the community, but that could not alter their generally accepted stature as classics of literature.[7] Laurier supported his minister in the controversy but the leaders of the Methodist and Presbyterian churches, the Moral and Social Reform Council, and the *Globe* all found Aylesworth unconvincing and the government's action in the Skill and King case just one example of a 'suspicious laxness in prosecuting such offenders ... [and a willingness] to pardon or release from prison ... vicious-minded convicts whose trade in life is more pernicious than a pestilence.'[8] For many Ontario Protestants the Skill and King affair and the fate of the Miller bill raised questions about the effectiveness of the Laurier government as a custodian of morality, despite its contribution to the better observance of the sabbath through the passage of the Lord's Day Act. Many of these were the same people in whom some doubts about the character of Laurier Liberalism had already been stirred by the autonomy crisis.

Yet another cause of alarm in Ontario was the application in Canada of the Vatican's decree, *Ne Temere*, which discouraged marriages between Catholics and Protestants and ruled them invalid unless performed by a Roman Catholic priest under special dispensation. Church courts of every Protestant denomination denounced the decree when it was used in Quebec to annul certain marriages performed by Protestant clergymen and to call in question some marriages in other provinces. Roman Catholics contended that the decree was simply a formal recognition that marriage was a sacrament that could only be valid when either party was a Catholic and if it were performed by the church, a view that the Quebec civil code rightly confirmed. But Protestants saw the ruling as an attack on civil liberties, a violation of the principle of equality before the law, and often as a gross insult to their clergy. Rowell was an active member of a special committee appointed by the Methodist General Conference to draft a statement on the subject. While less inflammatory than the utterances of many individual Methodists, the committee's pronouncement was altogether firm: 'We maintain that any and all attempts to give effect to the provisions of this *Ne Temere* Decree, to the disturbance and ruin of duly-constituted families, must meet our firm resistance and cannot with us, as a matter of sacred conscience and civil and religious right, be tolerated.' Since the British North America Act gave power over the solemnization of marriage to the provinces, the Methodist statement called on all the provinces 'to enact, if not already in existence, and enforce, such measures as shall forever confirm the validity of marriages duly solemnized by law; and thereby resist and check these foreign aggressions.'[9] The Laurier government refused to be drawn into the dispute and the issue was submitted to the courts. But the government's neutrality did not prevent the controversy from arousing old fears in Ontario about the ecclesiastical pressure to which Catholic politicians might be subjected.

Of themselves, these episodes involving morality and religion were not major political issues, but at a time when the Laurier government could expect to suffer from the natural decline that usually accompanies a long term of office they created additional tensions within the Liberal party.

Rowell was brought into active politics again by the issue that made all other causes of dissension among Ontario Liberals seem insignificant. Initially, the news that Canada had at last won from the Americans the free trade in the fruits of forest, farm, and fisheries sought by both Liberal and Conservative governments ever since Confederation appeared to be an economic and political triumph for the Liberals. Even some of the Conservative leaders conceded this immediately after the announcement from Laurier's minister of finance, W.S. Fielding, in late January 1911 that Parliament would be asked to approve a reciprocity agreement covering natural products traded between Canada and the United States. But in a matter of days Conservative strategists had realized how many Canadians already feared, or could be persuaded to fear, reciprocity. Within three weeks there was ample evidence that a good many opponents could be recruited from among Liberals, especially in Ontario. In mid-February, at a meeting organized by the Toronto Board of Trade, reciprocity was put to a vote and rejected 302 to 13. There were many more than thirteen Liberals present; the result was a dramatic indication of the feeling against the agreement among Toronto businessmen of both parties. Three days later the Liberal revolt came to a head with the publication of an anti-reciprocity manifesto from eighteen prominent Toronto business leaders; although most of them had not been active in party affairs they all considered themselves Liberals.[10] The group was broadly representative of banks and railways, trust and insurance companies, and manufacturing and merchandising enterprises. In declaring that reciprocity would destroy the east-west trade on which the Canadian economy had been established with so much struggle, that the agreement would inevitably be extended to include manufactured goods, and that the political independence of Canada would be threatened by the development of such close commercial dependence on the United States, the manifesto set out the main outlines of the great debate that preoccupied Canadians for the next seven months.

With every issue of the *Globe* and every lunch hour talk downtown it became clearer to Rowell that few of Toronto's leading citizens were lining up on the side of reciprocity. In Toronto, Senator Cox was almost alone among major business figures in supporting the trade agreement, and his assurances to manufacturers that there was no danger that free trade would ever be extended to their goods were falling on deaf ears. The opponents of reciprocity included many Liberals and independents whom Rowell knew well and whose capabilities he respected – Clifford Sifton, Sir Edmund Walker, president of the Canadian Bank of Commerce, the powerful financier, E.R. Wood, the president of the T. Eaton Company, John C. Eaton, D.C. Cameron of Winnipeg, W.T. White of the National Trust, J.W. Flavelle of the William Davies Company, and John Willison, who from the very first had made the *News* a formidable voice against reciprocity. But he could not share their judgment about the proposed trade agreement. A life-long advocate of freer trade as a means of gaining larger markets for Canada's primary produce and a lower cost of living for the average citizen, Rowell welcomed the abolition of tariffs on natural products. Not every director of the *Globe* had found it possible to do so, but in the end the paper stood behind official Liberal policy; so did the *Star*, and both Macdonald and Atkinson campaigned actively for the agreement. The chief support for reciprocity came from labour and agriculture, and the leaders of the trade unions and farmers' organizations were loud in their praise of the new tariff policy. Although fruit and vegetable growers objected and some factory workers feared that their jobs would be endangered if free trade in manufactured goods were brought nearer, the Liberals claimed a very solid following among farmers and city wage earners.

Early in the public discussion of the agreement Rowell joined a committee formed by the Ontario Reform Association to provide pro-reciprocity speakers for meetings throughout the province and placed his own name on the panel of those available.[11] Every day it became clearer how hard the pro-reciprocity speakers would have to work and how weak was the Liberal party organization. The Conservatives were making increasing and devastating use of the utterances of President Taft, Representative Champ Clark, and other American leaders to spread the impression that powerful American groups saw the institution of reciprocity as the crucial step toward the annexation of Canada. Clearly, many Canadians were already persuaded that the national interest, the interests of the major industrialists and financiers, and their own were identical.

Rowell made his first public declaration on reciprocity two weeks after the publication of the manifesto of 'The Eighteen.' The residents of Richmond Hill in North York listened to an address that set the pattern for the many speeches he made throughout the province in the months following. Taking as his starting point Lloyd George's description of the reciprocal trade agreement as 'a triumph of common sense,' he dealt one by one with the objections raised by the manifesto of the Liberal rebels. Against the charge that the government had no mandate to enter into such an agreement he placed the history of the efforts of both Liberal and Conservative governments during the past half century to secure a similar arrangement and asserted that Laurier had been elected in 1896 with a mandate to secure a reciprocal agreement if adequate terms were assured; the people of Canada had since re-elected Laurier three times, and thus that mandate had never been withdrawn. As for the argument that Canada had in Britain as large a foreign market as she could supply with agricultural produce, this ignored the fact that Canada was only at the beginning of her history as an exporter of grain and there was a limit to how much more wheat Britain could consume. But reciprocity would increase the market on the North American continent from the eight million people of Canada to ninety million. There were those who denied that the United States could in practice become a significant market for Canadian wheat, since the Americans themselves were exporters of grain; but had that not been so to an even greater extent during the reciprocity of 1854–66, when Canada had found a very profitable agricultural market in the United States? Rowell accused opponents of reciprocity of ignorance of the developing pattern and strength of Canadian trade: already Canadian bankers were making loans in the United States in amounts which in some years had exceeded the total paid-up capital of all the banks in Canada; in 1910 the Canadian mining industry sold 85 per cent of its surplus production in the American market, while lumbermen shipped 67 per cent of their foreign exports south of the border. And this brought him to 'the wildest and most unreasonable' feature of the opposition to reciprocity. 'Nobody has suggested any tendency to disloyalty on the part of either the bankers, the miners or the lumbermen. Even the manufacturers last year sold about 50 per cent of their surplus products to the United States. It must have been advantageous to them or surely they would not have run the risk of having their affections alienated from England by going into this market.' Farmers were in a different situation, since they disposed of only 13 per cent of their surplus in the United States. Why should that market be denied them, and why should trade on their part endanger the future of the nation any more than that carried on by other economic groups in the community?[12]

Rowell had no reason to yield place to anyone in feeling for the British connection, and it gave him some pleasure to demonstrate that the flagwavers who so ardently opposed reciprocity were ignorant not only of the economic facts of life but of the state of the Empire. Canada's enormous increase in trade with Britain in the past decade and the much greater increase in trade with the United States had been accompanied by the growth of 'a sense of national self-consciousness and of Imperial relationship quite unknown to us fifteen or twenty years ago ...' This growth was demonstrated in the very concrete evidence of the British preference, Canadian participation in the war in South Africa, and the establishment of a Canadian navy. At the same time there had been a drawing-together of all the English-speaking peoples; the signing of the Boundary Waters Treaty, the settlement of the long outstanding fisheries dispute between Canada and the United

States by the Hague Tribunal, and now the reciprocity agreement must all be understood as part of a growing co-operation among the various branches of the English-speaking race. Canadians were beginning 'to realize the great part their country may play as an integral part of the Empire, helping to unite the English-speaking races in sympathetic and practical co-operation for the preservation of the peace of the world and the maintenance of our Christian civilization against possible dangers in the Far East.' Most of these great movements had been adversely criticized by the very people who were now criticizing the reciprocity agreement and crowning their earlier errors with the grossest disservice to their country by suggesting to the world that 'the loyalty of Canadians is a purchasable quantity and depends upon trade advantage.' On the contrary, the loyalty of Canadians 'rests upon a deep-seated and personal attachment to our laws, our institutions, our form of government and the British crown.' Canadians had no desire to sell their political future, but that was the impression critics of reciprocity were conveying to Americans. Further, they were also encouraging the thousands of Americans who were settling in Canada to believe that 'they need not forswear allegiance to the Stars and Stripes, but that some day the Stars and Stripes may wave over Canada and thereby they are creating an impression which may be most disturbing and disintegrating in the days to come.'[13]

The general content of Rowell's defence of Liberal policy was no different than that of hundreds of other apologias delivered across the nation, but his presentations of the case were distinguished for their clarity, to which his capacity for using the statistics of a complex subject in a manner accessible to laymen contributed greatly, and by the passion with which he maintained the pro-Canadian and pro-British credentials of Laurier Liberalism.

In the spring of 1911 Rowell journeyed to England for meetings of the Continuation Committee of the Edinburgh Conference, of which he was treasurer and a member of the executive. Shortly after Rowell's return to Canada Laurier responded to the continuing obstruction of the Conservatives in parliament and to their cry 'let the people decide' on the reciprocity issue by announcing the dissolution of the House and the calling of an election for September 21.

After a family holiday at Honey Harbour on Georgian Bay, Rowell was ready to re-enter the fight over reciprocity, although not to the extent of accepting a suggestion that he be the Liberal standard-bearer in North Toronto.[14] As he travelled the province from Brockville to Sarnia in the campaign the immediate commercial advantages of reciprocity took second place in his argument. Increasingly he emphasized the baneful effect of a high tariff on the structure of American society and on the economic prospects of the American people, and drew the lessons in the American experience for Canadians. The ever-increasing control of combines and trusts over the lives of Americans meant that 'twenty to twenty-five men substantially control business operations in the United States.' If Canadians wanted a more equitable distribution of wealth than prevailed south of the border they would not secure it under a Conservative government dominated by the great financial concerns of the nation represented by Clifford Sifton.[15]

A secondary but by no means unimportant issue in the election was Canada's place within the Empire and especially her responsibility for naval defence. From the first Rowell had supported Laurier's policy for the development of a distinctive Canadian navy that could be placed at Britain's service in time of war at the discretion of the Parliament of Canada. That policy was consistent with Rowell's desire to see an extension both of Canadian responsibility and of Canadian autonomy within the Empire. Although he sometimes wished that Laurier's elaborations of his assertions that 'When Great Britain is at war, Canada is at war' were less open to the interpretation that he accepted that fact reluctantly, Rowell was in essential agreement with Laurier's steady refusal to enter into more formal agreements for imperial co-operation, and had approved Laurier's resistance to Sir Joseph Ward of New Zealand and the other centralizers at the imperial conference earlier in the year.[16] A prime reason for defeating the Conservatives in the election was their failure to state a naval policy. The party that had so often claimed to be the 'British party' had formed an alliance with Henri Bourassa and his Quebec Nationalists, and presumably was therefore committed to the Nationalist rejection of a Canadian navy and every other form of responsibility for the defence of Canada and the Empire. Yet the Tories dared to say that the Liberals were unfaithful to British traditions. Rowell's reading of the record proved that 'Liberals are true Loyalists, not merely lip Loyalists. Who gave us British preference? The Liberals. Who gave us the Imperial penny postage? The Liberals. Who sent the first Canadian contingent to cover itself with glory by aiding Britain? Sir Wilfrid Laurier. Who refused to send a contingent to aid Britain in the Egyptian campaign? Sir John A. Macdonald.'[17]

Thus the economic, social, and imperial interests of the nation demanded that the demonic Borden-Sifton-Bourassa coalition be rejected. 'In order to find a parallel in history for such an unnatural and unholy alliance one has to go back to the days of ancient Rome when Caesar, Pompey, and Cassius, with their divergent aims and ambitions, formed an alliance called "The First Triumvirate" to get control of the Government of Rome.'[18]

But most of the electors of Canada, especially in Ontario, had not so learned their history, or the lessons of the present. Convinced by a highly organized and well financed Conservative campaign that they had prosperity enough, that reciprocity threatened economic and political arrangements that had served them well, and that Laurier Liberalism was a doubtful custodian of the interests of pro-British Protestant Canadians, the electorate returned 133 Conservatives and only 88 Liberals. In Ontario the Liberals now held only 14 seats to the Conservatives 74. The twenty-first of September 1911 was the gloomiest day in living memory for Ontario Liberals. They had lost Canada because they had lost Ontario, and the national party Laurier had built lay in apparent ruin.[19]

In mid-October, only three weeks after the Liberal debacle, Premier Whitney of Ontario announced that he would shortly seek a dissolution of the Legislature. Since his government had been in office only three and a half years and had enjoyed the largest majority in the history of the province, the coming election seemed obviously timed to take advantage of the current disarray of Liberalism. To many Liberals and Conservatives alike that appeared hardly necessary, since the provincial Liberal party, even without the recent catastrophe, was in desperate straits. It had not recovered any sense of purpose since the downfall of 1905. After Ross's resignation George P. Graham had led the party for a brief seven months before his departure for a cabinet position in the Laurier government. His successor, an able Owen Sound lawyer, A.G. Mackay, was a hard worker and an excellent debater, but the party had made little progress under his leadership. In some quarters Mackay was felt to be too exclusively concerned with the interests of rural Ontario to the neglect of the cities; the temperance wing of the party found him wanting, as did enthusiasts for the public ownership of utilities. Now, with an election in the offing, he faced charges concerning his personal morals; although the accusations were made by a woman in a mental hospital, described by Mackay as 'absolute blackmail,' and never heard of again, Mackay felt obliged to resign from the leadership.

On the day that the dissolution of the Legislature was formally announced and an election called for 11 December, three hundred members of the Reform Association of Ontario were gathered in Toronto. Their first business was to appoint four representatives of the association to meet with the seventeen members of the party caucus in the Legislature to agree on a recommendation for the leadership. The position had already been offered unofficially to Mackenzie King, whose defeat six weeks earlier in North Waterloo had just relieved him of his duties as minister of labour in the federal government. But King felt that his ambitions were unlikely to be served by leadership of a small and disunited provincial opposition; if things went unexpectedly well, he might become premier of Ontario in four years time, 'but what after all is that?'[20]

Rejected by King, the party turned to Rowell and confronted him with one of the most difficult decisions of his life. At first neither he nor Nell found the proposal attractive; it would alter their lives greatly, leaving him even less time with his growing family. His health was excellent at the moment, but he had always to remember the warnings he had received from time to time of the limits to his physical strength.[21] His law practice would necessarily suffer, and although it was never his ambition to make as much money as he could, the financial sacrifice involved could not be altogether overlooked. The party was willing to pay the new leader $5,000 a year. Rowell declined the salary but welcomed the assurance that funds would be available for a private secretary and increased office assistance at party headquarters.[22]

He was still intensely interested in the issues of federal politics, especially imperial relations, but in recent years he had become increasingly concerned with the broad fields of social legislation and economic development that lay within provincial jurisdiction. The official census, just reported, showed that the urban population of Ontario had increased by nearly 400,000 in the past decade, while the rural population had declined by 50,000. With the necessary vision, Ontario might be saved from the slums, the poverty, and the inequalities of opportunity that he had found so depressing in the older industrial cities of Britain. But he had to admit that the chances of coming to power and having an opportunity of implementing policies were remote, barring some unforeseen and dramatic change; it would require years of uphill work to rebuild the party from the lowest point in its history. The Conservatives were in exuberant good health, and although Sir James Whitney was sixty-eight and might be expected to relinquish the premiership before very long, the party gave every appearance of being able to survive a change of leadership without undue strain. Apart from provincial considerations, any contribution Rowell could make to the rebuilding of the party in Ontario would also help to repair the fortunes of the federal Liberals. He might even prove to be the effective Ontario leader and lieutenant Laurier had needed for so long.

Could the work and the sacrifice be worth anything he might achieve? 'Nothing has given us more thought or prayer,' wrote Nell, 'for we realize that it may mean a turning point in our lives and may commit us to public service as we have not been before.' In the confidence that it was 'the right thing' he assumed the leadership of the Ontario Liberal party on his forty-fourth birthday.[23]

In the six weeks until polling day little could be done to remedy the party's deficiencies. Mackenzie King, who had agreed to serve as president of the provincial party organization, and the rest of the executive agreed with Rowell that he should announce as limited a platform as he could reasonably get away with, concentrate on keeping the seats the party now held, since that was all that could be expected, and then prepare to fight again another day.[24] The temperance plank in the platform was the most difficult of all. He had not changed his own views on total abolition and was at the moment a vice-president of the Dominion Alliance. He had accepted the leadership after assurances that the party was ready 'to take advanced ground on the question of temperance as well as other questions of social reform,' but there had been no agreement as to what precisely that ground would be.[25] He knew that many of his supporters, including those of his own household – for his sister Sazie was now national president of the Women's Christian Temperance Union – would be disappointed if he failed to come out immediately for total abolition of the bar. But to do so would be to commit the party to his own personal views without adequate discussion with his colleagues[26] and might prove so divisive as to end all hope of achieving any reform at all. The first announcement of the platform in the new leader's official *Address to the Electors*, published a week after his acceptance of the leadership, therefore advocated only the immediate substitution of a simple majority for the three-fifths vote now required for the adoption or repeal of local option and promised that further measures for the suppression of the liquor traffic would be presented to the people at the next election.

Much of Rowell's platform concerned northern Ontario. A number of prominent Liberals had advised him to capitalize on Whitney's strategic error in failing to present specific plans for the further development of that area.[27] His knowledge of the northern part of the province was one of his assets as party leader, and the advice fell on well-disposed ears. The platform promised the establishment of a Department of Immigration and Colonization under a minister of the crown who would devote his full time to securing more settlers, better roads, and more schools in the north. No settlement of the continuing dispute about the Ontario-Manitoba boundary that failed to give Ontario a good ocean port on Hudson Bay would be accepted by a Liberal government, and the Temiskaming and Northern Ontario Railway would be extended to the bay. An amended law would make mining titles more secure, and an eight-hour-day law for underground miners would be passed.

Revealing the considerable influence that the ideas of Henry George exercised among Ontario Liberals, but without fully adopting the single tax, the platform declared that the demands of social justice necessitated legislation to permit municipalities to put a lower tax on improvements than on land values or to abolish taxes on improvements altogether. Heavier taxes would be levied on railways to make them bear a fairer share of the costs of the economic development from which they benefited so greatly. A Liberal government would also expand the publicly owned hydro system more rapidly, especially in rural areas, and would place the telephone system under public ownership. A royal commission would look into the causes of rural decline, and city voters were promised a special study of health problems in the industrial centres of the province, a workmen's compensation act modelled on that of Britain, more industrial training schools, and the encouragement of town planning. A provincial civil service commission would be set up and appointments to the civil service would henceforth be made only after competitive examinations wherever this was feasible. 'Such trusts, mergers, and other combinations of capital as stifle competition, increase the cost of living and impair political independence' would be combated by legislation. Steps would be taken to prohibit corporation contributions to election funds, and to require the publication of all campaign contributions, and a public prosecutor would be appointed to handle charges of electoral corruption.[28] It was a platform fully in accord with the 'progressive' spirit currently dominant in North American politics generally.

Unlike Whitney's platform, Rowell's had something to say about bilingual schools, which were currently being investigated for the government by Dr F.W. Merchant. In effect, the Liberals reaffirmed the position the party had taken when the last session of the Legislature had given unanimous approval to Conservative G. Howard Ferguson's resolution declaring that English must be 'the language of instruction and of all communication with the pupils in the public and separate schools ... except where, in the opinion of the department [of education] it is impracticable by reason of the pupils not understanding English.'[29] Now Rowell promised to implement that resolution through 'the provision of adequate training schools [and] a sufficient supply of competent teachers ... to ensure under proper regulations that the pupils in every school ... shall receive a thorough English education.'[30]

The platform, admitted even by its authors to be a 'stand pat' effort, was naturally open to charges from Whitney that it was 'a skimpy chicken,' hatched from a list of things the government had already done.[31] But for all that, Rowell's platform had a good reform ring to it in its pledges of remedies for electoral abuse, its taxation policy, and its acknowledgement of the new needs of the cities. Unexciting, perhaps, but a platform from which a respectable campaign could be fought.

In the existing condition of the party, finding a seat in the Legislature for the new leader was not without difficulty, because there were few seats a Liberal could be sure of winning. The problem was resolved when Dr Andrew MacKay, the member for North Oxford, agreed to step down in Rowell's favour. It would have been hard to find a safer seat than the riding of Sir Oliver Mowat and Andrew Pattullo, with its record of unbroken Liberal victories, both provincially and federally, ever since 1867. But there was considerable opposition to an outside candidate[32] and Rowell approached the nomination meeting in Woodstock with some apprehension, as he later confessed to an audience whose warm welcome 'to one not their own' had proven his fears entirely unfounded.[33]

The Liberal campaign was officially launched at a Massey Hall meeting on 14 November. If enthusiasm were any gauge, Rowell's success was assured. The doors were closed long before the proceedings were to begin and hundreds were turned away. The platform group included few active or eminent politicians, but Senators Jaffray and Cox, W.A. Charlton MP, J.E. Atkinson of the *Toronto Star*, Dr Macdonald, Stewart Lyon, and J.F. Mackay of the *Globe*, and James Ryrie, E.R. Wood, J.W. Curry, and G.G.S. Lindsey were on hand. After Mackenzie King had discussed the social and economic condition of the province and Dr Macdonald had contributed some of his customary generalized Gaelic inspiration, Rowell concentrated on the government's failure to develop northern Ontario more rapidly, on the need to ensure an English education for all Ontario children, and on explaining his temperance policy.[34]

Nell, confident in a new black velvet dress and hat, shared a box with King's mother, Atkinson's wife and daughter, Mrs E.R. Wood, and the wife of Rowell's partner Tom Reid. It was a fine vantage point for studying the effect of the new leader's speech, and she was satisfied that she was not alone in thinking that he had spoken splendidly.[35]

The organized temperance movement was less pleased. Although Rowell had repeated his pledge to present a new policy at the next election, 'not in the form of a referendum, but as the policy of the party, upon which we will stand or fall,' that was not enough. 'There was a right thing to do. He has not done it,' charged the secretary of the Ontario Alliance, Rev. Ben Spence.[36] But Rowell remained unperturbed, convinced that, however it might appear to certain extremists, his position was 'the only right one' he could take.[37]

Another group, one that included many prohibitionists, had been cheered by Rowell's acceptance of the leadership, although most of its members were unable to support him at the polls. The Canadian Suffrage Association queried every candidate in the election about his views on women's franchise, and received from Rowell the encouraging reply expected: so far he had not had time to confer with his colleagues on this subject, but he had followed the debate on women's suffrage, especially as it had developed in Britain, and was personally 'prepared to give it most sympathetic consideration.'[38]

As the campaign was carried onto the hustings Nell accompanied him whenever she could to protect him from his absent-minded tendency to forget to dress for the cold of late fall and from failure to get enough rest. His chief platform assistant was Mackenzie King. King thought Rowell 'a man of true power and moral earnestness,' having hardly an equal in Canadian public life 'so far ... as his character and ability as a man is concerned,' and he was pleased to support him.[39] Nor was King unaware of the advantages to his own career of becoming better known in the province. For Rowell the interest of Laurier's former minister of labour in labour and industrial questions could be useful in helping to educate Ontario Liberals to take a greater interest in new social legislation. Speakers of equal distinction and experience were hard to find in this campaign; King attributed their scarcity to the desire of 'all the other men to keep out of the fight, not to be identified with a second loss.'[40] Whether for that reason or otherwise, Laurier sent his regrets at his inability to assist, while paying tribute to Rowell's 'thoroughness in everything ... his high principles, eloquence, and nervous force.'[41]

Party organization was minimal. Not only were many workers exhausted or disheartened by the federal defeat but there were even some Liberals, powerful 'machine men,' who had little interest in furthering the political fortunes of a leader so vocally hostile to their methods. King believed that this element hoped to see Rowell and himself 'wiped out' and were standing aside to watch the debacle. In any case, that kind of help was not wanted in building the party Rowell wished to create. Money was hard to raise; at best, an election close on the heels of the most expensive federal campaign in the history of the nation was bound to present unusual financial problems, and the party treasury was able to find for the whole provincial campaign only a sum equal to that spent in a number of individual ridings in the federal contest.[42]

Reciprocity dogged Rowell's campaign in other ways too. The opposition made much of his eminence as a corporation lawyer and painted him as the servant of the American companies developing the Sault Ste Marie area, companies whose garnering of Canadian money would have reached into the millions had the treacherous reciprocity policy been accepted.[43] He saw little profit in threshing the old straw of the federal campaign again nor in going out of his way to deal with implications that support of the Ross government by so outstanding a moral reformer demanded some explanation. The recent Liberal past was best ignored.

With a government well content to let general prosperity and a record of competent administration fight for it against a weak opposition the campaign was a quiet one. No major issue emerged, although the bilingual schools question was discussed as frequently as any other. But this issue cut across party lines. The attorney general, J.J. Foy, a Roman Catholic of Irish origin, declared for nothing but English in Ontario's schools, thus allying himself with the Orange wing of his party. The minister of public works, Dr J.O. Reaume, stated that as a French-speaking Canadian he could confidently support Premier Whitney's view that all children should learn English and those whose native tongue was French might be taught in French in the early grades. Liberal attempts to make capital of this conflict inside the cabinet scarcely carried the ring of conviction, for while A.G. Mackay in his strongly Orange riding of Grey North argued for no language but English, Rowell told an audience in North Bay, where there were many French Canadians, that while all children should learn English 'the state has no right to say that these same children should grow up without further knowledge of the language which they first lisped at their mothers' knees.'[44] In his own solidly English-speaking riding Rowell's emphasis was somewhat different. There he stated that there was no excuse for schools where only French was taught and called on Whitney to decide whether he agreed with Mr Foy or Dr Reaume.[45]

As an unexciting campaign drew to a close there were still seventeen constituencies where no Liberal candidate had been nominated and the Conservative would go in by acclamation. Either Rowell or King had spoken at least once in every constituency where there was a contest, but often it was impossible to feel that they were doing more than just keeping the campaign going.[46] By polling day, 11 December, all that could be hoped for was that the party be not utterly routed. But the news that began to flow into Rowell's committee rooms in Woodstock was very much better than that. He was personally elected in North Oxford with a majority of over five hundred over his Conservative opponent, Robert Lockhart, a local farmer. There were two Liberal gains, to make a total of twenty-one seats, and an encouraging increase in the popular vote, although the government still had a majority of nearly four to one in the Legislature. Rowell found no cause for complaint; a little ground had been gained and now the long-term task could be taken up.[47]

DON QUIXOTE ROWELL GOES ON THE WAR PATH.

Toronto *News* 21 November 1911

7
Leader of the opposition

As Lieutenant Governor Sir John Gibson opened the Thirteenth Legislature of Ontario on 7 February 1912, the leader of His Majesty's Loyal Opposition was well aware that he and his little band of followers put no great fear into the hearts of the Conservative hosts on the other side of the House. Like himself, more than half of the Liberal members were sitting in an elected assembly for the first time; whatever their experience in other forums their skill in parliamentary debate, like his, was still unknown. Several men had served one or two terms in the Legislature, including the former leader, A.G. Mackay; so had William Proudfoot, a Goderich lawyer and that relatively rare phenomenon – an ardent Anglican prohibitionist; T.R. Atkinson, highly successful in the town of Simcoe as lawyer and tombstone maker and renowned beyond as a crack marksman of the militia; T.R. Mayberry, a prosperous retired dairy farmer from Ingersoll; R.J. McCormick, farmer and single taxer of Lambton East; and Damase Racine, a small-town merchant from the dominantly French-Canadian riding of Russell. Only two of the group around Rowell could be considered seasoned politicians – Samuel Clarke, a Cobourg merchant and veteran of the Patrons of Industry who had held his seat since 1898, and C.M. Bowman, the Southampton leather and lumber manufacturer who was again serving as party whip.

Already in the discussions in caucus Rowell's awareness of the difficulties of building a new party had been fully confirmed. Pledged to a program of advanced social legislation to combat the evils of industrial society, he found himself the leader of a group that was essentially the hard core of the old rural Grit party of the late nineteenth century. His party's strength lay in the rural ridings of the western part of old Ontario and was augmented by a scattering of seats east to Glengarry and north as far as Rainy River. Not a single dominantly urban riding had returned a Liberal. True, Rowell expected to have the support of the member for Hamilton East, Allan Studholme, the sole representative of the Independent Labour Party in the House, but that could scarcely give the party an urban wing. A group of farmers, small-town lawyers, and merchants was unlikely to generate much enthusiasm for legislation in the interests of industrial communities, unless through a frankly opportunistic recognition that it might win votes in the larger cities where the party so obviously needed new support. But they could scarcely claim to speak for the cities.

In the fulfilment of at least one of his aspirations a party strong in rural areas was an asset, albeit perhaps a mixed one. Temperance feeling had always been strongest in rural Ontario and local option had enjoyed greater support in the towns and smaller cities than in the large urban centres. With the exception of the four French-speaking Roman Catholics, all the Liberal members were Protestants, with Presbyterians the most numerous and Methodists a close second. Not all Protestants could be counted active prohibitionists but there was a strong nucleus of temperance men in Rowell's group and the rest were likely to be open to pressure from their overwhelmingly Protestant constituents among whom temperance sentiment had been growing for so many years. But as Rowell well knew it was in the cities that liquor still cast its greatest blight and it was there that the next round of the battle must be won. A party based on the rural vote could provide a springboard for the attack, but that was all. If prohibition were to be effective it must have the support of more city voters and they must be offered strong temperance candidates in future elections.

His maiden speech was made in a situation well defined by the tradition that the chief function of the opposition in the debate on the speech from the throne was to draw attention to the weaknesses in the outline of the government's program for the session. That was fortunate, for it helped to conceal the continuing controversy over policy within the Liberal caucus, especially on the temperance issue. For the present he could safely emphasize the silence of the throne speech on the administration of the Hydro Electric system, on the unsettled Manitoba-Ontario boundary, on funds for the development of northern Ontario, on the sale of liquor, and on bilingual schools, without himself having to state more than the most general position on any of them.[1]

Why, Rowell enquired, was Whitney not proceeding to place the Hydro Commission under the control of a minister of power, a plan on which he had invited the verdict of the people in the recent election? The Liberals had opposed the proposal as infringing the rights of the municipalities, who were the real owners of Hydro, and jeopardizing the independence of muncipal governments in their relations with the provincial administration. Rowell had no difficulty in interpreting Whitney's failure to implement his earlier scheme as a Liberal victory.[2] But while Liberal and independent criticism may have had some effect, the victory in fact belonged mainly to Adam Beck, the chief architect of Hydro, chairman of the Hydro Commission, and minister without portfolio in the Whitney cabinet. Beck was adamantly opposed to any attempt to make Hydro a department of government, and later in the session he secured approval of a bill which extended the powers of the Hydro Commission and left it independent of direct government control.[3] In general Rowell and the Liberals supported Beck's bill, although they argued that the municipalities should have a representative on the commission and were critical of what they held to be the inadequate definition of some of the new and extensive powers.[4] But however the Liberals might hark back to the dying days of the Ross government when they had passed the first bill for the establishment of publicly owned power, or whatever claims they might make for the constructive nature of their continuing interest in the subject, the enormous prestige of the venture was garnered by Beck and the Whitney administration that had executed the program. No amount of Liberal talk could destroy the political advantage accruing to a regime under which electric power had been switched on in twenty-six municipalities during the past two years and would be made available to as many more very shortly.[5]

In decrying Whitney's failure to specify the funds which would be allocated to the development of northern Ontario, Rowell accused the government not only of neglecting to outline an appropriate economic policy for Ontario but of blindness to Ontario's essential contribution to the growth of the whole nation. Only if northern Ontario, and most immediately 'the clay belt,' were adequately settled and developed could the key province of the Dominion play her destined role in binding together east and west.[6] At the very next sitting Whitney announced his intention of asking the Legislature for authority to borrow five million dollars to be used for the colonization and development of northern Ontario, a move which left Rowell with little to say except to ask whether the amount was large enough.[7] Later, the opposition charged the government with failure to safeguard the important principle of parliamentary control over detailed expenditures from this fund, but no significant changes were effected as a result.[8]

An inadequate understanding of Ontario's role in the total life of the nation was also revealed in Whitney's handling of the long-disputed question of the northern section of the boundary between Ontario and Manitoba. Whitney had hoped to make some definitive progress on the matter with the new Conservative Borden government in Ottawa before the opening of the Legislature, and his failure to do so was a source of anxiety to him.[9] Whether Rowell fully appreciated the extent of Whitney's embarrassment or not, it would have been politically foolish to have failed to ask questions about the government's apparent failure to attend to the province's interests,[10] although in fact members of both provincial parties were agreed that the vital core of the whole dispute was the guaranteeing to the province of a site for a port on Hudson Bay suitable for ocean-going vessels. When Whitney was unable to give any satisfaction on the boundary question, Rowell moved a resolution declaring that Ontario's northerly boundary, like those of the four western provinces, should be the sixtieth parallel; only that limit would secure to the province her natural hinterland. Such a settlement would place the mouths of both the Nelson and Churchill rivers inside Ontario's bounds, and therefore Ontario should meet Manitoba's objections to this by agreeing that the northwest corner of the boundary would run down the middle of the Churchill River, thus giving Manitoba an opportunity to build an ocean port.[11] The Liberals were not in a very strong position on this issue; when Whitney detailed in the Legislature his government's earlier correspondence with Laurier over the boundary settlement it made plausible the Conservative contention that much of the fault for the delay in reaching agreement could be laid at Laurier's door. A week later Whitney read to the House the text of a resolution settling the boundary on lines that had been proposed in 1908 and giving Manitoba nearly all she wanted. The boundary between Manitoba and Ontario was to run northeast from a point near the fifty-third parallel to Hudson Bay at the eighty-ninth parallel, leaving Ontario with a strip five miles wide from that point to the mouth of the Nelson River.[12]

The ensuing Liberal attempt to censure the government for carrying on negotiations on such an important matter without consulting the Legislature and for ineffective presentation of Ontario's case at Ottawa was a mere formality, and the settlement was approved on a straight party vote while Whitney congratulated the Legislature for having foiled Liberal attempts to set Ontario and Manitoba against one another.[13]

The Liberals had stirred some public interest in this boundary dispute but they gained no great advantage. In an era of unprecedented prosperity, with most of northern Ontario still undeveloped and many of her resources as yet unknown, Liberal charges that Whitney's policy had deprived the province of forty thousand square miles of valuable land were powerless to excite the average Ontario voter.

Of much greater potential force was the Liberal position on taxation. Tax reform was a live issue in both parties, despite the strenuous efforts of Premier Whitney to stem the tide. In keeping with his election promise, Rowell introduced a bill to give municipalities local option in lowering taxes on improvements and raising them on land. At the same time a Conservative member, J.A. Ellis of Ottawa, had before the Legislature a private bill for the gradual abolition of all assessments on improvements at the will of the ratepayers in the municipalities. Whitney objected to both bills, and indeed tended to look on all the schemes for taxation reform that were urged upon him by successive delegations as dangerous expressions of 'Henry

George socialism.' However, he could not ignore the subject entirely and before the session was over the two bills and the whole question of tax reform had been referred to a special committee of the Legislature for study.[14]

During this session the Liberal party was less than aggressive about proposals for social reform. Rowell introduced an eight-hour-day bill for all underground workers, as an alternative to a government proposal ensuring the same hours only to actual miners, but both bills were given a six-month 'hoist,' ostensibly to allow for the study of the principles involved.[15] A Liberal bill to establish a civil service commission met the usual fate of opposition proposals.[16] During debate on three private bills to give the vote to women in various property-holding categories Rowell declared publicly for the first time his support for women's suffrage, beginning with the municipal franchise, but made it clear that this was not yet official party policy.[17] All the Liberals supported the most limited of the bills, as did a few Conservatives, but Premier Whitney declared that the question was 'a dead issue' since it was of little concern to the women themselves; if the franchise were ever extended to women it could not be given only to some but would require 'opening the flood-gates and allowing all the sisters in.'[18]

The general direction Rowell wished his party to take was indicated during the debate on the budget. Allan Studholme, the only labour member of the Legislature, had had a good deal to say about the failure of the government to give due concern to the welfare of workingmen. Rowell identified himself with Studholme's remarks and looked forward to the time when there would be additional labour representatives. He had no doubt that such representation had been good for Britain and for many European countries, and it would be good for Ontario and Canada. 'No one can be satisfied ... when we recall the statement made by the honorable member for East Hamilton, that the average wage of the workmen of Canada – skilled and unskilled – only amounts to $535 per annum ...' especially when that wage was contrasted with 'the conditions of ... reckless extravagance under which some of our citizens live ...' If the labouring men of Ontario would only display Studholme's 'ability, persistence and enthusiasm' there would be several labour representatives in the Legislature.[19] Although it was not spelled out, Rowell's meaning was clear; if a future labour group chose to support the Liberals, or better still to join them, it would give the party a welcome push. Could Rowell have guaranteed that future labour representatives would be of Studholme's stripe his purposes would be well served indeed; not only had the sixty-six year old stovemounter been an active trade unionist and single taxer in both Britain and Australia before settling in Hamilton twenty years ago, but he was as well a Methodist, a prohibitionist, an advocate of women's suffrage, and a vice-president of the Dominion Council for Moral and Social Reform.

Not until near the end of the session was Rowell able to bring his party into agreement on a liquor policy. Some members counselled leaving the matter until the next session, while others advocated the holding of a party convention and a full-scale debate of the subject. The latter course was full of danger, and Rowell could reasonably feel that the convention of the previous fall, while it had not chosen him directly, since that was the work of the group in the Legislature, had accepted him as leader with at least a general awareness of where he wanted to take the party on the liquor issue. Moreover, if a firm policy were announced now it would rally the organized temperance forces who were for the present reserving judgment on the Liberals, and would provide time for a thorough program of education to secure acceptance of the Liberal policy before the next election. Therefore Rowell pressed for a decision now, and eventually even the most reluctant members of caucus agreed: the abolition of the bar was to be official Liberal policy.

As Rowell's opening remarks in the Legislature declared, it was in large measure for this hour that he had come into public life, and his speech matched the occasion; even those most hostile to its intent agreed that it was delivered with power and eloquence. Declaring that civilized opinion everywhere was against the three great evils of modern society – the opium trade, the liquor traffic, and the white slave traffic – he drew on the authority of science, economics, the church, and common sense, and produced a mass of statistics to prove the relation between liquor and industrial absenteeism, crime, insanity, and pauperism. Although the abolition of the liquor trade was good in itself it had also to be understood as the prerequisite for other reforms; no lesser authorities than the British labour leaders John Burns and Arthur Henderson had indicted the bar as a serious barrier to the progress of workingmen. Anticipating the frequent charge that to abolish the bars where most of the drinking population got their liquor, while leaving the shop and club licences to serve the wealthier groups in society was undemocratic, Rowell left no doubt that in the end every outlet must be closed. To abolish the bars at once would strike the liquor evil at its most vulnerable point; the shops and clubs could then be dealt with by local option. By his own admission, a good deal had been accomplished under local option, a concession his opponents were quick to seize upon as justifying its continuation. Of 811 Ontario municipalities, 444 were at present dry, and another 118 would be so if a simple majority were enough to win local option contests. Such wide support for the temperance position was a clear indication that the people of Ontario were now ready to take the next big social advance open to them and do away with the public bar forever.[20]

Following Rowell the party whip, C.M. Bowman, spoke vigorously of the benefits conferred on his own town by local option, declaring it to be the best thing that had ever happened to Southampton; the lot of all citizens was improved and one merchant reported that his business had increased by 25 per cent under the dry regime. William Proudfoot and Samuel Clarke then performed, in keeping with their long devotion to the temperance cause, and were joined by William McDonald, R.J. McCormick and Hugh Munro, the carriage manufacturer from Glengarry riding. Alan Studholme also spoke in favour of abolition of the bar, but declared that he would hold Rowell to his promise to promote the abolition of club licences as well; otherwise, the destruction of the bar was class legislation.[21]

Rowell had forecast in his pre-election declaration of policy that the liquor interests and the Whitney government would respond to the Liberal platform by proposing the abolition of 'treating' in bars, a custom which was generally agreed to be a cause of much excessive drinking and attempts to exercise political influence. He was shortly proven right. Whitney declared his acceptance of everything the Liberals said about the baneful effects of liquor; indeed, that story was known to every school child, and every civilized government accepted the duty of doing whatever it could to mitigate the evils of the trade in strong drink. Whitney pointed with satisfaction to the progress in Ontario under local option, which had made much of the province completely dry. Rowell's policy would simply transfer drinking from bars to the shops and other illegal places, and encourage the growth of a vast illicit liquor trade.[22] Despite his vigorous rejection of Rowell's solution, Whitney revealed the great pressure put upon him by the temperance wing of his own party in fear that Rowell's policy might attract many temperance Conservatives[23] when he agreed that his government might take one further step – the abolition of treating. Rowell argued that the abolition of treating was an idle gesture, since the measure could not be enforced unless a policeman were stationed in every bar; its ineffectiveness made it quite acceptable to the liquor traffic and the Conservative advocacy of this 'compromise' only confirmed Liberal contentions that the liquor interests were in league with the Conservative party.[24]

Rowell's motion was defeated, and Whitney's, giving a very general commendation of the abolition of treating, was passed. These were straight party votes, with the significant exception that two of the French-speaking Liberals voted with the government. As many outsiders suspected, enthusiasm for the abolition of the bar was not unanimous on the Liberal side of the House.

Throughout the session Rowell made repeated attempts to get the government to declare a policy on bilingual schools. At first, Whitney pleaded the necessity of waiting until the completion of the Merchant Report, but the question entered a new phase when the report was presented to the Legislature on March 6. On the whole, Dr Merchant's investigation confirmed the observations of Bishop Fallon of London, the *Toronto Star*, and numerous other critics. In 80 per cent of the separate schools in eastern Ontario, and in 90 per cent of the public schools and rural separate schools in the northern districts, Dr Merchant found that French was used in teaching all subjects except English; English was treated simply as one subject among others. In many areas the professional qualifications of the teachers in these schools were minimal and some had so slight a knowledge of English as to be doubtful teachers of the language. In short, it was revealed that while there were a few schools that might properly be called 'bilingual,' most were really French schools. Although the report was appreciative of the difficulties of achieving good academic results in schools where time must be spent on promoting competence in two languages, it concluded that the bilingual schools were 'lacking in efficiency' and that most of their students were leaving school, often at a very early age, 'to meet the demands of life with an inadequate education.'[25]

On four different occasions after the tabling of the Merchant Report Rowell asked the government for a statement of government policy now that the facts were known, and was always informed that one would be forthcoming in due course.[26] Finally, half an hour before prorogation, Whitney had an announcement. He reaffirmed the government's adherence to the resolution of the previous session prescribing a knowledge of English for all Ontario school pupils, and outlined plans for additional inspection of schools to assure adequate testing of progress and enforcement of the regulations. Henceforth, state aid to schools would be contingent on the employment of teachers able to instruct in English, and no text books other than those authorized by the Department of Education would be used. Outlining what was eventually to form the core of the department's official ruling, 'Regulation 17,' Whitney declared that 'instruction in English shall commence at once upon a child entering school, the use of French as the language of instruction and of communication to vary according to local conditions upon the report of the supervising inspector, but in no case to continue beyond the end of the first form.' When questioned, the premier explained that first form meant the first two years of school, but no hard and fast rule could be laid down. Rowell enquired whether the new policy meant that Regulation 15, which provided that French or German might be used as a language of instruction in certain areas, was in effect being superseded, and was told that it was not for the present. Noting that this seemed to mean instruction in French was to continue, Rowell observed that there was much to be said for doing so; at the same time he commended Dr Merchant's suggestion that French be made a subject of study in all public schools as it was already in the high schools.[27] Thus both parties had taken a highly cautious approach to a potentially inflammable issue. As the Toronto *World* viewed it, 'Sir James had performed the sword dance awkwardly enough, but apparently without cutting his feet. Mr Rowell had pirouetted on eggs without cracking a shell.'[28]

But Rowell was not as eager to leave this issue dormant as he seemed to some observers. A week after the end of the session he devoted to the school question most of an address to a Liberal gathering in Toronto. Charging that the Department of Education had long known what the Merchant Report revealed, he accused the government of insincerity and lack of courage. He doubted whether the provisions for inspection in the new arrangements were adequate, although he believed that if the government pursued its announced policy sincerely and persistently the whole character of bilingual schools would be changed for the better. The big question was whether the government would do so. Resting on one of the privileges of opposition he did not say precisely what he would do himself.[29]

In mid-May, Toronto society was agog in anticipation of a nine-day visit from the governor general, HRH the duke of Connaught and the duchess, and their daughter, the Princess Patricia. A vice-regal visitation was always an event in loyalist Toronto, but the occasion was given added significance when the governor general was a member of the royal family, the third son of Queen Victoria, and the brother of the reigning monarch. Even those elements among Toronto opinion, including the *Star*, which had earlier expressed a strong preference for the appointment of a commoner as the Crown's representative[30] had been somewhat disarmed by the duke's first visit to the city the previous autumn and now accepted him without marked suspicion that his presence would encourage unhealthy aristocratic sentiments in the community.

Nell Rowell did not always welcome the additional social obligations that her husband's entry into public life had brought to them both, and initially she was only modestly enthusiastic about the royal visit. Like other prominent Methodists in the city, the Rowells were not in attendance at the duke's first official act in the city – the opening of the spring season of the Ontario Jockey Club at the Woodbine race track – and derived no particular satisfaction from the news that 'Heresy,' a horse owned by the Dyment brothers, long active in the Liberal party, won the King's Plate.[31] They had feared that the dinner given that night by the royal couple at Government House, to which the leader of the opposition and his wife were invited, would be 'all race and society people,' but it proved to be 'much more congenial,' since the thirty guests were mainly cabinet ministers, politicians, judges, professors, and members of the clergy. Wearing a new cream satin dress, Nell's curtseys before the royal hosts, well practised beforehand amid regret that she had not learned the art in her youth, felt less awkward than she had feared; at least her husband assured her later that they looked no different from the rest. Seated at the head table Nell had ample opportunity to observe all the details of the occasion. Approvingly, she found the dinner elegant but not ostentatious, the champagne adequate for those who cared for it (no cigarettes were offered to the guests), and the royal ladies' attire simple and in excellent taste. 'I hope' she commented in reporting the event to her sisters-in-law 'their simplicity of dress will steady some of our wealthy people for I am sure their gowns were not any better than anyone else's and their jewels are official almost.' Altogether, the Rowells had 'a splendid time' and would be 'glad to go [again] at the next chance.'[32]

The next chance was less socially select and came when four hundred members of the Empire Club and their wives celebrated Empire Day by entertaining the royal party at dinner in Convocation Hall. Somewhat reluctantly, for they had 'always made it quite an occasion with fireworks and "refreshments"'' the Rowells gave up their usual celebration of Empire Day with the children to take their places at the head table and to listen to the governor general discussing the necessity of building up the various races of Canada into a people unified by devotion to the Empire and crown.[33] Finally, there was the royal garden party at Benvenuto, the residence of the railway magnate, Sir William Mackenzie, with whom the vice-regal party was staying. Then Toronto's spring social season returned to its normal pace.

Rowell's immediate and pressing task for the summer of 1912 was party organization and the related mission of making himself and his policies better known to the people of the province. Plans had to be made at once to ensure that Liberal agents in every riding attended to the revision of the voters' lists that had been ordered after the census of 1911, so that all eligible Liberal voters would be on the lists and 'phoney' Conservative names eliminated. Three full-time party organizers were in the field: D.H. Walkinson in the north, W.F. Summerhayes in the eastern ridings, and W.H. Adams, general secretary of the Ontario Reform Association, in the central and western sections of the province. Among them, they were to visit every riding several times during the spring and summer; frequently, they experienced difficulty in finding a local Liberal executive and sometimes had to start afresh to organize new executive committees; often they could do little more than to make sure that someone, usually a local Liberal lawyer, was attending to the voters' lists.[34]

In many ridings the barrier to creating an active local party organization was still the pervasive apathy arising from the party's unhappy experiences at the polls during the past year, but in some, notably in northern Ontario, there was marked discontent over the temperance policy.[35] And in southern constituencies the members of the Ward Six Liberal Association of Toronto were not alone in decrying the manner in which the temperance policy had been adopted. Even some of the most ardent abolitionists declared that the party would be stronger had a provincial convention been given an opportunity to endorse abolition, and they demanded that no further radical steps be taken by the leadership outside a party convention. In the end, ward six Liberals, in common with numerous Liberal organizations elsewhere, supported the temperance policy unanimously,[36] but they left more than a suspicion among outsiders that unanimity was usually an attempt to present a bold front to the world rather than an outpouring of undivided conviction. Yet there was no doubt that the temperance cause was gaining ground in both parties. The Conservative *Mail and Empire* went so far as to declare that if Rowell's campaign succeeded in gaining enough public support, the Whitney government, with its usual responsiveness to the popular will, would abolish the bar.[37]

In London at the beginning of a series of summer speaking engagements Rowell put this indirect suggestion of a possible bipartisan policy to the test by challenging Whitney to give up his 'ineffective and inefficient substitute' for abolition and join with him in the auguration of Ontario's golden age.[38] But no Conservative hand was extended to grasp this opportunity, and Rowell therefore continued his campaign to persuade the electors that only his party had serious intentions of temperance reform.

At the same time he was busy enlarging the party's interest in northern Ontario. At the end of July a group of Ontario Liberals, nearly one hundred strong, made a six-day tour of the north. Each constituency was invited to send one representative Liberal, and the party was completed by the addition of several Liberal journalists and a number of prominent Liberal businessmen, including J.E. Atkinson, A.E. Ames, James Ryrie, William G. Jaffray, and R.S. Gourlay, president of the Toronto Board of Trade. Depleted Liberal coffers and, as Rowell explained, 'Sir James' threatened anti-treating legislation' dictated adherence to the principle of each man paying his own fare of about fifty dollars.[39] From their special train on the provincial government's Temiskaming and Northern Ontario Railway the tourists from the south saw all the major centres from Cobalt to Cochrane, visiting silver and gold mines, inspecting the agricultural developments in the Clay Belt and at the provincial experimental farm at Monteith, and discussing the area's needs with managers and miners, businessmen and farmers.[40] After the northern tour Rowell embarked on a week's intensive cultivation of his own riding. Taking his family with him in a rented automobile, a mode of transportation still novel enough to excite some public comment, he made the kind of village-to-village campaign through North Oxford that had been impossible in the short time before the election. Choosing the centre of his riding, Woodstock, for a major pronouncement on social legislation, he addressed himself to the workingmen in the furniture and hardware factories, carriage works, boiler plants, and other small industries in the town, and later in print, to workingmen throughout the province. It was the fullest statement of a social philosophy that he had yet made from a political platform. Its central premise was easy to grasp: 'We have in the past been greatly concerned in the production of wealth. We must now devote more attention to the question of the distribution of wealth; because on its distribution so largely depends the welfare of our citizens.'[41]

Rowell contended that the most urgently needed social legislation in the province was, as the recent Liberal election platform had proclaimed, a new Workmen's Compensation Act. The existing act, placed on the statute books by the Mowat government in 1885, no longer met the needs of industrial life, and its perpetuation left Ontario much behind nearly all the civilized world – Britain, Germany, Russia, all the other self-governing colonies of the Empire, and a majority of the Canadian provinces. Under the operation of the present Ontario law, with its severe limitations on the type of accident covered, not more than 20 per cent of the victims of industrial accidents were entitled to compensation for injuries suffered at work. Even when a workman was entitled to collect compensation he could rarely stand the expenditure necessary to pursue his case in the courts against his employer and the wealthy insurance company with which the employer was usually insured against such liabilities. As Rowell had seen it in operation, the present law did more to provide employment for lawyers and insurance companies than compensation for workmen. Yet, despite the admitted need for a new law, the Whitney government had procrastinated in coming to grips with the problem ever since 1907 when a bill that had proved unacceptable to both employers and employees had been withdrawn from the Legislature. In lieu of legislation Whitney had appointed a commission to acquire information about measures in other countries – information which a responsible government should have had in its possession – and then to consider the whole problem in Ontario. Although the interim report of the commissioner, Chief Justice Sir William Meredith, tabled in the Legislature at the last session, had declared bluntly that the present law was 'entirely inadequate' there was reason to doubt that the government intended to enact a measure equal to the prevailing conditions; if it did, it would have the full support of the Liberal opposition.[42]

The underlying principles of an acceptable workmen's compensation scheme would begin, in Rowell's view, with an acceptance of the fact that industrial accidents were 'apparently ... one of the sacrifices which our modern civilization demands as a condition of our industrial progress.' That being so, why should the victims of industrial accidents bear the whole loss, as was nearly always the case in Ontario now? 'If modern industry demands this sacrifice, why should not the industry bear the cost? In the past we have been jealous for the rights of property and property should be protected ... by law, but the rights of humanity have not been sufficiently recognized and protected. For the future these rights must receive greater emphasis, and whenever we must choose between the two, the rights of humanity must prevail.' If industry bore the cost of compensation for accidents it would increase the cost of production, and that increase would, rightly, be passed on to the community as a whole. 'The community now seeks to bear the cost through public or private charity of those in absolute need. But workmen and workwomen should not be dependent on uncertain charity for that which they should enjoy as a right, as industrial workers working for the good of the whole community.'[43]

Beyond that, adequate legislation and factory inspection would seek to prevent industrial accidents, but when they did occur there must be no necessity to establish blame for the accident; it mattered not to the families of injured workmen whether a crippling or fatal accident was the fault of the worker or his employer. Occupational diseases must come under the act, as they did not at present. An employee or his dependents must be enabled to secure the compensation to which they were entitled without recourse to litigation. Rowell concluded that with her superior resources and the experience of other industrial communities to draw on, notably that of Britain and the state of Washington, Ontario should have the most advanced and generous workmen's compensation in the world.[44]

Neither the Canadian Manufacturers' Association nor the Trades and Labor Congress would have taken exception to most of Rowell's argument: that was clear from representations the two bodies had made in recent months to the Meredith commission.[45] But full acceptance of his claim that industry should bear the cost of compensation would resolve the major disagreement between industry and labour on this subject. Although he did not say so specifically, Rowell's whole presentation of the matter seemed to imply that the employees, contrary to the current contention of the employers, should not be required to contribute to the compensation fund.

Rowell's prescription for an improved lot for the workingman did not end with workmen's compensation. He urged his Woodstock audience to support the Liberal party in pressing for the establishment of a provincial Department of Health with sufficient funds to enable it to devote ample thought and money to the prevention of disease. The now dormant Bureau of Labour should be revived to carry out investigations of working conditions and the government should provide positive leadership in preventing the growth of the kind of living and working conditions that blighted the lives of millions in the big cities of Europe and the United States. The province urgently needed a new Department of Labour and Public Health headed by a full-time minister of the crown, a man in full sympathy with the masses of the people and devoted to making Ontario one of the most civilized communities in the world instead of one of the most backward.[46]

The education of a different group in the community was the purpose of a dinner at the National Club to which Rowell invited a number of Ontario business leaders to meet four visiting Britons. Sir Thomas Whittaker, a Liberal member of the British Parliament and president of the United Kingdom Provident Institution, one of the major insurance organizations in Britain, was in Canada, like another of the guests, Henry Holloway, a leading building contractor and Wesleyan layman, to assess investment opportunities for business capital. But for this evening Sir Thomas was primarily the social reformer, the former chairman of a parliamentary committee whose work had resulted in the Trade Boards Act of 1909, which established minimum wages in some of the lowest paid trades in Britain. Whittaker explained that the extension of the principle of the minimum wage was both just and inevitable, as was the growth of contributory insurance schemes to help all workers during sickness or unemployment and to care for the indigent aged.[47] The other guests, Mr Isaac Mitchell and Sir George Askwith of the British Board of Trade, had come to Canada to study the operation of Mackenzie King's Industrial Disputes Investigation Act of 1907. Askwith, by virtue of his contributions to the settlement of the great railway and dock strikes of the past year, had recently been appointed chief industrial commissioner for the British government. Whatever he may have heard from Toronto businessmen about labour conciliation procedures in Canada, Askwith was left in no uncertainty about the attitude of organized labour. Attending the annual meeting in Guelph of the Trades and Labor Congress of Canada, he learned that the Congress had agreed to urge the immediate repeal of the Industrial Disputes Investigation Act.[48]

By the early autumn of 1912 Rowell looked back on his first year as party leader with some satisfaction. From the detaching distance of Lake Mohonk, New York, where he was attending a meeting of the Continuation Committee of the Edinburgh Conference, he replied to Mackenzie King's request for an assessment of their party's situation: 'On not less than six or seven matters of first rate importance has the Government abandoned its old position & adopted ours or some substitute therefore.' These included hydro-electric administration and rural extension, the development of northern Ontario, taxation, temperance, the control of tuberculosis, the eight-hour day for miners, and workmen's compensation.[49] There was encouragement too in the tax reformers' enthusiasm for Rowell's position on taxation: the single taxers who predominated in the Tax Reform League of eastern Ontario applauded their president, Stewart Lyon of the *Globe*, when he commended Rowell heartily as 'a most ardent advocate' of tax reform.[50] Moreover, his temperance policy had, not surprisingly, received enthusiastic endorsation from a host of Methodist, Presbyterian, and Baptist church courts and from an impressive list of individual clergymen and educators. The *Christian Guardian*, forsaking its usual political neutrality, left no doubt in the minds of its readers that their Christian duty lay in support of the Liberal temperance platform.[51] Never had the organized temperance forces in Ontario been more vigorous or better financed; the educational fund of the Ontario branch of the Dominion Alliance had increased from $14,000 to $55,000 in four years, it had ten full-time field secretaries at work and in the past year it had sponsored three thousand public meetings.[52] But over all this activity there hung, as always, a large political question: how many voters would forsake their normal party preferences on a single issue when it came time to go to the polls?

Two imminent by-elections for which the party was ill-prepared provided a partial answer to that question. Rowell was anxious to put up a strong fight in both North Waterloo and East Middlesex but his determination was not matched by the riding executives. In the former, the local Liberals failed to persuade a strong candidate to run and thereafter were too discouraged to nominate anyone else;[53] two independents were allowed to provide the only opposition and the government retained the seat easily. East Middlesex Liberals 'mixed matters up almost as badly,' Rowell complained to King. The entry into the contest of William Sutherland as an independent candidate pledged to temperance reform made the Liberals reluctant to oppose him; and instead they agreed to endorse Sutherland if he would declare his commitment to the Liberal platform of the abolition of the bar. It took Sutherland so long to come to the right conclusion that by then, ten days before election day, Rowell was unhappily aware that 'the Liberals have lost their enthusiasm and the Temperance people have lost faith in him ... it looks like a very difficult situation.'[54] For the duration of the brief campaign Rowell gave his undivided attention to the battle. There was only one issue: would East Middlesex gain 'the proud distinction of leading this province in ... wiping out the bar.' As if preparing to accept defeat he added: 'But no matter what you do it will not stop the progress of the fight, for the moral sense of Ontario is against the open bar, and the open bar is going to go.'[55] It was as well to be prepared; in the result the Liberal majority of 540 achieved in the election of a year before was almost exactly reversed in favour of the Conservatives.

Despite his day-to-day preoccupation with the affairs of the provincial party Rowell was much concerned with the developing agitation in Toronto over Canadian responsibility for naval defence. Borden's election had been followed by a long Conservative silence on the naval issue, while from Britain came reports, official and unofficial, of mounting anxiety over the Empire's capacity to meet the threat of the growing German navy. Many Ontarians, both Conservative and Liberal, were dismayed by Borden's procrastination and behind the politicians, notably among business and professional men, there was continuing discussion of the defence question. One of the first public manifestations of the strength of this agitation and of its bipartisan character was a largely attended meeting of the National Club when two of its members, Rowell and T.W. White, spoke on imperial problems; White, one of 'the Eighteen' who had departed from the ranks of Toronto Liberals over reciprocity, was now Borden's minister of finance. In one of the most positive statements to come from a member of the government in some time White expressed his absolute confidence that the Parliament and people of Canada would do their share in imperial defence and anticipated the next step in imperial organization as some form of federal union of the Empire. While expressing 'very great satisfaction' at White's assurances about the willingness of Canada to assume its defence responsibilities, Rowell's emphasis was different: improved communications, the Imperial Conference, and the creation of the Imperial Council of Defence could all be valuable instruments for imperial unity, but only if the autonomy of the Dominions and the voluntary nature of their co-operation in matters of common concern were fully respected. He made no direct reference to imperial federation, but clearly he was no more enthusiastic about it than he had ever been.[56]

During the summer of 1912, while Borden and several of his ministers were in London for discussions with the British Admiralty, enthusiasts for a bipartisan naval policy were at work in Toronto, Winnipeg, and several other centres on a series of resolutions which they planned to issue as a memorial calling for a non-party naval policy. Rowell was a member of the original group of twenty or so Toronto men who accepted the invitation of G. Frank Beer, a Liberal manufacturer, to work on the problem; the others present included editors of all the Toronto daily newspapers, Sir Edmund Walker, Sir William Mackenzie, J.W. Flavelle, W.E. Rundle, and D.B. Hanna. Atkinson would have been just as pleased if the meeting had never been held,[57] but like Winnipeg's Liberal editor, J.W. Dafoe, he participated in the drafting of the memorial in the hope of preventing it from becoming an expression of 'the Toronto jingo vein' committing 'hundreds of Liberals ... to policies that would compromise them in the future.'[58] Macdonald of the *Globe* felt even more strongly, and, unlike Atkinson, refused to sign the memorial, in keeping with his view that it was not only impossible but undesirable even to try to take important issues out of politics; a non-partisan policy, he warned, would remove the vital question of defence from the control of the Canadian people.[59]

There can be no doubt that Rowell found the memorial, at least, unobjectionable. He had long favoured Laurier's plan for the creation of a Canadian navy, to be placed at the service of the Empire in time of need at the discretion of the Canadian Parliament. In effect, the memorial endorsed that plan as the country's permanent naval policy, while leaving room for the immediate emergency cash contributions for additions to the British navy that seemed likely to become Conservative policy. But Rowell's signature did not appear on the published document, an omission which can be attributed either to sentiments in him similar to Macdonald's or to the desire of the organizers of the movement to underline its representative and non-partisan character by keeping it free from association with leading politicians of both parties.

Shortly after his return from Britain, Prime Minister Borden was entertained by the Toronto Board of Trade at a non-party banquet, said to be the largest dinner ever held in Canada. On the floor of the new Mutual Street Arena fifteen hundred men sat down to eat, while an audience of ten thousand listened to the speeches from the surrounding tiers of seats. After Premier Whitney and the Toronto members of the federal cabinet had lauded Borden's great services to Canada and to imperial unity during his two months in Britain, the prime minister emphasized his belief that in England he had spoken, and had been accepted, not as the leader of one party, but as the representative of the whole Canadian people; in that capacity he had been confident in promising that Canada would not fail the Empire in her hour of need. Although declaring that his experience in Britain had convinced him that there was indeed an emergency in imperial defence, he declined to make any comment until the convening of Parliament on the form Canadian assistance would take.[60] Rowell and J.E. Atkinson were the two Liberal speakers of the evening. Borden welcomed, as 'a strong imperial speech,' Rowell's rhetorical question to Britons: 'As Canadians, as a self-respecting, liberty-loving, virile people, shall we not say the time has come when we must bear our share and take up our burden with you?'[61]

While Toronto was entertaining Borden, Laurier was embarking on his first extensive speaking tour of Ontario since the great defeat of a year before. During his visit to the western part of the province Rowell joined him for a series of meetings in Woodstock which brought together fourteen thousand Liberals, all told, from several counties. Under the unmistakable warmth of the welcome accorded 'the old chief' the seventy-one-year-old Laurier turned on all his old charm and eloquence. The response was enough to persuade Rowell that 'if the trade agreement with the United States were out of the way Sir Wilfrid would make very large gains in Ontario at the next election.'[62] Fortunately, the trade question was at least dormant, but defence was not. At one of the Woodstock meetings, where he shared the platform of the Opera House with Laurier, Rowell decried Conservative talk of an emergency naval policy as 'side-tracking'; the real problem was Canada's permanent policy. In contrast to the Conservatives, the Liberals had a policy in their commitment to the establishment of a Canadian navy. Laurier had 'blazed the path of Canadian participation in Imperial naval defence' and 'pioneered the way not only for to-day but for generations yet to come. The policy of Borden is to talk loyalty; the policy of Laurier is to practise it.'[63]

A month later in a speech to the Montreal Reform Association Rowell again charged that the Conservatives had no policy. Privately he admitted that the resignation of the Quebec Nationalist, F.D. Monk, from the Borden cabinet because of his rejection of the Conservative naval policy then being shaped would help Borden in English Canada by taking a good deal of the punch out of the charge that the government was dominated by the Nationalists,[64] but that line of attack was still worth using. Clearly the Conservative party could not have a policy: 'How,' Rowell asked, 'can it reconcile the irreconcilable elements within its own bosom? How can it reconcile any action it may take with the pledges it made to secure

Nationalist support in Quebec against the Liberal government in Ontario and other parts of Canada?' He offered no precise prescription for action, but declared that it must be prompt, 'not because of any so-called "emergency," but because action is overdue and our own self-respect will no longer permit us to let the mother country bear our responsibilities.' Canadian defence policy should 'not be formed in response to the spirit of militarism. Our navy is not for aggression, but for the defence of our coasts and the protection of our trade routes; for the maintenance of the traditions and ideals for which our British system of government and our flag stand.'[65]

On this occasion, as on several others in succeeding months, Rowell used the statement of the former British Conservative prime minister, A.J. Balfour, to the Imperial Conference of 1911 as his text for discussing the method by which imperial relations, including the determination of naval responsibility, should be conducted. In Rowell's view Balfour's pronouncement was 'entirely satisfactory' to Canadian Liberals as 'the frankest recognition by a statesman of Great Britain ... so far ... of the status of the self-governing Dominions.'[66] Balfour looked forward to the day when the continuing evolution of the British Dominions would 'build up something which the world has never yet dreamed of – a coalition of free and self-governing communities who feel that they are never more themselves, never more masters of their own fate, than when they recognize that they are parts of a greater whole, from which they can draw inspiration and strength.'[67]

ROOT AND BRANCH REFORM

Toronto *Globe*
17 October 1912

Rowell's approach to the naval problem left the way open for him to approve almost any form of Canadian contribution. Thus, when Borden introduced his government's proposal for a $35 million contribution to build additional ships for the British navy he did not identify himself with the denunciations of Laurier, the *Globe*, and much of the rest of the Liberal press, or with their claims that on the evidence provided by the British Admiralty itself there was no emergency and the organization of a permanent Canadian navy should therefore be advanced. The worst that Rowell could say about Borden's naval bill was that it did not go far enough since it failed to provide for the manning and maintenance of the ships that were to be built with Canadian money.[68]

As the parliamentary debate on the naval aid bill wore on through almost four months to its final passage by the newly instituted use of closure, Rowell gave no indication of his attitude to the determined adherence of the Liberal opposition in the House of Commons to the creation of a distinctly Canadian navy. On only one aspect of the new policy did Rowell voice any apprehension: what were its implications for Canadian autonomy? Borden had made it clear that Canada's participation in imperial defence must be accompanied by new forms of consultation within the Empire on the foreign policy of which defence was an instrument, but he had given no hint as to how consultation was to be worked out in practice. Rowell favoured the principle of consultation; he did not share the *Globe*'s view that Borden's interest in a common imperial foreign policy was 'treason to what is most significant and most far-reaching in Canadian history.'[69] But he had firm views on how consultation should be conducted, or at least on how it ought not to be conducted. He was disturbed by the knowledge that at the meeting of the Committee of Imperial Defence held in 1911 foreign policy had been discussed in a manner that gave cause for alarm lest the committee take over some of the policy-making discussions until then carried on in the Imperial Conference.[70] Such a development would have most disquieting consequences for Dominion autonomy, as Rowell elaborated in an address given in Owen Sound the day after the Commons approved Borden's policy of financial contribution. The defence committee was 'an unrepresentative and irresponsible body' created by the British prime minister and responsible only to him. Such a body could fill a useful role for its overseas members by acquainting them with the facts of the defence picture but anyone who thought it could 'constitute the nucleus or starting point for some form of closer Imperial organization, misreads and misunderstands the temper of the people of the overseas Dominions.' Canadians were satisfied with the Imperial Conference as the vehicle of consultation; in the future, a Canada many times larger would not be so satisfied. But let the future generation devise its own policies to suit its own needs. Many things might be different by then: 'Europe to-day is an armed camp. Before another generation this ruinous policy may have made Europe bankrupt, or the idea of international arbitration may have so grown as to change the whole problem of defence.' This being so, it was unfortunate that a question as important as imperial relations was being thrust upon Canadians amid partisan feeling on the naval question that made it difficult for them to examine the alternatives on their merits.[71]

In Rowell's view there were four main options: independence, the formation of a 'new central organization or body to control the external affairs of the Empire,' the continuation of the present relationship, or the development of 'a great co-operative alliance between the free nations of the Empire.' There were many who held that only the first two were live options; but under new conditions might not a great British alliance be a possible choice? Calling to the support of his argument the British colonial theorist, Richard Jebb, whose books, *The Imperial Conference* of 1911 and *The Britannic Question* of 1913, he seems to have studied carefully, Rowell warned that any attempt 'to force the pace' would destroy the creative possibilities of the future. 'Just as the British cabinet system, unrecognized has grown out of the needs and exigencies of administration to be the most powerful organ of government under our constitution, so I believe in the Imperial Conference we have the nucleus of an Imperial body, which, if we are but true to the genius of the British people, may develop to meet the needs of the future, and with the Crown and the Throne may constitute the central and unifying organization of the Empire.'[72] Such a policy, pragmatic and gradual, offered no dramatic solution to imperial problems, but it was consistent with his reading of British history and his understanding of the Canadian experience.

'The nerve of the working class!' Toronto *Globe* 29 March 1913

8
Abolish-the-bar

The opening of the Legislature in early February 1913 revealed an opposition of somewhat more reforming temper and fighting spirit than a year earlier. Rowell was absent from the House for the first week with an attack of influenza; an aggressive Liberal attack on taxation during the throne speech debate was therefore led by the able member for Middlesex West, J.C. Elliott. The Liberals were emboldened in their demands for a lower rate of taxation on buildings, businesses, and incomes by the wide public clamour on the subject. In recent weeks taxation had become an even more sensitive issue for the government because of the defection of two Ottawa papers normally friendly to the Conservatives; the *Citizen*, whose managing editor, Wilson Southam, was a vice-president of the Single Tax League, and the *Journal* both asserted that Conservative resistance to tax reform had become a sufficient reason for a change of government.[1] On his first day in the House, Rowell came vigorously to Elliott's support and it was soon evident that the Liberals had got under the premier's skin. Whitney once again gave the impression that he did not understand, or had no interest in, this kind of economic question, for he allowed other members of his party to make the undoubtedly arguable economic case against the Liberal proposals. The premier himself resorted to guilt-by-association tactics: the whole Ontario tax reform movement was 'Henry George Socialism' promoted by 'Southam ... who worked for Sir Wilfrid Laurier in the fight for reciprocity ... and who does not believe in anything that other people believe in ...' What self-respecting citizen, asked the premier, could support a movement heavily financed by 'the unutterable Joseph Fels?' The Philadelphia soap manufacturer, single tax leader, and Zionist, had drawn large crowds to recent meetings in several Ontario centres and had been given an interview by the premier. Whitney also held it against the tax reform movement that it had as one of its leaders the assistant editor of the *Globe*, 'Mr Stewart Lyon who does not think it possible for a Tory to be a good man.'[2]

Tax reform, Rowell retorted, was 'no more a Henry George theory' than the indubitably respectable report of the British royal commission on housing of 1885. He quoted at length from the British report to demonstrate the evils of a taxation policy that allowed land to lie idle, militated against the restoration of agricultural land to cultivation, encouraged city slums by failing to provide any incentive for the construction of better housing, and thus contributed to the miseries of both rural and urban populations. Under the present system of taxation in Ontario, Rowell argued, it was possible for a man to hold his land for an increase in value far exceeding the yearly tax and sell it at a higher price, the increase in value being due solely to the improvements made on adjacent properties by his more industrious neighbours whose enterprise was then rewarded by a higher tax rate.[3] But all that the Liberals gained from their efforts to relieve the burden of taxation on industry was a government promise to clarify the meaning of a section of the Assessment Act.

At long last the government introduced a draft bill for a Workmen's Compensation Act. It made employers responsible for all accidents except those caused by wilful misconduct among over 400,000 Ontario workers who would be eligible for minimum average compensation of $4,000.[4] The Canadian Manufacturers' Association quickly denounced the bill as unworkable and preposterous and the rate of compensation exorbitant; at such a rate, the manufacturers contended, the argument for contributions from the workmen themselves was irrefutable, although the draft bill placed the whole cost on the employers.[5] Before long, Whitney withdrew the bill under a barrage of protests that the measure would add so much to operating costs that Ontario manufacturing concerns would be unable to meet competition, notably from Quebec where labour costs were already lower.[6] Pressed by Rowell to declare when the bill or an alternative would be reintroduced the premier replied that it would not be during that session.[7] The opposition's silence on the measure, especially on the question of workmen's contributions, suggested that at least some of the Liberals were not altogether unhappy with the result.

Rowell was a little more aggressive when he tackled the role of combines and monopolies in the province. The currently operative legislation was the British Statute of Monopolies of 1897 which the provincial legislature had declared in that year to be in effect in Ontario. Rowell wanted to know why the government had dropped the case against the alleged 'tack combine' in Toronto which had been investigated as long ago as 1905. 'Corporations in Ontario ... will not be different from those in the United States until we have a vigorous and efficient enforcement of the law,' Rowell asserted.[8] Later in the session, J.C. Elliott asked why only one member of the Stamped Ware Association, the hardware manufacturers, had been fined the small sum of $1,000 in 1912, while all the other companies investigated had gone free of penalty, and why prosecution of the Grocers' Guild for alleged combinations to control certain food prices had recently been dropped.[9] The government had a ready answer to these questions: like the federal Combines Investigation Act the provincial statute left the decisions to investigate and to prosecute to the attorney general's department, and in all these instances the government pleaded insufficient evidence to warrant prosecution.

When the government introduced a bill regulating conditions and hours of work for certain employers in factories, shops, and office buildings, the Liberals gave the measure close criticism. The bill broke little new ground, being largely a consolidation of existing statutes and Rowell attacked it as entirely inadequate for a progressive industrial society, demanding that it be replaced by measures based on modern principles of factory regulation and inspection.[10] Later he introduced a series of specific amendments to the government bill: provision for the appointment of additional women as factory inspectors; a prohibition against employing children during school hours or for more than eight hours a day; the raising of the legal age for the employment of children from twelve to fourteen years; a requirement that no employer be permitted to hire anyone under fifteen unless the prospective employee could produce a certificate of ability to read and write; a ban on the employment of youths or young girls in properties below street level; and the empowering of inspectors to prohibit the employment of any child or youth whose health was deemed to render him unfit for the employment in question.[11] These amendments formed a program of factory legislation significantly in advance of the government's measures, but they were all lost.

The same fate attended Rowell's motion for the revision of the administration of the laws affecting labour. The existing system was loosely organized: the Bureau of Labour, established in 1900, exercised its limited and ill-defined functions under the Department of Public Works, while the Factory and Workshops Act was administered by the Department of Agriculture, and the welfare of miners was attended to by the Department of Lands and Forests. J.E. Atkinson of the *Star* was the original framer of the motion Rowell presented to the Legislature for the amalgamation of all agencies concerned with labour under the supervision of a full-time minister of labour. Atkinson's proposed resolution had the prior approval of James Simpson and Fred Bancroft, president and vice-president of the Trades and Labor Congress of Canada, who believed that administrative reorganization was an essential preliminary to remedying the serious defects of Ontario's law regulating conditions of labour, especially among women and girls.[12]

A broader approach to labour questions informed Rowell's later demand for the appointment of a commission to investigate the whole problem of conditions of labour and the well-being of wage earners in the province. In Ontario, one of the wealthiest communities in the world, there were gross inequalities in the distribution of the fruits of industry he contended, and it was becoming more and more difficult for a workingman to maintain a home and raise a family in decency. Only careful research into existing conditions by a group of qualified commissioners could lead to valid remedies of the situation.[13]

Speaking for himself only and not for the party, Rowell was prepared outside the Legislature to declare to the Men's Union of Earlscourt Methodist Church what some of those remedies should be: he would follow the institution of workmen's compensation with a system of social insurance designed to offer the workingman some protection against the economic disabilities imposed on him and his family by sickness, unemployment, old age, and death. Present wage levels made it impossible for workers to do anything to shield themselves against these afflictions; while social insurance must not become an alternative to better wages, it would do much to enhance the dignity and comfort of thousands of citizens.[14]

Once again the House debated women's franchise in various forms, with Rowell supporting bills to give the municipal vote to property-owning women both single and married and to confer the parliamentary franchise on all women qualified to vote in municipal elections. Again these measures enjoyed the endorsement of most Liberals, and a few independent Conservatives, but were still far from becoming law. Once more the Liberals endeavoured to censure the government's development of New Ontario, and again decried the delayed extension of hydro service into rural areas.

No episode of the session received as much publicity as the allegations of improper and corrupt conduct brought against Whitney and the provincial secretary, W.J. Hanna, by William Proudfoot. For a time it appeared that 'the Proudfoot charges' would reveal serious chinks in the armour of the premier who was 'bold enough to be honest,' and perhaps would act as an antidote to the long hangover of corruption charges from the Ross era under which the Liberals had for so long suffered. Proudfoot, Rowell, and several other Liberals demanded that a royal commission investigate Hanna's alleged receipt of a $500 contribution to the Conservative election fund of 1908 in return for the settlement of certain claims arising from a government contract for supplies for the provincial prison farm at Guelph. The government majority rejected this procedure and the charges were referred to the House Committee on Privileges and Elections. Rowell and the eight other Liberal members of the committee found that their interpretation of the evidence differed sharply from that placed upon it by the twenty-nine Conservative members.

The result of several stormy sessions involving a variety of procedural controversies was two reports, majority and minority, in which favourable and unfavourable conclusions were drawn on strict party lines. In the end, while it appeared that Hanna could fairly be charged with indiscretion, there was little to persuade the uncommitted that the provincial secretary or the premier was guilty of gross corruption.[15] Rowell remained convinced that the investigation had been a farce and publicly declared his belief that a more independent tribunal would have reached a different verdict.[16]

Early in the session Rowell reopened the liquor question by challenging Whitney to introduce his promised anti-treating legislation. The Liberals had by no means changed their minds about the inadequacy of such a measure but were prepared to support it as a step in the right direction. Whitney sidestepped this test of his sincerity by capitalizing on the government's victory in the East Middlesex by-election. At least half of the big Conservative majority there, Whitney claimed, was the work of Liberals who objected to their party's 'abolish-the-bar' policy. He further declared that the failure of the Liberals to run candidates at all in three, more recent by-elections was an admission of the divisions amongst Liberals on the liquor issue. Whitney found the relation of the Liberal leader himself to the liquor trade highly ambiguous: as a director of the *Globe*, Rowell had money 'pouring into his pockets' from the liquor advertisements published in the paper. Whitney read from a recent editorial in the *Christian Guardian* decrying a policy that allowed the *Globe* to accept such advertisements while at the same time waging editorial war on the sale of liquor.[17] The premier's hearty delight in subjecting Rowell to this kind of goading was shared by many members of the Legislature, for Whitney was not alone in feeling a strong distrust of 'men who pose as moral reformers and endeavour to draw a line between themselves and the rest of the community.'[18]

For Rowell it was all rather awkward. There was no denying the party's by-election failures. While he was able to announce that he had resigned as a *Globe* director six weeks earlier, that did not take the barb out of Whitney's next question, whether he had also sold all his shares in the company to free himself from 'that tainted money.'[19] But at least there was no open break in the party ranks and the 'abolish-the-bar' resolution was again defeated on a straight party vote.

The response of the voters to the Liberal temperance policy continued to be discouraging. In a South Lanark by-election where Rowell kept the abolition of the bar at the centre of his campaign the Conservative majority of the previous election was somewhat reduced but the government candidate was still decisively returned. In Grey Centre the victory of T.B. Lucas at the previous general election had been so resounding that the Liberals decided not to waste their energies in opposing him in the by-election necessitated by his appointment as provincial treasurer. But they approached North Grey, long one of their own strongholds, with optimism. A.G. MacKay's decision to escape the blight of scandal and to leave Owen Sound to build a new legal and political career in Edmonton precipitated a mid-summer election which Rowell fully expected to win. Highlighting 'the Proudfoot charges' and their temperance policy, and with a candidate who had the official endorsement of the Political Action Committee of the Ontario Alliance, the Liberals put every ounce of effort they could muster into the North Grey contest, only to find that they polled twelve hundred fewer votes than two years earlier and lost the seat to a Conservative who had made no promises on the liquor question, save to support the government.

For Rowell it was a severe political blow because of its possible general effect on 'the temperance cause and the other movements we are advocating – the defeat in itself is not so important but it will no doubt materially affect the public mind & they are apt to conclude that the people do not desire our policy of "abolish the bar" ... in political life ... they forgive anything if you succeed; the only thing they do not forgive is failure.'[20] Personally, he was not depressed: 'If a man were fighting simply for political preferment these defeats would mean much more than they do to me. As long as I do what I believe is right & in the public interest my conscience is clear and I can leave the results with Providence. I am going to forget about these things and have a real good summer in England.'[21]

Sailing from Montreal on the ss *Megantic* and enjoying a sightseeing visit to Quebec City, his memory went back to his trip to Quebec thirteen years earlier with Mary and Nell and to its happy outcome. 'Insofar as you helped me secure a wife,' he wrote his sister, 'I cannot be grateful enough for the one Providence has given me. Nell is a jewel.'[22] Regrettably, Nell was not with him now, but she and the two children were to join him later in England.

As usual this was to be a working holiday and he was armed with letters of introduction and plans to assist him in learning all he could about social and political conditions in Britain. In the past seven years under the 'New Liberalism' of the administrations of Sir Henry Campbell-Bannerman and H.H. Asquith, Britons had taken their first decisive steps toward the welfare state, and Rowell was eager to study the operation of the new legislation at first hand. With Lloyd George, chancellor of the exchequer and prime initiator of the National Insurance Act, he discussed the scheme that had given all workingmen some protection against sickness, and a few of them a buffer against the economic devastation of unemployment. Lloyd George was more impressed by Rowell's ability and sincerity than by any other Canadian public figure he had met, with the exception of Laurier.[23] Sidney Buxton, president of the Board of Trade, was a helpful informant on social insurance and labour legislation, and from John Burns, president of the Local Government Board, he had an account of the working of the Housing and Town Planning Act. The only Methodist in the government, Walter Runciman, minister of agriculture, was glad to explain the work of his department, as was Herbert Samuel, the postmaster general, 'a very able young man,' Rowell judged, 'a Hebrew. There are three in the government. There appears to be no real prejudice against them over here and this is as it should be.' After dinner with Sir John Simon, the solicitor general, Rowell understood why Simon was regarded as one of the most brilliant young men in Parliament and likely to become prime minister: 'I do not know that I have ever met a more attractive personality.' The foreign secretary, Sir Edward Grey, and the colonial sceretary, Lewis Harcourt, more than lived up to his advance impressions of them. With several Nonconformist members of Parliament he had lengthy discussions of social reform: T.R. Ferens of Hull, whose success in Reckitt and Sons, dyers, had enabled him to become one of the most generous Methodist philanthropists; J. Allen Baker, the Quaker engineer and promoter of the extension of tramways in London, who was currently endeavouring to improve relations between Britain and Germany through exchange visits by churchmen of the two countries; and Arnold Rowntree of York, a member of the Quaker family of cocoa manufacturers and reformers who held the controlling interest in the Liberal Radical weekly *The Nation*, an independent exponent of 'the New Liberalism' to which Rowell had been a subscriber for some time. All this, together with many interviews with members of the civil service in several government departments, especially those concerned with the administration of the recent social legislation, provided a fresh fund of useful information for the future.

At a choral service in Westminister Abbey on a Sunday morning, after he had been joined by Nell and the children, a dramatic reminder of one of the liveliest social issues of the day occurred. Suddenly, as the prayers were being sung, they heard, above the voices of the choir and of Dean Ryle, another well sung supplication that began, 'God Save Mrs Pankhurst.' The refrain was chanted several times before the vergers managed to expel the intruders, a 'choir' of about twenty militant suffragettes. Later that day Mrs Pankhurst's followers staged a wild meeting in Trafalgar Square, and mounted police soon patrolled the district.

The whole family enjoyed a few days in the Lake District and a visit to the site of Joseph Rowell's farm, 'The Breakings.' The house was gone now, and the Rowell property had been absorbed into a larger farm. Rowell's purchase of his grandfather's clock from local residents provided a cherished memento of the family past – one that he had long wanted to possess. Before taking ship at Liverpool, Rowell visited nearby Port Sunlight, the company-owned housing development for workers in Sir William Lever's soap works. That experiment, along with the impact of his visit earlier in the summer to Letchworth Garden City, the new town created since 1904 by a private company and now housing more than eight thousand persons, stirred his thinking about housing as no other experience had done and sent him home confirmed in his conviction that adequate forethought could prevent the growth of unhealthy and unsightly slums in industrial communities.[24]

The political situation in Ontario had not changed during Rowell's two-month absence. On the day of his return the Conservatives won yet another by-election in which temperance had again been the dominant issue; the Liberals had not expected to win East York, but it was discouraging to have made no significant inroads on the Conservative majority.

Shortly after, in a by-election in Peel where Rowell and his party again endeavoured to keep the temperance question to the fore, their program was rejected, although there was some satisfaction in a reduced Conservative majority. More was at stake for the Liberals three weeks later in the opportunity to redeem East Middlesex, lost only a year earlier. Their candidate was a firmly declared temperance Liberal and the party hoped desperately to recapture the seat as proof that the people of Ontario were ready to abolish the bar. By this test they were not, although there was a substantial cut in the Conservative majority. To his sister Mary who had just gone to Wesley College, Winnipeg, as a lecturer in French and dean of women, Rowell reflected on the result.

> East Middlesex was to some extent encouraging but in others very much the reverse ... If I did not keep optimistic the whole party would be sick of the issue because of the apathy and indifference of Christian men who have made so many professions but when it comes to action are apathetic, indifferent or even hostile. Business interest or party affiliations control their actions. The encouraging features are the open support we received in East Middlesex from a few Conservative temperance men and the fact that for the first time the WCTU took part in the fight though their entrance was at such a late date it did not materially affect the result. 'God's in His heaven, all's right with the world', & in his own time matters will work out right.[25]

Nell was also increasingly busy in public affairs. In her second term as national president of the YWCA she was actively concerned in that organization's social work among women and girls and in its campaigns for women's suffrage and for stricter regulation of working conditions among female factory workers. With the founding of the Women's Liberal Club of Toronto she became its first president and subsequently assisted in the formation of similar clubs in other centres. She very soon acquired a reputation as a graceful and effective speaker, especially accomplished in interpreting to women's groups the need for increased social legislation and its effect on their families.

With the opening of the 1914 session of the Legislature in mid-February, social welfare was the main theme of Rowell's contribution to the debate on the speech from the throne. In a proposed amendment to the speech Rowell charged the government with failure to meet the problems of unemployment and low wages which had beset the province with the slackening of the boom of the past decade, and once again he proposed the establishment of a Department of Labour under a full-time cabinet minister.

In one major area of reform, progress was made when the government reintroduced, amid renewed cries of 'socialism' and 'economic ruin' from business groups, its controversial Workmen's Compensation Act. The act was almost identical with the draft presented in the previous session and retained the non-contributory aspect so obnoxious to the Canadian Manufacturers' Association.[26] The government was loud in its claims that the measure was one of the most advanced pieces of social legislation in any country in the world and far ahead of the British act in the scale of compensation – a judgment in which so good a Liberal as Joseph Atkinson fully concurred.[27] The Liberal opposition in the house found no difficulty in voting for it. The labour interests had every reason to be pleased with the act, which went into effect on 1 January 1915 despite the continuing protests of the CMA, and in this matter at least they had no reason for thinking that they would have obtained better treatment from a Liberal government. Despite all their agitation for workmen's compensation the Liberals gained little political kudos from the achievement.

A measure which Rowell had advocated in his first appeal to the electors became law in 1914 with the passage of a bill to regulate election campaign contributions. Henceforth, any liquor licensee or member of a liquor trade association, any public contractor, or any corporation or official of a corporation who contributed funds to aid or prevent the nomination or election of any person to public office was subject to a fine equal to the contribution made, or not less than $100.[28] Since no provision was made to subject party accounts to public audit the possibilities of enforcing the law were slight, but it was a gesture in the right direction and enjoyed Liberal support.

Developments on the liquor front gave the Legislature some of its liveliest moments during this session. When a Conservative member, G. Howard Ferguson, read to the house a letter written six months earlier by Gustave Evanturel, Liberal member for Prescott, to the secretary of the Ontario Licenced Trade Association, the Liberals were confronted with the first public revelation in the Legislature of dissension within their ranks on the temperance question. Evanturel's letter invited the hotelkeepers to pay him $10,000 to supplement his sessional indemnity and keep as their spokesman 'the only MPP in the Ontario House who will place himself openly against the policy of Rowell and the restrictions to the trade brought from time to time by the government.'[29] Rowell was on his feet immediately to declare that Evanturel's opposition to the official party policy

N.W. Rowell 1900

Nell Rowell 1897

on this issue was well known but that could not justify his writing such a letter; in effect, Rowell read Evanturel out of the party, a move that was formally endorsed by the Liberal caucus at its meeting the next day.[30] Shortly, Evanturel appeared in the Legislature in the role of penitent, regretting his 'thoughtlessness and foolishness' and explaining that when he wrote the letter he had not fully understood the meaning of his action.[31] But Rowell was determined to take decisive action against the dissident member, and with the co-operation of the officials of the Prescott County Liberal Association Evanturel's resignation from the party was secured;[32] for the remainder of the session he sat as an Independent.

A few days after this episode the Liberals tried to produce proof of their frequently reiterated charges that the Conservatives enjoyed relations of a doubtful character with the liquor interests. In what was soon known as 'the Snider case,' C.M. Bowman charged in the Legislature that W.K. Snider, provincial licence inspector and a former Conservative party organizer, had been used by the Conservatives to help defeat the prohibition forces in local option contests in January 1914 in the counties of Peel, Welland, and Huron. Many Liberals had long believed that the provincial secretary, W.J. Hanna, whose department had general jurisdiction over licensing, had an understanding with the liquor interests; now their chance to expose the worst had come. One Huron county lawyer informed Rowell that the hotelkeepers were prepared 'to tell all they know about Hanna's connection with them' in retaliation for Hanna's announcement that no more licences would be issued in the county.[33]

But nothing was proved. In sworn affidavits both Hanna and Snider stated that the charges of improper agreement between the government and the liquor interests were completely unfounded and government influence had never been used anywhere against the adoption of local option. Bowman's resolution of censure was defeated on a straight party vote and was replaced by a Conservative motion commending the government for its great work in reducing the evils of liquor.[34] The Liberals had no reason to feel that the political impact of their charges against Snider outweighed that of the Evanturel affair.

During the session there was frequent discussion in caucus of the party's position on temperance. Many Liberals thought their party's appeal to temperance sympathizers would be increased by immediate advocacy of outright abolition of all liquor shops as well as of bars, while others were strongly opposed to such a move.[35] In the end it was decided to adhere to the present policy: once more the abolish-the-bar motion was introduced in the Legislature and defeated, while Rowell promised that in the next election there would be one fundamental issue facing the people of Ontario: 'Shall the organized liquor forces in this province triumph against the forces of a common Christianity?'[36]

When a general election was called for the end of June 1914, Rowell was the leader of a markedly more spirited and better organized party than the one that had been suddenly precipitated into the election of 1911. Active preparations for this contest had been begun early in the spring and in many ridings were carried forward by local party organizations that had been considerably revived in the past two and a half years. To this renewal of activity and confidence the central party office had made important contributions, although much still remained to be done to strengthen party organization. Thanks to a committee headed by A.E. Ames, a secretarial fund of $5,600 a year had been raised. It was enough to pay an experienced young Liberal journalist, Main Johnson, to act as secretary to the leader, plus the salary of one full-time stenographer and half the salary of another stenographer shared with Rowell's law firm. These added resources, together with the continuing services of the general secretary of the Ontario Reform Association, F.G. Inwood, and his office, had made it possible to issue better and more frequent press releases, to promote the organization of Liberal Clubs in fifty-two centres, to unite them in the Liberal Club Federation of Ontario, and to further their effectiveness through the services of a Speakers' Bureau and an Information Bureau. A successful effort had been made to enlist the active participation of young men in the Liberal clubs, and the formation of Women's Liberal Clubs had been begun; so far there were only three active women's groups – the one presided over in Toronto by Nell Rowell and others in Hamilton and Wiarton – but there were many individual members across the province who assisted in local organization, publicity, and canvassing. For the immediate requirements of the abolish-the-bar election A.E. Ames had raised a special fund from among men who were especially interested in prohibition, including a few independent Conservatives such as J.W. Flavelle. Ames's chief assistants as money-raisers were Thomas Findley, general manager of the Massey-Harris Company and an active Presbyterian layman, and F.H. Deacon, a stockbroker and prominent Methodist.[37]

It was too soon to judge whether the new quarters of the Ontario Club on Wellington Street, opened a year earlier, had yet fulfilled the purpose outlined by its president, P.C. Larkin, president of the Salada Tea Company of Canada, as 'a meeting place for the members of the party in the best financial positions that would strengthen their political leaning, in consequence opening their purses to meet the monetary needs of the party.'[38] But already it was established that 'the most elaborate and comfortable of any strictly political club in Toronto' had lived up to its boast of having one of the finest culinary establishments in the city and that many of its members had been undeterred by the convictions of their party leader in their enjoyment of the club bar. When Rowell had been twitted in the Legislature about his connection with 'the official bar of the Liberal party' he had replied that the

Ontario Club was a purely social club, that he was not one of its officers, and that the club had no voice in forming the policy of the Liberal party.[39]

True to his promises, Rowell made abolition of the bar the major issue of his campaign: 'That for which the organized Temperance and Christian forces of the Province have worked and prayed for for years is now within their reach, and it rests with them to say whether the open bar shall be continued or forever wiped out,' his election manifesto declared.[40] The organized temperance and Christian forces of Ontario had never been more actively involved in party politics than they were now. The official courts and church papers of the Methodist, Presbyterian, and Baptist denominations declared that abolition of the bar was a moral issue that should cut across party ties and urged their members to vote for prohibition candidates; in practice that meant supporting Liberals, Independent Temperance Liberals, and a handful of Independent Conservatives. In this campaign it was not unusual for Conservative clergymen, usually Methodist but sometimes Anglican, to appear on Liberal platforms to declare that on this one issue and for this election they were supporting Rowell and the abolition of the bar.[41] A new force outside the churches, but drawing largely on the Protestant denominations for its membership, the Ontario Young Manhood Association, threw itself into the Liberal campaign. The association was said to include many youthful Conservatives among its seventy-five thousand members,[42] who were exhorted to work for the election of Liberal or Independent Conservative temperance candidates. At the same time the leaders of the Canadian Suffrage Association urged the election of the Liberals as the party that would bring the political equality and the social reforms desired by the women of the province and by all progressively minded voters.[43]

The Liberals allowed only three seats to go to the Conservatives by acclamation and were given one themselves in Glengarry, an indication of the party's increased strength since the previous general election. Where necessary – and usually it was not – the central party organization tried to ensure that the Liberal candidate in every riding was a strong temperance man. In a dozen ridings candidates endorsed by the Liberals bore no Liberal tag but ran under the banners 'Independent Temperance,' 'Independent,' or 'Temperance.' Most of these men were relative strangers to party politics but the labels they bore testified to their preoccupation with the one great issue. In two ridings, Victoria North and Norfolk South, the Liberals threw their support behind 'Temperance Conservatives' who were running against official Conservative nominees, and in Norfolk North the Conservatives allowed a Liberal and an Anti-Temperance Liberal to fight it out between them. In Prescott the dissident Gustave Evanturel's attempts to secure the official Liberal nomination were matched by Rowell's equal determination to prevent him from doing so. Rowell urged the federal Liberal members from the area, G.P.

Graham and Edmond Proulx, to use their political influence in the riding to thwart Evanturel, and for a time he planned to attend the nominating meeting in Prescott in the hope that his presence would stiffen the opposition to Evanturel. But the outcome of the nominating convention seemed very uncertain, and Rowell was unwilling to have to repudiate Evanturel from the platform before a hostile crowd if he were to win the nomination;[44] it was safer to remain in Toronto and await the result. In the end, the local Liberal executive confirmed its earlier repudiation of Evanturel, who continued to seek Rowell's endorsation, arguing that he was still a good Liberal, would support the party on every issue, and was the only man who could hold Prescott for the party. Evanturel charged that the official candidate was the choice only of the local riding executive, as the voters' response to his own independent candidature would shortly prove.[45]

The Conservatives campaigned to the end on their record of 'clean government' and put great trust in the remarkable economic growth of the past decade to work for them. They were forced to fight with very little direct assistance from their leader, for an ailing Premier Whitney was able to appear before the electors only once during the campaign. Whitney had never enjoyed much reputation as an orator, but it was generally agreed that his address to the audience that packed Massey Hall was one of the finest of his career. Dealing at length with the liquor question, he reiterated the defence used by his party throughout the campaign; under the Conservative administration of the policy of local option the number of liquor licences had been reduced from 2,800 to 1,600; further progress in this direction could only be retarded if the matter were made a party issue as the clergymen who were turning their churches into 'party committee rooms' seemed determined to do.[46] The government dramatized its claims of service to the temperance cause in a widely distributed 'temperance map' illustrating the progress of the abolition of the bar under local option and the three-fifths majority clause.

As the campaign entered its final week Rowell and his family made their headquarters at 84 Vansittart Avenue in Woodstock, the residence Rowell rented to give him a closer connection with his own riding. He had found interest in his campaign gratifying in the last three weeks of extensive travel throughout the province, and his addresses had frequently drawn the largest crowds attending provincial campaign meetings in many years. Mackenzie King and J.A. Macdonald had once more given him great assistance on the platform, but again no prominent federal Liberal from Ontario had come forward to help. Nell was completely caught up in the campaign. After much persuasive talk she and a few others had managed to call a meeting of Liberal women in Woodstock, and there was now a possibility that a group of women would undertake the distribution of abolish-the-bar leaflets to every house in the city. She had found that 'the leading ladies ... are not favouring this but will not oppose the others doing it.' Elsewhere, the women were less hesitant and many centres had active campaign committees for the first time. 'In Toronto it is simply splendid the work they are doing, personally canvassing, etc. I am just so glad I took my courage in my hands a year ago and started the first meeting.' Could they win? Nell could not quite predict a Liberal victory but it was encouraging that 'the betting men are staking no money on the government ... You see I can write of nothing else' she explained to her sister-in-law in Switzerland.[47]

At the last big Liberal rally in Toronto, attended by four thousand people and presided over by Rev. Father L. Minehan, the city's leading Roman Catholic prohibitionist, several of the speakers who joined in declaring 'our principles are our politics' were Conservatives. Everything depended on persuading thousands of other temperance Conservatives to desert party loyalty for one great principle. There, and in his final statement in the press, Rowell based his appeal on only one issue. The fight was clear and simple: 'You have on the one hand organized Christianity, and on the other hand the organized liquor interests.'[48] Ontario's day of decision was at hand.

But Ontario was determined to keep its bars, fiercely so, it seemed. The Conservatives were swept back into power with a majority reduced by only three seats. The standing now was 83 Conservatives, 26 Liberals, and 2 Independents – Allan Studholme in Hamilton East and Gustave Evanturel in Prescott. The Liberals had gained eight seats including three of the five new seats being contested for the first time. There was no comfort in the reduction of Rowell's majority in North Oxford from the 560 of 1911 to 113, nor in the slight reduction in the Liberal share of the popular vote in the province; the Liberals had 43 per cent of the vote, the Conservatives 54 per cent. Ironically, in a 'temperance election' the largest majority in the province was polled by the financier and distiller, G.H. Gooderham, the Conservative candidate in South-West Toronto. Obviously, thousands of Ontario electors had failed to vote as their religious leaders had urged. Whitney rejoiced in the total humiliation of 'the demagogic clergymen' and deplored the lasting harm they had done both to the temperance cause and to the influence of the churches.[49]

The day after the election Rowell was off to the woods of Maine for two weeks of trout fishing with G.A. Warburton, general secretary of the Toronto YMCA, and W.P. Gundy, both hard workers in the campaign. As he returned to his legal practice and the affairs of the party he was 'not discouraged or downhearted. I am somewhat disappointed that is all ... I was surprised that more men did not put principle above party. It was their failure not mine that is responsible for the result so I have no regrets. I did my best & left the results to the people and Providence.'[50]

During the weeks after the election there were persistent rumours, especially in the Conservative press, that the decisive rejection of the Liberal temperance program could only mean Rowell's early resignation. If Rowell himself had any such thought he was not encouraged in it by Mackenzie King, J.E. Atkinson,

Stewart Lyon, A.E. Ames, W.P. Gundy, or the rest of the Liberal strategists and workers who had been his counsellors for the past three years. King told a North York Liberal that Rowell had 'brought the party out of the slough ... and transformed it into a fighting force which believes both in its cause and in itself'; the change augured well for Ontario Liberalism, both provincially and federally.[51] King assured Rowell himself that he had 'in magnificent fashion wiped out all the legacies of the past ... and laid a solid moral foundation for constructive and progressive reform in the nature of social service.' Admittedly, there was much questioning within the party about the wisdom of continuing with the present temperance policy, but King had firm views on the subject, views in which he said Laurier heartily concurred: 'You have put the bar in its proper place as an obstacle of social reform in every direction ... We have won back to Liberalism many of the best men of the Province. We have placed in their true relationship the liquor interests and the Conservative party, and the parties now rightly stand before the public as representative of interests which are diametrically opposed. Social wellbeing versus selfish interests ... the more clear the line of demarkation is made through time the better.'[52]

As he contemplated the group he would now lead in the Legislature Rowell could find one striking improvement over the pre-election party: earlier the Liberals had held only one riding, his own, with a dominant or significant proportion of urban voters. Now, in addition to North Oxford, they had captured Windsor, Brant South (Brantford), Wellington South (Guelph), Peterborough West (Peterborough), and both the Ottawa seats. These additions scarcely added up to a sweep of the cities, but they did give the party a foothold that might be used to extend its appeal to more urban dwellers. All the urban representatives were new to provincial politics, although several had extensive experience in local government. Among them, Samuel Carter, mayor of Guelph and manufacturer of knitted goods, appeared to be the strongest addition to the party caucus. Reared in the English co-operative movement in Nottinghamshire and now president of the Workingmen's Co-operative Society and chairman of the Light and Heat Commission in Guelph, Carter had been one of the earliest advocates of the public ownership of hydro-electric power in the province and was an active Methodist and prohibitionist.

The new Legislature that met for the first time in mid-February 1915 saw the debut as premier of William Hearst, former minister of lands and forests, who had succeeded to the Conservative leadership on the death of Whitney early in the preceding autumn. The temperance forces entertained some optimism about Hearst as an ally in their cause; a Methodist and a participant in a number of local option campaigns in Sault Ste Marie in his own riding, he was personally a 'temperance man.' How far he could take his followers was uncertain, but he was believed to favour much stricter control of the sale of liquor than many members of his party.

The advent of the war had given the prohibitionists a new weapon in their armoury. Abolition could now be argued as an economy that would save grain for more vital purposes and a reform that would produce the sober population, both in and out of uniform, that alone could fight the war with maximum efficiency. Rowell had already challenged Hearst, two months after the latter assumed the premiership, to join him in a non-partisan measure imposing prohibition, including the closing of shops and clubs as well as bars for the duration of the war.[53] Now, when he renewed the offer in the Legislature it met with the same resistance as before. But in the rising tide of sentiment that saw prohibition as a patriotic commitment Hearst was under a great deal of public pressure to do what his natural inclinations dictated and he therefore embarked upon a new policy. A bill was introduced to place the administration of the liquor laws under a five-man commission with wide powers to regulate hours of sale in accordance with local conditions and to cancel licences for violations. Rowell and the Liberals denounced the plan as a complete evasion of the problem and in a series of amendments they tried at least to tighten up the laws which the commissioners would be empowered to administer. These included attempts to get bars and clubs closed at 7 PM, and, failing that, at eight, then at nine, and finally at ten. After the defeat of all these amendments, plus another to substitute a simple majority for the three-fifths clause in local option contests, the government plan was adopted at the end of a long and stormy session of the Legislature lasting until five o'clock in the morning.[54]

The announcement of the names of the five members of the new Licence Board was heartening to temperance advocates. The chairman was J.D. Flavelle, a Lindsay businessman and brother of J.W. Flavelle, and the vice-chairman was W.S. Dingman, publisher of the *Stratford Herald*; the other members were Frederick Dane, a former commissioner of the Temiskaming and Northern Ontario Railway, John A. Ayearst, the present provincial licence inspector, and George T. Smith, a mining recorder. All but Ayearst were Methodists, and Flavelle and Dingman had long been vocal about their temperance sympathies, and continued to be so in their new positions.

Temperance was not the only cause aided by the advent of the war. The vigour with which women rallied behind the war effort strengthened the argument for granting them full rights of citizenship, but any hope that Hearst might take a different attitude from Whitney was dashed when Liberal members again introduced bills to give the municipal and provincial franchises to all property-owning spinsters and widows. Like Whitney, Hearst contended that the majority of women did not want to vote; and even if they did he was not convinced that their influence would be entirely beneficial.[55] Rowell was more than ever sure that it would. With temperance sentiment visibly increasing, it was evident, he told the Legislature, that 'if the municipal franchise is extended to married women Local Option will be carried in municipalities where it is now defeated by a small majority.' Moreover, quite apart from the good influence women would exercise, it was manifestly unjust to allow corporations to have a vote in municipal money by-laws, as they had, while denying any vote at all to half the population. Could it be shown that women had done any great harm to the province since they secured the franchise for the election of school boards, and unmarried women and widows the municipal vote?[56] But this reform too had to wait its time, although obviously it could not be long.

At the first meeting of the Liberal caucus in the autumn of 1915 the party took a step Rowell had long urged by committing itself to the closing of all clubs and shops as well as bars for the duration of the war, none of them to be opened until after a referendum at the conclusion of the war. The battle would now be assisted by a new non-partisan organization. The 'Committee of One Hundred' was an attempt to take the temperance question out of party politics once and for all and press the fight for total prohibition to an early and victorious conclusion. Although Rowell recognized that its program was, in effect, the Liberal program, he endeavoured not to spoil the non-partisan image of the Committee of One Hundred by claiming its policy as identical with the Liberal platform. In fact, Liberals had been the chief initiators of the committee, with Sam Carter, W.P. Gundy, and Rowell all playing important roles behind the scenes. When the birth of the new Committee of One Hundred was formally declared in mid-October it was claimed that half of the prominent citizens who made up its membership were Conservatives. Its officers were men who had taken little active part in politics and included Judge E.P. Clement of Berlin, president of the Mutual Life Assurance Company as chairman, and James Hales, a lawyer and former Toronto alderman as vice-chairman. Before long the services of G.A. Warburton, who had already proved his organizing ability as a highly successful YMCA secretary, were secured as executive secretary. The committee arose from the conviction of the prohibition forces that public opinion was fast approaching the condition that the Dominion Alliance, the WCTU, and their supporters had laboured so long to create, and that abolition feeling was almost as strong among Conservatives as among Liberals. Even the House of Bishops of the Church of England had gone as far as urging voluntary abstention from drink as a patriotic duty. If Conservatives could be shown a way of supporting prohibition without appearing to espouse a Liberal policy they would do so.[57] The Conservative cabinet was believed to be still divided on the prohibition question, but privately Premier Hearst gave the One Hundred considerable encouragement.[58]

Rowell was confident that the campaign of the Committee of One Hundred would have an effect on the government: the most he counted on was ' a referendum on fair terms ... it is a foregone conclusion what will happen.' With the situation developing well in several other provinces too, he felt that 'the tide is running strongly our way and I hope the result may be a dry Canada in the near future. It looks very much like it now.'[59] Just after the New Year he went south for a week's holiday at Clifton Springs, Virginia, with Nell and her parents, satisfied that in the forthcoming session of the Legislature the government would bring in some advanced proposals.

The hour of Ontario's salvation was even nearer than he believed. The speech from the throne at the opening of the 1916 session of the Legislature announced the government's intention of submitting the prohibition issue to the electors, the time and precise method of doing so to be indicated later.[60] The Committee of One Hundred saw this as a call to redouble its efforts to secure signatures to the petition it had for some time been circulating demanding total prohibition. The campaign ended when ten thousand people paraded to the parliament buildings with banners, floats, and a student chorus to present the results of the petition to the premier. Judge Clement informed Hearst that 852,562 persons in Ontario had signed the prohibition petition; of these, 348,166 were male British subjects over 21, while 477,396 were women and young men who were minors – but none was under the age of 18; the eligible voters who had signed the petition constituted over 73 per cent of those who had voted at the last provincial election and nearly 48 per cent of all those on the voter's list.[61] The accompanying address lauded the steps so far taken by the government to curb the consumption of liquor and pledged the support of the petitioners if the administration were to initiate prohibition by legislative act instead of by the anticipated referendum.[62]

The activities of the Committee of One Hundred produced a counter organization of anti-prohibitionists – the Personal Liberty League. It was flooding the province with literature designed to convince the public that prohibition was an undemocratic infringement of the rights of the individual, that it should not be forced on the province in the absence of 100,000 voters serving overseas, and that the effects of liquor on health were not as had been claimed: did not the British army issue two and one-half ounces of rum a week to its soldiers to increase their physical stamina? Moreover, the League claimed that beer, which had a very low alcoholic content, was 'the poor man's drink'; any measure which deprived the workingman of his beer was class discrimination. Added to all this were the difficulties of enforcing prohibitory legislation, difficulties so great that several American states had abandoned prohibition. The views of the Personal Liberty League, if not always the organization itself, had the support of most of the labour organizations, the commercial travellers, the hotel keepers, and, of course, the brewers and distillers. The latter had strong convictions about the detrimental effects of prohibition on provincial tax revenues, on investors in breweries and distilleries, and on the general economic prosperity of the community.[63]

The struggle to which Rowell had given so much was drawing to a climax, although he did not occupy the place he had once aspired to hold, as the undoubted leader of the crusade. It was W.J. Hanna, the provincial secretary, who introduced the Ontario Temperance Act: the sale of all intoxicating liquors, including beer, in bar rooms, clubs, and shops would end 16 September 1916. Henceforth there would be no legal sale of any kind of liquor except for medicinal and sacramental purposes, and that only on the prescription of a physician or the order of a clergyman.[64]

Hearst emphasized that prohibition was a war measure, that the government had given up the idea of a referendum because of the difficulties of holding one in wartime and because it was evident that public opinion was in favour of prohibition and would approve its introduction by act of the Legislature. Although the premier suggested that prohibition would prove 'a blessing to thousands in our province to-day who are battling manfully against their appetites for strong drink' he stressed its value in helping the province to contribute more worthily to the war effort through money saved for more constructive purposes and through greater efficiency and fewer hours lost in drunkenness in industry. As for those who talked of their personal freedom, the premier asked: 'Is this a time to talk of personal liberty, to think of our pleasure, our appetites, our enjoyments, when the civilization of the world is hanging in the balance and the very foundations of liberty are tottering and dependent upon the strength of Great Britain and her allies in the field and on the high seas?'[65]

Every member of the Legislature answered 'no' to that question, none more honestly than the leader of the opposition: Ontario was dry by the unanimous vote of the elected representatives of the people. It was politically and humanly impossible for Rowell to allow the occasion to pass without mention of the long Liberal fight for this day. He recalled earlier occasions when he had pleaded with the government to join with his party in realizing the dream that today had come true. Much of his deeply felt satisfaction had to be enjoyed in private; he remained sceptical of the genuineness of the conversion of many Conservatives and believed that Hearst had only been able to keep the numerous dissenters in his own party in line because 'there was nowhere for them to turn. They could not come to us because we were supporting the Prime Minister.'[66] Looked at in the perspective of history over the past fifty years he found the action of his party almost unique: 'I do not believe you will find a case where the Opposition, either Liberal or Conservative, has been more generous or helpful to a Government in a great public measure which the Opposition had itself advocated and which the Government had opposed. In fact, I do not know of any parallel case unless it be that of Confederation itself.'[67]

With liquor banned the way was prepared for a great age of reform in Ontario.

9
Ontario and Quebec at war

While Rowell was bringing his party to agreement on a liquor policy and presenting his general platform of social reform the bilingual schools issue simmered. After the promulgation of Regulation 17, with its restriction of the use of French as a language of instruction to the first two years of school, the government had reinforced its operation with Regulation 18, declaring that any school failing to comply with the official language policy would forfeit support from public funds and its teachers would be liable to suspension or cancellation of their certificates. Amid rising protest from French Canadians in both Ontario and Quebec, the Ottawa Separate School Board had announced that it did not intend to enforce Regulation 17.

While Whitney was buffeted about between an odd alliance of militant Protestants and the Irish Catholic clergy of Ontario who approved his policy on the one hand, and French-speaking clergy and Conservative politicians at Ottawa fearful for their party's fortunes in Quebec on the other, the Ontario Liberal party pursued a watchful silence. Only once during the 1913 session of the Legislature was that silence broken and then only by two French-speaking Liberal members. Gustave Evanturel, Liberal member for the riding of Prescott, regretted the absence of any reference to the language issue in the speech from the throne and demanded the publication of letters from Bishop Fallon to members of the cabinet, letters which he believed would reveal a 'conspiracy' by the Irish clergy and the Whitney government against the Franco-Ontarians. He called also for the resignation of the French-speaking member of Whitney's cabinet, the minister of public works, Dr J.O. Reaume, whose support of the government's policy indicted him as a traitor to the interests of his race. Later, Evanturel and his colleague, Zotique Mageau of Sturgeon Falls, charged that some of the admitted academic difficulties of the bilingual schools were due to their receipt of an unfair share of school funds, and they demanded that this wrong be righted.[1] But the government refused to be drawn into battle, a strategy which was assisted by the failure of the opposition to endow the protests of Evanturel and Mageau with any status other than that of the view of private members.

In the autumn of 1913 the controversy threatened to reach the boiling point when the government reissued Regulation 17 in a slightly modified form. The chief inspector of schools was now given power to permit the use of French beyond the first two years of studies where he deemed it necessary to the pupils' academic progress, and to allow the study of French for more than the one hour a day originally permitted in certain schools, provided that this did not interfere with the study of English. Theoretically, at least, this seemed to invite circumvention of the original policy through potentially numerous exceptions to the rules, although the minister of education maintained that there had been no essential change of policy.[2] As proof of its intention to enforce the law the government soon announced that the Ottawa Separate School Board would be cut off from receipt of public funds because of its refusal to submit reports or admit inspectors during the past year.[3]

Rowell broke a lengthy silence on the bilingual question during a fall by-election campaign in the riding of Peel after several Conservative challenges to state his policy. Paying tribute to the importance of the French-speaking population of Ontario, who now numbered 250,000 and constituted 10 per cent of the total, Rowell chastised the government for the neglect that had produced the conditions revealed in the Merchant Report, again rehearsed the conflicting statements on the subject from members of the cabinet, and asked whether it was any wonder that much of the Conservative press and the Orange Lodges felt betrayed and outraged by the revised Regulation 17, when Whitney had promised that he would stand by the original formulation. At the same time French Canadians felt that they were the victims of bad faith as well. In contrast to the vacillation of the government, Rowell claimed that the Liberal policy was still the same as it had been before the last election: 'English is the language of this continent. It is the official language of this province. Our French Canadian fellow-citizens will agree with us that any child in this province who does not at school acquire a good working knowledge of English is handicapped in the struggle of life ... What we are concerned about is that they should master English and not that they should be ignorant of French.'[4]

Despite the efforts of both parties to avoid it as far as possible, the school question inevitably became the second issue in the abolish-the-bar election campaign of 1914. By this time Ottawa was the centre of the controversy; there the English-speaking members of the Separate School Board were at loggerheads with the French majority on the board over the latter's refusal to enforce Regulation 17. When the French-speaking section of the board tried to pass a city by-law allowing it to issue debentures to raise money for new schools to be operated independently of the Department of Education's language regulations, the English-speaking group obtained an interim court injunction preventing this move and calling on the government to enforce Regulation 17. On the eve of the election the Supreme Court of Ontario was beginning its hearings on the validity of the injunction.

The position of the parties on the bilingual schools was ill-defined enough to cause confusion during the election campaign among at least some of the leading Orangemen in the province. W.R. Plewman, editor of the Orange *Sentinel*, believed that Whitney had betrayed an essential position in the modifications of Regulation 17 introduced the previous year and was beginning to think that the Liberals were sounder on this issue as well as on temperance. Plewman's father-in-law, H.C. Hocken, publisher of the *Sentinel*, mayor of Toronto, and a staunch Conservative, thought Rowell had been less than forthright on the language problem and could see no reason for preferring the Liberals. When Plewman and Hocken discussed his attitude with Rowell directly, he told them that there was no excuse for doubt about his position; he had stated it on many occasions, but he promised to do so again.[5]

Shortly thereafter Rowell went further than ever before in attacking the modifications made in the original Regulation 17 and implied that they gave more scope to the French language than should be tolerated. The fundamental principle to be kept in view was that 'this is an English-speaking Province and an English-speaking Province it will remain. The regulations of the Education Department should be framed and the Department administered in full recognition of this fact.'[6] Plewman was satisfied, but when Hocken, finding it impossible to exhort Orangemen to depart from their traditional Conservative allegiance, refused to publish his editorial declaring so in the *Sentinel*, Plewman resigned. Two days before the election Plewman issued an appeal to the Orangemen of Ontario to vote for the Liberals: 'We are on the verge of the greatest political upheaval in the history of Canada. The bar will be banished and the English language will be preserved if we vote against those who, last September and since, spurned the power of our illustrious order.'[7] At the same time *Le Droit* of Ottawa, which had been established to fight for French-language rights, hailed the Liberals as the protectors of the French tongue.[8] Most of the French-speaking voters of Ontario appeared to agree with *Le Droit*, for they defeated the Conservative Dr Reaume in Windsor, elected two new French-speaking Liberals, and were apparently crucial in returning Liberal candidates in a few additional ridings. Five of the six French-speaking members of the Legislature were now Liberals. Franco-Ontarian voters had given the Liberals a vote of confidence which might well prove a mixed blessing.

That the bilingual issue occupied so little of the time of the new legislative session of 1915 was no indication of its current importance. In Ottawa the French and English sections of the Separate School Board were still deadlocked and the former was fighting the Department of Education in an endeavour to run schools outside the jurisdiction of the department. As a result, many local schools were in practice closed to English students while others were closed entirely, despite an order of the Ontario Supreme Court that all the schools be opened and only qualified teachers employed. Among French Canadians in both Ontario and Quebec, resistance to Regulation 17 was revealing a solidarity that cut across party lines and was strong enough to unite, on a common platform in Montreal, the Nationalists, Henri Bourassa and Armand Lavergne, the Conservative Senator A.C.P. Landry, Liberal Senators Raoul Dandurand and N.A. Belcourt, and Archbishop Bruchési and other churchmen to launch a campaign to raise funds for 'les blessés d'Ontario.'[9] Three weeks later Cardinal Bégin published an open letter to Archbishop Bruchési defending the inalienable right of every race to its own language and affirming the 'noble duty of the French and Catholic province of Quebec to assist with all its influence and all its resources those who suffer and struggle until full justice shall be rendered them.'[10] Within days, the Quebec Legislature gave unaimous approval to a resolution deploring the situation in Ontario and asserting that Ontario's legislators were deficient in their understanding and application of traditional British principles relating to minorities.[11]

Few Ontarians accepted the repeated declarations of the premier and other Conservative leaders that no religious issue was involved in the bilingual question. Most English-speaking citizens were firmly convinced that the spread of the French language was synonymous with the extension of the power of the Roman Catholic church and the increasingly active participation of the clergy in the opposition to Regulation 17 reinforced their fears. That these fears among Protestants would lead to a campaign against separate schools was the motivating force behind the stand taken by many English Catholic clergy in Ontario. Father Michael Whalen's open letter in reply to Cardinal Bégin was the most dramatic expression of their view. The Ottawa priest blamed the growing racial war on *Le Droit* and on extremists in both political and religious circles, and he questioned the right of the Quebec clergy to speak for the Roman Catholic church:

We deny that the French-Canadian raiders on the school system of Ontario have a right to declare, in the name of the Catholic Church, a religious war on the government of this province. We protest against their dragging religion into their language agitation; we protest against their identifying their cause with that of the Separate Schools; we reprobate their methods as un-Catholic. We assert that only the united Catholic Hierarchy of Ontario has the right to declare a Province-wide religious war against a law or regulation of the Ontario government. The United hierarchy has not done so.[12]

In the face of the increasing heat generated by the bilingual issue, and realizing the danger that the controversy could become emmeshed in racial tensions aroused by Canadian participation in the war in Europe, Ontario's politicians naturally tried to avoid further embroilment in it. There was no mention of the question in the Legislature until it was forced upon the attention of the members during the debate on the estimates of the Department of Education when it was revealed that 190 bilingual schools had been excluded from provincial grants of funds because of their failure to conform to the language regulations.[13] A few days later, when the government sought to pass a bill giving itself the power to set up a commission to take over the duties of the Ottawa Separate School Board should that body continue to defy the Department of Education, the only questions raised about the policy came from French-speaking Liberals and from J.C. Tolmie of Windsor and Hugh Munro of Glengarry whose constitutents included substantial members of French Canadians. Toward the end of the debate Rowell declared again that there could be 'no objection to French Canadians acquiring the best possible knowledge of their mother tongue' in the schools once the primary objective of ensuring an English education for every student had been achieved. Despite their strong criticism, the French-speaking Liberal members did not go so far as to divide the House on the establishment of the commission to resolve the situation in Ottawa.[14] Once again open schism had been avoided.

The bilingual schools controversy entered a new phase when the Supreme Court of Ontario gave its judgment in the Ottawa Separate School Board's appeal against the earlier court order to reopen the schools. In delivering the unanimous judgment of the court, Chief Justice Sir William Meredith observed that he could find nothing to support the Ottawa board's view that the use of the French language in Ontario was guaranteed either by constitutional or natural right. Therefore, in the court's view, Regulation 17 was constitutionally valid.[15] A week later an order-in-council placed the Ottawa separate schools under the jurisdiction of a three-man commission, as stipulated in the recent measure passed in the Legislature.

With every round won by the Ontario government, French Canadian resistance stiffened. The French Canadian Education Association and other organizations continued to receive funds, often from the remotest Quebec villages, for the war on the Ontario front. The question of financial contributions to this cause came to a head with the Quebec Legislature's approval of an amendment to a bill authorizing the city of Montreal to make a gift to the Patriotic Fund by enlarging the scope of the provisions to permit gifts to educational funds either inside or outside the province. The wider frame of reference was approved with only three dissenting voices[16]; to many Ontarians it seemed that Quebec municipalities were being actively encouraged to intensify a most regrettable agitation in their province.

Rowell was profoundly disturbed by the action of the Quebec Legislature which he could only view as an unwarranted intervention in Ontario's affairs by another province. After much thought he decided that he would have to make a statement on the matter in the Ontario Legislature, although he was reluctant to take such a step for fear it would provide the Quebec Nationalists with added ammunition in their campaign against recruiting. That would be detrimental not only to the country but also to the Liberal party. It was only fair that he inform Laurier of what he proposed to do: 'I must make clear our position, that the question is one which must be settled by the people of Ontario ... alone; that minorities must depend on the sense of justice and fair play of the majority in all matters under our constitution.' Rowell intended to accompany his defence of Ontario's right to control her own educational policies with a proposal for the appointment of a three-man commission to study how Regulation 17 had worked out in practice; he thought that a commission composed of the Roman Catholic Archbishop of Toronto, Neil McNeil, for whose fairness and acuteness on public issues Rowell had the highest regard, plus an Ontario French Canadian, and President Robert Falconer of the University of Toronto should report on the present situation and make proposals for future policy. In further elaboration of his own position Rowell told Laurier:

I cannot depart from the position which I have always taken since I became leader of the Liberal party that it is the duty of the state to see that every child in the province receives a good English education and that consistent with this requirement, where the parents of the children desire that the children should also study the French language, there should be no objection on our part to their doing so. The practical difficulty is to ensure the first without appearing to unduly interfere with the second, and the difficulty is greatly increased by the extravagant and entirely unwarranted claim put forth by the Nationalists with reference to the right to use the French language in this province.[17]

In response, Laurier agreed 'heart and soul' with Rowell's definition of the duty of the state to the children of Ontario but he would express part of it more strongly: 'I would substitute for the words "there should be no objection on our part to their doing so," that "the law should provide that they may do so."' He was in entire agreement with Rowell's proposed commission, believed Archbishop McNeil an excellent choice, and as the Ontario French Canadian suggested Monseigneur Latulippe, bishop of Temiskaming, who held extreme views on the bilingual question and therefore represented a position that must be considered in any attempt to settle the issue.[18]

Although Laurier had maintained a public silence on the bilingual question there was no doubt in his mind about the correct Liberal stand on the matter. It was the policy adopted by Oliver Mowat forty years earlier, one that could be readily understood and simply stated: all children in Ontario must learn English, but they must learn French as well if their parents wish. However, 'this is exactly what is denied by Regulation 17 ... That seems to me absolutely tyrannical.' Laurier shared with many other French Canadian Liberals in Ottawa a special alarm about section 4 of Regulation 17 which appeared to them to mean not only that the teaching of the French language was subject to certain restrictions throughout the province, but that it was not to be taught at all in schools where it was not being taught in August 1913. Clearly this would preclude teaching in French in schools established after that date.[19] Although Rowell agreed with Laurier that the wording of the clause was not entirely clear, he was 'inclined to take the view' that Laurier's interpretation was correct and this was what the Legislature intended. Further, he thought it unlikely that an amendment to alter that intention could be passed in the Legislature at the present time.[20]

Soon, Rowell introduced his proposal for a commission to examine the operation of Regulation 17, prefacing his motion with a strong affirmation of Ontario's absolute right to control education without outside interference and regretting the government's inability to secure a sufficient number of qualified bilingual teachers. Predictably, the acting minister of education, Howard Ferguson, simply dismissed the proposal with the assertion that the government understood the situation well enough without a report from another commission.[21] Given the public temper in the province, and in the absence of pressure from the federal Conservatives on their Ontario colleagues, Rowell had never really expected any other outcome.[22] He had made the maximum gesture his own convictions and the attitudes of the people of Ontario would allow him to make. It was too little to bring even a temporary relaxation of tension within the Liberal party.

Now Ontario Liberals were apprehensive about rumours that the federal Liberal party would publicly endorse some form of interference in Ontario's domestic affairs, possibly by the introduction of a motion of censure in the House of Commons. Rowell hastened to inform Laurier that public opinion in Ontario would be inflamed by the introduction of any resolution referring to Ontario's educational policies.[23] Laurier's reply hinted that the decision had already been made; over the implacability of Ontario Liberals he had to record his 'strong disappointment. If the party cannot stand up to the principles advocated, maintained and fought for by Mowat and Blake ... it is more than time for me to step down and out.'[24]

In a lengthy argument on the problem Rowell and Laurier vied with one another for pre-eminence in faithfulness to 'the Mowat tradition.' They could readily agree that Mowat had stood for two principles – provincial rights and justice for minorities, but they parted company on the meaning of these principles when applied to the current dispute. Laurier recognized the correctness of Rowell's contention that there were no formal constitutional guarantees for the French language in Ontario, but he found many precedents for representations to provincial legislatures by the federal Parliament, often with beneficial results. But Rowell rejected federal intervention of any kind on an educational question as constitutionally invalid. Further, in the present situation any such action would be politically dangerous because it would assist the Conservatives in their current campaign to divert attention from their incompetence in handling the war effort by exploiting the racial issue. He appreciated to the full, he told Laurier, 'the injustice of such a campaign and how unfair it is that the Tories should escape the full responsibility for nourishing the Nationalist movement.' As for the suggestion that Laurier should step down, that was 'unthinkable. You are the one man in Canada who, if in power, could unite the whole people of Canada in doing their whole duty in this war ... There is only one place for you and that is the place of leadership.' In standing his ground against the Nationalist movement Laurier might well do 'the greatest work' of his life and lay the basis for better relations between the races in the future.[25]

To a further plea from Laurier that Ontario at least hear the appeal of a minority Rowell could only reply that it was the cause of the greatest regret that further reflection had not shown him anything that he could usefully add to the views he had already expressed to Laurier.[26]

Even as Rowell's letter was being written Ernest Lapointe was introducing in the House of Commons a resolution that 'this House ... while fully respecting the principle of provincial rights and the necessity of every child being given a thorough English education, respectfully suggests to the Legislative Assembly of Ontario the wisdom of making it clear that the privilege of the children of French parentage of being taught in their mother tongue be not interfered with.'[27] Laurier supported the resolution with one of the finest of his great orations:

I appeal, not to passion or prejudice, but to the sober reasoning and judgment of my fellow-countrymen of all origins. I discard at once all reference to constitutional arguments ... I do not ... invoke the cold letter of any positive law ...

I am of the old school of Mowat and Blake, the parent school of Provincial Rights. By that doctrine I stand. The province of Ontario, and Ontario alone, will and shall determine for herself the decision. Yet is it forbidden by the code of the new converts to the doctrine of provincial rights that I stand at the bar before my fellow-countrymen of Ontario and make my plea? Is it forbidden that I respectfully present the petition of a humble servant of French origin?

I know there is in the province of Ontario a sense of irritation at the position taken by some of my fellow-countrymen of French blood in the province of Quebec ... It is true, alas, that there are in my province men of French origin who,

when France is fighting the fight of heroism which stirs the blood of mankind, remain with their blood cold, who tell us: 'No, we will not lift a finger to assist Britain in defending the integrity of France, but we want our wrongs to be righted in Ontario.' Wrongs or no wrongs, there is a field of honour; there is a call of duty.

Referring to the recent adoption by Willison's Toronto *News* of the slogan 'One language and one language only,' Laurier asked where the British Empire would be if that doctrine had been applied around the world:

It is because British institutions everywhere have carried freedom and respect for minorities that England is as strong as she is today ...
Now I come to the point where I want to speak to my fellow-countrymen in the province of Ontario. When I ask that every child of my own race should receive an English education, will you refuse us the privilege of education also in the language of our mothers and our fathers? ... Is that an unnatural demand? Is that an obnoxious demand? Will the concession of it do harm to anybody? ... I do not believe it; and, if we discuss this question with frankness, as between man and man, in my humble opinion, it can yet be settled by an appeal to the people of Ontario, I do not believe that any man will refuse us the benefit of a French education.[28]

Reading Laurier's speech the next morning in the *Globe*, Rowell admired its fine spirit and the accomplished oratory but did not change his mind. The eleven Liberal members of Parliament from the west and one Ontario man had voted against the Lapointe resolution, but all the rest of the Liberals from Quebec, the Maritimes, and Ontario had supported it. There had been a break in government ranks too, with five Quebec Conservatives supporting the resolution.

Later that day Rowell received a letter Laurier had written him just before his speech in the House: 'You and I have reached a line of cleavage which – I so judge from the tone of your letter just received – is final and beyond redemption ... I write with a heavy heart. The party has not advanced; it has sorely retrograded, abandoning position after position before the haughty onslaughts of Toryism.'[29]

In the next few days Rowell learned how close the Ontario Liberal representatives in Ottawa had been to voting against the Lapointe resolution. They were in favour of conciliation, but thought that Laurier's failure to understand the strength of feeling in Ontario made him blind to the inexpedience of the resolution. When told of their attitude and informed that they would nevertheless vote for the resolution out of their regard for him, Laurier had said that that was too much to ask and announced his intention of resigning the leadership. In consternation the Ontario Liberals had sent word to 'the Old Man' that they would support the resolution and persuaded him to withdraw his resignation.[30]

As for his own relations with Laurier – 'final and beyond redemption' – had it really come to that? Rowell 'read and re-read' Laurier's most recent letter, 'each time with increasing regret. I confess I cannot quite understand it (he replied). You agree with me that the policy to be pursued in connection with these schools must be settled by the Government and the Legislature of this Province, and the question of the policy to be pursued is therefore a matter with which the political parties in the Province have to deal ... I cannot surrender my convictions without surrendering my right to the leadership of the Provincial Liberal Party.' Moreover, surely Laurier could understand that if on a question so vital as education the provincial party 'were to surrender its view to the views of the party leaders at Ottawa, it would not only be doing what I believe to be wrong in the Province, but it would be committing political suicide.'[31]

Laurier's suggestion that the party had lost ground in Ontario and the implication that this was due to Rowell's leadership was puzzling to Rowell; for it was at variance with the many expressions of appreciation he had received from Laurier. Rowell had no hestitation in asserting that the provincial Liberal party had been rebuilt on 'a solid democratic basis' and by 'pressing to the front legislation dealing with the amelioration of social conditions and the improving of the lot of the average man' had become stronger than it had been for many years. 'You speak of the attitude of the party in Toronto. I do not know just what you include in this term. I only accept responsibility for my own views, as publicly stated, or as embodied in my correspondence with you ... I cannot think that there has been anything harsh or unsympathetic in anything I have said or written. If there has been, it was not so intended; it was a fault of expression and not of the heart.'[32]

Rowell's letter was never mailed; on learning that Laurier would arrive in Toronto the next day for urgent talks with himself, Atkinson, Lyon, and a few others, he set it aside in favour of the opportunity to present its content to Laurier in person. After two days at the Ontario Club and a series of talks with leading Liberals, Laurier departed in the conviction that the Lapointe resolution would not hurt the party in Ontario 'if our friends have the courage to maintain that it is right. This, however, will not be done in Toronto, and all the damage which we will suffer will come from that direction.'[33] The biggest problem in Toronto, in Laurier's diagnosis, was the Liberal press; if it were 'courageous and met the situation squarely, no harm would result from the bilingual question' but that was more than he expected.[34]

In reaching the gulf which now separated them on the school question, Rowell and Laurier had both followed 'correct' constitutional arguments and, from within their own differing political perspectives, they were both 'right' politically. Rowell's natural inclinations and convictions, personal and political, accurately reflected Ontario's vision of itself as an English-speaking province. Once the Conservative party had committed itself to restrictions on French language instruction in Ontario's schools, it would indeed have been political suicide, as Rowell argued, for Ontario Liberals to add to their many problems by adopting a 'weaker' position than Conservatives on the language issue. The 'Protestant conscience' to which Rowell's whole reform program was designed to appeal was not amenable to proposals for the extension of French influence – and inevitably Roman Catholic influence – in the province. Even had Rowell's own views on the language issue been less firm than they were, the party could not afford to jeopardize its already precarious political strength by the adoption of a policy out of tune with the dominant temper of the Ontario electorate.

Nor did Laurier and the federal Liberals have much room for manœuvre. Their primary concern was to maintain their hold on the allegiance of French Canadians, since 1896 the most stable element within the federal Liberal party, and all the more important since the defeat of 1911 had severely diminished Liberal support in English Canada, notably in Ontario. With the party's Quebec base increasingly undermined by Bourassa and the Nationalist movement, it was impossible for Laurier to be other than vigilant on behalf of the French minority in Ontario.

Altogether, Rowell and Laurier were in an impasse for which there seemed to be no solution. Although Toronto Liberals were unwilling to maintain positively that Laurier's attitude was right, they were prepared to cease making an issue of it in public. Beyond a few relatively unimpassioned assertions of Ontario's right to control her own affairs, neither the *Globe* nor the *Star* had much to say about bilingualism for the time being. Two weeks after Laurier's visit to Toronto Rowell gave a dinner at the Ontario Club for 150 leading Liberals from all parts of the province. The discussion was devoted to post-war social problems, concluding in a decision to carry out a systematic investigation of a variety of social and economic problems in the province, and also to the question whether the party should hold a convention soon or at the end of the war. Not a word was heard about bilingualism.[35]

Subsequently, several developments offered some hope that there would be no further wrangles over the teaching of French in Ontario schools. In the autumn of 1916 Pope Benedict xv issued the encyclical, *Commisso divinitus*, the Vatican's answer to the many appeals forwarded in the past six years by both French and Irish Roman Catholics for vindication of their positions in the bilingual dispute. The Vatican declared that Ontario children should have 'a thorough knowledge of English' but that there must also be an 'equitable teaching of French for French-Canadian children.' It admonished the Catholics of the Dominion to act with moderation and to 'remember that the one thing of supreme importance above all others is to have Catholic schools, and not to imperil their existence.'[36] The English-speaking bishops were well satisfied with the pronouncement, but their French colleagues felt otherwise. The inability of the Quebec Nationalists to find any encouragement in it was evident in the silence of Bourassa and *Le Devoir*.[37] A week after the publication of the encyclical the Judicial Committee of the Privy Council handed down judgments in the two cases referred from the Ontario courts: the legislation that circumvented the Ottawa Separate School Board by establishing the Ottawa School Commission was *ultra vires*[38] but Regulation 17 was *intra vires*; Ontario had won the essential point. Although their Lordships regretted that the regulation was 'couched in obscure language' so that it was 'not easy to ascertain its true effect,' they found that it was only denominational and not language privileges that were guaranteed under the BNA Act, and the Department of Education therefore had a free hand with language teaching.[39]

Despite the reluctance of many French Canadians to accept defeat, it appeared for a time that the bilingual issue was settled and controversy would now die away. Perhaps a new era was to find its symbol in the visit to Toronto early in 1917 of a group of French Canadians under the auspices of the 'Bonne Entente' movement. Organized three months earlier when a number of prominent Ontarians had visited Quebec, the Bonne Entente movement was in part an attempt to save the Liberal party from the destruction with which it was threatened by the widening abyss between the two races and partly a device to restore the trade of English-speaking manufacturers in Montreal, damaged by French Canadian hostility toward them. Participation was by no means limited to Liberals, but they were its most active spirits in both provinces. The Toronto leaders included A.E. Ames, J.H. Gundy, J.M. Godfrey, and Dr G.H. Locke, all Liberals, and S.R. Parsons, vice-president of the Canadian Manufacturers' Association, a Conservative. During the Toronto visit the chairman of the Quebec section of the movement, Sir George Garneau, received an honorary degree from the University of Toronto, and Premier Sir Lomer Gouin vied with Hearst and Rowell in supporting national unity and the war effort.[40]

But Senator Landry and other officers of the French-Canadian Education Association of Ontario were not members of the Bonne Entente, and when they declared a fight to the death against Regulation 17,[41] the Orange Order replied with a threat to campaign for the total abolition of separate schools if the bilingual agitation continued.[42] When the Legislature was convened the government still had to find some way of enforcing Regulation 17, especially in Ottawa. Its solution to the problem was to introduce a bill to appoint another commission to take over the duties of the Ottawa Separate School Board if it persisted in its resistance. The government apparently believed that the terms of the new bill were sufficiently different from the earlier measure to pass the scrutiny of the courts. Rowell had serious doubt about the constitutionality of the bill, and he said so in the House.[43] Yet it was impossible to vote against it, as he explained to Laurier:

It appears to me that after the Ottawa School Board has taken the matter to the Privy Council and Regulation 17 has been declared constitutional, they should loyally accept the decision and carry out the law. We cannot put ourselves in the position of appearing to excuse non-compliance with the law.

Many of our members think the bill ... is deliberately introduced with a view to laying a trap for us, and that if we opposed it they would go all through the country in their campaign trying to link us up with the opposition of the Ottawa School Board to the regulation. We cannot permit them to put us in this position.[44]

All the members of the Legislature supported the measure, save for the five French-speaking representatives.[45] The voting was the same on a further bill to charge the Ottawa Board $300,000, the amount spent by the government when it was operating the schools under the now unconstitutional commission. Again, Rowell did not like the bill and made a mild protest against charging the Ottawa Board in this fashion, but he and all the English-speaking Liberals voted for it.[46]

Laurier was astonished at these two measures; he thought the first 'an impudent re-enactment' of a law already rejected by the highest court, the second an even more obvious 'violation of all principles of equity and justice,' since the city of Ottawa was to be assessed expenses illegally incurred. He had no comment on Rowell's explanation of the political necessity of supporting both measures.[47] The time had passed when Laurier expected the majority of Ontario Liberals to act on what he recognized as Liberal principles.

Throughout their long disagreement over the language issue, Rowell and Laurier, unlike many Canadians, both French and English, had understood the language question and the recruiting problem as two separate issues and had done everything in their power to present them in that light. By the spring of 1916 events were in train that made it increasingly unlikely that the general public would isolate the two issues and more and more difficult even for men of good will to do so.

10
Democracy versus militarism

Although Rowell was not uninformed about the European power struggle that had been developing for so long, the actual outbreak of hostilities in August 1914 was a distinct surprise, as it was to most Canadians. From the first he entertained no doubt that the war must be fought to a finish and Canada must assist in full measure. He explained to his sister, who had managed to make a hasty departure from France for England just before the outbreak of hostilities: 'The whole war is a terrible reflection upon our modern civilization but I think it must go on until the allies win a decisive victory over the Germans, or over their government for I cannot think that all the German people wish this terrible war.'[1]

Rowell's spontaneous response to the opening of hostilities was echoed by most Ontarians of both political parties. Within ten days of the declaration of war, and even before the Dominion Parliament had passed the bill establishing the Canadian Patriotic Fund to collect monies for the support of dependents of men volunteering for overseas duty, the Toronto and York Patriotic Fund Association had been formed with Sir William Mulock as president, E.R. Wood as treasurer, and Sir John Willison as chairman of the publicity committee. In the current economic slump there was a good deal of pessimism about the possibility of raising the $500,000 that the committee estimated as Toronto's share of the national fund during the next year. But within a month Toronto and York County had raised $900,000.[2] While the provincial government made a gift of 250,000 bags of flour valued at $700,000 to the British government, every city, town, and village in the province was beginning the collections for Belgian relief, the farm production drives, and the Red Cross meetings that soon became part of the lives of thousands of Canadians.

No institution in Canadian society responded more vigorously to the demands of the war than the Methodist church. The General Conference of the church, meeting in Ottawa two months after the declaration of war, evidenced the spirit that characterized the church until the end of hostilities. Rowell had been forced to play a somewhat less active role in church affairs since his entry into politics but he was still a delegate to the General Conference and a member of four of its committees – missions, education, church property, and civil rights and privileges. As a member of the latter he assisted in drafting for adoption by the Conference a resolution of loyalty which emphasized the English origins of Canadian Methodism, affirmed the righteousness of the British cause, and pledged support to the 'Motherland' in her hour of trial.[3] Among all the many reports submitted to the Conference, perhaps that of the Committee on Social Service and Evangelism most displayed the influence of the war. While supporting the war as a crusade to aid the weak, it asked whether the carnage in Europe might be due to the church's excessive interest in creeds and ritual, to the neglect of teaching the love of neighbour. Already the bill for the war, it was noted, was enough to endow twenty universities or twenty schools of applied science for the betterment of human life. The war overseas must not be allowed to detract from the struggle for social justice in Canada where 'Kaiserism in commerce and industry is yet to be conquered.' Deploring a growing 'autocracy of wealth' the report advocated a social system where 'men shall have to earn what they own, and shall be compelled to use what they own for the public good.' Commending a growing sense of stewardship among some of the wealthy, the report found among others 'a patronizing paternalism which seeks to do for the needy what a juster social order would enable them to do for themselves. Paternalism may do for the weak, but it will not develop the strong, free man in Christ Jesus, who stands to work out his destiny in the complexity of social relations in which he finds himself.'[4]

Equally acceptable to Rowell's ears was Laurier's address to the Methodist Conference on the meaning of the war: 'The sword will not be put back in the scabbard until this Imperial bully has been taught that his scrap of paper is a solemn obligation, and that solemn obligations between nations, as between individuals, must be observed.'[5]

From the beginning of the war Rowell took a prominent part in the work of the Patriotic Fund, the Red Cross, and the recruiting campaign. By the time Colonel Sam Hughes had transported the thirty thousand men of the First Division from the chaos of Valcartier Camp to the mud of Salisbury Plain and the Second Division was being organized, Rowell was declaring to a Montreal audience that Canada must put one hundred thousand men in the field,[6] a figure frequently mentioned by other public figures as well. A few weeks later he asserted that Canada must raise forces in proportion to those of Great Britain; Canada's share would be one-sixth of Great Britain's war effort; if the mother country sent two million men into battle, as now seemed probable, Canada should send three hundred thousand.[7] Few Canadians were thinking in such large figures, and many cherished the illusion that the war would end by Christmas or at least by the summer.

Increasingly, the constant theme in Rowell's presentation of the war to Canadians was the opportunity and responsibility of proving themselves full-grown members of the Empire by making sacrifices equal to Great Britain's. But he saw the military struggle as something more than an occasion for the expression of a mature Canadian nationalism or the payment of a debt to a generous parent. Just as the glory of Britain had been the steady enhancement of the rights of Parliament ever since the days of Cromwell, so the tragedy of Germany was the failure of the Social Democrats to prevail over the Prussian militarists, with the result that two great empires now faced each other in a struggle between democracy and militarism in 'the supremest conflict democracy has ever faced.' In that conflict Canadians had as direct as interest as any free people. Since democracy meant just as much to Canadians as it did to Britons it must be defended by equal participation in the war. Nine months after the outbreak of war Rowell found Canada falling far short of equal sacrifice. She should have had more than 350,000 men under arms; the city of Birmingham, with a population only slightly larger than Toronto's, had sent over sixty thousand men, more than the whole of Canada would have contributed to the struggle when both Canadian divisions were at the front. A first step in remedying this situation would be a truly non-partisan approach to recruiting and the establishment of a national recruiting committee composed of members of both political parties, as had been done in Britain, so that Canadian leaders could stand together on common platforms to inform the people more fully of the issues of the war.[8]

Privately, Rowell entertained little hope that Canada would meet her responsibilities under the present Conservative leadership. Two days in Ottawa in connection with a hearing before the Supreme Court of Canada brought him political gossip that confirmed his own impressions of the government's capabilities:

> Sir Robert Borden is an amiable man with good ideals but without decision of character, the courage or the outlook to fill the position of premier at this time, and his good name is used as a cloak and a shield for policies and practices in administration – by men like Rogers who largely dominate him – which are entirely discreditable. It is almost a tragedy that Canada should be afflicted with such a government at this time. One result of their incompetence and timidity is that Canada, the best able of all the Dominions to help in this struggle, has done the least. The response of the people of Canada has been magnificent. They have done it all without any real [leadership?].

At the same time an evening's private discussion with Laurier enhanced his admiration for the whole-hearted support the Liberal leader had given the war: 'Canada little knows the debt she owes him. The more I see of him the more I admire him and the more I appreciate the service he has rendered and is rendering in this grave hour.'[9]

In that spring of 1915 Canadian troops had their first major encounter with the enemy. At the end of April, during the second battle of Ypres, young Canadians but recently recruited withstood the superior forces of the German professional army in the face of the enemy's first extensive use of poison gas and despite the flight of two French divisions that left an undefended four-mile gap in the Allied line. The British generals, press, and political leaders were full of praise for the Canadians whose subsequent actions saved the day by covering the otherwise exposed flank of much of the British army and averting what might have been a disaster for British arms. Here was cause for pride and a final answer to those who doubted whether Britain really needed Canada at her side. But no great tide of patriotic fervour swept the country over the victory at Ypres; pride was tempered by a painful realization of the human costs of war. Over seven hundred young men lay dead in Flanders; more than 2,100 were wounded and 2,500 missing. In thousands of Canadian homes the war took on new meaning.

By the autumn of 1915 the common platform that Rowell had advocated six months earlier had become the order of the day as political leaders and prominent citizens forgot party affiliations and joined in recruiting drives. Borden had returned home from England in September convinced that the British Empire would be unable to organize its full strength for another eighteen months and that Canada must prepare for a long war and the sending of many more troops. In the accelerated recruiting drive which followed, no other political leader in the province appeared more frequently than Rowell. His Conservative opposite number was often Sir George Foster, Borden's minister of trade and commerce, who rated Rowell as one of the most effective recruiting speakers in the country.[10] More and more, Rowell hammered at the theme that Canada had not begun to do her duty. While France had exceeded the safe limit of 10 per cent of the population enlisted, and Britain was rapidly approaching the same position, Canada had enlisted only 2 per cent. Canada must begin to pull her weight by doubling her armed strength immediately.[11]

The government's announcement late in 1915 that the armed forces would be increased to 250,000 was welcome news to Rowell and the signal for a renewed devotion to recruiting throughout the province. But there was no rush to the colours. The easiest days of recruiting were over, the Third Division would be infinitely harder to enlist than the First and Second, and in the face of a steady decline in enlistments there was much talk of 'the recruiting crisis.' Rowell had no doubt that there was a crisis and that it was due mainly to a failure of leadership in Ottawa. While individual effort would help, what was most needed was a clear statement from the government as to how it proposed to get the additional one hundred thousand men it had promised, he told an audience of his constituents in

Woodstock. The country was deluged with organizations, public meetings, and exhortations, but there was no central government plan which alone could make these well-meant efforts effective. But the government was not solely responsible for the lag in recruiting. Rowell laid a good deal of the blame at the door of the many unco-operative businessmen who had suffered nothing, but rather had benefited, from the relief from social and industrial problems that the war had brought. That situation must end: there must be some sacrifice from those at home and business-men must reorganize their affairs so that men would be released for battle duty. Here again the government had given no leadership.[12]

No change of leadership was in sight. The life of Parliament was due to expire in the autumn of 1916 and Laurier, while rejecting Borden's proposal for an address to the king requesting an extension of Parliament until after the war, had agreed to an extension for one year. The country was, for the present, saved from a wartime election. For that Rowell was grateful, but the continuation in office of a govern-ment whose direction of the war effort he increasingly questioned was a large price to pay for political peace.

Despite his growing concern with recruitment, Rowell did not abandon his interest in Ontario's social problems. Indeed, as the war continued he became increasingly convinced that only a determined effort to create a better social order could justify the appeal to men to sacrifice their lives on the battlefield. At the outbreak of the war he had been giving a good deal of thought to the widespread unemployment in the province, the consequence of the economic slump felt across the country, and was engaged in a careful study of the recent book on unemployment by William Be-veridge, director of Britain's government labour exchanges and a principal drafter of the British unemployment insurance legislation. By the autumn of 1914 the Ontario government was apparently willing, as it had not been when Rowell proposed it in the Legislature that spring, to appoint a commission to investigate unemployment. In anticipation of government action and perhaps out of fear that the proposed investigation would be too narrow in scope, Rowell took a somewhat unusual initiative for the leader of the opposition when he called together a non-partisan group of interested persons to discuss the scope and methods desirable in a study of unemployment. His invitation to dinner at the National Club was accepted by J.S. Willison, Archbishop Neil McNeil of the Roman Catholic diocese of Toronto, Archdeacon H.J. Cody of St Paul's Anglican Church, W.P. Gundy, president of the Toronto Board of Trade, Alan Studholme, the labour member of the Legislature, James Simpson, the socialist president of the Trades and Labor Congress of Canada and a member of the Toronto Board of Control, Frank Beer, the president of a private venture, the Toronto Housing Company, and two Univer-sity of Toronto professors, the mathematician A.T. DeLury and Gilbert Jackson, an economist who had recently come to Canada on his graduation from Cambridge University.[13]

Six weeks later, when the government appointed the Ontario Unemployment Commission, the new body looked very like Rowell's dinner party. Sir John Willison was chairman, W.P. Gundy, treasurer, Gilbert Jackson, secretary, and Archbishop McNeil, Archdeacon Cody, Professor DeLury, and Frank Beer were among the members. The other members were Rev. Dr Daniel Strachan of the Presbyterian church, W.K. McNaught, a former Conservative member of the Legislature, W.L. Best of the Locomotive Engineers representing labour, and Joseph Gibbons of London. Subsequently, a Toronto journalist, Marjorie Mac-Murchy, was appointed joint secretary with special responsibility for matters relating to the employment of women. Rowell was generally pleased with the composition of the commission, although he regretted his failure to secure the inclusion of two official labour representatives. Rowell and Gilbert Jackson had several discussions of the frame of reference of the commission and agreed that it should examine the causes and consequences of unemployment and investigate measures for reducing it and for providing systematic relief in cases of enforced unemployment.[14] Rowell was disappointed when Willison outlined the commission's task to the public omitting any reference to the provision of relief to the unemployed.[15] The omission seemed to rule out consideration of any scheme for unemployment insurance, which Rowell had hoped the commission would study seriously.

The commission undertook its study at a difficult time. The industrial situation was extremely fluid early in 1915 for the pre-war unemployment had grown worse, owing in part to the dislocations created by the war. Rapidly changing conditions threatened to make information quite out of date by the time it was compiled. Moreover, there was some hostility, or at least a lack of co-operation, from the 1,637 factories whose management was associated with the Canadian Manufacturers' Association and who were asked to supply information to the commission; only 651 replied in the form requested. Despite this the commission was able to carry out one of the most systematic investigations of an economic and social issue ever attempted in the province.[16] By the time it submitted its report to the Legislature early in 1916 the talk was all of manpower shortages, 'unemployment' almost a forgotten word, and many of the commission's recommendations apparently unnecessary, at least for the present.

Rowell's interest in recruiting and in the shape of post-war Canada took him on a trip to western Canada in the early summer of 1915. His immediate purpose was to give a series of addresses on Canada's role in the war to Canadian Clubs in several western cities and to study social legislation, especially liquor regulations, in the western provinces. He had no intention, he insisted, of making any political speeches. But under present circumstances any speeches by a prominent politician, especially if they urged greater participation in the war, were bound to have political implications, and to bring their author considerable public attention, a fact that was clearly recognized, and approved, in the *Globe's* editorial offices.[17] The trip was also assumed to have political significance, whatever Rowell's intention, by one Montreal Liberal who learned of it. A. Kirk Cameron, president of the Metal Shingle and Siding Company and participant in several other Montreal businesses, was a frequent visitor to western Canada and an active 'back room' Liberal. For some time Cameron had been promoting endeavours in Montreal and Toronto to organize the younger members of the Liberal party across the country and to introduce them to one another. Rowell's trip would serve that purpose, but it would be even more effective, in Cameron's view, in creating 'the impression that the Liberal party of the future will be well manned by clean bright men of industry and ability'[18] if Rowell were accompanied by two or three other younger Liberals. As a result of Cameron's last-minute negotiations through Stewart Lyon of the *Globe*, Rowell was joined in Winnipeg by two Montrealers – A.R. McMaster, an able thirty-eight-year-old lawyer, and S.W. Jacobs, an eminent criminal lawyer and a leader in the Jewish community across Canada.

McMaster and Jacobs were soon enthusiastic about the Ontario leader's prowess on the platform, whether before a Canadian Club, the Methodist congregation who heard him discuss the effects of the war on the Mohammedans, or the great temperance banquet in honour of Premier Walter Scott's recent closing of bars and clubs throughout Saskatchewan when McMaster found Rowell 'splendid, humorous, genial, eloquent, almost inspired.'[19] McMaster clearly had the air of a man with an eye out for a future leader of the Liberals of Canada. Sam Jacobs gave that impression even more strongly when he told the *Globe* on his return to Toronto that 'Mr Rowell simply swept the West with his reform speeches ... it was the opinion of many of those to whom I spoke that in the Liberal leader of Ontario the progressive forces throughout the Dominion will find a champion capable of maintaining the best traditions of Liberalism.'[20] The Conservative press both east and west was quick to use the success of Rowell's western tour as the basis for predicting his early advent to the leadership of the federal Liberal party. Rowell himself was well removed from the scene of these speculations. At the conclusion of his speaking engagements Nell had joined him for a holiday, first for some climbing at the Alpine Club in Banff and then at their Okanagan fruit farm.

During the ensuing autumn of 1915 McMaster and Jacobs invited Rowell to address the Montreal Reform Club and made further attempts to bring together eastern and western Liberals, notably at a consultation of party leaders and workers arranged by Cameron and McMaster in Ottawa. Rowell was unable to attend but sent his secretary, Main Johnson, instead.[21] The Ottawa conference agreed to establish a National Liberal Advisory Committee to direct the work of studying and recommending party policy and preparing for the next election. But for weeks Laurier took no initiative in arranging for the calling of the committee and considerable anxiety developed among the promoters of the idea over the delay.[22] Cameron began to entertain the suspicion that Laurier, Sidney Fisher, Rodolphe Lemieux, and some of the other members of the Liberal hierarchy feared that the new blood and the new ideas that would be brought into party councils if the committee were formed as suggested would be 'detrimental to the interests of their own selfish projects.'[23] Eventually the committee was organized and held its first meeting before the end of 1915; its fifty-six members, drawn from all parts of Canada, were assigned to a number of subcommittees on a variety of subjects. Rowell was appointed to the committee on technical education and industrial training under the chairmanship of Mackenzie King. Although he was not a member of it, Rowell also followed closely the work of the subcommittee on social legislation headed by J.E. Atkinson. In two months' time Atkinson's committee was ready with an interim report recommending that the Liberal party commit itself to national schemes of health and unemployment insurance, old age pensions, mothers' allowances, federal workmen's compensation, and minimum wage laws.[24] For Rowell it was a program that inspired confidence in the future of the Liberal party and of Canada and one to which he could give enthusiastic support. Above all, it was a guarantee of the better life the men in the trenches so richly deserved.

At the beginning of 1916 Borden announced the government's intention of increasing the Canadian armed forces to five hundred thousand, a figure that Rowell had publicly advocated the previous summer in Victoria.[25] Although Rowell welcomed this decision, he found it difficult to see how the government expected to raise so many men; it still had to find fifty thousand of the 250,000 authorized the previous summer, and there was no suggestion of any reorganization of recruiting methods nor any hint that the administration was even thinking of going back on its repeated promises not to resort to conscription. It was becoming increasingly evident that the minister of militia, Sir Sam Hughes, was one of the biggest obstacles to a vigorous and united war effort. Almost every time the minister displayed his Napoleonic temperament in some impetuous utterance he contributed to the decline of public and cabinet confidence in his suitability for his position and to the wonderment of both friend and foe about the considerations which could possibly compel even the gentlemanly Borden to retain him in his position. Hughes' dogmatic defence of the Ross rifle did little to counteract the recurring reports from the front of the rifle's tendency to jam under heavy use or to refute the resulting allegations that the young men of Canada were being sent to the front with defective arms. When the Liberals demanded an investigation of the operations of the Shell Committee, which operated under authority of the minister of militia, they believed that their charges that Hughes had mishandled shell contracts to secure profits for his old friend Colonel (Honorary) J. Wesley Allison would finally substantiate the charges of maladministration against Hughes. Enough preliminary evidence was presented to force the Borden government to appoint a royal commission, which began its investigations early in the spring of 1916. In the meantime there were growing complaints about shortages of labour or misuse of manpower from manufacturers, labour leaders, and farmers and charges that Canadian nickel was reaching the Germans through the United States. But despite all the difficulties and doubts men came forward at the rate of about thirty thousand a month for the first three months of 1916; at that rate the country would be able to honour its promise of half a million men. But by May enlistments for the month fell to fifteen thousand and in June to less than eleven thousand.[26] Meanwhile, the losses at the front, such as the nearly two thousand dead, wounded, or missing suffered by the Second Division in the single disastrous battle of St Eloi, underlined the need for reinforcements for the existing divisions. Moreover, although meaningful figures on recruitment seemed difficult to obtain, certain facts were made public that fired English Canadian tempers. In the Senate the Conservative brigadier general James Mason presented statistics on enlistment showing that although there were in Canada three times as many Canadian-born males aged 20 to 44 as there were British-born males of the same age, the British-born had by the end of 1915 produced 63 per cent of all recruits, while the Canadian-born accounted for only 30 per cent. No one found these revelations exceptional; it was natural enough that the many men who had recently come to Canada from 'the old country' would respond to Britain's need. But a source of acrimony lay in Senator Mason's further breakdown of his figures and the confirmation of the growing belief of English Canadians that French Canadians were failing to do their share: although French Canadians constituted 40 per cent of the men of military age they had so far supplied only 4.5 per cent of the enlistments.[27]

A charitable interpretation of these statistics in Ontario was not encouraged by the current utterances of Nationalists like Armand Lavergne, who told the Quebec Legislature that 'every French Canadian who enlists fails to do his duty ... If the Germans are persecutors, there are worse than Germans at our very gates ... every cent that is spent in Quebec to aid enlistment of men is money stolen from the minority in Ontario ... I ask myself if the German regime might be favourably compared with that of the Boches of Ontario.'[28] As Rowell pointed out to Andrew McMaster, 'it would be hopeless to endeavour to convince the people of Ontario that Quebec has done all that she might have done or should have done in connection with recruiting.' The blame rested largely on the federal government because of 'the encouragement they gave the Nationalists in 1910 and 1911, and their complete failure of evidence of any leadership in Quebec or, for that matter, in any other part of Canada at the present time.'[29]

N.W. Rowell 1917

Nell Rowell 1918

Could the province of Ontario do anything to compensate for what was lacking in the leadership provided by the federal government? That was a question Rowell had considered for many months. During the legislative session of 1916 he decided that, despite the limitations on what a province could do to effect a truly national mobilization, Ontario could do more. After prior consultation with Premier Hearst, Rowell presented to the Legislature a resolution providing for the establishment of a provincial committee composed of members of both parties and private citizens whose advice and experience would be useful in 'assisting in the work of recruiting men for the CEF, ensuring a sufficient supply of labour for the agricultural interests and the necessary industrial operations of the Province; and in promoting thrift and economy among the people, thereby strengthening our financial position during the war and preparing for the period of reconstruction after the War.'[30] Rowell quickly complied with Hearst's request that he draft an outline of a bill to establish the Committee on the Organization of Resources, but he was distressed when Hearst displayed no speed in securing passage of the bill and appointing the committee.[31] When it was constituted, the committee consisted of the lieutenant governor, Sir John Hendrie, as chairman, Hearst and Rowell as vice-chairmen, and seven members of the Legislature drawn from both parties; Dr A.H. Abbott, a former University of Toronto psychologist, was appointed executive secretary. When Hearst found that urgent business in his home riding prevented him from attending the first meeting of the committee and from co-operating with Rowell in calling together a representative group of men to hear Lionel Curtis of 'The Round Table' discuss the British organization of resources, Rowell informed him in no uncertain terms that he was failing to give the committee's work the priority it deserved. Nor would he accept Hearst's proposal that implementation of the plan to appoint men from outside the Legislature should be postponed.[32] After several conversations the two men agreed that the Manufacturers' Association and the Ontario Trades and Labour Council be asked to name one representative each as promptly as possible; in addition there were to be representatives of the various military districts in the province and seven additional members, four to be nominated by Hearst and three by Rowell. Rowell proposed[33] to nominate Arthur T. Little, a London wholesale drygoods merchant, W.E. Rundle, general manager of the National Trust of Toronto, and J.M. Godfrey, a Toronto lawyer and president of the Canadian National Service League, which had three months earlier begun to urge the Borden government to adopt some form of national selective service. Godfrey was personally committed to conscription and had recently been urging Laurier to come out in favour of it.[34]

The difficulties he had encountered in getting the Ontario Committee on the Organization of Resources under way was only one more of the many experiences which added to Rowell's puzzlement and distress over the lack of any compelling sense of urgency about the war among his fellow countrymen. Their attitude was still in marked contrast to the more disciplined vigour of the British people who were showing the world, he told a St Catharines audience, how a nation could be mobilized.[35] He had followed with approval the formation of Asquith's coalition government in May 1915, which included the appointment of Arthur Henderson as the voice of labour and the aggressive Lloyd George as minister of munitions. In January 1916 Britain had instituted conscription of unmarried men and in April of married men as well; all this had been accompanied by increased taxation of a kind that the Canadian government appeared not even to contemplate. Yet Rowell was no less convinced than he had been at the beginning of the war that this was as much Canada's war as Britain's.

That there were other North Americans who ought to make the war their own was also the implication, although never the specifically stated message, of several addresses Rowell gave in the United States. Polite convention precluded his telling the Americans what their foreign policy should be, but any careful listener could see his meaning through the impassioned exposition of the reasons for Canadian participation. The National Laymen's Missionary Congress in Washington DC at the end of April 1916 gave him an audience of Americans from across the continent. That the purpose of the war was the creation of a more Christian society and a world without war he had no doubt:

I recently saw the statement in the report of your committee on Industrial Relations that 2 per cent of the people of the US own 60 per cent of the property, 33 per cent of the middle class own 35 per cent and 65 per cent own but 5 per cent. I have no figures for my own country, but they would indicate the same tendency ... I want to ask you this. Do we, as Christians, think this is a Christian division of property?
Three fifths of the men who have gone from my country to fight in the war are manual laborers ... Do you think when these men, who have poured out their life's blood to save the homes, the property and the liberties of those who remain behind return home, they will be content through the years to come to take this minimum proportion of the property which they have helped to preserve, and would it be Christian on our part to ask them to do it? ... In this great hour in human history every Christian man in America ... can make his life tell perhaps as life has never told in the course of human history.[36]

Nothing but his intense desire to study the British and French war efforts at first hand and to see conditions among the Canadian troops overseas could have reconciled Rowell to a trip to Europe that would take him away from his wartime responsibilities in Canada and separate him from his family for many weeks. It was especially hard to leave Nell behind just then; she had not been well since the birth six weeks earlier of their son, Frederick Newton Alexander, and he would have preferred to be nearer at hand. But Britain's need and Canada's honour called. His unofficial advisers among Toronto Liberals were anxious that he make the trip. They trusted him to unearth more reliable information than could be gleaned from the conflicting reports and charges to which they were daily subjected about affairs in Britain and at the front; some of them, notably P.C. Larkin, had raised a fund to help finance his journey. He was well armed with letters of introduction to members of the British government and civil service and assured by Prime Minister Borden that he had requested the Canadian high commissioner in London, Sir George Perley, to do everything in his power to secure a relaxation of the regulations which normally prevented civilians from visiting the fighting front in France.[37]

At the end of June he sailed from New York on the ss *Kroonland* of the American Red Star line with his secretary, Main Johnson, Geraldine Wright, wife of his nephew Ward Wright, who was now a major on active duty with the Canadian army, and their five-year-old son, Peter, who was soon, at least in the estimate of an admiring uncle, the most popular passenger on board. The several babies on board never failed to remind him of the infant at home and of the baby's mother, for whom he was preparing several long letters for immediate mailing from Liverpool. 'Dearest Nell' was never long out of mind and he many times enjoyed taking out the photographs of her and the children. 'Two things one greatly regrets to see have marked this voyage,' he told Nell. 'Several of the women on board openly smoke cigarettes on deck. This appears to me to be the limit. I could stand the actresses but among others I see one of our Col's wives who is travelling with a baby in arms & two or three small children going over to see her husband ... I cannot stand those who do it although Mr Johnson certifies that ... some of them are exceedingly nice and very clever. The other is Sunday games. This is the first voyage I have taken on which shuffle board is played on Sunday – I am glad to say though by only a limited number.'[38]

The quarters he and Johnson took up in the Savoy Hotel in London were more luxurious than Rowell thought appropriate in wartime, but it was too late to make a change. His first impression that London was not much more changed by the war than Toronto did not survive his first sight of the ambulance trains bringing in the wounded from France and a visit to a military hospital. During a day at Bramshott Camp where the Fourth Division was in training he had his first encounter with Canadian soldiers overseas and met a number of sons of Toronto friends. For the present there seemed little possibility that a civilian would be allowed to go to the front. The Canadians were still actively engaged in the Ypres salient, while further south, in the opening weeks of the great battle of the Somme, the British and the French were engaged in some of the heaviest and costliest fighting of the war. Trying to be patient, he visited old friends and learned all he could about the organization of the civilian war effort in Britain.[39]

Suddenly, after two weeks in England, he was informed that plans were made for him to visit the front if he could leave the next day. Appointments speedily cancelled, he and Johnson left London for Folkestone and then crossed the channel to Boulogne. There the wounded were being brought in from the casualty clearing stations and placed in ambulances for the steamer to England. 'Each man had two tags, one fastened to each shoulder, giving his name, number of his regiment and nature of his wounds ... Thus they are labelled and packed like goods.'[40] By midnight they had arrived at the quarters of the commander of the Canadian Corps, Lieutenant General Sir Julian Byng, where they were to stay. Rowell's itinerary was planned by a distinguished soldier from Toronto, Colonel C.H. Mitchell, who personally escorted him on many of his visits – to a school for snipers, an exhibition of bomb throwing at a bombing school, hospitals and casualty clearing stations, the various branches of the engineering services, and meetings with chaplains, both Roman Catholic and Protestant. On a visit to Ypres his guide was Captain Talbot Papineau, grandson of Louis-Joseph Papineau, cousin of Bourassa, and junior law partner of Andrew McMaster. Papineau's regiment, the Princess Patricia's Canadian Light Infantry, had been in the front line during the struggle for Ypres and in several engagements since then; of the original strength of his battalion only twelve men and one officer – Papineau – now remained. A Toronto friend, Captain J.M. Macdonnell, in civilian life a junior officer with the National Trust, took Rowell out to watch the night bombardment of the German trenches near Ypres. Meetings with other friends and acquaintances or their sons were frequent – Sir John Willison's son Walter, and Irving Hearst, the premier's son, were among them – and he was gratified to see each of his three nephews, Ward and Douglas Wright and John Langford, looking fit and well.[41]

An unexpected privilege was granted when he was permitted to visit the front line trenches at dawn in the company of Brigadier General Robert Rennie, who explained the principles of trench warfare and showed him the craters near St Eloi, Sanctuary Wood, and other battle sites already famous at home. As he moved about he heard a great deal of criticism of the inadequacy and unsuitability of the training and of the frivolous life led at Shorncliffe by officers who should have been at the front, and many complaints about the deficiencies of the Ross rifle. On his last night at the front he had a frank talk with the commander of the First Canadian Division, Major General Arthur Currie. Currie also was highly critical of Shorncliffe and the Ross rifle and urged the absolute necessity of 'trusting the general staff and of eliminating politics from all appointments and promotions in the army.' As he was driven to Paris, the chauffeur, a young man from Windsor, gave him the same last word he had heard from so many others: 'Urge the men to enlist & come over and help.'[42] Rowell needed no urging; no four days of his life had made such a profound impression on him: 'I could never have properly understood or appreciated what our Canadians are doing had I not visited the front. Truly war is Hell and it is more so today than ever but our Canadians are doing magnificently. I was never prouder of our men in the trenches, but they need reinforcements. What they are asking is more men & less politics ...'[43]

In Paris the British embassy had been alerted to Rowell's interest in the domestic organization of the French war effort and had arranged a round of visits. He was struck by the fact that many French convalescent hospitals were also industrial training centres: 'Everything possible is being done to fit men for the life of peace after the war. One could not but contrast this with what we are doing or failing to do in Canada.' Also in marked contrast to Canada were the enormous munitions factories where nearly all the workers were women, ranging in age from eighteen to fifty: 'As one saw these women toiling ... 10 hours per day making shells for their husbands & brothers & for their country one could not but feel an affection and almost a reverence for these patriotic women ... how little we have done compared with France.'[44]

At the Ministry of Works and Social Services he gathered information on social insurance, wartime labour laws, and health measures. He especially valued two long discussions with Raphael Georges Levy, professor of political economy at the Sorbonne, on working class movements in France and the role they were likely to play after the war. He was surprised to find that Levy was 'a temperance man' and fairly representative of members of the French anti-alcoholic movement: 'The forces behind it here are quite different or at least not quite the same as with us. The moving spirits are social reformers, men interested in the social and economic aspects of the question as it affects the future of France.'[45] Was there here a suggestion that this might be a more creative approach to the matter than the fanaticism of some Canadians whose political support he had enjoyed?

He extended his stay in Paris longer than he had planned in the hope that his application for a permit to visit the French battlefields would yet be granted; the extra time was well spent and every day brought some additional useful knowledge. 'I never missed a university education as much as now,' he told Nell. 'I am taking post graduate work without the preliminary foundation. And how I wish I could speak French. It is most unsatisfactory working through an interpreter, though Mr Johnson is very good and a great help ... What a great privilege I am enjoying these days. It is a far cry from the country school to what I am now seeing but I hope to make good use of it all for the benefit of Canada when I return.'[46]

At last the military permit came through, and almost exactly two years after the beginning of the war he was touring part of the enormous battleground of the Marne, scene of the struggle he believed had 'saved civilization. It compelled the Germans to retire and it gave the Allies time to prepare for the final contest ... one could not but feel that this was sacred ground.' As he was leaving Paris, one question dominated his mind: 'How can we help France more in the unparalleled sacrifice she is making in the cause of liberty.'[47]

Returning to England he took up the investigations and interviews that had been interrupted by the visit to France. On his last night in Paris he had dined with Britain's most powerful press lord, Baron Northcliffe, proprietor of both the *Times* and the *Daily Mail*, one of the moving spirits behind the creation of the coalition government, and a critic of Prime Minister Asquith. Now he also sought out the views of Lord Burnham, proprietor and editor of the *Daily Telegraph*, Geoffrey Robinson, editor of the *Times*, and J.A. Spender of the *Westminster Gazette*. From these and other discussions with men outside the government he was well aware of the heavy criticism to which Asquith was being subjected for failure to prosecute the war with sufficient zeal. He held consultations with several members of the cabinet – Lloyd George on munitions production, Sir Herbert Samuel on the operation of conscription, Arthur Henderson on labour problems, Austen Chamberlain, secretary for India, Lord Robert Cecil, and Asquith himself. The former home secretary, Sir John Simon, whom he had so much admired on his previous visit, explained the position of the fifty Liberals who had refused to support compulsory military service and his own resignation from the cabinet as a protest against its adoption. From all that he could learn Rowell concluded that Asquith was still 'the biggest man they have got and the sanest and safest.'[48]

After delivering a public lecture at Oxford on Canada's war effort, as arranged by A.L. Smith, the master of Balliol, he was the weekend guest at the nearby country estate of Sir Lewis and Lady Harcourt where he enjoyed the family of four children and an opportunity to discuss imperial relations with the former colonial secretary who was now Asquith's minister of works. A rather different view of empire dominated the discussions of the following weekend which Rowell spent at Cliveden as the guest of Major and Mrs Waldorf Astor. It was a 'Round Table weekend' for which his reading on board ship of Lionel Curtis's recently published *The Problem of the Commonwealth* had prepared him well. The other guests included Philip Kerr, editor of *The Round Table*, R.H. Brand, MP, the British representative on the Imperial Munitions Board in Canada, Geoffrey Robinson of the *Times*, and Lionel Hitchens, all of whom had been members of 'Lord Milner's Kindergarten' in South Africa more than a decade earlier. Like other visitors to Cliveden, Rowell found Nancy Astor 'exceedingly bright and clever. Has the offhand manner of the American girl'; and of course he applauded her devotion to the work of the Canadian hospital on the estate.[49]

During several days spent in the Midlands he visited munitions plants in Manchester, Leeds, and Sheffield; as in France he was impressed by the extensive use of female labour in the factories and by the acute concern everywhere with the shortage of labour. His main purpose in going to Scotland was to have a brief holiday with Sir Andrew and Lady Fraser and to see the naval construction on the Clyde and part of the fleet in the Firth of Forth. Thereafter he suddenly decided to go to Ireland for two days to satisfy his curiosity about the troubles there. The most memorable part of his brief stay in Dublin was a long talk with George ('A.E.') Russell, the nationalist poet and social reformer, whose knowledge of the conflicting views of his fellow countrymen provided Rowell with an excellent survey of the current Irish scene. In Belfast he was entertained by the lord mayor at a luncheon of leading citizens, 'all Unionists and strong anti-Homerulers,' and was exposed to another version of Irish politics by the chairman of the board of directors of the nationalist paper, the *Irish Times*. It was a most enjoyable and informative two days.[50]

The whole trip had taken at least a month longer than he had planned, but he had no doubt that it was very much worthwhile. He could claim no expert knowledge of the many problems he had examined, but he had acquired a broad picture of the whole structure of the British and French war effort and of Canada's part in it, a perspective possessed by no other Canadian civilian, not even the prime minister himself.

11
The full current of
the world's life

Rowell's first obligation on returning to Canada was to explain what he had seen and heard in France and England during the past two months. To Borden, 'the only man who can deal with the situation at the present time,' he immediately sent a long report. On the whole, he told the prime minister, he had found the Canadians ready and fit and deserving of the high praise they received in both Britain and France. Yet he was bound to report some serious deficiencies: he was glad to learn that during his absence the Ross rifle had been replaced with the Lee-Enfield for all Canadian troops, but he had also found that the Oliver equipment issued to the men in Canada was being replaced with English equipment when they got to France, surely a wasteful procedure. He had also been told that many Canadian-made machine guns were defective and had to be replaced by others made in Birmingham. And everywhere he had heard complaints about the training given Canadian officers both in Canada and at Shorncliffe. Army medical authorities had told him that a very high percentage of the Canadians arriving in England were physically unfit and should never have been accepted for service: 'I was told that the matter was so grave as to become a serious scandal.'

In the trenches Rowell had been distressed to find it a commonly held belief that army appointments and promotions were very often made for personal or political reasons. There was much bitter feeling among those at the front over 'the surplus of highly paid officers ... in England drawing good salaries.' Many officers thought that a good deal of the mismanagement and political influence could be laid at the door of Sir Max Aitken, who had been appointed by Sir Sam Hughes as Canadian war records officer and 'eye-witness' in France. Rowell made no claim to have investigated any of these matters thoroughly; he was only passing on to Borden information from 'thoroughly reliable and entirely disinterested' men. 'The whole situation seems to suggest a lack of proper co-ordination between the management of affairs in Canada, Great Britain, and at the front; and that in the interests of efficiency and of the well-being of our men ... a radical change is needed.' He was not suggesting that any action be taken on the basis of his report, but he urged Borden to go to Britain and France as soon as possible to see the situation for himself, or, failing that, to send a Conservative 'as disinterested and public-spirited as Mr Flavelle, head of the Imperial Munitions Board, or a man of like standing.'[1]

Borden's reply was rather cool and defensive, even sharp, as he asserted that the question of the Ross rifle had been settled six months ago and that no Oliver equipment had been issued for eighteen months. For most of the criticisms he had an answer. The question of appointments had been 'under consideration for some time.' Borden made no mention of Sir Max Aitken but said that overseas organization had already engaged the attention of the government and he hoped for an improvement in the near future.[2] That was as far as a prime minister could go in admitting to an opposition politician his troubles with the arrogant and inflexible Sir Sam Hughes and his appointees.

On the public platform there was no hint of the criticisms Rowell had addressed to the prime minister. Travelling widely throughout the province, he tried to inspire pride in the Canadians overseas by recounting their exploits on the field of battle and assailed the argument that Britain and France had not yet made their maximum effort and that Canada should do no more until they had. Never had a civilian leader given Canadians at home a more complete or vivid picture of the daily lives of the men overseas; their training and organization, their carefully guarded passage across the Atlantic and the English Channel, their life in English camps and at the front, their medical and chaplaincy services, and the care bestowed upon their graves were all fully explained. Frequently, especially before women's groups, he referred to his talks with the sons or husbands of members of his audience and urged the women to appoint themselves as recruiting officers to secure the men without whom the sacrifice of those now in France might be in vain.[3] Several addresses, including one to the Victoria College alumni, were devoted almost entirely to an account of France's solitary defence of civilization in the days before Britain could get her armies to the continent and to praise of the qualities of her contemporary leaders, Joffre, Briand, and Poincaré.[4] He spoke often of the organizing genius of Lloyd George in the production of munitions and the rallying of Britain's financial resources, attributing much of this success to Lloyd George's willingness to reach out beyond party to draw on the services of hundreds of businessmen and scientists who had only been waiting to be shown how their skills could best be used. The meaning of this for Canada was unmistakable.

Frequently he emphasized, as in his first address on his return to Toronto, to the

Men's Canadian Club, the effect of participation in the war on the national outlook of the men overseas and on the future role of Canada in the world: 'Our men who went to the front, however provincial or limited may have been the outlook of some of them, have now become citizens of the world. This war has deepened our sense of nationality and enlarged our sense of destiny. We have swung out into the full current of the world's life, and whether we view with satisfaction or alarm the position in which we find ourselves we can never retrace our steps.'[5]

Rowell's story was heard in person by thousands of Ontario citizens and several hundred Montrealers; many more read it. Naturally, the *Globe* and the *Star* gave full coverage to a Liberal leader's overseas impressions, but the Conservative *Mail and Empire* and the *News* were equally attentive. Always he expressed the conviction that if the people were told the facts, as he was trying to tell them, they would respond with enough men to keep Canada's four divisions up to strength. But, supposing they did not, what then? He made no direct reference to any method of recruitment except the voluntary one, but early in October 1916 at Woodstock he spoke of the call of 'the larger citizenship.'[6] His tone alarmed both Laurier and Lemieux: was he hinting at coalition, conscription, or both? Laurier determined to have a frank talk with Rowell the next week during the convention of the Federation of Ontario Liberal Clubs in London.[7]

Rowell had not seen Laurier since his return from Europe. They had several discussions in London and most of a day together in Toronto afterwards, when Laurier's fears about the direction in which Rowell might be moving were eased.[8] In his convention address Rowell dealt mainly with provincial issues, especially post-war legislation to protect the workingman, and he identified himself fully with the charges of several Ontario Liberals concerning the handling of nickel by both provincial and federal governments. There was no further talk of 'the larger citizenship.'[9] His few days in Ontario convinced Laurier that Liberal fortunes were improving rapidly; gone was the despair he had expressed five months earlier over the effects of the bilingual issue: 'It is absolutely manifest that we are making serious headway. Unless the government is reconstructed by the elimination of Sam Hughes, the situation would seem to be hopeless; and even without Sam Hughes it would not be much better.'[10]

Borden soon dealt with the problem of Hughes. At long last, in the face of a final act of insubordination from his minister of militia, who had announced the establishment and personnel of a Canadian Military Council in London well before cabinet approved the plan, Borden demanded and received Hughes' resignation. Now it might be easier for some Liberals at least to co-operate with the government.

One interpretation of Hughes' long overdue dismissal saw it as part of Tory preparations for an election, although the air was also full of talk of coalition or an extension of the life of Parliament. Rowell reported to Laurier that the Conservative desire for an election was growing and with it the determination to fight the contest on racial lines. One of the signs was the very full reporting of Nationalist speeches in Toronto papers, as evidence that the government was doing its best with recruiting in Quebec against the most implacable opposition. To offset the effect of this propaganda Rowell suggested that an effort be made to secure fuller coverage in the Toronto Liberal press of recruiting speeches given by Quebec Liberals. Laurier was somewhat piqued by Rowell's letter. If the Liberal press in Ontario thought Quebec speeches should be more fully reported all that was necessary was to go ahead and print them. Scores of Quebec Liberals had made dozens of recruiting speeches: 'No notice of them was ever taken by your press in Ontario. Now that the Nationalist members make speeches for consumption in the English-speaking provinces they are carefully reported by the Tory press.'[11]

If Rowell's report of the growing danger of an election on racial lines was intended to imply that either coalition or an extension of Parliament were preferable to an election, he did not make this explicit at the moment. Yet all around him Toronto Liberals were discussing coalition. Atkinson's *Star* had been advocating it editorially for months, hoping for a coalition led by Laurier but believing that the vital interest was to secure non-party prosecution of the war. The *Globe* walked more warily in the presence of coalition talk, but it clearly wanted an improved war effort.

Just before Christmas, Borden and R.B. Bennett wound up a cross-country tour to persuade Canadians of the merits of the government's recently instituted National Service plan with a meeting in Toronto. Rowell was Borden's chief supporter on the platform; as on many earlier occasions he urged the signing of the national registration cards to assist in the government's manpower survey and presented the immediate needs of the armed forces. Those needs were daily growing more acute; enlistments had fallen from one thousand a day early in 1916 to a mere trickle of about three hundred, far too few to maintain the strength of the four Canadian divisions at the front. In Toronto, Bennett was once again explicit about the government's rejection of conscription and emphasized the voluntary nature of the National Registration scheme; a united, voluntary manpower policy was the only alternative, he declared, to 'civil war, riot, and insurrection.'[12] But the men were not coming forward; the labour unions were hostile to the National Registration, which they feared as a preliminary to conscription; industrialists and farmers complained that their vital contributions to the war effort were undermined by indiscriminate recruiting; and French Canada drew ever more within herself.

Early in 1917 Rowell urged Laurier to enter a national government. Such a move would unite Ontario Liberals behind him, whereas an election fought amid the racial passions the Tories would stir up in Ontario would create a rift from which the party and the nation would suffer for years to come. If Borden did not invite Laurier to help form a national government but asked for an extension of Parliament, Laurier should agree only on condition that a national government be formed.[13] Laurier was increasingly disposed to feel that most of the English-speaking Liberals who were offering him so much advice were really trying to tell him that he was no longer useful because his racial origin was against him, although they never came out and said so:

> The situation is simply this that the government has been constantly losing ground, but a good many of those dissatisfied, and perhaps all, do not want to entrust the direction of affairs to a leader of French origin. Analyze the situation any way you please and tell me candidly whether this is not at the present moment the true and only difficulty. The constant appeals which have been made on that ground by *The News, The Telegram*, the *Orange Sentinel*, and some other papers of the same ilk have produced their effect, all the more so that the defence on our side has lacked vigour ... The very fact that you and so many of our friends in Toronto are looking to a coalition is abundant proof that my usefulness is gone.[14]

Rowell categorically denied that the true cause of Ontario interest in national government was Laurier's racial origin. The cause was discontent with the prosecution of the war by the present government, a discontent that was abated, but not eliminated, by the resignation of Hughes. The majority of Ontario citizens 'are supremely concerned ... that Canada should do her part worthily and they place this higher than any party consideration.' They believed that Ontario and Quebec could only be united in a whole-hearted effort by a government including leaders from both provinces: 'When you suggest that the proposal means that your usefulness is gone, I say again unhesitatingly, no. The proposal is predicated upon your continuing to render the state large and invaluable service – perhaps by reason of the very difficulty of the situation the most valuable service you have ever rendered.'

He entirely agreed with Laurier's contention that he could not be expected to enter a government without knowing precisely its composition and program. Rowell hoped for an administration half of whose members would be chosen by Laurier; 'the old element' in the Conservatives could not then dominate. If the powerful forces in the cabinet opposed to coalition prevented Borden from making such a proposal, then Laurier would be the master of the situation when Borden asked for an extension of Parliament: 'If you then put the proposition squarely before him that the nation's need at this time is the strongest possible government ... and not a party government ... you have the country with you.' Rowell was at some pains to argue that his own decision to urge national government had no direct relation to the campaign being carried on by Atkinson through the *Star* nor to the opinion which Stewart Lyon of the *Globe* had slowly formed. But the fact that they had all come to essentially the same view was indicative of the general movement of feeling in the province:

I need hardly say to you that nothing has stirred me more deeply in all my life than this world-war. I hate war and all its brutalities with all my soul. You have repeatedly and impressively stated the issue. It is a struggle between two civilizations, two conceptions of government, two great ideals. Because I believe this to be absolutely the case I have thrown myself unreservedly into this struggle. When the war broke out, or shortly after, every one of my nephews then of military age enlisted and is serving with the colours. It is because the satisfactory issue of this struggle seems to me to be so vital to the welfare, not only of Canada but to our humanity, that I feel we in Canada should subordinate every party and personal consideration to attaining the supreme objective of a just and lasting peace.

Rowell freely admitted to Laurier the great difficulties in forming a national government, but the alternative was tragedy – 'an election in which racial feelings would be stirred to their depths and in which an appeal would be made to our worst side rather than to our best.' If the government won, Quebec would be embittered, and if Laurier came to power with a solid Quebec behind him 'you know what the feeling and attitude of the majority in this province would be.'[15] Laurier remained unconvinced by arguments for active co-operation with the Conservatives, believing that an election was both desirable and unavoidable within the next six months. If Ontario Liberals would only meet the race cry squarely, he told Stewart Lyon, Rowell's fears of its effect in Ontario would not materialize. Laurier believed that ought not to prove impossible because he had 'done nothing for which any of my friends should apologize.'[16] Although talk of a coalition or national government persisted in the press and among certain politicians, Laurier continued to believe that general enthusiasm in the country was slight. But whatever its actual strength he thought it good strategy 'to make no opposition to the movement, because it shows dissatisfaction with the present government. The Tories are putting forth every effort to discount it and therefore, on the whole we must reap some advantage from it.'[17]

Despite his concern with the war effort and the lack of leadership from the federal government, Rowell was still the leader of a provincial party, and it continued to receive much of his attention. During his absence in Europe two unusual events had occurred – the Liberals had won two by-elections, one in North Perth and the other in South-west Toronto.

When the North Perth by-election was called just before he left Toronto, Rowell had thought, in keeping with his general reluctance to fight by-elections in wartime, that the party ought not to contest it. But the local temperance Liberals in the riding felt that the government candidate was shaky on the temperance question and wanted a fight, although the Conservatives had won the seat in the last four elections. The Liberals therefore nominated Wellington Hay, a Methodist grain buyer from Listowel, to oppose John Makins, a farmer and an Anglican. During the campaign Hearst charged that the liquor interests were working against him out of anger over his passage of the Ontario Temperance Act.[18] G.A. Warburton of the Committee of One Hundred believed that this was true and publicly endorsed the Conservative candidate.[19] The local Liberal organizer, himself a temperance man, declared that the party had received no open assistance from the liquor interests, although he believed that 'a goodly number of the hotel people supported Mr Hay ... quietly among their own following.'[20] The Liberals carried even the most doubtful area, the city of Stratford, and in the riding as a whole turned the previous Conservative majority of over a thousand into a majority for themselves of over five hundred. Rowell resented Warburton's intervention in the election, but he believed that the result proved the truth of what he had always contended: once prohibition was a fact and the liquor interests could no longer gain any special advantage by supporting one party their baneful influence in politics would be removed and elections would be decided on other issues.[21]

The lesson of the second by-election was not so clear. Initially, the provincial executive had been opposed to contesting South-west Toronto, left vacant by the death of J.J. Foy, the attorney general, but again local Liberal wisdom decreed a fight.[22] The Conservatives nominated James Norris, who frankly differed from his party in favouring the granting of beer and wine licences but was nevertheless officially endorsed. The Liberals chose a well known and eloquent corporation counsel, H. Hartley Dewart, KC, who had recently been in the public eye for his attacks on the nickel policies of both provincial and federal governments, which were allegedly permitting Canadian nickel to reach German armament factories. Although he was the son of a former editor of the *Christian Guardian* it was no secret that Dewart had slipped from his Methodist moorings in his own attitude to liquor. In his acceptance speech Dewart made the government's ineffectiveness in organizing Ontario's contribution to the war effort the great issue. Prohibition could not be an issue, since 'Hearst and Rowell have agreed on a policy which ... is already on the statute books. I was not responsible for it, but ... as the Liberal policy I accept it. If you ask my view, I tell you I reserve to myself in case of emergency, the right to observe my independent judgement.'[23] Two additional candidates took firm stands on prohibition: Gordon Waldron, assistant editor of the farmers' paper the *Weekly Sun*, running as an independent Liberal, opposed prohibition, and J.M. Connor, a Social Democrat, supported it.

Dewart's equivocal attitude to the party's official temperance policy made him unacceptable to Liberal headquarters, notably to C.M. Bowman, who was acting leader in Rowell's absence, and to Atkinson; he therefore received no official assistance from the party.[24] Through the *Star*, Atkinson supported Connor, the Social Democrat, as the only candidate solidly committed to prohibition; the *Globe* refused to support anyone. Atkinson looked on the South-west Toronto contest as crucial for the party's future and was disgusted that certain Liberals who had earlier supported prohibition when it was good politics to do so were now aiding the liquor interests in their 'attempt to break the party in two. These men ought to see that the party is almost out of the woods, thanks to the adoption of prohibition by Hearst ... the Liberal boat having practically reached the other side of the stream what kind of sagacity is displayed in this violent rocking performance? ... To allow it to be even suspected that the Ontario Liberal party is weakening with regard to Rowell or prohibition would lay the party in ruins in this province for years to come.'[25] Dewart was obviously 'weakening,' for he fought his whole campaign without once mentioning Rowell's name; instead he directed attention to the nickel issue, the recent riot at Camp Borden, and the ineptness of both federal and provincial Conservative governments in the prosecution of the war. On election night the 'Dewart Liberals' were jubilant: a Liberal had won a Toronto seat in the provincial Legislature for the first time in twenty-six years.

Did Dewart's victory represent a Liberal revolt? Many Liberals thought so. Harry Anderson of the *Globe's* editorial staff saw in it nothing so drastic but found it significant that Dewart had won 'the strongest temperance ward in the city' and a riding that 'gives the second largest Tory majority in the city normally, and sends the biggest number of Toronto soldiers to camp and to the front.'[26] Another Liberal, freelance journalist H.F. Gadsby, told Laurier that the victory represented 'the revolt of red blooded Ontario Liberalism against the little group of herring-gutted bigots who would run this country like a Sunday School class ... The best thing about the South-west Toronto election is that it ripped open the pink tea crowd ... Atkinson is a pious rattlesnake ... a Liberal only from the ears up – he doesn't feel our principles in his heart. If he can't get his own way he aims to create trouble for the Liberal party by making an alliance with the socialists. He keeps two of them in his employ – Jimmy Simpson and Bancroft.'[27] Rowell's old rival for the East York nomination, Peter Ryan, also thought 'the Dewart revolt' would prove of lasting significance as having served notice that 'the boys won't tolerate men of Whispering Joe's class. Atkinson very plainly told a good loyal friend of yours [Laurier's] that he was more concerned in Rowell than in your success. Now I like Rowell very much but you cannot run a victorious Liberal party by the agency of Bible class exhorters. We have grown restive under it ... The boys ignored the "Holy Willies" ... and won a brilliant victory.'[28]

Laurier was too good a politician to be drawn into a conflict within a provincial party, but he allowed himself the observation that 'it looks as if public opinion in Ontario were silently, but none the less certainly, shaken up ... I have no fault to find with our friend Joe Atkinson if he is more concerned with the success of Rowell than with the success of Laurier. This is a matter of friendship, and we are living in a free country.'[29] Nevertheless, Laurier believed and hoped that the end of the era of battle over temperance was in sight. 'Our friend Rowell has gone as far as he could, or should in his policy of "Abolish the Bar." When he fell behind the Hearst government on the question of Prohibition, he might have remembered that Prohibition for the last forty years has been, to his certain knowledge and to mine, a football which the Tories managed more cleverly than the Grits ... I am not without hopes that the present situation in Ontario will be a lesson for all, and will teach us that men are neither angels nor demons, but beings endowed with some faults, and, much more, many qualities of heart and mind.'[30] If this last bit of homely wisdom was intended to talk Gadsby out of some of his implacable hostility to the Toronto 'uplifters' it was only temporarily effective.

Rowell drew a firm lesson from Dewart's victory: it was more than ever necessary to stand resolute in his liquor policy. He knew that there was some agitation within the party to put Dewart into the party leadership, but it came from only a minority and was no great threat. He had no illusions about Dewart's views on prohibition, but he was certain that Dewart was sharp enough to see the political advantages of formal acquiescence in official policy until the promised referendum at the end of the war.[31] But Dewart would bear watching, and everything possible must be done to safeguard the party from his influence.

To Rowell's regret it proved necessary to fight two more wartime by-elections early in 1917. The first, in West Simcoe, excited only mild interest. The Conservatives stood on their general record; they were rather vague in their own position on prohibition but charged that the Liberals were receiving support from the liquor interests. Rowell was satisfied that this was not the case and denied the charges forcefully,[32] but he was not surprised when the Conservatives retained the seat with a comfortable majority.

In North-west Toronto, W.D. McPherson's entry into the cabinet as provincial secretary necessitated his seeking re-election. Rowell wanted to let the seat go to McPherson by acclamation; he believed him to be one of the ablest men in the government and the riding was a 'temperance riding' where there was no danger to the temperance cause. Moreover, he thought it politically inexpedient to enter a Liberal candidate, since there was no chance that he could win and a defeat would be a break in the appearance of growing strength created by the recent victories in North Perth and South-west Toronto. But partly because of those triumphs the local Liberals wanted a contest they believed they could win. Rowell sent a friend to the nominating convention to try to prevent a decision to contest the seat. He was outmanœuvred and had to report back to Rowell that the meeting was a very representative one and strongly in favour of putting up a fight, not primarily on the liquor issue, but on other aspects of government policy.[33] The Liberal nomination went to James G. Cane, an officer of the Commercial Travellers' Association, an organization far from friendly to prohibition. Cane had personally supported Rowell's liquor policy at the 1914 convention of the party, but Rowell felt it necessary to warn him that he must make absolutely certain that no funds from liquor interests should get into his campaign fund. He feared that such an attempt would be made so that charges of insincerity could then be laid against the Liberal party. Rowell stated categorically that if anything of this kind happened he would immediately repudiate Cane and withdraw official party support.[34]

A few days before the voting in North-west Toronto G.A. Warburton of the Committee of One Hundred issued a statement on the election which more than hinted that the Conservative party, the party that had given the province the Ontario Temperance Act, was the true temperance party.[35] Rowell found this blow almost incomprehensible: 'Nothing has happened since I entered public life that has hurt me more than what I feel to be the unfairness and injustice of your statement.' It was the Liberal party that had created the Committee of One Hundred initially, and while Rowell had no desire to minimize what the government had done, nobody who knew the story of the temperance movement in Ontario could accept the implication that the temperance cause was safe only in Conservative hands. Was it not true that Warburton really feared that unless Hearst remained at the head of the government the temperance cause was lost as far as the Conservative party was concerned? If this were so, he asked Warburton, 'why do you seek to make the Liberal party the scapegoat and not the real parties whom you do not trust?'[36] Warburton contended that he was not attacking the Liberals but supporting McPherson, because he believed that Cane, like Dewart before him, was being backed by the liquor interests. He regretted that Rowell did not seem to understand that 'the liquor element is really working with certain elements in the Liberal party at the present time.'[37] Rowell could find no evidence for this; with Dewart as his chief platform support, he campaigned actively on Cane's behalf, majoring on the temperance question while Dewart handled the nickel controversy and other issues connected with the war. Rowell's belief that North-west Toronto was a safe Conservative seat proved justified when the government held it with a majority of over eighteen hundred votes.

Now it was time to attend to the work of a new session of the Legislature. The Liberal party caucus, most of whose members had individually supported the provincial franchise for women, was now prepared to make the female franchise official party policy and a major item of business for the session. In the throne speech debate Rowell regretted the absence of any reference to the subject in the speech and moved an amendment calling for the introduction of such a measure. The premier was obviously taken aback by this development, and quickly asked the speaker to declare the amendment out of order on the ground that the subject was already on the order paper. Perhaps Hearst had intended to put it on the order paper, but it was not there. The Liberals were irate when the speaker, after considering the matter for five days, granted Hearst's request, and they appealed to the House against the speaker's ruling. The House upheld the speaker on a straight party vote, and Hearst subsequently introduced his own bill to extend the franchise to women. The premier, who had a year ago deplored the same proposal as introducing a divisive element among the women that would distract them from their splendid war work, now handed them the vote as a reward for their great patriotic services. Little wonder that there was much puzzlement over the government's sudden conversion. Could it be that pressure had been brought to bear from the federal Conservatives, who were already considering ways of allowing women to vote in the next federal election on the assumption that most of them would support conscription if it were presented to them?[38] Or had Ontario Tories, noting the granting of the female franchise in Manitoba and its imminent approval in the other western provinces, simply acquiesced in the trend of the times and made certain that they would be given credit for the inevitable?

Whatever their motives, the Conservatives had once again stolen the Liberal thunder. It was hard to bear. Rowell underscored the suddenness of the government's change of heart, pointed out that Liberals had been supporting suffrage measures in the House ever since 1912, and reviewed the extensions of the franchise in Ontario since Confederation to demonstrate that all the major advances had been the work of the Liberal Mowat government. Although technically the enfranchisement of Ontario women had become government policy Rowell was not prepared to allow all the credit for 'this great, radical, democratic measure' to be garnered by the Conservatives who had so consistently opposed it.[39]

There was not one member of the House to oppose it now. To Rowell it seemed logical that anyone who could vote ought also to be eligible for election to the Legislature. That principle, he pointed out, was recognized in the franchise bills passed or likely to be passed in the western provinces, in Australia, in the United States where the first woman had just been elected to Congress, and in Ontario and Britain in relation to school boards. But Hearst thought the revolution had gone far enough; he dealt facetiously with Rowell's further remarks on the special knowledge of family and social problems and other qualifications which intelligent women would bring to the House and retreated behind the assertion that women did not want to sit in the Legislature.[40]

During this session the Liberals mounted a major attack on the government's nickel policy, a vital wartime issue since three-quarters of the world's supply of nickel was produced by the International Nickel Company of Sudbury. It was now two years since Rowell had first raised questions in the Legislature about conditions that seemed to inhibit maximum production of an essential war material and were apparently allowing nickel to reach the Germans via refineries in the United States, and he had demanded that the ore be refined in Canada, and sales controlled by Canada.[41] At that time Premier Hearst had promised a royal commission, subsequently appointed, to look into the affairs of the industry. Addressing the General Reform Association of Ontario in the fall of 1916, Rowell had urged that the province take over both nickel production and sales, contending that this was the only policy able to satisfy Canadians that their sons were not being killed in Europe by weapons made from Canadian nickel.[42] Now, three months later, the Liberals introduced a resolution calling for public ownership of the industry.[43] The government took refuge behind the impending report of the royal commission, which in due course rejected public ownership while encouraging the program of refining within the province on which International Nickel was already embarked. Before the session ended, taxes on profits from nickel mining were increased, but not to the extent that Rowell and his followers thought desirable.[44]

Willingness to fight wartime by-elections was not the only sign of the 'politics as usual' mentality that Rowell increasingly deplored. On his return from overseas he had hoped to find a well organized and functioning provincial Organization of War Resources Committee, eager to profit from all he had learned about the organization of the civilian war effort in England and France. Instead he found that despite his earlier pleas to Hearst nothing had been done in his absence to complete the constitution of the committee. The representative men to be appointed from outside the Legislature had not yet been asked to serve. Throughout the fall of 1916 Rowell protested to Hearst, but the committee continued to mark time, apparently waiting for action from the federal government and some understanding of how provincial plans could fit into the broader scheme. But even after the establishment of the National Service Board the committee had failed to consider its relation to the new plan.[45] Early in 1917 Rowell concluded that the government had no intention of proceeding with the committee.[46] Hearst made no attempt to explain the eight-month delay. He accused Rowell of a 'desire to criticize and complain rather ... than to help and co-operate in a common object' and of leaning toward 'generalities ... hopes or aspirations' as substitutes for 'any concrete proposition for effective work.' Hearst took no responsibility for failure to call the committee; the lieutenant governor, acting in his capacity as a citizen of Ontario like every other member of the committee, was the chairman. Hearst had understood that Rowell was on the committee in the same role and not as an opposition critic.[47] Rowell had not thought that this was Hearst's view of the committee, although he would be glad if its work could go forward on that basis. Since Hearst's letter had helped to clear up the situation and they both agreed there was still useful work for the committee to do, the first step was to go ahead and constitute the committee as planned.[48] As his four nominees Rowell chose W.E. Rundle and A.T. Little to represent business, William Dryden of Brooklin representing agriculture, and Walter Rollo of Hamilton representing labour.

Once functioning, the committee encouraged the growth of local war committees in every community and district of Ontario and through them promoted co-operative vegetable gardens, urged city men to help with the rural harvest, made loans available to farmers to assist them in increasing their acreages, and advertised widely the virtues of increased industrial production and thrift in the home. An assessment of the value of the committee was difficult, but it could hardly be rated an outstanding success in non-partisan wartime endeavour, even when all due allowance was made for the absence of national policies that might have enabled it to define its own work more effectively.

Rowell's continuing concern with the recruiting problem led him to conclude early in 1917 that the immediate needs of the armed forces could be met if the Militia Act were put into force. From the men thus called up for the defence of Canada he thought it would be possible to obtain enough volunteers for overseas service.[49] His first public presentation of this solution to the manpower crisis was made in the village of Thamesford in his own riding in mid-February: under the Militia Act he would call up all unmarried men and widowers aged eighteen to thirty without children, with exemptions for men whose services were absolutely essential in agriculture and munitions production. At the same time female workers should be used much more extensively in factory work. How else could repetition be prevented of the all too typical experience of one battalion in whose recruiting campaign he had taken part. After a year's recruiting the battalion still had less than seven hundred men, having lost over four hundred through desertions and discharges for physical unfitness. Recently, the battalion had conducted a week's intensive recruiting campaign and secured the names of two hundred young men who, in the opinion of the local recruiting committee, were not essential in civilian life and should enlist; at the end of the week only three of the men had enlisted.[50]

But the Militia Act was not invoked, nor was any other decisive action forthcoming from Ottawa. Rowell continued his appeals for voluntary enlistments, not because he believed they would bring much practical result, but simply because there was no alternative. As long as the military authorities arranged recruiting meetings he could not refuse to help. It was obvious that the government's only recent initiative, the attempt to raise a Civil Defence Force for home service to release troops in Canada for overseas services and provide a pool from which men might be persuaded to enlist was a dismal failure.[51] And while the capture of Vimy Ridge by the Canadian Corps in that spring of 1917 brought Canada the applause of the allies and much satisfaction at home, it also enlarged the casualty lists and underlined the need for replacements at the front.

Amid the gloom at home Rowell found two sources of good cheer in the outside world – the American entry into the war and the Russian revolution, destined he was sure, to be 'one of the great landmarks in human progress.'[52] Perhaps there was also a source of some optimism in the knowledge that Sir Robert Borden had gone to Britain to study allied war needs for himself. Rowell chose the eve of Borden's return from London to make a blunt pronouncement on the state of the nation. To a Woodstock audience he declared that it was now evident beyond doubt that voluntary recruiting was a failure and could not supply the men to meet Canada's existing commitments.[53] Two days later in an address to the Canadian Club of North Bay he gave his first public call for a coalition government. Citing northern Ontario's record of enlistments as proof of the unity which could exist between English and French, he entirely rejected a suggestion that only the Anglo-Saxon population should be taken into account when comparing Canada's war effort with that of the other Dominions: 'I believe the whole people of Canada will loyally accept any measures which any government in which they have confidence, may declare to be necessary to win this war.' Obviously that could not be the present government, at least not without radical reformation.[54]

Privately he had little hope that Borden would initiate any major reform of his government. If, instead of adequate measures, Borden asked for another extension of Parliament, what should the Liberal response be? He could not agree with a Nova Scotia Liberal member of the House of Commons, A.K. Maclean, that a wartime election was so abhorrent that it must be avoided no matter what the cost: 'If Sir Robert Borden will not reform his government, if we are to have another year or two of the same indecision, incapacity, and graft, I would not want to say there should be an unconditional extension of the parliamentary term.' In the event of an election the Liberals must promise to form a truly war government; there would be no point in putting out the present government without guarantees that the new one would prosecute the war with greater vigour. He still hoped an election could be avoided, but the terms for doing so must be acceptable. Looking at the situation from the point of view of provincial politics he admitted that he had very strong reasons for wanting to postpone an election: if a provincial election were held in Ontario before a federal contest he believed that the Liberals would win; but after a federal election in which the Conservatives would make the race issue dominant and would carry the province with a substantial majority, the prospects of the provincial Liberals would be most uncertain.[55]

The immediate choice facing Liberals was made plain sooner than Rowell had expected. On his return from England Borden wasted no time in announcing to a reassembled Parliament that the government would shortly introduce a plan of 'compulsory military service on a selective basis' to raise at least fifty thousand, and probably one hundred thousand, additional men. Despite the regrettable absence of any accompanying plan for government reorganization Rowell had no doubt that Borden must be supported in this measure and believed that most English-speaking Liberals would agree with him in that. The crucial question was the response of Quebec Liberals. He placed his view of the proper course of action before Rodolphe Lemieux, Laurier's principal strategist in Quebec. While admitting the long list of charges against the Borden government, Rowell contended that in the interests of winning the war and maintaining national unity these failures must be treated as a thing of the past and the new measure supported because it was right.

If Quebec now stands aloof on this vital issue it appears to me we face the most serious racial differences which have confronted us for a generation. If, on the other hand, Quebec comes in and cordially supports proposals to raise the necessary men by compulsion, we will at once have the answer to this campaign against the province of Quebec. It is open then to prove your statement that the failure to secure larger numbers of recruits has been due to local conditions plus the nationalist movement and the incompetence of the government.[56]

Lemieux was entirely unconvinced: Borden was simply playing into the hands of 'the firebrands of both Ontario and Quebec.' The Quebec situation was admittedly complex; not the least of the factors in it was the natural grievance against 'the Toronto Tory Government,' that, 'casting aside the Mowat tradition, enacted Regulation 17 against the English-French schools – *and not against the English-German schools.*' Moreover, Borden's whole procedure was undemocratic, since he had failed to consult Parliament before promising half a million men. The Borden government, in Lemieux's view, was motivated by political considerations and hoped to use the conscription issue to keep itself in office. Lemieux joined Laurier and many other Quebec Liberals in advocating a referendum on conscription. If a majority of Canadians approved conscription, Quebec, as a law-abiding province, would not have to be 'bullied into the ranks.' But Lemieux was not so sure that 'outside of a few centres' conscription was very popular: 'An act of "selective conscription" administered by the present discredited government, without a referendum, will, in my humble judgement, create a serious situation not in Quebec alone but all over Canada.'[57] Rowell granted that Lemieux might be right about the government's political motives, and he fully agreed that Borden should have consulted Parliament more often, especially on every decision to increase the Canadian forces, but this was all irrelevant now. Rowell was at a loss to see how a referendum would secure men. 'It may be that conscription is not particularly popular in any part of Canada. I do not know. But my view in reference to it is not determined by its popularity, but by ... its necessity.' He could see no alternative to compulsion except failure to reinforce the men at the front: 'This alternative for me is impossible and I believe it is impossible for the great mass of our people in Canada irrespective of race, if they once thoroughly understood the situation.'[58]

In the last few days of May the rumours from Ottawa were of political changes pending, but none of them gave Rowell much confidence that the demands of the hour would be met, as he admitted frankly to his sister:

> It is a tragedy the way the Government has mishandled the situation and we are in danger of national disunion because of their incompetence. Sir Robert Borden has been a dismal failure as Prime Minister. He appears to be dominated by Rogers and the machine element for whom party is everything and country wholly secondary. Sir Wilfrid has reached such an age and the condition of his health is such that I fear he cannot give the country the leadership it needs and demands and it would be almost impossible for any French Canadian under existing conditions to meet the situation unless he could carry his province on conscription and it is said no one could. I do not know enough of the Quebec situation to have an independent opinion on the matter. This last report of Judge Galt should surely mean Rogers' dismissal and not only Sir Robert's mishandling of the war but his retention of Rogers in his government and his chronic indecision should mean his retirement also, though I fear it will not. If both Sir Robert and Sir Wilfrid retired it would leave the way clear for a national or war government which to my mind is the only solution which will ensure united and effective action, and it will require an exceptionally strong government to do this ... I hope this week may see a change in Government which will promise better things for the future. If Sir Wilfrid retires as it appears quite probable he will, I think Mr Graham will succeed him'[59]

In Ottawa, when the British foreign secretary, A.J. Balfour, addressed a joint session of Parliament there were replies from both Borden and Laurier. Rowell found it easy to express to Laurier his satisfaction that 'on a great historic occasion' he had so eloquently expressed the sentiments of the Canadian people.[60] 'England, great at all times, was never greater than at this moment,' Laurier had declared. 'Canadians stand to-day prouder of the British allegiance than we were three years ago.'[61] How could Laurier hold attitudes toward the war apparently so like his own and yet come to such different practical conclusions? Perhaps, he suggested to Laurier, his own distress over the manpower problem was due to his experience overseas; that made him 'feel more keenly over the situation than those who have not had a similar opportunity.' Surely Liberals must either accept conscription or suggest some other means of securing reinforcements?[62]

Laurier was nettled by Rowell's comments on the depths and possible uniqueness of his anxiety about the current scene. 'I think you may be sure that it is no less painful to me, and perhaps, more, as I have more responsibility than any other in the unfortunate position in which we are.' He was just as eager as Rowell to reinforce the men overseas, but only by voluntary enlistment. Any form of compulsion would create 'a line of cleavage in the population ... for which I will not be responsible.' The cleavage would not simply be one between Quebec and the rest of the country; Laurier's correspondence convinced him that 'in every other province there is amongst the masses an undercurrent which will be sore and bitter if at the present moment a conscription law is forced upon them.' As for his own position in Quebec, he had affirmed when he introduced his naval policy and in the face of vicious attack from the Nationalists, that a Canadian navy would not be a first step toward conscription and that service in it would be voluntary, as in the army. His total opposition to conscription had been very fully stated then: 'Now if I were to waver, to hesitate or to flinch, I would simply hand over the province of Quebec to the extremists. I would not only lose the respect of the people whom I thus addressed, but my own self-respect also.' Laurier said he had been approached to join a coalition but had found the terms unacceptable. He continued to favour a referendum, which he believed would go in favour of conscription. Although it would not be easy, he would devote all his energy to persuading the people of Quebec to accept the verdict of the majority and adhere to the law.[63]

Shortly, from the Liberal member of Parliament for Lambton West, F.F. Pardee, Rowell learned the terms of Borden's offer to Laurier.[64] The prime minister had proposed that a coalition government be formed to pass the Military Service Bill, but that the measure be put into effect only if the people approved it at an election. But Laurier had held out for a referendum before passage of the bill, and it looked as if that would mean the end of the matter. Believing as he did that coalition was the most important immediate objective and not a final decision about recruiting methods, Rowell joined Pardee in urging Laurier to tell Borden that he would enter a coalition pledged to make one more effort at voluntary recruitment, the new government to decide what further measures should be taken if that failed.[65] But there was to be no coalition. Even when Borden offered Laurier what amounted to a veto on the entire membership of a coalition cabinet,[66] Laurier was adamant. The enforcement of conscription was the central purpose of coalition, he believed, and that he could not accept. On 7 June, with the publication of an exchange of letters between Borden and Laurier, the public was informed of the negotiations and their failure.[67]

12
The larger citizenship

Now the country was full of rumours that Borden would go behind Laurier to ask other Liberals to join a coalition. Rowell was embarrassed when 'a Liberal leak' let out the news that Willison had assured Borden that Rowell would be willing to join a coalition.[1] On 9 June at a large meeting of Toronto Liberals chaired by S.J. Moore and called at the signed request of forty-eight prominent party members, 'to force the party's hand' according to P.C. Larkin, Rowell urged the immediate introduction of conscription.[2] Two days later, while Borden was introducing the first reading of the Military Service Act making all male British subjects in Canada aged twenty to forty-five liable to conscription, Rowell joined Premier Hearst, two of his cabinet ministers, and several Liberals at a large non-partisan public meeting in calling for conscription and a renewed war effort.[3] He made no mention of coalition; if conscription could be put through with a good measure of Liberal support that would be acceptable; the party would be divided but it might be spared the destruction that seemed to stare it in the face.

But ideally Rowell still wanted coalition. He hoped and believed that Borden would shortly approach George P. Graham, the senior member of Parliament from Ontario, with a coalition proposal. In the strongest terms Rowell urged Graham to accept. Graham thought that most of his constituents were opposed to conscription, although he was personally in favour of it, so that he vacillated and tended to see the merits of Laurier's referendum while admitting there was little chance that the House would pass any motion to hold a referendum. Rowell had no confidence that a referendum would go in favour of conscription unless the race issue were exploited in such a way as to set the whole of English Canada against Quebec, a calamity to be avoided if at all possible. If Graham would act on his convictions that tragedy would be avoided, Rowell urged, and it would be the finest hour of Graham's public career.[4]

A long exhortation to Graham to do his public duty had a more immediate personal application than Rowell realized. The next day Sir John Willison, intruding on the quiet of a Sunday afternoon, called at Rowell's home as the emissary of Sir Robert Borden with an invitation to Rowell to join a coalition government, one-half of whose members would be Liberals who would share equally in policy-making and administration and would have an opportunity to put forward 'almost any reasonable suggestions regarding the personnel of the new cabinet.' Rowell's immediate reaction was that the offer should be made to Graham rather than to himself. A genuine coalition could only be formed by men who were able to command parliamentary support; that automatically ruled out a provincial politician. Moreover, he had no desire to leave his present responsibilities as leader of the provincial party, especially since he believed that the party's prospects were now brighter than they had been for many years. Willison and Rowell were agreed that two objectives were 'paramount to all others which should determine our conduct at the present time ... first, winning the war; and second, preserving our national unity.' The order of these priorities was of the utmost significance and came to the heart of the matter: Willison believed that the government would have almost no support on conscription in Quebec, and he doubted that conscription could be enforced there if it were passed. At the same time he agreed with Rowell's contention that it would be extremely difficult to have a stable, united government unless Quebec were 'influentially represented.' For the moment Rowell could see no way through the dilemma created by the conflict between these two objectives; all he could do was to promise to discuss his future course with Graham and F.F. Pardee. However, if, as Willison thought, the Ontario Liberal members of Parliament had already been consulted through Pardee and had rejected coalition, there could be little doubt of their attitude. But perhaps the coming week in Parliament would clarify the situation.[5]

The next afternoon Borden presented the Military Service Act for second reading, and Laurier countered with a proposal for a referendum, thus initiating an intense debate lasting for nearly three weeks. Willison called again briefly and Rowell asked for definite answers to two questions. Had a proposal similar to the one made to himself been made to Graham? If it had not, he urged that it be made immediately. Had Borden ever stipulated that the Hon. Robert Rogers must remain in any coalition cabinet or that he must be appointed high commissioner to London? Rowell believed that one or the other promise had been made to the 'Minister of Elections'; if so, coalition was out of the question.[6] While Willison was securing answers to Rowell's queries, Graham and Pardee arrived in the city for a meeting at the Ontario Club with twenty-five of the city's leading Liberals. For Rowell it was a heartening occasion since all but two of those present were in favour of coalition and the enforcement of conscription.[7] There followed a long discussion with Graham and Pardee when Rowell outlined the proposal Willison had put to him. The two federal Liberals had indeed been approached by Borden, but they understood that they were being invited as individuals to join the government and had therefore declined in the belief that the question could be dealt with only by the whole party or by a substantial group within it; but they favoured coalition if an acceptable basis could be found.[8]

Shortly, Willison came to Rowell's house bearing assurances that no guarantees had been given to Rogers about his future, and that the coalition offer made to Pardee had been made to him as chief Liberal whip in the House, and was therefore an 'official' approach, not a personal one as Pardee seemed to think. Despite the confusion on this latter point, it was now evident that the possibilities of coalition with Ottawa Liberals had been exhausted at least for the present. Asked whether he would go to see Borden, Rowell told Willison that he could only do so if he received 'such a direct summons or invitation from the Premier that I could not properly refuse to go.'[9] Willison already had Borden's summons in his hand asking Rowell to come to Ottawa in 'the immediate future' to discuss 'a subject of public importance.'[10] Since Rowell already had plans to leave that night to attend to Exchequer Court business in Ottawa, he could easily comply.

Over breakfast the next morning Borden advanced to Rowell essentially the same proposal he made to Laurier.[11] He repeated his assurances that the personnel of the cabinet must be satisfactory to both sides, again answering Rowell's objections to Rogers. On some points he now went further than he had with Laurier: he was willing to retire from the premiership if that would aid in the formation of a genuine coalition government that would carry out the conscription policy,[12] and he suggested that if no group of parliamentary Liberals would join Rowell in entering a coalition he would look for prominent Liberals not then active in politics.[13] Both agreed that the Military Service Act should be put into force and, coalition or not, a general election must be held soon.[14] Rowell determined to see Laurier and other Ottawa Liberals in one more effort to find some basis of co-operation. Later that morning in the presence of Graham and Pardee, Rowell asked Laurier if he would 'make a public declaration that if a majority of the members elected to a new House of Commons, whether Liberal or Conservative, were in favour of conscription, he would accept this as a mandate from the people to put the conscription law in force, and if called upon to form a government ... would do so on this basis, undertaking to put the law into force and to secure the reinforcements required to maintain our divisions at the front.'[15] He was profoundly disappointed, although scarcely surprised, by Laurier's negative reaction and returned reluctantly to Borden with a pessimistic report on prospects for any further overtures to Laurier.[16] Of one thing his interview with Borden had convinced him: the failings of the present government were not due to any lack of sincerity or genuine concern in the prime minister for a greater war effort. Once again it was necessary to face the prospect of proceeding without Laurier.

Returning to Toronto he pondered a discussion he had had in Ottawa with W.G. Mitchell, the provincial treasurer of Quebec, and W.R. McDonald, another English-speaking Quebec Liberal. To the latter's suggestion that Quebec be exempted from the operation of the conscription law, Mitchell had replied that Quebec would resent this even more than its application.[17] Exempting Quebec from conscription was no solution, as Rowell knew full well; whatever Quebec might think of the proposal, it would be howled down in English-speaking Canada, where the determination 'to make the French do their duty' provided much of the emotional force behind the growing conscription movement. But raising the question with Laurier at least served to prolong his dialogue with his party's leader, a dialogue that was becoming increasingly unrewarding. There was no solution to the present dilemma, Laurier replied, as long as conscription remained a condition sine qua non of Canadian participation in the war. He was daily less in favour of coalition, especially as he now believed that 'certain railway interests' were actively promoting it.[18]

Rowell decided to go to Ottawa again. The western Liberals – Arthur Sifton of Alberta, J.A. Calder of Saskatchewan, A.B. Hudson of Manitoba, and J.W. Dafoe – were in the capital, and Clifford Sifton had just issued a manifesto calling for the immediate formation of a coalition conscription government.[19] There now seemed to be a real possibility that a group of western Liberals would be willing to enter a coalition; in that case, the question of Ontario's representation would need reconsideration. As he stepped off the night train from Toronto on the morning of 6 July, Rowell learned that the Military Service Act had passed second reading at five o'clock that morning, with 118 members in favour and 55 against. All but ten of those opposed were from Quebec, while only eight Quebec members had voted for the bill. Only two Ontario members, Charles Murphy of Russell and Edmond Proulx of Prescott, were opposed. The long awaited vote had indeed cleared the air, revealing a division on racial lines that was almost complete.

With his written rejection of Borden's earlier coalition offer in his brief case,[20] Rowell embarked on yet another attempt to achieve the one goal that could save the war effort, national unity, and the Liberal party – the conversion of Laurier to conscription and to a coalition government that would implement conscription. Going over much old ground with Laurier, Rowell contended that thanks to the impact of the munitions industry on the economy 'Canada has profited the most and suffered the least from this war of any of the nations of the empire.' Surely then, in the face of current reports that England was calling all available men and France was near the breaking point, her morale saved only by the entry of the United States into the war, the least Canada could do was to maintain her divisions at the front at full strength. As for the alleged activities of the railway interests, he would like further information about them; but whatever they might be, they should not influence anybody's attitude toward coalition because the only valid consideration was the prosecution of the war. Could Laurier not at least refrain from disapproving of a coalition that might include some of the conscriptionist Liberals in the House of Commons? The alternative was a bitter racial campaign that would make relations between Ontario and Quebec even worse. Rowell found a parallel and a solution to the present crisis in the experience of Liberals fifty years earlier: 'Brown and Mowat and McDougall joined the then government to make Confederation possible. The Liberals of Quebec opposed Confederation and the coalition government which advocated it ... Each respected the conscientious convictions of the other ... and when Confederation was accomplished ... they ... joined hands in a union which has bound the Liberals of the two provinces together from that day to the present time.'[21]

Laurier found the example of Brown and Confederation irrelevant: Brown had finally been offered an opportunity to implement a principle for which he had long contended – representation by population – and which his opponents had all along rejected; Brown would have been false to his old cause had he declined. But now Rowell was asking him 'to accept a coalition either actively or passively to carry out a principle which I have been opposing all along.' It was an impossible proposition: Rowell and his friends failed to understand how difficult the situation had become for Quebec Liberals.

Since the vote on the Conscription Bill in which English-speaking and French-speaking Liberals so badly split, my friends in Quebec represent to me that our position is desperate and one or two have already expressed the opinion of the Nationalists that we should not send another man to the war nor spend another dollar. They represent to me, and with great reason, that we have to fight at once the Nationalists at one end, the English-speaking Liberals at the other and the Tories everywhere.[22]

Rowell was alarmed by Laurier's reference to the influence of the Nationalists on some Quebec Liberals; he had not realized that things had gone so far, although the essential unity of French Canadians on conscription was evident in the conduct of their representatives in Parliament: 'The friends in Quebec to whom you refer must have entirely forgotten what you have so repeatedly and so eloquently stated is the issue in this war ... as a life and death struggle for the preservation of democracy, and ... to save all that Liberalism has fought to accomplish.' If Laurier were to give in to those Liberals whose opinions were similar to those of the Nationalists, English-speaking Canadians could come to only one conclusion: 'that the Liberal Party in Quebec is in effect striking its flag, to some extent at least, to the Nationalist movement. While it is preserving the name Liberal, is it not largely accepting the Nationalist policy?'

Against Laurier's charge that Ontario Liberals looked at the situation only from their own point of view, Rowell asserted that he and his colleagues were more than willing to meet Quebec halfway: for example, he knew of no significant groups of Ontario Liberals who were unwilling, even at this date, to make another effort at a whole-hearted voluntary recruiting campaign, 'with intent to use compulsion only if that failed,' either under a coalition or a Liberal government if one were elected. But Laurier and the Quebec Liberals had refused this compromise, without proposing any alternative plan for getting the necessary men to the front.[23]

Rowell's argument with Laurier was not conducted in ignorance of the facts of French Canadian history: he knew how slight had been the political and cultural ties between Quebec and France over many generations. Yet, like many English Canadians, he failed to understand the full significance of French Canada's separation from Europe. Such was the intensity of Rowell's own emotional response to the call to defend all that Britain had contributed to the world that he found it impossible to comprehend how appeals for aid to France in her struggle to preserve French civilization could fall so largely on deaf ears in French Canada.

Again, like many English-speaking Liberals, Rowell was also the captive of his own high assessment of Laurier's capacities as a political leader and especially of his interpretation of the politics of 1896. On this reading of history, Laurier's political genius had enabled him to persuade French Canadians to accept a settlement of the Manitoba school question that they had no natural inclination to find agreeable; if only Laurier would say the right word now, French Canada would follow him again. Intellectually, Rowell understood that Quebec society was not so monolithic that Laurier was a virtual dictator who could lead his people where he would, and he understood the meaning of Bourassa and the Nationalists for the nation. But Rowell's passionate commitment to a maximum Canadian war effort made him incapable of seeing clearly the reality of the political threat to Laurier posed by the Nationalists and the conscription issue. Moreover, Rowell's view of politics as a struggle for the realization of principles encouraged him to believe that Laurier could and should take a stand that Rowell believed, erroneously, would alter the moral climate in Quebec. But Laurier, in sharp contrast to Rowell, was a political animal to the core – and he was still the leader of a *federal* party.

In his final effort to win Laurier to conscription Rowell did not rely entirely on verbal argument. He hoped that the federal politician in Laurier would respond to a display of strength demonstrating conclusively that the majority of Ontario Liberals were conscriptionists. But it was not easy to arrange the desired manifestation of feeling. When he proposed to George Graham the holding of a meeting of the executive of the Reform Association of Ontario, or, better still, a convention of the whole association, Graham demurred on the ground that either meeting could only produce a display of bitter dissension. Rowell replied that a measure of disagreement was already obvious; but there was no point in hiding the fact that the two Ontario Liberals who had voted against conscription represented a small minority of Ontario Liberals and that 'those who oppose conscription are the dissenters from the Liberal policy of this province.' That fact must be publicly advertised, for there would be 'no hope for the Provincial Liberal party for a generation unless that is frankly the attitude of the Liberals of the province ... and of the Federal Liberal party.' The logic of the position held by Graham and Pardee, Rowell urged, must surely lead them further than simply voting for conscription in the House: they must also give positive leadership in the formation and articulation of Ontario Liberal opinion.[24] Graham seemed incapable of dealing with Rowell's argument on grounds either of principle or of the politics of the situation. He still believed that conscription was right, but pleaded that his relation to Laurier as 'the closest adviser of the Prime Minister for years, with all that implies' was the origin of 'the almost unbearable position in which this decision places me.'[25] Graham's ambivalence was becoming increasingly hard for Rowell to tolerate. Clearly, at least for the present, Graham was incapable of decisive action.

Although he had thus far failed to secure a demonstration of Ontario Liberal opinion, Rowell found developments at Ottawa encouraging. On the morning of 17 July the twenty-six conscriptionist Liberals in the House of Commons met together under the chairmanship of A.K. Maclean of Nova Scotia and framed 'a confession of faith,' which Pardee described to Rowell as 'not as strong as it might have been but ... the best that could be got without another break.'[26] The conscriptionist Liberals in the Commons were clearly becoming a political force. That afternoon Borden introduced his motion to ask the British Parliament to extend the life of the Canadian Parliament until 7 October 1918, making it clear that if the opposition as a party voted against it he would not proceed with the implementation of the motion and there would be an election. Graham immediately moved an amendment, declaring that there were subjects more important than the extension of Parliament. Consideration of the prime minister's resolution should be deferred until the government produced adequate plans for organizing the war effort, equitable taxation to pay for it, and measures to control the cost of living.[27] All but one of the Liberals, Dr Michael Clark of Red Deer, supported Graham's amendment, which was lost by a mere seventeen votes. Laurier then took up the attack on extension, asserting that an old Parliament with twenty vacancies that proposed to endorse so crucial a measure as conscription and had denied the people a referendum on the question had turned British institutions into 'Prussian institutions' and must be replaced speedily.[28] Borden's extension motion carried, with Dr Clark again the only defecting Liberal, but in keeping with his announced intention Borden did not act upon it. Both parties now began to prepare for the fray.

Although Rowell preferred an election to an extension of the life of the present Parliament, the prospect of an appeal to the voters in the current condition of the Liberal party only reinforced his appreciation of the merits of coalition. As long as the date for an election was not announced there was still room for manœuvre, although Borden was now clearly in an awkward position with his own party, for Liberal unity in the rejection of extension could be interpreted by the anti-coalition Conservatives as proof that the Liberals with whom the prime minister had been negotiating were not acting in good faith. But the door to coalition was not entirely closed.

Now Rowell pinned his hopes on the meeting of federal Liberal members and federal candidates Pardee had called for 20 July in Toronto. As a provincial Liberal Rowell could not attend the gathering, but he, Pardee, and Graham held a consultation in Rowell's office the day before and agreed that since Laurier was irrevocably against conscription the majority of English-speaking Liberals would have to act on their belief in conscription whatever effect this might have in Quebec. They expected that during the coming week Borden would renew his coalition offer on a fifty-fifty basis to the conscriptionist Liberals in the House, and they were unanimous in believing that such an offer could not be refused without compromising the party before the country. It was understood, at least by Rowell, that the meeting of the following day was for consultation only, that final commitment for or against coalition would be left open, and that no conclusions would be reached or public statements made afterward.[29]

On the morning after the meeting, Rowell, in Woodstock for the weekend, was astonished on opening his copy of the *Globe* to read a statement from Graham on the deliberations of the previous day. He was shocked to see any report at all, but its content was even more distressing. According to Graham's statement, the meeting had urged another voluntary effort before any resort to conscription, declared against parliamentary extension, asserted the impracticability of coalition with the Borden government, and announced that Liberals would fight the next election under Laurier's leadership.[30] What confusion or treachery motivated Graham?

Rowell wasted no time in protesting against Graham's adoption of a position 'wholly opposed to the line of action we had all agreed was both in the nation's and the party's interests,' and contrary to the professed personal convictions of both Graham and Pardee:

how is it possible for men to be both for conscription and against it at the same time? How is it possible for men to stand behind our men at the front and promise them conscription ... and at the same time, in effect, declare that you are going to help form a government opposed to conscription?

This declaration ... weakens Canada's position as a belligerent power in this struggle with Germany, discourages our men at the front and jeopardizes the future of the Liberal party in Ontario. And it appears to me it strikes a severe blow at the sincerity of the Liberal conscriptionist members.[31]

Graham had not waited for Rowell's reaction before giving him his own version of what had happened: although he and Pardee had stated firmly at the outset of the meeting, as agreed, what the group's policy should be, 'there was an avalanche that could not be stemmed' and 'the almost unanimous and enthusiastic view of the candidates was the very opposite.' Sir Wilfrid was the only leader they would think of; there was 'absolute unanimity against a coalition *now* no matter what might be said or done after an election.' All but three or four of the men present thought that the members of the House who had voted for conscription had done so hastily and without sufficient awareness of the true state of public opinion in Ontario.[32] The situation was scarcely clarified by the denials of Pardee and Hugh Guthrie in the House of Commons concerning the accuracy of Graham's statements to the press; both men still claimed that they were conscriptionists and desired a national government if a proper basis for it could be agreed upon.[33]

Whatever Graham was up to, the whole episode had done nothing to create the impression that Ontario Liberals were united behind conscription. Rowell was depressed and more than ever convinced that it had been a mistake not to have held sooner the conference of provincial Liberal leaders he had earlier advocated. Now, lamenting the situation to J.W. Dafoe, it seemed to Rowell essential to bring the provincial leaders together 'if the Liberal party is to be saved from breaking up into separate factions or if it is to be saved from committing itself to a course of failing to support the war, disastrous alike to Canada and to the party.' Rowell offered to go to Winnipeg to meet with the three prairie Liberal premiers immediately after the consultations they had already planned in preparation for the forthcoming western Liberal convention early in August. Even if such a meeting failed to agree on a policy concerning coalition, which was of 'secondary importance' in Rowell's mind, it might 'keep the Liberal party straight on the issue of winning the war.'[34] But western Liberals were on their guard against 'intervention' from the east, a mood derived partly from their suspicion of Sir Clifford Sifton, whom many westerners, with good reason, looked upon as an agent of eastern financial interests. Consequently Dafoe thought there was no point in consultation with anyone from Ontario until after the western convention.[35]

In his growing anxiety Rowell found no consolation in his most recent communication from Laurier. It was clear to both men that their political association was drawing to an unhappy conclusion. 'You and I are old friends,' wrote Laurier 'and while it seems to me we are drifting more and more apart, I would be sorry if anything that was said between us at this time were to mar our actual friendship or future relations.' Rowell's last letter had revealed a misunderstanding of the position of Quebec Liberals: Laurier by no means suggested that they were being carried away by Nationalist sentiment; rather, they were fighting it by insisting that Canada was in the war to the end and in continuing to urge voluntary enlistment. He had only been trying to show Rowell 'the discouragement in which we are placed to fight it, by the attitude of our English-speaking Liberals.'[36] The next day the conscription bill passed its third reading by a vote of 102 to 44.

Rowell had no difficulty reciprocating Laurier's sentiments concerning their personal relations. 'It is' he wrote 'with the deepest possible personal regret that I find myself compelled to differ from your judgment and conclusions on an issue of such vital importance. I cannot but think that we look at the war from quite different viewpoints, and this being so we reach quite different conclusions ... I have little hope of the results of a voluntary effort which did not have the possibility of compulsion at the end in case the voluntary effort failed. ... you used the expression you are against compulsion to the last. This is the most crucial difference between us.'[37] The gulf between them was now fully admitted as unbridgeable.

The cause of coalition was not aided by the publication of the report of the federal royal commission investigating the charges against Robert Rogers. Setting aside the findings of two earlier provincial commissions, the new report exonerated Rogers of the charges of improper and corrupt dealings in real estate connected with the Manitoba Agricultural College. The belief that the findings of the new commission were intended to save the political skin of the minister of public works, and to some extent that of the whole Borden administration, was not confined to ardent Liberals. For Rowell the new report was 'a national disgrace' and 'a palpable subterfuge,' impossible to reconcile with his own impression of Borden's sincerity and honesty. Undoubtedly it was now more difficult for Liberals to contemplate a coalition under Borden's leadership. Yet for all that Rowell retained the estimate he had held of Borden since his interview with him in June as 'the one man in the government ... who most appreciates the seriousness of the crisis and who probably is most able to deal with it from the Conservative standpoint.' This being so, he wished Atkinson would desist from his current editorial line in the *Star* decrying the formation of a coalition under Sir Robert. Although this was undoubtedly the view of a large section of Ontario, it was not in the public interest to undermine Borden's prestige and make it harder for him to handle his own party. With Ontario Liberal editors generally, Rowell was well satisfied. They had just held a meeting and with only one dissenting vote, that of the editor of the *London Advertiser*, had adopted a statement on the war calling for conscription of men and wealth, a progressive income tax, control of profiteering, the nationalization of munitions plants, and more food production and personal thrift. Declaring that the Borden government had proved its inability to lead Canada, the Liberal editors advocated a war government representing both parties.[38]

The uncertain state of affairs in the Liberal party made it difficult for Rowell to make up his mind about his relation to a group which was anxious to make him its spokesman. The 'Win-the-War' movement was the mid-1917 incarnation of the Bonne Entente movement of late 1916 and the National Unity movement of early 1917; ostensibly non-partisan, its leaders were mainly Liberals. At the end of May it had sponsored a convention in Montreal under two slogans: 'Win-the-War' and 'l'unité nationale.' Although the National Unity Convention had fallen short of espousing conscription, its proposals for a more intensified war effort had had little appeal to French Canadians and had contributed nothing to the gathering's publicly professed aim.[39] Now the Win-the-War League planned a Toronto convention for early August under the sponsorship of a number of men of both parties, none of them at the moment active in politics. John M. Godfrey, a Toronto Liberal lawyer and president of the league, and the journalist, Arthur Hawkes, assumed the work of organization. With the Military Service Act now through third reading and shortly to become law, the league was attempting to create a public opinion favourable to the formation of a coalition and the avoiding of an election. Early in their planning, Godfrey and Hawkes had tried to get Rowell to commit himself to their program and to agree to address the coming convention, but he had put them off. He was still, as earlier, anxious to have a coalition before an election if an acceptable basis could be worked out. But he had never publicly committed himself to that course and he would not do so as long as there was even a faint chance that the Liberal party as a whole could be brought to accept conscription. His hesitance exasperated some of the Win-the-War Liberals and encouraged the rumour among them that his reluctance to 'go over the top' revealed his anxiety about taking any step that might jeopardize his prospects of succeeding to the Liberal leadership in the event of Laurier's resignation.[40]

In the end, Rowell did address the convention of eight hundred delegates but regretted his decision before the evening was over. As chairman, Godfrey declared that Laurier no longer had the right to lead Canadians and called for a new war-party to support a national government. Then the Liberal member of Parliament for Wellington South, Hugh Guthrie, proclaimed that Borden was the only man who could form a national government and denounced Quebec for its recruiting effort. Following Sir William Hearst, Rowell called for conscription and a national government representing all sections of the nation as offering the only solution to the nation's current difficulties; he did not come out unequivocally for a coalition before an election but appeared to assume that a general election on party lines would be fought in the autumn and that from the new Parliament a truly representative national government should be formed. As in many earlier speeches, a large part of his address was devoted to argument for a much stiffer tax on corporations engaged in war production and for a heavier tax on large incomes than was proposed in Canada's first income tax bill, which had just been introduced in the House of Commons. Before it adjourned, the convention passed resolutions endorsing the immediate enforcement of conscription and the formation of a nonpartisan government that would then seek an extension of parliament.[41] Although he welcomed any demonstration of support for conscription, Rowell had to agree that his own fears and those of other Liberals that the convention would serve no good purpose had been justified; far too much had been said too unequivocally. Guthrie's conduct in attacking Quebec and approving Borden's continued administration of the nation's affairs was puzzling; Rowell accepted neither as a legitimate position for an Ontario Liberal to take. Public attack on Laurier and splintering off from the party by individual Liberals could do nothing but harm to the party and little good to the country.[42]

Soon Rowell was receiving disconcerting reports from Main Johnson, who was in Winnipeg as his personal observer at the Winnipeg convention of Liberals from the four western provinces. From the first, Johnson had the impression that the convention was absolutely united in hostility to Borden and to any continuation of a regime under his leadership, that there was general rejection of Sifton's role in Liberal affairs, that a majority of the delegates were behind Laurier, and that probably a majority, perhaps as many as 90 per cent, he later concluded, were opposed to conscription.[43] Given Johnson's pessimistic reports, the final conclusions of the convention, while far from Rowell's earlier expectations, came as a relief. A resolution describing Laurier as 'the greatest of all Canadians' anticipated the early unification of Canada under his 'matchless statesmanship' in the prosecution of the war. The conscriptionists were defeated in their attempts to secure an outright commitment to compulsory military service but some of them accepted the war resolution that eventually passed because they thought its advocacy of 'the taking of all steps necessary to maintain the strength of Canada's armed forces' implied conscription, or at least left the door open for it. Coalition was not endorsed, although there was the suggestion that a national government under Laurier might be desirable after a Liberal election victory.[44] Clearly Rowell's Winnipeg friends were not representative of western Liberals as a whole, and their enthusiasm for conscription and coalition had misled him about the state of opinion in the west. But at least the convention resolutions urged a maximum war effort and they did not preclude either conscription or coalition.[45]

A wartime election now appeared inevitable. That prospect was not altered by the meeting convened by the governor general, the duke of Devonshire, at Borden's request just as the Winnipeg Liberal convention was concluded. In the presence of

G.P. Graham, Lord Shaughnessy, Sir Lomer Gouin, Sir George Foster, Sir Clifford Sifton, and Archbishop Mathieu, the Roman Catholic bishop of Regina, Borden offered Laurier a version of coalition slightly different from his earlier proposal: after the immediate formation of a coalition government there would be an extension of Parliament for six months in return for a suspension of the operation of the Military Service Act while a united appeal for recruits was made. But Laurier stressed the importance of a Parliament with a fresh mandate from the people, and the conference ended without any tangible results.[46]

On 14 August Rowell asked Willison to transmit to Borden his letter of 6 July, which had now received the approval of the western Liberal leaders, formally rejecting Borden's coalition offer to him.[47] Whatever part Rowell took in the coming election would be as a Liberal, pledged to the enforcement of conscription by a national war government to be formed after the appeal to the voters.

With the federal party approaching a state of chaos, it was almost a case of every Liberal for himself in the late summer of 1917. Although Rowell was committed to fighting an election on party lines if necessary, he kept an ear to the ground for the rumblings of any shifts on the political scene. A few reverberations were coming out of the west where discussion of the meaning of the recent Winnipeg convention had never ceased. The resignation of Robert Rogers from the federal cabinet in mid-August removed a large obstacle from the path of Liberals who were well disposed toward coalition. Within a week of Rogers' departure two thousand Liberals in South Winnipeg repudiated Laurier's leadership, declared for national government without an election, and heard Premier T.C. Norris pledge his support for Sir Robert Borden as the leader of a coalition.[48] But J.A. Calder, Arthur Sifton, T.A. Crerar, and A.B. Hudson were unwilling to see Borden continue as first minister of a coalition. They suggested that Sir George Foster, Chief Justice Lyman Duff, Sir Adam Beck, or Sir William Mulock would have their support. Acting on his belief that the western Liberals sincerely believed a change of leadership would greatly strengthen coalition in the west, Borden submitted his resignation to the Conservative caucus in favour of Foster, only to have it heartily rejected. Assured by Sir Clifford Sifton that the opposition of the western Liberals to his leadership was irrevocable, plagued by strong resistance to coalition from many of his colleagues, and close to complete nervous exhaustion, Borden decided to drop all negotiations until after the prorogation of Parliament.[49]

The fluidity of the situation among western Liberals encouraged Rowell to continue to work for a conference of provincial Liberal leaders favourable to conscription, and he urged A.K. Maclean to convene it. Even if the western leaders were unable to come, a consultation among the rest might at least do something to work out a much needed policy before the coming general election.[50] But Maclean was prepared to take the decision of the western Liberals as final and feared that the conference proposed by Rowell could only be divisive and 'end in compromising positions.'[51] Pardee, recalling the conference of Ontario Liberals six weeks earlier and the more recent Winnipeg gathering, was 'somewhat frightened of conventions.'[52] At the moment no Ontario conscriptionist Liberal could forget the catastrophic results of the recent deliberations of federal Liberal candidates in the province, for they were all too painfully blazoned across the pages of the Conservative press. The extended notes of what had been said by every speaker, taken by Charles Murphy for private circulation among a select group of Liberals,[53] had somehow reached the front page of the Toronto *Telegram*. Murphy's transcript of the proceedings revealed marked confusion on conscription, a willingness on the part of many candidates to jump whichever way was most likely to win the election, and a considerable devotion to Laurier's leadership.[54] Borden's comment on these revelations was typical of the reaction of many Conservatives and ashamed Liberals: 'Plainly they had no thought but party advantage.'[55] Conscriptionist Liberals and the Ontario Liberal press decided that the only defence against the damage wrought, albeit a poor one, was silence.

Rowell persisted in his efforts to get A.K. Maclean to take some lead in rallying Liberal opinion. His task was made much harder by the government's introduction in the House of Commons of one of the most unusual franchise measures ever passed by a democratic Parliament. Under the Wartime Election Act, strongly advocated by Borden's solicitor general, Arthur Meighen, all persons of enemy-alien origin naturalized since 1902 were to be disfranchised unless they had sons, grandsons, or brothers in the Canadian forces overseas, while the franchise was conferred on the wives, widows, mothers, sisters, and daughters of men serving overseas.[56] The measure was a blatant attempt to fix the conditions of a Conservative victory in the coming election, for most of the men disfranchised were supporters of the Liberal party, which had been in office when they migrated to Canada, and it was assumed that they would not vote for a more vigorous war effort against their native lands. At the same time, the new women voters were expected to support conscription. With the exception of Hugh Guthrie, all the members of the Liberal opposition resisted this tampering with the franchise, but by the thrice-repeated use of closure it was enacted. Rowell did not like the measure; it was 'in many respects ... another act of folly and grossly unfair,'[57] and he had no doubt about its purely political motivation. Unfortunately, it added greatly to the difficulties of Liberals who wanted to find common ground with the Conservatives.[58]

Rowell was convinced that it was now impossible to form a coalition before an election even if it were desirable, and of that he was uncertain. He analysed the political scene for Premier H.C. Brewster of British Columbia, the most hesitant about coalition of the four western premiers.

If as a result of the general election we have in the new House of Commons Conscriptionist Conservatives, Conscriptionist Liberals and anti-conscriptionist Liberals – no one group strong enough to form a government – I have good hopes that the men from Quebec would accept the situation, and rather than pursue the policy of isolation would join in forming a government which would enforce conscription ... If Sir Wilfrid should be called upon to form a government, and if the Liberal Conscriptionists maintained their principles, he could only form it on the basis of accepting conscription ... If a majority of anti-conscriptionists was elected to the House Sir Wilfrid could not undertake to enforce conscription and might be compelled to repeal it. It is idle to suggest that this would bring peace to Canada. It would open to us one of the gravest chapters in our country's history, for the people of Canada who have given their loved ones for the sake of Canada in this war, and the men who have gone to the front and offered their lives in Canada's defence, would for a generation at least, resent with all the power at their command, what they would honestly believe to be the sacrifice of our bravest and best men, and the cause for which they are fighting, to suit the views of those who themselves did not and would not go to fight.[59]

In mid-September Rowell left on a trip through the west. Its declared object was to attend to the affairs of his British Columbia fruit ranch, and he consistently refused all invitations to give public addresses, save one to the Vancouver Canadian Club on the recruiting situation. But politics were never long out of his mind nor of the awareness of those who learned that he was in the west. He stopped off in Winnipeg at the request of A.B. Hudson for talks with the western Liberals, Crerar, A.L. Sifton, and J.A. Calder, who had just informed Borden that they would, after all, enter a coalition under his leadership. There he learned that earlier reports of Laurier's imminent resignation were unfounded and that the belief that Laurier would remain in the leadership was a partial reason for the growing enthusiasm among the Liberals of Winnipeg for Union Government, as coalition was now known there. Doubtless a realistic appraisal of the electoral scene that confronted conscriptionist Liberals, now that the Wartime Election Act was on the statute books, also helped many of them to appreciate the merits of Union Government. With a significant number of normally Liberal voters removed from the lists by the new franchise act, and with the likelihood that in most ridings a conscriptionist Liberal would have to compete, not only with a Conservative but also with a Laurier Liberal, the outlook for conscriptionist Liberals was bleak. 'They all tell me,' Rowell reported to Pardee, 'that the feeling for a Union Government is growing every day ... There is much less protest against the Franchise Act on the part of the Liberal electors than they anticipated.'[60] Rowell agreed to join the four prospective western Liberal members of a coalition at their conference with Borden in Ottawa in the first week of October. But there was still time for him to go to the Okanagan and to get a sense of the political atmosphere further west.

His subsequent talks with Premier W.M. Martin of Saskatchewan, W.M. Davidson, editor of the Calgary *Albertan*, and Premier Brewster and Senator Hewitt Bostock of British Columbia, and his encounters with a great variety of westerners, convinced him that the political picture, especially in Alberta and British Columbia, was 'very similar to Ontario. Very different views are entertained by real good men and all is uncertainty.'[61]

On his return to Toronto there was again news that Laurier had actually resigned, but these tidings were shortly corrected. Briefly, in the face of assurances from many Liberals that under an English-speaking leader the party could win the election, it had seemed that Laurier would resign; but under a barrage of protests from other elements in the party, and faithful to the dictates of his own pugnacity, Laurier had determined not to give up the fight.[62] He was expected in Toronto shortly after the conclusion of talks with his friends in Montreal. At the home of P.C. Larkin, Rowell took part in discussions of the basis on which the party would fight the election. Laurier was still adamant in his opposition to conscription. For Rowell the final parting of the ways had come: he informed Laurier that if the western conscriptionist Liberals went into a coalition on a fair basis and in sufficient numbers to preserve their identity as a Liberal group, he would go in too.[63]

In Ottawa, Borden had resumed his efforts to form a coalition, and two Liberals, Hugh Guthrie from Ontario and C.C. Ballantyne of Montreal had 'jumped the gun' and joined his ministry. When Rowell learned that Calder, Sifton, Crerar, and Hudson were in the capital as planned, Rowell was uncertain whether he should await their summons or Borden's, or go to Ottawa immediately. Consulting members of the group with whom he had first discussed conscription nearly a year earlier – W.G. Jaffray and J.F. Mackay of the *Globe*, A.E. Ames, J.H. Gundy, J.E. Atkinson, Thomas Findley, and his partner, Tom Reid – he found that most of them thought he should go to Ottawa immediately to take whatever part was open to him in the decisions then being made, and they were unanimous that he should enter a Union Government if invited. He left on that night's train for Ottawa and arrived to receive Borden's call the next morning to a discussion of the structure of a new government.[64] The chief difficulties were over personnel; and one of these was of special concern to Ontario. Since George Graham had decided to stay with Laurier, F.F. Pardee was now the senior Ontario Liberal in the House of Commons who might be willing to enter a coalition, and Rowell wanted him in. But Borden found this difficult because Pardee's earlier hesitance over conscription had raised doubts about his sincerity among some prominent Ontario Conservatives.[65] Rowell also emphasized the importance of labour representation in the cabinet, stressed the desirability of establishing a War Council within the cabinet, and expressed his disapproval of the Wartime Election Act, thus adding to the pressure on Borden from some of the western Liberals for the repeal of the act.[66]

The lengthy conferences extending over three days, the waiting, and the uncertainty were wearing. Rowell found little enjoyment in rehearsing recent events and the current crisis as he saw them with a visitor to Ottawa, his friend, J. Allen Baker. This British member of Parliament, true to his Quaker pacifism, was opposed to conscription and strongly in favour of Laurier. 'I am very fond of [Baker] and it was not pleasant to have to tell him how strongly I dissented from his views on the question of conscription and how impossible it was for me to support Sir Wilfrid on this issue. I am commencing to realize what it will mean no matter which way I go but one can only do the thing which he believes to be right and trust the future to Him who holds the future in his hands.'[67]

In the early morning hours of 12 October it was settled that the three western Liberals – Calder, A.L. Sifton, and Crerar – and General S.C. Mewburn from Ontario, would enter a coalition; they wanted Rowell to be sworn in with them at noon that day. Still he hesitated, uncertain whether the minimum conditions on policy and representation had been met. The big question remaining was Maritime representation; it appeared that at least one and probably two of F.B. Carvell, A.K. Maclean, and Premier Murray of Nova Scotia would join, but none of them was as yet finally committed.

The general conditions of the coalition were acceptable. Regrettably, there were to be no concessions on the franchise act, but there would be ten Liberals in a twenty-two-member ministry. If the Maritimers were part of the Liberal section of the coalition the Liberal Unionists could not be considered a mere Liberal splinter group: that was of the utmost importance not only for the effectiveness of the Union Government in winning the confidence of Liberal voters and in prosecuting the war but also for its bearing on the future of the Liberal party and on the careers of those who joined the new government. Although Pardee was not to be a member of the government, Rowell had Borden's promise that he would get the first Liberal cabinet position that became available for Ontario.[68]

The position Rowell himself was offered as president of the Privy Council and vice-chairman of the new War Committee was more than satisfactory. The prime minister was normally president of the council, and the proposed division of labour was intended to symbolize the equality of Liberals and Conservatives in the new government. Rowell had urged the division of the cabinet into two committees, as had been done in Britain earlier that year, and the proposal was accepted; there was to be a War Committee composed of ministers whose departments were most closely involved in the war effort, and a Reconstruction Committee concerned mainly with post-war problems. Officially, Borden would be chairman of both committees but it was understood that the vice-chairmen would be responsible for the activities of their committees. In his work with the War Committee Rowell might have as much influence on Canada's war effort as any man in the country. It almost seemed that this was the task for which he had been preparing himself ever since the beginning of the war; it was precisely the kind of opportunity for service he had sought and, as well, a staggering responsibility in the exercise of which he was bound to be judged in the light of his own sharp criticisms of the past war effort. It was a call not to be refused: he would go in.[69]

With his swearing in as a minister of the crown, the welcome addition of F.B. Carvell of New Brunswick and A.K. Maclean of Nova Scotia to the government, and the first meetings of the new cabinet, Rowell was eager to give his undivided attention to the work of the War Committee. But first he must bid official farewell to his political associates of the past six years. At a meeting of his colleagues in the Legislature and the provincial Liberal candidates in the last election, Rowell presented his resignation as leader of the Liberal party in Ontario. In accepting the resignation the gathering was entirely noncommittal about his action. Although it passed a resolution affirming the party's adherence to 'the progressive policies' followed under his leadership, there was no mention of the war or of Union Government. Certain individuals expressed their appreciation of his services to the party, but the meeting did not tender the vote of thanks normally accorded to a retiring leader. For the moment the provincial party was endeavouring to prevent the intrusion of federal issues that might divide it as sharply as the national organization was divided.[70]

His break with Laurier required formal recognition. Rowell wrote lamenting the absence from the new cabinet of a strong Liberal leader from Quebec, regretting that their paths must diverge for the present and recalling appreciatively Laurier's remarks during the summer about the preservation of their friendship.[71] Laurier was polite but terse. Since he was ignorant of the conditions on which Rowell had entered the government he could not judge their validity, but whatever they were he doubted that anything could alter his regret over Rowell's course: 'I have too much respect for your convictions to allow an action which I cannot approve to interfere with our old personal relations, and I sincerely wish you success in everything except politics.'[72]

On her first weekend visit to Ottawa after the formation of the new government Nell Rowell found it 'a lonely place now ... The official Liberals don't want us nor do the Conservatives, so our social circle is very limited.'[73] The feeling accurately reflected the position in which Rowell had placed himself. Many Canadians were unable to believe that his motives were as straightforward as his public utterances suggested. Among Conservatives there was some disposition to feel that Rowell found it expedient to join them because his advocacy of a variety of unpopular policies had made life uncomfortable and the future unpromising for his ambitions within the Liberal party. Of course, Conservatives were not incapable of expediency. One of the merits of coalition in the eyes of some Conservatives was the opportunity it provided for sharing the responsibility for the enforcement of conscription, while others were uncertain about whether they could win an election on their own.[74] There were those, especially among anti-conscriptionist Liberals, who interpreted Rowell's actions as a campaign to succeed Laurier in the leadership of the Liberal party.[75] Undoubtedly many Liberals, notably the Toronto group who had supported him ever since his entry into provincial politics, saw him as a possible candidate for the leadership of the federal party. And a more independent observer, Sir John Willison, who had long since severed his relations with the Liberal party, had never ceased to look on his protégé of the election of 1900 as a potential prime minister.[76]

Yet no one who knew the story of Rowell's conduct within the Liberal party and of his strenuous efforts to win Laurier and, failing that, Graham and Pardee to the cause of conscription and then of coalition could reasonably accuse him of 'plotting' to usurp Laurier's position as leader. Although Rowell had eventually come to the point where he thought the party and the country would be better served by another leader, he was precluded from thinking of himself in that role by the political realities of the time. Even had he been able to make a place for himself in the federal arena it was clear that no Liberal caucus or convention held amid wartime tensions, or in any forseeable future after the war, could conceivably have elected Rowell as leader once he had vigorously espoused conscription. English Canada was less united in favour of conscription than French Canada was in opposing it, and thus, even in Ontario, Rowell could not readily have found a sufficiently solid base for a bid for national leadership. In placing himself in the forefront of the conscription movement in Ontario he had not compromised his integrity whatever his detractors might say, but he had severely limited his future political prospects. Understanding this full well, he was not perturbed. As he had explained so often, he supported conscription not because it was popular, but because it was 'right.'

Men whose primary allegiance was to party found it hard to believe that some men were actually devoted to principles and policies above party. They therefore sought an explanation of Rowell's actions outside his professions of commitment to a maximum war effort and often thought they found it in personal ambition or desire to serve 'the railway interests' or other corporations. The truth was much simpler, although the set of attitudes and emotions that lay behind Rowell's wartime priorities was far from simple. In entering the Union Government Rowell made no deals with anyone. The only absolute condition of his adherence to the coalition was that the Military Service Act should be enforced and the whole war effort organized with maximum efficiency. As Mackenzie King, carefully keeping himself outside the conscription controversy and planning his own future, observed of Rowell's part in the Union Government negotiations: 'To him conscription is *everything*.'[77] Other issues, although they might be affected by the new government, were entirely secondary.

Rowell's single-minded devotion to the ideal of a maximum Canadian contribution to the war in both men and resources was rooted in his nationalism. Just as Bourassa, and in some degree Laurier, expressed a French Canadian or Quebec nationalism, so Rowell was the voice of an English Canadian or Ontario nationalism with its own distinctive vision of Canada and of Canada's relationships with the world beyond her shores. Although shared by many English Canadians across the country, the roots of that vision lay in the loyalist traditions of the Maritimes and Ontario, with the centre of its political expression in Ontario. During the war Rowell became the perfect embodiment of an earlier tradition of Canadian nationalism combined with an imperial sentiment characteristic of an influential group of English Canadians in the later nineteenth century, notably George Monro Grant and Sir George Parkin. As for them, so for Rowell there was no essential conflict between devotion to the values of the British Empire and a profound national feeling distinctly Canadian. Rather, it was through the preservation and transformation of the Empire that Canada would be enabled to make her unique contribution to Christian civilization.[78] Therefore, in the circumstances of the first world war the imperative was to save that empire and that civilization from destruction. Rowell's insistence on 'equality of sacrifice' was based on two firmly held convictions: the first, that Canada's interests both moral and material, no less than Britain's, were threatened by the possibility of defeat in the war; and the second, that Canada's full contribution to the war effort would demonstrate the autonomy and influence she increasingly claimed within the Empire. Presented with Methodist enthusiasm, Rowell's wartime rhetoric and actions aroused in fellow citizens of kindred attitudes and emotions 'the sense of power' so long characteristic of Ontario nationalism and imperialism. If French Canadians were unable to respond to the call of 'the larger citizenship,' that was regrettable, but their failure could not be allowed to prevent the realization of Canada's destiny.

13

Saving civilization at the polls

When Rowell and his new colleagues began their work as members of the cabinet of the Union Government, one of their first moves was the publication of a twelve-point statement of war policy. When shown Borden's draft of it, Rowell urged that the omission of any reference to the government's determination to invite the participation of labour in its counsels be corrected.[1] But in the end no reference to such an intention was made, an omen perhaps of how hard it would be to create a new administration less devoted to the interests of business and to the philosophy of 'business as usual' than the old Borden government had been. The declaration committed the government to the immediate enforcement of the Military Service Act, the extension of the Civil Service Act and the abolition of patronage, women's franchise, 'adequate taxation' of war profits and incomes, a progressive immigration policy, effective care of demobilized soldiers, 'co-operative management' of the railways, reduction of public expenditure and the encouragement of private thrift, limitations on excessive profits, hoarding, and rising prices, 'the encouragement of co-operation' among agriculturalists to reduce prices to the consumer, development of natural resources 'with the co-operation and assistance of the State in every reasonable way,' and 'the maintenance of good relations between employers and employed and such conditions of employment as will assure suitable standards of living among the labouring classes.'[2]

What would such generalities mean in practice? It was of the utmost importance, not only to the war effort but also for the winning of the coming election, that their meaning be demonstrated speedily. Most of the matters demanding immediate attention were the concern of the War Committee under Rowell's direction. Associated with him on the committee, with Borden as nominal chairman, were the

Liberal Unionists General Mewburn, F.B. Carvell, and A.L. Sifton, and the Conservatives Sir Thomas White, C.C. Ballantyne, C.J. Doherty, Sir Edward Kemp, and P.E. Blondin, one of the two French Canadians, both Conservatives, in the new government. Food control was an urgent concern and Rowell was given supervision of the work of the food controller, W.J. Hanna, the former Ontario Conservative cabinet minister who had been appointed to the position four months earlier. Although on paper the food controller had extensive and rather arbitrary jurisdiction over the sale, distribution, prices, and conservation of food, very little had been accomplished, and the press of both parties were declaring the food control program a farce. In the next few weeks further modest steps were taken toward greater conservation of food supplies but with the exception of the lifting of the ban on the production of oleomargarine and the licensing of the sale of cereal grains, they were largely voluntary and did little to meet the public outcry for price control.

Equally pressing problems arose from the administration of the Military Service Act. During the summer of 1916 the Department of Justice had established provincial boards of selection, local exemption tribunals, and military boards across the country, but nobody had been called to report and there was still much confusion about the application of the conscription law. At its first meeting the new cabinet passed an order-in-council that required the first group of men in Class 1 – single men and widowers aged twenty to twenty-two without children – to report, and the machinery established for the administration of conscription was put to the test. The War Committee of the cabinet was responsible for laying down the broad principles on which the act was to be administered, notably the definitions of categories of men to be exempted,[3] although wide discretionary powers rested with the judges who presided over the local exemption tribunals.

Plans for the organization of industry and heavier taxation of war profits also occupied much of Rowell's thought during these first days as a member of the government. He already knew that in his general views in these matters he had the support of the group of Toronto Liberal financiers who had urged him to enter the government. When W.E. Rundle, president of the National Trust, offered more specific advice, it was bound to be carefully considered, for there was no businessman in Canada for whom Rowell had greater respect and none was a closer personal friend. Rundle advocated the pooling of the assets, personnel, and property of the railways to limit their drain on public funds and to make their policies publicly accountable, government control of prices of coal, iron, and steel, and a reduction in food prices, however slight, 'to steady public opinion and help it to accept the greater sacrifices that are coming.' Those sacrifices should include heavier income taxes, nominal on small incomes but very much higher on incomes over $5,000, and the extension of the war profits tax introduced the previous summer. 'Much as we all dislike taxation, those of us who can must pay,' wrote Rundle.[4] Rowell's friends in the editorial offices of the *Star* and the *Globe* were insistent in their public demands for more government direction in the nation's economic affairs and counted heavily on him for their realization. The first duty of the Union Government, said the *Globe*, was 'to strike at the cause of popular discontent by demonstrating that it has the intention and the will to lay a firm hand on the machinery of Big Business, and make it work for the State.'[5]

Rowell had both the intention and the will, but would they prevail among his new colleagues? The most immediate test brought Rowell into a new relationship with Sir Joseph Flavelle, his colleague of many years on Methodist committees and a valued friend, vice-president of the Robert Simpson Company, and president and controlling shareholder of the William Davies Company, meat packers. Of the several investigations of food prices conducted during the spring and summer of 1917 by the acting commissioner of the cost of living, W.F. O'Connor, none had attracted so much public attention as the examination of the operations of the cold storage companies, and one of the largest of these was the William Davies Company. Although the commissioner had found that the business of ten leading storage companies was conducted legally and usually without excessive accumulation of profits, he suggested that a 'tendency' toward excessive profits on beef and butter deserved the attention of the food controller. His report contained several hints of information still uncovered and showed that while profits on individual items were often not excessive the sheer volume of sales through British war contracts had yielded greatly increased profits for the largest companies.[6] The suspicion that Flavelle had used connections formed through his chairmanship of the Imperial Munitions Board to secure British contracts for the William Davies Company, his recent receipt of a baronetcy, and the contrast between an earlier public declaration that 'the profiteers ought to go to the hell to which they belong' and the current revelations of his company's profits, made Flavelle the centre of public resentment over the rising cost of living. During the two weeks before the formation of the Union Government, officials of the William Davies Company were appearing before the royal commission appointed to pursue some of the unanswered questions in the O'Connor report. Flavelle's position in the public esteem was not improved by his testimony that he had 'no qualms of conscience' about accepting the profits he had made during the war, which he frankly agreed were very large.[7]

Flavelle had been an early and vocal supporter of Union Government, but now, as he awaited the submission of the report of the royal commission, he was worried and sought an interview with Rowell, who had been appointed chairman of a special committee of the cabinet to deal with the report. The meeting was not reassuring to Flavelle, and he left with the conviction that the government was preparing for 'discriminatory action' against the William Davies Company. In Flavelle's view that would be the effect of the new taxes the government was apparently considering, since they would bear most heavily on the larger companies. It was unfair, Flavelle protested, to penalize the large companies whose volume of business made them more efficient. His own 'much wronged company' was suffering from 'the ugly temper' and 'spirit of bitterness' that was distracting the whole country from 'constructive work,' and the government would be well advised to 'introduce the minimum of interference in the natural activities of the businesses concerned.'[8] Rowell was not deterred. His committee worked out a new scale of taxation, which the *Globe* reported would allow not more than a 2 per cent profit on total annual sales and not more than 7 per cent on capital invested.[9] For the present there was no official announcement of the new taxation, but what it might mean to the William Davies Company was suggested when the royal commission's report was made public: in its best year, 1916, the company had made 5.32 per cent on sales and 80 per cent on investment.[10] On the day of the release of the report Rowell wrote to Flavelle making clear the government's intention of proceeding with the limitation of profits. Rejecting Flavelle's suggestion that the new government was being forced to carry through a policy begun in haste by the former administration, Rowell assured him that the Union Government would have taken up the question of war profits quite apart from the investigation that had already been launched. Rowell felt that Flavelle misunderstood the spirit in which the government was acting, asserted that the public interest must outweigh all other considerations, and reminded Flavelle that until now he had always, to Rowell's certain knowledge, agreed with the principle of government regulation of essential industries.[11] But, for the moment, no action was taken against the packers. Did the necessities of the coming election dictate both a public indication of determination to control packing house profits and a postponement of specific measures?

From the end of October, when the election was announced for 17 December, the demands of the forthcoming campaign consumed more and more time and energy while, to Rowell's great frustration, the work of the War Committee was partly set aside. The preparation of the election manifesto provided Rowell with one opportunity to chart the emphasis of the government's policy. In general, he approved the original draft prepared by Sir John Willison, chairman of the Unionist Publicity Committee. However, there were a few slight changes and two significant additions he wished to have made.[12] One involved the brief, general reference to increased taxation. He suggested a further sentence, which appeared in the final document: 'In order to meet the ever-increasing expenditure for war purposes, and also to ensure that all share in common service and sacrifice, wealth will be conscripted by adequate taxation of war profits and increased taxation of incomes.'[13] The other concerned labour's role in the war.

Progress in securing better relations with labour had been too slow in the first few weeks of the new government's life to suit Rowell. In keeping with his promise to

Rowell to bring a labour man into the government, Borden had appointed as minister without portfolio Senator Gideon D. Robertson, for many years an official of the Trades and Labor Congress of Canada. At the same time it had been agreed that the Liberals would have the privilege of nominating an undersecretary of labour, but so far no appointment had been made. Rowell was urging that D.A. Carey of Toronto be given the job; besides representing labour, Carey would provide a voice for Ontario's Irish Catholics and help to satisfy their complaints that they were not adequately represented in the government.[14] Carey had been active in the Trades and Labor Congress since before the turn of the century and was one of the group of Congress executive members who had prevented the annual convention in September 1917 from urging its members to active resistance to conscription. Although the Congress had been persuaded not to incite disobedience to the law, it had reiterated its earlier condemnation of the principle of conscription and as further evidence of its dissatisfaction had passed a resolution favouring the formation of an Independent Labour Party in Canada.[15] The immediate manpower crisis and the obvious disaffection of much of the labour movement, in addition to Rowell's settled disposition to see labour assume a larger role in political life, made it seem urgent to promote a more positive attitude toward labour than the recent Conservative administration had demonstrated. He advised Borden to devote a whole section of his manifesto to labour, paying tribute to labour's patriotic part in the war, noting the large proportion of workingmen who had gone to the front, pointing out that 'it is the right of labour to receive new and larger recognition than ever before' and that the appointment of a labour man to the cabinet and the proposed addition of another labour leader as undersecretary were 'an earnest of the New Day.'[16] But other members of the cabinet were unwilling to go so far, and when the manifesto appeared it contained only the original brief reference to labour.

Agreeing on a manifesto was by far the easiest part of the election preparations. The most difficult was the effort to secure Liberal and Conservative co-operation in placing Union Government candidates in the field. In recent months Rowell had had many discouraging revelations of the strength of party feelings in a time of national peril, but the worst was yet to come. A few days after the birth of the new government, he and Dr J.D. Reid, minister of railways and canals and long Borden's political manager for Ontario, were put in charge of sorting out the eighty-two crucial Ontario seats. Since Quebec was almost certain to be solidly for Laurier and the west was considered uncertain, the fate of the Union Government might be settled in Ontario; it was therefore vital that Conservatives and Liberal Unionists co-operate fully in the province. Yet that essential co-operation was inhibited by the awareness amongst politicians of both parties that Ontario was also crucial for their long-term futures. Conservatives and Liberal Unionists knew they had lost Quebec for some time because of their stand on conscription, and Ontario's post-war political importance was thereby enhanced. At dissolution the Conservatives held seventy Ontario seats and the Liberals twelve. The Conservatives were reluctant to give up any of this advantage; just how reluctant became clear to Rowell when he had his first discussion of the Ontario seats with Reid on 18 October.

When the government was formed Rowell and Borden had agreed that there could be no hard and fast rule about how the Unionist candidates should be chosen but in general selection would be the work of joint conventions of the local Conservative and Liberal organizations. Rowell was willing to take the chance that in such a procedure a reasonable number of Liberals would be nominated. Where no joint convention was possible and two conscriptionist candidates were in the field, Rowell would allow them to fight it out without interference from the government. Reid found this 'too absurd to discuss,' since 'it would practically prohibit the government from taking any part in the elections in Ontario.' Rowell soon learned that Reid, unlike Borden, was incapable of understanding the new government as a genuine coalition but looked on it as a Conservative government which some Liberals had entered, probably for highly nefarious purposes. Reid proposed that every sitting Conservative member should have government endorsation and that the Liberals who had voted for conscription in the House and supported Union Government should be endorsed. He was altogether opposed to Rowell's plan of urging candidates already nominated by either party to withdraw in order that a joint convention could be held. Reid would encourage joint conventions only in ridings where sitting members were not running again. In short, Reid proposed to maintain the party status quo. Rowell was equally opposed to automatic recognition of the sitting member, believing that the election of 1911 did not provide a fair basis for determining representation six years later under war conditions. Moreover, there was the very practical consideration that an agreement that confined Liberal Unionists to the twelve seats they now had would convince thousands of Liberals that the price of coalition was too high and they would refuse to support the Union Government at the polls. Rowell held out for a minimum of twenty seats for Liberal Unionists. Two days of discussion of the Ontario seats yielded only deadlock, and Rowell and Reid were forced to appeal to Borden to arbitrate.[17]

Borden's full and generous commitment to coalition on equal terms enabled him to appreciate Rowell's dilemma, but the prime minister had little success in bringing Reid around. Reid persisted in the suspicion that Rowell was simply being obstructionist and that having succeeded in breaking up the Conservative organization ostensibly in the interests of co-operation, the Liberals would 'bolt' on nomination day. Even if nothing as dramatic or drastic happened, failure to resist Rowell's demands, Reid argued, would give the public the impression that Rowell was the dominant factor in the new government and that it owed its existence to his Liberal supporters. This would alienate a host of Conservatives and there would then be many straight Conservative candidates in the field. In the final result not more than half the Ontario members in the new House of Commons would be Conservative Unionists and the Conservative party would be severely damaged for years to come.[18]

The realization that Reid's jealous partisanship was shared by much of the grass roots of his party in Ontario gave many Liberal Unionists some anxious moments about the fate of the enterprise on which they were embarked. The president of the Toronto Conservative Club, Dr Norman Allen, was cheered enthusiastically when he told the members of the club that Union Government was unnecessary to win the war and that in joining it the federal Conservative leaders were allowing the Liberals to appear as the true defenders of the national interest; the meeting refused to endorse the government.[19] A few days later the Central Committee of the Ontario Conservative Association voted 'to have no truck with the Liberals' and only reversed the decision after 'a straight talk' from Sir George Foster.[20] Incidents like this throughout the province and the growing evidence that many Liberals remained loyal to Laurier forced Rowell to abandon his hope that joint conventions could be held to nominate candidates. It was now all too evident that there were very few ridings in which a joint convention could be convened, and the government would therefore have to endorse one or more of the candidates chosen by party conventions. Faced with this disagreeable prospect Borden and Rowell agreed on three principles which should govern the decision to endorse a given candidate: the general political history of the riding, the attitude of the sitting member to conscription and Union Government, and the relative chances of the candidates in carrying the riding against any opponents of the government.[21]

This agreement was reached only after two weeks of lengthy meetings almost every day, but it was far from being the end of the matter. When the discussion of specific ridings was resumed Rowell found Reid just as suspicious and determined as ever. In an attempt to resolve the difficulties Borden asked the other Conservative ministers from Ontario – Sir George Foster, Sir Edward Kemp, and Sir Thomas White – to attend the consultations and Rowell was joined by F.F. Pardee and Lloyd Harris.[22] Finally, the Liberal bargainers reluctantly accepted the principle of recognizing the sitting member as the official government candidate.[23] However, that still left some room for manœuvre since there were a good many ridings in which the previous member was not running again. Well before nomination day, 19 November, agreement was reached on most of the seats, but several were the cause of acute dissension until the last minute.

Rowell's own difficulties in finding a constituency where he could enjoy the support of members of both parties came as a surprise, but for a time they caused him little concern.[24] Initially, his closest friends and supporters wanted one of the Toronto seats for him; although Foster co-operated, they were disappointed.[25] An all-night meeting of Liberal and Conservative officials in the Albany Club failed to secure an opening for Rowell because every one of the Conservative riding associations threatened to run a straight Conservative candidate against him.[26] Thereafter there were discussions with local party officials in several rural ridings; in both North and South Oxford and in Brant the government candidates already endorsed refused to resign in Rowell's favour; for a time North York seemed likely, but further investigation revealed strong enough support there for Mackenzie King, who after much manœuvring and uncertainty had decided that he was with Laurier, to rule it out. Halton was also considered, but W.D. Gregory, the Laurier Liberal candidate, presented too great a threat.[27] A way out of what was becoming an alarming situation was found when the Liberal candidate in Durham, V.T. Bartram, agreed to withdraw, and the Conservative nominee, Colonel R.A. Mulholland, was persuaded with the help of a promise of an appointment to the Senate to do likewise.[28]

Rowell went to his nomination meeting in the village of Orono in some trepidation because there were rumours of continuing resistance to his candidacy. But when all but fifteen of the four hundred Liberal and Conservative voters from the district supported Colonel Mulholland in his formal nomination of Rowell it was clear that there would be no revolt. The audience was cool at first, but Rowell had not gone far in his acceptance speech before he knew that he was winning his listeners.[29] When a heckler called out: 'What are you now – a Grit or a Tory?' the answer came back like a shot: 'You can call me whatever you like. I care not whether you call me Grit or Tory or Unionist. For the sake of the men I have seen fighting for Canada and pouring out their very life blood on the fields of France and Flanders, I am willing to be called anything if I can help them.' At this the audience rose to its feet, and he was unable to go on until the cheering subsided. When he could proceed he elaborated on his experiences in France; the choice facing the electors was Union Government and support for those boys in France or virtual withdrawal from the war. In that decision local party differences were as nothing compared with 'the gulf that separates the Anglo-Saxon people from cruel Prussian militarism.'[30]

For Liberal conscriptionists in Ontario the campaign was formally inaugurated at the Hamilton Win-the-War Convention early in November when four hundred men and women, most of them party workers from all parts of the province, were in attendance. The speakers, Rowell, S.C. Mewburn, F.B. Carvell, and Lloyd Harris addressed the gathering in the Royal Connaught Hotel from a platform adorned with a great scroll reading 'Our Country First.' Appropriately, in view of the government's announcement that it would extend the franchise to women, 'the audience was dotted with ladies busily engaged in patriotic knitting, and repeated cordial expression was given to the new order, under which all ... [would] share the duties and privileges of the state.'[31] Rowell's chief task again that evening was to justify his own abandonment of strict party allegiances and to persuade his fellow Liberals to be 'big and manly and patriotic' and to 'surrender party prejudices but not ... principles' in supporting Union Government. He had been slow to realize just how much opposition to the crossing of party lines there would be in the Liberal party. Now he took full advantage of this opportunity to explain his own course to a broadly representative group of Liberals.

I have no apology to offer for joining my fellow Liberals in going into the Union Government, but had my refusal induced others to refuse, had the Unionist Government failed, and military service been defeated, had our men not been backed up at the front, I could not have forgotten through all the days that may be to come that failure in this critical hour of our country's difficulty. That was the issue I had to face: to be true to my conception of duty and the gallant soldiers fighting our battles, or yield to the appeals of my party associates and keep straight within party lines. If I have done wrong, if I have erred in the course I have taken, history will be my judge; and I place myself in the hands of history and the people of Canada.

Returning now to the analogy he had drawn privately to Laurier, Rowell asserted that 'there is not a prouder moment in history than when George Brown forsook his party and joined with his antagonists to achieve Confederation.'[32] The implied comparison was even less valid now than when he had first made it. It was true that George Brown had forsaken his strictly Grit allegiance to join with Conservatives in the coalition of 1864 to promote the union of British North America, but the Upper Canadian Protestant had done something more radical than abandon a party label: he had bridged the gulf between his own English followers and the French-Canadian Roman Catholics whose influence he had feared and denounced for so many years.

Before it ended, the Hamilton meeting of conscriptionist Liberals elected the chairman, G.G.S. Lindsey, as permanent head of an executive charged with the general direction of the Liberal Unionist election campaign in Ontario. In this manner an open conflict within the executive of the Ontario Reform Association, which the Unionists feared would have proven dominantly Laurierite in a show-down, was avoided. The nucleus of a Liberal Unionist election machinery was thus formed and launched on a sea of troubles. More effective in the Liberal Unionist cause was the 'Citizens Union Committee,' an outgrowth of the Committee of One Hundred, which had remained in existence after the passing of the Ontario Temperance Act to serve as the watchdog of a dry Ontario, and in particular to prepare for the promised post-war plebescite.[33] In the meantime, by the decision of its executive, the committee's efficient organization, including the indefatigable executive director, G.A. Warburton, was placed at the service of the Unionist campaign. Although it was officially non-partisan, as in its previous incarnation, the committee's most active members were Liberals and its energies were directed mainly to bringing other Liberals to support the Union Government. Whatever the Liberal Unionist campaign in Ontario lacked it was neither money nor press support. The vast majority of the wealthiest Liberals in the province were behind the government. A cause nourished by financiers like Ames, Wood, Gundy, and F.H. Deacon and by their equivalents in the major cities throughout the province was unlikely to languish for lack of funds. With the exception of the London *Advertiser* and some of the rural weeklies, the entire Liberal press joined the Conservatives in Ontario in urging victory for the Unionists.

The Unionist campaign in Ontario gathered momentum during the last ten days of November when Borden toured the province, beginning with a meeting in Massey Hall in Toronto where he was supported by Rowell, Premier Hearst, and the president of the University of Toronto, Sir Robert Falconer. Borden stressed the government's determination to administer the Military Service Act impartially in every section of the country and promised further representation for Ontario Liberals and for labour in the cabinet. When Rowell rose to speak he was given an ovation while the band of the 48th Highlanders played 'The Maple Leaf Forever.' His address was chiefly a defence of Liberal support of the government: there was no alternative for anyone who believed that Canada must not quit the war.[34] Until the end of the month he was Borden's chief platform assistant in more than two dozen communities in the western and central sections of the province, although he was not present at the chaotic Kitchener meeting which refused to give the prime minister a hearing.

Despite all the resources being poured into Ontario the prospects of the Unionists often seemed bleak. There was no effective headquarters organization able to overcome the continued bickering of Conservatives and Liberal Unionists; there was great discontent over the manner in which the local tribunals were exercising their powers under the Military Service Act; and the farming community was believed to be almost unanimously opposed to conscription. Reluctantly, Rowell agreed to the proposal that Sir Clifford Sifton should take over the direction of the campaign in Ontario. His anxiety about the dangers of associating Sifton with the Unionist cause in this capacity was underlined when Rowell learned that Sifton was to share an office with Frank Cochrane, minister without portfolio in the government and a Conservative politician whom many Liberals ranked not far behind Robert Rogers in the mastery of dubious practice. Unable to see Sifton himself,

Rowell dictated a memorandum and dispatched his secretary to read it into the deaf Sifton's famous ear trumpet. Rowell reminded Sifton of how very unpopular he was with the majority of the voters, especially in the west, of how badly his name was received at the western Liberal convention, and of how much his trip to the west at that time had assisted Laurier. Nothing but more harm could be done if it became known that he was working so closely with Cochrane that they shared an office. It was strong medicine, but Sifton took it well and accepted Rowell's advice that he direct the Ontario campaign as unobtrusively as possible from his room in the King Edward Hotel in Toronto.[35]

Anxiety about Ontario was a major reason for the cabinet's decision to clarify the status of farmers under the Military Service Act.[36] Throughout the campaign, government speakers had declared that men actively engaged in food production would be exempt from military service. In most districts this policy had been broadly interpreted, but not always, and there was much criticism of its application. Now, under an order-in-council passed two weeks before the election, any agriculturist who had been refused exemption by a local tribunal was given the right of appeal directly to the minister of militia and defence and assured that there was little doubt it would be granted. The move did nothing to appease the leaders of farm opinion, whose views were faithfully represented in the *Weekly Sun*'s attribution of the exemption policy to sheer fright about the election result.[37] The labour vote also remained a cause for uncertainty. The Independent Labour Party, led by the former Ontario Liberal, Walter R. Rollo of Hamilton, was running a number of candidates of its own and in other ridings had endorsed the Laurier standard-bearers. Many labour voters were believed to be pro-Unionist, but how many there would prove to be was anxiously debated.

From other fronts the news of Unionist fortunes was unequivocal. The pronouncements of the leading women's organizations and the willingness of their officers to speak from government platforms confirmed the earlier assumption that women would work for conscription and those who had a vote would support it at the polls. Although there was no mention of prohibition in the government's platform, Rowell found that the Liberals who had supported him most vigorously in the abolish-the-bar campaign were usually those who were now the most ardent Liberal Unionists,[38] and this group included many women who were about to vote for the first time. If Protestant church members heeded their church courts and the sermons they heard on Sundays there was no doubt that they would vote for Unionist candidates. Among the clergy none were more outspoken in support of the government than the Methodists. The Methodist Ministerial Association of Toronto and hundreds of Methodist preachers in their pulpits throughout the province proclaimed the conflict as a redemptive war and support of Union Government a Christian duty. The Unionist publicity committee made extensive use of 'An Open

Letter on the Duty of the Hour' by Rev. Dr S.D. Chown, the general superintendent of the Methodist church, backing the conscription of both men and wealth and citing Rowell as a patriotic Liberal whose example should be emulated.[39]

As the campaign entered its last two weeks Rowell found his energies taxed to the limit. In co-operation with the ministers of militia and justice, Mewburn and Doherty, he spent many hours trying to correct the maladministration of the Military Service Act by local tribunals whose 'excessive zeal' had led them to act with 'great stupidity,' with results that were often unfair to individuals and harmful to the government's prestige.[40] But the most insistent call was from the public platform. As always his speeches were a combination of detailed argument and impassioned appeal to the emotions of his audience. Increasingly he thought it necessary to answer the charges of the Laurier Liberals that he and the new government were 'the servants of the big interests.' On the contrary, he contended, 'not only is it the strongest war government we can secure, it is also the most radical and progressive government since Confederation,' as its legislative program would soon demonstrate. All the most progressive elements in Liberalism in both Ontario and the west were behind the government. In contrast, the Laurier Liberal leaders in Ontario, Hartley Dewart and Gordon Waldron, had placed themselves at the head of the most reactionary forces in the Liberal party.[41] He tried to counter the feeling, rarely expressed in public but nonetheless influential, that Canada should not introduce conscription until there were proportionately as many Americans at the front as there were Canadians. Rowell maintained that this attitude did less than justice to Canada's national spirit and would assist German propagandists in weakening the American war effort. But there was also an economic argument that he feared too many Canadians ignored. The Canadian war effort depended heavily on raw materials and other supplies imported from the United States: 'Now I ask you what would happen if Canada decided to quit the war and let the United States bear the burden? Might not the people of the United States say "If Canada is no longer prepared to fight side by side with us, we should retain the essential materials at home in order to be more efficient ourselves and more vigorously prosecute the war." And if the United States refused to issue licenses for export to Canada ... the whole industrial fabric would be paralyzed.'[42] The implications of the paralysis for manufacturers and workers for both the present and the future were obvious.

Many times he discussed the military situation in Europe: plainly Germany's withdrawal from the eastern front after the collapse of Russia and the concentration of her forces in the west, coupled with the desperate need for British and French assistance to the Italians, had created a severe military crisis. If Canada were to do its share, its four divisions must be maintained by the impartial enforcement of conscription in every part of the country.

The decision on the seventeenth of December is a decision to go on with the war or a decision to quit the war ... When you go to mark your ballot it will decide not so much between Tory and Liberal, not so much between Sir Robert Borden and the members of his cabinet, and Sir Wilfrid Laurier, important as that may be, but when you cast your ballot you are helping to decide the future of Canada, the future of our empire, and the cause of human liberty ... It is the struggle of the lower against the higher. It is the struggle of the Pagan belief against the Christian and in the hearts and souls of the men and women of Canada between now and the seventeenth of December must go on a similar struggle. Your patriotism, your sense of duty calls you to do the noble, the great, the heroic thing no matter what it may cost you ... You must fight that struggle in your own heart, and in your own conscience. For a man in casting his ballot reveals to his God his own character.[43]

During a series of meetings with Sir William Hearst in northern Ontario Rowell had a painful experience of one of the costs of wartime politics. In the riding of Temiskaming he appeared reluctantly on the platform in the interests of Frank Cochrane, the government candidate, against whose influence he had just warned Sir Clifford Sifton. The Liberal-Labour candidate, Arthur Roebuck, was not only a conscriptionist, but he shared Rowell's interest in social and industrial legislation and had been one of his staunchest supporters in the last provincial election. It was difficult to answer a New Liskeard Liberal, an official of the Temiskaming and Hudson Bay Mining Company, who contrasted Roebuck, 'frank, fearless, intelligent, and honourable beyond all question ... always for the rights of the people as opposed to special privileges,' with the character of Cochrane who he believed was probably 'a greater menace to the public life of Canada' than Robert Rogers, for reasons which he was sure Rowell understood perfectly well.[44] But only the Union Government would enforce conscription; for Rowell that overriding fact settled such personal and political dilemmas for the duration.

At the beginning of the campaign the Unionist leaders had made few direct references to French Canada, but as the cause seemed to falter there was more disposition to become aggressive toward Quebec. When Borden discussed the question with Rowell and White they agreed that henceforth the attitude of Quebec should be treated more fully in the press and on the public platform.[45] Until then Rowell had said nothing about Quebec, except what was implied in his repeated insistence that conscription would be enforced impartially throughout the country. Now, in a carefully prepared address at North Bay, he was more direct. Why was the attitude of Quebec toward the war so different from the rest of the country? Obviously it was not due to any fundamental cowardice or unwillingness among French Canadians to defend the nation: the fine response of the French-speaking citizens of North Bay and the fighting record of the Royal 22nd Regiment from Quebec gave the lie to any such charge. Rather, Quebec's stance must be due to ignorance of the facts, an ignorance that Bourassa and his Nationalists and the majority of the Quebec clergy were determined to maintain. 'In this attitude they were undoubtedly encouraged and abetted by the members of the religious orders from France who found asylum in Canada and used that asylum to undermine Canada's strength in the struggle. It is a misfortune that they did not follow the example of the priests of the Catholic Church in France, who threw themselves into the struggle of their people to preserve their national existence, and by their courage and sacrifice won for themselves a new place in the hearts and affections of the French people.'

Had Laurier been twenty years younger, Rowell was confident he would have fought and triumphed over 'the sinister influence' of the Nationalists instead of taking the position that to support conscription would be to hand Quebec over to Bourassa. In fact there was now no distinction between the policies of the two leaders, he declared: Bourassa endorsed Laurier's referendum, claiming it as his own and asserting that the Nationalists asked only to assist Laurier in ousting 'this government of national treason.' It was a tragic situation, but the choice was clear: 'The people of Canada must choose between a government composed of the leaders of both political parties in all the provinces of Canada save one, or a government brought into existence by the Nationalist-clerical reactionaries of the Province of Quebec ... So long as the people of Quebec deliberately isolate themselves from the rest of Canada by refusing to join in the common sacrifice, just so long will they erect barriers between the races which can only lead to disunion and disaster.'[46]

Compared to the diatribes against Quebec and Laurier in which many Unionist candidates indulged, this presentation of the condition of the nation as Rowell viewed it was moderate indeed – and in spirit unlike the editorial in Willison's *News* that had recently described Laurier as 'nothing more than a play-actor, a demagogue, a charlatan and a mountebank.'[47] Rowell had not lost his distaste for an election fought on a crude race cry, but he had cast in his lot with men who were uninhibited by any vestige of loyalty for a respected French Canadian leader, and the excesses had to be tolerated for the sake of the great cause. Increasingly, as 17 December drew nearer, the Unionist publicity committee under Willison's direction played on the racial theme in the thousands of newspaper advertisements, pamphlets, and posters that the committee in its affluence poured out. 'Is a United Quebec to Rule All Canada?' 'Who Shall Spend the Proceeds of the Victory Loan? Is it to be used in support of Canadian men at the front, and to bring war orders to Canada? Or is it to be handed over to Laurier and Bourassa?' On 15 December a full page advertisement in the newspapers of the province warned: 'A Solid Quebec will Vote to Rule All Canada. Only a Solid Ontario can Defeat Them.' And elsewhere readers were told 'It Rests with You – You Have the Vote for the Boys – or the Kaiser.'[48]

Although Unionist fortunes appeared to be improving in the last ten days of the campaign, Rowell and the men around him in Toronto and Ottawa were uncertain and fearful of the outcome until the very end. While Rowell's chief anxiety was for the fate of the government, he was also apprehensive about his own prospects in Durham. There, the Laurier Liberals, partly at the instigation of W.L. Smith of the *Weekly Sun* who hated Rowell's ideas on social legislation for urban workers and was hostile to a greater war effort, had nominated G.W. Jones, a life-long Conservative and president of the county's telephone system.[49] The managers of the Laurier-Liberal campaign in Ontario devoted a sizable part of their meagre resources to ensuring that if Rowell won it would only be with the most strenuous effort.[50] Consequently, Rowell was forced to spend far more time in his own riding than he had originally intended; Ward Wright and Main Johnson, who were in charge of the campaign in Durham, decided that it was essential to keep the provincial organizer, W.C. Rean, in the riding for nearly a month, despite the desperate need for his experience in the central office. It was intolerable even to contemplate the loss of influence in the government for the whole Liberal Unionist contingent that would ensue from Rowell's defeat, and his position therefore had to be assured at any cost.[51] He spent the last two days of a long, cold campaign in Durham among the voters of Newcastle and Bowmanville, where he found little to cheer him, and in an unusual mood of criticism, which its victims attributed to extreme fatigue, he had some severe comments about the organizing endeavours of Wright and Rean on his own behalf.[52]

He spent election day in Toronto, mainly in discussing law with his legal partners.[53] About four o'clock he went home, 'neither elated nor depressed, but in a tired, quiet mood, prepared for any result.' The earliest returns were soon coming in: the Toronto ridings were secure; then came the news that he had a safe lead of five hundred votes in Durham. After dinner he and Nell went to his office in the Canada Life Building on King Street to receive the returns as they were reported by telephone from the headquarters of the Citizens Union Committee downstairs. By nine o'clock there was no doubt that Ontario had come through more strongly than he had dared to hope; so had the west, and the government would have a substantial majority. Leaving his office with Ward Wright and Main Johnson he set out on a round of visits in the centre of the city. The first call was at the University Club, which was almost completely Unionist in sympathy and had furnished many workers and speakers in the campaign. The predominately legal company present gave Rowell as warm a welcome as the club's austere atmosphere permitted, and after a short speech he moved on to the *Globe* office. The walking was difficult, for the city had just had the heaviest snowfall in decades. As Rowell and his two companions ploughed their way through the drifts and the jostling crowd there were many stage whispers, 'There's Rowell himself,' from citizens who were evidently surprised to see him behaving so much like themselves. In front of the *Globe* a small and silent crowd was gathered reading the bulletins displayed on the building. As Rowell read the news he gave an astonished exclamation, and understood the reason for the silence: Sir Wilfrid Laurier was personally defeated in Ottawa. The victor was Dr J.L. Chabot, the only French Canadian supporter of the government elected. Laurier would still have a seat, for Quebec East had once again returned him handsomely. But Rowell had expected him to win Ottawa as well; it was a measure of Ontario's commitment to the war that he had not.

Inside the building Rowell had a brief conference with Stewart Lyon, and then the two men climbed out a window overlooking Melinda Street onto a fire escape. The crowd below gave them a mixed reception; many were 'die-hards' and one created a commotion by calling out 'Renegade Rowell.' The ensuing barrage of catcalls from both sides nearly drowned out Rowell's expressions of pride in Toronto and Ontario and his tribute to the women workers in the campaign. In the *Star* editorial offices he received a warm but quiet, almost solemn, welcome from Atkinson and a group of prominent Liberals. Again there had been no preparations for a speech and there was no platform; with Atkinson holding his coat tails in a firm grip lest he lose his footing on the icy cornice Rowell let himself through a window to address a much larger and friendlier crowd than the one he had just left at the *Globe*.

Visits to the *Globe* and the *Star* on election nights were an old habit. But from here on, as he began the rounds of the Conservative papers, he was in new territory. In the office of the *Mail and Empire* a large group of Conservatives stood up and cheered noisily on his arrival. When he stepped onto the platform outside, the thousands of people who blocked Bay Street for some distance broke into wild cheering and under the stimulation of this reception Rowell spoke vehemently of the meaning of the Union Jack that floated above his head. Further up Bay Street in the *News* office there were only a few people around Sir John Willison and the editor. After they had greeted Rowell the band on the balcony stopped playing long enough for a brief speech to a small gathering of people outside.

Stopping in at the office of the Citizens Union Committee Rowell found W.E. Rundle, J.H. Gundy, G.A. Warburton, E.R. Wood and G.H. Wood, President Falconer, and a number of prominent businessmen and their wives listening to the returns and rejoicing in the predominance of Unionists elected everywhere but in Quebec, and in the news that Rowell now had a majority of nearly four thousand in Durham. The last newspaper to be visited was the *World*, where the publisher, Rowell's Conservative opponent in his first election campaign in 1900, W.F. ('Billy') Maclean, was celebrating his huge majority in South York and welcomed

Rowell in high spirits. Late in the evening he went to the National Club where 'a big crowd of respectable, prominent business men ... gave him a real touch of the "conquering hero."' The club's rules were violated as Frank Beer and Main Johnson 'rushed downstairs, opened the mysterious door between the men's and women's quarters and released some dozen women who were patiently waiting for their husbands to take them home. For a few moments they were thoroughly dazed and showed no indication that they appreciated their good fortune. Gradually, however, light dawned ... and they rushed ... through the door, across a corner of the men's washroom, and up the stairs to the lounge where, on the fringe, they were allowed to hear Mr Rowell.' Thus did equality of the sexes, at least in wartime, come to the National Club.

On his way home he stopped again at the *Globe* for the latest returns and to issue a statement to the press. Ontario had elected sixty-four Unionist Conservatives, eight Liberal Unionists, and ten Laurier Liberals. Across the country the government would have a majority of at least sixty and perhaps more when the soldiers' votes were counted. Laurier had carried all but three of the Quebec seats but had won only twenty outside the province. Only 20 per cent of the people of Quebec had supported the government, compared to 61 per cent in Ontario and 53 per cent in the country as a whole. The verdict was more decisive than Rowell or any of his colleagues had expected.[54] Ignoring his own public assertions that Laurier was no longer the master of Quebec, he told a *Globe* reporter that if Quebec would loyally accept the verdict of the people as Laurier had pledged, and if French Canadians would now fight for their country, Canada would enjoy a unity previously unknown; 'the whole matter is in the hands of Quebec. This is now the hour for reconciliation.'[55]

PART THREE

14
The organization of victory

On the day after the election, J.E. Atkinson, J.H. Gundy, J.F. Mackay, W.E. Rundle, Tom Reid, Ward Wright, and Main Johnson were gathered in Rowell's living room on Crescent Road. There was only one topic of discussion: What to do about Quebec? Atkinson, on whose initiative the group had been assembled, wanted those who had worked to win the election to 'join now in a big, decisive scheme' to secure French-Canadian co-operation for the duration of the war.

Rowell was the only man in the room who shared Atkinson's view of the urgency of the matter; the rest were disposed to let matters take their course for the present or to counsel punitive action to teach Quebec a lesson. The immediate issue was the filling of the two cabinet vacancies left by the defeat of the two French-Canadian members of the previous Borden administration, P.E. Blondin and A.J. Sevigny. A majority favoured adding F.F. Pardee to the cabinet at once as a step toward realizing the equality of representation for Conservatives and Liberal Unionists that Borden and Rowell had repeatedly affirmed during the campaign. Atkinson was convinced, however, that filling even one of the vacant posts with an Ontario man would further antagonize Quebec and argued that both positions should be held open while a determined effort was made to get some outstanding and truly representative French Canadian such as Ernest Lapointe to join the government. Rowell thought Lapointe the ablest French Canadian in the House, after Sir Wilfrid himself but was not able to overcome the resistance to Atkinson's suggestion. Rundle reminded the company vehemently that Lapointe had moved the objectionable resolution against Regulation 17 in the Commons in 1916; how could such a man be incorporated into the government? It would be unwise, Rundle argued, to make hasty overtures to the French Canadians: they had only themselves to blame for the lack of ministerial representation since they had defeated all the government candidates in Quebec, except for three English Canadians from Montreal. He inclined to the view that filling at least one of the vacant portfolios with an English Canadian would demonstrate to French Canadians how isolated they were and would help 'to bring them to time.' Gundy, who had suggested earlier in the day that the formation of a coalition government in Ontario, the abolition of separate schools, and the abandonment of the element of bilingualism at present tolerated in the province might be desirable next steps, now proposed that some of the more outspoken 'anti-war' parish priests in Quebec should be thrown into jail. The group was agreed that the local curés, many of them influenced by members of orders expelled from France, had been a most important factor in deterring recruiting, and that their hostility to French Canadian enlistments was dictated largely by fear that young French Canadians who went to Europe would be tainted by the anti-clericalism of France and return to Quebec in a less docile temper than before. Rowell failed to see how the situation would be improved by the jailing of priests; instead, he advocated seeking the advice of Cardinal Bégin and Archbishop Bruchési on how the climate in Quebec could be improved. In discussing the merits of approaching Laurier and Lord Shaughnessy, they tended to agree with Mackay that Shaughnessy's large business interests in every part of the country gave him a long-term vital interest in the establishment of good feeling that outweighed any result that could be achieved by an appeal to the aging Laurier's transitory concern for the immediate political aspects of the situation. Moreover, Shaughnessy was believed to have great influence with the Roman Catholic church.

No possible avenue of approach was overlooked in considering methods to persuade Quebec to accept the Military Service Act quietly and deliver her quotas of men. Perhaps the Royal 22nd Regiment, the courageous 'Van Doos,' should be brought home to tell their own story to their compatriots? Would greater use of brass bands, following the example of the British recruiting mission in the USA on which Ward Wright had served, produce more patriotic fervour? Or should selected Franco-Americans from the New England states be imported to bolster the war spirit in Quebec? By the time he left for Ottawa later that night Rowell had received no conclusive advice, and he and Atkinson were still of the opinion that a conciliatory approach to Quebec was likely to yield better results than a belligerent one.[1]

Among his fellow cabinet ministers Rowell found a strong feeling that the best contribution to the healing of racial division would be to forget the election campaign as quickly as possible. Borden's parting advice to the cabinet, as he left for a three-week vacation in Virginia to recover from the near collapse he had suffered at the end of the campaign, was that in the next few weeks members of the government should make no public reference to the situation in Quebec and the English-language press should be urged to ignore the subject.[2] Rowell, whose selection as acting prime minister during Borden's absence again underlined Borden's desire to emphasize the equality of the Liberals in the cabinet, agreed with his colleagues to handle the Quebec situation by avoiding any action directed specifically toward French Canada. For the present it was to be assumed that Quebec would now shoulder her responsibilities in winning the war.

After a brief Christmas holiday with his family in Toronto, Rowell took up the work of the War Committee. Loring Christie, legal adviser in the Department of External Affairs, had been appointed secretary, and detailed plans were now laid to enlist the more active participation in the war effort of business, labour, and women and to institute more effective organization of production and distribution of food and essential raw materials.

The most pressing concern of the War Committee was the manpower problem. As chairman of the committee, Rowell worked with the minister of labour, T.W. Crothers, in issuing invitations to representatives of organized labour to meet with members of the federal and provincial governments in mid-January to discuss the more effective use of the nation's human resources. The response from labour was not as enthusiastic as the government had hoped. Although the Trades and Labour Congress of Canada sent four of its top officials – J.C. Watters, P.M. Draper, James Simpson, and Fred Bancroft – and although twenty-six representatives of individual unions were also present on 16 January, all were from Ontario and Montreal. A gathering that included none of the more radical western unionists could scarcely be considered a national conference of labour. Rowell presided at the opening session and made it clear that any decisions reached would have the status only of 'advice' to the government. Thereafter J.C. Watters was elected chairman of the discussions, which were adjourned on the third day to allow some of the members to go to Washington to investigate labour problems there and to give the government a chance to formulate concrete proposals and secure wider representation from Canadian labour. When the conference resumed on 29 January several Maritime and western labour leaders were in attendance.

Most of the tentative proposals advanced by the government were rejected by the labour spokesmen. Rowell's eagerness to secure their approval of the appointment of a labour man as undersecretary was thwarted by the unionists' refusal to establish such a formal tie with any government of whatever political composition. While no individual could be prevented from accepting such a position, the conference refused to give its blessing to the plan or to agree that anyone who accepted the position could be considered a direct representative of the unions. Similarly, labour opposed government proposals to consider the importation of Chinese coolie labour, to conscript for farm work men physically unfit for the army, and to close down non-essential industries to release men for other work. The latter suggestion produced a lengthy discussion of the distinction between essential and non-essential industries and ended with a request that the government provide a workable definition so that the question could be considered again. The labour position throughout was based on the assumption that there was no shortage of labour in Canada but only faulty distribution; redistribution must not be secured by any form of industrial or agricultural conscription. The only points of real agreement were approval of the national registration of man and woman power and of the establishment of government labour exchanges, and an understanding that labour should have 'fair representation' on all government committees concerned with demobilization and reconstruction.[3] In failing to produce the degree of co-operation he had hoped for, the conference had done little to make Rowell's tasks easier.

During the next month the government made several announcements on labour policy. There would be no conscription of men for farm labour and no importation of coolie labour for the present, but a national registration would provide an inventory of human resources and information about the kind of labour used in various industries, while the War Trade Board, which was soon to be appointed, would classify Canadian industries in order of priority.[4] There was to be no conscription of enemy aliens for agricultural or industrial work for the present because it was deemed impossible to use this type of labour except under military supervision.[5] Finally, an order-in-council announced the establishment of a cabinet subcommittee on labour under the chairmanship of Senator Gideon Robertson. The only other minister on this committee was J.A. Calder, minister of immigration and colonization, the other eleven members being persons from various centres and occupations, including two labour leaders and one woman. Under the direction of the cabinet this board would conduct a national registration of human resources.[6] Rowell and Senator Robertson tried unsuccessfully to have J.E. Atkinson added to the committee. Atkinson wanted the terms of reference enlarged to include an investigation of 'the social and economic condition of the working population of Canada with a view to recommending legislation calculated to increase the well-being of the masses of the people.'[7] Whether because the cabinet refused to expand the committee's function or for some other reason, Atkinson was not appointed.

The mobilization of industry proved to be no easier than the co-ordination of labour. Early in January the War Committee sent a delegation representing government and business interests to Washington to examine methods of war organization in the United States and to make recommendations concerning suitable plans for Canada. The government's initiative received some prodding and full co-operation from the Canadian Manufacturers' Association. With the increasing involvement of the United States in the war the American conservation list had become so extensive that licensing and export restrictions on materials imported from the United States affected a large number of Canadian industries, many of which were engaged in war production. On some raw materials the United States had placed export embargoes that severely restricted Canadian production. Although the United States was endeavouring to maintain its exports to Canada of such vital materials as iron and steel and other items used in the manufacture of munitions, many Canadian manufacturers laboured under shortages of supply, confusion over the changing American restrictions, and generally unstable business conditions. The CMA believed it would be beneficial to the war effort and to the profit of its member industries if applications for Canadian imports from the United States could be channelled through a government-appointed board and sorted into some order of priority.[8]

A move toward facilitating Canadian-American trade and war production was taken early in February with the appointment of a Canadian War Mission in Washington, headed by Lloyd Harris (of the Massey-Harris Company and innumerable Canadian enterprises) who had heretofore represented the Imperial Munitions Board in the American capital. The other members of the new mission, which was to work closely with the British War Mission, were F.A. Rolph, head of a large Toronto lithographing firm and a former president of the Canadian Manufacturers' Association, Ross H. McMaster, manager of the Montreal operations of the Steel Company of Canada, and A.H. Scott, a Montreal importer. A few days later the government announced the establishment of a War Trade Board as a subcommittee of the War Committee. Its scope, at least potentially, was greater than had been envisaged by the Canadian Manufacturers' Association: it was to have direction of licences for export and import, to keep records of the country's stock of raw materials and manufactured products, to establish distinctions between essential and less essential industries, to investigate and make recommendations concerning production and trade, and to work closely with its counterpart in the United States. The actual powers of the new board were not clearly defined. Apparently most of its activities were to rest on the voluntary co-operation of business but the order-in-council establishing the board also ordered it 'to undertake and carry out such supervision as may be necessary of all industrial and commercial enterprises and by co-operation with producers to prevent waste of labour, of raw materials and of products' and 'to direct priority in the distribution of fuel, electrical energy, raw materials and partially finished products.'[9] These clauses could be interpreted as providing for a wholesale mobilization of the nation's productive resources under government direction: but it was noteworthy that the government was given no means of dealing with those who might resist its recommendations, and the announcement a few days later of the personnel of the board provided little evidence that the government intended to exercise a heavy hand over business. Sir George Foster was to serve as chairman and Frank P. Jones of Montreal, president of the Canada Cement Company, as vice-chairman. The other members were J.H.

Gundy, C.B. McNaught, a Toronto insurance broker and coal company president, and J.W. McConnell, Montreal financier and managing director of the St Lawrence Sugar Refineries; C.A. Magrath, recently appointed food controller, and Hormisdas Laporte, chairman of the War Purchasing Commission, were to serve as ex-officio members. One of the board's first acts was the imposition of an embargo on a limited list of luxury imports ranging from the more expensive brands of automobiles to paintings and other works of art. At least at the outset it seemed that the board might justify Rowell's criticism of it – that 'it looked to be a rather conservative board,' one that might prove 'afraid to plunge into radical measures.'[10]

On Gundy's appointment to the War Trade Board Rowell agreed to share with him the suite that he had taken early in the New Year in the Roxborough apartments in Ottawa. Since Gundy would be away a good deal the arrangement would not prevent Nell from visiting frequently. After prolonged consideration it had been decided not to disrupt the family by selling the Crescent Road home; unfortunately that meant Rowell would see little of Nell and the children. But that was a price of the war, and his family life was less affected by the conflict than that of many men whom he met every day.

His regard for Gundy's ability and integrity did not prevent Rowell from disagreeing with him. The continuing question of the limitation of packers' profits was only one of several issues connected with government regulation of business on which they had a difference of opinion. Two months after the election the government still had not proceeded with its declared intention of limiting packing house profits to 11 per cent on capital invested. The packers, through their principal spokesman, J.S. Maclean of the Harris Abattoir of Toronto, were united in their complaints against the government's policy and determined to keep the restraints placed on them to a minimum. A particular point at issue was the packers' insistence that 'capital invested' should be interpreted to include 'borrowed capital.'

Gundy pleaded the cause of the packers with Rowell and in particular defended their definition of 'capital.' During a lengthy discussion in their apartment Gundy argued that the exclusion of borrowed capital would discourage expansion of an industry that was vital to the war effort. Future Canadian investment in the packing industry might be diverted to Chicago where the American government accepted the definition of capital favoured by Gundy and the packers. Rowell, pale and wan with fatigue, lay on a couch all evening rubbing his head at frequent intervals but was still capable of answering Gundy 'with a fire which blazed out from his tired frame.' He was unable to see why the packers should feel so hard hit: they had a most important advantage in the security of their markets. Moreover, the government was quite willing to discuss plans for making funds available for necessary additions to plant to companies that might find it difficult, with curtailed profits, to borrow in the ordinary market. But for Rowell broader issues of social policy took precedence over the financial effects of taxation on the packers. Believing that both the public interest and its own electoral success would be served by a policy of restricting profits, the government had made election promises that made it absolutely clear that 'capital' did not include borrowed money. Now that the government was securely in power with an overwhelming majority, how could it possibly say to the people that it did not mean what it had said? Moreover, it was impossible to be tender toward businessmen when young Canadians were losing their lives. 'The state was conscripting men, and taking their lives, but every time [it] began by taxation or otherwise to affect the profits of business interests, there was a great hue and cry.'[11]

Nor could Rowell approve of Gundy's assurances to Gordon Macgregor, president of the Ford Motor Company of Canada. Earlier that very day Gundy and Macgregor had agreed that purchases of non-essential automobiles would have to be curtailed and that a comparatively heavy tax on every motor car manufactured or imported would be sufficient to achieve that end. Rowell was not opposed to this policy for the moment, but he thought it unwise to suggest to any business a limit of control or taxation beyond which the government would not act. 'We must win the war,' he declared heatedly 'and we shall not be stopped by business or any other interests, however powerful they may be. If I think a thing should be done, I'll urge its adoption no matter whom it may hurt.'[12]

His disagreement with Gundy became even more intense when Rowell launched into a discussion of the significance of the growing unrest among labouring classes throughout the world, leaving no doubt that he sympathized with them in large measure and was prepared to see substantial changes in the organization of society to meet their just grievances. The problem of unrest in Canada was currently embodied in a strike in the Drumheller coal mines. In the face of threats of violence the Mounted Police had moved onto the scene with a machine gun. Since the Mounted Police were under the general jurisdiction of the president of the Privy Council, Rowell had earlier that day been endeavouring to have the machine gun removed. It had been placed there without his knowledge through some misunderstanding in the chain of command governing the force, and he was fearful lest it encourage rather than deter an outbreak of violence and bloodshed. Gundy had a ready panacea for the Drumheller unrest and similar upheavals: 'What those miners want is for some Christian to go among them and show them how to live decent, quiet, and orderly lives – a man like Warburton. It's Christianity they want.'[13] Such a blunt avowal of the usefulness of religion as 'the opiate of the masses' was unacceptable to Rowell. He was unaccustomed to thinking of Christianity as a sedative, and his social and political sense was too sophisticated to permit acquiescence in such a simple solution to a complex problem. Gundy made no headway with Rowell. Before long, an order-in-council limiting packers' profits to 11 per cent was passed; borrowed capital was not included in the sum on which profits were estimated.[14]

In accord with his wish to expand opportunities for women to share in the war effort, Rowell and the War Committee arranged a Women's War Conference, which brought seventy-five delegates representing all the major women's organizations in the country to Ottawa at the end of February. Among them was Rowell's sister, Mrs Gordon Wright ('Sazie') who was serving her tenth term as national president of the Women's Christian Temperance Union. Rowell presided at the opening session which heard an address from the governor general and elected as chairman Mrs H.P. Plumptre of Toronto who had been active in several voluntary wartime organizations and in the campaign to elect the Union Government. Since their role in the war effort was less controversial than labour's, the women proved easier to handle than the labour representatives a few weeks earlier. Rowell was well satisfied with the result and believed that a number of the resolutions passed by the conference should receive the government's serious consideration. The women suggested methods for the more extensive use of womanpower in the current labour shortage, urged the establishment of a training program for women in farm work and certain trades, called for compulsory measures to ration food, requested the government to establish a federal department of health to promote child welfare and assist in the control of venereal disease, and expressed appreciation of the recent federal legislation banning the importation into Canada of liquor over $2^1/_2$ per cent proof, a measure intended to support existing provincial and Dominion legislation.[15]

The early weeks of 1918 provided Rowell with an opportunity to test his conviction that the Canadian people would rise to a more creditable war effort if only they were better informed. The Department of Public Information, created the previous autumn with the journalist, M.E. Nichols, as director and George Locke of the Toronto Public Library as assistant director was attached to the Privy Council office. It was charged with keeping the public informed of the progress of the war and of the program of the various government departments concerned with the war, and with publicizing the Canadian war effort in allied countries, especially Britain and the United States. In addition, the preparation of the *Daily Record*, the bulletin issued to overseas troops and previously under the control of the Department of Militia, had been transferred to the Department of Public Information. To handle the expanding work of the Privy Council office, Rowell added an assistant secretary for himself, John Allen, son of a former minister of Metropolitan Church, while another of Rowell's former associates in the Metropolitan Sunday School, Vincent

Massey, was appointed to prepare literature for the Department of Public Information. On a weekend visit Nell observed 'there are so many of the Metropolitan here ... and Methodists generally.'[16]

The first session of the new Parliament was to meet in mid-March 1918. The government prepared for it with its strength increased since the election by the final result of the overseas soldiers' vote. Ninety per cent of the soldiers as a whole, and 94 per cent of those from Ontario, had voted for Unionist candidates. Twenty-three seats had changed hands, and there were now one hundred and fourteen Conservatives, thirty-five Liberal Unionists, and eighty-six Laurier Liberals. By the loss of Nipissing and South Perth the Laurier Liberals from Ontario had been reduced to eight, and the government supporters increased to seventy-four. Since there were still only eight Liberal Unionists from Ontario, Rowell's continuing concern for equalization of cabinet representation by the addition of F.F. Pardee evoked little response from his Conservative colleagues. J.D. Reid remained adamantly opposed to the addition of another Liberal unless Rowell could perform a feat whose difficulty Reid, in his continuing misunderstanding of the drastic step the Liberal Unionists had taken in joining the coalition, failed to comprehend. He wanted Rowell to persuade a Quebec Liberal to enter the cabinet, chiefly because the absence of a Catholic Liberal left the Conservative Unionists open to the criticism that they were pro-Catholic. There were only half a dozen Roman Catholics in the government's entire following, and Reid thought it politically dangerous for the Conservatives to furnish another Catholic cabinet minister in addition to C.J. Doherty.[17] Rowell had no time to waste on attempting the impossible; there were no cabinet changes for the present.

In a series of cabinet meetings to plan the work of the session Rowell fought for the extension of the federal prohibition laws for one year after the end of the war. He believed that this was essential to encourage sobriety among the returning soldiers and to create a suitable atmosphere for the tasks of post-war reconstruction. He was hopeful that the extension would reinforce the various provincial temperance regulations and persuade the Canadian people to remain 'dry.' For a time Rowell was apprehensive lest most of the cabinet succumb to pressure from groups who wanted prohibition to cease with the war,[18] but in the end the government came down on the right side.

That battle won, Rowell went to Toronto and was immediately sent to bed for a week in the hope that this would allow him to recover from his extreme fatigue before the opening of Parliament. After that, his doctor decreed, he would have to learn to take things more easily than he had since he entered the government: no man could work all day and most nights until close to midnight without finding nature in revolt against such abuse. He went up to Ottawa for the opening and took his place in the front row on the government benches. Unknown to him, two of his Liberal Unionist colleagues, Carvell and Calder, with whom Borden had discussed the seating arrangements, had suggested that Rowell should be placed in the second row. They were 'not very appreciative of him,' Borden observed,[19] but neither personal inclination nor political sense allowed him to consider for one moment placing the president of the Privy Council anywhere but in the first row.

On the second day of the session the debate on the reply to the speech from the throne inevitably brought an attack on conscription and the conduct of the recent election from Sir Wilfrid Laurier and a defence from Sir Robert Borden. Their tone was moderate; clearly both leaders wanted to forget the excesses of the election campaign. At the end of the afternoon sitting exhaustion forced Rowell to go home to bed. At ten o'clock at night when he was discussing business with Main Johnson he received a phone call from the house reporting that Charles Murphy, a former member of the Laurier cabinet and now a Laurier loyalist, had just concluded a two-hour denunciation of Rowell in the House.[20] The next day, as he read the verbatim account of the official debates he was in no doubt that he was the victim of one of the most vitriolic attacks in Canadian parliamentary history.

Regretting that in the past two days nobody in the House had exposed the government's deliberate resort to appeals to racial and religious passion during the election campaign, Murphy proposed to compensate for this neglect by making Rowell the chief object of his attention. Murphy professed to discern in the whole conscription movement and the Unionist election campaign an anti-Catholic, anti-French, anti-Laurier plot to deceive the Canadian people, 'the crowning infamy' being the use of Protestant pulpits as 'political cockpits' and the attempt to convince the new women voters that the most important agency of German diplomacy was the Roman Catholic church. Turning to Rowell's call for sacrifice, he challenged the credentials of one who, Murphy suggested, had become wealthy through his work for the Ross government, had only become leader of the Ontario Liberals on condition that he be guaranteed against personal loss through the 'secretarial fund,' and had made his carefully calculated and much advertised trip to the front in 1916 at the expense of his friends. Where was the sacrifice? The career of Newton Wesley Rowell, declared Murphy, was an example of the same 'cult of commercialized Christianity' practised by John Wesley Allison and Joseph Wesley Flavelle. Murphy's strongest language was reserved for Rowell's 'conspiracy' to overthrow Laurier and for his 'slanderous attack' in North Bay on members of the French religious orders, the truth of which Rowell had never attempted to prove despite several public challenges to do so.[21]

To his secretary's eye that morning Rowell, though pale and worn, seemed 'as cool and calm as ever' and 'not the least perturbed at the attack.'[22] Rowell thought the personal charges were not very important: among those who knew him they could do no harm and in many other quarters Murphy's reputation as a professional Irish Catholic and the very violence of his language would discredit him. The two matters of moment were Murphy's unconvincing defence of the French religious orders and his charge of conspiracy against Laurier. In the interest of the Union Government's public relations Rowell was at first disposed to believe that these two matters should be dealt with soon and he began to prepare a statement. That was not difficult: the record of his leadership and his procedures in the organization of the Ontario Liberal party were straightforward and well known and approved by a majority of the officers and leading figures in the party. So also was his conduct in the negotiations leading to the formation of the Union Government.

If he were to make a reply what form should it take? Had Murphy performed the normal courtesy of giving him notice beforehand that he intended to refer to him that night, Rowell would have been in his place in the House despite his fatigue and could then have answered on the spot. In order to prevent further violent talk J.D. Reid had moved adjournment immediately at the conclusion of Murphy's diatribe. Under House rules the matter could not be discussed again during that session unless Rowell rose on a point of privilege and thus secured a chance to rebut the charges. Borden thought that would be the soundest response to 'a very brutal & savage attack.'[23] Atkinson and Stewart Lyon were also inclined to think that he should reply, but nearly everyone else who was consulted or offered advice – Calder, Crerar, Vincent Massey, J.F. Mackay, F.H. Deacon, C.M. Bowman – thought otherwise.[24] The more Rowell considered the matter the more he felt that to answer now would simply be helping Murphy feed the racial and religious antagonisms undermining the war effort. He decided that he might reply some time in the future; in the meantime both he and the government would have to suffer whatever loss of prestige the attack had brought.

There could be no doubt about Murphy's purpose in launching the attack: he wanted to make the cleavage in the Liberals complete and permanent at both the provincial and federal levels and to ensure that Rowell could have no place in post-war Liberal politics. The Laurier Liberals were distressed by Rowell's obvious influence in the government and by the recent election of William Proudfoot, a 'Rowellite,' as interim leader of the Ontario Liberals.[25] It was no accident, as Rowell observed, that Hartley Dewart was in the gallery of the House to witness Murphy's attack,[26] because he and his friends were intensely interested in its outcome and had assisted Murphy in its preparation. Indeed, Murphy had been trying to collect incriminating evidence against Rowell ever since the election. His research had been disappointing. Instead of finding proof, as he had hoped, that Rowell's overseas trip in 1916 had been financed by the unpopular Flavelle he had learned that most of the money had been put up by P.C. Larkin, a useless piece of information since Larkin was in his own camp. He had been unable to unearth anything specific about his victim's association with the Ross government or the Lake Superior corporation and had no evidence whatever that Rowell had ever received a penny from the secretarial fund.[27] But the possible uses of innuendo and 'guilt by association' were almost unlimited, as Murphy's attack had so amply demonstrated, and his friends rejoiced. 'Rowell is a dead one,' declared Andrew Haydon, an Ottawa lawyer and active Laurierite. 'Rowell is beyond hope of resurrection ... certain ... men sitting in the National Club the following day ... looked ... as if a load of manure had been dumped on them,' wrote a Toronto supporter.[28] In a different quarter, Rowell's cabinet colleague, Sir George Foster, confided to his diary that Murphy's attack 'pleased most of Laurier's followers and some of ours.'[29]

Was Laurier a party to the attack on Rowell? If Laurier knew that something was brewing it is unlikely that he condoned it. From the beginning he had treated the Liberal Unionists as 'erring brothers' who would come home in due course. Yet his general toleration of Liberal Unionists did not prevent Laurier from being puzzled by Rowell's influence in the country: Rowell seemed to have 'carried with him only a small minority of the party, but that minority constitutes the most powerful element, all the wealthy men in all the large centres. The rank and file have no use for him.' Laurier conceded Rowell's 'eminent parts and abilities,' but observed that 'his personality does not seem to have gone deep into the community. What he has of influence seems to arise from the fact that the big interests have pinned their faith on him and push him on, and in return he will be the champion of the big interests.'[30] But this view did not dispose Laurier to wage war on any Liberal Unionist. The political tension at home and the new peril overseas arising from the Russian military collapse meant that 'both the tactical and the patriotic course' was to allow 'a free hand to the administration both here and at Toronto.'[31] Such counsel had no effect on Dewart and Murphy.

Two days after Murphy's oration Rowell was well enough to appear in the House briefly, but he took no part in the debate save to answer a question, during the discussion of the government's bill to extend the operation of the Civil Service Commission concerning the appointment of M.E. Nichols as director of public information. In outlining the functions of Nichols and his office Rowell made the most of this opportunity to laud the work done by the Department of Public Information both at home and overseas. But he was clearly not at his best; even though he had shouldered no major responsibilities for the early days of the session it was increasingly evident that he could not go on without a rest. Reluctantly, at the urging of Borden, his doctor, and Nell, he agreed that he and Nell would go to the Clifton Inn at Niagara Falls for ten days, returning to Ottawa after Easter.

The news from the front made it even more than usually frustrating to be off duty. On the first day of spring, the Germans, now freed from any effective resistance on the Russian front and anxious to end the war before American forces could be fully involved, launched their long-expected offensive on the western front. Thrusting into Picardy against British and French troops more thinly dispersed than at any time since the beginning of the war, the Germans within five days were threatening to cut off the British divisions from their French allies. The appointment of General Foch, the hero of the Marne in 1914, as commander-in-chief of the allied forces was a symbol both of the plight of the allies and of their determination to endure. Like everyone else, Rowell realized that this was the great crisis of the war. He found it 'difficult to think of anything ... but the situation on the western front.' Every dispatch from France made Murphy's attack and the political vindictiveness it represented seem at once more tragic and more inconsequential and confirmed him in his decision not to reply.[32]

On his return to Ottawa after Easter Rowell was still fighting the influenza he had contracted during his rest cure in Niagara Falls, and for the next two weeks he carried on only with difficulty. It was no time for relaxation: through frequent and lengthy cabinet meetings and in sessions of Parliament lasting into the early hours of the morning the implications of the outbreak of armed resistance to attempts to enforce conscription in Quebec City were being debated. There had been rioting in the Quebec capital, in Laurier's own riding, from the evening of 29 March until 2 April. The dispatch of a Toronto battalion to reinforce the military forces already in the city did nothing to calm the mob, and before order was restored four civilians were dead, many more hurt, fifty-eight arrested, and five soliders wounded. On 3 April Borden's speech to the Unionist caucus on the situation in Quebec and the government's determination to administer the conscription act impartially won Rowell's warmest admiration, and produced demands from some members for the imposition of martial law in the province, demands which Borden successfully resisted. The next day the government issued an order-in-council regularizing the administration's action in using troops to quell the disturbances in Quebec, granting it wide power to take similar action anywhere in Canada, giving the minister of justice power to suspend the operation of *habeas corpus*, and subjecting any male found guilty of taking part in a disturbance occasioned by opposition to the Military Service Act to immediate conscription even if he were a member of a normally exempt class.[33] When it was presented to Parliament this measure produced conflicting criticisms of the methods used in the enforcement of conscription. Some of Borden's own followers, notably H.H. Stevens of Vancouver, complained that the regulations were administered more firmly in other provinces than in Quebec, while Laurier and other Liberals contended that the recent riots had been due to the character and actions of certain officials charged with the enforcement of the law. Still, Laurier urged obedience to the law of the land.[34]

Within a few days the news from France was somewhat brighter. The tide had by no means turned, but the German drive had been slowed down and Amiens still stood in French hands. The Canadian Corps had not been involved in the recent heavy fighting, but the casualties in the British divisions had been enormous and there was no doubt that the Canadians would soon again be in the thick of it. Then it would be difficult to maintain even the present four divisions, let alone increase the Canadian effort. Rowell felt that it was imperative to find more men immediately, but where were they to be found? Logically, the place to get them was in Quebec. He believed, as Borden explained to the House, that the Military Service Act was being administered formally in Quebec in the same way as in other provinces, but since public opinion was hostile, the functioning of the tribunals of first appeal for exemptions produced different results. All the government could do was to bring all exemption cases before central appeal judges for review as expeditiously as possible.[35]

In Rowell's view the church, the press, and the political leaders of Quebec, with few exceptions, had all failed to give their people proper leadership. Rowell advised, although the rest of the cabinet were not convinced, that the religious leaders of Quebec should be summoned to a conference at which the government would put the issue to them squarely. They should be told forthrightly that however ancient the original source of the rights enjoyed by the church in Quebec, those rights would be gravely imperilled if the people of Canada, and especially the thousands of returning soldiers, felt in the end that Quebec had done far less than its share in the present crisis. The church should realize the danger it was in from the fact that there were already suggestions in the press and other quarters that the Treaty of Paris of 1763 should be revised.[36]

Through translations of editorials from the Quebec press and of speeches of public figures provided by Main Johnson, Rowell was well aware that in recent months even *Le Canada* and *La Presse* had abandoned their earlier positive attitudes and were now beginning to outdo Bourassa's *Le Devoir* in their hostility to English Canada and the war. Nor were matters being improved by such articles as one in *Le Petit Canadien*, the organ of the Société Saint John Baptiste, by Gustave Beaudoin, who declared that French Canadians were determined to see their duty 'in the universal conflict from the ... standpoint of our own interests, in this sense that in order to continue to defend "the cause of civilization and justice" – read here the cause of others – we do not believe we have the right to impair seriously the energies we shall so greatly need to ensure our French survival.' Rowell found even more incomprehensible the utterance of the chief justice of Quebec, Sir Horace Archambault, who told the French military mission that had recently visited Canada that 'the French Canadians have not blindly precipitated themselves into the abyss ... because they did not consider it to be their right to break the work of a century and a half of strife and to destroy the sacred temple of French hopes in America.'[37]

That such statements represented the true mood of the majority in Quebec Rowell had no doubt. He was even more aware of the growing restlessness of English Canada, centring in resentment towards Quebec and, increasingly, towards the government that permitted such unsatisfactory enlistments from east of the Ottawa. English Canadians found it more and more difficult to see why their young men should give their lives to preserve the privileges and liberties of Quebec, if Quebeckers themselves would not join the fight. Clearly, a means of raising more men must be found, and speedily. And it must be a method that would draw in more French Canadians.[38]

The cabinet was soon discussing two main alternatives. Either the present selective draft of all men in Class I under the Military Service Act – (single men aged eighteen to thirty) – should be extended to Class II (single men aged thirty to forty-five) or exemptions should be cancelled within Class I. Rowell estimated that by cancelling all exemptions for men aged twenty to twenty-four in Class I enough reinforcements could be secured to last six months. The chief disadvantage of this procedure was that it would take many men from farm work all across the country. Its strongest feature was that for the first time it would produce a substantial number of soliders from Quebec; that could not be said for calling up an older group, for marriages were earlier in Quebec than elsewhere and most of the men over twenty-four would be married.[39]

In common with the rest of the cabinet Rowell was also considering the desirability of stringent regulations forbidding any discussion in the press of the causes or conduct of the war or of the administration of conscription and other war measures, and of anything tending to work against 'the unity of Canada.' He came to the conclusion that new regulations were unnecessary; a section of the Military Service Act already gave the Canadian government more extensive powers to regulate the press than any conferred on the wartime governments of either Britain or the United States. So far, the Canadian government had not used these powers. Rowell was reluctant to think that it might be necessary to use them, and he had not been enthusiastic about recent suggestions that Le Devoir should be suppressed. In any case, that paper and Le Canada as well could be silenced under the present law. As the minister in charge of the Department of Public Information, Rowell would have a large responsibility in the enforcement of any censorship against statements detrimental to 'the unity of Canada.' New regulations would almost certainly earn the hostility of the radical and Liberal Unionist press, some of which would doubtless be directed against Rowell himself. And there might be large and perilous difficulties in administering such censorship: 'Suppose the French papers for some reason ... quite within the range of possibility, should ''be good'' and ... that certain

Ontario papers, the Toronto *Telegram*, for instance should fall within the law. Could the government suppress the *Telegram* and leave entrenched *Le Devoir*, no matter how "good" the latter might technically be at the time?' It was comforting to have so specific and practical an argument to support his continued resistance to a step that he found illiberal and repellent.[40]

Apart from the content of any new regulations on the draft or on censorship there was also the debatable question of how they should be instituted, whether by Parliament or simply by order-in-council. There had been a great deal of protest in Quebec, and some complaints in English Canada, notably from the Toronto *Star*, against the government's increasing use of orders-in-council. Rowell was strongly opposed to changing the operation of the Military Service Act by mere order-in-council: in Britain 'it was always parliament which decided these things,' he argued; and since Parliament was actually in session at the moment it would be folly to ignore the House. Moreover, he believed that decisions coming from Parliament would carry much greater weight than any merely emanating from the government. But he was unwilling to risk any delay that submission to Parliament might entail. If the opposition were to delay the bill, then the present military emergency warranted the use of closure after a stated period for debate of the measure.[41]

The cabinet and the government caucus agreed on an order-in-council, contingent on the assent of both houses of Parliament, giving the government sweeping powers to abolish all exemptions for any age and any class. In an accompanying statement the government announced the immediate abolition of exemptions for single men aged twenty to twenty-two years inclusive. Although that did not cover as large a group as Rowell would have wished, it was a step in the right direction. The cabinet's decision on censorship was less agreeable; perhaps that was why Borden found that Rowell made 'a poor fist' of a draft statement explaining new restrictions on the press to the public. Eventually, after Borden had appointed Meighen and Calder to assist him, Rowell had the statement ready.[42] The irony inherent in his having to explain to representatives of the press regulations concerning their future operations that he himself had opposed did not escape him.[43] The principle of cabinet solidarity, especially in a wartime coalition, produced strange anomalies.

The next day Parliament met in an unprecendented secret session whose chief purpose was to impress Canadians with the gravity of the Allied position. Borden hoped that the exercise would offset the 'inevitable lagging of interest' in so long a struggle and 'perhaps aid in awakening a better spirit in Quebec.'[44] Whatever else it may have achieved it did nothing to blunt opposition criticism. The day afterward, Rowell was subjected to bitter attack during the debate on the estimates for the Department of Public Information. Rodolphe Lemieux disputed Rowell's contention that the department was ensuring better publicity for the Canadian war effort both overseas and at home.[45] Since the Canadian press was the best in the world before the establishment of the department, Lemieux failed to see why it needed assistance. It was the *Daily Record*, sent to the Canadian men overseas, that drew the greatest opposition ire. Appealing over Rowell's head to the prime minister, Lemieux asked what hope there was for national unity when public funds were spent for 'publications in which one-half of the people of Canada are being libelled and slandered.' From Witley Camp in England, Lemieux's son had dispatched to his father a bundle of copies of the *Daily Record* 'containing the vilest statements about my right hon. leader and about French Canadians generally ... The *Record* did its work in the trenches in the last campaign. Drop it, for heaven's sake.' Borden replied that he would like to see such issues if they existed and supported Rowell's contention that the men overseas were highly appreciative of the *Daily Record*.[46]

For the first month of the session Rowell had taken little part in the proceedings of the House of Commons but had confined himself to answering a few questions about matters under his jurisdiction. Not until the opening of the debate on the revision of the Military Service Act and the cancellation of exemptions did he deliver a major address. Borden had introduced the measure in a lengthy and effective speech outlining the current military situation and giving the most up-to-date figures on enlistment, which showed that of 147,505 native-born Canadians now overseas 16,268 were of French descent. The prime minister's purpose in citing these statistics was obvious and was underlined by his closing appeal to the press and public in both sections of the country not to indulge in recriminations but to unite in a war effort worthy of the whole nation.[47]

Laurier followed Borden with an attack on the government's method of extending conscription as yet another example of 'Prussian autocracy.' The abolition of exemptions was dishonest, he charged, since half or three-quarters of the members on the government side of the House 'were elected upon the direct or indirect pledge that the farmers in their constituencies would not be amenable [sic] to military service.' Now, on the eve of seeding, the government proposed to withdraw up to fifty thousand men from farming, men who would arrive in Britain and France too late to be of any use in the present crucial fighting. Perhaps the real reason for this policy rested not on military requirements but on political necessities: the government had won the election on the slogan 'You must not allow Quebec to rule Canada.' Now the idea, although not often publicly expressed, was 'We must make Quebec fight.' Once more Laurier rehearsed the social and historical reasons for the failure of French Canadians to feel as involved in the war as most other Canadians; these, plus the Conservative alliance with the Nationalists and the faulty recruiting methods used in Quebec explained the result. But even now, an appeal to reason and imagination would succeed just as the slow process of education had brought wartime Quebec to a position similar to the rest of Canada on prohibition. 'A piffling speech,' Borden thought privately.[48]

When Laurier sat down, Rowell was on his feet as the second speaker for the government. He faced Laurier with substantially the same arguments that he had presented over so many months before the split in the party. From behind a deferential and far from bitter demeanor toward his old leader, there emerged a firm declaration that Laurier had no solution to the immediate problem. The answer to Laurier's questioning of the necessity of the government's extension of the draft lay in General Currie's order of the day of 27 March in which he informed the Canadian army of the steady retreat of British troops before superior German numbers; and since then the military situation had grown worse. How did Laurier propose to stop the Germans? How could anything he had suggested 'protect the homes ... and the people of Canada if the German force broke through, compelled Britain to conclude a peace, destroyed her navy, and crossed the ocean to invade our country? ... it is a real danger.' Those who continued to argue that the war should now be left to the Americans, at least until they had made a contribution in proportion to the rest of the Allies, were obscuring the fact that this was Canada's war as much as any country's.

He rejected Laurier's contention that Canada should give priority to food production: 'Our duty is not to send food or men, our duty is to send food and men.' As for the charge that the government had broken its pledge not to conscript the farmers, there was another pledge that took precedence over everything else: 'If there was one clear pledge the government made to the country, if there was one clear mandate the government received from the country it was that Canada should maintain our divisions up to strength and provide adequate reinforcements.' No one could accuse the government of acting without serious consideration of the food problem or in ignorance of the possible political consequences. The new measure would affect every constituency in Canada. He was well aware that the government's action would be very unpopular and would bring suffering and sorrow to many homes in his own rural riding. But a government that could be dissuaded from the right course 'when the sanctity of every home in the land is imperilled' would not deserve the confidence of the people.

Comparison of Canada's war effort with those of other countries was even less satisfying now than during the election campaign. Taking the number of men actually overseas, Canada had 5 per cent of her population in the battle, compared with Britain's 12 per cent, and still Britain was asking her people for another half million men. Canada would have to send another one hundred thousand men to the front to equal Australia's record and another seven divisions to equal New Zealand's. In spite of its acute racial divisions even South Africa had done more than Canada. Rowell admitted that Canada's agricultural commitments meant that comparisons of men could not be absolute, but he was confident that with better organization, with the immediate closing down of non-essential industries, and especially with public acceptance of the demonstrated willingness of Canada's women to be more actively involved in agricultural and industrial production the armed forces could be increased without jeopardy to munitions and food supply. His comments about the greater use of woman power, bolstered by glowing accounts of what he had seen of women workers in Britain and France, and his reference to closing down non-essential industries went further than any cabinet minister had gone on either subject until now. Coming from the vice-chairman of the War Committee these statements seemed to foretell a more vigorous mobilization of civilian workers.

As for national unity, France, with one-sixth of her population enlisted, provided the most impressive model. 'I would that from Atlantic to Pacific, we should all be imbued with the spirit of France, and that, with her, we might cry, "Until death or victory."' He had no more doubt than Laurier about the essential fighting spirit of the French Canadians. Unity at home could be achieved in the same way as it was at the front: 'by marching together to a great objective, seeking to serve and to sacrifice together ... [If] the sons of Ontario and Quebec go forth to fight for the homes and liberties of Canada ... and mingle their blood in a common grave, the men who return ... will put an end to racial strife in this country.' But above all, 'right must triumph. The cause of liberty must prevail. Canada will not stain her glorious record; Canada will add a new and glorious chapter to her history; Canada will fight to the last for the sacred cause of liberty, of British freedom, for civilization.'[49]

Rowell was well satisfied with the reception accorded his speech from the government benches: the prime minister felt that he had been ably supported by a 'strong and eloquent' presentation,[50] and the Unionist press generally described it as one of the best of his career. 'The ice now being thoroughly broken' Rowell expected to feel more at home in the House.[51] When the bill passed by a vote of 114 to 65, four Laurier Liberals voting with the government, its principles were embodied in orders-in-council cancelling all exemptions in the twenty- to twenty-two-year class and requiring the registration of all unmarried men of nineteen years and those who were twenty before 13 October 1917. In council Rowell urged that the latter group should be called up immediately, on the grounds that they would be needed very soon and their training should begin now. Moreover, an immediate decision would relieve a great deal of uncertainty and anxiety among farmers. But a majority in the cabinet took the view that this policy would immediately alienate more farmers than absolutely necessary, and Rowell's argument was rejected.[52]

Had Rowell's program been adopted he would have been confronted with an even more irate delegation from the United Farmers of Ontario than the one that soon appeared before the War Committee to protest the cancellation of exemptions. Getting no satisfaction from Rowell and an adamant committee the farmers proceeded with their plans for a mass demonstration in Ottawa. Within a week, five thousand Ontario and Quebec farmers, headed by the Quebec minister of agriculture, descended on the capital and threatened to enter the House of Commons by force after the prime minister refused their request to appear there.[53] Rowell was well aware that the farmers' enthusiasm for increased production owed something to the unprecendented prices currently paid for farm products as well as to patriotism, and he recognized some justice in their contention that farm labour should not be conscripted until non-essential industries were closed. Thus, through J.H. Gundy, he renewed his efforts to impress on the War Trade Board the absolute necessity of coming speedily to a definition of non-essential industries and of mapping out a plan for the utilization of more women in factories, possibly by directing that only women be used for certain classes of work.[54] But the War Trade Board had thus far shown little sign of ability to move quickly on anything.

In the wake of the abolition of exemptions it became increasingly difficult for the Department of Public Information to carry out Rowell's instructions for a more intensive presentation of the government's policies to the farming community. The director of the department, M.E. Nichols, tried to secure the co-operation of Peter McArthur, the most respected and best known farm columnist in the country. McArthur, although willing at least to listen to a justification of the government's case, in the end proved typical of all the farm editors and columnists whom Nichols approached. 'They all reflected the view' he told Rowell in explaining his difficulties 'which they say is a conviction on the part of the farmers that notwithstanding military developments since March 21, the peril of hunger among our allies is greater than the peril of the defeat of our armies.'[55] Unfortunately, the farmers found support for their conviction in the literature being issued to them by the Department of Agriculture and the Canadian Food Board. Rowell took steps to have the emphasis of these publications altered so that all departments of the government would present a united front.[56] At the same time he arranged to have all the farm periodicals publish a special message he had secured from Lloyd George stressing the immediate priority of reinforcements over food in the Allied war effort.[57] But despite these efforts there was little change in the tone of the farm press or of the constituency it served.

At least there was some reason for satisfaction in the reception accorded the abolition of exemptions in Quebec. There was no repetition of the earlier riots, and the government was hopeful that a change of sentiment was developing in the province, a change which the English-speaking press was urged to foster by moderating its statements about Quebec.[58]

During the session there were other questions of policy in which Rowell took a keen interest, although he bore no major responsibility for them. The government's measure to extend the operation of the Civil Service Commission to the thirty-five thousand members of the outside service in addition to the five thousand in the inside service was the realization of an objective that had been high on Rowell's list of priorities when he entered the government, as it had long been on Borden's. This reform, Rowell told the House, was 'the most radical ... civil service reform that has ever been made on this continent, at least, and I think I am safe in saying that it is the most radical that has ever been made at one stroke in any country.[59] Together with the expansion of the jurisdiction of the War Purchasing Commission to purchases by all departments of government, in addition to those directly concerned with war supplies, a long forward step had been taken in the elimination of patronage from the public service. And as an extension of the democratic spirit and an important advance in Canada's constitutional status, Rowell was enthusiastic about the government's proposal to request that the crown cease to confer titles on Canadians except by consent of the Canadian cabinet. In a rare moment of agreement with his former leader he supported Laurier's call for those who already held hereditary titles to join in making a bonfire of them.[60]

As the acting minister of finance, A.K. Maclean, began the preparation of the Union Government's first budget Rowell hoped for a scale of taxation that would make equality of financial sacrifice a greater reality than it had been thus far. He was alarmed by reports that Maclean's view of the desirable rate of taxation fell far short both of the scale originally suggested by Borden and of what he himself thought necessary, especially on incomes over $25,000.[61] In the end, Maclean's budget reduced exemptions from personal income tax from $3,000 to $2,000 for married persons and from $1,500 to $1,000 for single persons, and the rates of taxation were increased moderately on incomes up to $50,000 and sharply on those above. A new war surtax was imposed, ranging from 5 per cent on incomes of $6,000 to 30 per cent on those over $200,000, and rising to 50 per cent on incomes of $1 million. Corporation income tax was raised from 4 per cent to 6 per cent, and the Business Profits War Tax was continued at increased rates.[62] Rowell would have gone further, but at least this was a step in the right direction.

During the later part of the session Rowell spent a good deal of time helping to work out the terms on which some of the increased revenues were to be spent. As chairman of the special committee of the House on pensions for disabled soldiers and for the dependents of those killed he presented a report on the last day of the session proposing the most generous pension scale provided by any of the Allies. Although many questions were raised, the essential points in the recommendations to the Pension Board for the treatment of Canadian war veterans were not controversial and the report was commended to the board without division.[63] This atmosphere of amity was a far cry from the bitterness and denunciation that had marked the beginning of the session.

15
The coronation of democracy

Early in the spring of 1918 Borden had tentatively invited Rowell to be part of the Canadian delegation to the meetings of the Imperial War Cabinet and War Conference during the coming summer. For a time Rowell was anxious lest his health prevent him from agreeing to an assignment he was eager to accept. By early May he was back to normal strength, and Borden announced that Meighen, Calder, and Rowell would accompany him to London. The choice was natural enough. Borden's inclusion of Rowell and Calder demonstrated once again the prime minister's determination to make his administration an equal partnership of Liberals and Conservatives. Moreover, Borden had a high opinion of Rowell's knowledge and judgment of imperial and foreign affairs. At the time of the formation of the Union Government he had come close to making him secretary of state for external affairs,[1] but in the end had followed the practice of attaching the office to that of the prime minister. Furthermore, on the face of it, it was logical for the vice-chairman of the War Committee to go to London to secure first-hand information on Allied war needs. Yet it had to be confessed that the usefulness of the War Committee was not readily demonstrated. It was not evident that the committee, from whose work Rowell had anticipated such positive results, had been responsible for the initiation of any war measures that would not have been adopted in any case. It had met only irregularly, and during one period of seven weeks Rowell had convened it only once. The committee's able secretary, Loring Christie, was hard pressed to find any justification for its perpetuation, since he could see in it no advantage over the traditional system of cabinet responsibility for major matters with reference of specific subjects to ad hoc subcommittees.[2] Perhaps some of the committee's ineffectiveness was due to the difficulty of getting information from

Britain on the total Allied war program, and, in so far as that was true, Rowell's trip might improve matters.

The logic of Rowell's attendance at the London meetings was not apparent to several of his colleagues, as Borden at least was fully aware. During the session a number of ministers had come to view Rowell's earnestness and his evangelical zeal for an increased war effort as evidence that he was 'a pusher and self-advertiser.'[3] His inclusion in the imperial delegation did nothing to diminish the resentment: one of his Conservative colleagues, C.C. Ballantyne, minister of fisheries and marine, was especially bitter at being overlooked in favour of Rowell, while the minister of militia and defence, S.C. Mewburn, also protested his exclusion.[4] Among the Conservatives, Sir George Foster, who as minister of trade and commerce had hoped to go to London to discuss post-war trade, was not surprised at Borden's choice: 'Of course Rowell goes. He dearly loves the limelight and Borden plays to his penchant.'[5] So strong was the feeling that the composition of the delegation became a subject of discussion in the cabinet, and the prime minister was required to justify his choice. Borden stood firm and the three colleagues he had originally chosen accompanied him to London, with the understanding that they would return around 1 July to be replaced by Ballantyne and Mewburn. Foster remained unpacified: 'There is a very strong feeling that Rowell pushed himself on the delegation and it is quite true. There was no reason why he should go except his desire to get into the limelight. Singularly enough the peculiarity is as much recognized on one side of the House as on the other.'[6]

The CPR steamship *Melita* was part of the convoy of thirteen vessels that sailed from New York on 27 May, the day on which, unknown to the travellers until they reached England, Germany launched an intensified campaign of submarine warfare against Allied shipping on the Atlantic. The *Melita* carried 2,500 American troops and a small group of civilians on a zigzag course through rough seas that lengthened the crossing to nearly two weeks. When the Canadian party disembarked at Liverpool the English press was full of the depredations of German submarines during the time their convoy had been at sea and the continuing German land offensive. The vigour of the German offensive on both land and sea suggested a long road to an Allied victory, despite the growing assistance of the Americans who had just sent their first two divisions into combat. As Rowell and his colleagues settled into their offices at 2 Whitehall Gardens and their suites in the Savoy Hotel in London the Germans sent eleven divisions against the Allied line west of the Oise River and advanced six miles before they were stopped by French forces, a further reminder of how far the war was from a successful conclusion.

Rowell needed none of these events to heighten his sense of urgency about the intensification of the Empire's war effort. With a slight suggestion that he felt an excess of agitation or zeal in his minister, Borden noted in his diary: 'Rowell began to bombard me with letters about various subjects.'[7] One of the subjects on which Rowell felt strongly enough to put himself in writing was the distinction drawn between the work of the Imperial War Cabinet and the Imperial War Conference. He could see no good reason for any division of responsibility: 'The meeting of the Imperial Conference should have been dignified by the consideration of the whole war situation and how the Dominions can best help to meet it.' As it was, the agenda of the conference, now revealed, called for discussion of civil problems and post-war issues, leaving war problems entirely to the Imperial War Cabinet, composed of the British War Cabinet, the Dominion prime ministers, and one additional minister from each Dominion. Rowell was convinced that if he were 'sidetracked' into the Imperial Conference his trip to London would serve no purpose: his duties with the War Committee at home made imperative his attendance at the body that would discuss the conduct of the war; post-war imperial problems, much as they interested him, were for the present of altogether secondary importance.[8] He seriously doubted whether the British government would in fact prove able or willing to provide the extensive information the Canadian War Committee needed to mount a more co-ordinated and effective war effort, but it was clear that if any body dealt with the subjects of his immediate concern it would be the War Cabinet. His desire to be the second Canadian minister, after Borden, in attendance at the War Cabinet was presented forcefully to the prime minister. Borden was unwilling to give Rowell exclusive right to accompany him to the cabinet, but proposed that he participate whenever matters pertaining to the work of the War Committee were to be discussed, an arrangement that Rowell found entirely acceptable.[9] While they would give the bulk of their time to the Imperial Conference, Meighen and Calder would thus have the chance to attend the War Cabinet occasionally.

In the few days before the meetings of the War Cabinet began, Rowell spent much of his time talking with the director of the newly established Ministry of Information, the Canadian, Lord Beaverbrook, and members of his staff, about the necessity of better liaison between London and Washington, and of Ottawa with both of those centres, in further Allied propaganda. Rowell was especially concerned, as he had been for many months, that Canada's story was being inadequately told among her allies. As one remedy, he had arranged before leaving home that Professor G.M. Wrong, the Toronto historian, should spend the summer in the United States on behalf of the Department of Public Information to increase American press coverage of Canada's 'ideals and activities in connection with the war.'[10] A proposal to which Rowell was entirely unreceptive came from Major Evelyn Wrench, charged with responsibility for war propaganda in British countries, that extra supplies of the propaganda literature prepared in Britain should be provided for Canadian consumption. This solution to the problem surprised Rowell. In the face of the British ministry's lack of sensitivity and its ignorance of the large volume of literature already produced by the Department of Public Information under his own direction, Rowell politely declined the offer in favour of the continued use of material prepared in Canada.[11]

The first days in London also brought consultation with the commander-in-chief of the Canadian Corps, General Arthur Currie, and with the overseas minister of militia, Sir Edmund Kemp. Their accounts of the catastrophic consequences of patronage and excessive concern for the promotion of career soldiers, and of disagreement between the British cabinet and the top military leaders, confirmed the Canadian ministers in their impression that there was still no well-formulated British strategy and that there was widespread 'incompetency, disorganization and confusion at the front.'[12] Not the least perturbing feature of Currie's presentation of the recent past was his contention that the sixteen thousand Canadian casualties suffered in the mud of Passchendaele had been in vain because British strategy had failed to follow up the costly gains made there. The Canadian ministers agreed that Borden should confront the British politicians with some home truths.[13]

On the second day of the conference, Borden, following full consultation with his cabinet colleagues,[14] delivered his indictment of the organization of the British war effort. The chief of the general staff, Sir Henry Wilson, left the room when Borden began, and the Canadians were gratified when Lloyd George, always happy to receive reinforcement in his own war against the generals, recalled Wilson to hear Borden's address. Borden asserted that Currie's account of Passchendaele and its aftermath and his strictures on many British generals for technical incompetence, which left them ignorant of such crucial matters as developments since 1914 in the uses of barbed wire, could lead only to the conclusion that 'the unfortunate results which have been obtained during the past year, and especially during the past three months, are due to lack of foresight, lack of preparation, and to defects of system and organization.' He was certain that as far as the Canadian forces were concerned there was nothing lacking in the quality of the men themselves. Borden was bold enough to suggest that some of the fault lay in the British refusal to appoint anyone but a professional soldier to a rank above brigadier general; the men with the greatest battle experience were often thus barred from participation in decisions on strategy. Had Canada followed such a policy she would have had few capable leaders at the top and Currie himself, a businessman before the war, would have been excluded. Borden could find no merit whatever in a policy that amounted 'to scrapping the brains of the nation in the greatest struggle of history.' But the Canadians would not allow the past errors of British leadership to weaken their resolve. 'We came over' Borden declared 'to fight in earnest; and Canada will fight it out to the end. But earnestness must be expressed in organization, foresight, preparation. Let the past bury its dead, but for God's sake let us get down to earnest endeavour and hold this line until the Americans can come in and help us to sustain it to the end.'[15]

Prime Minister W.F. Massey of New Zealand supported the Canadian charges fully, declaring that at Passchendaele his countrymen had been 'simply shot down like rabbits' because of British ineptness in the over-all direction of the operation.[16] Rowell was more than satisfied with Borden's performance and was confident that 'his frankness and force ... will stir things up here.'[17] The immediate result of Borden's initiative was the establishment of a subcommittee of the War Cabinet, composed of the British and Dominion prime ministers, to make a thorough study of the steps needed to win the war. Although the committee prepared a report it was quickly outmoded by the events leading to the early conclusion of the war.

Every day in London reinforced Rowell's impression of the urgent need for shaking things up and demonstrated how difficult it would be to get the information he needed for the War Committee. Clearly he could not do so if he had to return to Canada at the end of June as he had planned and hoped to do, and he and Borden agreed that he should remain in England instead of returning when Mewburn and Ballantyne arrived.[18] He was increasingly distressed by the apparent casualness in high places and concluded that 'they are not accustomed to do business over here as expeditiously as we do.' At least he had learned enough to be satisfied that the Allied need for men was without doubt greater than the need for food, and that Canada had done the right thing in deciding to cancel exemptions even at the risk of hampering farm production.[19]

At the end of June a recess in the sittings of the War Cabinet gave the Canadian cabinet ministers an opportunity to make a five-day visit to France. Of the four Canadian divisions, only one was in the line, and most of the Canadians in France had been enjoying a rest from fighting for the past three months. The Second Division had just left the front, having been replaced by the Third. Shortly after his arrival at General Currie's headquarters Rowell asked to be taken to see one of the units in the Second Division, the Royal 22nd Regiment of Quebec. He was escorted by the brigade commander, Brigadier General J.M. Ross, son of an old Liberal party worker in the village of Embro in Oxford County, who assured Rowell that there was no better body of men under his command than the French Canadians of the 22nd Regiment. Later that day he attended the church parade of the Fourth Infantry Brigade, 'the Ontario Brigade,' with General Robert Rennie, who had been in command of the brigade on his previous visit two years earlier. 'It was one of the most impressive services I have ever attended,' he told Nell during a lengthy account of his time in France. 'They were drawn up out in an open field, every man a veteran. They had just come out of the line after three months hard work. The sky above was perfectly blue, the country side beautiful in the summer sun – and as these men sang our familiar hymns I confess a lump arose in my throat. All through the service you could hear the sound of the guns.' Accepting General Rennie's invitation to say a few words to the men, Rowell 'reminded them that at home in all the churches of Canada the people were on that day ... thinking of and praying for them ... that we wished them Godspeed and a safe return.'

Canadians who would never return lay in their thousands in nearby cemeteries. He placed flowers on the graves of the sons of several friends, including that of G.P. Graham's only son. Fortunately, all of his six nephews then in France had survived, and in visits to additional Canadian units he was able to meet each of them, as well as scores of other young men whom he had known at home and to whose parents he would report on his return to Canada.

In Paris, Borden and Rowell attended a meeting of the Supreme Allied War Council. The two Canadian ministers were introduced to the council by Lloyd George and they remained to listen to the discussion of current Allied war strategy. Rowell was much impressed by 'the solidarity and strength (though Latins)' of Prime Minister Clemenceau, Foreign Minister Pichon, and Marshall Foch of France and by Orlando, premier of Italy, and his foreign minister, Sonnino. This 'unique and impressive assembly' offered a ground of hope for the future: 'If nations can form a league and meet around a common council table to wage a war, they can also form a league to maintain peace. We must pray that such a result will follow this cruel war.'[20]

Returning to London, Rowell was distressed to find that the War Cabinet, as well as the Imperial Conference, was much concerned with post-war imperial relations. He was still firm in the view that the first task was to win the war; otherwise the problems of imperial reorganization might be resolved in catastrophe. But the British government was insisting on discussion of imperial issues, and therefore they could not be ignored entirely. Rowell's chief contribution was to encourage Borden to stand on the intent of Resolution 9 of the Imperial Conference of 1917 – that constitutional relations within the empire should not be dealt with until after the war. He had no objection to making immediate changes of procedure where they would facilitate the prosecution of the war or when they would merely give formal recognition to a position already held by the Dominions. Thus, before the war conference he gave strong support to plans which he had already discussed at length with Lord Beaverbrook for the establishment of an imperial news service. Rowell stressed the value of such a service in stimulating the Dominions' war effort through the provision of more adequate information about their respective endeavours, and underlined the primary role that must be assigned to the press rather than to the direct action of government in establishing the service.[21]

Similarly, like Borden, Rowell supported Hughes' proposal for the improvement of communication between the Dominions and Britain by the abandonment of the practice under which Dominion prime ministers communicated with the British government through the governors general and the Colonial Office. His own view on this subject went rather further than the proposal that was eventually agreed upon. He would confine the questions dealt with directly through the prime ministers to those connected with the work of the Imperial War Cabinet. Each Dominion should appoint an assistant secretary to the War Cabinet, who would have access to all official papers; only in this way could there be full participation of the Dominions in the direction of the war effort. Rowell thought it a natural corollary of these developments to press for a definition of the position of the governor general that corresponded more closely to current practice: the governors general should cease to represent the Colonial Office and should have the same relation to their respective governments as had the king to the British government. In what seemed to be a reference to a future peacetime equivalent of the War Cabinet he proposed that governors general should be appointed by 'the imperial cabinet.'[22] Rowell anticipated considerable British resistance to the suggestion about the redefinition of the position of the representative of the crown in the Dominions; apparently Borden also recognized this difficulty and therefore did not advance the proposal. When Lloyd George presented a resolution on channels of communication for the consideration of the Imperial War Cabinet, his three proposals made no reference to the governor general.

Asked by Borden to comment on the resolution, Rowell found the first two sections entirely acceptable, since they provided for direct communication between Dominion prime ministers and the British prime minister on matters which the former deemed important and for Dominion representation at Imperial War Cabinet meetings by a cabinet minister from each Dominion when the prime minister was not in London. Unfortunately, there was no specific provision for the appointment of assistant secretaries from the Dominions as he had advocated. The third part of the resolution Rowell rejected quickly and firmly: he was certain its plan for the immediate appointment of a committee of British and Dominion representatives to consider the future organization of the Empire would not be approved by a majority of Canadians, and he urged Borden not to acquiesce in any such discussions; until the end of the war it would be better for each government to consider the matter independently.[23] Delegates from the other Dominions took a similar view, and Borden told the War Cabinet that there could be no discussion of constitutional changes until after the war.[24]

The eagerness of the British government to push the Dominions into new paths also seemed to be indicated by a sudden announcement in a luncheon speech from the colonial secretary, Walter Long, that the War Cabinet had approved a scheme for trade preference within the Empire. The Canadians were astonished since they were well aware that the question had never been discussed at any sessions they had attended. If Long's intention was to force the issue, Rowell regretted his action and urged Borden to refuse to discuss the subject at the present time: 'We have always insisted on maintaining our own fiscal independence, and in this case we should take the ground that this ... [is] a matter for the British Government and not for the Imperial War Cabinet. If they should choose to give us this preference well and good, but to have it announced as a decision of the Imperial War Cabinet might lead to misunderstandings between Great Britain and the Dominions.'[25] The matter was disposed of satisfactorily within a few days when Borden declared publicly that Long's announcement was made on behalf of the British government only and that imperial preference was not being discussed by either the Imperial War Cabinet or the Imperial War Conference.[26]

Only slightly less controversial was Australia's proposal to the Imperial War Conference for the post-war establishment of an Imperial Court of Appeal. Here Borden called on Rowell's legal knowledge to argue that there were already too many appeal courts open to Canadians and they were in no need of yet another. Canada was satisfied with the treatment Canadian cases received from the Judicial Committee of the Privy Council, Rowell asserted. If there was any desire for a change it was in the direction of the limitation of appeals: 'There is a growing ... opinion that our own Courts should be the final authority.'[27] Finally, Hughes and Borden prepared a resolution, which the Canadians could support without committing themselves, asking the British government to investigate the feasibility of an Imperial Court of Appeal and, if found practicable, to submit a plan to the Dominions for their consideration.[28]

Rowell was equally convinced that there should be no discussion of a plan prepared by the British Admiralty, on instructions from the Imperial War Conference of 1917, for the peacetime development of a unified imperial navy under an imperial authority of undefined character. Initially, Borden and C.C. Ballantyne, Canada's minister of naval service, were prepared to consider naval issues in a broad context, although they were agreed that the Admiralty's current proposal for a single navy was impossible. However, they were willing to consider a plan for joint control by Britain and the Dominions in wartime. Rowell feared that Borden was not sufficiently concerned about the manner in which Canada's control of her navy should be handed over to the imperial authority. Borden considered this a mere technicality. Rowell saw it as an act charged with symbolic significance: the transfer of authority must not take place automatically, but only by the action of the Canadian government, a method which would constitute 'a fuller recognition of our right to control our own affairs.'[29] It was soon evident that all the Dominions save Newfoundland agreed that a single navy was quite impracticable, and Borden informed the Admiralty that there was no point in discussing the proposition.[30] To

Rowell's relief the whole naval issue was left for examination after the end of the war.

Since Rowell was preparing to leave for Canada at the end of July he would miss the last meetings of the Imperial War Cabinet when there was to be discussion of British proposals on the terms of peace. Borden showed him the documents with a request for comments. One report in particular caught Rowell's attention – the report on the question of the disposal of German colonial territories. Noting that Canada, alone of the British nations, had no territorial ambitions and that among the other allies only the United States was in a similar position, he concluded that 'we would appear therefore to have a special responsibility to keep in their supreme place the moral issues for which we entered the conflict, and not permit the issue to become one for the acquisition of territory, however desirable this might at the time appear.' He had no doubt that the parts of the Empire directly concerned would like to have adjacent German territories, but that was not a cause to justify prolonging the war; Canada must declare herself against the acquisition of territories by any part of the Empire.[31]

Right up until his last day in London, Rowell spent most of his time outside the sessions of the War Cabinet and War Conference trying to get the information he needed for the work of the War Committee at home. In discussions with the minister of munitions, Winston Churchill, the food controller, J.R. Clynes, Lord Milner, secretary for war, and Sir Auckland Geddes, minister of national service, and in numerous government departments, he tried to get answers to his questions about British needs and plans for the future.[32] The net result was far less than satisfying. To the assistant secretary of the War Cabinet, L.S. Amery, he expressed his disappointment frankly: he had been unable to discover any comprehensive plan for using the Allied superiority in manpower and munitions to achieve victory. Declaring that 'the conduct of the war is the most gigantic business enterprise to which the mind of man has ever been directed' and admitting all the uncertainties that might upset the best laid plans in so vast an undertaking, he could still find no excuse for the failure of Allied military advisors to produce a program for victory, and he implied that British politicians must be condemned for their failure to extract one from the military experts. The questions raised by Borden nearly six weeks earlier at the opening of the Imperial War Cabinet meetings had not been answered, and most of them had not even been discussed. Rowell conceded that he had acquired some useful information in England, but it was insufficient to permit him to make any clear recommendations to the War Committee in Ottawa on the future mobilization of Canada's resources. Under the present 'policy of drift' the war could be lost or unnecessarily prolonged. 'If we fail' he told Amery 'it will not be because the rank and file of our armies have proved unequal to their task, but in spite of the dauntless courage and heroic achievements of our soldiers. It will be a failure of leadership and organization.'[33] There was no need to spell out the large share of the responsibility that would have to be borne by British statesmen.

His extended stay in Britain left him pessimistic about the quality of much of English life. After a dinner at Buckingham Palace for the overseas politicians he sent Nell a full report of the carefully organized informality of an occasion that permitted all the guests to chat with the king and queen and Princess Mary. George v, while 'not imposing looking' struck him as 'a very agreeable man who tries to do his duty as he sees it and to get a reasonable amount of enjoyment out of his life as he goes along.' Queen Mary was undoubtedly 'queenly looking. She would be a striking figure anywhere and impressed you as solid, serious, sensible, I should say wholly out of sympathy with the smart set here.' Princess Mary appeared as 'a good wholesome unspoiled English girl entirely lacking that smart or pert quality so often seen in your young girls to-day and which – unconscious as they may be of it – is such a real handicap to them.' Altogether he decided that 'the influence of the court on the life of the nation would be good, like that of Queen Victoria. They exemplify the domestic virtues.' But he had serious doubts about whether that influence would prevail: 'The more one sees of social life over here among many people who are supposed to be leaders the less one likes it and the more one thinks they need some real moral renewal to give them real moral enthusiasms. The smoking among women is more widespread than I had imagined and drinking wine etc. has of course become the custom.' At the end of a long letter it was one o'clock in the morning. But, he told Nell, 'when we are chatting together time does not count – not for us at least.' Yet he had counted exactly the days that must pass before he could sail for home.[34]

The country to which Rowell returned was noticeably more restless than the one he had left two months before, and it was becoming daily more critical of the Union Government. There was still much criticism of the abolition of exemptions and extensive resistance to it. Of the seventy thousand exemptions cancelled across the country, about thirty thousand were in Quebec. Everywhere there were many men who had failed to report, and in Quebec the proportion amounted to more than half of those who should have reported.[35] A few of the defaulters had been prosecuted, but the task of pursuing so many men was formidable, and on 2 August the government had declared an amnesty until 24 August. Defaulters or deserters who came forward by that date were assured that they would not suffer penalty for their earlier negligence: after that they would be subject to the judgment of courts martial. When the amnesty expired, only about ten thousand men had taken advantage of it, and the burden of enforcing the Military Service Act still rested heavily on the government. Many citizens who wanted a more aggressive war effort were criticizing the preoccupation of so many cabinet ministers with affairs in Britain, while opposition Liberals who merely wanted to embarrass the government, took up the cry. Even the *Globe* and the *Star* joined in the clamour of much of the press that Rowell and the other ministers had been in England too long.

Obviously it was time for the Union Government, and for the president of the Privy Council in particular, to do some political fence-mending. Within a week of his return Rowell had arranged to give three addresses in his own riding. By the time he appeared before the electors of Durham in Newcastle the Canadian Corps had taken a crucial part in the battle of Amiens. He tried to make the occasion a patriotic gathering rather than a political meeting. This latest achievement confirmed what Rowell had heard on every side overseas: the Canadian Corps 'is the finest single fighting unit on the Western front' and General Currie 'one of the outstanding generals of the war.' He renewed his pledge that as long as he remained a member of the government he would do everything in his power 'to see that adequate reinforcements are provided to carry on the work for which so many have given their lives.'[36] The next day at Port Hope his main purpose was to explain Borden's continued absence from Canada as essential to the nation's interest in imperial and international affairs and in accordance with the judgment of all his cabinet colleagues.[37] Finally, at Millbrook, Rowell gave a detailed defence of the major policies of the government in the ten months since its formation: 66,542 men had gone overseas during that time, all but seven thousand of them conscripts, and Canada had thus been able to keep her divisions up to full strength, with the result that Canadian casualties in the heavy fighting of recent weeks had been much lower than among the forces of the other Allied nations. At home the money market had been stabilized by the regulation of the sale of securities and the success of the Victory Loans. The prohibition on imports of non-essential goods had also helped to provide the funds advanced to Britain for the purchase in Canada of munitions, ships, and food. Government control over certain aspects of industry and over fuel and food supplies had made the war effort more efficient. The economic burdens of the war had been more widely spread, he told an audience composed mainly of farmers and their wives, by a business profits tax 'said to be the highest imposed on business in any of the nations in the war.' By its prohibition legislation the government had destroyed an enemy that Lloyd George had described in 1915 as Britain's greatest – drink – and had thereby contributed to the defeat of the other two enemies, Germany and Austria. And the future democratic basis of the government of Canada had been broadened by the granting of the franchise to all women.[38]

Rowell's activities on the public platform involved him once more in open battle with the more militant Laurier Liberals. Murphy and the group around him who had made Rowell their chief target were well aware of the good impression that his hard work and debating ability had made on the House of Commons;[39] they may also have feared that his participation in the Imperial Conference would further add to his prestige. After Rowell's Newcastle speech Lucien Cannon and C.G. Power, law partners and Liberal members of Parliament for Dorchester and Quebec South respectively, protested to Rowell and sent copies of their letter to the press, thus beginning an exchange that was widely publicized in Ontario and Quebec for the next two weeks. Noting Rowell's references to the necessity of providing adequate reinforcements for the troops now overseas, Cannon and Power professed to see in them a forecast of 'a new levy of Canadians for service at the front.'[40]

Rowell could see no reason for misunderstanding or misconstruing his speech. He had not suggested a new levy but had merely reiterated the government's determination 'to stand behind its mandate from the people to back up the men at the front.' Cannon and Power might more usefully employ their time in encouraging the ten thousand defaulters in the military district of Quebec to report before the expiration of the amnesty. Since Power had enlisted early in the war and had 'fought gallantly at the front,' Rowell could reply 'cheerfully' to him. Cannon's position was different. During a by-election in Quebec at the beginning of 1917 Cannon was reported to have said that Canada had done enough in the war, and his statement had been reprinted in the German press. 'The people of Germany were thus encouraged to believe that the people of Canada ... were no longer willing to fight against Prussian militarism, which would destroy your race and language, if it could, which has desecrated the altars of your Church in Belgium and left ruin and devastation in its path wherever it has gone.'[41]

If Cannon and Power hoped that their letter would elicit a reply that would permit them to rekindle the fires lit by Murphy then Rowell's call to atonement gave them their chance. Cannon now took up the cudgels alone. Rowell had not answered his questions on manpower, he charged, nor had he said when 'the government would stop tearing up the constitution and ruling the country by Order-in-Council.' Questioning Rowell's figures on defaulters in Quebec, he contended that there were no more than elsewhere, and those were due to government blunders and to the Conservative-Nationalist alliance of 1911, to which Rowell had become a party by joining forces with Borden and his Nationalist colleagues. The old charges that Rowell had led in 'the plot' to betray Laurier were rehearsed again, followed by the suggestion that it was unseemly for the president of the Privy Council to get his information on the Dorchester by-election from the German press. Cannon's control of language was fully demonstrated as he directed his attention to Rowell's warning that Germany would destroy his race, language and religion. 'What were you thinking about? my race! your papers publish every day gross insults against it; in your speeches you purposely revile it. My language! you hope it will no longer be heard on the lips of our French-Canadian children in Ontario. My religion!' Despite Murphy's eloquent defence of 'the French religious now dying for their country ...

remorse has not yet wrung ... an apology from your sectarian heart. I pray you! Do cure your audacity!'[42]

Rowell could see no value in the continuation of this public squabble, and his reply was brief. Cannon's second letter would merely confirm the public in the view that he was opposed to backing up the men at the front. His position was the same as Bourassa's, 'with this great difference, that he [Bourassa] does not put them forth as being the sentiments of a Liberal, but frankly and openly as a nationalist.' Since the nation was engaged in a war and not a general election Rowell would not reply to Cannon's 'long and discursive political polemic ... The question of reinforcing our divisions ... was settled by the people of Canada in December last and all patriotic and public-spirited citizens may be expected to co-operate in carrying out the law.'[43]

Cannon's outburst was perhaps the least worrisome expression of hostility to Rowell and the government because there was nothing new in his charges. Much more alarming was the evidence that Union Government was losing people who had once been friends. The war news was growing steadily more heartening; early in September 1918 the Canadians added to their battle honours in the great struggle for Arras as the Allied armies moved steadily forward toward the Hindenburg Line; every day more Canadians dared to hope that the war would be over before the year's end. As the hope grew and the pressure to maintain a unified war spirit began to decline, the defects of the government, real and imagined, mounted.

On Borden's return from England Rowell pressed upon the prime minister the necessity for better publicity for the government to steady the public temper. When Borden agreed with his proposal that the immediate need would be met by a booklet 'wholly free of political bias' outlining the record of the Union Government, to be prepared by the secretary of the War Committee, Vincent Massey, Rowell followed up the suggestion by urging the establishment of a Union Government publicity office.[44] Such an agency was even more vital to the present government than the Liberal and Conservative press bureaus of the pre-coalition years, since the Union Government had no traditional party loyalty on which it could count for support. As 'a firm believer in the use of the press in creating public opinion,' Rowell urged the importance both for the government and the public interest that the public should have 'the correct version of the facts ... justifying the course of the government.'[45] He might also have added that while all members of the government had reasons for wanting a better press it was a matter of political life and death for the Liberal Unionists. They had burned their bridges as no Conservative had had to do in joining the coalition, and if their public turned against them on a large scale their political careers would be seriously threatened. But the complications inherent in Rowell's plan for a government publicity office were very great and the rest of the cabinet were even more aware of them than Rowell himself. The inevitable opposition charge that the Union Government publicity office and the Department of Public Information would be synonymous would be difficult to refute. Furthermore, the move proposed by Rowell would lead many observers to the conclusion that a new and permanent Unionist party had been formed; on that subject the members of the cabinet were uncertain and divided; it was not a problem that had to be faced until after the war and for the present it was best to shelve it.

In the meantime Rowell saw two steps which the government must take immediately. The first was to remedy some of the admitted deficiencies of the work of the War Committee by the establishment of a government department modelled on the British Department of National Service. Convinced by his investigations overseas that the British pattern of organization was applicable to Canada, Rowell urged that this procedure would produce a more systematic attack on the whole problem of the distribution of manpower than any that the Canadian government had yet been able to make.[46] A second demonstration of decisive action should be given, he proposed, by proceeding with the nationalization of the Grand Trunk Railway, whose board had for several months been refusing to accept the purchase price offered by the government. 'The Gordian knot' of the railway problem would be cut if the government took over the railway and operated it under the War Measures Act, leaving the question of compensation until later. Moreover, if the right type of top-ranking business and railway men were appointed to manage the public railway system it would give convincing proof of the feasibility of government ownership of railways and reflect credit on the Union Government.[47]

By the middle of September 1918 there was no longer any doubt about the outcome of the war. Increasingly, the government and the people of Canada were thinking of the new problems they would face with the advent of peace, although few believed that there could be an armistice before the end of the year. In mid-September Rowell set off on a three-week trip through western Canada to examine the administration of the Royal North West Mounted Police, which was under the jurisdiction of the Privy Council office, to arrange for more active measures to counteract anti-war propaganda in the west, especially in British Columbia, and to attend to his Okanagan interests.[48] His experiences on the prairies and the Pacific coast did nothing to weaken his conviction about the need for a Union Government publicity office, for there was clearly great hostility to the government everywhere. He urged Borden to come west himself, or at least to send one or two cabinet ministers as soon as possible.[49]

During Rowell's absence the attention of the cabinet was directed to the west by the receipt of a report prepared by C.H. Cahan, the Montreal Conservative lawyer who had been asked in the spring of 1918 to investigate subversive activities in Canada. Cahan's lengthy submission showed extensive operations by Bolshevik organizations across the country, especially in western Canada.[50] Two weeks later an order-in-council banned organizations advocating the overthrow of government or private property by force, and fourteen parties or groups were specifically named as henceforth illegal.[51] Rowell had no quarrel with the intent of this measure, and he commended it to the members of the Women's Canadian Club of Vancouver. It would be particularly useful, he asserted, in enabling the government to deal with any infiltration of members of the International Workers of the World from the United States. The iww had been declared illegal south of the border and its president, Eugene V. Debs, had just been sentenced to ten years in prison for seditious utterance. If it were true, as rumour had it, that some of the iww leaders were planning to transfer their activities to Canada they would find no asylum, Rowell assured his audience, 'for they are the worst enemies honest and patriotic labour can have, and the government will be as vigilant in reaching and punishing them' as the American government. Of the loyalty and determination of the vast majority of Canadian workingmen he had no doubt: they would 'come through' in the same spirit as the Canadians who were now locked in a life and death struggle with the German army.[52]

Due to his absence from Ottawa Rowell had not seen the list of organizations included in the government ban, and he was surprised and distressed when he learned that it included the Social Democratic Party of Canada. Immediately on his return to the capital Rowell protested to the minister of justice, C.J. Doherty, that there was no reason whatever for banning the sDP, 'an organized labour party to which many of the leading members of labour belong,' and which should enjoy 'the same right of meeting, association, and of propaganda as any other political party in Canada possesses.' Moreover, he urged the cabinet to re-examine the general provisions of the ban to see if they were not broader than necessary and 'liable to an interpretation which would include associations which are neither revolutionary nor unpatriotic.'[53] Doherty had been assured by the commissioner of Dominion police only four months earlier that there was 'nothing sinister' about the sDP.[54] Now, when Doherty raised the question of the sDP, Cahan, who had just been appointed director of the newly established Public Safety Branch of the Department of Justice and was charged with policing activities under the War Measures Act, remained adamantly convinced that the sDP was a revolutionary party, an exponent of international socialism, and an opponent of the continuation of the war.[55] When the status of the sDP remained unchanged Rowell renewed his objection, this time going over Doherty's head to the prime minister. He had studied the history and constitution of the party and had concluded that there could be no justification for continuing a ban against 'a recognized political party.' 'If we wish to combat their ideas there is only one way to do it, and that is by combatting them in public argument or propaganda.' A policy of repression was not only contrary to the public interest, but also to the interest of a government which could not afford to alienate 'the progressive elements in the community, who, while out of sympathy with the programme of the Social Democratic Party, still insist on freedom of thought and freedom of speech on social and economic questions.' That his argument was all too well founded was proven by an editorial in that day's *Ottawa Citizen* listing the respected public men in other countries who had been associated with the SDP. That was only one example of the legitimate hostility that would be directed at the government if it persisted, especially just at the end of the war, in suppressing a democratic party that had existed unmolested in the country for over ten years.[56] Later, when the question was discussed in council, Rowell was supported strongly by T.A. Crerar who contended that the SDP was very like the British Labour party and clearly within the democratic tradition. Despite that, Crerar charged that Cahan seemed to have made the SDP the object of his special attention: its headquarters in Winnipeg had been raided and broken up, its executive in Toronto had felt it necessary to disband and to destroy its literature, and thereafter four of its members, along with other party members in Ontario, had been arrested.[57] Rowell and Crerar prevailed, and within a few days the SDP was explicitly excluded from the list of banned organizations.

Rowell found another item in government policy deficient in execution, although not in intention. While he was in the west an order-in-council was drafted prohibiting strikes and lockouts during the war.[58] He was back in Ottawa in time to agree to its proclamation, which he did in the belief that leaders of organized labour had been consulted and had agreed to what he fully recognized as 'drastic action.' As soon as the measure was announced there were loud outcries from labour leaders. Tom Moore, president of the Trades and Labor Congress of Canada, denounced it as tantamount to 'the abolition of the foundation of industrial liberty,' and denied that there had been any prior consultation with labour. Senator Gideon Robertson, vice-president of the Telegraphers, and chairman of the labour committee of the cabinet, responded with a statement declaring that the government was guilty of no breach of faith with labour, that the order only formalized agreements reached at the conferences held with labour leaders earlier in the year, and that it applied with equal force to lockouts by employers. Anyway, he asked, how could labour's interests be seriously infringed by a government which had appointed labour representatives to eight committees concerned with the war effort?[59] The labour leaders were not mollified; for most of them, Robertson's defence of the government was further justification of the caution that had led the recent annual convention of the Trades and Labor Congress to refuse to compromise labour's independence by making an official nomination to the office of undersecretary of state for labour, the office that Rowell had been so eager to establish.

Despite labour's rejection of the undersecretaryship Rowell believed that since the formation of the Union Government some progress had been made in establish-

Parliament Hill, Ottawa, 11 November 1918

TOO LATE!

A Solid Quebec
Will Vote to
Rule All Canada
Only a Solid
Ontario Can
Defeat Them

Citizens' Union Committee

Unionist electioneering, 15 December 1917

ing a better relationship between government and labour. At least this year the annual meeting of the Trades and Labor Congress had not debated the advisability of outright resistance to conscription as the convention of 1917 had done, nor was there now as much talk of a general strike as there had been then. But any advance seemed to be jeopardized now, and Rowell thought that the administration had been put in an extremely difficult position that made some explanation imperative.[60] No satisfactory explanation ever came, labour continued to protest, and the issue was only resolved with the coming of peace and the revocation of the order.

While Canadians were being exhorted to put one more Victory Loan over the top and many schools were closed and public meetings cancelled across the country in an effort to check the killing influenza epidemic sweeping Canada along with the rest of the world, the news from the front grew daily more cheering. By 7 November the Toronto *Globe* announced in large headlines: 'Hun, Hat in Hand, Waits on Foch.' On the night of 10 November the Canadian Corps took the town of Mons to complete its part in the great Allied advance that ended the war. To many Canadians it seemed fitting that their men should have carried the war back to the scene of the first engagement between the British and the Germans more than four years earlier. At the same time they were satisfied that their prime minister was already on his way to Europe, confident that the sacrifices of Canadians on the field of battle would assure his country of a voice in the shaping of peace.

In Ottawa on 11 November the president of the Privy Council presided at a service of thanksgiving on Parliament Hill. Rowell told the quietly jubilant but sombre audience of politicians, members of the armed forces, veterans, and general citizenry who stood in the cold rain under a dark sky: 'To-day marks the close of the old order and dawn of the new. It is the coronation day of democracy.'[61]

16
The new order

'The Hohenzollerns, the Hapsburgs, and the Romanoffs ... have all gone ... In the struggle to preserve our own freedom we have given freedom to these other peoples ... we have made the world safe for democracy abroad.' Ten days after the armistice Rowell was in Massey Hall addressing the International Patriotic Rally organized by the Empire Club of Toronto. As the welcome of the chairman, Lieutenant Governor Sir John Hendrie, and the addresses of Governors James Cox of Ohio and C.H. Whitman of New York testified, the gathering was planned as a celebration of Anglo-American unity in the achievement of victory. Rowell, representing the government of Canada, struck a mildly discordant note by emphasizing the primacy of the Royal Navy in maintaining the vital freedom of the seas during the war. His remarks reflected the widespread feeling in Britain and the Dominions that in some quarters the Americans were credited with having won the war almost single-handed, and that President Wilson's commitment to the principle of post-war freedom of the seas was altogether too vague to be reassuring. Rowell's declaration that Britain should and would insist on an interpretation of freedom of the seas consistent with the interests and obligations of her worldwide commonwealth was greeted with enthusiastic applause. But most of his address concerned the outlines of a new democracy at home, a theme that was perhaps not quite what the sponsors of the meeting had expected.

A gathering that included many influential Torontonians offered a platform for the presentation of Rowell's conviction that the principles to whose triumph overseas Canadians had contributed so fully must be expressed in the solution of social and industrial questions at home; otherwise the war would have been in vain for most Canadians. 'The form which that expression will take will largely depend upon the attitude which public men, leaders of industry and labour, assume at the present time.' By its part in the war, labour had won 'the right to a new place in ... political, industrial and social life ... and the frank recognition of this fact will broaden the basis and strengthen the foundation upon which our democratic institutions rest.'[1]

Two days later Rowell elaborated the means by which democracy could be made safe in a sermon in Metropolitan Church in commemoration of one hundred years of Methodism in Toronto. Quoting the assertion of the English rationalist historian, Lecky, that Methodism had saved England from the horrors of the French Revolution, Rowell asked whether the new day of democracy would arrive in Canada in the way it had come to England or as it had in France and Russia and as it might yet come in Austria and Germany, through revolution? In Russia the pre-revolutionary identification of the church with the old autocracy made it no more worthy of the confidence of the Russian people than the political leaders of the old order; consequently, in the present revolutionary chaos in Russia the church was powerless to serve as a rallying point around which order and justice could be established. Similarly, in spite of the intellectual achievements of German theologians, the German church had lost its moral enthusiasm, had justified German crimes in the war, and was in the minds of most liberal reformers associated with autocracy. Thus there was little religious idealism in contemporary German socialism; indeed, one development within German socialism had produced Russian Bolshevism, 'which is essentially materialistic in its conception of life and simply means the substitution of hand workers in control of the Government of the country for the autocracy that previously ruled.' German conduct during the war had shown conclusively that knowledge and science were only a curse to man unless controlled by moral and religious ideals. The war could also teach the world another important lesson, 'the fact that our humanity is essentially one.' The ultimate irrelevance of national boundaries meant that the murder of an Austrian prince sent Canadians to die across the sea and 'Spanish influenza,' originating among the impoverished peoples of Central Europe, brought death and misery to Canada.

Above all, Rowell declared, in terms typical of the post-war idealism of Canadian Methodists, the war had 'vindicated the moral conscience of the race.' The willingness to sacrifice and the moral indignation aroused by the horrors perpetrated by Germany had 'produced a passion for righteousness and justice, a determination that the wrongs would be righted and the guilty ones punished ... and that moral energy and enthusiasm which has sent men forth to die emanates from the teaching and preaching of the gospel of Christ.' Only the Christian church could give the leadership needed in passing from the old order into the new.[2]

Probably few Methodists would have disagreed with Rowell's comments on the social order in European countries, but to be more specific about the Canadian scene was to contribute to the controversy currently raging in the church and which a month before had produced a great deal of heat in the meeting of the Methodist General Conference. As finally accepted by the Conference, the report of the Committee on Evangelism and Social Service asserted that labour ought to have a share in the management and the profits and risks of industry. Pointing to co-operative stores, factories, and steamship lines in Britain as models of 'democracy in industry,' it denounced the company town as a menace to democracy because its citizens were robbed of their freedom of social and political action. Further, the report advocated a national system of old age insurance 'in which the annuity paid shall be based upon the average earnings of the country each year of a man's effective life,' and 'the nationalization of our natural resources, such as mines, waterpower, fisheries, forest, the means of communication, and public utilities.'[3]

Rowell was nominally a delegate to the General Conference, but his public duties had prevented him from attending most of the sessions and he had taken no part in the debate on the disputed report. Did it represent his way into the new order? His own comment on the new Methodist social program left room for more than one interpretation:

> While we may not all agree with just the form in which it is expressed, I believe all thoughtful and wise students must agree with the spirit behind that expression ... In the new day that is coming I trust we will not be afraid of more collective action than we have had in the past ... and do not let us be terrified by names ... Can we continue to justify capital in any form, exercising its power to limit and repress the rights of those who may chance to come under its control. The very spirit which prompted us to fight this war ... must mean that Governments and people alike will be prepared to control the power of the strong for the defence of the weak in every walk of life ... I venture to think that in the days that lie ahead there will be much less of competition and vastly more of co-operation as between employers and employees ... if there are employers who do not recognize this fact they are sinning against their own interests.[4]

What did the words of the Methodist layman mean when translated into specific proposals by a member of a coalition cabinet? Rowell had had a chance to work this out over the last weekend in October when he had discussed social and industrial questions with 'the Toronto friends' who had encouraged him to join the Union Government, most of whom were active Methodists. Post-war problems would be even more difficult than those of the war, they had all agreed, and the people of Canada would not be in a normal condition after the strain of four years of war. If the situation were met without adequate plans nobody could predict what might happen. On the basis of his Toronto discussions Rowell outlined for Borden a program for early action by the Union Government, one which he believed was definite and constructive enough 'to quicken the imagination of all patriotic citizens' and prevent immediate reversion to old party loyalties.

First of all, the government should proceed with its railway policy by taking over at once both the Grand Trunk and the Grand Trunk Pacific railways, preferably with their agreement but without it if necessary. The services of these two railways, along with those of the Canadian Northern and the Intercolonial, must be co-ordinated under the strongest management available, and a development program begun to enable the publicly owned system to compete with the CPR. The government railways could be used to assist in the transition to a peacetime economy if orders for rails and rolling stock were placed with the steel companies now, so that there would be a minimum break in their operations when munitions production ended.

Rowell was thoroughly behind the initiative already taken by the government to extend Canadian overseas trade and stimulate the domestic economy through a shipbuilding program to provide merchant fleets for the Great Lakes and for all the main routes of world shipping. This must be accompanied by deepening the St Lawrence and Welland Canals so that standard-size ocean vessels could navigate as far as Fort William. But he would go still further: under the supervision of a peacetime equivalent of the War Trade Board, and in connection with the government railways and steamships, he would establish 'a trading company with the principal Canadian importers and exporters as shareholders' to promote the development of foreign trade. To facilitate this expansion the government should encourage Canadian banks to establish branches in Africa, South America, and the Far East.

Another area of direct government action should be the expansion of the hydro-electric potentialities along the St Lawrence and at Niagara and other sites, under a government board composed of the best businessmen who could be secured for the public service. In making the proposal that the federal government enter this field Rowell clearly had no doubt that such action was within its constitutional power.[5]

Rowell now renewed proposals in areas whose importance he had been urging on Borden for several months – housing and public health. In housing he wanted the federal government to make substantial funds available to the provinces for loan to the municipalities as housing subsidies, and to establish detailed standards for facilities included, quality of building, and garden areas. Recalling his pre-war visits to the new garden cities of England, he told Borden that only someone who had seen these developments could 'adequately appreciate what it would mean ... if the government were to carry out a comprehensive housing programme.'[6]

During the summer the government had sounded out the provinces to ascertain their receptivity to a system of federal housing loans. Ontario was the most interested province; the Hearst administration had already established a housing committee under the chairmanship of Sir John Willison, empowered as a temporary measure to make available to municipalities loans at 5 per cent from a fund of $2 million, on condition that the municipalities put up funds as well and that certain specifications regarding total costs and sites were met.[7] But the question had remained unsettled for many months. Several of Rowell's cabinet colleagues, including the most influential Ontario Conservative and minister of finance, Sir Thomas White, were less than enthusiastic about subsidized housing, especially if it were to involve the federal government.[8] But Rowell was unwilling to let the question drop.

The Dominion government should also take a direct part, Rowell urged, in promoting the health of Canadians by creating a federal Department of Health to work in co-operation with provincial departments. Army medical examinations had shown how great was the wastage of manpower because of ill health. Improved health would be a contribution not only to the well being and happiness of individuals but to the whole post-war economy. And, more immediately, there was the large problem of mounting a nationwide attack on the control of venereal disease; already the incidence of this disease had increased notably with the return of numbers of men from overseas, and it was bound to get worse with general demobilization.

In co-operation with the provinces the Dominion government should at once work out a comprehensive scheme for improving facilities for technical and agricultural education, including more programs of practical training in the high schools along lines outlined in the current British Education Bill. And for the longer term a vigorous policy to encourage immigration was needed to keep the economy expanding.

The labour committee of the cabinet should begin immediately to study means of developing more co-operative relations between labour and capital. The system of federal labour exchanges established at the last session of Parliament should be extended to diminish the impact of the economic dislocation that the closing of the munitions plants and the return of the soldiers was bound to bring. A federal eight-hour day law should be enacted for the whole country, to be shortened if extensive unemployment developed. And, in consultation with the provinces, the federal government should develop a scheme of old age pensions, and unemployment and sickness insurance.

Altogether, Rowell's program constituted intervention by government, and especially by the federal government, in the economic and social life of the nation on a scale unprecedented in Canada. The necessities of war had already accelerated such intervention in some fields; Rowell proposed to withdraw from none of them and to make the experience of the war years the springboard from which a new welfare state would be created in the coming decade. He had no illusions about the magnitude of the tasks he outlined. The building of the new Canada would require a vast reorganization and expansion of the administrative machinery of government and the recruitment to the civil service and to administrative boards of the best brains of the country. It would mean government expenditures of a size unknown in peacetime. Here again, the wartime experience could be capitalized upon; he was confident that 'the people of Canada have had such a training during the period of the war in lending money to the Government that we could secure the necessary funds from them to carry out a great constructive development policy.' A society that had proven its capacity to mobilize its human and material resources for war could surely do as much to assist its citizens in creating the better world for which the war had been fought.[9]

Some of Rowell's articles of policy were shortly being discussed in cabinet and it was agreed to establish a Department of Health.[10] But any delineation of an extensive legislative program hinged on the settlement of the question of the continued existence of the government. Should an administration formed specifically as a win-the-war government remain in office after the signing of the armistice? Rowell had no doubt about his course for the next few months and he readily joined the other Liberal Unionists in assuring Borden of their intention of remaining in the cabinet. That settled, an effort was made to strengthen the cabinet and to effect some minor reorganization. At last it was agreed to bring in F.F. Pardee as an additional Liberal, but he had no desire to join what might well prove to be a dying ministry.[11] Nor was it a propitious moment for renewed efforts to secure French Canadian representation. That question had not been forgotten since the failure of Rowell's attempt to interest Dr H.S. Béland, the Liberal member of Parliament for Three Rivers, who had just been released from three years in a German prison camp and had returned to Canada on board the ship that brought Rowell home from England.[12] Unfortunately, no French Canadian candidate for cabinet membership had since been found. Nor was Borden now able to make any more progress with cabinet reorganization. Rowell agreed to accept the portfolio of Trade and Commerce, but Calder put up such strenuous objections that Borden withdrew the offer and made it instead to C.C. Ballantyne, who turned it down.[13] In the end there was no cabinet shuffle and the members all remained where they were.

Decisions within the Union Government could do nothing to prevent speculation and manœuvre among Laurier Liberals. At least some of the activity among the Liberal opposition was known to Rowell through Atkinson who was still in frequent communication with P.C. Larkin. Laurier thought that Rowell had gone 'clean over to the Tories,' especially in supporting the understanding that Laurier believed the Borden government had made at the Imperial Conference the preceding summer to give assistance to British protectionists. If that were so, said Laurier, 'the line of cleavage between us is final and irrevocable ... the moment protection is introduced in Great Britain with a view to bargaining for favours between the Mother Country and the colonies, that moment will be the signal of disruption.'[14] Atkinson, through Larkin, assured Laurier that Borden and Rowell both had precisely his own view on imperial preference, but if Great Britain offered Canada a trade preference for reasons of her own, Canada could not refuse it, although she would certainly take no initiative. Laurier found it difficult to accept these assurances, although he admitted that his assessment of Rowell's position on imperial preference was derived partly from inference from the fact that 'he has aligned himself with the big interests who .. are promoting the policy.' More than that, Laurier admitted that 'on the whole, I believe him to be a tory in his very bones. I confess that I may be prejudiced. His last campaign and his appeals to the passions of his audiences against Quebec was vile, and this perhaps may have biased my judgment. I do not believe that I have ever been carried from my moorings by prejudices, and I will be only too glad to be convinced of my error, if really I am in error.'[15] Larkin himself thought the Liberal party could get along well enough without Rowell were it not for the women's vote, which he admitted he had unwisely discounted in the last election. 'It is an unknown quantity and he is the kind of man that can affect it. He appeals so strongly to sentiment and they are so ignorant of economics.'[16]

When Atkinson raised with Rowell the questions that concerned Laurier, Rowell was astounded at such misunderstanding, pointing out for Laurier's eventual attention his opposition not only to imperial preference but to 'any form of centralization within the Empire' and stating that, far from being identified with 'the big interests,' he was in fact openly attacked by them as the author of the act limiting packers' profits. As reported by Larkin, the most important part of Rowell's conversation with Atkinson was in the Liberal editor's remark that 'if Mr Rowell was to be ostracized, then of course his friends would be also, ... a threat that if the Party was not going to make room for Mr Rowell, then it would not get the support of Mr J.E. Atkinson and the *Star*.' Larkin was sure that Atkinson would change his attitude if it once became clear that Rowell was on the losing side.[17]

In the weeks immediately after the armistice the Murphy-Dewart Liberals renewed their campaign to control the post-war Liberal party. They were adamant in the belief that the return of Rowell was to big a price to pay for the *Star*'s support,[18] despite the fact that they had been trying for over a year to obtain a reliable journalistic mouthpiece in Ontario.[19] At the same time the Murphy group had intensified efforts to get Ontario Liberals organized in three regions, one advantage of which was to reduce the control of Toronto, whence most of the 'traitors' and their money had come.[20] Now Murphy was trying to prod Laurier into holding a series of organization meetings, including a national convention, as quickly as possible before the break-up of the Union Government and the return of the

Unionists began. Only thus could he hope to keep control of the party firmly in the hands of the 'loyalists.' Much to Murphy's disgust, Laurier preferred to delay, and at the organization meeting of the Western Ontario Liberal Association held ten days after the armistice the Liberal leader's reference to a future national convention included no indication of its probable date.[21]

The camp of the Laurier Liberals was not the only scene of preparation for the renewal of party warfare. No one conversant with the workings of the Conservative party, least of all Borden, was in any doubt about the purpose of the banquet staged in Toronto on 28 November in honour of the leading Conservative opponent of coalition, Hon. Robert Rogers. The rousing reception accorded by six hundred Ontario Conservatives to Rogers' appeal for a return to normal party politics was evidence that many Conservatives were eager to break up the present government.[22] If Rogers had his way Rowell would be the first Liberal to go, for no group of Liberals was so much hated by his wing of the Conservatives as Rowell and the 'uplifters.'

More distressing to Liberal Unionists than developments among either Laurier Liberals or Conservatives were signs of discontent among their own supporters, notably on the prairies. By the end of November the former Liberal premier of Saskatchewan, Walter Scott, who had earlier supported the coalition, came out in the pages of his paper, the *Moose Jaw Times*, against the continuation of the present administration, and the cry that the government had outlived its usefulness was taken up by other elements in the Saskatchewan Liberal press. But for the moment there was no significant revolt among Liberal Unionists in Ontario, and Rowell was under no pressure to reconsider his position. The movement among some of his cabinet colleagues, led by Meighen, to try to put a stop to the developing political uncertainty by announcing early in the new year the formation of a permanent Unionist party, held little appeal.[23] He would continue in the government as a Liberal Unionist until there was some clear reason to change.

This was the position he declared in his most important political statement in the weeks immediately following the peace, made before an audience of his own constituents in Bowmanville on the anniversary of the victory of the Union government at the polls. Reviewing the government's legislative and administrative achievements during its year in office, he found them more impressive than those of any other government in Canadian history. Clearly it was the imperative duty of that government to carry on, against all appeals to party until the men returning from the front had resumed their places in civilian life.

For some weeks he had been looking for an appropriate occasion to reply to Murphy. The patriotic considerations that had dictated silence until the end of the war no longer held, and there were increasingly persuasive political reaons for speaking. A rebuttal of Murphy might help to lessen the effectiveness of his Liberal enemies' attempts to keep alive the religious and racial divisions of the war, and thus in due course might contribute to the revival of a genuine Liberal party, although at the moment that revival seemed a long way off. He found the immediate occasion for a reply to Murphy during a report to his own constituents on the first year of Union Government.

He would reply, but he saw no reason to apologize. He had said only what Bourassa and everyone else knew to be true – that the majority of the French Canadian clergy supported Bourassa in his opposition to conscription. In order to make political capital, certain opponents of Union Government had suggested that his remarks 'covered the members of religious orders who were French reservists ... who when called to the colours ... returned to France and fought as members of the French army.' At the time of his address he had not known that French priests in Canada were liable to military service and he had therefore made no special reference to them, but his attitude to all who had fought for France had been unmistakably clear. Had he paid a specific tribute to the members of the French clergy in Quebec who had gone home under the law of France to serve in the army he would also have pointed out how privileged were the clergy under the Canadian law that exempted them from compulsory military service and have observed that 'this imposed an additional obligation upon them to respond to the call of Canada, and to oppose and not to support Mr Bourassa.' The trouble, Rowell affirmed to his constituents, was not that he had misrepresented anybody but that he had 'told the truth about the situation then existing in the Province of Quebec.'

Distasteful as it was, Rowell thought it necessary to deal with 'other absurd and idle tales.' These included the story about his financial relations with the Ontario Liberal party. In fact, he had declined the salary of five thousand dollars offered by the party when it invited him to become leader; he had lost several thousand dollars a year in income because of the time he had devoted to public service, a fact that would not be worth mentioning save for the accusations that had been made.

The last story he must dispose of was that the Liberal Unionists were traitors to Laurier and Rowell had entered the Union Government because he was disappointed over his failure to oust Laurier from the federal leadership. The absurdity of this was clear to anyone who would look at the record: he had broken with Laurier on 'grave matters of public policy' about which there was no secret whatever and about which there had never been anything but the utmost frankness between himself and Laurier. Concluding with his well loved comparison between George Brown and his followers in 1864 and the Liberal Unionists of 1917, Rowell declared his conviction that Canada, during the present government's year in office, had not only assisted in overthrowing German autocracy but had 'laid anew the foundations of Canadian national unity on the solid basis of the common obligation of every citizen to serve the state in the hour of his country's need.'[24]

Now for a few days he could be in Toronto for a family Christmas. Langford and Mary were home from boarding school for the first time since they went away in the autumn – Langford to St Andrew's College, Aurora, and Mary to King's Hall in Compton, Quebec, where her father had been assured the instruction in French was excellent. In this first peacetime Christmas he looked forward, hopefully, at the end of the war to end war, to a world in which the message of peace on earth had a unique meaning.[25]

Although Rowell's immediate duties in the weeks just after the armistice involved him mainly in domestic politics he paid close attention to imperial and foreign developments, and in particular to the role that Canada would play at the Peace Conference. When the prime minister and his party set out for London the possibilities for Canadian participation were undefined, although it appeared that the British government assumed that the Dominions would form part of the British delegation. A majority of the Canadian cabinet, none more so than Rowell, was convinced that Canada must have separate and distinct representation. Whatever the decision, Rowell and Borden were agreed that it would be impossible to carry public opinion in favour of Borden's presence in London over any extended period of time unless Canadians were better informed about the work of the ministers who were overseas than they had been the previous summer during the meetings of the Imperial War Cabinet and Conference. Borden was glad to accept Rowell's proposal that the government send J. W. Dafoe of the *Manitoba Free Press* to London to supply the Canadian press with a first hand account of the Peace Conference.[26] As an architect, and still enthusiastic supporter, of Union Government and as an ardent exponent of Canadian autonomy and of Wilsonian principles for the post-war world, Rowell could scarcely have found anyone whose reporting was more likely to have so desirable an impact on his readers. At the same time Rowell tried to expedite plans for the establishment of a Canadian publicity office in New York, so that Canadian views on the Peace Conference would be circulated in the United States.[27]

Did Canada *have* any views? Among the few Canadians who took an active interest in international affairs there was some doubt. Professor G. M. Wrong urged upon Rowell the desirability of providing the Canadian representatives at the conference with the assistance of a group of Canadian scholars studying the problems of peace similar to the American 'House Committee.' Rowell saw some merit in the idea, but Borden rejected it on the grounds that it was unnecessary for the Canadian delegation to duplicate the studies made available to it from the British Foreign Office.[28] Wrong found Borden's reaction indicative of 'the truly colonial attitude of mind.' The fact that 'English officials' were studying the proposed peace treaties did not mean that 'we should have no mind of our own respecting them.' For Wrong it was 'humiliating that we have had no voice at all in shaping official opinion in respect to British ideals of peace.' He had to admit that it was perhaps too late to work out a Canadian position on such questions as the future of Alsace-Lorraine, the boundaries of the many Slavic nations, or the frontiers of Italy. But Wrong feared that Canada was going to the Peace Conference 'as a colony not as a nation.'[29] Rowell did not accept Wrong's distressing conclusion; he was confident that Canada had views and that they would be as forcefully expressed at the Peace Conference as they had been at the imperial meetings of the previous summer 'if Canada is represented as the government believes it should be.'[30]

In principle, Rowell agreed with Wrong that it would have been valuable to have a group of Canadian scholars assisting the Canadian delegation, but at this late date all he could suggest was that perhaps one or two university men, possibly Wrong himself and President Falconer of the University of Toronto, might be appointed to keep in touch with the House Committee and the Foreign Office and make information more easily accessible to Borden and his colleagues.[31] Borden supported his continuing resistance to such an arrangement with the opinion of Loring Christie that the 'somewhat mysterious committee of professors,' the American 'Inquiry,' was merely a collector of information lacking access to the most secret State Department materials and so unrelated to the actual machinery of government as to be of very little use in the formation of policy.[32] His experience in London was constantly confirming Borden's conviction that no Canadian advisory group could rival the services of the Foreign Office; nor had he found reason to believe that British information was coloured to prejudice Canadian interests in any way. Indeed, Borden affirmed that Canadian concerns were limited, confined mainly to 'the solution of such problems as the League of Nations, disarmament proposals, indemnities and economic arrangements.' In his own staff, already much larger than that of any of the other Dominions, he had all the assistance he needed.[33]

Rowell was at one with Borden in his analysis of the character of Canadian interests in the peace settlement. They were also fully agreed that, however Canada's views were formulated, they must be expressed as independently as possible. Thus Rowell was perturbed when Borden cabled from London complaining of the contrast between the frequent reports in the London press of demands in Parliament and popular demonstrations in Australia for separate representation at the Peace Conference, and most of the dispatches from Canada, which only quoted 'stupid editorials suggesting Canadian delegates should return immediately' and seemed to 'virtually propose that Canada shall be unrepresented.'[34] Rowell hastened to reassure Borden that such dispatches did not represent Canadian opinion, and he immediately took steps through certain key members of the Canadian press to make sure that British papers, and in particular the *Times*, through its Canadian correspondent, Sir John Willison, was provided with more frequent and vigorous presentation of Canadian interest in separate representation.[35] And the cabinet tried to arm Borden for his discussions on this subject in the Imperial War Cabinet with affirmations that it was even more strongly in favour of distinctive Canadian representation than when he left Canada.[36]

The appearance of cabinet unity in the pursuit of status did not mean that Rowell found all of his colleagues as single-minded on this subject as he would have liked them to be. Their diversity of opinion was evident in discussions about when the next session of Parliament should be called and whether Borden's presence was essential. A minority of the cabinet were disposed to think that there should be no further session until after an election. Although Rowell could understand the growing public demand for an early election to which some of his colleagues were responding, he could see no reasonable alternative to the present administration in the months immediately ahead. He urged Borden to repeal the Wartime Election Act at the first opportunity and thus to remove a source of grave misgiving among Liberals and a possible basis for charges that the Union Government intended to fight another election on the franchise of 1917. If the government could not agree to repeal the Act at the next session the matter should be left to the judgment of individual members of the House in a free vote.[37] In any case, Rowell was convinced that Parliament must meet very soon, early in February at the latest. Any other course would leave a coalition formed for wartime purposes open to serious and wholly justifiable criticism on constitutional grounds and would give the impression that the government was afraid to meet the Commons. An early session would supply what the government's reputation most urgently required, 'evidence that it knows what it is going to do and ... has the courage to go ahead and do it.'[38]

The decision was not entirely to Rowell's liking: Parliament would not meet until 20 February; but that seemed the earliest date by which a useful legislative program would be ready for presentation, a decisive consideration. Many members of the cabinet, notably Meighen, thought that Borden should come home for all or most of the session since no service that he could render in Europe, whatever Canada's status, could equal the usefulness of his leadership at home.[39] For Rowell the question of Borden's return hung on the decision about Dominion representation at the Peace conference. As 1918 drew to a close no decision had been reached, due largely to the preoccupation of the British members of the Imperial War Cabinet and Conference with the current general election, which was to return Lloyd George's coalition with a staggering majority. If Canada were not given 'direct full representation' Borden should come home at once and let the British government understand clearly the reason for his departure. Rowell was in no doubt that in this feeling he represented the majority of the Canadian people. But it was inconceivable to him that Canada would be denied what she had won on the field of battle. Nor was it only national pride that would be hurt. 'It does not require much vision'

Rowell wrote anxiously to Borden 'to see the political possibilities and implications of such a position. Certainly the prestige of Union Government would be impaired, and it might affect your own.' Impatiently he awaited a resolution of the question, understanding full well that Great Britain and the United States would decide it; if either completely rejected the Dominions' claims there would be no Canadian representation.[40] Two days later, when the papers carried a London dispatch suggesting that the Dominions would probably be given the status accorded the smallest nations at the Peace Conference, Rowell thought the proposal an insult. Canada's position, he cabled Borden, should not be assessed as that of a nation of eight millions, but of fifty millions, 'and thus, potentially at least, one of the Great Powers.' That future, plus the record of Canada's troops, justified her in demanding a status 'equal to that of any other representative of [the] Britannic nations or of [the] American nation.'[41] By mid-January Borden and Foster were in Paris to occupy the two independent seats awarded Canada and to serve on the panel of British Empire delegates. Canada and the other Dominions, save New Zealand with one seat, had the same representation as Greece, Portugal, Hejaz, and China, among others, although none of the other 'two-delegate' powers had contributed as much in men and resources to the Allied victory. Canada had her place in the sun.

Unfortunately, as Rowell soon discovered, most of the world, including some Canadians in high places, neither knew nor cared about this change in the ordering of international politics.[42] At least half the members of the cabinet in Ottawa felt none of Rowell's satisfaction in Borden's acceptance of the position of chief British delegate at the proposed conference with the various factions of Russians at Prinkipo on the Sea of Marmara, but continued to believe that the prime minister's time could be better occupied in Ottawa, or at least in consideration of the major issues of the peace settlement.[43] Nor did the rest of their colleagues see as much reason for regret as did Borden and Rowell in the failure of the Canadian delegates to persuade the other Dominion representatives at the Peace Conference to renounce their claims to adjacent German colonies. However, Rowell accepted the agreement to put the colonies under a mandate of the new League of Nations as the best compromise obtainable.[44]

Clear evidence of the general ignorance of Canada's new position in the world was evident in the news of the Peace Conference appearing in Canadian newspapers. Rowell complained to Borden that the papers were filled with dispatches by American correspondents who played up Wilson's role, paid some attention to Lloyd George and Clemenceau, but rarely mentioned Borden or Canada. Dafoe's reports were excellent, but being commentaries rather than straight news they were less sensational than the American dispatches and failed to hit the headlines. Canadians ought to be able to get more news of their own country's position, and they ought to get it as quickly from Canadian sources as from American news services. Rowell proposed that one or two Canadian reporters now in London be asked to go to Paris to cover the conference from a vantage point other than the semi-official position held by Dafoe.[45] Borden promised to see what could be done from Paris, but six weeks later Rowell was still making the same complaint.[46] The new nationalism seemed doomed to defeat on the public relations front. To the end of the conference Rowell tried to improve Canadian news, but had little success. As the deliberations in Versailles were nearing their conclusion he took great pains to ensure that when the peace was signed the initial eight-thousand-word summary of the treaties would be put on the cables for Ottawa and Washington at precisely the same time and that, for this occasion at least, the Canadian Press would try to match the usually speedier distribution services of the Associated Press in New York. Reluctantly, however, he accepted Borden's opinion that the government would not be justified in spending $90,000 to have the whole text cabled directly to Ottawa. It would have to go through New York.[46]

During Borden's absence from the country Rowell became the leading apologist for a development in Canadian external policy much harder to justify than Canada's role at the Peace Conference. The sending of four thousand Canadians to assist in the Allied intervention in Russia was not easy to explain to anyone, least of all to a war-weary public.

It had all started when he arrived in London for the meetings of the Imperial War Cabinet and had first learned of the British desire to secure American co-operation in a joint military intervention in Russia with the purpose of reopening the eastern front, which had collapsed with the Russian signing of the Treaty of Brest-Litovsk with the Germans. If the Germans could have been re-engaged in Russia it was hoped that they would then have had to relax their attack on the hard-pressed Allied forces on the western front. For three months President Wilson had withheld his consent to such an operation, and the British were contemplating unilateral action if they could find the additional troops required. The Canadians were sounded out on their willingness to help. At the beginning of July the British, despairing of American aid, decided to act and ordered a regiment stationed in Hong Kong to embark for Vladivostok to relieve the Czech garrison there, which was believed to be in imminent danger of being overcome by a force of former German and Austrian prisoners of war reputedly armed with weapons supplied by the Germans. Once rescued, the Czechs would assist in the larger British aim of opening up the eastern front.[47]

Apparently Borden had already given the British reason to hope that a Canadian force would be provided for Siberia, because within a few days the head of the British military mission in Washington was in Ottawa discussing arrangements for Canadian participation.[48] Rowell and the Canadian minister of militia, General

Mewburn, were soon in conference with British military officials, and Rowell assured the war office that matters could be 'satisfactorily arranged.'[49] Rowell also took part in discussions with London representatives of a Russian trading company who outlined possibilities for the development of Canadian trade in Siberia, but he appears to have been much less taken with this idea than Borden, who became increasingly caught up in the vision of a vast Canadian trading enterprise in Siberia.[50]

The Canadian ministers in London were not disposed to rush into the venture. Many questions were raised about the securing of recruits, their duties, and their command that had to be answered. And there was a large political problem: as long as the Americans rejected intervention the whole situation was awkward for Canada because, as always, Canadian politicians had no desire to be caught in a conflict of policies between Britain and the United States. The dilemma was not resolved when the Americans announced in mid-July that they would not participate in military intervention in the internal affairs of Russia. President Wilson could not espouse a policy that would violate his treasured principle of 'self-determination.' The United States would, however, assist in the rescue of the Czechs. As expected, Japan would also participate in the operation and would provide the bulk of the force. Now both Britain and the United States were in effect intervening, but for quite different reasons: Britain to open the eastern front, the United States simply to help the beleaguered Czechs who were skirmishing with the Bolsheviks from the Urals to Vladivostok. Also alarming was the decided possibility of dissension between the Americans and the Japanese and Japan's invocation of the Anglo-Japanese alliance; where would Canada be then?

When Rowell returned to Ottawa from London in early August he found a confused cabinet. Unfortunately, nothing he had learned in London enabled him to clarify the subject for his colleagues. Rowell now had doubts about proceeding and cabled Borden that if it were decided to go ahead with Canadian participation the precise relationship of the Canadian forces to those of the other Allies, as well as the purpose of the whole operation, would have to be defined and explained to the public.[51] How often in the weeks ahead he was to wish that such a definition had been forthcoming! General Mewburn was even more reluctant, arguing that Canada must not become involved in another theatre of war where the purposes of the Allies, especially the American objective, was so confused and predicting violent objection to the policy throughout Canada.[52] Borden swept aside the questions raised by his colleagues in Ottawa. They had no effect in the face of his national pride, which made him reluctant to refuse the British request for aid, and his increasing absorption in the fantasy of a Canadian trading empire in Russia. Evidently the pleasant prospect of expanding Canadian commerce obscured the harsh facts of the continuing political and military struggle within Russia. With little enthusiasm, and on the understanding that a Canadian economic mission would be sent to Siberia as well as a military force, the cabinet agreed to accept Borden's view. Brigadier General J.H. Elmsley was appointed commander of the Canadian force, but only after a controversy with the War Office was it established that his actions were to be directed from Ottawa and not from London.[53]

Shortly afterwards, when Rowell made his first public comment on the expedition in an address to his own constituents in Durham, he made no mention of Canadian trade with Siberia. He presented the venture as simply a move 'to co-operate with the Allies in assisting the Czecho-Slovaks and the Russian people, who are courageously battling against Germany's efforts to dominate and control Siberia, as she already dominates and controls Western Russia.'[54] Subsequently, during his 'public relations tour' of western Canada, he spoke frequently on the record of the Union Government and on the Russian situation, notably to six Canadian Club audiences in centres from Winnipeg to Vancouver. Soon after his return to Toronto he told the Men's Canadian Club that young Canadians were going to the aid of the heroic Czechs, but now he identified the Bolsheviks as the enemy. By helping to overthrow them and to establish 'a truly Russian government' Canada would participate in the highly desirable objective of helping Russia to find her liberty-loving, deeply religious soul and become one of the great new democracies of the century. Finally, he moved on to the more general ground of the significance in the twentieth century of the more than half of the human race who lived around the rim of the Pacific Ocean, a significance which Canadians must not fail to appreciate. Canada was entitled to have a voice in all the developments on the northern Pacific and it was of the utmost importance to her that 'our nearest neighbours across the Pacific shall be a country developed by ... a people free, loving democracy, the Russian people,' and not by Germany.[55] He was now well established as the government's foremost spokesman in the public defence of the expedition to Siberia. It was an unenviable position.

With the coming of the armistice the Canadian role in Siberia became more debatable than ever. At first, Rowell shared the reaction of his colleagues in Ottawa and was inclined to believe that an already sceptical public would refuse to tolerate the dispatch of further groups of Canadians to join the eight hundred who had already arrived at Vladivostock.[56] The publicity given the appointment of a five-man economic mission headed by C.F. Just and financed by an initial government credit of $1 million for the opening of trading operations in Siberia had done little to make the total enterprise more popular. In London Borden was unmoved by the hesitance of his colleagues at home. He had now found a positive political purpose in the venture: British forces were needed to stabilize the newly formed anti-Bolshevik government in Siberia and since Britain could not supply the troops at the moment Canada should do so. But the possibility that the Canadians would be involved in any serious fighting was slight, he assured the cabinet, and the prospect of future trade with Siberia still seemed bright.[57]

Borden's argument that the troops should go forward as planned was unconvincing to White, Crerar, Ballantyne, Calder, and Reid. Not unreasonably, they had difficulty seeing the value of opening the eastern front now that the war was over. However sound the other reasons for Allied intervention might be, they saw it as 'a task for nations more immediately interested in the finances of Russia' and were alarmed by the political consequences of persistence in a policy so manifestly rejected by the majority of press and people. Rowell became the chief defender of Borden's position.[58] When Borden insisted that he and the three cabinet ministers who were with him in London – Foster, Sifton, and Doherty – felt strongly that withdrawal would be a breach of promise to Great Britain that would leave 'Canada's present position and prestige ... singularly impaired,' the entire cabinet, with the exception of Crerar, took a more favourable view and agreed to proceed with the expedition as planned, provided that the force be recalled within a year of the armistice or the draftees who constituted 36 per cent of the force be replaced by volunteers.[59] Assured once again that Canada must honour her obligation to Great Britain, Crerar acquiesced, but without the least enthusiasm. Rowell was under no illusions about the heavy burden placed on the Department of Public Information in defending this decision, but he assured Borden optimistically that the Canadian people would 'support all reasonable Governmental action provided they are kept fully informed of the reasons therefor.'[60]

But that was just the problem. In the weeks following, Rowell found it impossible to present a reasonable justification for the continued presence of Canadians in Russia. His task was not made easier by the unexpected appearance in the press, on the very day of the cabinet decision to proceed with the expedition to Siberia, of a dispatch announcing the arrival of Canadian troops in the Archangel area of Northern Russia. Although the cabinet had given general approval to the War Office for the dispatch of a few Canadians to that sector there had been no public announcement. By cable Rowell pleaded with Borden for an immediate and intelligible explanation of Allied and British policy toward Russia. When the answer came it was of little use, since it could not be published without endangering the mission in which 450 Canadians were assisting British and American forces in trying to prevent the Bolsheviks from seizing arms and ammunition supplied to the previous Russian government from Britain.[61] Responding to renewed pleas from Ottawa for a statement of British policy, Borden persuaded the colonial secretary to provide his impatient and sceptical colleagues with a copy of a recent statement prepared for British military and civil representatives in Vladivostock and Archangel. Rowell read it with hopes that were soon dashed. It was an equivocal document. While disclaiming any campaign against Bolshevism and any desire to establish a particular political system in Russia, it referred to British commitments to the new anti-Bolshevik regimes in certain parts of Russia, as well as to the Czechs, and praised those 'who are resisting on the spot the invasion of militant Bolshevism.'[62] Using the part of the dispatch that rejected any political purpose for the intervention, Rowell prepared a draft of a public statement and sought London's approval for his proposed use of a secret document.[63]

The misgivings that still affected most members of the Canadian cabinet were mounting again with every new piece of evidence suggesting that there was no reason for continued Canadian participation except the honouring of a promise that had involved Canada in furthering some British scheme whose purpose, in so far as one could be discerned, was apparently political rather than military. Any public admission that this was the situation would surely bring pointed comment on the discrepancy between the government's claims for Canadian autonomy and the apparent practice in relation to the Siberian affair. And any identification of Canada with an anti-Bolshevik mission was bound to alienate further the labour movement and many other elements in the community whose good opinion the Union Government undoubtedly needed. After a flurry of enquiring and protesting telegrams to Borden from various ministers in Ottawa the prime minister told his colleagues at home that they should reach their own decision, although he clearly hoped that continued Canadian participation in the expedition might be made more palatable by his assurances that the Canadians were in little danger of suffering any casualties, since it was understood by the British that they were not to be moved 'up country' from Vladivostok without Ottawa's consent and without full clarification of the role they were to play if they did move inland. After extended deliberation the cabinet decided to permit the further dispatch of the Canadian troops who were ready to go to Siberia, but stipulated that they must not engage in any military operation without Ottawa's explicit consent and must all be brought home by spring.[64]

Even before this there had been tension between the head of the British Military Mission in Siberia, General Knox, and the Canadian commander, General Elmsley. But they were in agreement in protesting to the War Office when they learned that because of Canada's refusal to allow her troops to move inland and her intention of recalling her force in the near future the War Office had decided to recommend the abandonment of the whole British operation in Siberia since the two British battalions involved would be quite useless without the support of the larger body of Canadians. The British War Cabinet rejected the War Office's recommendation, and the Canadians remained in Vladivostok on the conditions earlier stipulated.[65] At this point, a month after his request, the colonial secretary refused approval of Rowell's proposed statement on Siberian policy on the ground that it would give aid and comfort to the Soviet government.[66] Perhaps it did not matter so much now if the troops were to come home soon, but for the next several weeks he continued to work on a public statement.

In the meantime Borden had decided that the whole Allied policy of intervention was futile. To the Imperial War Cabinet he proposed that the various Russian factions should be invited to a conference where the Allied nations could 'bring pressure, if necessary, upon them to restrain them and control aggression, and to bring about conditions of stable government.'[67] Lloyd George took up the idea and secured the support of the other major powers for the Prinkipo Conference. In this move Lloyd George did not enjoy the wholehearted support of all members of his cabinet. As part of their campaign to keep the British committed to intervention, A.J. Balfour, the foreign secretary, and Winston Churchill, secretary for war, tried to persuade Borden to reconsider his views on early Canadian withdrawal, arguing that if the Allies remained in Russia for a few months longer Bolshevik power would collapse. If Allied intervention ended they feared that the Bolsheviks would over-run the whole of Russia and then combine with the Germans to menace the world, and especially the British position in India. Borden was unconvinced by the British statesmen's dramatic portrayal of how much of the world's fate hung on the continued presence of some four thousand Canadians in Vladivostok and was certain that the Canadian people as a whole would share his reaction to any proposals for further military action on their part. Borden's increasing awareness of the complexities of European politics was reflected in his report to his colleagues in Ottawa of discussions with Balfour and Churchill: 'Russia must work out her own salvation which may take years. If Bolshevist power crumbles other governments will probably fight each other for some time to come.' Moreover, he could see no reason for believing that a Bolshevik government was more likely than any other kind of Russian government to join forces with the Germans.[68] It was soon evident that numerous difficulties, not the least of which was the refusal of the various Russian governments to attend, would mean that the Prinkipo Conference would never be held. Meanwhile, Borden insisted that the Canadians in Siberia must go home, and now stipulated that they must be withdrawn by April.

None of the frequent dispatches that appeared on Rowell's desk made the work of the Department of Public Information any easier in the face of steady public clamour either for immediate withdrawal of the Canadians from Siberia or for some explanation of the policy that kept them there. Borden's firmness in trying to extricate the country from the Siberian confusion could not be publicized. And his most recent account of his stand against Balfour and Churchill had been accom-panied by a request for another postponement for at least two weeks of any official comment.[69] Once again, Rowell put aside his draft statement. It was a necessity that could do no good for the Union Government or for the member of the cabinet who had been most vocal in supporting Canadian involvement in the intervention in Russia.

17
Recrimination and reform

As Rowell sat among his cabinet colleagues in the Basilica of Notre Dame early in 1919 at the state funeral of Laurier, his old leader was almost 'the chief' once more. For a moment the most ardent English-Canadian nationalists were united with Henri Bourassa and Armand Lavergne in paying tribute to the Canadian who had few rivals in the affections of his fellow countrymen and only one competitor, Sir John A. Macdonald, as an architect of the nation. Without the man whose personality and speech had graced Parliament for forty-five years, who had led the Liberal party for nearly thirty-two of those years – fifteen as prime minister – Canada would never be quite the same again. It was not only the end of the war that marked the close of an era.

Just two days before Laurier's death Rowell had spoken briefly with him after a meeting of the Ottawa Canadian Club; Laurier had seemed well and intensely interested in the subject of the day – the future of the Yugoslavs in the resettlement of Europe. Although the most suspicious Laurier Liberals would have found it hard to believe, the Union Government had not hesitated for a moment in embarking on the arrangements that made Sir Wilfrid's funeral what Rowell rightly described as 'one of the most imposing and impressive sights ever seen in Ottawa.' The service in the Basilica, with its splendid music and the participation of the members of the hierarchy and dozens of lesser clergy, stirred Rowell to reflect on Laurier's relations with his church: 'The clergy did not fail to make it a great Roman Catholic function and they praised Sir Wilfrid's devotion to the church. He may have been [devout] lately but he certainly was not in his earlier years. I never heard a man speak more frankly of the narrowness and intolerance of the clergy in Quebec or more firmly of the necessity of not giving way to their views.'[1]

The changes in the immediate political scene arising from Laurier's death were almost entirely favourable to the Union Government, and the administration could face with confidence the new session of Parliament now beginning. Although the Unionists had had no fear of defection from their ranks serious enough to force an election in the near future, they now enjoyed the added protection of uncertainty within the opposition. The Liberals would be unlikely to display marked vigour until the party's future was settled by the selection of a new leader and the adoption of a program. In the rather weak speech of D.D. McKenzie, whom the Liberals had chosen as House leader for the current session, it was evident that the party hoped that in the next few months many Liberal Unionists would return to the fold. 'Let me tell my good friends' McKenzie declared 'that the war is over. The light is in the window for you; the latch string is on the outside and you are all welcome.'[2] If Charles Murphy and Lucien Cannon had their way the welcome would not extend to Newton Rowell. That did not bother Rowell: for the present there was little on the other side of the door that could attract him, and he was not disposed to try to lift the latch.

As the government benches anticipated, the debate on the speech from the throne was but a few hours old before the opposition had launched an attack on Borden's long sojourn in England and France. Ernest Lapointe charged that in addition to neglecting Canada's vital interests at home the prime minister was acting unconstitutionally in changing Canada's position in the Empire without parliamentary authority. The Confederation 'treaty' had not empowered the federal government 'to delegate any of its powers to another body without the consent of the parties to its original contract.' If he were not so delegating powers, what did Borden mean when he said that the calling of the Dominion prime ministers to the Imperial War Cabinet and Conference the previous summer was 'a great step in the constitutional development of the Empire?' Did a recent announcement that the Imperial War Cabinet would continue as a permanent organ of the Empire represent a change? Apparently the Round Table group believed that it did. According to Lapointe its members were jubilant, knowing that an Imperial Cabinet would lead to the achievement of their ultimate aim, the establishment of an Imperial Parliament.[3]

As acting minister of external affairs Rowell made a lengthy statement on imperial relations and endeavoured to answer Lapointe's queries. It was not an easy assignment. Attempting to refute the charge that the government had effected a change in Canada's status without parliamentary authority he contended that nobody had challenged Borden's statements in Parliament on the usefulness of the sessions of the Imperial War Cabinet, and since then a general election had been held. 'So ... whatever may be the constitutional relationship arising out of the presence of representatives of Canada in the Imperial War Cabinet that relationship has the assent of the Canadian parliament and the Canadian people.' He did not deny that Canada's status had changed, but it had changed only in the direction of increased autonomy. 'The Imperial [War] Cabinet does not deal with a single question which in the past has been dealt with by the parliament of Canada.' When challenged on his interpretation of the election Rowell had to admit that this issue had played no significant part in the campaign, but he explained that this was only because everyone took the principle of imperial consultation for granted. Lapointe was not satisfied. In a normal cabinet a member resigned if he disagreed with his colleagues; what would happen in that case in the new Imperial Cabinet? Rowell had no direct answer, but stressed the responsibility of each delegate to his own cabinet at home and tried to underplay the logical constitutional questions, to which recent developments undoubtedly gave rise, by a strong statement on the necessity of extending Canadian autonomy. He found it inconceivable that the House could believe that Canadians should continue 'in a position where we have no voice in questions of foreign policy on the issues of peace and war.' There were only two ways in which Canada could acquire a voice: 'She can have it as an independent nation, or by co-operation with the nations that now form part of the British Empire.' The latter was the only reasonable course. That agreed on, the precise constitutional definition would have to await the next Imperial Conference and the subsequent approval of that definition by the Canadian Parliament.[4]

Whatever the formal definition of the new status was to be, Rowell could point to several proofs of its reality: the recognition accorded the Dominions at the Peace Conference, the anticipated invitation to the Dominions to sign the peace treaty in their own right, and the probability that Canada would become a charter member of the new League of Nations whose constitution was now being drafted. He made no attempt to conceal the responsibility accompanying these developments. 'Every nation that signs the covenant of the league pledges itself to maintain the territorial integrity of the others as against outside aggression.' Surely this must be seen as 'one of the most momentous questions to which the statesmen of this country can devote their attention.' Could anyone then doubt the necessity of Borden's presence in Europe to make the Canadian influence felt in a gathering that was even more crucial than the Congress of Vienna?[5]

Three weeks later the opposition was again on the attack on the subject of imperial relations and forced Rowell to reiterate what he had said earlier about Canadian autonomy and the Imperial Cabinet. During this discussion the Liberals launched the heaviest of several attacks on the Siberian expedition, with Ernest Lapointe and C.G. Power leading the way. Hermas Deslauriers, member for the Quebec riding of St Mary, had declared that sending Canadian troops to Siberia could do nothing but 'implant throughout Russia the hatred of everything Canadian, thus endangering Canada's future in ways we have not space to dwell on ... The crime is more than all on the head of N.W. Rowell ... Yes, the President of the Privy

Council is the only one among the ministers who was so bold as to not only defend what is being done but further to try to get some kudos out of it. On the Judgment Day I prefer to be in the place of the last Publican, of the greatest sinner rather than in that of the "First Layman" of a great church, a man whose hands will be red with the blood of his fellow-citizens sacrificed in a nameless cause.'[6]

Under the questioning of Lapointe and Power, Rowell was forced to admit that the decision to send troops to Siberia had initially been made while he and Borden were attending the War Cabinet and the proposal that Canada participate had originated with the British ministers, although he was quick to point out that the size of the Canadian contingent had been determined by Canada. The Liberals scarcely needed to elaborate on the implications of these revelations: if this was an example of the consequences of the increased status Canada had acquired through representation in the Imperial War Cabinet, it was something she could very well do without.[7]

It was no easier to meet Power's demand for an explanation of the general reasons for Allied intervention in Russia, but Rowell gave three main objectives: to keep Germany at least slightly occupied on the eastern front and therefore unable to devote all her forces to the hard-pressed western front, to rescue the Czechs for service on the western front, and to prevent permanent German control of the Russian provinces acquired in the Treaty of Brest-Litovsk, containing fifty or sixty million people, great industrial centres, and the finest farming land in Russia. Under further questioning Power forced Rowell to agree with him that allied intervention had left the threat of German territorial gains in the east unchanged. But Rowell would not accept the implication that the whole intervention had therefore been a failure and asserted that at least the Germans had been prevented from using their genius for organization to make Russia a great force against the Allies. Power remained unconvinced and continued with an exposition of the confusion evident in the whole Allied position in Russia.

When pressed further about the reasons for Canadian participation in this ill-conceived venture, Rowell declared that the Canadian ministers in London in the summer of 1918 had felt that they could not refuse the British request for aid in Siberia because all the other Dominions had sent proportionately more men to the front than Canada. At the time, Britain had thrown all her available men into the struggle in France, down to mere youths of eighteen and could do no more. 'We took the position we did because of the critical situation which existed at the time, and in this I am speaking for myself, I am sure the same is true of my colleagues – I have nothing whatever to regret in the action then taken.'[8]

Power's renewed charge that any reasons for Allied intervention that may have existed in the late spring of 1918 had disappeared by the time the Canadians were despatched to Siberia was hard to meet. Rowell could only admit that Japan,

France, Italy, and Britain all had their troops in Siberia before Canada, the Canadians having been delayed 'owing to conditions prevailing in Canada.' He also admitted the government's enquiry about release from its obligations when the armistice was signed and the subsequent decision to go ahead 'owing to the critical situation in Russia' and Britain's inability to send a contingent at that moment. What else could Canada have done? 'Could we as Canadians say that when ... the Supreme Council considered it essential that troops should be maintained there, Canada should be the first one to quit and refuse to take her share? That is not the part Canada has played in this war, and it was not the part the government was prepared to have her play.'[9]

But to the opposition national honour was not enough. Was Canada now at war with Russia? Power wanted to know. 'There are several governments in Russia with which we are not at war,' Rowell replied. Was Canada at war with any government in Russia? Unwilling to reveal fully the government's own doubt on this point, and unable to say publicly that the Canadian troops were under orders not to proceed inland from Vladivostok, Rowell could only say that 'so far as the Canadian brigade is concerned we are not in contact with the forces of any Government with which we are at war.' Thomas Vien then took up the cudgels for the opposition and tried to get Rowell to say explicitly that the Canadians were sent to Siberia only because no other Allied troops were available. Rowell refused to fall into this trap; that it was a trap was evident in Vien's next statement that surely the United States, whose sacrifices were so much smaller than Canada's, could have provided the four or five thousand troops required for Siberia; instead, Canada had done more than her fair share, Vien charged, because her relations with the Empire had dictated a policy not in keeping with Canadian interests. Rowell was vehement in his denial: 'I desire to put myself on record as absolutely dissenting from my honorable friend's view. I desire to join issue squarely and fairly on that question.' The Americans had sent all they had agreed to send; if Canada had defaulted on her obligations Britain might well have been forced to call out more schoolboys. Power made one more attempt to find out what Russians the Canadians were pursuing, apparently in an attempt to secure an admission that it was the Bolsheviks, an admission that would have been extremely unpopular with labour and liberal opinion in the country. But now Rowell was not prepared to repeat what he had said outside the House in the previous autumn about the necessity of routing the Bolsheviks. He drew the discussion to a close by declaring that he had said all the military situation would permit.[10]

Within the severe limitations imposed by the confusion of the total Allied position and the further complications attending Canadian involvement Rowell had outlined the government's policy as well as possible and had defended it with conviction. None of his cabinet colleagues envied him the task. Politically, the less any member of the government was publicly associated with the Siberian debacle the better; there were too many Canadians, and by no means only French Canadians, who agreed with Dr Béland's later summary in the House, that Canadian participation in the Siberian expedition was 'a political error, a military mistake, and a wanton extravagance.'[11]

Most of Rowell's work in the current parliamentary session was more congenial than the defence of the Siberian affair. For three months before the opening of Parliament he had been hard at work on measures that represented the first instalment of the program of social legislation that was now his chief concern. The new measures were the least contentious features of the program he had outlined to Borden – only those on which it was easiest to secure the cabinet's agreement – but at least they were a beginning. The first was a bill to establish a federal Department of Health, in Rowell's view 'one of the most important features of the Government's policy during the period of reconstruction,'[12] a recognition of a new concern for the health of industrial workers and an acceptance of the principle that 'although in the past emphasis has been placed on property, in future emphasis must be placed more largely on life.'[13] He had no difficulty in presenting statistics to show that there was much to be done in the control of preventable disease and death: more than half the men given medical examinations under the Military Service Act were rejected as physically unfit, and the infant mortality rate in Canada was much higher than in most western countries. In some Canadian cities 25 per cent of the babies died during their first year; in Glasgow, with its slums, the infant mortality rate was 111 per thousand compared with 224 per thousand in Ottawa![14]

In noting the variety of organizations, especially among women and labour, that had petitioned the government to establish a Department of Health, Rowell observed that the cabinet had also received a joint deputation on the same subject from the Trades and Labor Congress of Canada and from the Canadian Manufacturers' Association. With the enthusiastic support of representatives of the Trades and Labor Congress, Rowell had originally proposed that the new department should be called the Department of Social Welfare. Although its initial activities would concern health in a specific sense, Rowell preferred the broader title and functions that would have included study of the causes of unemployment and its remedies, supervision of the government's housing program, and responsibility for the distribution of government literature on health and on social insurance, 'in order that the public might be fully seized of the results of these measures in other countries.' Unfortunately, there was less than total agreement even on his own side of the House on the provision for such a 'propaganda' role for the department and much vociferous opposition from the Quebec members about ill-defined provisions for the extension of federal influence in welfare legislation, a field that lay primarily within provincial jurisdiction.[15] C.G. Power wanted to know whether 'social welfare' would include prohibition and other invasions of private life and suggested that in Canada there was some difficulty in agreeing on a standard of social welfare: was the standard to be socialistic, Bolshevik, Methodist, Presbyterian, or Catholic?[16] In the face of these objections Rowell did not press for the more inclusive title, and after due assurances had been given that in many areas the main functions of the new department would encourage co-operation among the provinces in preventive health measures and that under the bill before the House there could be no infringement of the rights of the provinces, the measure was passed without significant opposition.[17] But much to Rowell's regret, the new Department of Health would not become an instrument for the creation of a new industrial order.

Rowell's interest in a federal housing program had led to his appointment as chairman of a cabinet subcommittee on housing whose other members were Robertson, Maclean, and Crerar. Some of the earlier opposition to federal involvement in housing had been overcome by the hope that a vigorous promotion of housing construction would reduce unemployment and stabilize the social situation during the first post-war winter.[18] Thus, before the end of 1918 the government had decided to extend its plan for loans to municipalities through the provinces for home building by increasing the amount available from $2 million to $25 million. A major task of Rowell's committee was to work out the details of the arrangement with the provinces. This proved to be difficult, especially in relation to Ontario where plans for a housing program were more fully developed than in any other province. Rowell spent many hours in negotiations with Premier Hearst and other representatives of the Ontario government until agreement was reached on the province's powers to administer the loans and the Dominion's right to supervise the kind and quality of houses erected and to require that no one with an income over three thousand dollars could live in the subsidized housing. After lengthy arguments and some misunderstanding with Hearst, Rowell was forced in the end to accept an agreement which left many more features of the program to the discretion of the provinces and assigned to Ottawa more purely advisory functions than he had at first planned or thought desirable.[19]

When Rowell presented his housing bill to Parliament he was merely asking for its approval of a government policy that had already been set in motion by order-in-council. Anticipating the criticism that housing was no concern of the Dominion government, Rowell emphasized that the bill was designed primarily to ease the problems of returning soldiers, a matter that clearly lay within the jurisdiction of the Dominion. But it would also benefit Canada as a whole by providing employment for as many as forty thousand people, setting a standard for workingmen's houses that would raise the general quality of work by other builders and enlarging that stable group of home owners who were the backbone of the country. Above all, it would lessen economic inequality: 'We cannot go on in the future with that unequal distribution of wealth ... which ... is in a very substantial measure responsible for the world-wide social unrest.' Rowell saw the housing program as a step toward the better world for which the war had been fought. Recalling his visits to many homes in the poorer districts of Toronto during the winter of 1914 when unemployment was high, he had 'no hesitation in saying that it is a disgrace that with all our natural resources and advantages such conditions of housing and poverty should exist.'[20]

Rowell was also well satisfied with the work of the parliamentary commission on pensions over which he had presided and whose major labour he now presented to the House in a bill to establish a permanent Board of Pension Commissioners to administer the pensions of returned soldiers and their dependents and to replace the pension scheme instituted under the War Measures Act with permanent provisions for the disabled and the bereaved. Rowell was proud that, like the temporary scheme it replaced, the new plan was at least as generous as any provided by other Allied governments. A few members of the House, while approving it as a whole, thought it a little too generous at one point. Who, members of the opposition wanted to know, were the 'unmarried wives' who were to receive pensions? When Rowell explained that they were common law wives D.D. McKenzie charged that to give common law wives pensions on the same basis as legal wives was to encourage immorality, while Rodolphe Lemieux and other French Catholic members denounced the proposal as hostile to the whole Christian tradition.[21] Rowell protested his complete agreement with everything Lemieux and other members said about the sanctity of marriage; but the war had created 'many unusual situations' and the proposal contained in the bill had seemed to Rowell and his committee the fairest and most humane way of handling a situation which did exist, whatever moral judgment one might make on it. Lemieux and Lapointe continued this brief debate on social ethics with pleas that the law must not recognize an unChristian standard. H.A. Mackie, Liberal Unionist from Edmonton, said the bill was in keeping with the New Testament attitude toward the woman taken in adultery. More daringly, Dr Michael Clark cited George Eliot as a fine example of a common law wife.[22] Lemieux's amendment to exclude common law wives from the pension scheme was defeated, and the bill was passed after it was agreed to delete the ambiguous term 'unmarried wives.'

It was dissension within the cabinet over the budget that finally brought Borden home from Europe. In the face of the growing militancy of farmers' organizations and their threats of direct political action to secure tariff reductions, the tariff question could no longer be avoided. Some minimum revision was necessary to enable the ministers from the west to remain in the government. For this reason, and in keeping with his general leaning towards 'freer trade,' Rowell supported the western cabinet ministers in their successful demand for the repeal of the British preferential war customs tax of 5 per cent, the abolition of the general war tariff of $7^{1}/_{2}$ per cent on foodstuffs, clothing, boots and shoes, cement, and a number of other articles, and a reduction of from 32 to 50 per cent on various kinds of farm implements.[23] In the House he asserted that this budget embodied the best features of the reciprocity agreement of 1911 and indeed gave greater reductions in the tariff on agricultural implements as well as free wheat and flour. Next year he hoped for a further reduction on food, but there could be no over-all tariff revision until that time. Even then, he insisted, he would oppose serious reductions on iron and steel, since it was essential that Canada be self-sufficient in those commodities.[24]

As he had stated publicly several times since the end of the war, Rowell was more interested in direct taxation than in the tariff. Within the cabinet he led a fight for the retention in the 1919 budget of the full Business War Profits Tax and an increased personal income tax.[25] This point of view carried the day: the Business War Profits Tax was renewed at the previous rate, while the corporation income tax was increased from 6 to 10 per cent on net income; the personal income tax remained at 4 per cent on incomes under $6,000 but on those above was increased in a rising scale from 8 per cent to 65 per cent on incomes over $150,000. Rowell felt that these taxes, together with the severe restrictions on packing-house profits and the government's food control policy, refuted opposition charges that the government had allowed the profiteers to run riot. He also rejected the suggestion that the Victory Loans were in the hands of the wealthy by pointing out that the 1918 loan had over one million subscribers and that most of the bonds were still in the possession of the original purchasers. Indeed, no country in the world had survived the war better financially, nor been more brilliantly served by a finance minister than Canada had been by Sir Thomas White. While it was true that the cost of living had risen sharply, this was part of the high cost of war suffered by every country, but less by Canada than by most.[26]

Among the recent measures Rowell wished to see established permanently was the wartime abolition of one form of patronage. He prepared and introduced the government's bill to establish a permanent purchasing commission of three members to purchase supplies for all government departments. Borden and Rowell both felt strongly that the adoption of this method during the war had saved the government large sums of money and eliminated much political patronage. But Rowell's assertion that the measure would allow a cut of three hundred in the number of persons normally engaged in purchasing for various departments was met by Liberal charges that the three commissioners would constitute an irresponsible bureaucracy enjoying excessively large salaries.[27] So great was the opposition to the measure on both sides of the House that it soon became clear that many members were completely unwilling to give up the well-proven political advantages of the extensive patronage involved in the pre-war ways of allocating government purchases. In the face of this strenuous resistance Borden and Rowell reluctantly concluded that it would be unwise to present the bill for third reading.[28]

For a time it looked as if Rowell would also see the defeat of a prohibition measure close to his heart. Borden introduced, and the House passed, a bill continuing the wartime Dominion prohibition legislation until the end of the current fiscal year, 31 March 1920. Thereupon, the Senate proposed to amend the measure to limit the law's operation to the period of one year from the Armistice, that is, only until 11 November 1919. The House passed the original bill again after a strong presentation from Sir Thomas White, but at the end of the session the attitude of the Senate remained uncertain. In the meantime Rowell had seen fresh reason for believing that the prohibition legislation was both morally and socially essential to the welfare of a restless nation.

The reality behind Rowell's many public descriptions of labour's demands for a better deal in the new world was dramatically illustrated in the Winnipeg strike. The most extensive industrial upheaval in the country's history put Rowell in an awkward position. On the one hand he had considerable sympathy for workers suffering from what he believed to be the genuine economic injustices behind the discontent; on the other hand he saw the maintenance of law and order as a prior condition for any reform, while as the minister responsible for the administration of the Royal North-West Mounted Police had had some direct responsibility for upholding that order.

The development of a serious strike in western Canada was no surprise to Rowell, thanks to his trip to the west coast the previous autumn and to his subsequent reading of the weekly reports of Commissioner Perry of the Mounted Police. To Rowell, as to the rest of the cabinet, British Columbia had seemed the most likely scene of a clash. But when the lieutenant governor of British Columbia proposed that the British government be asked to send a cruiser to the west coast to assist in keeping order, Rowell's nationalism made him agree entirely with Borden's rejection of the idea. Borden called it 'one of the most absurd' he had ever heard.[29]

As matters turned out, it was Winnipeg, in the heart of the continent, far from possible rescue by any naval force, that proved to be the centre of post-war upheaval. A strike among workers in the metal trades of that city developed into a general strike that eventually took thirty thousand workers from their jobs in the largest industrial upheaval the country had ever known. At least one servant of the Borden administration derived some measure of satisfaction from this development: C.H. Cahan, the government's investigator of subversive activities, complained to Borden that during the prime minister's absence in Paris 'the radical and revolutionary element in the country has, without any restraint ... been perfecting plans for a general strike throughout Canada'; his attempts to inform Borden's cabinet colleagues of the true state of affairs had been treated with 'contemptuous indifference.'[30] As a professed sympathizer with labour and a defender of the Social Democratic Party Rowell was no doubt one of the prime offenders in Cahan's eyes.

The Winnipeg strike was a severe test of Rowell's frequently expressed sympathies with labour. His responsibility for the Mounted Police from the first involved him directly in the implementation of the government's early pledge to assist the provincial and municipal authorities in the maintenance of order. The first day of the strike, on Rowell's authority and after consultation with General Mewburn, a squadron of RNWMP returning from overseas was dispatched to Winnipeg for demobilization to assist the troops already stationed there should need arise.[31] The next day Rowell made his first public statement on the situation in Winnipeg. In the House of Commons he rebuked the Winnipeg postal workers who had joined the strike and promised the full support of the government to all federal employees who remained at their posts; while rejecting the right of public service workers to join a sympathetic strike, he made no comment on strikes against private business.[32]

Although he was silent in public on the issues of the strike, Rowell followed closely the developments of the next three weeks in Winnipeg, where his colleagues Meighen and Robertson were investigating the situation. In mid-June Rowell delivered a lengthy rebuttal to repeated opposition charges of government failure to check the rising cost of living. He left little doubt that he was in substantial agreement with the Citizens' Committee of One Thousand in Winnipeg, whose most prominent members included several leading Liberal lawyers whom he knew and respected – his cousin J.B. Coyne, Isaac Pitblado, E.K. Williams, and A.L. Crossin among others. The Citizens' Committee had initially declared its neutrality in the strike but had shortly pronounced the walkout a Bolshevist revolution and proceeded to rally and co-ordinate the anti-strike forces of the city. In its publicity against the strikers, the Citizens' Committee, vigorously supported by John Dafoe and the *Manitoba Free Press*, alleged that the 'alien' or 'foreign' element in Winnipeg had a large role in the strike. Such charges conveniently ignored the fact that most of the strike leaders came out of the British labour movement. The impression that the upheaval in Winnipeg was but the first manifestation of a Moscow-inspired plot to take over the country was strengthened by a rash of strikes in several other cities, although none of them reached anything like the proportions of the troubles in Winnipeg.

Rowell did not deny that the high cost of living was a factor in industrial unrest in Canada, but he found the chief cause in 'the deep and vital currents of social and economic unrest moving labouring people throughout the world.' One of these currents, he told the House, was Anglo-Saxon and democratic in origin; it believed in co-operation between capital and labour, espoused constitutional methods and persuasion, and asked for certain specific reforms – an eight-hour day, a living wage and a large share in the joint product of labour and capital, a larger voice in the control of industry, and more adequate provision against unemployment – all measures on whose reasonableness and justness there was general agreement. Another stream of unrest bore the economic and social theories of Karl Marx, 'developed under the blighting influence of German autocracy,' proclaiming inevitable and irreconcilable conflict between capital and labour and the establishment by force of the dictatorship of the proletariat. The way forward for Canada, Rowell asserted, could lie only in the application of the first of these social philosophies and the establishment of co-operation between labour and capital. There were more Marxists in Canada than most Canadians would probably believe, Rowell charged. 'I know it. I have the responsibility for administering the Royal North-West Mounted Police and for months I have had weekly and sometimes daily reports on the conditions. We know what these men are saying in secret. It is not necessary to tell you what they say in secret; it is only necessary to tell you what they say in public.' He found and quoted at length a clear example of subversive utterance in the resolution passed the preceding March by the Calgary convention of the One Big Union, with its expression of determination to establish 'a proletarian dictatorship,' and to effect 'the transformation of capitalist property to communal wealth.'[33]

At the same time Rowell urged Canadians not to allow the seriousness of the present situation to prevent a just discrimination between 'men seeking to overthrow constituted authority, and the sober, serious leaders of the [labour] movement.' Nor should it be forgotten that the western extremists had been defeated in the last annual convention of the Trades and Labor Congress of Canada by responsible men who represented the tradition of Samuel Gompers in American labour. There were some who urged the government to take more drastic action, forgetting that 'the only way you can successfully defeat error is by teaching the truth.' The Canadian people must make it clear that they did not countenance the radical views of the OBU but were determined to take a more constructive approach to the industrial question. Unfortunately, many persons were being anything but helpful during the current troubles: 'The man who within this House or this country delivers inflammatory speeches charging the government with profiteering and being friends of profiteers is playing into the hands of these very Bolsheviks, and it would only be a certain measure of justice if the first property confiscated were his and he were put to do the manual labour that is required in Russia.' Equally unhelpful were those who ascribed to the federal government all the blame for failure to keep law and order in industrial relations throughout the country, ignoring the fact that this area was primarily the responsibility of provincial and municipal authorities. But again he reiterated the federal government's determination to back up those authorities to the full limit of its power in the current situation.

What was the solution? The long-run answer, as Rowell saw it, was 'to do justice, and more than justice to the legitimate demands of labour. We must put the honest, patriotic, public-spirited leaders in a position to successfully combat the extremists in their own ranks by showing that the Government and people of this country have dealt fairly and squarely with them.' While noting with implied approval that workers everywhere were asking for 'a larger voice in the control of industry' and 'a larger share of the joint product of labour and capital,' and observing that at the Peace Conference the statesmen of the world had agreed that such demands were 'in spirit just,' he made no reference to the issue at the heart of the Winnipeg strike – the demand of the Metal Trades Council for recognition as the collective bargaining agent in dealings with employers in the metal and foundry industries.[34] As long as there was any reason to believe that Marxists and devotees of the OBU were influential in the leadership of the strike he could speak only in vague generalities of his sympathy for labour.

Rowell's stance might win approval from the executive of the Trades and Labor Congress of Canada, which had refused to endorse the strike in any way, but it was unlikely in the atmosphere of the day to win acceptance in many quarters of the trade union movement for Rowell or for the Union Government as friends of labour. The Liberal opposition seized the opportunity to question Rowell's credentials as a democrat, a labour sympathizer, and an exponent of national unity. Ernest Lapointe and Lucien Cannon led the attack, denouncing the association of the president of the Privy Council with the Wartime Election Act, conscription, control of the press, and the government's methods of dealing with the Winnipeg strike – all of them measures, they declared, not unlike those Rowell condemned in Russia. Rowell's oratorical treatment of events in Winnipeg was an attempt to set the stage for the election that was imminent, according to Cannon: 'I am very much afraid that the revolution may not be as actual as the minister has depicted it, but the war in Europe being over he feels it is necessary to have a small local war so as to permit him to repeat his familiar arguments.' In short, said Cannon, Rowell had become 'a great Canadian Tory,' who had good words for the profiteer and the manufacturer, but none for labour.[35] The French Canadian Liberals clearly had no intention of dropping their vendetta against Rowell. Whatever members of the House thought about this licking of old wounds, Cannon's comments on labour sounded strange to some ears; for it was not Rowell or any other member of the government but the Liberal house leader, D.D. McKenzie, who only a few days before had proposed the abolition of the right to strike.[36]

The government's determination to maintain law and order was expressed in the passing of a bill, from first reading to royal assent in a single day, 6 June, providing for the deportation of Canadian citizens under special circumstances. It was also visible in the arrest of ten strike leaders in the early hours of 17 June and in the events of 21 June in Winnipeg. Since the RNWMP were major participants in the latter episode, 'Bloody Saturday,' Rowell spoke for the government in the House on the affair. He asserted that the strikers who had refused to respect the mayor's ban on parades had resorted to violence first, that they wrecked a street car, hurled various missiles, and finally fired on the police, and that the officer in command of the Mounted Police gave the order to fire on the strikers in self-defence. Paying tribute to the coolness, courage, and patience of the police, while regretting the casualties, Rowell declared that 'the sooner all classes recognize that it is the intention of the Federal Government and of the provincial and various municipal governments in Canada to maintain law and order and to protect life and property, the more speedily we shall reach a common understanding in relation to all matters affecting the public interest.' By the time Rowell made these statements the strike had been abandoned; he gave general approval to the collective bargaining arrangements agreed to by the three Winnipeg firms against whom the metal workers had first struck, observing that this definition of collective bargaining was the same as the one already in use in Canadian railway companies.[37]

The Union Government could look with satisfaction on the fact that there had been so little violation of law and order during the strike. This was due more to the non-violent intentions, moderation, and good sense of the strikers than to the wisdom of the Dominion government.[38] The strike did nothing to shore up a weakening government or to enhance the prestige of any of the cabinet ministers involved in it. From one side there was criticism charging too little action to quell the strike, and from the other denunciation of 'repressive measures.' All that Rowell and his colleagues could hope for now was that they might be spared such trials in the months ahead.

The unrest in Winnipeg spurred on the work of the Royal Commission on Industrial Relations, which the government had appointed early in April, and ensured the early submission of its report to Parliament. The commission was constituted of men representing three groups: the public was represented by Chief Justice T.G. Mathers of Manitoba, chairman, Hon. R. Smeaton White, publisher of the Montreal *Gazette*, and Charles Harrison, a North Bay railway conductor and Labour Unionist member of Parliament. The employers had a voice through Carl Riordan, manager of a large pulp and paper firm, and Frank Pauzé, president of a lumber company, both from Montreal, while Tom Moore and J.W. Bruce, members of the executive of the Trades and Labour Congress, represented labour.

The commission's terms of reference had given it broad scope in investigating industrial relations in Canada, and the report submitted to Parliament on 1 July demonstrated that the commissioners had ranged widely and not hesitated to make their recommendations specific. The report proposed early legislation to fix minimum wages for women, girls, and unskilled labour, and an eight-hour day and one day of rest weekly for all workers. Immediate investigation of the merits of proportional representation and of various schemes of state insurance against unemployment, old age, and sickness were recommended. Further, the commission supported the right of workers to organize and join unions of their own choice and the right to collective bargaining. In considering the control of industry the report paid some attention to the Whitley works committees and industrial councils set up in Britain since 1917 and to the 'Colorado Plan,' which Mackenzie King had helped to initiate in the Colorado enterprises of the Rockefellers, and recommended the adaptation of these schemes to the Canadian industrial scene; a government bureau should be established to promote the development of industrial councils. While the commissioners asserted that they were 'under no illusions as to the Industrial Councils constituting a universal panacea for all industrial troubles,' they believed that 'nothing but good could come from their establishment in all industries where a considerable number of work people are employed.'[39] By comparison with present industrial practices in Canada the report was somewhat radical, or at least potentially so, depending on the extent to which the recommendations were developed in practice. Rowell was well pleased with its general direction and reported to Borden his substantial agreement with its recommendations.[40]

Resistance to the report by many members of the business community was foreshadowed in the refusal of two members of the commission to sign the document. White and Pauzé submitted a minority report denying the existence of poverty or unemployment on any significant scale in Canada, making no mention of minimum wages or collective bargaining, emphasizing the difficulty of administering schemes of social insurance in a federal state, and stressing the possible dire effects of such schemes on the morale and productivity of workers. The minority report declared flatly that the Whitley plan would not be practicable in Canada, although it conceded that the Colorado plan might be.[41] This judgment was apparently based on the belief that the former granted more participation in the government of industry to workers than was actually the case in Britain, and that the latter permitted only company unions. Obviously, the path to industrial reform would not be a smooth one; there was less agreement on 'the reasonableness and justness' of certain measures than Rowell had so confidently declared during the Winnipeg strike.

As Parliament moved towards prorogation Rowell was forced to consider again his own position in the Union Government. Crerar had already resigned from the cabinet, contending that the tariff reductions in the recent budget failed to meet the needs of western Canada. Twelve western Liberal Unionists, plus Pardee and Fielding, had deserted the government to sit with the Liberal opposition. In the face of renewed pressure from those Conservatives and the few Liberal Unionists who wished to form a permanent Unionist party without delay, Rowell continued to urge adherence to the status quo. To do so was not easy: in addition to the general political considerations making this a difficult position to defend, Rowell was bothered by the attitude of the *Globe*. For some months that newspaper, while favouring the continuation of the Union Government, had often been lukewarm to the administration and on occasion had displayed what Rowell felt was close to outright hostility towards himself. Rowell was at a loss to understand the *Globe*'s coolness: what had happened to the warm assurances of support from the *Globe*'s president, W.G. Jaffray, and key members of the editorial staff that had encouraged him to enter the Union Government? With the coming of peace Stewart Lyon had urged Rowell to remain in the government and to accept even heavier responsibilities. Rowell was confident that he had consistently advocated policies to which the *Globe* was committed and felt strongly that his record in the government merited something better than unfair dispatches and editorial comments. For some time he had wondered whether part of the explanation lay in Jaffray's sudden recollection of what he deemed an excessive bill for legal services from Rowell. Although experience with Jaffray gave Rowell reason to feel that 'it would be futile to attempt to eradicate the prejudice,' he had thought for some time that he must try to get to the bottom of the matter.[42] When the *Globe* published an editorial[43] approving Crerar's resignation and implying disapproval of Liberals who remained in the cabinet he decided to have it out with Lyon.

The situation was worth a long and carefully prepared letter to Lyon. If the Union Government was still needed, asked Rowell, why was the *Globe* making a hero of Crerar? Rowell could easily find grounds for differing with his colleagues and withdrawing from the government, but such a course would do exactly what Crerar's action had done: 'It has not only affected the government to some extent, but it affects the stability of all government. The "Reds" in the west are hailing it as the first step toward the crumbling of the Government, and it is hailed with satisfaction by every enemy alien in Canada, every pacifist, every socialist and every enemy of the established order and of Canada's full participation in the war.' Referring to his almost single-handed fight in the cabinet against any reduction of the Business War Profits Tax and for an increased income tax, Rowell contended that his stand on taxation and his position on the tariff were both more in line with the *Globe*'s thinking than Crerar's. Perhaps, Rowell suggested, the editorial office was being influenced less by principle than by an awareness of considerable public hostility to him, arising from his record on prohibition and conscription. If he had been a straight Liberal he would have been supported as he had been as Liberal leader in Ontario. But 'the Liberal press seems afraid to defend a Liberal who is in the Union Government.'[44]

Lyon's reply was sharp: the *Globe* had never promised uncritical support of the government, and Lyon had made it clear to Rowell in Ottawa the previous November that there could be no permanent Union Government. The specific issue on which the *Globe* had been most critical of Rowell personally, according to Lyon, was Rowell's vote against the Mowat amendment to the Railway Act during the previous session. Lyon charged that this aligned Rowell with 'the Mackenzie-Nicholls ring' of exploiters, whose company, the Toronto Power Company, would deprive the people of Toronto of the ownership of their own city streets. Further, Lyon objected to the continuation of the war surtax of $42^1/_2$ per cent on many essential articles, and he believed the income tax rate too low to be of much significance. Both of these features of the budget illustrated the government's total failure to tackle the high cost of living. Lyon saw even less hope of reform if the government continued in office after an election, which he believed the protectionists and corporations wanted to bring on before the Wartime Election Act lapsed. 'The strongest forces behind the government,' he asserted, 'are absolutely hostile to any material change in the tariff ... they are hostile to national ownership of railways ... and they are plotting and planning to make the government ... a reactionary "Big Interest" Government, even though it may be necessary to preserve the name of Unionism.'[45]

Rowell agreed that there had never been any understanding that the *Globe* would support the government indefinitely, and he fully expected the editors to exercise their freedom to criticize specific measures at any time. But he was astonished to find that in Lyon's eyes his years of fighting for public ownership had been wiped out by one vote in Parliament. He was certain that he had acted correctly in refusing to support the Mowat amendment and in voting instead for Dr Reid's motion ruling that the rights granted to the Toronto and Niagara Power Company in its dispute with the city of Toronto must not be exercised without the approval of the Board of Railway Commissioners. In the circumstances this was the best safeguard of the public interest obtainable, since the Senate would almost certainly have rejected the Mowat amendment and then the power of the corporation would have remained unlimited. Rowell declared that the war surtax was a source of essential revenue; it was a temporary measure and he agreed that a new policy must be formed shortly, but it was not practicable to give the matter the necessary attention at the moment. As for an election, no responsible person was advocating an early election; the only thing that could precipitate one was conduct like Crerar's on the part of other members of the government, but of that there was fortunately no sign.

Rowell saved his greatest force for the refutation of Lyon's charge that the 'Big Interests' dominated the government. The two major forces behind the present administration were the Liberal Unionists, especially those from western Canada, and the Ontario section of the Conservative party. The Liberal Unionists had taken a strong stand for a downward revision of the tariff, and if that revision were not carried out the government would fall. The Liberal Unionists were clearly neither powerless nor reactionary as Lyon had contended. The 'Big Interests' were in fact fighting the government, and the *Globe* was in a rather odd relationship to them: 'The *Montreal Star*, which is hostile to national ownership is hammering the Government on one side ... while the *Globe* which *stands* for public ownership is hammering us on the other. Is that fair? I have been too closely associated with politics for the past twenty-five years not to know the attitude of Governments toward corporations and I know that no Government in Canada has ever fought against corporate influence in the largest sense as vigorously as the Union Government.' The proof of this was in the government's relations with the corporate interests generally thought to be most influential with governments – the railways and the liquor interests. Despite the hostility of both the CPR and the Grand Trunk and all opponents of public ownership, the government was going ahead with its policy of national ownership of railways, while the Laurier Liberals, to whom the *Globe* was now giving some support, were opposing public ownership. The assumption of the liquor interests that they were invulnerable to Dominion regulation had been disproved by the Union Government's prohibition measures. The fact that the Senate seemed determined to kill the bill extending prohibition had no bearing on the government's determination to fight the liquor interests. Finally, there were the regulations imposed, after strenuous resistance, on the packers, regulations under which they were still operating and which were 'the most onerous ever imposed by any Government on any industry during the war.'

The *Globe*'s attitude was doing nothing to improve the awkward position in which Rowell found himself within the government: 'Measures which I have pressed strongly upon my colleagues, some of which they have not been very anxious to accept but which they have accepted as being in the public interest, even though it meant the alienation of their friends and supporters, have brought no strength to the government from those who have been the strongest advocates of them.' Some of his colleagues were now saying to him: 'It is the same old story over again. You do these things; you get no support for them – nothing but kicks and cuffs ... the Government cannot carry on in a democratic country in that way.' Rowell could hardly blame his associates for this view, although he did not share it: if one saw politics as an arena in which to do battle for certain moral and social objectives, kicks and cuffs were only to be expected. Rowell stressed to Lyon that he was not pleading for exemption from criticism, but only that Lyon ascertain from him the facts of matters in which the *Globe* was interested before it launched attacks on himself or the government.[46] Apparently Lyon had no answer to these complaints since he made no reply. The answer was conveyed through the editorial columns of the *Globe*: in the next weeks the paper became even more critical of Rowell and the Union Government.

Meanwhile, at the end of June, Rowell attended a lengthy government caucus, the first since Borden's return from overseas, where the future of the coalition was considered. The decision to continue along the general lines outlined by the prime minister was concurred in without much dissent except on the part of a few western Liberals and one from Ontario. The program agreed upon left room for the extension of present policies or for marking time and avoided any mention of the most contentious issue, the tariff.[47] Borden believed that the caucus had gone a long way in agreeing to the formation of a new party, and this was the impression given the country by most of the press, but that was not Rowell's understanding. Rowell had agreed with the rejection of Borden's offer to resign, and he had agreed to a fall session of Parliament to deal chiefly with the ratification of the peace treaty and with the railway and prohibition questions; beyond that he remained uncommitted.[48]

After the caucus Borden turned once more to Rowell for proposals concerning the social program the government should now carry out. Rowell immediately consulted with J.E. Atkinson, who proved to be of little assistance. Although Atkinson was appreciative of the 'progressive programme' put through by the Union Government, he believed that nothing more could be expected from the administration because the Conservative party would inevitably, and soon, re-assert its control over the leaders in Ottawa. He was convinced that the reforms he and Rowell had at heart could not be served by Rowell's permanent association with 'non-progressives.' But he did not advise Rowell's withdrawal from the government at present; like Rowell he could see no other political home. 'I am looking to the West and to an awakened Labor mind for the renaissance.' But until it came he would have to sit on the cross benches of neutrality; in this frame of mind Atkinson had no specific reforms to suggest.[49]

Atkinson's pessimism did not deter Rowell from trying to push the government in the desired direction. While Rowell was satisfied that some of the policies he had suggested the previous autumn had been implemented, he urged Borden to consider further those that had not. He pointed out that most of his proposals in the industrial field, on which no action had yet been taken, were covered by the majority report of the Royal Commission on Industrial Relations. He advocated government adoption of this report in principle, its implementation where the federal authority had power, and consultations with the provinces to secure the adoption of recommendations lying within provincial jurisdiction. And another attempt, he believed, should be made to make the Dominion prohibition legislation permanent, subject to its repeal by the provinces; this would place responsibility for the perpetuation of prohibitory legislation squarely on the provinces.

Rowell stated bluntly that the tariff issue could no longer be bypassed. The tariff should be revised as far as possible in the direction of increased British preference 'consistent with the maintenance of our essential industries,' and the policy of 'free food' should be applied to Britain. The good relations between east and west on which any effective Canadian government must rest could not be secured without substantial tariff reductions. In 'a very large list of staple commodities ... it appears to me almost incredible that many of our most important industries could not carry on their business successfully on a substantially lower tariff.' On what basis should an industry's capacity for bearing a lower tariff be determined? He did not find the answer unduly difficult to see. The decision must be made with reference to the position of the worker and to the protection of the consumer, neither of which had been adequately considered in the past. 'Any industry which enjoys the benefit of state protection through a protective tariff should not be permitted to say that it is not able to pay a living wage or to provide such a standard of comfort for its workers as would appear to be just and reasonable, and any industry which did not do so might have its production withdrawn for it cannot justify its continuance.' The recently established Board of Commerce, which was to administer the new Combines and Fair Prices Act, might be the body to deal with the problem, but in any case he was strongly of the opinion that 'the Government should consider the question of the limitation of profits of all industries which greatly profit by the tariff.'

Once more Rowell emphasized 'the industrial question' as '*the* problem which the nations of the world must face in the immediate future.' The workingman was demanding not only a larger share of the fruits of the joint production of labour and capital but also a recognition of his importance by the establishment of 'joint control of industry.' The biggest question facing all democratic statesmen was 'how to promote such a good understanding between employers and employees as will make possible co-operation in the management and control of industry.' He doubted that the situation could be met simply by the establishment of minimum wages, but for the present he had no solution to offer. Again he observed that the implementation of his social program would accelerate the increase in public business that had occurred during the war and would necessitate 'a radical change in the machinery of Government.' It would also require the reform of the Senate by the adoption of some method of selection that would produce a body more 'consistent with the spirit of our time.'[50]

Rowell seemed to assume that the measures proposed would find acceptance among all, or nearly all, men of intelligence and good will. He did not explain how the medicine could be got down the throats of the members of the Canadian Manufacturers' Association, the Chambers of Commerce, Boards of Trade, and of most of his cabinet colleagues. That it would not be swallowed without a struggle was already evident in the minority report of the Royal Commission on Industrial Relations. It was also evident in the attitude of the businessman and fellow Methodist whose contribution to the organization of the war effort Rowell admired as much as that of any man in Canada, Sir Joseph Flavelle. Flavelle's wartime experience, especially with the packing-house industry and the Imperial Munitions Board, led him to conclusions very different from Rowell's on the subject of government intervention in the economic and social life of the nation. Flavelle was convinced that reconstruction must depend largely on business leadership and not on government and plans like Rowell's must be resisted because they would rob the individual of opportunities to do what he should do for himself. In these opinions Flavelle was probably representative of most of the business community.[51] To meet such opposition a plan of battle as well as an objective was needed, but Rowell did not have one. Despite his long association with businessmen he was naïve about the realities of economic power in Canadian society. His liberal Methodist idealism, with its optimistic assessment of human nature and its egalitarian hope for the salvation of all men, allowed him to believe that rational appeals to the self-interest and good will of members of the business community would persuade them to support social reform. But idealism was not enough.

18
No light in the window

Amid the work of the busy days before prorogation and the discussions about the future of the Borden administration Rowell had given only passing attention to the coming convention of the Ontario Liberal party. He fully expected that the gathering would confirm William Proudfoot in the leadership after his eighteen months as acting leader and that a platform similar to the one on which the party had stood under his own leadership would be reaffirmed. Now the incredible had happened: the convention had rejected Proudfoot and Major the Rev. J.C. Tolmie as well, and had elected none other than Hartley Dewart as provincial leader! 'The Ontario Liberal party has committed suicide,'[1] Rowell told the defeated leader. 'If our policies had been just the opposite of what they were, he would have been a very suitable leader.'[2] Proudfoot himself was not surprised; for many Liberals, support of Union Government had weakened party affiliations, so that most of the people who were currently attending local Liberal gatherings were Laurier Liberals. Local riding associations had appointed a disproportionate number of Laurier Liberals as delegates, and the resulting convention had been unrepresentative of Ontario Liberalism. Unfortunately, no explanation could negate the result: the provincial party was now in the hands of the Murphy-Dewart clique. The prospects for Liberalism in Ontario were dim indeed: 'Co-operation between Liberal-Unionists and the Liberals of Ontario who believe that Temperance and Social Reform are paramount ... and the Murphy-Dewart Liberals,' who would undoubtedly enjoy the full support of the liquor interests, was out of the question.[3] In particular, Rowell found it 'incredible that the Liberal women will follow an anti-prohibitionist leader, or that women who demand social legislation and high ideals will rally behind the choice.'[4] He found little solace in the fact that it was the insistence of the women that had secured the inclusion in the party platform of a commitment to 'progressive temperance legislation.' Such a statement might mean anything; what was really required was a pledge to sustain the Ontario Temperance Act in the referendum that the Hearst government proposed to hold at the time of the forthcoming provincial election. In any case, whatever the plank on temperance, who could believe that it would be honoured under Dewart's leadership? There was little that could be said to comfort disgusted former colleagues in the Legislature like T. Scott Davidson of North Brant who asked Rowell: 'Can you answer this question? How could the delegates at the Convention ... when they passed so strongly on the action of the Senate re Prohibition turn right about face and select Dewart as leader? It beats anything I ever saw or heard of. You know as I know the shape we have seen him in the House. Enough said. "Consistency thou art a jewel."' [5]

Atkinson was equally dismayed about the short-term prospects of the party, but he was hopeful for the future. He could see only 'political insolvency' under Dewart's leadership. 'Why the people should put Hearst out to put him in' was beyond Atkinson's understanding. Henceforth, his motto, and the *Star*'s would be 'measures not men,' and he would wait for the better elements who still constituted a majority in the party to react to the disintegration that he was sure would soon set in. 'I have hope' Atkinson assured Rowell 'that Philip sober will after a little repent the choice of Philip drunk. But there may be a year or two of the spree.' [6] Briefly, Rowell contemplated the formation of a union prohibitionist government in Ontario in which the prohibitionist Liberals would join with Hearst in keeping Ontario dry. [7] But whatever the merits of the idea there was little he could do from his present position to rally the discouraged ranks of true Ontario Liberalism.

One thing he could do was to make a statement on the position in which Ontario Liberal Unionists now found themselves. He chose to do it in the form of a letter addressed to one of his Port Hope constituents with whom he arranged for its publication in the *Bowmanville Statesman*. Soon the letter was reprinted in newspapers across the province, and a lively debate was precipitated on editorial pages and in correspondence columns.

Rowell began by regretting that divisions of opinion over the conduct of the war that had not divided the provincial party in the past three years had done so now. The misfortune, he charged, was due to 'the illiberal and intolerant attitude of one section of the party' led by Hartley Dewart. Dewart had not only opposed the formation of the Union Government but 'in co-operation with Mr Murphy, he led all the diverse elements in our population in Ontario hostile to Union Government and Canada's war policy and put forth his utmost efforts to defeat both.' In another respect as well Dewart was in a minority in the Liberal party, Rowell contended, for he was opposed to 'the overwhelming majority' of the party on the temperance issue and was, in fact, the 'rising hope' of the liquor interests. What was the proper course of action now for Ontario Liberal prohibitionists? They could make sure that the Ontario Temperance Act was sustained at the forthcoming referendum, and in electing a new Legislature they could see to it that 'men are elected and a government ... secured in sympathy with the law.' Although he made no mention of the Conservatives, Rowell was clearly suggesting that it might be possible to achieve this end only through support of the Hearst government; for he declared flatly that he could not see how Liberal Unionists and prohibitionists could support a leader 'opposed to their war and temperance policies.'

Turning to federal politics, Rowell attacked the right of the forthcoming Liberal convention to speak for the party. The convention had been called, not by the Liberal members of the House of Commons, but merely by one section of the Liberals in the House. That group represented a majority of the Liberal party in only one section of the country, Quebec. Outside Quebec a majority of the Liberals in Parliament were Liberal Unionists. Although a few Liberals who supported Union Government might attend, 'the convention will not be in a position to represent or speak for the Liberals who supported Union Government.' In these circumstances every Liberal Unionist must decide on his course, remembering that if the present government were to fall there would be an election neither side of the House wanted. That nobody in the House wanted an early election was evident in the agreement reached by the government and the opposition during the recent session that it was unnecessary to proceed with a new franchise bill at that time. As a result, there was no franchise act in force under which a peacetime election could properly be held. It was thus the indisputable duty of Liberal Unionists to support the government during this period of reconstruction, especially since several major items of business, notably the formal consideration of the report of the Royal Commission on Industrial Relations and the approval of the peace treaties, were not yet completed.[8]

While Ontario Liberals contemplated this advice in the pages of their daily papers Rowell was on his way west to the Okanagan with his family. He looked forward to the first extended holiday he had had since the formation of the Union Government, although in the unsettled state of political affairs the duration of his respite seemed uncertain. Just how unsettled matters were was shown in his conversations with several Winnipeg friends. He was forced to conclude that 'Union Government in the west is at present unpopular to put it mildly.' Although the western political scene was discouraging, there was nothing in it to give him reason for altering his conviction that Borden should go ahead with government reorganization and should outline a policy for the next year or two. But he still believed that there must be no Unionist party.

Since leaving Ottawa he had considered the question of a new party more thoroughly than ever before and had decided that Liberal Unionists would have greater influence in the country and in the government in the promotion of 'genuinely progressive measures' if they continued to be known as Liberals. 'Personally,' he told his Liberal Unionist cabinet colleague from Saskatchewan, J.A. Calder, 'I shall always call myself what I am and intend to remain – a Liberal. I am not prepared to turn over to the unprogressive and reactionary group who now constitute the Opposition, the right to claim the benefit of being the sole possessors of the Liberal name and the Liberal tradition.' If a majority of the cabinet decided that a Unionist party must be formed, then Rowell was firm in the procedure that should be followed. The prime minister should formulate a policy, invite colleagues to join him, and then go to the country as a Union Government. A permanent Unionist government would have no mandate to govern and should appeal to the country at once. Indeed, this necessity to seek a mandate from the electorate was itself an argument against the immediate formation of a Unionist party, since there was general agreement that there could be no election at the present time.[9]

Rowell was only just beginning to enjoy the sunshine of the Okanagan summer when the Ontario newspapers began to arrive bearing news of reactions to his 'manifesto' to Liberal Unionists. The most important, and one that caused him grave concern, was an editorial in the *Globe*, 'Mr Rowell Crosses the Floor.'[10] Although he had ceased to be under any illusion about the *Globe*'s hostility to continuation of the Union Government, he was not prepared for such a strong personal attack. The core of the paper's complaint was that 'the Liberals of Durham who voted for Rowell gave him no authority to destroy the historic party ... by agreeing to a political merger with the Conservatives.' The next day the editors explained that the *Globe*'s inability to abandon principle and follow Rowell into a new Unionist party, which 'must remain essentially the old Conservative party under the disguise of a name less likely to repel the progressive west,' did not mean that it had espoused Dewart's cause. There was no connection between the policies of the federal and provincial parties, according to the *Globe*, except that there might be some truth in the allegation that Dewart had been chosen leader to punish those who had 'deserted' Laurier. In any case, Dewart had not yet declared himself on the major provincial issue, the liquor question. In support of the implication that Dewart might still emerge as a strong prohibitionist the paper featured a denial from Dewart of any connection with the liquor interests. At the same time Dewart attacked Rowell's control over the press through the Department of Public Information, noting that Rowell was evidently finding his authority inadequate for controlling the Ontario Liberal party.[11]

Rowell immediately asked Atkinson to point out in the *Star* that 'nothing more is implied in my letter than is expressly stated. No Union Party has been formed ... to support high protection and the big interests ... I am and always will continue a Liberal and democrat opposed to the big interests as against the masses.'[12] The

Star responded as requested,[13] as well as to Rowell's plea that its comment be put on the Canadian Press wires across the country as the *Globe*'s charge had been.

Even more surprising to Rowell than the *Globe*'s attack was the attitude of M.A. James, publisher of the *Bowmanville Statesman* and one of the most influential Liberals in Rowell's constituency. Although James agreed that the choice of Dewart had been a mistake, he believed Rowell's attack on the convention's decision was an even greater blunder since it would help to perpetuate differences within the party at a time when it was highly desirable to bury the hatchet. Although he did not like to do so, James was forced to conclude on the basis of everything he could learn that Dewart did in fact enjoy the support of the majority of Ontario Liberals.[14]

Since the *Globe*'s editorial had been widely reprinted throughout Ontario and beyond, Rowell decided to reply in a lengthy letter to the paper. Again he asserted that he remained a Liberal, exactly what he was on the day the electors of Durham sent him to the House of Commons. In claiming to be a Liberal he meant that he was 'a real progressive, and not a so-called Liberal, who may be a reactionary.' Perhaps, he went on, the *Globe* would answer a series of straight questions about its own position. Did the *Globe* believe that the Union Government, and Rowell with it, should give up its endeavours to ensure the continuation of the prohibition orders-in-council, to abolish patronage, and to establish a publicly owned railway system, and instead join the Laurier Liberals in opposing all of these measures? Why was the *Globe* not supporting the government in its policies for securing co-operation between capital and labour, for controlling prices and profits, and for enhancing Canada's participation in the councils of the Empire and the world? Was it possible that the *Globe* could think that 'the government should turn over the solution of these problems to the present Opposition in the House of Commons?' On every one of these questions Rowell outlined a position that both he and the *Globe* had held.[15] It was a presentation of past and present politics that the *Globe* could not easily refute.

The *Globe*'s rebuttal was assisted by ammunition provided by the Conservatives when the *Mail and Empire* published an 'inside account' of a secret meeting of the Central Conservative Association of Toronto at which H.C. Hocken declared that in future it would be impossible to separate Rowell and Borden. The assembled Toronto Conservatives found this entirely agreeable as long as Rowell accepted the traditional policies of the Conservative party, the most important being the National Policy of Sir John A. Macdonald.[16] The next *Globe* editorial glowed with satisfaction at this proof of the negligible influence Rowell would have in the government unless he ceased to be a Liberal.[17] In any case, the editors argued, the Union Government had finished its task of winning the war; now Rowell was sponsoring a new party with neither platform nor principles. Had he forgotten that the bill validating the prohibition orders-in-council had been rejected by a Conservative Senate, or could he deny that many of the Conservatives with whom he was now yoked were opposed to both public ownership and the abolition of patronage? The *Globe* was in no doubt that 'if the alternatives are the creation of a permanent Unionist party dominated by Conservative politicians and carrying out Conservative tariff policies or an immediate general election, there are few Liberal Unionists in Ontario who would not prefer to have the political atmosphere cleared by an election.'[18] Obviously the *Globe* could not be convinced that Rowell's alternative was a viable one. Even the *Toronto Star*, although it declared its adherence to Rowell's program and promised support for liberal measures under any party's sponsorship, was lukewarm in its acceptance of the existing political order.[19]

From his side, Dewart kept the controversy going by renewing his charges that Rowell had conspired with Hearst during the war to end the normal functioning of the party system in the province and was guilty of intrigue against Laurier. For a while Rowell debated whether this was the moment to publish a lengthy statement he had been preparing for some months detailing the circumstances of his entry into the Union Government. But when Premier Hearst issued an emphatic denial that there had been any negotiations between himself and Rowell some of the charges were satisfactorily refuted; the rest could wait until the fall session of Parliament when the opposition would no doubt again open the question of his relations with Laurier.[20]

While Rowell was on holiday Borden announced two new appointments to the cabinet: Sir Henry Drayton gave up his position as chairman of the Board of Railway Commissioners to become minister of finance when Sir Thomas White was forced to retire to attend to the improvement of his health and his private business; and Dr S.F. Tolmie, taking the portfolio of agriculture, strengthened cabinet representation from British Columbia. Although Rowell regarded both these appointments as good ones, the fact remained that both men were Conservatives; their accession to the cabinet did nothing to answer Liberal Unionist criticism of Borden for his failure to equalize representation. The prime minister was, it was true, tackling that problem rather dramatically by an attempt to woo some prominent Quebec Liberals into the cabinet. Rowell had discussed this possibility with Borden and other ministers before he left Ottawa,[21] and was therefore not surprised to hear that Borden was conferring with the premier of Quebec, Sir Lomer Gouin, and with Rodolphe Lemieux, Ernest Lapointe, Jacques Bureau, and others. Borden reported that some of them were willing to join the government but were 'rather afraid of the public opinion they have created,' found Regulation 17 still a stumbling block, and would want Borden to persuade the Ontario government to modify it.[22] Rowell's observation on the progress of the negotiations was short and caustic: 'In view of all that Lemieux and Lapointe have said about Union Government one can appreciate what they say about public opinion but miracles never cease.'[23] In the end the Quebec politicians decided to take no action until after the Liberal convention. Perhaps it was just as well; while the inclusion of French-speaking representatives in the cabinet would strengthen the administration in its weakest point, the presence of one or more of the most conservative Quebec Liberals would also present difficulties for Rowell. Colleagues noted for their protectionist views and their hostility to public ownership of railways could scarcely make the cabinet more congenial to him.

As the opening of the convention on 5 August approached there was much discussion among rank-and-file Liberal Unionist supporters about the attitude they should adopt toward the deliberations. Some were disposed to participate in the convention or to support it publicly in order to pave the way for the eventual reunion of the party, even though the Union Government might continue for some time yet. Other Liberal Unionists desired informal consultation between the two wings of Liberalism before the convention. Rowell agreed that such a meeting was desirable; he also believed it to be impossible. 'It takes two to co-operate' he pointed out to the editor of the *Bowmanville Statesman*, and there had been nothing but hostility towards the Liberal Unionist leaders from the Laurier Liberals 'who deliberately seek to destroy the reputation of the Liberal Unionists to further their own political ends.' On their side, 'the Liberal Unionists ... have acted throughout with the greatest moderation ... They have, beyond what was reasonable, accepted insult and attack by men who, not only did not take part in the war themselves, but sought to get into power by organizing all the pro-German and anti-British elements in the country. Do you think that the Liberals who sacrificed personal comfort and personal friendships to help in forming Union Government and save Canada should, hat-in-hand, go to the men who failed Canada in the hour of need?'[24]

Rowell did not return to Ottawa from British Columbia until just after the conclusion of the Liberal convention but relied on press reports and the comments of friends in forming his impressions of the gathering. For the benefit of his colleague, A.K. Maclean, who was holidaying in England, Rowell put some of his conclusions on paper. It had undoubtedly been a Laurier Liberal Convention; the few Liberal Unionists who had attended, apart from the eight Liberal provincial premiers, had been kept in the background and made to feel rather uncomfortable. Thus F.F. Pardee had been nominated for one of the twenty-seven Ontario positions on the resolutions committee but had not been elected. As for the oratory, 'the speakers reached their greatest triumphs when they denounced Liberal Unionist members of the Government ... [but] only three or four speakers made any personal references and on the whole the speeches were kept within reasonable bounds.' The convention had been a marvel of organization. 'It operated with machine-like precision; no one had a chance to speak or to present an idea who was not on the set programme; and the Opposition Liberals present received the proposed policies with great enthusiasm and went away happy.' Rowell was uncertain of the effect the choice of Mackenzie King as the new leader would have on the country, although he was confident that King's war record would tell against his effectiveness. What of the new Liberal platform adopted at the convention? Rowell was not disposed to take it very seriously. '[It] is undoubtedly designed to secure the largest possible number of votes. It is certainly a platform to get in on.'[25]

Yet much of the new Liberal platform could well have been drawn up by Rowell himself. The sections on social and industrial reform, as drafted by Mackenzie King, were in substance an 'Atkinson-Rowell program' and were entirely in keeping with the majority report of the Royal Commission on Industrial Relations. The resolutions on 'freer trade,' on the need for Dominion legislation on liquor control to bring about complete prohibition, and on the desirability of continuing business and personal income taxes were all in keeping with Rowell's frequently expressed views. There was a serious flaw, it was true, in the Liberal plank on the railway question. The convention had straddled the fence on that issue by criticizing the government's execution of its policy while avoiding any commitment on the principle of public ownership. The emotional overtones in many of the speeches against Imperial centralization were very different from Rowell's more positive statements on the tie with Britain, but the resolution itself was completely consistent with his views.[26] The new Liberal platform, if taken at its face value, could easily have provided a bridge for Rowell's return to a reconstituted Liberal party. But he had no confidence in the sincerity of the men or the interests controlling the party. Nothing at the convention had increased his desire to leave the government.

Rowell's scepticism about the new Liberal platform and his uncertainty about the future character of Mackenzie King's leadership did not prevent him from sending a friendly note to the new Liberal leader. After congratulating King on the opportunity he now enjoyed to serve his country, Rowell observed that 'while we may not agree on all questions of policy I am sure we can agree to disagree.'[27] The months ahead would reveal how much agreement was possible. About Hartley Dewart, he felt more strongly. When Rowell journeyed to Toronto briefly to participate in ceremonies admitting the Prince of Wales as a bencher of the Law Society of Upper Canada he passed Dewart in Osgoode Hall without greeting the new provincial leader. Nor did Dewart make any effort to break the silence.[28]

With the Liberal convention over, the time was ripe for a conference of Rowell's leading Toronto supporters. As he had done so often, he first had a long session with Atkinson. The editor of the *Star* would have preferred to see Rowell at the head of the federal Liberal party, but since the heritage of wartime animosities made that impossible he had decided to back Mackenzie King.[29] Atkinson could no longer see any point in supporting the Union Government, and he urged Rowell and all Liberal Unionists to return to party lines. But most of the group that later assembled in the home of F.H. Deacon to discuss Rowell's future course disagreed. This 'very fine company ... [of] old and warm personal and political friends,' Rowell told Nell, included most of the men who had urged him to enter the Union Government two years earlier. J.H. Gundy, J.F. Mackay, A.E. Ames, E.R. Wood, S.J. Moore, and Atkinson were all there, as were several other prominent Toronto Liberal Unionists: Thomas Bradshaw, insurance executive, stockbroker, and leading Canadian actuary, W.G. Watson, an officer of the Toronto General Trusts Corporation, and Robert McKay and J.L. Ross, both lawyers and experienced party workers. Early in the discussion it became clear that no one favoured the creation of a formal Unionist party. But only Atkinson and Bradshaw urged early reunion with the Laurier Liberals. All the rest, with the exception of Robert McKay who was uncertain of his course, were adamant in their refusal to return to the Liberal party under Mackenzie King 'or under any men or with men who failed Canada in the supreme crisis.'[30] Moore hoped that generally improving economic conditions and the recent actions of both the Canadian and American governments in endeavouring to control profiteering and lower prices on the necessities of life would shortly redound to the credit of the government, and rally the Liberal Unionist voters of 1917 behind a continuation of the present administration.[31] Ames was as appalled as anyone present by the utter unacceptability of the only alternatives open if the Liberal Unionists disbanded – absorption by Conservatives or Laurier Liberals – and clung tenaciously to the conviction that both fates could be avoided if the government resolutely pursued the program that Rowell had been urging on the prime minister in recent months.[32] The same course of action was strongly supported by Rowell's law partners, S. Casey Wood and Tom Reid. Despite the opposition of Atkinson, whose opinions he had no inclination to treat lightly, Rowell's Toronto consultations confirmed him in his preference for remaining with the government.[33] Within a few days Atkinson brought Rowell and Mackenzie King together over dinner at the Ottawa Country Club.[34] If Atkinson was seeking a political rapprochement, he was disappointed. The only immediate result was that Rowell received an autographed copy of King's prescription for industrial peace, *Industry and Humanity*, which he had already read with interest when it was first published nine months earlier.[35]

As always over the past twenty-five years, Sir John Willison was concerning himself with Rowell's political career and in more than one conversation urged him to remain with the government permanently. Later, Willison wrote to underline the soundness of his advice: 'an extraordinary change ... in the public attitude towards you is taking place and ... in my judgment there is no position you may not attain if you remain in public life. You will not misunderstand me if I suggest that ... there are few competitors for the first places.' Willison expected and welcomed the formation of a permanent Unionist party, most of whose members and supporters, perhaps as many as 85 per cent, would inevitably be Conservatives. He did not much care what the new party was called, and agreed with Rowell that '"Conservative" is not a good name for this country.' Indeed, he was not convinced that either 'Liberal' or 'Conservative' had any meaning in Canada: 'Laurier was a Tory. Borden is a Liberal.'[36] Rowell's experience had fully verified the truth of this description, which was why he was prepared to remain with the prime minister for the present. But he was far from convinced that he should drop the Liberal label now, or ever.

In the weeks after the opening of the special fall session of Parliament Rowell had ample reason to believe that his effectiveness in the government was far from ended. He had never been in more frequent consultation with Borden, and he had an abundance of opportunities to present the merits of his social program to a sympathetic prime minister. There was satisfaction for him as well in the implementation of policies agreed on earlier, notably in the appointment of the Board of Commerce from whose labours Rowell hoped for a significant decrease in or at least stabilization of, consumer prices. And plans were under way for a National Industrial Conference to bring together sixty representatives each from business and industry to consider the recommendations of the report of the Royal Commission on Industrial Relations. Further, Rowell again urged on Borden the importance of financial aid to returned university students.[37] He again raised the question of taxation of war profits with a plea for serious consideration of a proposal that would have amounted to post-war conscription of wealth as thorough as any that had been advocated during the war: the government should tax Canadians 'to the extent of the actual increase in their wealth ... during the period of the war.' No one would then have profited materially from the conflict. In the west, especially, Rowell had found much more enthusiasm among veterans for this measure than for the additional $2,000 bonus for veterans currently being advocated by the Great War Veterans' Association. He was not unaware that 'the difficulties ... would be enormous ... and they may be insuperable'; but he was convinced that there was 'a real measure of justice in such a proposal.' He thought it not impossible that at least some important elements in the business community might accept it. He was encouraged in this view by his discussion with 'so sane and conservative a man' as R.T. Riley, one of the most versatile and successful businessmen in Winnipeg. Riley thought it 'a just and feasible proposal ... and that in the interests of business it would be much better that they should now have the definite burden which they must pay fixed, than to be compelled to look forward to an indefinite charge upon profits and earnings as a means of paying Canada's war obligations and carrying on the business of the country.'[38] So radical a proposal was beyond the bounds of

Borden's 'Liberalism,' and there is no evidence that it ever came before cabinet.

Even on measures being discussed in cabinet and caucus there was a distressing lack of agreement. This fact was somewhat obscured from the public by the earlier announcement that the special fall session of Parliament was being called to deal with the peace treaties. But Rowell had always thought it important that the government should announce a sufficiently comprehensive program to inspire confidence among the electorate that the Union Government was still functioning decisively. To his regret, the speech from the throne, the shortest in Canadian parliamentary history, mentioned only one subject, the treaties. It was vital that in the next few weeks the dissension within the coalition should be resolved so that measures to which he assigned the highest priority – the nationalization of the Grand Trunk, the renewal of the prohibition law, and the extension of soldiers' gratuities – could be passed.[39]

Unity in the cabinet and caucus was not assisted by the illness that forced Borden's absence from Parliament after the first week of the session. Although the prime minister still conferred with his colleagues at home, with none more frequently than with Rowell, he was unable to give the leadership so urgent at the moment. But when Borden offered to resign only Meighen supported the suggestion. Rowell, along with the rest of the cabinet, was convinced that Borden's resignation would be a catastrophe; Borden must remain at the helm, at least nominally, while he took an extended holiday.[40] This arranged, Borden departed for West Virginia leaving Sir George Foster as acting prime minister. Under the seventy-two-year-old Foster, tired and grieving over the recent death of his wife, the government would have to struggle on as best it could.

In Borden's absence Rowell and A.L. Sifton were the chief government interpreters in Parliament of the peace treaty, and more importantly, of Canada's new role in international affairs. By signing the peace treaty in her own right, Rowell declared, Canada had taken the last great step forward into nationhood. But it was easier to hail the new status than to define it precisely in the face of questions from members of the opposition, some of whom declared that Canada was not a sovereign nation and had no right to sign the treaty, while others bemoaned the loss to London or Geneva of the autonomy that already existed. What was the difference, they wanted to know, between 'approval' and 'ratification,' between 'legal right' and 'constitutional right,' between 'neutrality' and 'non-participation?' Some members of the House were visibly annoyed by Rowell's rather superior attitude during the discussion of these subtleties and by his assumption that such simple distinctions could be grasped easily by anyone only slightly brighter than D.D. McKenzie. McKenzie's suggestion that Canada was not a nation and no action of her Parliament could make any difference in the binding effect of the treaty on Canada had kept him awake one night, Rowell told the House, while he contemplated McKenzie's ignorance of both Liberal and Conservative policies ever since 1858. He treated the more ably presented arguments of Lapointe and Fielding with greater respect, but in the end he failed to produce any wholly logical explanation of the mystery that enabled the British Empire to be one body, yet five nations.[41]

Before his illness Borden had begun to present to the House the new responsibilities Canada had undertaken in joining the League of Nations. He had refused to answer questions about the truth of newspaper reports that at the Paris Conference Canada had protested against Article 10 of the League Covenant, which required all League members to come to the assistance of any other member nation under attack. Rowell now claimed that many Canadians were placing far too much emphasis on Article 10 because it was the subject of controversy in the United States. To do so was to miss the point, Rowell contended. The real heart of the Covenant was in Article 12, binding all signatories to submit their disputes to arbitration and thus implementing the primary object of the League, the prevention of war. 'In ninety-nine cases out of one hundred' war would thus be avoided. 'Men will get together and talk things over, and they will settle their disputes.' Article 10 was simply an extra 'insurance feature.' Implying that he was less than entirely enthusiastic about this provision himself, Rowell admitted that 'it is a Covenant upon which ... there are honest differences of opinion, and there may have been in the Peace Conference. But it is part of the League; we cannot help it; we must take it as part of the whole Covenant.' The acceptance of Article 10 meant no infringement of Canadian autonomy, as critics alleged. Canada could be involved in action against an aggressor under Article 10 only with the agreement of the Canadian Parliament, which alone had power to raise Canadian troops. Thus the power of the League Council under Article 10 was 'only advisory.' Moreover, if the Council decided to request a military contribution from Canada towards any League action, Canada would automatically become 'a country of special interest' and be entitled to a seat on the Council without whose unanimous consent no action could be taken.[42]

Before he took his seat Rowell returned to the theme which had run through all his remarks on the new pattern of imperial relations and on the League, a theme with which he was so preoccupied that like nearly all the participants in the debate he had paid no attention at all to the terms of the post-war settlement itself. The fact of Canada's enhanced stature among the nations of the world overshadowed every other significance. Paying tribute to Borden and Sifton, Rowell asserted that their representation of Canada's interests at the Peace Conference had crowned the nation's contribution to the war. On behalf of their countrymen they had signed a treaty that would affect Canada 'not only to-day with her eight millions of people' but in the future when she would have 'from twenty-five to fifty millions, when Canada is not only one of the greatest powers on the Pacific, but one of the great powers of the world'; and in the League of Nations there was the hope of peace 'not only for a generation, perhaps, but for a century to come.'[43]

Although Rowell's exposition of Canada's new position in the world won the admiring approval of A.R. McMaster as a statement of the true Liberal doctrine on colonial evolution to full autonomy, nothing could diminish the efforts of other opposition members, notably Lucien Cannon and Rodolphe Lemieux, to show that Rowell had departed from that doctrine and from his own previous policies. Quoting from his pre-war public statements on imperial relations, they charged that Rowell had become 'an advocate of the Curtis plan and the Milner policy, which is jingo Imperialist policy.' Under that new order Canada would, by her membership in the Imperial Council, be swept automatically into future British wars and by her participation in the League into wars involving countless other nations. And Rowell called this progress![44] The chief effect of the whole debate on Rowell's thinking was simply to confirm him in his conviction of the dangers of allowing the conduct of Canada's external relations to fall into the hands of the opposition party.

His feeling towards that group was scarcely improved when Joseph Archambault, member for Chambly and Verchères, attacked the government's failure to control the cost of living. The president of the Privy Council, Archambault charged, was the arch defender of the profiteers, the Flavelles and the Gordons, and 'had shown more grit in defending a profiteering company' than he had the year before in the House when the member for Russell made 'precise accusations against him.'[45] Here was the opportunity to reply to Murphy on the floor of the House. Rowell was well prepared because he had been working on a draft of a lengthy statement of his share in the events leading up to the formation of the government and had reviewed it with both Willison and Pardee and more recently with his cousin in Winnipeg, J.B. Coyne.[46]

Before turning to Murphy's earlier charges he defended himself and the government on the cost-of-living issue. His own and the administration's resistance to the liquor, railway, and packing house interests, the activities of the cost-of-living commissioner, and the appointment of the Board of Commerce were fully expounded. Altogether, Rowell contended, the Canadian government's program for finding a solution to the problem of high prices was far ahead of anything being done in Britain or the United States. He stoutly denied that he had ever defended a profiteer, and although he was not at liberty to announce that he had pressed the matter on Borden, he did declare that 'if it were possible I should like to see a situation in which all profits made by men during the war – the amounts by which they increased their wealth over the wealth they produced before the war – were turned into the public treasury.' Before leaving the subject of profiteers he had something to say about Sir Joseph Flavelle, who, he believed, had received far less appreciation than he deserved at the hands of the Canadian people. He did not intend 'to discuss the question of the bacon business'; but he would not withdraw one word of what he had said earlier in the House about Flavelle's services as chairman of the Imperial Munitions Board, services that the nation would one day assess accurately. In the meantime, 'the public man who is afraid because of some cheap criticism of doing justice to a man who has rendered such great service to the country would be unworthy to occupy a seat in this House.'[47]

Proceeding to the allegations of the member for Russell, Rowell observed that Murphy was not in the House: had he known that he would be discussing this subject that day he would have favoured Murphy with the customary notice that he proposed to speak of him, a courtesy Murphy had not extended to him in March 1918. For eighteen months he had refrained from answering Murphy for fear of increasing racial and religious tensions in the country, and only on the cessation of hostilities had he defended himself before the voters of his own riding. But now that his silence had been the object of taunts from the opposition he would answer in the House once and for all. Meticulously, he described the establishment and purpose of the secretarial fund. Murphy knew that his assertions about the secretarial fund were false, Rowell charged, but 'either he, or those associated with him, or the Liberal information bureau ... had his speech printed and distributed throughout Canada ... Is that what a public man has the right to expect from even his bitterest opponents on the other side of the House?' Murphy had gone so far as to say that the secretarial fund was raised for the purpose of supplanting Laurier. On the contrary, Rowell claimed, 'one might say ... that it was raised to prevent embarrassment to Sir Wilfrid.' Since some members of the federal Liberal party had been unwilling to identify themselves with the policy of 'abolish-the-bar' and the 'advanced social programme' of the Ontario party, it had been agreed that the provincial and federal parties would each work through their own organization, co-operating as much as possible.

Neither in this nor in the negotiations leading to the formation of the Union Government had there been any conspiracy. At every step he had kept the chief Liberal Whip, F.F. Pardee, informed, a fact that he was sure Pardee would have verified were he not absent from the House at the moment. If Laurier were in his old place in the House he too would tell the same story, a story that would one day be told in full when his correspondence with Laurier could be made public. In the meantime, he quoted a sentence from a letter Laurier had written him just before his entry into the Union Government in which the Liberal Leader referred to his respect for Rowell's convictions and expressed the hope that their acute difference of opinion would not mar their 'old personal relations.' All the evidence showed, stated Rowell, that 'I never questioned his sincerity in the course he took, and I am perfectly sure he never questioned mine.'

Finally, Murphy's repeated assertions that he had slandered the Roman Catholic church and the whole French Canadian race in his address in December 1917 had to be met. Rowell read key excerpts from the speech and found nothing that required retraction. His tribute to the work of priests in France, which he now repeated, made it clear that he was not belittling priests in general; had he known that the members of the French orders who had come to Canada were liable for military service, he would have included them in his favourable comments; as it was, he accepted Murphy's figures on the war record of this group and only regretted that 'their splendid example was not used by him and more of his associates to appeal to others of their own religion, to inspire them to similar service,' as Bishop Fallon of London had done.

Again Rowell drew a comparison between the Upper Canadian Liberals in 1864 and the Liberal Unionists of 1917 and closed with a portrayal of the dire consequences of the defeat of conscription and failure to support the men at the front: 'There would have been created in Canada a religious and racial cleavage which decades would not have healed. And it will stand to the everlasting credit of that distinguished man, Sir Wilfrid Laurier, that when the verdict was given at the polls ... he strongly urged his compatriots in Quebec to accept the verdict of the people.'[48]

The Liberal whip, J.A. Robb, was immediately on his feet to congratulate Rowell on his change of heart concerning the people of Quebec, a change he found hard to reconcile with the methods used by Rowell as chief campaign and advertising manager of the Union Government election campaign in Ontario. Robb adamantly refused to accept Rowell's denial that he had anything to do with organizing the advertising and read a number of anti-Quebec excerpts from government advertising during the campaign as examples of 'the sort of stuff the President of the Privy Council was putting out in 1917.'[49] Thus did the opposition serve notice that Rowell's rebuttal had changed nothing on the other side of the House. The 'light in the window' for Liberal Unionists was not intended to shed its beam as far as Rowell. Even on his own side some resented his reading the excerpt from Laurier's letter because many members had more than a suspicion that it did not represent the whole of Laurier's opinion of Rowell.[50]

During this special session a few measures for which Rowell bore major responsibility were adopted with little resistance. For the first time he was in the House as minister of health, a position he had occupied since 1 July. After he had worked out the broad lines on which the department was to function the actual work of organization had been done by the newly appointed deputy minister, Dr J.A. Amyot, whose career as an authority on public health and later as a member of the Canadian Medical Corps had made Rowell anxious to secure his services. In the House Rowell outlined the scope of the new department, stressing that its activities could be carried on, from both constitutional and practical necessity, only in close co-operation with the provincial governments. The measures passed by the federal Parliament in this field would probably be few; for the moment the only bill Rowell had to present was one to restrict further the sale of certain drugs. After he had produced figures to show that prohibition had not increased the use of these drugs, as some opponents of prohibition were charging, the measure went through easily.[51]

Similarly, there was only mild opposition comment on Rowell's presentation of a bill to amalgamate the Dominion Police with the Royal North-West Mounted Police under the name Royal Canadian Mounted Police. To D.D. McKenzie's doubt about the need for such a force, since Nova Scotia had always got along very well without one, several western members replied with tributes to the work of the Mounties among aliens. And in Rowell's mind the role of the Mounted Police in the Winnipeg strike was still the prime example of the usefulness of the force; their presence had prevented serious bloodshed and their very existence was 'a safeguard against disturbance.' Questioned as to why the militia, whose size had recently been doubled, was not sufficient to maintain order throughout the country, Rowell replied that the militia had been doubled on paper but not in practice. In any case, he thought it 'wiser to have that reserve in the form of a police force rather than in the form of a larger military force than we need otherwise maintain. It ... is less likely to give offence and create irritation if the force available for maintaining order is a police rather than a military force.' Under probing from the opposition he admitted that under the bill before the House the RCMP could legally be used in any province by the Dominion government but that the government intended to adhere to the present policy of intervening only on the invitation of provincial governments, except in cases in which the RCMP was charged with the enforcement of Dominion laws, i.e. with matters relating to aliens, the policing of the international boundary, customs and inland revenue, Indian affairs, government railways, and the post office.[52] Thus clarified, the bill passed without division.

Rowell's presentation of a bill to amend the Department of Soldiers' Civil Re-establishment Act produced more discussion, but the effectiveness of opposition criticism was severely limited by its failure to propose concrete alternatives to government plans. When the government declined to increase cash gratuities to returned soldiers Mackenzie King launched a long attack on the administration's handling of veterans' affairs, but while asserting that the question of further gratuities had not been considered carefully enough, he refused to commit himself to the principle of increased payments. Rowell did not enjoy answering questions on the government's failure to provide financial aid to university students whose education had been interrupted by war service. His failure thus far to convince the cabinet of the necessity of such assistance continued to be a source of great regret to him. All he could say in the House was that the government was considering this debatable question in which he admitted a deep personal interest.[53]

Much to Rowell's satisfaction it proved possible to proceed with the government's program of railway legislation when the Unionist caucus agreed to government acquisition of the Grand Trunk Railway. In Parliament most of the cabinet were either absent or silent on the railway question. Illness prevented the prime minister from being present to support a measure embodying principles of public control of railways which he had held for many years.[54] Once again Rowell found himself in full agreement with Borden on a major issue of public policy. The task of presenting the railway bill to the House fell formally to J.D. Reid, as minister of railways, but the chief and highly skilful pilot of the legislation was Meighen. Rowell had a grasp of the legal and financial subtleties of the complicated measure superior to Reid's and equalled only by Meighen's. During a debate that occupied the House almost exclusively for more than two weeks he spoke frequently on matters both of principle and of detail. Like Meighen, Rowell argued for the bill as the only common sense business solution to the railway problem. Government ownership was economically and politically preferable to the only other alternatives: liquidation of the road with consequent waste of the investment in the company to date, or acquisition by the CPR, a solution unpalatable to the Canadian people, who were unwilling to see the whole transportation system controlled by one big corporation. Unlike Meighen, who had no particular commitment to the principle of public ownership, Rowell argued for the bill on that principle. This was his distinctive contribution to the debate, and it caused not a little distress among some of his less enthusiastic colleagues on the government benches.

Against those who contrasted the success of the CPR with the troubles of the present government railway system, Rowell pointed out that few railways anywhere had been subsidized by public money and lands as the CPR had been. And why did Canada already have some publicly owned railways? 'They are in the hands of the government not because of any failure of government ownership but because of the failure of private ownership.' The Canadian public would receive no adequate return from the investment of millions of dollars because of the duplication of lines that had been permitted to grow up under private ownership. 'This condition of things is due not to public ownership but to private ownership of railways in this country.' The explanation of the immediate plight of the government railways was clear: they did not form a transcontinental system. However, if the Grand Trunk lines in Ontario and Quebec were added, they could become a paying proposition, a fact that explained the present bitter opposition of the CPR. The private railway interests and the opposition in the House were well aware that if they could prevent the incorporation of the Grand Trunk into the government railway system they would 'make government operation of railways in Canada a colossal failure and would enable the private interests from one end of the country to the other to say that public ownership could never be a success in Canada.' Future acceptance of the whole principle of public ownership of utilities in Canada might therefore hang on the fate of the Grand Trunk bill. Rowell was convinced that the present government had proved that publicly owned railways could be operated free of political interest by an independent board of business and railway experts. As for efficiency, even if it could be proven that public ownership was slightly less efficient than private, he would support it because of the elimination of patronage it facilitated. 'If there is one thing that has bedevilled the public life of this country it has been the influence of railway corporations.' In an extended lecture on the social values of public ownership Rowell contended that 'we will educate our people to the higher responsibilities of citizenship and to distinterested public service only as we trust them with these important responsibilities.' To deny that a public utility could be well operated was 'an absolute distrust of the people.'[55] To his gratification Parliament decided to trust the people; the measure to nationalize the Grand Trunk became law.

Throughout the session Rowell had urged in council the necessity of reintroducing the bill on Dominion prohibition, but a majority of members argued that the measure should wait until after the Ontario provincial election lest it influence the outcome of the election or the referendum on the Ontario Temperance Act. The result of those contests on 22 October was astounding to victors and vanquished alike. Although the continuation of prohibition was approved by a vote of nearly two to one, the Hearst government, which had led Ontario into its dry state, failed to secure a majority. To the relief of Rowell and all prohibitionist Liberals, Hartley Dewart was also unable to form a government, and the premiership therefore devolved on Ernest C. Drury of the United Farmers of Ontario who formed an administration of farmer-labour members. Although this was not a development that Rowell had anticipated, it was one in which he saw considerable hope for progressive legislation. But briefly he feared that Hearst's defeat would make his cabinet colleagues even more reluctant to support any temperance legislation. Foster put the dilemma succinctly in his diary: 'We are having trouble with a lot of our Ontario men – mad at Hearst's desertion by the temperance people for whom he imperilled his political future. What rank ingratitude.'[56] Yet in spite of this evidence of the growing unpopularity of temperance legislation the caucus and cabinet agreed to proceed with the bill drafted by Rowell. This decision may be attributed not only to the enthusiasm of cabinet ministers like Rowell and Foster but also to the limited nature of the legislation itself. It gave no direct powers to the Dominion government but simply amended the Canada Temperance Act to allow the Dominion to arrange for any 'prohibition province' that requested it to hold a referendum on the importation of intoxicants into that province; machinery was thus set up through which the provinces could continue certain of the regulatory functions which the Dominion government had exercised during the war. In the closing hours of the session, and under the reluctant sponsorship of Doherty, the temperance legislation was passed.

While the special session was drawing to a close Rowell was 'shining at Washington,' as Foster remarked with perhaps a suggestion of jealousy.[57] With the minister of labour, Gideon Robertson, Rowell was representing the Canadian government at the inaugural conference of the International Labor Organization. Canadian labour's spokesman was P.M. Draper, secretary of the Trades and Labor Congress, and the employers were represented by S.R. Parsons, president of the British American Oil Company. Well known both as a Conservative and as a Methodist layman, Parsons had recently received considerable publicity for his outspoken hostility to the radical pronouncements of the General Conference of his church on the social order.

The Canadian delegates to the conference went to Washington with the National Industrial Conference called by the Canadian government just behind them. What had happened at Ottawa did not augur well for Canadian unity in the councils of the ILO. Although the Ottawa conference had been impressive in the broadness of its representation, the delegates could come to little agreement. Officially, the conference approved unanimously the formation of industrial councils on the model of the Whitley councils in England, but the discussion revealed sharp differences between employers and employees on the structure and function of these bodies. The union representatives were absolutely opposed to any new form of organization that might weaken existing labour organizations and had no thought of giving up their present unions to take part in industrial councils of uncertain powers. On the other hand, many employers were hostile to the government's sponsorship of the idea of councils, fearing that it simply meant government blessing on the growth of unions. A more open clash developed over the adoption of the principle of collective bargaining and over the eight-hour day, and the conference ended without any agreement whatever on these points.[58] Confronted by these evidences of the gulf between Canadian employers and organized labour, the government had found it politic, amid all its other uncertainties, to refrain from initiating a parliamentary discussion of the report of the Royal Commission on Industrial Relations.

In the first meetings of the new ILO there were inevitably many constitutional points and questions of procedure to be resolved. Rowell was active in this side of the work of the conference, especially in his capacity as chairman of the commission on applications for admission of new members. Taking a 'strict constructionist' view of the ILO constitution, he contended that membership was coterminous with membership in the League of Nations. He could accept no other reading of the constitution and was insistent that any departure from its clear meaning would jeopardize the whole future of the ILO. Draft conventions from a conference not legally constituted would be readily challenged and the work of the new organization thereby invalidated. In due course a compromise with the 'loose constructionists' was reached, one which Rowell was satisfied did not prejudice the constitutional foundations of the ILO.[59]

The basis of the conference's deliberations was the labour section of the Peace Treaty which had noted several areas of urgent concern. The conference had no great difficulty in agreeing on a draft convention on the working hours and conditions of women and children and on more adequate factory inspection, but the general adoption of an eight-hour day proved to be much more contentious. The representative of Canadian employers, S.R. Parsons, played a considerable part in sharpening the controversy when he announced that he could not associate himself with the report submitted by the majority of the employers' representatives, a report which accepted the principle of the eight-hour day and the forty-eight-hour week in industry under certain rigidly specified conditions. Parsons' opposition was total and amounted to a rejection of the whole concept of the ILO. When economic conditions varied so greatly throughout the world it was impossible to make relevant suggestions for hours of work applicable to all countries. Further, he asserted, the world was not suffering from long hours but from underproduction, especially of food and clothing; reduction of working hours could only accentuate the world's dire need for more consumer goods. In any case, this was an economic problem; Parsons feared that 'if we try to settle it in our legislative halls in a political way, it will receive a political and not an economic answer. The more business interests of any country get into the hands of the government and politicians the more difficult it is to keep out influences that should never come between one class and another in any country.' The ILO should drop its attempts to make recommendations on hours of work: 'If we attempt this it is the surest way of wrecking our civilization, and we have the best civilization to-day that the world has ever seen. Let us take care of it and mend it here and there, but not attempt to destroy it.' Parsons believed that limitation of hours would be a special hardship on new industries in the less industrialized countries like Canada. And a further problem for Canada was the great uncertainty about whether the United States would join the League of Nations and the ILO: 'It would be suicidal for us, their small neighbour ... to agree to what they had not adhered to ... Until the United States has spoken Canada must keep silent.'[60]

The workers' delegates also objected to the majority report of the employers on the grounds that the conditions attached to acceptance of the eight-hour principle were so severe that in practice they meant opposition. Rowell was less than pleased by the reactionary pronouncements of Parsons and alarmed by an apparent impasse between workers and employers that threatened to become so acute that nothing would be accomplished on what he believed to be the most important question under discussion. In an effort to save the situation he moved that the eight-hour issue be referred to an especially appointed commission of representatives of employers, employees, and government which should be asked to bring in an agreement that had some chance of securing the necessary two-thirds majority. The conference agreed to this procedure and Parsons, Draper, and Robertson were chosen to represent Canada.[61] During this interval Parsons consulted with several of his business acquaintances in Canada, while Rowell went off to New York to confer with Borden about the attitude he should take if Parsons continued his resistance.

In two weeks' time the commission presented its report on a draft convention for an eight-hour day and a forty-eight-hour week. Obviously there was at least one member of the commission who did not agree with its work. Parsons was first on his feet, declaring that Canadian employers would not accept the convention. After the British labour leader G.N. Barnes had pointed out rather sharply to Parsons that the ILO had no power to force Canadian application of the convention, implying that Parsons had obstructed the conference long enough, Rowell took the floor. Although he had earlier indicated that the Canadian government was well disposed towards the eight-hour principle, he now delivered a direct rebuttal of Parsons. As representative of Canadian employers Parsons had very properly presented certain views, but 'in the last analysis the Governments in the different countries must determine what the policy of the country shall be,' and both representatives of the Canadian government would vote for the convention. Rowell's comments on the bearing of American attitudes on Canada's actions had special point because five days earlier the United States Senate had rejected the Versailles Treaty and the League of Nations. He wished to disabuse the conference of any ideas it might have gathered on this subject from Parsons or from the American press, which was assuming that Canada would not act unless the United States did so: 'The action of the Government of Canada in these matters does not depend on the action of the Government of the United States. It has not in the past. It will not in the future.' The Canadian Parliament had already approved the treaty, including the labour clauses and the League Covenant, and intended to 'carry out, in spirit as well as in letter, the obligations it has assumed.'[62]

Although the draft was passed, the Washington convention had provided one more demonstration of the reluctance of Canadian employers to contemplate even moderate changes in their operations. Obviously, a great deal of public education was needed, and to that end Rowell delivered during the next weeks a number of addresses on the organization and aims of the ILO. He stressed the unity of view that had prevailed at Washington among Canadian representatives of government, capital, and labour on 'the great majority' of the recommendations before the conference, an approach which was perhaps intended to play down Parsons' contribution to the deliberations. Always, in an evident bid for the ear of the business community, he declared that to oppose the class war of some labour extremists with a claim for class domination by capital would not bring peace to the world: 'The real friends of law and order and constituted authority are those who join with the legitimate leaders of labour in an honest effort to rectify the wrongs of the past and to secure as speedily as possible the establishment of social justice.' Frequently too, he defended Canada's policy against those who said she should not have moved ahead of the United States. He was certain that just as the United States had followed Canada into the war, she would in time enter the league and the ILO. In the meantime, Canada had secured 'the moral leadership of the continent by the part she has taken during the past five years.'[63]

19
An honourable discharge

Although the special autumn session of 1919 had been more productive than Rowell had at first believed likely, it had not been a happy experience for most of the members of the government. The silence of certain ministers on government measures was widely and rightly interpreted as a sign of something less than unanimity within the cabinet. At the end of October, J.D. Reid was in such despair over the chaos within government ranks that he doubted the administration could hold together for another two weeks until prorogation.[1] Nor was morale improved by the results of eight fall by-elections: Sir Henry Drayton went in by acclamation in Kingston, and S.F. Tolmie won in Victoria against a Labour candidate, but in four seats widely distributed – two in Ontario, one in Saskatchewan, and another in New Brunswick – the new Progressive farmers' party carried the day. Mackenzie King was allowed to go in by acclamation in Prince, PEI, and Ernest Lapointe was elected in Laurier's old seat, Quebec East. When Borden returned at the end of November from his rest cure it was not surprising that he had even more difficulty than before in finding new blood for the cabinet: prospective candidates were reluctant to face by-elections amid such uncertain political winds.

The cabinet was also beleagured by ill health. As winter set in, Ballantyne, Sifton, Reid, Burrell, Kemp, Foster, and Doherty were all suffering either from specific disabilities or from sheer exhaustion.[2] Most serious of all was the failure of Borden's holiday to restore his strength; his doctors now advised that he must retire or risk complete physical collapse. Once again, Rowell thought that Borden's retirement would mean the end of the coalition, and he emerged as the leader of a group in the cabinet determined to prevent it.[3] Over Meighen's vigorous opposition it was agreed that Borden should retain the premiership and take a year's vacation.

Rowell believed that he would not actually be away more than four or five months. Certain correspondents in the press gallery more than hinted that Rowell was motivated by personal ambition.[4] They suspected that if the government could hang on for a time he hoped it would recover in public esteem and he would then become prime minister. The suspicion was unjustified; Rowell was well aware that many of his policies were unacceptable to most of his Conservative colleagues and perhaps to some of the Liberal Unionists as well. That was clearer to him now than ever. And the prospect of a change of views within the cabinet seemed slight. There was little sign that the present cabinet would move to institute heavier taxation or significant reductions in the tariff, or that it would implement the recommendation of the Royal Commission on Industrial Relations. And now his colleagues had definitely rejected financial assistance to student veterans, despite the well documented arguments of President Falconer of the University of Toronto and a committee representing the universities. A large majority of the cabinet, including Borden, thought it impossible to assist one group of veterans and not others. Rowell could not understand this position: other veterans could secure work and start earning immediately, whereas returned students had to disburse funds at once in order to continue their education. Moreover, the nation needed all the highly trained men it could produce in the near future, especially if the social policies Rowell advocated were adopted. Returned students who were unable to complete their university degrees would have 'a sense of grievance and injustice suffered' that would not be in the public interest. Rowell felt so strongly about this that he was obliged to tell Borden that he could not 'conscientiously defend the action of the Government on this question should it ever come up for consideration in the House or elsewhere.'[5] Despite the frequency with which his name was mentioned in press speculation about a new leader he was not an active candidate. The only question he had to face was how long he could remain in the government.

He was anxious to discuss the situation thoroughly with J.W. Dafoe and tried to persuade the Winnipeg editor to come to Ottawa. But Dafoe and his paper had adopted a position of 'detached, watchful waiting,' and he was unwilling to become involved in the crisis of the government whose formation he had assisted. Dafoe was well satisfied with the government's wartime performance, but now it seemed to him to have no policy and to be simply drifting. He was sure that if an election were held soon it would give the Liberals the largest group in Parliament, although not a majority. He would not welcome that result any more than Rowell. If the Unionists could adopt a definite program, including the adoption of a tariff for revenue, which 'would do more good than anything else,' it might emerge as a minority moderate party with some influence. As for himself, Dafoe was looking with increasing favour on the farmers' movement, although he had given it no formal endorsement. He disliked its 'class characteristics' but he could not oppose a platform containing so many planks for which the *Free Press* had argued over the years.[6] Dafoe was not much help at this point, beyond confirming Rowell's own growing feeling of frustration.

As 1919 drew to a close, Rowell lost a battle within the cabinet to have federal prohibition measures continue beyond the end of the current calendar year. By order-in-council the government had repealed the operation of the War Measures Act as of 1 January 1920, although it made exceptions of several regulations controlling certain business activities. Rowell wanted to have the federal prohibition laws included in the list of exceptions. To exclude them was, he argued, a betrayal of Borden's promise to the House eighteen months earlier that these measures would not be repealed until a year after signing the peace. Peace had not yet been officially proclaimed and repeal should not come until a year after that date. As recently as six months before, he pointed out, Parliament had voted to continue the measure by a margin of seventy-one votes, the largest majority the Union Government had ever received on any question. Further, he was confident that there was general agreement in the country that the maintenance of the prohibition laws would promote stability in a time of great social unrest. The strength of temperance sentiment had been overwhelmingly demonstrated in the recent Ontario referendum, and he was sure that in every other province except Quebec a similar appeal to the people would have resulted in the same verdict. As it was, he feared that the repeal would greatly weaken the effect of the legislation of the recent autumn session, since it would facilitate the flooding of dry provinces, especially Ontario, with supplies of liquor from Montreal. He had nothing but praise for Borden's own attitude on the liquor question but that did not weaken his feeling about the end result.[7] Nobody would believe that Rowell had acquiesced in repeal, which made this an embarrassment both to him and to the govenment as a further indication of disunity in the cabinet.

He was distressed also by knowledge accidentally acquired from a passing reference by Reid that the government was in the midst of negotiations for the purchase of certain subsidiary assets of the Canadian Northern Railway from Mackenzie and Mann, from whom the government had acquired the Canadian Northern in 1918. Rowell was annoyed on two counts. He thought the negotiations ought not to have been entered into at all, and he objected to their having been carried so far without his knowledge. He was absolutely opposed to any further dealings with Mackenzie and Mann unless they were essential for the completion of the publicly owned railway system. If the purchase must be proceeded with, the government should procure an independent valuation quite unconnected with officials of the government railways, many of whom had had earlier connections with the two railway magnates. The company must not receive a dollar more than could be obtained in the open market, and the approval of Parliament must be secured before the government gave any firm commitment to purchase.[8] This procedure was not only businesslike and honest, it was also a political necessity. Nothing would do more to confirm the frequent charges that the Union Government was the servant of 'the big interests' than the suspicion that some obscure and probably nefarious arrangement had been made with Mackenzie and Mann. No purchases were made from that quarter in the months following Rowell's protest.

Once again, preparations for the opening of a new session of Parliament at the end of February required agreement on a legislative program. Rowell believed that in recent weeks public regard for the government had taken a turn for the better and that many persons in both parties who had shortly before favoured a return to old party lines had changed their minds.[9] Yet it was clear that the demand within the Conservative party for the abandonment of the coalition had by no means died. That was evident in the increasing activity of two of the leaders of this movement, Robert Rogers in the west and G. Howard Ferguson, the Conservative leader in Ontario. This demand was a major cause of difficulty within the cabinet in reaching agreement on a policy statement. Some work had been done on this before Borden's departure, and the result had been a statement that assumed the continuation of Union Government and outlined a very general policy. But just before the opening of the session Rowell was alarmed to find that a majority of the cabinet were prepared to revise the statement to declare publicly that the work of the present government was finished and that a new party should be formed. Protesting, Rowell secured the agreement of his colleagues that the new policy would not be made public until Borden resumed the active premiership or a new prime minister was chosen, since a new policy must be acceptable to its permanent leader.

Rowell found the statement of policy deficient on at least six counts. There was no reference to the constitutional conference that should be held as soon as possible to define imperial relations more precisely, nor was there any suggestion whatever that the government had, or intended to have, a naval policy. Rowell still wanted an effective Canadian navy, as he had for more than a decade. No attention had been paid to the maintenance of recent civil service reforms or to the extension of efforts to abolish patronage in government, while the labour plank had been so watered down as to be entirely lacking in any positive declaration of principles on industrial problems. Finally, the approach to taxation reflected an undue emphasis on taxation of consumption as compared with taxation of wealth: 'We have not yet taken from the men of means in Canada a sufficiently large percentage of the money required for carrying on the public service of the country.'[10] He still wanted a revision of the tariff, although he did not think this as important as several of the other matters.

Rowell no longer had any doubt about the influence he could expect to exercise in the government. This was the parting of the ways, although the manner of his departure from the cabinet had yet to be determined. When Calder and Reid journeyed to New York to meet Borden en route from England to further recuperation in South Carolina they handed him a letter from Rowell announcing his intention to resign whenever it would be least embarrassing to the government. That would probably be when Borden retired, or, if he did not retire, when he reorganized the government on reassuming active leadership. In any case, Rowell did not see how he could remain beyond the end of the present session of Parliament. Initially, Borden was surprised by this development, since it seemed somewhat inconsistent with Rowell's repeated efforts to maintain the government. Yet he could take no exception to Rowell's statement of his case.[11]

Rowell was confident that Borden would agree with his assertion that Union Government had represented 'the progressive forces of the nation' and had enacted 'more real progressive legislation of a far-reaching character than any other Government in Canadian history.' Yet it could not be denied that this legislation was too advanced for many of the government's supporters in Parliament and the country. The resulting restiveness among many Conservatives, together with the emergence of the farmers' movement and organized labour as independent political forces, was rapidly changing the political life of the nation. In these circumstances Rowell believed that the new party proposed by his colleagues would attract 'the most conservative elements in the population outside of Quebec, and probably there also, and ... would inevitably become the real Conservative Party of Canada.' He recognized that there was a very important place for such a party in the Canadian political system, but he did not belong in it. 'You know' he told the prime minister 'from our many conversations on social and economic questions, particularly those relating to the distribution of taxation and to labour, that I believe in much more radical policies than are likely to be adopted by a Government depending for its support upon the Conservative forces of the nation ... When, therefore, the time arrives for making a declaration that Union Government has finished its work, I think I may fairly ask for an honorable discharge to resume the practice of my profession.'[12]

As he took his place on the treasury benches for the first session in the new Parliament buildings and his last as a cabinet minister he was in a diminishing company of Liberal Unionists. Mewburn and Maclean had both resigned from the cabinet in recent weeks, leaving only five of the ten original Liberal members – Calder, Sifton, Guthrie, Ballantyne, and himself. The presence in the House of the eleven members of the new National Progressive Party, led by his former colleague, T.A. Crerar, was another visible reminder of the unsettled political situation. Rowell expected the session to be relatively uneventful. Given the limited areas of agreement within the cabinet, the government could not embark on any highly controversial measures, and the Liberal opposition was in a similar condition.

Although the government side of the House lived in mortal dread of the day when the Liberals would launch a tariff motion,[13] that peril never had to be faced. The Liberals, who were not proving particularly impressive under the leadership of Mackenzie King and who were increasingly concerned about proper strategy vis-à-vis the Progressives, were evidently not disposed to rock the government on the tariff or any other issue.

Early in the session's business the House endured Murphy's regular attack on Rowell. This time it was longer, lasting almost the entire three hours of an afternoon session, and more virulent. Rowell replied at once. In the course of the exchange the speaker was forced to remind Murphy several times and Rowell once that they were 'exceeding the rules as well as the amenities of debate' when they accused one another of lying. Altogether Murphy's diatribe was a masterly demonstration of what an angry and articulate Irishman could concoct out of his own black prejudices and clever appeals to the post-war anxieties and hostilities of various sectors of the electorate.[14] In its way, it was all somewhat flattering; so much attention suggested that Rowell's reputation, despite Murphy's best efforts, was still flourishing enough to require demolition.

Murphy 'was heard in silence mainly by his party,' and Rowell was 'strongly sustained by our men who looked upon the attack as unwarranted,' Foster observed. When Rowell rose immediately after the evening recess to make a one-hour reply he 'gave him his own back in kind.'[15] The reception given Murphy's address by his own colleagues in the opposition was 'the best evidence to the House and to the country that the men who know him best trust him the least,' Rowell suggested. One after another he answered most of the specific charges, usually in detail. It was distasteful to have to prove that he had never been paid a cent from any fund for his services to the social and political causes in which he believed, that he was not a tax evader, and that he had not made his career out of 'usurping' the positions and responsibilities of other men. As for the North Bay speech, to which Murphy had returned once more, Rowell asserted that he had long since made clear the meaning of his remarks on that occasion.

Rowell concluded with a general eulogy of Union Government and of the Canadian troops.[16] This was perhaps unfortunate because there were many Canadians both in and out of Parliament who were by now very bored with this kind of oratory, however justified they might believe it to be. Yet probably this latest encounter with Murphy had done him no harm. Foster noted that 'the House it was plainly seen was sorry for the episode and wants no more,'[17] and Borden's secretary reported that most of King's followers 'openly deplore Murphy's unbridled personal attack on Rowell who gains steadily in public esteem if not in personal popularity.'[18] Still, there was at least some humiliation in a situation that made it necessary for Rowell to reply as he did. Willison implied this when he conceded that 'it was, I fear, necessary that you should answer Murphy. But ... you do not need to defend yourself again against his charges ... Murphy has lost and you have gained greatly by the controversy.' Rowell had no doubt about his attitude; whatever Murphy might do next he was through with it.[19] Regrettably, only death could silence Charles Murphy.

With his refutation of Murphy out of the way, Rowell was able to turn to the next business – his presentation to Parliament of the peace treaty with Bulgaria. Since nobody knew or cared very much about Bulgaria and the objections to Canada's involvement in any treaties at all had all been stated in the previous session, ratification followed without delay. Indeed, the whole session was marked by the absence of major legislation, and even on the most important measure – a bill to provide for a new peacetime franchise – there was substantial agreement among most members, although a few members obviously still found difficulty in reconciling themselves to the permanent enfranchisement of women.

During a session when domestic issues proved less amenable to constructive treatment on his part, Rowell was able to devote much of his energy to fulfilling his responsibilities in Borden's absence as acting secretary of state for external affairs. Most of his public addresses during the late winter and early spring of 1920 dealt with the League of Nations. During much of this time he watched events in Washington with growing anxiety. A further attempt was being made in the United States to secure Senate endorsation of the League Covenant with the fifteen reservations sponsored by the Republican Senator Henry Cabot Lodge. One of the reservations embodied the Lenroot resolution of the previous autumn and would have exempted the United States from adherence to any action or report of the League Council or Assembly in which more than one member of the British Empire had cast a vote. The Canadian attitude to this provision expressing the widely held American view that the Dominions were not separate nations and should be represented only as part of the British Empire had already been made clear in the United States, notably when an opponent of the resolution read into the *Congressional Record* a statement by Borden. Rowell was troubled not only by the American misinterpretation of Canada's position but also by apathy on the subject in Canada, and he was determined to do what he could to change both attitudes.

During the second Senate debate Professor G.M. Wrong was in the United States and was in frequent contact with ex-president William Howard Taft, a friend of many summers at Murray Bay. Although Wrong's nationalism had been greatly strengthened by the war, he was disposed to think that Canada ought at least to consider renouncing the right to election to the Council in order to facilitate American acceptance of the League, and he endeavoured to present Taft's view on the matter to Rowell. Taft contended that Canada would never be elected to the Council and her insistence on the right was 'a mere question of vanity.' Playing on

Britain's gratitude for their part in the war, the Dominions had 'extorted' from London the 'anomalous concession' of separate representation. In Taft's view the position accorded the Dominions in the League had created the largest single difficulty, not excepting objection to Article 10, in getting the United States into the League.[20] Taft's attitude, which was shared by many American leaders, was both puzzling and entirely unacceptable to Rowell. Canada could not disclaim the right to election to the Council 'without recognizing that we were inferior in status to the other members of the League' he told Wrong. 'It greatly surprises me that men like Mr Taft do not recognize that the presence of Canada in the League and on the Council, if she should ever be elected – should help to forward the very ideals of justice, liberty and world peace which the United States professes to hold so dear.' He did not intend to say it in public (although many American friends of the League had) but he noted that 'everyone knows that in an acute controversy in which the United States was profoundly interested she would control the votes of a large number of the Central and South American countries. She should be the last nation in the world to offer objection to Canada's position.'[21] Canada would not be a banana republic if Rowell could prevent it.

He had no doubt that he spoke for the vast majority of informed Canadians, and he instructed Wrong to show his present letter to Taft:

The Lenroot resolution will be looked upon by the Canadian people as a deliberate affront to Canada and the other Dominions, an affront given to placate Sinn Fein and Pro-German sentiment in the United States. If the final decision of the American Government is in favour of the Lenroot resolution either in its original or its modified form and by reason of the action of other members of the League the ratification in this form goes into effect, Mr Taft and others who are sincerely interested in a good understanding between Canada and the United States and the different branches of the Anglo-Saxon race, should realize that such action may seriously impair the good relations between our two countries for years to come.

You ask what Canada will do if such a reservation is adopted. There is no question as to what Canada will do nor any question what the other Dominions will do for they feel just as strongly – some of them more strongly, if that be possible – on this matter. She will not only not approve the reservation, but she will protest against it. Under no conditions will she accept it.[22]

Three days later Rowell told an audience of war veterans in Ottawa that if the American Senate approved the Lenroot resolution and won its acceptance by the other powers, Canada would withdraw from the League. The feeling behind the public sentiment was revealed to his old friend Sir James Aikins, now the lieutenant governor of Manitoba. 'I must say ... that the cool assumption that the United

States is entitled to tell us how and when we shall adjust the internal relations of the different portions of the British Empire is another illustration of the amazing self-conceit of even the best intentioned American who seems to think it his prerogative to settle the affairs of the North American continent.'[23] Nor was he overwhelmed by Taft's petulant observation that 'of course if Canada wishes to "bust" the League ... Canada will have to take the responsibility.'[24] He found it hard to believe that Taft was serious in suggesting that 'we will be responsible for wrecking the League because we will not relinquish the position we already have in the League to humour the United States. Germany might with just as good grounds, have said that Belgium was responsible for the war and all the consequences that followed in Belgium because she did not efface herself when Germany requested the right to march through. It does not appear to me to be possible to argue with men who hold such views.' The solution seemed evident: 'Why does not the United States come in and then ask to amend the Treaty in reference to voting rights, if she thinks it should be amended? I am afraid that the Republicans are much more concerned about the political advantage of getting the Irish and pro-German vote than they are about the League of Nations and that Mr Taft has permitted himself to be unconsciously influenced by this sentiment.' But whatever the explanation he recognized that 'the situation is most difficult and embarrassing and we must therefore move with great caution.'[25]

A further question involving Canadian-American relations was the proposal to establish a separate Canadian diplomatic representation in Washington. The matter had been under consideration by the Union Government ever since its formation, and Rowell had discussed the government's intentions in the House of Commons in the late spring of 1919. He had justified the establishment of a permanent Canadian mission in Washington mainly on two grounds: it would help to consolidate and continue the work of the Canadian War Trade Mission in Washington that had brought so much new business to Canada, and it would enable Canada to act as an interpreter between the United States and Britain. At that time there had been no opposition to the proposal in the House. Rowell had answered Lemieux's question about the status of the Canadian representative and his relation to the British ambassador to the United States with the information that Borden was currently working this out in London but that his personal opinion was that on purely Canadian questions the Canadian representative would deal directly with Washington and on others would act in consultation with the imperial government.[26]

Subsequently, the government had several times parried opposition attempts to secure details of the negotiations everyone knew were being continued. There was good reason for the government's silence: in October 1919, Borden and Rowell had drafted a dispatch to the colonial secretary, Lord Milner, outlining the form that Canadian representation at Washington should take and had received what they thought was a satisfactory reply. The Canadian minister was to be attached to the British embassy but would be the normal channel of communication between Ottawa and Washington.[27] The extended character of the negotiations was due at least in part to the reluctance of the Foreign Office to accept the Canadian definition of the status of Canada's minister.[28] In April 1920 when Rowell went to Washington he found that R.C. Lindsay, the chargé d'affaires at the British Embassy, and F.L. Polk, the American undersecretary of state, shared a different understanding of the status of the Canadian minister from his own. This was revealed during discussions of the announcement that was to be made of the establishment of Canadian representation in Washington. 'They strongly preferred' Rowell reported to Borden 'an announcement that would indicate that the so-called Canadian representation simply meant some internal re-arrangement of the Embassy staff in which Great Britain and Canada alone were interested, rather than an important departure that would enable Canada to deal direct with the [United States] government through her representative, though the representative was a member of the Embassy staff.' Rowell rejected the approach of the British and American spokesmen ostensibly on the ground that to acquiesce would have been politically embarrassing for the Canadian government. It was also true that to have accepted it would have been to agree to something less than the full and public recognition of the new Canadian position in the world he was so eager to demonstrate. If all reference to direct dealings with the United States was left out there were bound to be questions in Parliament, when it would be necessary to make clear that in fact such dealings were intended. In Rowell's view it was very much better for all concerned to make a public announcement containing 'all that was essential to be stated' and thus avoid several possibilities of misunderstanding.[29]

Indeed, the opposition, although not opposing the establishment of representation in Washington, was severely critical of the secrecy with which the negotiations had been carried on and greatly exercised by the proposal that in the absence from Washington of the British ambassador the Canadian minister would take charge of the whole embassy. Although Mackenzie King was engaged in getting his party 'out of the wrong lines of the last session' on imperial relations and had no objections to Canada's new claims to nationhood, he still agreed with the more conservative and cautious Fielding in seeing in this arrangement the possibility of conflict between Canada and Britain or perhaps of more centralization of imperial affairs.[30] Rowell swept aside protests about possible conflicts over matters of concern to both Canada and Great Britain with eloquent declarations about the common interests of the two countries and assurances that their differences could never be severe and could easily be worked out in practice.[31] Yet many members of the House were dissatisfied with the information they had been given on representation at Washington, and when Borden rejected Lemieux's request that the correspondence on the subject be tabled, the government was sustained by a margin of only five votes, the narrowest it had ever received.

The first budget presented by Sir Henry Drayton proved to be less controversial than Canadian-American relations, largely because it avoided the most contentious issue, the tariff. The position to be taken on the tariff in the budget was sharply debated in cabinet and caucus, and the final decision to leave it absolutely unchanged was reached only two days before the budget was brought down. Most of the cabinet members thought that the tariff was paramount. Rowell still believed that several other matters were 'equally important.' He therefore resisted the pressure for a tariff declaration, contending that to alter the tariff at all would be a reversal of the caucus decision five months earlier when it had been agreed that questions of policy, leadership, and permanent organization would all be considered together, if and when Borden retired. If the cabinet insisted on discussing the tariff, Rowell more than hinted, then he and the other Liberal Unionists would have to reconsider their course of action.[32] In the end the budget speech promised only a commission to study tariff revision.

The chief innovations in the budget were the imposition of a new luxury tax of 10 to 50 per cent to be paid by purchasers of a variety of goods and a sales tax of 1 or 2 per cent to be paid by manufacturers and importers. Rowell was sure this was a step in the right direction; but he was not pleased that the rates of personal income tax and corporation tax remained stationary and the business profits tax, although retained, was to apply only on profits in excess of 10 per cent rather than the previous 7 per cent and the taxation rates in various categories above 10 per cent reduced.

In one of the major speeches of his first term as leader of the Liberal opposition in Parliament, on a Fielding amendment calling for an immediate tariff reduction, Mackenzie King tried to tear apart the budget and generally to discredit the Union Government's record. Instead of 'a people's budget' the government had brought down 'a profiteer's budget' that left 'war-accumulated wealth ... practically unmolested,'[33] a sentiment not far from Rowell's own criticism of his colleagues' too timid approach to taxation. Rowell thought King's three-hour oration was 'not a bad speech but for its length. He covered all the territory from Dan to Bersheba [sic].'[34] Following King immediately, Rowell covered a good deal of territory himself in an hour and three-quarters. He had decided to make a hard-hitting defence of the government's record and endeavoured to demonstrate with chapter and verse that, contrary to King's allegations, the special wartime activities of the government had been carried on at reasonable expense in relation to the services performed. It was a 'serious irresponsibility' on the part of the opposition to suggest that the government was badly out in its accounts. The apparent discrepancy, he explained, could be understood by a careful study of the accounts and was due to the fact that one thousand boxes of vouchers from the paymaster general of the Canadian Army had still not arrived from England when the auditor's report was prepared. Rowell's call for a public retraction on this point precipitated a bitter exchange between himself and his old antagonist across the floor, Lucien Cannon.

As for the tariff, Rowell taunted the opposition that the vague demands of the Fielding amendment were a vote of want of confidence in the tariff resolution of their recent convention and insisted that in supporting the Liberals the Progressives were also voting against their own platform. He produced a long array of statistics to show that in two years 'the Liberal-Unionists in co-operation with their Conservative colleagues' had reduced the tariff burden of taxation by an amount twenty times greater than that afforded by the Liberals in their fifteen years in office after 1896. Rowell left no doubt in the minds of his hearers that he favoured the recent increases in other forms of taxation that were partly responsible for reducing the importance of the tariff as a source of revenue.[35]

Afterwards in the corridors he received the plaudits of many government supporters, some of whom thought it was the best speech he had made since entering Parliament. He did not rate it that highly himself, although he thought it one of his best. Never had he received more congratulations from his cabinet colleagues; especially valued was the comment of the usually silent Sifton, who pronounced it the best speech he had heard since coming to Ottawa.[36]

As Parliament moved laboriously toward prorogation, with many night sittings that sometimes lasted into the daylight hours, Rowell felt that on the whole it had been a good session. Some useful legislation had been put through, and there had been no obvious division within government ranks. He was disappointed that it had proved impossible for the government to agree on the reintroduction of the earlier bill to make the War Purchasing Commission permanent; too many members of the government caucus were still opposed to a reform carrying such practical political consequences.[37] The most notable feature of the session had been the presence of the Progressives in the House. Throughout, Rowell treated the members of the new party with respect and made it clear that when he denounced the Liberals as the reactionary party he was not including the farmers' group. They might be 'a little too radical perhaps,' but they were 'moving ahead along certain progressive lines.'[38] On one occasion he noted that the UFO-Labour government of E.C. Drury in Ontario 'had done very well in a great many matters.'[39] This was only one sign that the farmers and the labour movement were drawing closer together and would prove a 'very formidable' force across the country and especially in the next federal election,[40] a prospect that aroused in Rowell more interest than anxiety.

Well before the end of the session Borden had decided that he must retire when Parliament was prorogued, and Rowell had reaffirmed his earlier decision to retire when the prime minister did. On the day before prorogation he invited the Liberal

Unionist members from Ontario to come to his office at the end of the afternoon sitting of the House, and he then announced his intention to resign from the ministry. All of the group except John Harold urged him to remain on the ground that his withdrawal would mean the break-up of the government. The next morning all the Liberal Unionist members of the caucus, again save Harold, were of the opinion that his resignation would threaten the existence of the administration. They did not share Rowell's attitude towards permanent fusion with the Conservatives and endeavoured to convince him that if he cared about stability at a time of national crisis he must reconsider his position and remain. For many of them the most recent manifestation of crisis had been provided in the results two days earlier of the provincial election in Manitoba, where the Liberal government of T.C. Norris held only a minority of seats, while thirteen Farmers and eleven Labour party members had been returned. Of the newly elected labour members, four had been in prison until two days before the polling, serving one-year sentences for their activities in the Winnipeg strike; and another strike leader had headed the polls in Winnipeg. At the moment the composition of the new government of Manitoba was undetermined, since no group was large enough to form a solid administration. Here was proof of the necessity for 'sane and progressive men of both parties' to unite. All Rowell could do was to promise that he would consult some of his friends outside the House, but he held out no hope that this would change his mind. In the meantime Borden's resignation as leader of the government party had been accepted, and the formation of a new National Liberal and Conservative Party was announced. 'It has been a trying and difficult day,' he wrote Nell. 'I wished several times I could have the benefit of your judgment but said and did what I believed to be right and that is all a man can do.'[41] His consultations with his Toronto friends and by wire with Dafoe, Coyne, and A.B. Hudson in Winnipeg yielded no advice that required a change of heart: there was agreement that the government was still worthy of general support but that with the formation of a new party he was under no obligation to stay in the cabinet.[42] Sifton, Guthrie, Calder, and Ballantyne had all agreed to continue in a new administration, but that could not alter his decision either.

One of Rowell's last acts as a politician was to remind Borden of conversations he had had early in 1918, at Borden's request, with their mutual friend of many years, Sir John Willison, about an appointment to the Senate for the Toronto editor who had frequently played an influential role in the shaping of Rowell's political career. In urging that Willison now be appointed to the Senate Rowell scarcely needed to underline Willison's qualifications; at the same time he proposed Senate appointments for two Ontario Liberal Unionist members of Parliament, General S.C. Mewburn, the recently retired minister of militia and defence, and E.W. Nesbitt of North Oxford. But Borden thought any such last-minute appointments on the eve of his retirement would be unwise and could only agree to pass on the recommendations to his successor.[43]

A majority of the cabinet favoured Sir Thomas White as Borden's successor, but he refused. Borden turned to Arthur Meighen and, after expending some energy in persuading certain reluctant members of the cabinet to accept this alternative, recommended that the governor general call on Meighen to form a government.[44] Rowell believed that Meighen was 'the logical leader' of the Conservative party,[45] and that conservative the new party would undoubtedly be. A few hours before he agreed to accept the leadership, Meighen called on Rowell in his office and issued a strong invitation to join his new ministry, assuring him that his strength in both the House and the country was greater than he imagined. Rowell showed him his letter to Borden of the previous February explaining his reasons for retiring. Nothing had changed. Although he admired Meighen's abilities the new leader was a Conservative, and Rowell could not feel that he belonged in his ministry. To Meighen's request that at least he retain his seat in Parliament until the next election, Rowell promised a reply in the autumn. He explained his position again to Sir Thomas White, who also tried to persuade him to enter the new government but, unlike Meighen, could find no fault in Rowell's logic.[46]

Through all these negotiations he was glad he had made his position clear to the caucus; that step had made the last few days easier. And now, he exclaimed to Nell, 'I am a free man again.'[47] In this mood he had no difficulty in withstanding a renewed appeal from Meighen to join his ministry. The new prime minister, stressing the artificiality of party labels and his understanding that Rowell took no exception to the government's legislative or administrative record, professed to find difficulty in grasping the reasons for Rowell's reluctance. 'In the extraordinary conditions of the present hour' Meighen wrote three weeks after Rowell's resignation 'I do profoundly believe that the real enemy camp ... is to be found, not in the official opposition, but in those extreme and dangerous elements ... who have little regard for the institutions which both liberalism and liberal-conservatism have held in veneration, who have their counterparts in the destructive forces of other less fortunate nations and who are becoming more and more the dominating factor in Canada among those who like to call themselves progressives.' Under these circumstances, Meighen urged, 'you could best exert your great influence in the direction you will want to exert it by association with the National Liberal and Conservative Party.'[48] There was no point in arguing with Meighen about the magnitude of the threat to Canadian institutions. Even if it were as great as Meighen imagined, Rowell was firm in the conviction that his part could not be played from within the Conservative party.

Despite his exultation in his new freedom he would miss many of his cabinet colleagues, none so much as Borden. There was more than mere convention in his expressions of regret over the conclusion of his work with the retiring leader, and the feeling was fully reciprocated from Borden's side. Referring especially to the aspect of their labours together that had mattered most to both men Borden told Rowell that 'since you entered the government nearly three years ago, the world has passed through great events and Canada's place among the nations has become assured. Looking back over these events you may truthfully and justly say "Quarum magna pars fui." ' [49] Rowell had indeed had a large part in events full of significance for Canada. But for the immediate future it seemed that he was to be an observer rather than a maker of history.

Among those who came to say goodbye to Rowell as he prepared to vacate his office was the undersecretary of state for external affairs, Sir Joseph Pope, whose career as a public servant spanned nearly four decades since he first became Sir John A. Macdonald's private secretary. Pope had not always approved of Rowell's views, and in particular he had no enthusiasm for nationalistic endeavours to enhance Canadian autonomy, but he regretted Rowell's departure from the government. Writing in his diary later that day, Pope compared Rowell with the long succession of ministers with whom he had worked and found him 'the best I have ever served under, at all times accessible, courteous, patient, and one who quickly and decisively made up his mind, an invaluable quality in a minister. I have little doubt we shall see him again down here.' [50]

PART FOUR

20
Canada in the League of Nations

Less than a week after Rowell's resignation from the cabinet he and Nell sailed from Quebec City for Liverpool aboard the CPR's *Empress of France*. They intended to go to Cornwall to rest in the summer sun and play golf for several weeks. But first they registered at Brown's Hotel, a quiet spot in Albemarle Street, to enjoy a few days in London. Once again they were struck by the economic disparities of the ancient city, now greatly accentuated by the post-war inflation. Walking through Piccadilly in the evening Nell observed the people 'arriving at the Ritz and other fashionable restaurants for dinner and making their way to the theatres. Every taxi ... seemed filled with people in evening dress and then we turned into the Park and saw the other side of life. The contrasts in this big city are terrible. It can't be right but how many centuries must elapse before it is, no one can tell. It won't change in a day.' Later, they had their own night out at the Ritz when they entertained Judge Lyman Duff of the Supreme Court of Canada and Mrs Duff at dinner to meet Sir John and Lady Simon.[1] The former Liberal home secretary and opponent of conscription had recently been demobilized after service on the headquarters staff of the Royal Flying Corps, but now the conversation was all of the shape of post-war British politics.

Their plan for a quiet country holiday did not long survive a visit with L.S. Amery, undersecretary of state for the colonies. Rowell's enthusiasm for travel to unfamiliar countries, especially within the Empire, was readily aroused by Amery's suggestion that he use this chance of a lifetime for a relaxed journey to South Africa. The trip would mean a longer absence from Toronto than they had planned, but the household at home was under the reliable supervision of Nell's mother and after an exchange of cables with her the decision was that they would both go. There was

barely time for some hurried shopping and collection of the many letters of introduction to prominent South Africans arranged for by Amery before the ss
Llanstephan Castle sailed from Southampton for Cape Town. It was the longest
voyage either had ever taken. Both were busy reading about Africa, and Nell
enjoyed several novels. Rowell was disappointed to find that the ship's library
possessed no volume of any value on David Livingstone, but he had supplied
himself conscientiously with volumes such as James Bryce's *Impressions of South
Africa*, the last volume of *The Times History of the Boer War*, and *Jock of the
Bushveld* by Sir Percy Fitzpatrick, a prominent Transvaal mining entrepreneur and
politician whom Rowell hoped to meet in South Africa.[2] Altogether, his reading list
constituted a rather official British view of the recent history of southern Africa.

Through L.S. Amery it had been arranged that they would be the guests of the
South African government. On docking in Cape Town they were greeted by Prime
Minister Smuts' secretary with an outline of the plans that had been made. Among
their first engagements was luncheon with Smuts and three other cabinet ministers
and their wives at the prime minister's official residence. To Rowell's regret
Parliament had just adjourned, and there was thus no chance to see the South
African House in action, but he made the most of every opportunity to meet leading
politicians. It was a lively time in South African politics. Smuts had been prime
minister for only a year and had just survived his first test at the polls. His South
African party had emerged as the second largest group, and with the help of the
Unionist party and the Independents Smuts had formed a precarious government
with a majority of four. The opposition Nationalists were calling for secession from
the Empire, and there was some sympathy for this movement from Smuts' following as well. Journeying north to Kimberley in the comfortable salon car provided by
the government railway, and then to Bloemfontein, Ladysmith, and Durban the
Rowells saw frequent reminders of the struggle to maintain the Empire in southern
Africa, from the remains of the Boer War blockhouses at strategic points along the
railway to the battlefields of Paardeberg, Ladysmith, and Majuba Hill, bright now
with spring flowers.[3]

A highlight of Rowell's stay in Cape Town was an interview with Chief Khama
of the Bamangwato of Bechuanaland. The ninety-year-old Khama remembered
David Livingstone well, had been converted by John Moffat, and was still
active in the Congregational church, which the work of the London Missionary
Society had established firmly in Bechuanaland. As an ardent prohibitionist Chief
Khama was happy to describe the benefits of prohibition, which had been maintained in his territory ever since he assumed the throne in 1872.[4] For Rowell the
interview was a moving testimony to the value of a missionary enterprise whose
history was well known to him. Another side of the white man's burden was
displayed when they were taken on a tour of the De Beers diamond mine at

Kimberley. After a morning spent viewing thousands of dollars worth of diamonds in various stages of processing they visited the compounds housing the native workers in the mine. 'There are about fifteen thousand employed and they all live in compounds where they must stay all the time,' Nell reported. 'The company certainly provides everything for their comfort and it is scrupulously clean but I should like to hear the side of the natives too. They certainly appear most happy and healthy.'[5]

Their closest view of native life was provided by three days in Maseru, Basutoland, as the guest of the resident commissioner of the protectorate, Colonel E.C.F. Garroway, and his wife. In honour of his Canadian visitors Colonel Garroway had gone to great trouble to stock a supply of 'Canadian Club.' The commissioner's realization after their arrival that whiskey was entirely unnecessary for the entertainment of his guests proved to be no barrier in the inauguration of a friendship which was to be carried on by correspondence over several years. Of special interest to Rowell was the French Protestant mission near Maseru, the largest missionary endeavour in Basutoland and one for which he had recently helped to raise funds in Toronto.[6] The complexities of the outside world's impact on the heart of Africa were well illustrated in the course of a visit to the paramount chief of the Basuto tribes, Chief Griffith. As Rowell and his party approached Chief Griffith's palace, he explained in a letter to his daughter Mary, 'we saw standing on either side of the road about 100 Basutos dressed in native costume ... They were litigants or witnesses who had come to have the cases in which they were interested tried. The King and his judges sit at the gate as in the days of scripture ... Almost all cases governed by natural law or custom are tried in this way ... It was a most picturesque sight and one I shall never forget for the Basutos are big fine looking men.' Equally memorable, but more modern in style, was the paramount chief himself, who received Rowell in a well furnished, western-style drawing room, wearing a dark tweed suit, coloured shirt, and black tie. Through an interpreter they discussed missions and education in Basutoland, and the chief explained his conviction that the welfare of his people would be assured as long as they remained under direct British rule and were not placed under the government of the Union of South Africa. Although the chief was enthusiastic about the work of missions in his territory, his relations with the churches had been complicated on at least one point. He had applied to both of the major Protestant denominations in the area, the French Evangelical mission and the Church of England, for admission to membership, but was informed in each case that he would have to give up all but one of his several wives. Thereupon he applied to the Roman Catholics and was accepted. Rowell recounted the story for his family in a tone that implied that the Roman Catholics had applied an acceptable practical wisdom to the problem: 'They married him to one wife according to the laws of the Church and closed their eye to the others ... and he is now a devoted Roman Catholic and is helping the Church in every way among his own people.'⁷

Since leaving Cape Town Rowell had been following political developments in South Africa with interest, especially in his numerous conversations with local politicians in Durban. When he arrived in Johannesburg it was still not clear that the new Smuts government would survive, and he was glad to have lengthy discussions with two of the ablest Unionists in the country – although they had been defeated in the recent election – Hon. Hugh Wyndham and Patrick Duncan. Both were Britons who had gone to the Transvaal as secretaries to Lord Milner and had thus been part of Milner's famous 'Kindergarten.'⁸ Duncan, whom Rowell found intellectually and personally congenial to a marked degree, remained an informant on South African affairs until Rowell's death, by which time Duncan had become governor general of the Union. A side trip to Pretoria included visits to the home and grave of Paul Kruger, leader of the Boer resistance movement in the Transvaal and president of the South African Republic. More of a pilgrimage was a stop to lay a wreath at the grave of General Louis Botha, who had died only a year before. Rowell held in high esteem the Boer leader who had turned from defeat by the British to become an architect of the South African Union and its prime minister.⁹

Moving north for an all too short week in Southern Rhodesia they spent a weekend at Victoria Falls. It was strange to find themselves being paddled by four husky Barotse in a Canadian canoe built at Lakefield, Ontario, to the island in the Zambesi where David Livingstone had first viewed the falls in 1855. In his journal Livingstone had noted that only on this occasion had he indulged his vanity by carving his initials on a tree; Rowell was thrilled to find the 'DL' still visible.¹⁰ Equally moving was his sight of the grave of Cecil Rhodes, to which they motored from Bulawayo:

> It is a spot one will never forget. In a grave cut out of the granite rock on a central mound in the heart of the mountains he lies in lonely grandeur and simplicity. The view from his grave is magnificent. On every side there is a blending of mountain and valley in such a variety of forms and colours as captivates you. Rhodes himself described the scene as 'the view of the world.' It is a fitting grave for one whose heart was in Africa and whose life – however mistaken he may have been in some of his acts – was devoted to the opening up of Africa and uniting it firmly to the British Empire.¹¹

The area around Salisbury, their last stop in Southern Rhodesia, with the orchards of the Mazoe river valley, fine vegetable gardens, and surrounding mountains, reminded both Rowells very much of the Okanagan valley in British Columbia. Of great interest was a native industrial mission run by Jesuits and generally conceded to be the most impressive mission in the vicinity.¹²

Originally they had hoped to travel through much more of British East Africa, but that possibility was ruled out by developments initiated before they left Canada. Meighen had then asked Rowell whether he would consider membership on the Canadian delegation to the first assembly of the League of Nations. While he was in Africa the invitation had been officially confirmed, and Rowell had accepted. Consequently he had to be in London early in November. The uncertainties of passenger sailings from east African ports meant that they could not adopt a tight schedule but must leave room for delays. The first was encountered when they waited for five days in Beira, Portuguese East Africa, for the overdue ss *Karapara* of the British India Steam Navigation Company. The delay was an opportunity to expand the steady flow of letters they had been sending home with lively descriptions of the changing colours and sounds of an African city quite different in atmosphere from any they had yet seen.[13]

The week's trip up the coast to Mombasa included welcome one-day stops in Mozambique and Zanzibar. Thanks to the attention of the resident commissioner of Zanzibar they were able to see a good deal of the island. They sought out the headquarters of the famed Universities' Mission to Zanzibar, with its native schools and hospitals surrounding the fine Anglican Cathedral, and visited the former Sultan's palace, now the site of the British administrative offices.[14]

From Mombasa they set out in the private car of the governor of Kenya on the twenty-four-hour train journey to Nairobi, where they had been invited to be the guests of the governor, General Sir Edward Northey. At Government House they found themselves part of a large house party, enjoyable enough, 'though they were not really congenial people,' Nell found. But there was compensation in their first experience of small game hunting, the many wild animals they saw, and their interest in a service commemorating the fifty-fifth anniversary of the death at the hands of the Kikuyu, of Bishop James Hannington, the first Anglican bishop of eastern equatorial Africa and once the subject of a Chatauqua paper by his sister Mary, as Rowell now recalled.[15]

On their return to Mombasa they found a long awaited cable with the results of Langford's matriculation examinations. To his parents' great disappointment he had secured only partial standing and would therefore not enter Victoria College that fall as planned. His father tried to take a positive view of this setback, and sought to point a lesson for the future:

We were very pleased that you had got a partial pass, though I must confess I expected you to get the whole examination. Mother who knew more about your work was hopeful but not as sanguine as I. We are so glad you tried. We know you worked well and that you are now back at school hard at work.

I only got a partial in my first school examination. It was the High School Entrance. I failed in spelling or rather dictation because of my spelling. I never could spell but the failure only made me more determined to win out and not to fail again. In future examinations I worked not simply to get through but to pass as high as possible and I never had another failure. I am sure you will feel the same and will do as I did.[16]

As the ss *Margha* steamed out of the Gulf of Aden and into the Red Sea, Rowell reluctantly gave up his plan to stop over at Port Sudan and travel overland to Khartoum and down the Nile. Nor would their rate of progress permit them to renew their impressions of Egypt, so that they decided to stay with the ship to its destination in Marseilles. The decision was entirely agreeable to Nell. The heat of recent days had restricted her enjoyment, and she felt increasingly drawn towards home. Her reading of the large collection of family letters awaiting them at Suez did nothing to appease her desire to complete the journey. Boredom was an affliction from which neither of the Rowells was likely to suffer, but having exhausted their own supply of books they were brought near to that condition by the deficiencies of the libraries on the ships of the British India Company. Nell reread Dickens's *Dombey and Sons* with pleasure, tried and gave up on George Meredith, and then resorted to 'reading the greatest amount of trash to put in time.' She persuaded Newton to try one of Baroness Orczy's *Scarlet Pimpernel* novels: 'He got quite interested in time and said it was as wild as the Arabian Nights which he now finds he has read enough of. He will have great sport in telling baby about it.'[17] More to his liking, and provocative of reflection concerning an enterprise in which he had played a minor role, was his reading of Carlyle's *French Revolution*:

One cannot but be struck with the many points of similarity between the French and the Russian Revolutions. One is also impressed with the futility of any outside nations thinking they can solve such a problem of government for the Russian people. The nations of Europe thought they could do it for France one hundred years ago. They tried and failed. So the nations will fail with Russia. She must work out her own salvation and settle her own form of government, though it be with much travail and shedding of human blood.[18]

In London at Claridge's Hotel they joined the other Canadian delegates to the League Assembly, Sir George Foster and C.J. Doherty, who were accompanied by Loring Christie, legal advisor to the Department of External affairs and in fact the department's entire professional staff. Since Nell was not quite well and Newton was uncertain how long he would have to stay in Geneva, they reluctantly agreed that she would return home alone. It was hard for him to let her go after three months of what had been a second honeymoon. When the *Aquitania* sailed for New York, Nell's stateroom was replete with flowers and fruit 'sent just for the selfish reason that you should not forget me and that in some form I should accompany you.'[19]

In the few days before his departure from London for Geneva, Rowell represented Canada in the consultations of the British Empire delegates and engaged in discussions with many individuals interested in the League. He took an active part in the sessions of the British Empire delegation, which were intended to put the representative of the Dominions and India in possession of information available to the British foreign office on various items on the agenda of the League Assembly. Often his questions were simply for clarification of information, but on several occasions he appeared as an anxious guardian of Dominion autonomy, careful that nothing should be done to feed the American charges that the British Empire delegates were one bloc enjoying six votes. With the same care he insisted it be clearly understood that the credentials of the Dominion delegates had been issued by their own governments and would be deposited directly with the League Secretariat.[20]

Rowell was greatly distressed to learn in London that Lloyd George would probably not attend the Assembly, since he thought it vital that the prime ministers of the great powers should contribute their prestige to this most important venture in the history of mankind. As always, Rowell was concerned about American opinion of the League. At the eleventh hour he urged the British prime minister to go to Geneva to demonstrate, especially to the sceptical Americans, Britain's belief in the importance of the organization. 'As Prime Minister of Great Britain' he told Lloyd George 'you have it largely in your hands to determine the character of this first meeting and the place of the League in the life of the world.'[21] The appeal was of no avail, and although Rowell had the highest opinion of A.J. Balfour, the British foreign secretary and leader of that country's delegation, and respected the other British delegates, notably the labour leader G.N. Barnes, he continued to regret the absence of Lloyd George.

Although Canada was far from being a great power, Rowell would have preferred to see the Canadian delegation headed by the prime minister, despite the fact that Meighen had shown no great interest in international affairs. After the prime minister, Borden would have been the ideal choice, but his poor health precluded any intense work for the present. Borden was gratified that Rowell was a delegate, partly because he felt uneasy about the leader of the delegation, Sir George Foster, who at the Peace Conference 'did not seem to have an adequate conception of Canada's status and nationhood.' 'I hope' the former prime minister wrote 'that the steps taken in advance ... to which you have contributed so much will not be lost.'[22] Rowell found his position slightly awkward. In his own view he was 'the third member' of the Canadian delegation. Foster and Doherty were still cabinet ministers; he had been included in the delegation because of his interest in the League and knowledge of international affairs, which was generally admitted to be without equal in the House of Commons. And Rowell had some fear that Foster had both personal and political reasons for wishing to minimize his role within the delegation. The test came when Foster allocated the responsibilities of the Canadians for the work of the various League committees. Rowell's anxiety proved unfounded; Sir George consulted his two colleagues fully, and Rowell was entirely satisfied with a division of labour which gave him primary responsibility for representing Canada on Commission I, on constitutional questions, and on Commission II, dealing with technical organizations, including those devoted to public health.[23]

As the Assembly convened, Rowell began the series of almost daily letters to Nell that kept her informed not only of the work of the formal sessions but also of the vigorous social life of the delegates. Rowell enjoyed the social occasions, always reporting home the name and sometimes the attractiveness of the lady whom he took in to dinner and the subject matter of his conversations with his neighbours at table.

The Canadians made their debut on the world stage at Geneva in what seemed to many observers a trivial drama. Brazil proposed that the Assembly appoint a committee to arrange for the laying of a wreath on the tomb of Jean-Jacques Rousseau, with the suggestion that the author of the *Social Contract* was the father of the League of Nations. The proposal to honour the great Enlightenment philosopher was offensive to Judge Doherty's Roman Catholic sensibilities, as well as to his understanding of proper Assembly procedure. While Doherty was securing the agreement of Foster and Rowell to speak against the resolution, it was adopted, so that by the time Doherty spoke he was protesting against a fait accompli. However, he made his point, and the president of the Assembly agreed that in future no such resolution would be sprung on the Assembly but must go through the appropriate committee. Rowell had a good deal of sympathy for Doherty's attitude and failed to see 'what we have to do with Jean Jacques in the Assembly of the League.' His sympathy suffered no diminution when members of the Assembly were asked to gather at Rousseau's tomb at 11:30 on Sunday morning. Foster, a good Baptist, wrote to the president that as they did not approve the action and especially deplored the holding of the ceremony at the hour of Divine Service none of the Canadians would attend. Rowell was tempted to ask his two colleagues to join him in proposing that on the following Sunday the Assembly should lay a wreath at the monument to John Calvin and John Knox at the University of Geneva, and the next week at the statue of some suitably chosen Roman Catholic, if one could be found in Protestant Geneva.[24]

While the Assembly was officially honouring Rousseau, Rowell attended the morning service at the Anglican Church, where the sermon gave rise to comments rather different from those he would have made ten years earlier. 'The chaplain' he told Nell 'is a good warm hearted Irishman but I do not think his sermon this morning would add to his popularity among the non Anglo-Saxon members of the Assembly if any were present. The point of his sermon was that the British people had been chosen by God to lead the world in progress and civilization ... I confess the older I get and the more I know of life the less I feel like saying of any nation it is Divinely called to lead the world and I think his Irish tact must have failed him when he decided to preach such a sermon when the League was in session.'[25]

As the work of Commission II began, Rowell found himself in sharp disagreement with its chairman, Tommas Tittoni, president of the Italian Senate and representative of his country on the Council of the League. Rowell had disliked Tittoni from the start, and in the meetings of the British Empire delegates in Geneva had opposed his selection as chairman, saying that it would be rather inappropriate to elect as chairman of the committee to deal with health matters a representative of a country that had signally failed to carry out the recommendations of the Council in regard to typhus.[26] But a more fundamental objection, which would not be publicly stated, was his impression that Tittoni was 'a real Machiavellian' who wanted to use the prestige of the chairmanship to further his aspirations to become premier of Italy. Rowell's judgment was confirmed when Tittoni made a lengthy opening address 'exploiting his own views and bringing forward the absurd proposal,' which an Italian delegate had presented to the founding convention of the International Labour Organization the previous year, that the League should redistribute the world's raw materials to the nations needing them. Rowell could scarcely wait until Tittoni sat down to put his dissent on record and to declare the proposal entirely outside the purposes of the League. After a few more clashes with Tittoni, Rowell concluded that 'there is an internal antagonism between us, a wide difference of views and of ideals and that we each recognize it. I regret that this should be so for the Committee deals with many matters in which I am personally interested and about which I imagine I have a more intimate knowledge than most of the members of the Committee.'[27]

The question of raw materials was not without embarrassment to Canada because of the nature of the British involvement, a fact Rowell had recognized for some months, ever since Great Britain had approved a resolution in the League Council calling on the Advisory Economic and Finance Committee of the League to investigate ways of securing a more equitable distribution of raw materials.[28] Much as he favoured, ideally, a common vote for the British Empire countries, Rowell did not allow the British action, implying that the subject was a legitimate one for League concern, to modify his quite contrary view. Because of a slight illness suffered by Foster it fell to Rowell to address the Assembly for the first time, without much notice and without notes, when Italy and Belgium brought the raw materials issue before the full Assembly. He used the opportunity to outline his understanding of the central purposes of the League and again found himself pitted against Tittoni.

At the outset Rowell stressed the necessity of making a clear distinction between the primary and secondary functions of the League. The primary function was the prevention of war through the provision of alternative means for the settling of disputes. In an obvious reference to ex-enemy states, he asserted that it was essential for all major powers to be admitted to the League as soon as they could meet the conditions prescribed by the Covenant. The secondary functions of the League were those covered in Article 23 of the Covenant and in certain items in the peace treaties, including matters connected with health, transport, and labour. The League must not promote any secondary functions not specifically included in the Covenant. An example of an illegitimate secondary function was discussion of the raw materials question, which was plainly outside the competence of the League as defined in the Covenant. Further, on practical grounds he contended that it was ridiculous for the League to concern itself with this issue. The degree of economic control required to redistribute raw materials would not be acceptable to any country, since it would mean loss of control of their own international affairs. 'On our side of the Atlantic' that would not even be considered, Rowell declared, and any suggestion that such a proposal might be taken seriously would settle forever the attitude of the United States to the League.[29]

Another area in which Rowell saw danger of confusion concerned the status of delegates to the League Council. Were they on the Council in a personal capacity or did their views represent those of their governments? In Rowell's view it was essential that they represent their governments and that their votes should commit those governments to action; otherwise the League would be no more than a debating society. Rowell concluded his first address with a declaration that Canada, free from centuries of European conflict, was a disinterested participant in the League, anxious only to end militarism and help Europeans to solve 'their problems.'[30]

When the chairman called on Tittoni to conclude the session the Italian representative rebuked Rowell sharply. He decried Rowell's categorical statement on raw materials and asked what would become of the League if everyone took such an uncompromising attitude? Economic problems were not simply internal matters; they were among the root causes of war, and therefore of vital concern to the League. And Tittoni, who represented Italy on the Council, rejected Rowell's view of the position of Council members. They were, he contended, even more than representatives of their countries: 'we are something nobler and greater; we are magistrates,' and therefore free to exercise personal judgment.[31] Despite Tittoni's vigour, Rowell had the satisfaction of seeing a majority of the delegates support the positions for which he had been the most vocal advocate.

In Commission I on constitutional matters Rowell again came into conflict with a leading European statesman. This time it was René Viviani, who had been president of France at the beginning of the war. The Commission, chaired by A.J. Balfour of Britain, appointed Rowell and Viviani as joint *rapporteurs*, and they took up its chief assignment, defining the relative responsibilities of the Council and the Assembly at points where this was not already established in the Covenant. At first all went smoothly. It was decided that a more or less precise definition should be attempted on the basis of principles on which Rowell thought all the members were agreed, and Viviani was asked to prepare a draft of a report. Due to a delay in translation of the material Rowell received it only an hour or so before it was to be presented to the full committee. Rowell found Viviani's draft unacceptable, and in this verdict Doherty strongly concurred. The chief point in contention was the question of concurrent jurisdiction where the League Covenant did not assign control specifically either to the Council or to the Assembly. Viviani proposed that in such cases the Countil should automatically have jurisdiction.[32] Although Rowell was not prepared to say that the Council should never have control he wished to keep open the widest possible range of influence for the smaller nations, and their voice was more likely to be heard in the Assembly than in the Council. After securing a postponement in the presentation of the report he tried to arrange a further discussion with Viviani or an opportunity to submit his views in writing. Viviani was very curt, declaring that he had not come to Geneva to play all year and that he had three other committees to attend and could not give the report any more time. Rowell's insistence on further discussion brought the suggestion from Viviani that he would drop out and Rowell could present his own report for discussion in the Council and Assembly.

This last was or may have been a gentle hint in view of his assumed ascendency [*sic*] in the Assembly – of what would happen to me if I presented a report and he attacked it. The whole incident was such a childish exhibition of petulance, bad temper and ill manners that I could not have believed that an Ex-Prime Minister of France could have so acted had I not been a party to it. I have been trying to get an explanation. The only one I can find is that he is the spoiled child of democracy. Very able as an orator, perhaps the best in France, very proud of his own work and very resentful of criticism or opposition. As I have, as we have, such a warm feeling for France I thought of the easiest way out and then sent a note to him saying that he should present the report as his own saying that I agreed with the four conclusions at the end but did not accept responsibility for the body of the report. This he accepted. Thus I thought the incident was ended.[33]

The members of the League secretariat were not satisfied to leave matters thus, and on their urging Rowell put his comments in writing and forwarded them to Viviani, although the latter had again protested that he could give the report no further attention. Despite his initial desire to see a precise definition of the respective powers of the Council and the Assembly, Rowell now concluded that it was unwise to press for further definition at the present time and thus run the danger of jeopardizing acceptance of the report. Shortly, Viviani agreed to amend the report as Rowell proposed and forward it as their joint responsibility.[34] Speaking to the report in the later plenary session of the Assembly Rowell explained that he desired to expand the powers of the Assembly while others did not. He made a virtue of necessity: the avoidance of a firm decision was in keeping with the traditions of those experienced with British constitutions and would foster flexibility within the Assembly.[35]

The same concern for the role of the smaller powers informed Rowell's stand on frequency of re-election to the four non-permanent seats on the Council. On his motion it was agreed that no non-permanent member could serve for more than two consecutive terms of two years and retiring members should be eligible for re-election only after a four-year interval. But it was when the report of the committee on technical organizations reached the floor of the Assembly that Rowell struck his greatest blow on behalf of the influence of the lesser, largely non-European, powers. He had, of course, been a member of that committee originally, and it was there that his first encounter with Tittoni over raw materials had occurred. After that, due to a conflict of schedules, he had exchanged places with Sir George Foster on Committee v on the admission of new states. When the committee on technical organizations produced a report that went forward to the Assembly with unanimous endorsement from delegates representing every nation in the League Rowell was in an awkward spot. He found the report alarming, but to say so in the Assembly meant opposition to a document Foster had approved. Nevertheless, Sir George's assertion that Rowell must speak as his conscientious judgment dictated eased the situation somewhat.

Rowell's chief objection to the report was that it left the way open for the immediate establishment of three new international agencies dealing with finance, transit, and health. Although Rowell believed that the establishment of these bodies might eventually be desirable and practical, he declared that under the Covenant such organizations could not be set up without prior international conventions entered into directly by governments and these did not exist.[36] He did not say so to the Assembly, but Rowell had evidence of what too great haste in setting up an international organization might mean. He had seen the preliminary papers for the Barcelona conference on the establishment of the permanent organization on transit and was convinced that the proposals had far-reaching implications for Canadian railway and ocean transport. He believed that Canada should be represented at the conference, but not without enough time beforehand for very careful consideration of the proposals.[37] Moreover, as he pointed out to the Assembly, the addition of three further annual international conferences would put a severe strain on the finances and personnel of the smaller nations, especially on those outside Europe. If the more distant countries were unable to play an active role the Europeans would control the organizations. The conviction that this was not good enough launched Rowell into the most outspoken of his lectures to Europeans. 'Like a breath of the Canadian winter – cold but invigorating'[38] he 'startled the diplomatists of the old world' with the 'liveliest emotion' of the Assembly:[39]

I am perfectly sure that the people of Canada are not prepared to turn over the handling of these problems to a European League or to a European Committee. It is not that we have not the greatest respect and admiration for the statesmen of Europe, but they do not understand our viewpoint. Why, we do not permit even the statesmen of the Mother Country, Great Britain, for whom we have respect, admiration, and affection ... to settle any of our Canadian affairs. We settle these ourselves. Much less are we prepared to turn over the settlement of these matters to a general European Committee. You may say that we should have confidence in European statesmen and leaders. Perhaps we should, but it was European policy, European statesmanship, European ambition, that drenched this world in blood and from which we are still suffering and will suffer for generations. Fifty thousand Canadians under the soil of France and Flanders is what Canada has paid for European statesmanship trying to settle European problems. I place responsibility on a few; I would not distribute it over many; but nevertheless it is European.[40]

Gabriel Hanotaux of France was immediately on his feet to protest that Europe had borne many burdens for the whole world and deserved more appreciation.[41] Lord Robert Cecil tried to pacify him while Rowell added that he had not intended to suggest that European statesmanship had caused catastrophe, but only that it had not averted it.[42] If he had spoken with 'undue warmth' it was only because he wanted to emphasize the desire of the smaller nations to co-operate fully in the work of the League and its agencies.[43] Privately, he was altogether happy with the result of his outburst, as he reported to Nell:

This unanimous report was overturned by the effect of my address to the Assembly. After I had spoken it was not possible to pass the report simply because I had pointed out the fundamental misconception on which it was founded. The chairman wanted me to move an amendment setting out my views. I said no I have no amendment to move. I have laid my position before the

Assembly. I have cleared my conscience. The President however knew he dare not submit the report to a vote as it would be defeated, so finally the debate was adjourned and the President named a Committee of the Assembly to confer with the officers of Committee No. 2 to try and reach an understanding and agreement. I was chairman of this committee of the Assembly. We met and finally agreed upon amendments which safeguard the position and protect all vital interests and yesterday and to-day the Assembly unanimously adopted the amended resolutions. The result is every way satisfactory.[44]

Taken together the amendments meant a year's postponement of any decision on the establishment of additional technical organizations and clarified the procedures under which the whole question should be considered. In Rowell's view he had won a victory on three fronts: The Assembly had been 'saved from committing a grave blunder which might have had serious results,' it had 'vindicated its right to review and fundamentally change a report though assented to by all the states through their representatives on a committee,' and Europe had begun 'to realize there is another viewpoint they must respect.'[45] Loring Christie feared that the victory had its price. Although entirely in agreement with Rowell's intention he reported to Borden that the execution of it was less than perfect.

I feel sure that Mr Rowell was touching something real when he opened a fight against the tendency here to rush these organizations and set them up in all their elaboration at once. He succeeded to the extent that what was done can now be regarded as temporary, tentative, and open to review in the future. He did it practically single handed. But in my view he marred the performance by some words that need not have been said in quite the way he said them. Some words about European statesmanship. They hurt and stung many people and caused resentment. It seems to me the case should have been based on the power and importance of the New World and the necessity to take account of our point of view.[46]

Another point at which Canada stood out against Europe was in her renewal of the objections she had already raised at the Peace Conference to Article 10, the clause in the League Covenant binding every member to come to the defence of any other when attacked. After Canada's failure to exclude Article 10, the Covenant had been presented to Parliament, defended by the government, and approved. During the discussion in Parliament Rowell had already made it clear that he did not see Article 10 as the heart of the Covenant and doubted that it would be called into force. He would have been perfectly content to leave matters at that, but Doherty was determined to pursue the question. Rowell had no strong objections in principle but he thought it inexpedient to press the issue, given current conditions in the United States. In view of President Wilson's defence of the Covenant as it stood, he feared that 'Wilson and his friends would think Canada had gone back on them though they stood by Canada on the question of voting rights. On the other hand Republicans might think it was a move to catch them.' However, he soon withdrew his objections once it was evident that the Assembly would be unable to deal with the matter during the current session. Doherty made his speech to the Assembly on Article 10 but Rowell said nothing on this subject.[47]

The committee on the admission of new states raised fewer issues of immediate concern to Canada than most of the others but Rowell found its deliberations full of interest. From the outset he had held the view that all ex-enemy states should be admitted to the League as soon as possible. Thus he sided with the majority on the committee and in the Assembly for the admission of Austria and Bulgaria. But he favoured the exclusion of the Baltic states whose relations with the currently unstable Russia made the powers reluctant to accept responsibility for guaranteeing their frontiers under Article 10. In opposing admission of the Baltic states, Rowell stressed Canada's special concern in any matter involving Russia with whom she shared Pacific interests and an Arctic frontier,[48] points that few Canadians and fewer Europeans had ever considered.

Rowell was in the minority led by Lord Robert Cecil that favoured the admission of Albania. Against the argument of the majority that Albania was not a sovereign state because she was under military occupation, and against the Italian contention that part of Albania had been promised to Italy in the secret Treaty of London, Cecil and Rowell argued that in international law Albania was a sovereign state. In the full Assembly they decided to try to reverse the committee's recommendation against admission, and thanks to a last-minute change of heart on the part of Britain and France they succeeded.[49] Rowell was aware that there was no obvious reason for a Canadian's intense interest in tiny Albania. He believed that the defence of Albania was a matter of principle. He hoped that President Woodrow Wilson's earlier opposition to the partition of Albania had settled the matter, but there remained an element of doubt.

> I hope[d] all danger was past but I made up my mind so far as I was concerned I would try to put it out of the hands of the powers to partition Albania or deprive her of her rights by admitting her to the League. Once admitted under Article x the other powers are pledged to guarantee her territorial integrity against external aggression ... I could not but be indignant at the thought that the great powers Great Britain, France, and Italy which with Russia and Austria had in 1912 guaranteed the neutrality of Albania should have agreed by the secret Treaty of London to partition this defenceless state. I am told Italy demanded it as part of

the price for entering the war. I do not know the truth of this statement but it is the only explanation I have heard. When the matter came up in the Assembly I did the undiplomatic thing of saying what I thought about this Convention. I said I could not recognize the legality, the justice or morality of an agreement between a group of powers to partition and dismember a weak and defenceless state without the consent of such state. Neither the British nor the French delegates liked what I said and perhaps I should not have said it, but after all we said about Germany violating the neutrality of Belgium I was shocked that the Allied powers should have put their names to a treaty to partition Albania whose neutrality they had guaranteed.[50]

At the Assembly's conclusion there was no doubt in Rowell's mind that its greatest achievement was the agreement to establish a Permanent Court of International Justice. He would have preferred to see a court with full compulsory jurisdiction, but even without that power he saw this development as 'a really great step in advance toward the goal of settling international disputes by reason rather than by the sword ... Once the court is set up if it is composed of able men who command public confidence public opinion will compel the great powers to move ahead and agree to compulsory jurisdiction ... If the Assembly had no other piece of work to its credit it would still be a great landmark in human progress.'[51]

He believed there was in fact much more to the League's credit. The first meeting of the Assembly had achieved enough to support the hopes of the League's friends and to modify the scepticism of at least some of its detractors. It was gratifying to have his own assessment of how much Canada had contributed to the deliberations confirmed by much of the press comment. He fully agreed with Sir George Foster's observation that 'the Canadian delegation taken as a whole ranked after that of Great Britain and France in the amount of work done and in their influence upon the work and decisions of the conference.'[52] Assessing his own role at Geneva for Nell he found cause for satisfaction.

I thought Sir Robert's absence would probably result in my taking a very subordinate part. It had just the reverse. I made my position in my opening address. It was wholly unexpected and it was only because of Sir Geo's illness that I spoke, and so on. If there be a Providence that shapes our ends – certainly with our training we should not doubt it – then events have turned out in such an unexpected manner that I have been able to do work and to influence decisions in a way I would not have thought possible. I shall tell you more when I get home about this side of it.[53]

The British press would not have found Rowell's estimate of his part in the

Assembly exaggerated. Wilson Harris, a British Liberal and a prominent Quaker whom Rowell had first met in 1908 at a New York meeting of British, American, and Canadian missionary societies at which West China Union University was founded, was in Geneva for the London *Daily News* and judged Rowell as 'among the eight or ten leading figures,' an opinion echoed by the *Manchester Guardian*.[54] The *Nation* of London, searching for leaders who had 'kept the ideals of a sane liberalism to the fore ... under the tacitly recognized leadership of Lord Robert Cecil' found only a handful – Mr Barnes of Britain, Dr Nansen of Norway, M. Motta of Switzerland, and 'one of the discoveries of the Assembly, Mr Newton Rowell of Canada.' And from a more conservative perspective the London *Daily Telegraph*, ranking the outstanding figures of the Assembly in order of the impression they made on most observers, put Rowell in fifth place after Viviani, Cecil, Balfour, and Bourgeois of France.[55]

From the beginning of the meetings Rowell had deplored the fact that no Canadian newspaper had thought the Assembly important enough to send a correspondent to Geneva. To help fill the vacuum he had done what he could to ensure that the activities of the Canadian delegation received maximum attention from the twenty American correspondents present by making himself available for interviews and by giving two dinners followed by an evening's discussion for groups of American newsmen.[56] Since the Canadian press took most of its reports from American news services it was important for the Canadian story to be well covered by the American reporters.

Whether influenced by his interpretation of events or informed chiefly by their own North American perception of the world, Rowell could have no complaint about the American journalists' reporting of Canada's part in the Assembly. Their dispatches reflected the private comment of the Associated Press correspondent that the Canadians 'had done more to put life and reality into the Assembly than any other delegation.'[57] Rowell in particular was given full credit for playing a directing role both in public debate and behind the scenes, and his impassioned reference to the fifty thousand Canadians under the sod was reported across the continent, from the *New York Times* to the *San Francisco Chronicle*, and from the Halifax *Herald* to the Victoria *Colonist*. Although it was recognized that the absence of the United States had automatically enhanced Canada's position, most of the reporters found it remarkable that Canada had emerged so forcefully as the moral leader of the Americas and the champion of the smaller nations.

Readers of the substantial coverage given the Assembly by most of the major Canadian newspapers saw their country portrayed as a new and not insignificant force in world affairs, and possessing a statesman well able to hold his own with the most distinguished European leaders. With the Assembly concluded, Rowell found it good to look forward to a less grinding pace. Although so entirely absorbing, the month in Geneva had proved exhausting, and he was grateful that his health had stood up so well. He had missed only one session, and that due to his duties as best man at the wedding of Sir George Foster. The seventy-three-year-old Sir George's Scottish bride was the daughter of a member of the British Parliament and was given in marriage at a quiet ceremony by A.J. Balfour.[58]

Rowell was disappointed that the Assembly had finished its business too late to allow him to get back to Canada for Christmas. From Paris he wrote holiday letters to each member of the family, with some good advice to the children for the New Year. 'May it be a very happy one' he told Mary 'but above all may it be a useful one. Life's greatest joy you will always find comes from serving others rather than self, trying to make others happy. Our Great Example "went about doing good." May this be the best of your life in making others happy.' For Langford there was the wish that the 'New Year may be good for you in every way – good in health, good in your studies and above all good in character building. This is the most important thing above all else.'[59] Four-year-old Frederick was still too young to profit from written counsel.

Rowell and Foster spent two days in Paris en route to London, partly in connection with the negotiation of a new trade treaty between France and Canada, a matter in which Foster as minister of trade and commerce had a close interest, but also to try to repair the damage done by Rowell's comments on European statesmanship. The French press had given his speech a good deal of unfavourable attention and had portrayed him and Canada as rather hostile to France, an impression he was sorry to have given and had not intended. When Rowell and Foster met the group of French politicians assembled at luncheon by Philippe Roy, the Canadian commissioner general in Paris, there was no direct reference to the offending speech. In brief comments both Canadians confined themselves to general appreciation of the French people and sympathy for their heroic fight to repair the ravages of the war. A more informal and forthright discussion of French opinion and European affairs in general was possible when Rowell renewed his acquaintance with the prominent French journalist, André Siegfried, whose book, *The Race Question in Canada*, published in 1904, had done more than any other work to inform Frenchmen about Canada. Siegfried told Rowell that he knew that the French government approved of the change Rowell had secured in the report of the Assembly's Committee on technical organizations.[60]

The necessity of putting in ten days in London until his ship sailed at the end of the month was no great hardship despite his nostalgia for home during the holiday season. Soon he had a busy schedule of engagements with a variety of public figures and old friends and some interviews on behalf of the Algoma Central Railway – a first step in his return to legal practice. He attended the House to hear Bonar Law and the leader of the remnant of Asquith Liberals, Sir Donald Maclean, on government financial policy, followed by A.J. Balfour's report on the League of Nations Assembly. 'It was interesting but I did not think he did justice to the subject.' That night he found a performance of J.M. Barrie's new play, *Mary Rose*, 'beautifully played but so very sad, too sad for me. You know my failing in that respect,' he observed to Nell.[61]

At a luncheon given at the House of Commons by the British Empire Parliamentary Association, Rowell met an old friend, Lady Nancy Astor, who had recently become the first woman to sit in the British House of Commons. Like many of his contemporaries, Rowell was attracted to Lady Astor's mixture of earnestness, wit, and gaiety, and he admired her convictions on women's rights, temperance, and the extension of educational opportunity. He gladly accepted her invitation to join the Christmas festivities at the Astors' country home, Cliveden. Viscount Astor was on the Atlantic on the way home from a business trip to the United States, and Lady Astor's Christmas house party was composed mainly of their immediate family and a number of her relatives, but there were a few outsiders, so that some thirty people, including ten young children, sat down to Christmas dinner.[62]

One of the house guests was the American ambassador to Britain, John W. Davis, and his wife. During a long walk with Davis through the Buckinghamshire countryside they discussed American attitudes to the League of Nations. The League also occupied part of Rowell's lengthy talk with Philip Kerr, Lloyd George's private secretary and a frequent guest of Lady Astor with whom he shared a religious interest that led to his conversion to Christian Science under her guidance. Rowell was encouraged to find Kerr agreeing that the greatest weakness of the League lay in the personnel of the Council and that it was vital to secure new and stronger representatives. Believing that Kerr had great influence with Lloyd George, Rowell pressed the point he had made before the opening of the Assembly: 'I made clear to him that I thought the PM had not given the leadership in the matter of the League and the Assembly which we had the right to expect from the PM of Great Britain and that the responsibility for the success or failure of the League depended more on the Government of Great Britain than any other factor.'[63] When they moved on to more general talk Kerr was as pessimistic about the future as anyone Rowell met in England. The only hope Kerr could see for the prevention of the total collapse of European society within five years was in the intimate co-operation of the United States, Britain, and the Dominions. Kerr had already made Anglo-Saxon unity his life's mission, and his commitment to that cause disposed him to be less wholehearted in his support for the League of Nations than Rowell would have liked.

Among Rowell's English friends it was not easy to find any optimism about the future of Europe, and only a few felt confident even about Britain's prospects. Rowell could contemplate Canadian problems with some sense of relief: 'I never felt so thankful that I am a Canadian as now. We have very great reason for gratitude. I believe conditions are better in Canada than in any country in the world. While we have these great reasons for gratitude we cannot turn a deaf ear to the cry of need – there are some movements to alleviate conditions in which we certainly should help.'[64]

21

Canada, the Empire, and the
new internationalism

When Rowell arrived home in Toronto he lost no time in returning to legal practice at 120 Bay Street. Although he would continue in the firm, he had decided not to participate in the general law practice of Rowell, Reid, Wright, and MacMillan, but to engage only in work as counsel. That would give him freedom to choose his cases and to some extent to control the expenditure of his time, so that he could work on behalf of the causes to which he was committed, and in particular to publicizing the League of Nations. Legal work was not slow in coming: the wartime industrialization of Ontario had done nothing to diminish demand for the services of a first-class corporation lawyer. Before long he was acting for the province of Ontario in what proved to be a long-drawn-out case concerning the timber rights in Quetico Park of the Shevlin-Clarke Lumber Company of Fort Frances, and for the Toronto Railway Company before the arbitration board determining the compensation to be paid the company by the city of Toronto when the city's transportation system passed into public ownership under the Toronto Transportation Commission. In view of the opinion he had held of the financial operations and political influence of Mackenzie and Mann there was irony in his advocacy in the winding up of one of their many interests.

Originally he was determined to resign his seat in Parliament at once, before the session scheduled to open in February, since he thought it impossible to do justice both to his duties as a member and to his endeavour to re-establish himself in his profession after more than a decade away from it. However, on Prime Minister Meighen's urging he agreed to remain for the session in order to take part in the discussion of questions arising from the League Assembly. But he felt bound to make it clear that he could not attend the sittings of the House regularly.[1]

The decision to remain in Parliament imparted renewed vigour to the continuing speculation in both the Liberal and Tory press about Rowell's political future. Scarcely any of the commentators, who were generally more appreciative of Rowell's qualities than they had ever been, believed that his public career was ended, and some prophesied an important role for him in the near future. Among these was John A. Stevenson, who informed the readers of the British weekly the *New Statesman* that in a Parliament where the government's majority was under twenty, Rowell might well be 'the controlling factor.' In Stevenson's view he had 'a small special following' in the House of Commons, he was probably the most effective speaker within its walls, and in the country at large he had 'immeasureably increased his prestige and popularity by his courageous indictment of European statesmanship at Geneva.' Now that Rowell had 'freed himself from the deadening atmosphere of the coalition' he had an opportunity to make himself a powerful force for 'real Liberalism' in Canada.[2] What neither Stevenson nor any of the other well-disposed editorial writers and correspondents explained was how he could make his influence felt, even had he desired to do so, under the existing political conditions. He had no more wish than before to join Meighen's party, which in effect had become the Conservative party, and no overture had been made to him from Mackenzie King's Liberals, nor was any likely to be made by a group in which French Canadians were so dominant. In any case, as everyone knew, there was bound to be a general election soon with results not easy to predict.

Speculation about Rowell's future was largely laid to rest when he released to the press a letter stating the conditions on which he was remaining in the House for the coming session. He stressed that he would interest himself mainly in external affairs, and although he affirmed that since he had been elected as a Liberal Unionist he remained one, his tone implied a certain detachment from the government.[3] His old supporters in the *Globe*'s editorial office found his position unsatisfactory, and denounced him once more for remaining so long with a bankrupt coalition and for continuing to give it even token support now.[4]

To one important aspect of Canada's external relations Rowell gave some attention immediately on his return from Europe. In the Council of the League of Nations, for whom did the representative of the British Empire speak? For Great Britain alone, or for the whole Empire? Early in 1920, while he was still a member of the cabinet, the government had approved and forwarded to London a minute pointing out that as long as the British Empire was represented on the League Council, Canada and the other Dominions should be consulted about who should be appointed.[5] As a result of his experience at Geneva Rowell now had second thoughts about the wisdom of that minute. He concluded that even with consultation as to the appointee, it was impossible to continue the present form of representation in the Council, and in London he had presented his view to Lord Milner, secretary of state for the colonies. Rowell pointed out that on at least two important issues before the League Assembly the representatives of one or more of the Dominions had adopted a position contrary to that taken by the British Empire delegate in the Council. There had been Canada's contention that the distribution of raw materials was not properly the League's concern, although Balfour speaking in the Council had approved the reference of that question to a League committee. And again, South Africa and Canada thought that the form under which the League system of mandates had been set up by the Council should have been submitted to the Assembly's committee on mandates, but Balfour had taken the opposite view. Rowell was convinced that the Canadian delegation, and Balfour as well, believed that the latter was speaking only for Great Britain, but it was still a fact that, officially, Balfour was 'the British Empire' delegate. The only solution, Rowell told Milner, was to make it clear that the British representative on the Council represented Great Britain only. Until such time as the League Covenant could be amended and Great Britain substituted for the British Empire as the state to be represented on the Council, the position could be regularized by a statement to the same effect from Britain and the Dominions.[6] Milner would have preferred to leave matters as they were, but Rowell had the impression that he understood 'the very obvious and practical difficulties' and accepted Rowell's position.[7]

One of those practical difficulties always before Rowell's mind was the continuing trouble many Americans had in understanding the present British representation in the League. To the League Assembly he had pointed out the significance of the independent stand taken by the Dominions vis-à-vis Great Britain, and he hoped that this would clear up some of the misunderstanding in the United States. Shortly after his return to Canada he visited New York to address the Canadian Club there on the subject of the League Assembly and was gratified to learn from Colonel Edward House, President Wilson's personal adviser, that the point had got across in some quarters. However, his discussions with several American leaders revealed that the matter was still not entirely clear. Thus, Senator Elihu Root, who was expected to become chairman of President Harding's commission on the League, still found the character of British representation a stumbling block and urged upon Rowell the necessity of an early ending of dual representation. Although Rowell tried to convince Root that the 'apparent inconsistency' did not represent any 'real inconsistency,' it was not an easy task.[8]

Rowell had not given up his preference for a 'consultative Empire,' but he could see no alternative in the case of representation on the League Council, and he urged Meighen to settle the matter speedily:

It seems to me quite impossible for Mr. Balfour or any other representative of the British Empire to keep in such constant touch with all Governments of the

Dominions as to enable him to voice their views in the Council and yet, if he represents the British Empire on the Council when he votes, his vote is the vote of the British Empire and should bind all the constituent nations. The matter is undoubtedly one which might create a most embarrassing and difficult situation unless it is cleared up.[9]

The prime minister was not convinced that the matter demanded early attention; indeed it was not clear that he understood Rowell's point. While agreeing that there was a certain anomaly in the present position, Meighen saw no need for immediate change. Since in practice the British Empire delegate did not profess to commit the Dominions without previous consultation he thought it best not to seek to clarify the position until some future 'general clearing up of our constitutional ideas,' possibly at the next Imperial Conference.[10]

As he contemplated his contribution to the coming session of Parliament Rowell was much influenced in his thinking about the League and especially about the prospects for American participation by his recent conversations with ex-President W.H. Taft, Colonel House, and Senator Root, and with Charles Evans Hughes, whose imminent appointment as secretary of state was common talk. The picture he derived from these talks with key Republicans was that President Harding would propose an alternative organization to the League as he had promised in his election campaign. Root and others would argue strongly for this knowing full well that it was impossible to set up another international organization at that date. Then, if Britain and France would treat the proposal with reasonable courtesy, while resisting it firmly, Harding would be able to say that the implementation of his promises to pursue international co-operation required him to find some basis for participation in world affairs that was acceptable to the other powers. In the end, Harding would sponsor American entry into the League, with reservations.[11] As prophecy Rowell's assessment fell far short of accuracy. In the meantime it explained the optimism he displayed in the House about the prospects for early American adherence to the League. Without being specific he implied that the acceptance of some American reservations concerning the League Covenant would be necessary and therefore acceptable.[12] Already, in New York, he had declared that Canada would have no objection to the United States entering the League without subscribing to Article 10, a position consistent with Canada's own attitude to that article.[13]

Since Sir George Foster, as chairman of the Canadian delegation, had already given the House an extensive report on the League Assembly, Rowell confined the rest of his remarks on the League to a systematic and eloquent discussion[14] of the problems and issues on which he had worked most closely in Geneva. His presentation won much favourable comment in the press and earned him a note of appreciation and thanks from the prime minister.[15]

No degree of eloquence seemed to have much effect on the doubting Thomases among the members of the Liberal opposition. Later, in the debate on approval of the protocol establishing the Permanent Court of International Justice, Rowell repeated the claim he had made in numerous public addresses that the formation of the court was the most important achievement of the first Assembly and supported Doherty in expressing the hope that the day would soon come when all international disputes would be subject to compulsory arbitration by the court. Much of the opposition's scepticism was embodied in D.D. McKenzie's question about how compulsory arbitration could be reconciled with national sovereignty. Rowell replied that there was no conflict, since the states would first *agree* to submit all their disputes to arbitration. Rowell's old antagonist Lucien Cannon offered the most strenuous objections to Rowell's contentions that the Canadian delegates at Geneva had been engaged in matters of great moment for Canada and the world. On the contrary, Cannon charged, they, and Rowell pre-eminently, had simply been encouraging Canada to meddle in dozens of affairs that were none of her business.[16]

W.S. Fielding exhibited a similar 'little Canadianism' when he renewed his objections to the appointment of a Canadian representative in Washington and asserted that it was enough for the prime minister to go to the American capital when major issues arose. Once again Rowell stressed the magnitude of Canada's present and future commercial dealings with the United States and the growing importance of the North Pacific in world affairs, which would mean that the two nations would soon have new and vital relations in that area, and urged that the Washington appointment be made without delay.[17]

Privately, Meighen and Rowell had been discussing a suitable appointment to Washington. They agreed that Borden would be ideal but his poor health continued to keep him in semi-retirement. Rowell himself had been mentioned frequently in the press, but there is no evidence that he was seriously considered; he had made it clear that his decision to return to the practice of law was firm. At Meighen's request Rowell assessed the qualifications of Sir Robert Falconer, president of the University of Toronto, for the post. Rowell had long held Falconer in high regard, thought him 'thoroughly alive to the importance and significance of our present constitutional development,' and after discussion with men who had worked with Falconer as an administrator concluded that there was 'no other body in sight who possesses the peculiar qualifications required to the degree Sir Robert Falconer does.'[18] To Rowell's regret the appointment was not made then, and none had been made when the Meighen government left office nine months later.

It was Meighen's presentation of the agenda of the forthcoming conference of prime ministers of the Empire that provided the occasion for Rowell's major address on the future shape of Canada's external relations.[19] Emphasizing the basis of 'absolute equality' on which the prime ministers would for the first time be meeting, he described their main job as preparation for the constitutional conference he hoped would be held in Canada, the senior Dominion of the Empire, and urged that provision be made for representation of opposition parties in all the delegations so that the discussions might transcend party lines. There should be only two items on the agenda of the constitutional conference: agreement on a declaration recognizing 'the constitutional position of all the Dominions as equal in status with the Mother Country as self-governing nations of the British Empire' and 'an outline of plans for consultation and co-operation between the Mother Country and the Dominions in matters of common concern to the whole Empire.'

What were the matters of common concern? At least they could not include the naval question because the destruction of the German navy and the League's commitment to further disarmament meant that 'no question of naval policy arises,' at least not until it became clear that disarmament had failed. Until that time, which all must hope would not come, Canada should take the position that she would not increase either her naval or her military strength. For the moment Rowell gave no indication of the matters of common concern but outlined general principles that should inform 'any recognized policy of the Empire as a whole': the Empire must hold no territorial ambitions, should commit itself fully to the settlement of all disputes through the League of Nations, and should work through the League and with the United States for a limitation of armaments; the Empire must refrain from making alliances outside the League, for if the leading powers began to make such commitments there would soon be 'a reversion to the old principle of the balance of power from which we had hoped that the war had largely freed us'; finally, the special interest of Canada in all questions arising between the British Empire and the United States must be fully recognized and the prime minister should insist that 'no question of real importance arising between the British Empire and the United States should be settled without consultation with Canada.' Rowell recognized that he was advocating no new policy, but with a Canadian minister in Washington it could be followed more consistently, and both Canadian and general imperial interests would be better served:

Even though it may be repeating what has been said more than once I reiterate, from the knowledge that has come to me during recent years, that we do understand the British statesmen and their point of view better than the people in the United States understand them, while at the same time we understand the American point of view very much better than the British statesmen do, and the greatest hope for permanent and cordial relations and the best possible understanding between the British Empire and the United States lies in Canada's acting as an interpreter and mediator between the United States and the Empire.

Canada's unique capacity for playing the role of interpreter and mediator would not mean that she would compromise her own interests. Rowell went on to make clear that not only must Canada be consulted in matters concerning her, but where 'the clear and paramount interest is Canadian' they must be settled on Canadian terms. 'It is going much further than we have gone before ... but it is a right and sound principle.'[20]

Against this outline of general principles for the conduct of British policy Rowell proceeded to discuss two specific problems, both of which illustrated well the practical difficulties involved in implementing the policy of imperial consultation he was advocating: German reparations and the renewal of the Anglo-Japanese alliance, which was to be discussed at the conference of Empire prime ministers. On the first, Rowell questioned the wisdom of Canadian government policy and of the British policy it resembled. On the second he set out a desirable Canadian policy, the one that was in fact pursued but had not yet been officially announced; on this he may have been 'flying a kite' for Meighen to test public reaction.

Rowell had first become actively interested in the reparations question as it affected Canada after the government's announcement on 27 February 1921 that the Canadian claim against Germany, as submitted to the Reparations Commission, amounted to a billion dollars, more than $6 million of which was to cover war pensions and separation allowances paid to Canadian veterans and their dependents by the Canadian government. The size of the claim was in keeping with the scaling upward of claims on Germany in which the Allies had been engaged for the past several months. After considerable investigation Rowell concluded that the increased reparations were outside the terms of the armistice and of the Spa Agreement of July 1920. From information he had received at the British Empire discussions preceding the League Assembly, from Loring Christie's replies to his enquiries on the subject, and from his reading of the *Times* he believed that what had happened was that Britain, rather than risk a breach with France, had succumbed to French pressure to raise the German indemnities beyond the amount the British statesmen really believed Germany could pay. Although Rowell could understand the French attitude, he thought the French people and their government were in no emotional condition to make 'a common sense judgment.' The claim that Germany was already in default on certain other obligations under the peace treaty could not make Allied behaviour either legally or morally correct. Pensions and separation allowances were clearly part of the cost of the war operation itself, as distinct from the damage done to civilians or their property, the latter being the only category covered under the armistice.[21] Since he believed the increased claims were 'wrong and without any adequate justification' and could 'only lead to grave trouble in the future,' he exhorted Meighen to abandon the announced policy of the Canadian government.[22]

Now, six weeks later in the House, Rowell seemed even more convinced that the increased claims against Germany were wrong. He quoted the distressing admission of the attorney general of Great Britain that they did not come under the terms of the armistice but were justified by the generally accepted right of victors to enforce treaties, which right was not limited to the express terms of the treaty itself. Rowell feared that the *Manchester Guardian* and the London *Observer* were right in their contention that the Allies were committing themselves to 'a programme which may involve a new war.' Canada must have no part in forcing Germany to pay one dollar more than she had agreed to pay in the treaty. To Rowell's mind the revised Allied policy was one more indication of the limitations of European statesmanship, and he saw in the proposed American participation in the continuing reparation negotiations the chief hope for an early and just settlement: 'As a result of the crimes and horrors of war' he told the House 'the blood of Europe is still too hot to secure a just and permanent settlement of the question.' It was highly desirable for the United States to take part in settling the controversy 'because she is able to take such a view as we in Canada would take, an absolutely just view from the standpoint of Germany, and, at the same time, a view wholly sympathetic to the Allies.'[23] Once more, North American detachment from European problems constituted a qualification for settling those problems.

More difficult and more immediate for Canada than the controversy over reparations was the question of the renewal of the Anglo-Japanese alliance. Early in February during his visit to Washington Rowell had talked with several Republicans close to President Harding, including Charles Evans Hughes, W.H. Taft, and Elihu Root and had subsequently conveyed to Meighen their strong opposition to renewal of the alliance.[24] Later, before a large audience at Queen's University, Rowell had discussed the Anglo-Japanese alliance at length and had argued against its renewal mainly on the general ground that alliances formed outside the League of Nations would undermine the League's authority and by encouraging a return to the old 'balance of power' politics would be detrimental to world peace. Secondarily he had contended that the conditions in the Far East which had produced the treaty in 1905 no longer existed and although American apprehensions about the threat posed to the United States by the continuation of the treaty were completely unjustified, their existence could not be ignored, least of all by Canada.[25] In the House it was the last consideration that Rowell emphasized strongly. He found it hard to understand why the United States should fear that in case of war in the Pacific she would find both Japan and Britain ranged against her, since, as he explained, under Article 4, which had been added to the treaty in 1911, neither signatory was obligated to go to war against any other nation with whom it had a general treaty of arbitration. Thus, in the event of a controversy between the United States and Japan, the British Empire would not be bound to intervene. Nevertheless, American mistrust of Japan was a fact, and the treaty was the basis for much ill will in the United States toward both Japan and Britain. Therefore, argued Rowell, Canada should oppose renewal of the treaty.[26]

In these parliamentary speeches on external relations the underlying assumption, not always made explicit, was that Canada was primarily a North American nation. Despite Rowell's continuing advocacy of a common imperial foreign policy achieved by consultation on reparations and more directly on the non-renewal of the Anglo-Japanese treaty, he had interpreted Canada's interests in a way that aligned her with the United States. He hoped that consultation and negotiation, sustained by all the powerful forces of emotion and interest making Anglo-Saxon unity so appealing on both sides of the Atlantic and with Canada playing a leading role, would produce agreement that would save Canada from any painful choice between Britain and the United States. But if consultation did not yield agreement within the Empire or between the Empire and the United States, what then? He did not answer the question, but the implication of his thinking was that North America would win.

In the months following his return from Geneva Rowell had far more to say outside Parliament about international affairs than within it. Scarcely a week went by without at least one public address, and often there were three or four. Usually the topic was related directly to some aspect of the League Assembly, always with a good deal of attention to Canada's role there and in the future, but sometimes the subject was South Africa or Canada's interests in the Pacific. Before gatherings of teachers, Boards of Trade, Canadian Clubs, students and faculty in universities, and general meetings of citizens in churches and theatres he expounded the promise of peace through the League and pleaded for a more informed Canadian public opinion on international affairs. His message was heard in numerous Ontario centres, and he spent the last ten days of February in the west, going as far as Edmonton, while early in May he was in Moncton, Saint John, and Halifax. No subject to which he had ever given himself was better suited to his oratorical skills than the League, and many a reporter commented on the effectiveness of the easy direct manner in which he informed and held his audiences on complicated issues and the earnestness and sincerity that drove home to the heart his call for commitment to a great cause. Nowhere did he arouse more enthusiasm than among university audiences, where the idealism and nationalism fostered by the war were strong. The prairie students at the University of Saskatchewan who awarded an ovation to his address on 'Canada's Status as a Nation' were only slightly less vociferous in their applause than the Maritime students at Dalhousie.[27]

As he travelled about the country Rowell was doing more than making speeches. In every centre he talked with men and women whom he hoped to interest in one of his major preoccupations – the formation of an organization to publicize and support the League of Nations. Before he went to England in the summer of 1920 he had begun to sound out prominent Canadians on the desirability of establishing such an organization, and he had discussed the project with several Toronto friends, including W.E. Rundle, A.J. Glazebrook, Vincent Massey, J.M. Macdonnell, Professor R.M. MacIver, Sir Robert Falconer, and J.S. Maclean, all of whom were members of an informal Toronto discussion group on international affairs, which Rowell attended when he could. Rowell had also corresponded with Lord Robert Cecil, the moving spirit in the already large and well financed League of Nations Union in Britain, and he continued the discussion with Cecil in Geneva. On his return from Geneva Rowell was more than ever convinced that a League of Nations Society was needed in Canada. During his absence his Toronto friends had done nothing in the matter, but in Montreal Warwick Chipman, a prominent lawyer, and Francis Hankin had developed their own plans. After discussions with them Rowell pulled the Toronto and Montreal schemes together, and it was agreed to establish a national organization.

The League of Nations Society of Canada was launched at an impressive founding meeting in Ottawa on 31 May 1921 under the chairmanship of the governor general, the duke of Devonshire. In attendance were Canadians from many centres and walks of life, and the speakers included Sir Robert Borden, Sir George Foster, Dr H.M. Tory, the president of the University of Alberta, L.P.D. Tilley, a St John lawyer and Conservative politician, G.S. Campbell, a leading Halifax businessman, and P.M. Draper of the Trades and Labor Congress of Canada. The meeting approved a constitution drafted by A.J. Glazebrook and Warwick Chipman and revised by Rowell, elected Borden as president, Rowell and H.S. Beland as vice-presidents, and Vincent Massey as secretary, and appointed a central executive committee with Rowell as chairman.

As the person chiefly responsible for organizing the meeting Rowell had good cause to feel that an excellent beginning had been made, and in the following year he gave much attention to the affairs of the League of Nations Society. With Rundle, Borden, and Massey, he helped to finance the early operation of the society, and his office was the scene of regular planning meetings of the executive committee. Among other enterprises, the group organized, largely on the basis of contacts made earlier by Rowell, an autumn speaking tour of the west by Sir George Foster. Through this and other activities branches of the society were started across the country.

From the outset there was more than one opinion as to the character and purpose of the League of Nations Society. A few of the Toronto men were old members of the Round Table who believed that their interest in closer imperial relations could be made more palatable to the public through the movement to support the League. Still others wanted the organization to become, like its British equivalent, a pressure group to influence government policy. Rowell was under no illusion about the lack of interest in the League among most Canadian politicians, including the prime minister, nor unaware of the outright hostility of some, but he thought it bad strategy to lobby the politicians directly. Originally he had been inclined to favour an organization devoted mainly to the study of international problems, similar to the Royal Institute of International Affairs in London, but was persuaded by his Toronto associates that there was more immediate need for general propaganda for the League and the awakening of an intelligent interest in international issues among a broad public. Once it was agreed that the society's function was entirely educational he successfully resisted all suggestions for making it anything else.

Rowell was in close and regular contact with the administrative work of the League of Nations Society until the end of 1922, when it was decided to move the national office from Toronto to Ottawa, a better base, it was hoped, for securing the interest of French Canadians. At that time O.M. Biggar became chairman of the executive, and although Rowell remained on the committee, thereafter he rarely attended any but the annual meetings.[28] But he continued to speak frequently under the auspices of the society, and much of his public activity served the society's objectives as he became increasingly recognized as outstanding among the few Canadians of the decade who were knowledgeable about international affairs. It was chiefly in tribute to the stature he had already demonstrated, notably at Geneva, that the University of Toronto conferred on him the honorary degree of doctor of laws at its convocation in June 1921.

No one in Canada followed more closely than Rowell the reports of the London meeting of prime ministers of the Empire that summer, and save for the rejection of the anticipated constitutional conference they were largely to his satisfaction. A long step forward seemed to have been taken in Dominion participation in the formulation of imperial policy with Meighen's success, against strong opposition from Britain, Australia, and New Zealand, in persuading the conference not to renew the Anglo-Japanese alliance. In the end, the whole problem had been put into the wider context in which it belonged, again largely on Meighen's urging, with an agreement to seek a meeting of all the major Pacific powers. When this proposal was joined with a similar one from the United States, plans were quickly set in motion for a disarmament conference in Washington within a few months' time. Thus the unity of the Empire had been preserved, and in this instance Canada had indeed served as interpreter between Britain and the United States.[29]

Meighen left the London meetings assuming that the Dominions would be represented in the British Empire delegation at the Washington conference. When an enquiry to Lloyd George concerning the agenda revealed that the British government had no such understanding, Meighen made clear Canadian expectations.

Subsequently, the British Empire delegation was expanded to include the Dominions, and Canada nominated Sir Robert Borden as her representative. To Canadian ministers the problem seemed to have been resolved, but not to Prime Minister Smuts of South Africa. In a telegram to Meighen just three weeks before the conference was to open, Smuts protested that the Dominions should not send delegates unless and until they received separate invitations from the United States, the hosts of the conference. If the Americans issued individual invitations it would prove that the United States finally accepted the equal status of the Dominions; without that, the newly won Dominion status would be seriously threatened.[30]

Confidentially, Borden requested Rowell's opinion on Smuts's contention. To Rowell, as to Meighen, the proposed arrangements were quite satisfactory. Although it was regrettable that the character of representation had not been decided at the London conference, Lloyd George's recent announcement on the composition of the British Empire delegation clearly recognized and protected Dominion status. In Rowell's view 'if Canada has distinctive representation at Washington as part of the British Empire delegation, then we have carried out both the letter and the spirit of the arrangement made in reference to the appointment of a Canadian minister at Washington and the diplomatic unity of the Empire is preserved.' In order to spell out in practice the position Borden had taken at Paris, 'in the official record of the Washington Conference it should appear that on the British Empire Delegation Sir Robert Borden represents Canada and each of the Dominion delegates represents his own Dominion, whereas the British delegates represent Great Britain and the portions of the Empire not distinctively represented.' He was not in favour of acting on Smuts's suggestion: 'We should not lose any ground we have gained; at the same time as long as our status is conserved I do not think we should thrust the issue forward unnecessarily at the present time when so much depends upon the success of the present conference.'[31] This was essentially the position Meighen also took – that the substance of representation was more important than the form. In the end the form was not precisely the same as it had been at Paris, since there was no separate Dominion representation, but only participation in the British Empire delegation. For Canada the result was an acceptable example of imperial consultation in action, with opportunity for Canada to play a modest part as an interpreter between Britain and the United States. The deliberations at Washington brought an end to the Anglo-Japanese alliance and agreement on a series of treaties and resolutions which limited naval armaments in the Pacific and endeavoured generally to establish political stability in the area. Although Canada was only indirectly involved in these agreements, any moves that promoted Anglo-American understanding and peace in the Pacific area were in her interests.

While the Washington meetings were in progress Rowell had an opportunity to present his views on the state of the world in a series of four lectures delivered to large audiences in Convocation Hall at the University of Toronto. The Burwash Memorial Lectures, sponsored by Victoria College to honour its late president, Nathanael Burwash, given by Rowell and later published as *The British Empire and World Peace*, were a well-organized summary of what Rowell had been saying across the country in recent months, and, as always, they were designed both for instruction and inspiration. More historical in their reference than some of his less formal addresses, they sketched briefly the development of the nation state, ideas about a world state, church-state relations in Britain, and the growth of responsible government and the rule of law in Britain and Canada, in a manner reflecting his admiration for A.V. Dicey, James Bryce, and the Cambridge Modern History. Reaching the present, he dealt in lengthy detail with the formal structure of the League of Nations and its initial achievements and with current constitutional arrangements and issues in the British Empire. The League, in Rowell's view, was not yet as representative of the world as it must become. Not only was the United States outside it, but so were two other major powers, Germany and Russia. It was to be hoped that another meeting of the League Assembly would not close without the admission of Germany, and when Russia had settled the character of her government, whether it be the Soviet form or some other, and applied for admission she too should be seated speedily.[32]

Throughout the addresses ran the theme that the success of the League depended in large measure on the opinion of the peoples of the world. That opinion must be informed by a recognition that the nation state was no longer adequate to meet the needs of human society: 'The intellectual, moral, and spiritual ideas of mankind recognize no territorial limits, nor any particular form of sovereignty. The achievements of science are not the peculiar possessions of any one people but are the common property of all men. Trade, transportation, and finance have all been internationalized, and war, pestilence, and famine, the three great scourges of humanity, refuse to be stopped by national frontiers.'[33] Given these facts, and the destructive power of modern weapons of war, a political organization to establish a peaceful world was essential to human survival.

What of those who argued that man had always fought, and always would, and practical men ought not to waste their time in the pursuit of schemes for world peace? 'Peace and not war is the normal condition of the civilized races of men. While war is as old as recorded history, in all civilized communities it has been looked upon as an evil, though in some cases a necessary evil.'[34]

What were most likely to be the causes of war in the future? In the past there had been four principal causes: dynastic, economic, religious, and racial. The age of dynastic wars seemed to be over, and 'the last great war has shown that no State can gain economically as a result of a great war, and therefore wars waged on economic grounds alone are not so likely to arise in the future.' There was hope that religious wars also belonged to the past.

> The ultimate and most pressing problem of international politics appears to be the racial one. ... [Britain] is now conducting in India the greatest of all her experiments in the realm of government, viz. to lead an Oriental people without any practical experience in the working of democratic institutions and without the political ideas which lie at the basis of such institutions in the path of democratic, responsible government ... If the British Commonwealth can solve the problem of co-operation between East and West, can bridge the gulf that racial difference creates and racial prejudices would tend to widen, she will have rendered one of her greatest services to the human race and one of her largest contributions to the peace and progress of all mankind.[35]

The problem of race was not confined to Europe's relations with Asia. He had seen another aspect of it in Africa where a genuine racial consciousness was growing among the black peoples and must be met in a spirit of brotherhood and a desire to see Africans take a full part in organized society.[36]

Rowell continued to look to the Christian church as the primary creator of the moral atmosphere in which problems in racial and international relations could be resolved. If he was somewhat less confident in 1921 about the prospects for 'the evangelisation of the world in this generation' than he had been before the war, more conscious of evil within Christian civilization and more aware of the variety of social movements and religions that might contribute to the growth of human brotherhood, he still assigned a special role to the church, and especially to the educational and medical work of the modern missionary movement. Nothing the Christian church was doing was more important than its contribution to the development of educated leaders in Asia. These men and women, Rowell believed, would increasingly be influenced by the growing nationalism in their own countries and would create self-governing churches that truly expressed the thought and character of Eastern peoples. Rowell's earlier appreciation of the central position of China had been nourished by his fifteen years as a member of the Board of Governors of West China Union University and he was continuing to take an active interest in that institution.

> If China could be organized and militarized in the next fifty years to the extent Japan has been in the past half-century, the German Empire under the Kaiser would be a weak military organization compared to China, and our whole western civilization would be in jeopardy. Japan during the past fifty years but followed the example of the so-called Christian Powers ... Is it not a matter for

serious reflection that the great military Powers which in modern times have menaced the world's peace have been the so-called Christian Powers? They have menaced the peace, not because they were Christian but because they were not Christian enough.'[37]

What was Canada's contribution to the new international order? It would not be found in a weakening of existing political ties. The unity of the Britannic Commonwealth displayed so effectively in the recent war was now 'the greatest existing bulwark against the onrush of the forces of unrest, disorder, and disorganization.' Its only rival was the United States, which thus far had failed to co-operate fully in stabilizing the international situation.[38] Through the Commonwealth Canadians enjoyed a world citizenship unique in human history and were 'the possessors of an inheritance ... vastly greater than that possessed by a citizen of Rome.'[39] Further, in Canada's relations with the United States there were constructive possibilities. One lay in interpreting Britain and the United States to one another, especially in enlightening the many Americans who had little understanding of Britain.[40] Another was the demonstration provided in the past one hundred years of Canadian-American relations that 'it is practicable for nations living side by side to settle all their disputes by peaceable means, even though such disputes affect territory and so-called questions of national honour,' and 'that it is possible for nations having a common frontier of 5,400 miles strictly to limit naval and land forces and military fortifications,' with untold benefit to both.[41]

Canada's own national life was of great potential usefulness to the wider world. Thanks to the diversity of peoples in Canada, and especially by virtue of having two mother countries, 'we can respect the view of those who differ from us.' Using 'race' in a different sense and in the Canadian context now, and apparently discounting Canadian experience during the recent war, Rowell declared: 'This diversity of racial origin in our people and the consideration which it has compelled public men to give to the varying points of view of different racial strains in our population have already appreciably affected the attitude of our public men on Imperial and international questions. They are more tolerant of those who differ from them and they speak with a greater sense of responsibility.'[42] If Canadians were to realize their high destiny as conciliators, an extensive program of public education was required.

During the following winter Rowell continued giving many addresses aimed at cultivating the Canadian sense of responsibility, to the extent that a heavy schedule of legal work permitted. Early in 1922 he had the satisfaction of a court judgment in favour of his client, the province of Ontario, against the Shevlin-Clarke Lumber Company. In some quarters the decision was seen as a condemnation of the administration of Howard Ferguson, minister of lands and forests in the earlier Hearst government, now succeeded by the United Farmers of Ontario–Labour government led by E.C. Drury, and the matter was the subject of debate in the Ontario Legislature and of much partisan discussion in the press. Even more extended were the lengthy arbitration proceedings in the Toronto Railway Company case, which continued to require a good deal of Rowell's attention.

Legal matters were temporarily set aside at the end of May when he set sail for Europe, accompanied by Nell, his sister Mary, and two of the children, Mary and Frederick. Langford was to spend the period of their absence in Toronto and at a summer camp in Temagami. They went directly to France, and spent the next six weeks there and in southern Germany, Belgium, and Holland. In St Wolfgang, Austria, Nell attended the World's Committee of the Young Women's Christian Association, the policy-making body of the international YWCA, while her sister-in-law was another of the four Canadian delegates. The main items on the committee's agenda included the work of the Y among girls and women in industry and among immigrants, both matters in which Nell had recently taken an active interest as acting president of the YWCA of Canada and chairman of its committee on industrial work among women.

In Paris, Salzburg, Munich, Strasbourg, Brussels, and Amsterdam there were visits to cathedrals, museums, and art galleries, with the occasional shopping expedition. Memorable for quite different reasons were Verdun, Rheims, Amiens, and the cemeteries in Vimy, Ypres, St Julien, and Sanctuary Wood, where they found many familiar names.[43] As usual, Rowell was talking to anyone who had interesting views to share, nowhere with more enthusiasm than in The Hague, where the Permanent Court of International Justice had begun its work just five months earlier; his best informant was Lord Finlay, the British judge on the court. In mid-July when they reached London there were meetings with several of his associates in the League Assembly. The Council of the League was in session on the mandates for Palestine and Syria. Among several debates he attended in the House of Commons Rowell heard one of immediate and practical importance to Canada and was present for the vote that lifted the embargo, in effect since 1892, on the import into Britain of live cattle from Canada. More long-range in their significance were the deliberations of the International Missionary Council, which Rowell attended in Canterbury. After that, the family group settled into the Carlton Hotel, high on the cliffs at Bournemouth, for three weeks. Frequent trips to London enabled Rowell to continue his discussions with friends old and new, several of whom became recipients of gift copies of the Burwash lectures, published in England early that month by the Oxford University Press.[44]

Two subjects of continuing interest to Rowell – the reparations issue, currently the subject of discussions in London among representatives of the Allied powers, and procedures for consultation within the Empire – were brought together when the acting British foreign secretary, Lord Balfour, issued a note to the Allied powers owing war debts to Great Britain, pointing out that the amount Britain must collect from them was closely related to the settlement of the sum owed to the United States by Britain as a result of wartime borrowing. In an attempt to bring reparations and war debts together in a broad approach to 'end the economic injury inflicted on the world by the existing state of things,' read the note, 'this country would be prepared (subject to the just claims of other parts of the Empire) to abandon all further right to German Reparation and all claims to repayment by Allies, provided this renunciation formed part of a general plan by which this great problem could be dealt with as a whole and find a satisfactory solution.'[45]

The possibility of some general settlement of this kind had already been discussed in many quarters. Rowell had no objection to the intent of the Balfour Note, but he knew how much hostility there was to any such scheme in the United States, and thought the note should not have been sent. Moreover, he had more than a suspicion that the Canadian government had not been consulted, and he had no doubt that it should have been. His letter of enquiry to Lloyd George's private secretary, Sir Edward Grigg, soon became less a request for information than a strong protest:

If the Canadian Government was not consulted then it appears to me it was a serious departure from the understanding that the Dominions should be consulted on matters of Foreign policy directly affecting their interests ... The whole incident ... certainly strengthens the conviction of the necessity of a Canadian Representative at Washington both in the interests of Canada and the Empire. Is not this the second case within a year where, on a question of prime importance to good relations between the United States and the British Empire, the British Government has either not been correctly advised as to the trend of American sentiment or has failed to appreciate the advice given? The other case I refer to was the renewal of the Anglo-Japanese Alliance where Mr Meighen rendered a real service in drawing your Government's attention to the real trend of American sentiment. Pardon me if I speak frankly, it is because I feel deeply ... There was no justification under the Armistice terms which included Mr Wilson's 14 points for imposing the payment of pensions and separation allowances on Germany. I say that though I was a member of a Government which was a party to the Treaty. It was a wrong to Germany and a wrong to France; to Germany because it violated the conditions upon which she laid down her arms and placed her obligations far beyond her capacity to pay: to France because it divided the

Reparations on a basis entirely different from the division which would have prevailed if the terms of the Armistice had been carried out. Where a wrong has been done there is only one way to right it and that is to do one's best to undo it.[46]

Having said so much, Rowell decided to send copies of his letter to two other places where they might do some good – to Sir James Masterson-Smith, permanent undersecretary of state for the colonies, and Robert G. Vansittart, secretary to Lord Curzon, the British foreign secretary.

Within two weeks of Rowell's return to Canada the 'Chanak incident' provided a dramatic illustration of the difficulties of achieving a common imperial foreign policy. When the Canadian government was suddenly asked to send a contingent to assist Britain in the defence of the Dardanelles against the Turks, although it had not been consulted in the British actions which led up to the contemplation of this drastic step, King said 'no,' while Arthur Meighen declared that he should have answered 'ready, aye, ready!' Rowell made no public comment, but the episode was clearly a blow to every devotee of imperial unity, and it underlined for him the urgency of establishing adequate channels of communication between Ottawa and London.[47]

In one area at least, progress was made in imperial relations with the signing of a halibut fisheries treaty by Canada and the United States early in 1923. This final step in the evolution of Canadian autonomy in the making of commercial treaties had political implications as well, a fact evident in the initial resistance of the British Colonial Office and the American Senate to Canada's signing without the signature of the British ambassador in Washington. The treaty had been negotiated, like many others, solely between the two countries immediately concerned. The Canadian government's insistence that the treaty was valid without a British signature as had heretofore been required was intended to assert Canadian responsibility for a matter that concerned only Canada and not the rest of the Empire, a principle Rowell had been expounding since the end of the war.

22
An observer of King Liberalism

With the prorogation of parliament early in June 1921, and the official announcement confirming that Rowell would not sit in the next session there was another
flurry of speculation about his future. Many editorial writers still found it hard to
believe that he would remain out of public life for long. The Conservative *Ottawa
Journal* was perhaps better able to give a judicious assessment of his career than
most Liberal observers, who were still endeavouring to heal wartime divisions. In
the *Journal*'s opinion Rowell had abilities which the nation could not afford to lose:

> Mr. Rowell has exhibited qualities all too rare in the public men of these times,
> qualities which, no matter from what standpoint judged, placed him in the very
> forefront of contemporary statesmanship in Canada ... no public man sacrificed
> more for the sake of his country's cause in the days of the war. Had he cared to
> stand aside, to put party before principle, the highest prize in the gift of the official
> Liberal party might have been his. He was, and, indeed still is, the logical
> successor to Laurier.
>
> As a member of the coalition he was, next to Sir Robert Borden, its most salient
> force ...
>
> His gift of eloquence, his industry, his earnestness, and above all, his extensive
> knowledge in the wider realm of world affairs, made him an outstanding figure,
> and not the least of his services were those which he rendered the Dominion on
> the constitutional and external stage.
>
> It was his misfortune, though it was not always to his discredit, that he was not a
> popular figure in the House. A Gladstonian Liberal in his foreign outlook, his
> Liberalism in domestic affairs was more of the Georgian type, frequently border-

ing on State Socialism, and this tendency toward paternal legislation frequently brought him to cross purposes with the government's followers, intensely individualistic in purpose.

Taken all in all, however, he was a splendid influence in public life, and Canadians of all parties and of none who value ability and character in public service will hear of his retirement with feelings of profound regret.[1]

Rowell himself had no feelings of regret at being on the sidelines of Canadian politics, especially when he contemplated the imminence of a general election. For him, electioneering had never been one of the more enjoyable features of public life. But despite his continuing preoccupation with international issues he remained a keenly interested observer of the domestic political scene, one that was currently filled with omens of change.

In the past year there had been growing political manifestations of the new social and economic forces at work in Canada since the end of the war, especially in the west. In Manitoba, the Liberal government of T.C. Norris, elected in 1920, continued in office only through the sufferance of nine farmer and eleven labour representatives. In British Columbia, Liberals under John Oliver were in power, but in the 1920 election contest independent candidates throughout the province had won nearly as many votes as the victorious party, although only four labour representatives had been elected to the Legislature. The Liberal regime of W.M. Martin in Saskatchewan subverted the entry of an organized farmers' party into provincial politics only by the calling of a snap election in June 1921. Two months later, sixteen years of Liberal rule ended in Alberta with the triumph of the United Farmers of Alberta. In Ontario the two-year-old Farmer-Labour government of E.C. Drury, despite a good deal of internal wrangling over the nature of the party and its policies, had proved more durable than even some of its leaders had expected. And on the national scene it had become clear by the end of 1920 that the farmers, represented by the Progressive Party under T.A. Crerar, were going to be a substantial force in federal politics.

Although Rowell was not in a position to offer any public support, the Drury government enjoyed his good will.[2] He preferred the Drury administration to any that could be imagined under a Liberal label in the current circumstances, although in his view the ousting of Hartley Dewart in the autumn of 1921 in favour of the temporary leadership of Wellington Hay, Liberal whip in the Legislature, represented a slight improvement in provincial Liberal fortunes. In two policies of Drury's aggressive attorney general, W.E. Raney, Rowell could find reason enough to support the UFO government. Raney had launched an attack on the 'profiteering' of Ontario jockey clubs in the operation of horse racing and was threatening to subject these activities to severely restrictive legislation. Further, Raney was the chief exponent of the government's commitment to the enforcement of the Ontario Temperance Act.

With the ending of the federal government's wartime ban on the interprovincial movement of liquor, the enforcement of the Ontario Temperance Act had become even more difficult than before. Under an amendment to the Canada Temperance Act, an amendment Rowell had been instrumental in securing, a provincial government could call a referendum to seek approval for provincial legislation to fill the gap left by Ottawa's abandonment of this type of regulation. Accordingly, the Ontario government called a referendum for 18 April 1921 to ask the voters 'Shall the importation and the bringing of intoxicating liquors into the province for beverage purposes be forbidden?' If the voters answered 'yes,' then a further measure, popularly known as the 'Sandy Bill,' prohibiting the receiving or transporting of liquor within the province, would also come into effect.

As the contending forces organized for the fray, the anti-prohibitionists or 'moderates' as they preferred to call themselves, rallied behind the Citizens Liberty League with Admiral Sir Charles Kingsmill as honorary president and I.F. Hellmuth KC as chairman. The speakers for the League included the provost of Trinity College, Dr T.C. Street Macklem, Professor Stephen Leacock of McGill University, Col. William Hendrie, president of the Ontario Jockey Club, and Tom Moore, president of the Trades and Labor Congress of Canada. The League, arguing that prohibition was a violation of individual liberty, did not support a return to the open bar but advocated government control of the sale of liquor and the promotion of 'true temperance' by education and example. To the detriment of their campaign, the anti-prohibitionists imported a well known American orator from Chicago, Charles A. Windle, who made a week's tour of the province before the League was forced to disown him in the face of revelations of his pro-German and anti-British pronouncements during the war.

The prohibitionists were better organized and financed than their opponents. In the Dominion Alliance, with its branches throughout the province, they already had bases from which to fight the campaign, and their supporters included many men of substantial means. In Toronto, where the battle was recognized as one of the toughest, the Prohibition Committee was chaired by C.L. Burton of the Robert Simpson Company; J.H. Gundy was finance chairman, and the campaign was directed by a Methodist clergyman, Rev. Peter Bryce. Like their opponents the prohibitionists also drew on American talent in the person of the famous temperance orator, 'Pussyfoot' Johnson, who spoke to large audiences in several centres before being so heckled by an audience in Toronto's Massey Hall that he could not continue his speech. The next evening in Windsor he was routed from the platform by a hostile crowd and had to be escorted by the police to safety across the American border.[3]

Shortly after this episode, and almost on the eve of the referendum, twelve thousand people gathered in the Mutual Street Arena in Toronto to hear Premier Drury, Sir George Foster, and Rowell pleading for a Yes vote in the referendum. All the speakers paid some attention to the arguments of the Liberty League, but the emphasis was always on the moral and practical advantages of life under the Ontario Temperance Act and the need to create conditions in which it could be enforced. The frequent and prolonged applause suggested that those on the platform were preaching almost entirely to the converted. Noting that this was the first time he had appeared on the same platform with Drury since he became premier, Rowell declared that 'this magnificent gathering typified the uprising of the people of Ontario, not against individuals, not against their fellow-citizens, but against the organized, legalized, liquor traffic.' He admitted that prohibition involved no sacrifice for total abstainers, while it did demand 'some measure of personal sacrifice from the men who are accustomed to take a social glass.' But in the past many such men had made that sacrifice out of concern for the common good, and Rowell was sure they would do so again.

Every voter ought to understand clearly that government control of the sale of liquor was not an issue in the referendum, Rowell explained, and those who suggested that a No vote would result in government control were simply misleading the public. The people of Ontario had rejected government control in 1919; now they were voting only on whether to prohibit the importation of liquor into the province. A vote in favour would make possible the continuation of a law that had resulted in a decline in drunkenness, crime, and poverty, had 'changed the character of thousands of homes from misery to comfort,' and had given 'new hope and new opportunity to tens of thousands of women and children. Is that not worth while?'[4]

The voters of Ontario decided that it was. In a total of 914,711 votes, prohibition was favoured by a majority of 171,000. Although some cities returned a majority of No votes, Toronto showed 82,397 for prohibition and 73,377 against. In the ensuing discussions of the result, women campaign workers and voters were accorded much of the credit, or blame, for the outcome. For Rowell this demonstration of the wisdom of women voters was a vindication of his advocacy of their enfranchisement.

On 1 September 1921, three months after the prorogation of Parliament, Meighen announced the anticipated general election for 6 December. At the outset of the three-month campaign Meighen made the tariff the major election issue, and it remained so until the end. This choice of fighting ground was confirmation, if any were needed, of Rowell's conviction that he did not belong in Meighen's camp. To be sure, the tariff was not without consequence, but as he had argued in the cabinet, it was not the dominant issue Meighen and some of the other ministers made of it.

For Rowell, 'the industrial question' was still more important to Canada than the tariff.

Clearly that question would get little attention from Meighen's Conservatives, nor was Rowell so naïve as to believe that the author of *Industry and Humanity* would make industrial reform central to the Liberal election program. Mackenzie King was in no position to do that, whatever his personal wishes. Ironically, the 'Atkinson-Rowell Liberals' of Ontario, by pressing the conscription issue during the war to the point of dividing the party, had prepared the way for French Canadian domination of the post-war party and the suppression by Quebec's natural conservatism of 'the Atkinson social program' as it was embodied in the Liberal platform of 1919. Moreover, conservative influences within the Liberal party were not confined to Quebec; few among the faithful in the present Ontario Liberal party were vigorous in urging King to take advanced positions. Quite the contrary. With a nearly solid Quebec behind him and much of the west going to the Progressives, King was concentrating his campaign on Ontario, the most industrialized province in the country. He was obviously heeding the advice he was receiving on all sides to reassure the Ontario business community that it need fear neither the introduction of too low tariffs nor radical social legislation at the hands of a Liberal government.[5]

As the long campaign moved into its final stages Rowell was delivering the Burwash lectures and enjoying the independence of a non-partisan platform. He was not soliciting votes and was free to speak his mind on 'the industrial question,' to which he devoted most of one lecture. He had been thinking a good deal about industrial relations, especially since the ILO convention, and had discussed the subject with some of his Toronto friends, notably Professor R.M. MacIver, whose recent book, *Labor in the Changing World*, questioned the wage system and advocated more co-operative forms of industrial production.

'Next to the racial problem the most difficult, perplexing, and menacing to World Peace is the industrial' Rowell declared. In a brief historical sketch he traced the growth of the specialization and mechanization necessary for the enormous productivity of modern industry, with its accompanying accumulation of wealth in the hands of the few. Quoting Professor MacIver he observed that in Great Britain two-thirds of the wealth was owned by one-seventieth of the population, while in the United States two-thirds was owned by one-fiftieth of the population.[6] To Rowell's mind these facts explained much: 'Apart from any theories which one may entertain as to the organization of society ... these conditions alone are ... abundantly sufficient to produce general, deep-seated, and permanent industrial unrest.' He proceeded with the utmost caution in words that seemed to imply some far-reaching changes might be necessary:

We must recognize that the wages system, which to many appears to be as natural and inevitable a part of the industrial organization of society as the Ten Commandments are of the moral law, is not only challenged by large sections of organized labour, but by many of our foremost economists who have devoted their time to the study of the industrial problem ... There was a time when the working man only demanded higher wages, shorter hours, and better working conditions. To-day an increasing number, even among the more conservative, deny that these are the real or the true objectives of labour. What labour demands, and they contend should have, is a real partnership in industry, that they should be no more under the power or subject to the control of capital than capital is of labour.[7]

Labour had suffered unjustly throughout the world, in Rowell's view, because of general reaction against the oppressive policies of the Russian government in trying to establish communism at one step. He believed, like many observers, that Lenin's recently announced New Economic Policy, with its restoration of many aspects of a capitalist economy in both agriculture and industry, was an admission on the part of Russia's leaders that their attempt to apply Marxian Socialism had 'hopelessly and terribly failed.' But it would be highly dangerous to conclude from this failure that 'capitalistic domination of industry, which is probably more strikingly illustrated in the United States than in any other industrial country,' was a solution to the industrial problem either. 'The capitalist who wholly ignores the just claims of Labour is as great a menace to just and stable peace as is the extreme Marxian Socialist.'[8]

Again, by helping to create 'an atmosphere of brotherhood and a spirit of service' the churches must take a leading part in working out a long-term solution to the problems of industrial societies. Rowell was under no illusion that this could be accomplished without considerable opposition. That there would be serious resistance to any attempt by the church to take specific stands on labour issues was currently being demonstrated in the aftermath of the great Pittsburgh steel strike of 1919. The Inter-Church World Movement, a co-operative venture among the major American Protestant churches, had issued a report on the strike that was almost wholly favourable to the strikers, especially in their demand for the abolition of the twelve-hour day and the seven-day week in the steel industry. According to the churchmen's report, the strikers had been forced into submission by the unscrupulous tactics of management in persuading the public that the strike was part of a Bolshevik plot. Many American businessmen had withdrawn their support from the churches and from the YWCA, or were threatening to do so, and employers' associations were loud in their demands that the churches mind their own business – which did not include labour-management disputes. Rowell found the churches' report on the strike thorough and fair, and he had no doubt of the foolishness of the policy of much of the business community: 'Such an attitude on the part of the Employers'

Organizations is as great a menace to industrial peace as Russian Bolshevism. It feeds Bolshevism ... if the voice of the Church, or of any other Christian organization, allowed itself to be silenced by money-power it would repudiate its Founder and cease to be Christian.'⁹

A long step forward toward a more co-operative spirit would be taken if employers and managers were to recognize their unique responsibilities. In an assertion that could well have come from a professed economic determinist Rowell declared: 'Human nature does not vary in capitalist and worker. The difference is in the different positions in which they find themselves under the present system ... Is it not, however, fair to say to men of capital, because of the advantages and opportunities which they possess for investigation and for consideration of all aspects of the problem, that the primary responsibility rests upon them of facing this impasse as between Capital and Labour and of seeking to find a just and feasible solution.'

Rowell believed that men of good will, both in and out of the churches, ought to be able to agree on certain principles, beginning with the propositions that the objective of organized society was not to produce wealth, but to develop 'a wholesome, healthy, and intelligent citizenship,' and that labour therefore could not be regarded as 'a mere commodity or article of commerce.' So long as the wages system prevailed, 'a living wage should be the first charge upon industry' rather than the meeting of demands arising from property rights. Every worker must have a weekly day of rest, normally Sunday, and reasonable opportunity for rest and recreation the rest of the week. Efforts must be made to avoid unemployment, but when these failed, workers must be protected from the ensuing financial loss and demoralization as far as possible. Child labour should be abolished and young people given more adequate opportunities to continue their education. Employees should have the right of association for any lawful purpose equally with employers, and both should join together in working out a system under which 'Capital and Labour would share, both in determining the conditions under which their joint efforts should be carried on and in the results of those efforts.' It was a program that implied radical change, not least in the suggestion that the wages system might not last forever.¹⁰

Through their approval of the peace treaties and their participation in the ILO many governments had already given formal assent to these general objectives, but only the mobilization of 'the public opinion of the world and the moral sentiment of mankind' could ensure their implementation. Canada was in a peculiarly favourable position to contribute to the solution of the industrial problem. With 'neither the extremes of poverty or wealth which prevail in other countries, nor ... the class distinctions and animosities characteristic of older civilizations,' Canadians need not repeat the mistakes of the Old World. How were those mistakes to be avoided? Fortunately, Rowell asserted, Canadian society was thus far dominated by neither capital nor labour, and there was 'a great body of public opinion ... outside the ranks of both Capital and Labour, strong enough, if it asserts itself, to see that justice is done to both and to require that each should do justice to the other.'[11]

Rowell's industrial program and his faith in the power of public opinion in the general community to bring capital and labour together on reform measures were both completely in accord with Mackenzie King's personal views. A week after Rowell's lecture King was prime minister of Canada, the leader of a government just one seat short of a majority. The major pressure on the new Liberal administration was obviously going to come from the sixty-five Progressives in the House. Although a few of them were concerned about labour issues, the first priority for the majority was a lower tariff. As far as the reformation of labour relations could be effected from Ottawa little could be expected in the near future. A great deal of education would be required to create the public opinion that would force King in the direction in which he seemed to want to move, and in that Rowell might have a part to play.

Like many another former Liberal Unionist, including his friend J.W. Dafoe, Rowell took a 'wait and see' attitude towards the government of Mackenzie King during its early years.[12] Occasionally he wrote to the prime minister on specific matters on which he had strong feelings, while eschewing any reference to such broad political problems as King's relations with the Progressives. One such question was civil service reform, a subject that had occupied much of his attention as a cabinet minister and one about which he had felt some apprehension while Meighen was in office. Rowell had protested to Meighen against Conservative proposals to amend the Civil Service Act in a manner Rowell feared would weaken the powers of the Civil Service Commission. Subsequently, the proposals were greatly modified by a committee of the House of Commons and no great damage was done. Now, to Rowell's astonishment, with Liberals in power the independence of the civil service seemed even more threatened. One of King's own backbenchers, C.G. Power (Quebec South), had introduced a measure to repeal the Civil Service Act on the ground that it was unconstitutional because the Civil Service Commission was responsible neither to a minister nor to Parliament. In the House, King had rejected so drastic an action, as had Meighen, but several members of Parliament had advanced the perennial arguments in favour of greater flexibility in making government appointments, arguments always open to the suspicion of being merely veiled pleas for a return to patronage. The whole question was referred to yet another special committee of the House. At this point Rowell wrote to King: 'I know all the difficulties of administration from the standpoint of a minister and his deputy. I organized the Department of Health under the new Civil Service law, and I can appreciate the advantage which a minister or his deputy feels he would have if he had greater freedom. But ... I believe the benefits of Civil

Service reform incomparably outweigh the disadvantages which arise from the lack of greater freedom on the part of ministers and deputy ministers.'[13]

King gave Rowell firm assurance that 'you do not feel more firmly than I do about the desirability of avoiding anything in the nature of a return to political patronage.' However, King believed that the power of the Civil Service Commission to establish categories of employment and to issue rules and regulations was so great as to hinder the work of the service and render it more costly than it ought to be. The current enquiry, King suggested, would 'clear up many differences between the Deputy Ministers and the Commission in a manner likely to be of service to both.'[14] To Rowell's relief, the committee's report was confined to extensive recommendations for improvements in salaries, pensions, promotion policies, and general administration.[15] The principle of an independent civil service was still intact, and in this area the King government would continue to enjoy Rowell's confidence.

His interest in China led Rowell to question the government's policy on Chinese immigration into Canada. Largely in response to anxiety in British Columbia about the increasing oriental population in the province, an anxiety that produced unanimity among the thirteen members of Parliament from the Pacific province, the government introduced a bill to restrict the entry of Chinese into Canada. Henceforth, only members of the diplomatic corps, children born in Canada of Chinese parents who wished to return, students, and merchants would be admitted. An apparently liberal feature of the bill was the abolition of the five-hundred-dollar head tax on Chinese immigrants, but the total effect of the measure would be severely restrictive. Rowell conceded that the existing legislation might need amendment, but he found the proposed regulations 'very extreme.' At the moment civil war rendered China 'politically helpless,' but that misfortune should not influence Canadian policy. Rather, 'we should do everything possible, consistent with reasonable protection of Canadian interests, to show our friendship for and sympathy with the Chinese people in their struggle to establish a stable government and to meet the new conditions which Western civilization compels them to face.' The problem was not one that concerned British Columbia alone, but 'a Canadian and international question of great importance.' The Canadian Chinese Association, many of whose members were Canadian citizens, wished to have the bill referred to a committee of the Senate so that they might present their views, a request Rowell commended to the prime minister.[16]

King was swift to defend his position on Chinese immigration, referred Rowell to his recent efforts in Parliament to impress the members with the international significance of the legislation in question, and assured him that arrangements were already under way to refer the bill to a Senate committee. But King implied that his main concern was with opinion in British Columbia and that there was little hope of major amendment.[17] Shortly, a Senate Committee was established and heard a number of representations on the subject, but the bill became law with little modification save a clause allowing the admission of the wives of merchants.

For a time in the spring of 1923 Rowell's personal world closed in upon him, bringing acute anxiety and finally the greatest sorrow of his life. At the end of Langford's second year in arts at Victoria College he developed blood poisoning from an infected cut. His generally excellent health, to which his prowess in university athletics had contributed, and the blood given by five of his university friends for the largest transfusion ever attempted up to that time on an adult in Toronto enabled 'Lanky' to rally briefly, but two weeks later he died. Langford had been planning to study law and to enter his father's firm, and was developing interests his father had hoped would later lead him into public life. Rowell rarely talked about himself or his feelings under any circumstances. Now there were only a few outside his immediate family who could comprehend the blow he had suffered. Parents who had lost a son in the war could appreciate what had happened. Among these were Sir John and Lady Willison. Rowell saw less of Willison now than before the war and was well aware that Willison believed that views like his own on Canadian autonomy were wrecking the Empire. Yet Willison's had been among the warmest of the many letters of sympathy, and Rowell responded less formally than to some others: 'We believe he still lives and in the larger purposes of God there is still a place for him to serve. It is this thought which gives us comfort when the clouds around seem so thick and dark. I feel I can talk to you because you and Lady Willison know and understand. As you say, one must just carry on, taking up life's duties and helping all one can.'[18]

One way of helping was to continue expounding the conditions of peace to the Canadian public. The reparations controversy, about which few Canadians were much exercised, remained the central issue for Rowell, one he continued to see as primarily a moral problem. But he always stressed the practical interest of Canadians in the removal of the greatest hindrance to peace and economic recovery in Europe through a settlement of the reparations question. 'Canada's prosperity' he told the Toronto Board of Trade 'is more affected by Old-World economic conditions than by any possible tariff or transport changes.' Germany needed between one and two billion bushels of wheat, while many other countries also required large amounts of grain, but under the present exchange situation they could not purchase it. If Europe were in a position to buy Canadian wheat, 'what would that mean on the western wheat crop alone? An additional $150,000,000 going into the pockets of western farmers. What would that mean to the manufacturers and businessmen of Eastern Canada?' Canada had as well a less readily calculable but infinitely greater investment in Europe in her contribution to the last war, 'an investment in the cause of peace – the greatest investment Canada has ever made.'[19]

To a packed meeting of the Canadian and Rotary Clubs of Guelph, Rowell

presented a detailed history of the reparations issue, concluding with a denunciation of the Allied decision to include pensions and separation allowances in the
costs of the war. Much of the unrest and instability in Europe was directly due, in
his view, to the mistaken policy of setting an amount for reparations that Germany
could not pay. He still believed, all subtle argument to the contrary, that this was a
policy in violation of the terms of the armistice:

> You may not agree with me, but I believe there is a moral purpose in the world
> and that right is greater than might. I believe Germany lost this war because she
> entered upon it and fought it through, leaving the moral factor out of account. In
> the last analysis we won the war because we were on the side of right, and we
> must profoundly regret that in the hour of victory we did not put into practice the
> principles for which our men fought and died. We have suffered ever since, and
> we will continue to suffer, perchance for generations, because in the hour of
> victory we were not true to the principles for which we fought in the war.

The European situation was not improving. In the column next to the Guelph
Mercury's report of Rowell's address was the headline 'Martial Law is proclaimed
in Ruhr Cities'; elsewhere was a brief reference to the imposition of martial law in
Bavaria in the face of a threatened revolt of German Fascists under one Adolf
Hitler. France's occupation two weeks earlier of the highly industrialized Ruhr area
in an attempt to extract from Germany the reparations France claimed the defeated
enemy had defaulted on added to the difficulty of a solution.[20] Since relations
between Britain and France had been increasingly strained over reparations, it was
not surprising that Britain refused to support the French action. Unfortunately,
Rowell could see no way that Britain could influence French policy effectively. The
only hope, and that a faint one, seemed to lie in the force of French public opinion,
which Rowell believed was not in sympathy with such an extreme policy.[21]
Six months later it was clear how forlorn that hope was. The German workers in
the Ruhr had resisted French coercion and industrial production had been brought
almost to a standstill amid an intensification of feeling in both France and Germany. Now Rowell looked forward to the Imperial Conference in the autumn of
1923, assuming that the reparations question would be discussed since it was of
concern to all parts of the Empire. He still believed that an approach along the lines
of the Balfour Note provided the best basis for 'a sane and just settlement,' and he
so advised Mackenzie King. To the prime minister he stressed above all the
necessity of resolving this most vexing problem soon: 'I know all that France has
suffered; I have been over the ground. I have the deepest sympathy with France in
her desire for reparations, but the present policy of her government does appear to
me to lead inevitably to European chaos and to ... a war of revenge in the future; and

in the meantime the nations of the world will be living in the same state of apprehension as they did for the ten years preceding the outbreak of the European war.'[22] While the Imperial Conference was in session in London Rowell told the Women's Canadian Club of St Catharines that the problems arising from the reparations situation were among the most pressing before the conference. Declaring that this was 'the first time that an Empire Conference had been held to consider the future peace of the world,' Rowell underlined the necessity for 'an agreement on an Empire policy.' Any agreement must be based on the three principles of justice, protection of the rights and interests of all parties, and provision for the economic rehabilitation of Europe. In Rowell's view these principles were embodied in the current British proposals for French withdrawal from the Ruhr and the reference of the whole reparations issue to a body of impartial international experts who would determine Germany's capacity to pay and would so advise an inter-allied conference called to agree on a final financial settlement. The soundness of the British position should make agreement by the Dominions and the adoption of a common policy a simple matter. Since France and Belgium had so far rejected the British view it was all the more necessary for the world to know that this was the Empire's policy and not only Britain's.[23]

What was actually happening in London was somewhat different than Rowell hoped and imagined. The opening remarks of the British foreign secretary, Lord Curzon, referred to 'the foreign policy which is not that of these islands alone, but that of the Empire.' The rest of the Conference was largely the story of Mackenzie King's successful attempt to make it clear that Canada would have none of the centralizing King believed was implied in those words. There was to be no 'Empire policy' on reparations or on any other international issue. The conference ended without any formal rejection of the 'single Empire policy,' but at the same time no recommendations were made for improved consultations. The vagueness of the resolutions finally agreed on was further demonstration that there was to be no revival of an imperial cabinet, but rather a return to the earlier style of imperial conferences of the Laurier era with the emphasis on discussion, not decision.[24]

Rowell had never argued for a permanent imperial cabinet, but the failure to devise improved methods of communication was a disappointment to him. His own solution was regular consultation at imperial conferences, supplemented by the steady exchange of information through the high commissioners for the Dominions resident in London. 'The high commissioners could assume ambassadorial functions, on as favourable a footing as representatives of foreign powers. Canada might entrust to her High Commissioner diplomatic functions, and be kept in constant touch with large matters of foreign policy that might affect the Dominion.' In addition he could see 'no reason why, either before or after the League of Nations Assembly, representatives of the Dominions could not meet annually with the

British Government representatives to discuss matters affecting the Empire as a whole.'[25]

No such step, nor any alternative method of consultation, was in the wind. Mackenzie King did not wish to devise methods of constant consultation. He did not wish to be consulted, since consultation implied the possibility of commitment to the policy under discussion. It suited King's vision of the Empire to affirm with slight variations from time to time that 'the governments of the Empire must confer; the Parliaments of the Empire, if need be, must decide.'[26]

Whatever disappointment Rowell felt in the results of the conference, he said nothing in public. On one score at least he could find no fault. Alternating with the meetings of the Imperial Conference there were sessions of the Imperial Economic Conference. Before the meetings, rumour had it that there would be an effort to establish a common system of imperial preference, and in any case Australia would demand a preference in the British market. Rowell did not believe it possible to work out a preference applicable to the whole Empire, and even if it were, he doubted that it would be in the interests of imperial unity. A better course, he advised King, was to adhere to the sound policy established by the Liberals in 1897 and maintained by the party ever since: if either Canada or Britain wished to grant the other a preference, 'whether as a matter of common understanding or as a matter of spontaneous action, that is all to the good.' Failing that, there must be no demands and no bargaining.[27] In London King was confronted by Britain's interest in a common tariff policy and by a willingness to bargain rather sharply on the part of Australia, New Zealand, and South Africa. As the result of a process of discussion that King was satisfied fell short of bargaining, some new preference arrangements were tentatively agreed upon for ratification by the Parliaments of the respective countries. But when it was suggested that an Imperial Economic Committee be established to deal with matters of common economic and commercial concern, Canada refused.[28] Before long the new preferences came to naught as well, although not through any Canadian action. The Conservative Baldwin government, which had dramatically abandoned party tradition to commit itself to protection and the accompanying imperial preferences, was defeated at the polls before the end of the year, to be succeeded by Britain's first Labour government, headed by Ramsay MacDonald and unalterably devoted to free trade.

Early in 1924 a sequence of exchanges between Ottawa and London cast some doubt on the effectiveness of King's representations to the recent Imperial Conference. In the sequel to Chanak, a settlement of relations between Turkey and the Allied nations was embodied in a treaty drawn up at the Lausanne Conference in 1922. Canada was not invited to that conference, and King, wishing to avoid involvement in matters he thought of little or no concern to Canada, had not questioned the omission. Subsequently it became clear that the British government assumed that the Dominions would want to sign the treaty, as at Paris. King had explained that as Canada had not been represented in the drafting of the treaty and had no vital interest in it, she would not sign, and this the British government accepted.[29]

Eighteen months later, when the new prime minister of Britain, Ramsay Mac-Donald, told Ottawa that he hoped Canada would agree to the ratification of the treaty, King replied that his government would not do so. In an admittedly complex situation, MacDonald proved to be entirely lacking in understanding of the new imperial arrangements, contending that Canada had been represented in the framing of the treaty by the British delegates and assuring the British Parliament that Canada would honour the obligations imposed by the treaty. In an intricate constitutional argument, King took the position that Canada was bound by the Lausanne Treaty in so far as it ended the state of war heretofore existing between Turkey and Canada; but beyond that, Canada was not involved and accepted no obligation other than whatever the Canadian Parliament might in future decide to accept. Among other things, Canada was thus refusing to commit herself to the defence of the Dardenelles. After several exchanges with MacDonald and under pressure of embarrassment at the prime minister's misrepresentation of Canada's position, King finally persuaded MacDonald to allow the Canadian government to publish part of the correspondence on the subject.[30]

Following these developments as well as he could from the press, Rowell was not alone in finding it all rather confusing. Without passing judgment on anyone or on either government, he wrote to King requesting information about the precise nature of Canada's stand and the reasons for it.[31] King sent him the recent parliamentary debates on the subject without additional comment and two months later forwarded copies of the published correspondence.[32] Evidence is lacking, but, given his general views, it can only be assumed that Rowell believed Canada should have participated in the Lausanne Conference in some way and in the ratification of the treaty. At the same time, the behaviour of the British government illustrated the continuing difficulties in educating British politicians about acceptable conditions of participation.

A much more straightforward issue, one on which neither King nor Rowell had any difficulty in taking a position, was the British government's failure to invite Canadian representation at the Inter-Allied Conference on the Dawes report on reparations. When the Canadian government insisted that it had a vital interest in this question, Ramsay MacDonald was forced to admit that he had agreed with the other powers that there would be only three British delegates. The best that could be salvaged was an agreement that the third British member would be chosen daily from a panel of Dominion representatives.[33] Rowell entirely approved of King's stand, first in seeking direct representation, and then in agreeing to a modification of the request in order to meet an immediate problem. But in Rowell's view 'the panel system, as operated at the London Conference, must only be a temporary expedient and should not be permitted to become a settled policy, as I cannot think it is a satisfactory solution of the difficulty.'[34] A permanent solution would require much thought and patience.

23
A new church and a
new commonwealth

Rowell was again a vigorous participant in the church union movement in which he had retained an active interest ever since his appointment in 1904 to the first joint committee of the Methodist, Presbyterian, and Congregational churches. Considerable progress had been made before the war, but by 1912 it was evident that a significant minority among the Presbyterians was opposed to union, although enthusiasm was general among Methodists and Congregationalists. During the war there had been a gradual cessation of debate as church members devoted themselves increasingly to wartime activities. At the same time the war greatly accelerated the spontaneous growth of local 'union churches,' notably on the prairies where competition among the denominations had been found especially injurious. Between 1916 and 1921 Methodists and Presbyterians, who were prepared to act independently in anticipation of the larger official union they desired, created more than six hundred union churches across the country and more were continuing to be born.

In the autumn of 1921 the joint committee of the three churches resumed its meetings, now augmented by representatives of the Council of Local Union Churches. Rowell was once more among the Methodist members. That he had lost none of his earlier enthusiasm for union was evidenced by his acceptance of the chairmanship of the subcommittee on law and legislation, composed of clergy and laymen of the participating churches. A Saturday meeting in Rowell's office in October 1921 to consider the retaining of counsel and the drafting of the legislation necessary to effect church union was the beginning of an involved and demanding assignment that commanded many more of his Saturdays and a great deal of his energy and attention for the next four years.[1] Both federal and provincial legislation was needed. Only the Dominion Parliament could incorporate a nationwide body with jurisdiction over the general property of the church, and only provincial legislation could deal with property rights of individual congregations and with civil rights in the provinces, such as the right to solemnize marriage. Rowell's committee retained the services of two Toronto lawyers, McGregor Young and W. Gershom Mason, to draft the federal bill and to work with the lawyers in charge of legislation in the various provinces. Great care was required to produce legislation in accord with the positions on doctrine and polity outlined in the Basis of Union to which the uniting churches would adhere, to deal with property claims so as to prevent endless litigation after union, and to protect the interests of dissenting congregations, for it was now clear that a minority of the Presbyterians would not be part of the new United Church of Canada. Ever before the unionist lawyers as a warning against imperfections in their work was the Scottish experience in the 'Wee Free case.' In 1900 when the Free Church of Scotland joined with the United Presbyterian Church to form the United Free Church of Scotland a tiny dissident group within the Free Church, the 'Wee Frees,' challenged the union with the claim that their church's constitution did not permit the change in doctrine that had allegedly taken place with the entrance into union, and that as adherents to the original doctrine they were entitled to all the church's property. This claim was rejected by the courts in Scotland but was subsequently upheld by the House of Lords. Such was the resulting turmoil in Scotland that in 1905 the British Parliament was forced to pass remedial legislation to settle the conflicting property claims. The architects of Canadian church union were determined to avoid a repetition of such tumult.[2]

By the autumn of 1922 Rowell's committee was ready to present the draft legislation for approval and amendment by the participating churches, and during the following year it was assented to in principle by the General Conference of the Methodist Church, the General Assembly of the Presbyterian Church, the individual churches of the Congregational Union, and the Council of Local Union Churches. After taking note of the various amendments suggested by these bodies, Rowell and his committee presented the final draft of the legislation to a meeting of the joint committee on church union in September 1923. Plans were laid for implementing the legislation after a period in which the majority of uniting Presbyterians were to endeavour to reach an accommodation with the 'non-concurring' members of their denomination.

Rowell's labours in the cause of church union were not confined to his legal work. In the autumn of 1923 began a series of rallies across the country to acquaint Canadian Protestants with the principles of church union. The usual pattern of these meetings featured addresses by representatives of the uniting churches, nearly always clergymen. Rowell, addressing several meetings in Ontario centres, was often the sole Methodist speaker, as at a Toronto rally in Massey Hall where he stressed the role of the new church as a 'uniting church,' the beginnings of a bigger church union movement in Canada and overseas. He looked forward to a union that would include the Church of England in Canada, pointing out that the recently formed United church of South India was already negotiating with the Anglican church there. Both at home and abroad the mission fields were the chief creators of Christian unity and they would be its foremost beneficiaries: 'Three hundred millions of people are asking that Christ be given a chance in China by the Christian denominations in other parts of the world healing their divisions in order to ... present a united testimony for Christianity.'[3]

At the end of April 1924 the union legislation was referred to the private bills committee of the House of Commons. So great was public interest in the bill that hundreds of visitors to Ottawa stretched the capacities of hotels to overflowing, and many never managed to find a place even for part of a session in the four hundred seats of the railway committee room where the hearings were held. Rowell was not in attendance but followed reports of the proceedings with close attention. The wide interest in the bill ensured extensive press coverage of the hearings, nowhere more thorough than in the pages of the pro-union *Toronto Star*, which had consistently treated church union as the most significant national development since Confederation and earned the praise of the unionists' publicity chairman for contributing more than any other newspaper in the country to the creation of the United church.[4]

The committee heard first from a group of pro-unionist laymen – T.B. Macaulay, president of the Sun Life Assurance Company of Canada, for the Congregationalists, Elmer Davis, a Kingston manufacturer, for the Methodists, and for the Presbyterians Sir Robert Falconer, an ordained minister of his church but engaged in lay activities as president of the University of Toronto. There followed a group of anti-unionist Presbyterians, led by Dr Murray MacLaren, Conservative member of Parliament for Saint John, New Brunswick. Observers were treated to a display of legal talent, as some of the nation's most eminent lawyers took the stand on behalf of the contending parties. Eugene Lafleur led for the anti-unionists, W.N. Tilley and Aimé Geoffrion for the pro-unionist Presbyterians, the latter observing that he was not a Presbyterian and clearly delighting in the 'catholicity' of his new-found mastery of the subtleties of the history and forms of government of the Presbyterian church. Finally, the clergy took the stage to debate the fine points of theology and church polity. On behalf of the unionist Presbyterians Dr Leslie Pidgeon, under close questioning, endeavoured to explain the differences between Calvinism and Arminianism and to show that the doctrinal statement in the Basis of Union was an adequate modern statement of the essentials of both positions. The Presbyterian minority, for whom strict adherence to the Westminister Confession, the Shorter Catechism, and their traditional form of church government, constituted the only valid vehicles for the expression of the Word of God, had a young and eloquent defender in Rev. Stuart Parker, whose accent betrayed his recent arrival from Scotland. Rev. James Endicott, a veteran prairie minister, replied with a typical Methodist answer to the charge of Parker and other 'antis' that the new church, oblivious to cherished precedents and beliefs, would be a creedless non-entity: What precedents had enabled John Knox and John Wesley to found new churches? Sometimes it was as necessary to set a precedent as to quote one. As for creeds, they were the work of men, statements to mark the church's progress in understanding, a guide to faith and not faith itself. Finally, Dr George Pidgeon presented a closely argued account of the history and significance of earlier church unions, with special emphasis on unions among Presbyterians in Scotland and Canada, with a view to demonstrating that Presbyterians had frequently changed not only their forms of government but even their confessions of faith.[5]

The hearings before the private bills committee traversed no ground not already familiar to Rowell but provided confirmation, if any were still needed, of the strength of the resistance among the minority Presbyterians. To prevent what they believed would amount to the destruction of their church, the non-concurring Presbyterians, like the 'Wee Frees,' had leaned heavily during the debate on the contention that despite its recent four-to-one vote in favour of union, the General Assembly did not have the constitutional power to 'exterminate' the Presbyterian church in Canada. So forceful was their resistance that after several days' work the private bills committee adjourned to allow counsel for the contending parties to work out compromises on several issues. The difficulties involved proved to be so great that the intended adjournment of three or four days lasted two weeks. Rowell called together the committee on law and legislation, and it was agreed to instruct the unionist counsel to assent to certain amendments, the most important being one permitting congregations to vote on entering the union during the six months preceding the coming into force of the act of union, rather than after that date. One point on which Rowell and his committee were adamant was the name to be used by the non-concurring Presbyterians: they might use any name they wished except 'The Presbyterian Church in Canada,' the only name they wanted.[6] To the union-ists the Presbyterian church was about to merge with other bodies to form a new church and that fact must be formally acknowledged.

With unionist and non-unionist forces bombarding members of Parliament with petitions and memoranda, the private bills committee resumed its sittings. Im-mediately, the Liberal member for Lunenberg, William Duff, moved an amend-ment, seconded by Gus Porter, Conservative member for Hastings West, that would prevent union from coming into effect until the Supreme Court of Canada had ruled on the power of the Presbyterian General Assembly to form any union with other churches. Hurriedly, the friends of union on the committee managed to secure the appointment of a subcommittee to confer with representatives of each side as to the precise legal implications of the Duff amendment in the hope that some other agreement could be reached which would prevent such a potentially danger-ous amendment from arriving on the floor of the House of Commons.

Rowell had not expected this alarming turn of events. It was all the more disturbing since rumour had it that the prime minister approved the Duff amend-ment and had so indicated to the Liberal members of the committee. In an im-mediate and lengthy telegram to King, Rowell expressed his incredulity that King would support an amendment that would 'kill the bill ... and block the great movement for Christian unity.' A major objective of going to federal and provincial parliaments before the consummation of the union, Rowell stressed, was to prevent a repetition of the strife attendant on the 'Wee Free case,' a consideration that had been taken very seriously ever since the establishment of the joint committee in 1904. Now it was proposed 'to overturn the work of twenty years ... and have years of litigation over the question.' Further, an important principle of religious freedom would be violated if Parliament, for the first time in Canadian history, refused to pass legislation requested by religious institutions after due debate and decision by their governing bodies. Rowell was confident that his church would 'never be a party to a bill which involves directly or indirectly litigation as to the capacity of a sister church to do its own thinking and to determine its own policy.'[7]

The next day an only slightly modified version of the offending amendment passed the private bills committee by a vote of twenty-seven to twenty-three. It was necessary now to consider Methodist strategy carefully. 'Both reason and instinct,' Rowell told the general superintendent of the Methodist Church, Dr S.D. Chown, led him to conclude that the amended bill was entirely unacceptable. If the bill went to the House as it now stood, there should be a move to strike out the amendment and any other objectionable changes that might be introduced, 'so that every member of the House will be put on record on the issue.' If that failed, then several reasons dictated withdrawal of the bill. Not only were there the lessons to be drawn from the Scottish experience but there was also grave doubt about the kind of union to which Methodists might find themselves a party. 'After years of protracted and bitter litigation' it was bound to be not the union on which the Methodist church had agreed, but 'some hybrid or emasculated union brought about not by our own action but the joint action of Parliament and the Courts.' Rowell believed strongly that it was not in the interest of either Methodists or Presbyterians that his church should involve itself in 'a domestic legal dispute in the Presbyterian Church over the right of that Church to do its own thinking and settle its own policy.' As for parliament, 'Its members are not our task-masters to oppress us, but our representatives to do justly and promote the public interest. If they take the responsibility, by their denial of religious freedom, of compelling us to appeal from them to the people whom they represent, or misrepresent, while I would regret it, I would not shirk from it; we would have a real issue in Canada transcending in importance any now dividing political parties and give us something worth fighting for.'8

Just at this point, to his great regret, legal business took Rowell to England. Fortunately, as he later learned, there was no extended delay in the passage of the union legislation, although the anti-unionists continued their fight. As arranged, the church union bill was introduced into Parliament by Robert Forke, leader of the Progressive party, whose members, most of them from the west, were unanimous in support of union and forceful in their advocacy of it before the House. Also eloquent and persuasive on behalf of the bill was the leader of the Conservative opposition, Arthur Meighen. The dissenter among the leaders of the three political parties, all of whom were Presbyterians, was the prime minister. King made it clear that since the union bill was a private one the government assumed no position on it, and he specifically denied the rumour that he had requested members of the Liberal party to follow him in his personal opposition to the bill. After two days of intense debate the Duff amendment was defeated easily, and thereafter the bill enjoyed relatively plain sailing. By mid-July it had been passed in the Senate and given royal assent, and the uniting churches were proceeding with their plans for effecting the union.

Appeals to the Judicial Committee of the Privy Council once again took Rowell to England for three months in the summer of 1924. This time Nell and her mother accompanied him. Shortly after their arrival in England they spent a day at the highly popular British Empire exhibition at Wembley where the Canadian pavilion was naturally of special interest. Among the exhibits, devoted mainly to the country's natural resources and material prospects, was the first exhibition of Canadian paintings ever held outside of Canada, in which painters of the Group of Seven were prominently featured. In contrast to the large body of Canadian opinion that found their work too experimental and crude, the Rowells were thrilled by it.

Three legal cases occupied much of Rowell's attention in England, one of them being the final round of the Toronto Street Railway arbitration in which the city of Toronto was appealing against the award determined by the arbitration committee in Canada. To Rowell's satisfaction and that of his clients, the city's appeal was dismissed and the amount awarded the company was slightly increased.9 The second case grew out of the failure of the Home Bank in 1922. In the aftermath of that failure charges of misconduct and negligence were brought against the directors of the bank. The government of Ontario had decreed that they should be tried by judge and jury, while the Ontario Appellate Court had sustained the directors' appeal for trial before the county court judge. The question of the form of the trial was then taken to the Judicial Committee of the Privy Council where Rowell acted on behalf of the accused directors and won a favourable decision. That fall the directors were tried before Judge Emerson Coatsworth with Rowell among the group of distinguished Toronto lawyers acting for the defendants. Six officials and directors were given sentences varying from two years to one month, but these decisions were later quashed by the Supreme Court of Ontario.[10]

In another case that engaged Rowell's sympathies as well as his talents, his client, the Lord's Day Alliance of Canada, supported by the Dominion government, was appealing a ruling of the Court of Appeal of Manitoba, which had declared valid an act passed in 1923 by the Manitoba Legislature to permit the running of Sunday excursions to resorts in Manitoba. In his presentation before the Judicial Committee, Rowell based his case against the Manitoba legislation primarily on the contention that the act in question related to criminal law and therefore fell within the jurisdiction of the Dominion. Their lordships rejected this argument and before the end of the year delivered a judgment sustaining the verdict of the Manitoba court.[11]

In that summer of 1924 British politics were even more interesting than usual. The first Labour government in Britain's history, under the leadership of Ramsay MacDonald, had been in office only four months and could remain there only with the support of Asquith's Liberals. Under these circumstances little radical socialist legislation was to be expected, and save for a housing act which increased state subsidies for houses built for lease at controlled rents, the new government's domestic record was unremarkable.

The Labour party had always been enthusiastic about the League of Nations, and on his arrival in England Rowell was gratified by all the indications that Ramsay MacDonald's government would honour Labour's verbal commitments by adopting positive policies towards the League. Among other hopeful signs was the likelihood that MacDonald, who was also foreign secretary, would attend the autumn session of the League Assembly. No prime minister of any member nation had so far attended an Assembly. If MacDonald did so, the League's supporters were confident that the first ministers of other major powers, notably France and Italy, would also attend, to the enhancement of the League's prestige and influence. Rowell hastened to inform Mackenzie King of these expectations, asserting that it would be 'a great thing for Canada and a real help to the Assembly' if King were to lead the Canadian delegation. Anticipating King's feeling that he might be occupied to greater political advantage in Canada than in Geneva, Rowell urged that 'the firm establishment of peace in Europe and the consequent restoration of economic stability would do more to promote the prosperity of the farmers of Canada and with that of all of Canada than any possible measures of a domestic character that you can devise.'[12] King thought otherwise, or did not estimate his own or his country's influence so highly. Since he had been overseas at the Imperial Conference the year before he could not contemplate an extended absence again; his first duty was to the Liberal party and the public meetings he must address.[13] That fall, when the League Assembly met, four prime ministers, from Britain, France, Belgium, and Denmark were in attendance. Mackenzie King was on a long tour of western Canada, his first since becoming prime minister, and Canada was represented at Geneva by Senator Raoul Dandurand and the minister of defence, E.M. Macdonald, neither of whom could be considered among the heavyweights of King's cabinet.

King's policies towards the Empire and the League no doubt received much attention in the two long discussions Rowell had with Loring Christie, now embarked on a financial career in London. Christie's influence in the formulation of the Borden-Rowell and Meighen policies of consultation and commitment had made it impossible for King to believe that he could be useful to a government that had adopted a more independent and even isolationist style in the pursuit of Canadian autonomy. Christie had therefore been given very little to do and by 1923 had in effect been forced to resign from the Department of External Affairs.[14]

Mackenzie King's detachment from European affairs notwithstanding, the prospects for peace brightened perceptibly in 1924. While Rowell was in London, British efforts to improve relations with France resulted in important talks between Ramsay MacDonald and Edouard Herriot, whose recent accession to the French premiership had allowed the emergence of more conciliatory attitudes to Germany than those dominant in France under Poincaré. Subsequently, the hoped-for inter-allied talks on the Dawes report were held, and by summer's end Britain, France, the United States and other powers concerned had agreed on implementation of the Dawes plan. In settling for five years the reparations to be paid by Germany and in endeavouring to stabilize the German currency, largely through a loan from the United States, the plan offered hope for the economic health not only of Germany but of the rest of Europe as well. Not the least encouraging aspect of these developments was the evidence of American willingness to make some commitment to the establishment of the conditions for peace in Europe. Returning to Canada at the end of the summer, Rowell found it easier than it had been a few months earlier to believe that the League of Nations might now live with some chance of being effective.

This mood of optimism was not long sustained. In the autumn of 1924 the Protocol for the Pacific Settlement of International Disputes, soon to be known as the Geneva Protocol, was presented to the Assembly of the League of Nations. The work of many hands, this document owed much to two members of the British Labour cabinet, Lord Parmoor and Arthur Henderson, who were both on hand for the Assembly's unanimous commendation of the protocol to the member states. Within a few days of its presentation seventeen League members had signed the protocol and its prospects seemed bright, although so far only one of the great powers, France, had concurred. The Geneva Protocol was a bold attempt to clarify and strengthen the League Covenant by prescribing compulsory jurisdiction by the Permanent Court of International Justice for justiciable disputes and compulsory arbitration for all disputes of a non-legal character. According to the protocol, willingness to submit a dispute to the court or to arbitration was to be the means of identifying an aggressor, who would be subjected to economic and military sanctions identical to those set out in Article 10 of the League Covenant.

This approach to world security and eventual disarmament was congenial to Rowell, notably in the compulsory jurisdiction assigned to the Permanent Court of International Justice, a provision he would have liked to see included in the League Covenant from the beginning, but it was scarcely in accord with Canada's annual effort in the League Assembly to escape from the allegedly 'unlimited liabilities' imposed under Article 10. The attitude Canada would adopt toward the protocol was not entirely clear from the address of her representative, Senator Raoul Dandurand, before the Assembly. Beginning in a tone reminiscent of Rowell's much publicized lecture to the Europeans at the first Assembly, Dandurand asserted that 'the three chief pillars of the protocol – "arbitration, security, and disarmament" – have been the basis of Canada's relations with her neighbours for a hundred years and would continue to be so ... We think in terms of peace, while Europe, an armed camp, thinks in terms of war.' Without referring specifically to sanctions, he added words later to become famous, or infamous, as the epitome of Canadian foreign policy between the two world wars: 'May I be permitted to add that in this Association of Mutual Insurance against fire, the risks assumed by the different States are not equal? We live in a fire-proof house, far from inflammable materials.'[15]

To Rowell and the rest of the handful of Canadians who knew or cared about the protocol and supported it, such words sounded ominous. They would have been apprehensive indeed about Canada's position had they known how accurately Dandurand's concluding remarks reflected the argument embodied in a memorandum prepared for Prime Minister King by the undersecretary of state, Dr O.D. Skelton, who had recently succeeded Loring Christie as the key figure in the Department of External Affairs and was attending the current League Assembly as adviser to the Canadian delegation. In terms typical of his approach to European and imperial questions, Skelton stressed Canada's good fortune in 'its comparative isolation and its friendly neighbours' and described the protocol as 'a League of European Victors ... distinctly a European affair. It would not protect Canada an iota. It is designed to safeguard the territorial gains of the winners in the world war.'[16]

A week after Dandurand's Geneva speech Rowell discussed the protocol before the National Council of Women in Convocation Hall at the University of Toronto.

Rowell was in no doubt that if the nations were willing to assume the obligations prescribed by the protocol, which he outlined in some detail, they would be going 'far beyond any attempt so far made to ensure the peaceable settlement of all international disputes,' and the protocol therefore ought to receive 'the most serious consideration' from the Canadian government and Parliament. Although the whole tone of his address implied general approval Rowell did not specifically urge Canadian ratification of the protocol. His restraint stemmed from his hope that there would be a common British Empire policy on the protocol, one not yet agreed upon. He admitted that such a policy would be difficult to work out because of the global dispersion of the Empire and the reluctance of its members to commit themselves to putting out every fire that might break out anywhere. In practice, Rowell believed, adherence to the protocol would not mean the assumption of such extensive obligations: 'In applying the military sanctions the theory is that the nations called upon to use military force would be the nations having some geo-graphical relation to the aggressor. Therefore ... you would not expect a nation in America to be called upon to suppress ... trouble in Europe.'[17]

Two days before Rowell's comments, Ramsay MacDonald's government met sudden defeat in Parliament, an event not enhancing prospects for British adher-ence to the protocol. Three weeks later the British voters had elected Stanley Baldwin's Conservatives to office. In the new government both the colonial secre-tary, Lord Amery, an active Round Tabler, and the foreign secretary, Austen Chamberlain, were dedicated enthusiasts of greater imperial unity. In his first speech on assuming office Chamberlain spoke in terms that set Mackenzie King on his guard and in tones that may have implied too much even to Rowell: 'The first thoughts of an Englishman on appointment to the office of Foreign Secretary must be that he speaks in the name, not of Great Britain only, but of the British Dominions beyond the seas, and that it is his imperative duty to preserve in word and act the diplomatic unity of the British Empire. Our interests are one. Our intercourse must be intimate and constant, and we must speak with one voice in the Councils of the world.'[18]

The Geneva Protocol was still being discussed when Rowell visited England early in 1925 to argue, successfully, the case of the government of Canada against the constitutionality of the Judicature Act of Ontario of 1924, which endeavoured to give to the provincial government the right to designate the judges who were to be assigned to the Appellate Division of the Supreme Court of Ontario and to choose the chief justice of that court.[19]

It seemed increasingly likely that Britain, due partly to the opposition of the Dominions, would not ratify the protocol. While Rowell was on board ship return-ing to Canada, a news dispatch reported Canada's rejection of the protocol, and by the time he reached Toronto the British decision, which in fact predated the

Canadian announcement, had been made public. Austen Chamberlain was able to tell the League Council and the world that Britain and the Dominions were united in their rejection of the protocol. Thus there was a common Empire policy, although its content was not entirely to Rowell's liking. He would have preferred 'to have seen the British Empire go further in support of the Protocol.' At the same time he was grateful for the 'clear cut statement' King had made before Parliament and had included in his message to the League Council. Having rejected a document so many other nations had approved, there was now, Rowell contended, 'a moral obligation on the British Empire to present to the next Assembly of the League an alternative proposal, and Canada's suggestions would appear to afford a sound basis for such an alternative proposal.' Those suggestions, he added 'more nearly meet my own personal views than the Protocol itself.'[20] The Canadian government's memorandum of rejection had reaffirmed support for the general principles underlying the protocol, except for what it held to be the 'rigid application of economic and military sanctions in every future war,' had professed willingness to assist in working out means of implementing those principles, and had offered to take part at any time in a general conference on disarmament.[21]

Already there were plans among the Europeans for the holding of a new conference to discuss alternatives to the contested features of the Geneva Protocol, plans that were accelerated by Germany's proposal for a seven-power guarantee treaty of mutual assistance designed mainly to relieve French fears of Germany. Rowell told the Empire Club of Toronto that Canada should participate fully in that conference, and he welcomed the British foreign secretary's intimation that the imperial government intended to ask the delegates from the Dominions to the next League Assembly to attend a pre-Assembly meeting in London in order to determine whether a common Empire policy could be agreed upon. Canada should advocate, as the basis of that policy: compulsory jurisdiction for the Permanent Court of International Justice, further consideration of methods for settling non-justiciable disputes apart from the application of economic and military sanctions, and the holding of a general conference on the reduction of armaments. Rowell was adamant that Canada should not adhere to any treaty unless she had been a party to its negotiation.[22]

Within six months the Locarno Conference was in session. Canada had no share in it since the Dominions were not invited to attend and they did not press for an invitation. Least of all did Mackenzie King seek Dominion participation, either as part of the Empire delegation or independently; if there were no participation there could be no ensuing obligations.[23] The core of the series of Locarno treaties concluded at the end of 1925 lay in the guarantees by which Britain, France, Germany, Belgium, and Italy agreed to maintain the present frontiers in western Europe. Germany was to be admitted to the League and given a permanent seat on the Council. Britain signed the treaties for herself alone, with a specific provision that they should not be binding on the Dominions without their consent. In the absence of thorough consultation with the Dominions, this was entirely as Rowell would have had it.

Rowell did not abandon hope that Canada might adhere to the Locarno treaties at some later date. As the treaties were being formally signed he told the Toronto Bankers' Educational Association that the agreements marked the end of the transition from war to peace and had 'so contributed toward European peace and stability that even if Canada did join the mother country in the execution of this Pact of Guarantee her obligations would prove less onerous than her obligations would be if there were no Locarno agreements.' Regrettably in Rowell's eyes, there was no provision for compulsory jurisdiction of disputes by the Permanent Court of International Justice, but there was some compensation for this in the assurance that the obligations assumed by the powers were to be carried out within the League framework. Although Rowell disclaimed any desire to lecture the government publicly he clearly implied that an instrument so vital to the establishment of peace in Europe should have direct Canadian support: 'We should not claim the status which we do claim and which has been cheerfully accorded us unless we are prepared to assume the obligations that such a status involves.'[24]

But the truth was that the whole Canadian experience in the months leading up to Locarno presented yet another trial of faith in the possibility of a common Empire foreign policy. Unaware that behind the scenes the Canadian government had committed itself even less than King's cautious public utterances indicated, Rowell remained in that declining minority in Canada who still cherished some hope that a common policy could be achieved.

With the opening bars of 'The Church's One Foundation' the assembly of eight thousand, on 10 June 1925 in Toronto's Mutual Street Arena, rose to receive the three hundred and fifty commissioners to the first General Council of the new United Church of Canada, entering in three streams representing the denominational traditions now to be joined. Among the Methodist commissioners, none save a handful of the church's executive officers had worshipped with so many congregations across the country as Newton Rowell, and none possessed in imagination a more vivid picture of the nation and world for whose service the new church was being created. With the signing of the instrument of union and a communion service conducted by clergymen of the three uniting churches, Rowell saw the culmination of twenty-one years of discussion and negotiation. Later that day fraternal delegates brought greetings from churches around the world. Fittingly, Rowell read an address from thirty-two prominent laymen of the Wesleyan Methodist church in Britain, several of whom Rowell had known over many years, including Sir Robert

Perks, Walter Runciman, and Arthur Henderson. Like many British Methodists, Perks, through whom Rowell had arranged to secure the address, remained privately less than convinced of the wisdom of the Canadian religious experiment, despite Rowell's efforts in several discussions to assure him that nothing essential was being lost in the union. In particular, the former 'member for Nonconformity' in the British Parliament, whose many business interests, notably the proposed Georgian Bay Canal, had brought him to Canada frequently, was concerned lest the loss of the Methodist name would make it even harder than before for Canadian Methodism to retain the allegiance of migrating British Methodists. But Perks reluctantly agreed to defer to the judgment of Rowell and others on the spot who must be better informed.[25]

Soon after the newly formed General Council of the church began its deliberations, Rowell outlined to the members the legal position of the council, discussed the constitutional framework within which it would function, and subsequently took a major part in the work of the committee on colleges and universities. Before concluding its business the council placed on record its unanimous appreciation of 'the unique services' rendered by the layman who had been pre-eminent among those labouring in the union cause and expressed gratification that Rowell's 'unique and intimate knowledge of the work of the uniting churches' had now been transferred to the United church.[26] The conclusion of the inaugural council by no means ended Rowell's legal services to his church; for the committee on law and legislation was as busy as ever, mainly with problems arising over the distribution of property between uniting and non-concurring Presbyterians. Over the next five years he attended many meetings on these contentious issues and was frequently consulted by committees and individuals across the country. And as always in the past, he continued to play a full part in several of the church's national committees and in the life of the Metropolitan congregation, now increasingly a 'downtown' church confronting the social problems of a rapidly changing community.

The new church safely launched, Rowell very shortly set off on a three-month Pacific tour, accompanied by his daughter Mary who had just graduated from Victoria College. En route he had some Canadian business to attend to. Early in 1925 he had assumed the presidency of the Toronto General Trusts Company, succeeding the late Sir Edmund Walker, and now he paid his first official visits to the company's branches in Winnipeg and Vancouver. With the group of leading business figures assembled at dinner by Sir Daniel McMillan, chairman of the company's Winnipeg advisory board, all of whom were full of comment on the anticipated bumper wheat crop in the west, he sensed once again that exuberant confidence in the Canadian future that he had always experienced on the prairies.[27] In Vancouver he enjoyed a fitting prelude to a Pacific voyage when his friend Chris

Spencer, a member of the company's local advisory board, and owner of the city's largest department store, took him to a dinner given by the Vancouver Board of Trade for a group of Chinese businessmen from Shanghai.[28]

Most of the passengers on board the RMS *Niagara* from Vancouver were Americans travelling to Honolulu or Australians returning from England via Canada. Rowell sought the company of the Australians, as always with the purpose of learning as much as possible about their country, and happily found no dearth of informative companions. A few hours out of Honolulu he received a wire from the chairman of the Institute of Pacific Relations, which was holding its founding meeting there, asking Rowell to address the delegates on the British Commonwealth and Pacific problems. Thanks to his willingness to accede to the request, his few hours in Honolulu gave him a brief glimpse of the proceedings and personnel of the institute which, as he was encouraged to learn, seemed likely to become a permanent organization devoted to the serious study of the Pacific area.[29]

The sea voyage had made a new man of her father, Mary reported home. Now rested and jolly, he was ready for the next stage of their trip.[30] The next two weeks in New Zealand and a month in Australia were typical Rowell 'holidays,' visiting points of interest and meeting government leaders, judges, lawyers, and every student of public affairs he could arrange to see. He was astonished to find how many New Zealanders anticipated Canadian union with the United States and both privately and publicly attempted to disabuse them of this idea: no significant body of Canadians, he asserted, wanted any change that would take them out of the Empire; Canada had a national consciousness and national ideals distinct from those of the United States.[31]

As before during his absences Nell received a full account of his activities and his observations on persons and places. In New Zealand he was impressed by the precision with which hours of work for hotel and other employees were regulated and publicly posted, the dominance of the small frame cottage in housing, and the great height of New Zealand door handles for which he vainly sought an explanation.[32] Not surprisingly in a country settled almost entirely by Britons he found British legal and parliamentary traditions persisting in more unadulterated form than in Canada, although a visit to the House of Assembly provided 'as dull an afternoon as we frequently have in our House of Commons.' A major contrast with Canada that interested him greatly was the strong Labour party, whose leader, H.E. Holland, he found intelligent and well informed, and supported by followers who were frequently described to Rowell as 'the ablest and most industrious group in the House.'[33] Nowhere in New Zealand, nor later in Australia, did he encounter the results of Charles Murphy's attempt to prepare the way for him. Murphy boasted that he had sent the last of the 250,000 copies he had printed of his Commons attacks on Rowell to selected editors and politicians in both countries.[34]

But this effort to destroy Rowell's reputation in the far corners of the Empire was of no avail. From the governor general, the chief justice, and the prime minister to parliamentary backbenchers and practising lawyers, New Zealanders and Australians treated the former president of the Canadian Privy Council as a welcome guest. Indeed, Rowell himself was overwhelmed by the hospitality elicited through a few letters of introduction and appointments arranged by the resident Canadian trade commissioners.

Many of his hosts in Sydney, Adelaide, and Melbourne thought the natural way to entertain a visitor to Australia was to take him to the horse races. To all invitations Rowell applied his expertise in polite refusal, acquired through a lifetime of declining alcoholic beverages, and was never once lured to the track. A strike of workers on the Queensland Railway disrupted his travel plans slightly and provided an opportunity for some comparative study of labour relations. He was struck by the fact that the vigorous action of the strikers in pressing their claims produced nothing like the strong reaction from the public that would have developed under similar conditions in Canada.[35]

Like many another Canadian Puritan he found Australian society less appealing than the more familiar and sedate pace of New Zealand:

Australia is a wonderful country and most attractive but I come back to Canada satisfied and thankful that my lot is cast there. They make money easier, much easier, I think than we do in Canada and they take life much more leasurely [sic]. They are adicted [sic] to sport. Horse racing is referred to as a great national industry. You see it everywhere and hear of it everywhere and with it goes gambling and the gambling spirit.

On the other hand the people are generous. They support hospitals and educational institutions generously and their hospitality is proverbial. Climate may account for some of their characteristics or for the development out here of more or less inherited characteristics of the race. You cannot help but like them. I have met some most interesting men and have formed one or two real friendships I believe just as we did in South Africa.[36]

From Sydney the Japanese *Aki Maru* took two weeks to reach Hong Kong, where he and Mary transferred to the CPR's *Empress of Russia* and thence to Shanghai for a tantalizing few hours before sailing for Nagasaki. Leaving the ship there, they proceeded across Japan by train with stops at Kobe, Kyoto, and Tokyo before picking up the boat again in Yokohama for the voyage back to Vancouver.

Although his first-hand contact with China had been so brief, no impression of his Asian trip was as vivid as his awareness that all the Pacific countries were increasingly conscious of the rapidly growing importance of China, notwithstanding the disruptive effects of the current civil war and the absence of any central government that could truly claim to speak for all of China. He made only three public addresses that fall, two of them on China. Speaking to the Canadian Club of Toronto on the date of the opening of the international tariff conference in Peking, he suggested that this attempt on the part of the major powers to agree on a basis for giving China more autonomy in the levying and collection of customs might have 'as important a bearing on the peace and stability of China as the Locarno conference had on that of Europe.' It was clear to Rowell that the time had come when the outside powers must realize that they could no longer force their will on China and that Chinese national aspirations must be treated with understanding and respect, with the qualification that existing rights and interests and the safety of foreign trade must be ensured.[37] He pursued his interest in these developments through an enquiry to the prime minister about whether the Canadian government was taking any part in the Peking Conference or intended to show any interest in the forthcoming Commission on Extra-Territoriality in China, both of which had arisen out of the Washington Conference of 1922 at which Canada had been represented as part of the British delegation. Both the tariff and extraterritoriality were of great interest to Canada, Rowell argued, the first because it affected Canada's great hopes for increased trade with China and the second because of its relation to trade and to the extensive work of Canadian missionaries in China.[38]

Rowell was distressed to learn from Mackenzie King that although the British government had enquired whether Canada wished to be represented at the Peking customs conference, on the same terms as at Washington, the primary reason for Canada's refusal of the invitation was that 'no one was available at that time who would possess the necessary weight to give effective representation for Canada.'[39] This admission propelled Rowell into a discussion of a problem he had thought much about in the past five years, and one on which he had made some preliminary moves while he was acting minister of external affairs in 1920. At that time he had sent Loring Christie to London for informal consultations with members of the British government and the Foreign Office on methods of reorganizing the Department of External Affairs in a manner appropriate to Canada's enlarged participation in imperial and international affairs. Shortly after, Rowell left the government, and since then little had been done. Without 'a real Department of External Affairs' it was 'nearly inevitable,' in Rowell's view, that Canada would be unable to respond satisfactorily to meetings such as the Locarno Conference or to attend to her interests in the Pacific.[40]

In a lengthy submission to King, Rowell began his argument with 'three or four more or less fundamental propositions covering our Imperial relations' on which he was sure he and the prime minister and 'the great majority of those who have given thought to the question, not only in Canada but in Great Britain, Australia, and

South Africa' would be agreed. These included maintenance of the equality of members of the British Commonwealth and of their unity under a common sovereign, a unity that could only be sustained by consultation and co-operation. The primary international objective of Commonwealth members must be the preservation of peace through the League of Nations and the Permanent Court of International Justice. Without a reorganized and expanded Department of External Affairs Canada would fail to make her full contribution to that objective.

He had no rigid opinion about the form the reorganization should take, but he thought the department needed not only an expanded staff but a specialized one. Thus, there should be 'one man in charge of Far Eastern matters, whose duty it should be to become thoroughly informed on Chinese and Japanese questions ... as far as it is humanly possible to be informed; and whose duty it should be to consider and report on all despatches received from the British Foreign Office or Colonial Office dealing with Pacific problems.' Another man should be responsible for Canadian-American and Anglo-American relations, a position of great importance especially when the long-awaited Canadian minister to Washington was appointed. A third man would be charged with all matters relating to the League of Nations, and a fourth would handle imperial affairs. It was absolutely essential that this reorganization be accompanied by more adequate consultation with the British government, and to achieve this Rowell renewed a proposal he had made to King earlier and had more than once discussed in public – the conferring of 'full diplomatic standing' on the Canadian high commissioner in London. Whatever diplomatic representative Canada appointed in London he should be one of the Canadian delegates to all assemblies of the League, and would sit on important League committees, thus providing continuity and making Canada's work in the League more effective.

Canada's failure to send a representative to the Peking Conference was only one episode that showed 'we have grown in status away beyond the growth of the machinery of government, and the most urgent thing in connection with our Empire and international relations is that we should bring the machinery of government up-to-date, so as to accord with facts of the present time growing out of our present status.' Moreover, if Canada did not exercise the right she had won to representation at such conferences, 'there is danger of our losing it.'[41]

King was highly appreciative of Rowell's 'informed and constructive comment,' especially since 'the number of men interested in the problems of government as distinct from the questions of party fortune is not as yet very great in Canada.' At the same time the prime minister's acceptance of Rowell's 'fundamental propositions' was accompanied by so many cautious qualifications that it amounted to something less than genuine agreement. 'Equality of status is, of course, an aspiration rather than a fact, and many people who might agree to it as an abstract proposition would oppose, and have opposed, efforts on the part of Dominions to remove some of the anomalies which still remain.' In King's mind there were two major considerations which must always qualify the application of the general principles Rowell was advocating: Since 'every self-governing part of the Empire has its own neighbours and its distinctive problems ... it must therefore in these respects have a foreign as well as a domestic policy of its own.' Further, when an issue concerned 'two or more parts of the Empire ... there should be consultation and discussion to ensure, if possible, harmony, and in appropriate cases unity, of action.' To the suggestion that the powers of the high commissioner in London be enhanced, King was as cool as he had always been. Regrettably, the idea was too often linked with proposals for an imperial council and a single foreign policy for the whole Empire, with implied threats to Canada's right to determine her own policy in Canada.[42]

Although Rowell agreed with King that the principles he had expounded might be open to more than one interpretation, he thought the prime minister was making matters unnecessarily complicated. There was no doubt in Rowell's mind that equality of status was 'very much more than an aspiration,' as Canada's position in the League and the ILO demonstrated. While logically there might be difficulties in working out 'the Constitution of the Commonwealth,' in practice these were less than appeared and need not infringe on the principle that Canada's policy must be settled in Canada. However, he urged, 'it is one thing to settle it in Canada without adequate information and consultation and it is another thing to settle it in Canada after full information and adequate consultation.'[43]

It was easy enough for King to concur enthusiastically on the need to enlarge the Department of External Affairs. His deputy minister, Dr O.D. Skelton, agreed that Rowell was essentially right in his assessment of the department's needs.[44] But again there was a significant difference in emphasis. Rowell saw the expansion of the department as an urgent matter demanding early and dramatic action if Canada's new status were to be realized in practice. King and Skelton preferred to advance slowly. Their differences reflected two divergent approaches to foreign policy. Rowell believed that Canada's new position should lead the nation into the assumption of new responsibilities, both within and without the British Commonwealth, and on occasion to positive leadership in world affairs. King and Skelton cherished status, but they tended to see it as an end in itself and were reluctant to confirm it by actions that might add to Canada's external obligations, especially if those actions were likely to damage internal unity. Essentially King and Skelton were isolationists who entertained no aspirations to lead the world in the paths of peace.

King pointed out that he had already appointed a permanent Canadian advisory officer in Geneva, that he had added to the Ottawa staff as counsellor Jean Désy, formerly a teacher of international law at the University of Montreal, and that he planned to add 'a promising young university graduate every year or two as the work of the Department grows.'[45] By the end of the decade he had appointed to the department three such young graduates – Lester B. Pearson, Hugh L. Keenleyside, and Hume Wrong. At the end of the thirties there was a further expansion but it was not until after the second world war that Canada's capacities for the conduct of her relations with the outside world assumed the dimensions Rowell had urged upon a reluctant prime minister.

24
Cleaning up the Liberals

Rowell's preoccupation with Canada's external relations put him in an even smaller minority than usual in the autumn of 1925, when complex domestic political developments held the Canadian stage. Returning to Toronto from Australia just as a federal election campaign was entering its concluding phase, he watched closely Mackenzie King's second appeal to the electors.

After more than four years performing a balancing act that satisfied neither eastern manufacturing interests nor western farmers, King had leaned slightly in the direction of the east by taking into his cabinet on the eve of the election two moderate protectionists – Herbert Marler, a wealthy Montreal businessman, and Vincent Massey, president of the Massey-Harris farm-implement firm. At the same time, although failing in his effort to entice the Liberal premier of Saskatchewan, Charles Dunning, to join his administration, King was at least assured of Dunning's energetic support in the campaign.[1]

The Liberals fought the election of 1925 on the record of the economies effected under their administration, vilifying Meighen in Quebec for his support of conscription and advocating a broad platform of a tariff for revenue. Once again, Arthur Meighen opted firmly for a clearly protective tariff as the remedy for the nation's ills, while the Progressives, more divided than in 1927, took up no significant new ground.

For the second time Mackenzie King failed to secure a clear majority, and the prime minister and seven of his cabinet ministers went down to defeat in their own ridings. If anyone had won the election it was Meighen and the Conservatives. They emerged as the largest group in the House, with 116 of the 245 seats, a gain of sixty-seven over the previous session. Although the Progressives were reduced from sixty-five to twenty-four, they now occupied a crucial position without precedent in Canadian political history.

Nowhere had the Liberals more cause for dismay than in Ontario. Even before the election they had held only twenty-three of the province's eighty-two seats. These were now reduced to twelve, while the Conservative representation from Ontario had risen from thirty-five to sixty-eight. The Progressives had been almost wiped out in the province, with only two successful candidates compared to twenty-two in 1921. Commiserating with the prime minister, and especially over his personal defeat in North York, Rowell could find only one bright spot in the Ontario Liberal scene: 'The disappearance of the Progressive Party in Ontario will make for clearer issues and greater stability in political conditions in the province. Ontario is without doubt protectionist in its point of view.'[2]

What should the Liberals do? Initially, Rowell assumed that in view of King's difficulties in carrying on in the last Parliament, he would not attempt to do so now under even more uncertain circumstances, but would resign. The governor general would then call on Meighen to try to form a government.[3] This assumption proved unwarranted. King soon announced that three alternatives were open to him (the last a move that would have been unconstitutional): he could resign, or meet the new House to test his support there, or advise the governor general on an immediate dissolution of Parliament and the holding of another general election. King had chosen to meet the House. Three weeks later the prime minister was in Toronto for discussions with leading Liberals, including Rowell, on strategies to be pursued to strengthen the party before the opening of parliament early in January.

Shortly after the election Charles Dunning had agreed to enter the cabinet, but not immediately. Rowell was enthusiastic about the addition of Dunning and hoped he would be given the immigration portfolio, a move that 'would be hailed as inaugurating a new era in western settlement.' On Dunning's next visit to Toronto Rowell planned to arrange a meeting with 'a group of men who have not been active with the Liberal party during the past five years but who would give you their confidence I am sure.'[4] One of these Liberal Unionists was W.E. Rundle of the National Trust, perhaps Rowell's closest friend, who believed the country's greatest need was a more vigorous immigration policy and who had been hoping for some time that 'the West would give us another Sifton.'[5]

Although the acquisition of a strong westerner acceptable to many Progressives was a decided gain, there remained the woeful weakness of the party in Ontario, which had not a single elected representative in the cabinet. A number of Rowell's Toronto friends and Clifford Sifton, who had not always been well disposed to him, believed that the addition of Rowell to the cabinet would go a long way towards filling the Ontario vacuum. As the opening of Parliament approached they were vigorously pursuing this objective with Mackenzie King's co-operation, although with no encouragement from Rowell himself. Apart from any other considerations his health precluded an election campaign that in the circumstances was bound to be unusually strenuous, and he was unwilling at present to make the financial sacrifices entailed in giving up his law practice again, especially to join an administration whose life might be short.[6]

Like many other Liberals Rowell was urging King to stabilize his position by negotiating a formal coalition with the Progressives and bringing their leader, Robert Forke, and one or two others into the cabinet.[7] Although Forke failed to persuade enough of his followers to agree to outright coalition they gave the government their informal support and enabled it to survive its first tests in the House. At the end of three weeks the public learned of the price the government was paying for Progressive backing when J.S. Woodsworth, the independent labour member from North Winnipeg, read to the House a letter from King pledging to submit to the present session of Parliament legislation establishing a system of old age pensions and expressing willingness to contribute toward provincial relief costs in times of heavy unemployment. This was a price King was personally quite willing to pay because the bargain pushed him in the direction he desired but had been reluctant to take in the face of opposition within the cabinet and party.[8] The measure was one that Rowell could also welcome, not only as a guarantee of at least temporary stability in government but also as the first step in the implementation of the social policies he had helped to formulate in 1916. So far King seemed to have forgotten these policies, even although they were part of the platform of 1919.

Efforts to find cabinet representation from Ontario continued. King decided not to risk defeat again in his native province and instead successfully contested the Saskatchewan riding of Prince Albert. Many Ontario Liberals still wanted Vincent Massey in the cabinet, but no seat he could reasonably hope to win could be found. Clifford Sifton renewed his attempts to persuade Rowell to join the government, an accession of strength Sifton evidently hoped would be accompanied by certain tariff concessions to Ontario woollen manufacturers that Rowell could be persuaded were necessary.[9] If the announcement of Rowell's appointment to the cabinet could be made simultaneously with the appointment of Dunning as minister of railways and canals the King administration would be given a greatly improved image in both east and west. But only the westerner came in. Shortly, the Ontario situation was resolved by the elevation of the member for Middlesex West, J.C. Elliott, as minister of labour and health.

A new cabinet minister was obliged by law at that time to go before the electors again for ratification in his position as a minister of the crown. Although Elliott had won comfortably over his Conservative and Progressive opponents in the recent general election, the Liberals took no chances of his losing the by-election, though opposed only by a Conservative this time. Rowell contributed to the vigorous and successful effort to ensure Elliott's re-election by issuing a statement, his first on domestic issues since his retirement from Parliament, in the form of a letter to Elliott intended for distribution to the press. Except for stressing to the electors of West Middlesex the necessity of having Ontario representation in the cabinet, Rowell dealt almost exclusively with the tariff question, to which the Conservatives were again assigning priority. Far more important than any theoretically 'right' tariff, in Rowell's perspective, was unity between east and west, and this could only be achieved on the basis of 'a moderate tariff.' In a concise summary of the national policy developed by both Macdonald and Laurier, Rowell observed that the country needed 'neither a high tariff nor a low tariff, but a stable tariff, so that our manufacturers and businessmen will know that they can take advantage of the returning prosperity in the confident assurance that their plans will not be upset by radical changes in the present tariff.' With transportation in Dunning's able hands, an immigration policy to extend settlement in the west, and a stable tariff, Canadians could expect a repetition of the prosperity of the Laurier years, the greatest they had ever known.[10] Like other Liberals who had supported reciprocity in 1911, Rowell had moved some distance on the tariff in acknowledgement of the country's growing industrialization, most notably in Ontario. And like many of his Toronto business colleagues he looked on the continued growth of western settlement as the secret of an expanding economy.

Elliott won the by-election and assumed his cabinet duties, but not for long. Following another three months of acrimonious debate and precarious majorities for the government, Mackenzie King was faced with a motion of censure for proven corruption on a large scale in the administration of the customs service. That the minister of customs, Jacques Bureau, was a French Canadian heightened the government's embarrassment by drawing attention to the party's heavy dependence on a province not noted for the morality of its political life.

Since the Progressives had always put clean government high on their list of priorities, they could scarcely be expected to continue to support the government in the face of the compelling evidence of corruption unearthed by a parliamentary committee of investigation.[11] Realizing this, King requested the governor general, Lord Byng, for a dissolution and was refused, since it was not clear that an alternative government was impossible within the present Parliament. King then had no choice but to resign. Believing that he had enough Progressive support to finish the business of the session, Meighen formed a ministry, but only by appointing acting ministers who, because they did not hold permanent portfolios, would not be required to resign their seats to seek re-election and thus liquidate the narrow margin of votes that would keep Meighen in office. Within three days this administration fell, thanks to one Progressive vote cast inadvertently, on a Liberal motion questioning the legality of Meighen's method of appointing his cabinet and implying it had no right to be in office.

These events furnished King with a better issue for the necessary election than any he had found in the two preceding contests. 'The constitutional crisis,' as King chose to call it, could be understood by every voter, or so King believed. The issue was simple: was Canada a colony or a self-governing nation? In refusing King's request for a dissolution of Parliament King sincerely believed that Lord Byng had violated a cardinal principle of responsible government – that the crown or its representative must always accept the advice of the prime minister. As King explained to Rowell at the beginning of the campaign, and as he was to reiterate from coast to coast in the next two months, 'What as Liberals we have contended for in Parliament and will now contend for in the country, is that the relations of the government to the King's representative in Canada should be in all essentials the same as the relations of the government to the Crown itself in the Old Land and that all our parliamentary proceedings should be governed by British constitutional practice.' Appealing to Rowell's combined nationalist and imperial sentiments, King earnestly solicited his active support: 'I do not know of anyone in Canada who can present the issue in its true light and in a light that will serve to strengthen the British Empire in all its self-governing communities better than yourself.' Rowell's greatest contribution could be made as an active protagonist in the battle, King insisted, urging him to become a candidate. King had two ridings in mind – North Oxford or North York – either of which he was sure Rowell could win. If the Liberals were returned to power Rowell would be assured of a cabinet position on the terms King had already discussed with him.[12]

The answer to King's proposal was easily given. For the past four months Rowell's doctor had permitted him to carry on his work only under strict regulations and on the understanding that he would take two months' summer holiday free of all responsibility. Even had the state of his health not settled the matter, it would have been difficult to lure him into the fray. His disposition to stay permanently out of politics had remained strong during the past five years. Further, he feared that the current campaign would take a decidedly disagreeable turn, especially in Ontario where feelings about the British connection were so strong, and he could only be glad that he was barred from the struggle. He agreed with King that Canadian parliamentary procedure should be governed entirely by British constitutional practice and hoped that the campaign could be 'kept on this sound principle.' But he very much doubted it would be:

I am sure we are going to face another attempt to repeat the campaign of 1911. It will be a flag-waving campaign and the Liberals will be charged with attacking the representatives of the Crown and desiring to secure a separation from the Empire ... Mr Meighen has accepted full responsibility for Lord Byng's action in refusing you a dissolution, and is undoubtedly responsible for all subsequent proceedings. The attack should be upon him and his view of the constitution rather than on

> Lord Byng ... Mr Meighen since called upon to form an administration has made I think about as many mistakes as a man could in such a situation, and I cannot see how he can hope to carry the country.[13]

As the summer election campaign began, Rowell followed it from the shores of Lake Simcoe where, in the interests of a stomach ulcer and general exhaustion, he rested, chopped wood, and tried to stay away from the serious reading proscribed by his doctor, indulging instead his fondness for P.G. Wodehouse.[14] Rowell's initial detachment from the election was challenged by James A. Robb, former minister of finance in the King government, who solicited Rowell's aid, suggesting that the current situation presented 'an exceptional opportunity ... to help unite those who believe in policies calculated to bind Canadians of the different Provinces closer together, and also to bring us closer to the Mother country.' A pronouncement from Rowell, Robb urged, would have 'a steadying effect not only throughout Canada, but also in London.'[15] After more than two weeks Rowell produced a lengthy comment on recent events that generally supported the official Liberal version but also implied a criticism of the Liberals that he believed Robb might not like. However, he told his nephew Ward Wright 'it is the best I am prepared to do. If Robb does not care to publish I think the Toronto Committee particularly Gundy Atkinson and Massey may wish to publish.'[16]

In Rowell's mind there were three distinct questions at issue: (1) the refusal of the dissolution to King and Meighen's acceptance of the task of forming a new Government, (2) the manner in which Meighen constituted his ministry and asked for supplies, and (3) the manner in which Parliament was dissolved. In considering the first question Rowell found it impressive that the King government had retained the confidence of Parliament long enough to succeed in 'passing through the House almost its entire legislative programme, including one of the most notable budgets in our history.' Then, faced with a motion of censure, King had sought a dissolution, which the governor general had refused. Had Lord Byng acted correctly? Rowell's whole argument, that Lord Byng had misunderstood his duty, rested on his conviction that legally and constitutionally Canada occupied a position of absolute equality with Great Britain. Recent events reinforced his regret that the post-war constitutional conference he had strongly urged had never been held. Had it been, and had the position of the crown's representative in the Dominions been clearly spelled out, a situation like the present one could not have occurred. But even without that formal action it was agreed by all that Canada was a self-governing Dominion and that British practice should prevail. According to Rowell's study of Anson's *Law and Custom of the Constitution* and A. Berriedale Keith's *Responsible Government in the Dominions*, the crown in Britain had never refused a prime minister's request for a dissolution since the time of George III.

Moreover, there was a recent precedent in support of his view, since the King had granted dissolution to the government of Ramsay MacDonald, 'although it represented a minority in the House and was defeated by a decisive majority during the first session of Parliament following a general election.' Thus, what Lord Byng had done in refusing the requested dissolution was 'to challenge the status of the Dominions in the British Commonwealth.' He had, although with the best of intentions, applied 'the colonial theory of the Governor-General's duties' rather than 'the modern theory and British constitutional practice.'

Meighen had also accepted the 'colonial theory.' For this he had no excuse, since he had repeatedly asserted Canada's new status and there was no doubt from his many public pronouncements that he fully understood its implications. If Meighen believed that British constitutional practice should prevail in Canada it was his duty, when consulted by the governor general, to have so informed him and to have confirmed King's advice. By failing to do so and by attempting to form a new government Meighen 'accepted full responsibility under our Constitution for the refusal of the dissolution and for maintaining in Canada the Colonial theory that in the exercise of the prerogative of dissolution the discretion rests with the Governor-General.' Thus, 'those who are opposed to the Colonial theory should make their attack on Mr Meighen's position and policy and not on the Governor-General.'

Moving to the awkward question of King's request for a dissolution while facing a motion of censure. Rowell argued that the position that the modern crown must act on all recommendations for dissolution given by a prime minister 'does not depend upon the merits of the issue in respect of which dissolution is asked, but it is because its refusal would inevitably draw the Crown into political controversy, and that is not deemed to be either in the interests of the Crown or the country.' This argument, he contended, was as sound and applicable in Canada as in Great Britain. Even if the King government had been defeated on the motion of censure, it would still have had the option of resignation or dissolution and an appeal to the electors if it thought the judgment of the House at variance with that of the country.[17]

If the ministry of the day had the right to recommend dissolution under all circumstances, what about the rights of Parliament? Among other things it had the right to pass on the customs report and the motion of censure before it was dissolved. The protection of that right, however, did not rest with the governor general, 'but with the people of Canada in the general election following dissolution.'[18] There was some doubt in Rowell's mind whether King was to be believed in his assertion that had he been given a dissolution he would have proceeded with the business of the House before allowing it to take effect, but that was not the issue. Privately, he confided that 'if Mr King had procured the dissolution of the House before the Customs report was finally disposed of and without having the bills already passed assented to and without asking interim supply, Mr King would have been defeated in the country, and I think properly defeated.' In short, King may have been on the verge of making a serious error but was perhaps saved from it by Lord Byng's refusal of dissolution. But what had not happened could not be an issue. The fact was that 'Mr Meighen has taken Mr King's place and has proceeded unconstitutionally. The House of Commons has condemned him for his unconstitutional course and instead of resigning he has appealed from the judgment of the House to the judgment of the Country.'[19]

Meighen's major offence, Rowell told Robb and the voters, was in constituting a 'shadow government' composed of ministers who were not 'real ministers' since they had not taken a valid oath of office and been re-elected by the people. And to make matters worse, this unconstitutional government had gone to Parliament for supply and had rightly been refused. What Meighen should have done when he was called on to form an administration was to ask for an adjournment to allow him to constitute his ministry and to secure the re-election of his ministers. Once re-elected he could have requested supply and completed the business of the session in an orderly fashion.

Finally, there was the question of the manner in which Parliament was dissolved. Rowell rejected the argument of those, including Mackenzie King, who contended that having refused King a dissolution Lord Byng should also have refused Meighen and granted the dissolution then to King. The governor general had acted incorrectly in relation to King but was correct in granting Meighen's request. 'It is for the people of Canada to consider and pass upon Mr Meighen's action in advising dissolution at the time and under the circumstances in which the advice was tendered and accepted.' But all was not right in the manner in which dissolution had been carried out. British constitutional practice, as Rowell understood it, required that when a Parliament in session was to be dissolved the king should prorogue it first and then issue a proclamation of dissolution. Meighen should have advised the governor general to give assent to the bills already passed during the session and then to prorogue Parliament 'in the regular and constitutional way and only after this was done to issue the proclamation dissolving parliament. The course pursued was without precedent: it was a grave departure from constitutional practice and it destroyed an important part of the work of the session.'

In short, for Rowell the situation before the voters was this: 'Mr Meighen by accepting responsibility for the Colonial theory of the Governor-General's duty and by appealing to the Country against the decision of the House instead of resigning has made under both British and Canadian Constitutional practice, the Constitutional question a paramount issue in the election.'[20]

All this was set out again for the voters in Sarnia three days before they went to the polls in Rowell's only public appearance during the campaign. Urging the re-election of W.T. Goodison, the Liberal member for West Lambton who had been a member of the Commons special committee on the customs administration, Rowell asserted: 'Mr Meighen is appealing to the electors against the action of the House of Commons for censuring him for violating its rights and privileges. We must decide whether we will support the House of Commons or Mr Meighen.' A wrong decision on this issue, Rowell warned, would undermine the whole political system. 'It was disrespect for parliamentary institutions and the laws enacted by parliament and the consequent lawlessness in Italy that made Mussolini possible.' Had King been given a dissolution and used it to escape facing the motion of censure as the Conservatives were so sure he intended to do, the people of Canada would have been right to defeat him. But 'Mr King did not do the acts complained of. If he ever intended doing them Mr Meighen did not give him the chance.'[21]

Later students of 'the King-Byng affair' have rejected the plebiscitary theory of democracy inherent in the position adopted by King, Rowell, and many of their contemporaries, finding it entirely foreign to the British parliamentary system. In the view of these critics, the assumption that constitutional issues can be settled by popular vote and that the people are the sole guardians of their democratic rights ignores the powers and responsibilities of both crown and Parliament.[22] But at the time, King's reactions were almost entirely those of the intuitive politician. His dominant motive was to avoid handing over the government to Meighen or giving him any advantage. Most of King's constitutional arguments were developed after the events they were intended to justify.[23] Since he was not a member of the government Rowell was less subject to the pressures of the moment. Although he was a careful student of the constitution it may be argued that the Liberal overcame the parliamentarian and the Canadian nationalist overwhelmed the constitutionalist in Rowell. However, Rowell had more than once shown that he was not always a good party man, and both before and after 1926 he demonstrated his capacity to disagree with Mackenzie King. There is no reason to believe that his interpretation of 'the constitutional crisis' was lacking either in candour or thoughtful judgment.

Despite the significance of the constitutional issue it was by no means the only one Rowell discussed before the voters of West Lambton. His election-eve address was in effect a review of the state of the nation. A primary cause for concern was Ontario's role in Confederation. Never since 1867 had the province had so little representation at Ottawa in either Conservative or Liberal governments. This situation must be remedied not only for the good of Ontario but for the health of the whole nation. Since the Tories had so little support in Quebec and would gain nothing in the west with their high-tariff program, only the Liberal party could be the vehicle of national unity. Mackenzie King had already demonstrated his capacity to lead such a uniting party, notably by adopting policies that had gradually brought the Progressives back into the Liberal fold.

Rowell found other achievements to the credit of the party. The substantial tax reductions of the recent Robb budget were needed and should be carried further. Despite the powerful detractors of the publicly owned railway system, the CNR had turned a large operating deficit into a handsome surplus and would continue to do so under the ablest minister of railways in the nation's history, Charles Dunning. Rowell was not so impressed with Liberal immigration policy, although he commended recent efforts to secure more settlers from Britain; but both the pressure of overpopulation in Europe and the needs of Canada demanded more vigorous policies in the future settlement of the prairies. Both parties must accept blame for the maladministration of the Customs Department, but the bulk of the responsibility rested with the Liberals, who should and would do a thorough clean-up of the mess.[24]

On the whole Rowell was reiterating the standard Liberal arguments of the campaign. In the face of the evidence, even more partisan Liberals had admitted their party's mishandling of the Customs Department. But Rowell's address was not entirely party propaganda. Few Liberals had been publicly critical of the government's immigration policy, and fewer had even hinted that King's favourable position in the constitutional dispute might be due more to good luck than to good intentions.

In Rowell's judgment, the Conservative defeat on 14 September 1926 should be considered at least in part a verdict on Meighen's unconstitutional behaviour. Yet a look at the popular vote made it impossible to conclude that the Canadian people had interpreted the election in those terms. Although the Conservatives had lost twenty-five seats, leaving them with ninety-one, their share of the total vote had declined scarcely at all and still stood at just over 46 per cent. At the same time, despite his additional fifteen Liberal seats, for a total of 116, King, with 43.7 per cent of the popular vote had received less than overwhelming popular approval. However, with the assured support of ten Liberal-Progressives and the probable adherence of at least some of the collection of UFA, labour, and independent members who made up the balance of the new Parliament, King had a clear majority and would be more firmly in command of his party and of Parliament than ever before. Of the fifteen newly won Liberal ridings, nine were in Ontario and three in Manitoba. In Quebec the Liberals retained their sixty seats, while Conservative representation remained at four seats.

Congratulating King on his 'remarkable victory,' Rowell noted with particular gratification the increase in Ontario Liberal seats from twelve to twenty-three as evidence of a Liberal unity in Ontario greater than any since the election of 1908. If matters were properly handled from now on, even more of the Liberal businessmen and manufacturers who had deserted the party in the reciprocity election of 1911 could be won back, and the Liberal party would regain its old strength in Ontario. Four factors, Rowell advised King, were of special importance in the achieving of this objective. 'The strongest man you can get' must be appointed minister of customs and given full powers and unlimited government support in cleaning up the Customs Department, and a Progressive or Liberal-Progressive should be taken into the government to demonstrate the government's stability. Ontario must have equal representation with Quebec in the cabinet, and there must be a clear announcement of the government's determination to maintain the present tariff structure in order to stabilize business conditions and induce the investment of more Canadian capital in Canadian enterprises.[25]

King believed that the strongest man he could get as minister of customs was Rowell himself. Not only would his appointment assure the public that the Liberals were serious in their pledges to clean up the department, it would also be popular with the influential group of former Unionist Liberals in Toronto whose substantial services to the party in the recent election required recognition, and it would symbolize the final healing of the wartime rifts. King urged Rowell to join the cabinet on the understanding that he would enjoy a free hand and King's wholehearted support in the reorganization of the entire customs service. Within a year he would be given one of the the two portfolios for which he had earlier expressed his preference – finance or external affairs.[26]

This proposal interested Rowell sufficiently to encourage him to dispatch J.H. Gundy to Ottawa to seek further details from King. He wanted unequivocal assurance that the key Quebec ministers – Lapointe, Robb, and Cardin – really wanted him in the government and would give their full support in the reform of the customs. He wanted to know whether there would be a Progressive in the cabinet, as he thought essential, and whether the other ministers from Ontario would include Charles Murphy. King was already worried about Murphy and well aware that he would be most unacceptable to many of his cabinet colleagues, several of whom seemed anxious to have Rowell in the government. At the same time he recognized that from within a cabinet that included both men, Murphy could not attack Rowell as he would undoubtedly do if he were excluded.[27] Assured by Gundy of satisfactory consideration of his concerns, Rowell went to Ottawa in a positive frame of mind: his discussions with the officers of the trust company had been satisfactory, and x-rays of his stomach had shown that his ulcer was healed and should cause no further problem. Although he would be reluctant to leave his many clients and Nell was opposed to a return to politics, he would do so if the opportunity for service were clear enough.[28]

King soon began to regret that he had gone so far with Rowell. Everyone to whom he had spoken, even those who had been keenest to have him in the government, were now wavering, and all had underlined King's own growing doubt about the possibility of getting Rowell elected in any Ontario seat. King summarized the situation in his diary: 'Rowell seems to have lined up against him nearly all the forces that count in the ridings we have won ... enough to swing against him in a campaign.' Irish and French Catholics were against him, and so was the German vote in other ridings. Then there were the anti-prohibitionists who would be reinforced by funds from distillers determined at all costs to prevent Rowell from investigating their affairs as minister of customs. Further, by leading the church union movement he had antagonized 'the Scotch Presbyterians who are the backbone of the Liberal party in Ontario.' Many Liberals had not forgiven him for having 'left his Party as leader in Ontario without conference with them in the first instance, and having deserted Sir Wilfrid.' As another burden he would have to 'carry all the opprobrium that exists in the minds of the Civil Service against Unionist Government.' And then there was Charles Murphy waiting to reopen old cleavages.[29]

With the help of J.C. Elliott and James Malcolm, Ontario members of Parliament who were shortly to join the new administration, King explained to Rowell that it would be 'too dangerous both for him and the Party to attempt bringing him into the Government at this stage.' Detecting in Rowell what he thought was a moment's disappointment, King suggested that he might render great service as counsel to the commission he would set up to pursue the investigation of the customs. To King's relief Rowell 'displayed a very nice spirit,' accepted the job, and remarked on how pleased Nell would be at this result. The next day King discussed with him the conditions under which he might enter the government at a future date when a suitable seat was found, but Rowell refused to commit himself. Then the two men resumed an earlier conversation about William James and psychological research.[30]

Although he would not be a member of the cabinet, Rowell was accepting a major role in cleaning up the mess in the Customs Department and, indirectly, in helping to refurbish the tarnished image of the Liberal party. The report of the special parliamentary committee that had produced the motion of censure Mackenzie King had been so eager to escape had revealed liquor smuggling and tax evasion, with the connivance of members of the department, on a grand scale. Although most of the known smuggling involved liquor going to the United States, a variety of manufactured articles was believed to be entering Canada illegally without payment of duties. Canadian manufacturers of competing goods, through the Commercial Protective Association and Boards of Trade, were demanding that the government ensure enforcement of Canadian laws. King could not ignore such revelations and had acted speedily on the committee's recommendation that the investigation be extended by appointing Mr Justice François Lemieux, chief justice of the Superior

Court of Quebec, as royal commissioner with powers to expand the probe. Before the election, hearings were conducted in Montreal and the Maritimes, and on his return to office King embarked on plans to enlarge the commission's personnel and work. Having failed to get Rowell as minister, he very much wanted him as chief counsel of the commission, where his acknowledged thoroughness and honesty would be of service to the investigation and a proof to the public that the government was in earnest in its desire to root out corruption.

Although King had immediate political reasons for wanting a thorough investigation, there was also an international aspect to the whole question which he stressed in his discussions with Rowell. The smuggling of liquor from Canada into the United States, where the Eighteenth Amendment had been in force since 1920, was making the maintenance of prohibition difficult in the border states. With the progressive abandonment of prohibition by the Canadian provinces, starting with Quebec and British Columbia in 1921, supplies of liquor were increasingly available in Canada, and customs officials on both sides of the border frequently co-operated in facilitating missions to satisfy the needs of thirsty Americans. An anti-smuggling treaty signed by the two nations in 1924 had proved ineffectual. The American government had since been endeavouring to secure an amendment binding Canada to forbid clearances to ships carrying liquor to American ports. Opinion in Canada on the subject was divided. Many Canadians could see no reason to render assistance in the enforcement of an American law, while others held that the promotion of friendly relations with the United States demanded Canadian co-operation. The parliamentary committee on the customs had recommended denial of clearance, but so far no action had been taken.[31]

In accepting the assignment as counsel in the renewed investigation, Rowell had insisted that he would work only under certain carefully specified conditions. The personnel of the expanded commission must be acceptable to him; he must have a completely free hand in the conduct of the investigation, and he must be assured of an adequate staff to do the job. In particular, he must have the assistance of R.L. Calder, who had acted as counsel for the parliamentary committee. Since Calder was bilingual, he would be in charge of the investigation in Quebec and the Maritimes. Further, after careful study, Rowell had concluded that a revision of the order-in-council appointing Lemieux as commissioner was essential if the scope of the enquiry was to be adequate. Finally, since many Liberals or Liberal appointees would be exposed in the course of the commission's work he wanted the absolute assurance of King and the whole cabinet, especially the new minister of customs, W.D. Euler, that no political interference would be tolerated. 'You know and I know' he told King 'that once the investigation gets into the heart of the situation there will be all kinds of pressure brought to bear upon the Government and upon the Commission to slow up ... rather than permit any interference with the most thorough investigation I would be compelled to throw up the brief and state my reasons for doing so. You will appreciate what this would mean.'[32] All Rowell's conditions were accepted. His letter containing his remarks about political interference was read aloud to the cabinet, and he personally drafted the new order-in-council to which the cabinet gave approval.[33] The two new members of the enlarged commission were entirely acceptable: Mr Justice W.T. Brown of the Court of King's Bench of Saskatchewan and Mr Justice William H. Wright of the Ontario Supreme Court. These new arrangements brought Lemieux's resignation and his replacement by Mr Justice Ernest Roy of Quebec. Adequate staff was guaranteed and the stage was well set for an all-out war against violaters of American prohibition laws and evaders of Canadian taxes.

Like earlier press reports that he might enter the cabinet, the announcement of Rowell's appointment as counsel to the royal commission stirred up a flurry of angry exchanges among the Murphy Liberals. They rightly understood that many of the leading Liberals in the Toronto business community who had been Unionists in 1917 were again influential in the party, and Rowell's rehabilitation was a symbol of reunification they could not tolerate. Murphy's conviction that Rowell and his friends were now in complete control of the Liberal party in Ontario took on paranoid proportions when King excluded his former colleague from the new cabinet. The subsequent appointment of Rowell to the customs investigation was seen by Murphy as a deliberate insult to himself and a sign that Irish Catholics in Ontario must reconcile themselves to the realization that they would never again receive any appointment, however lowly, from a Liberal administration.[34]

Unity within the Ontario Liberal party became a pressing objective when the Conservative premier of the province, G. Howard Ferguson, called a general election for 1 December. In office since the defeat of the UFO-Labour government of E.C. Drury in 1924, the Ferguson administration at dissolution held seventy-six of the 111 seats in the legislature. The main issue in Ferguson's campaign was his proposal to repeal the Ontario Temperance Act (OTA) in favour of government sale of liquor. An independent government commission would administer the system, issuing permits to citizens over twenty-one for the purchase of liquor, wine, and beer.

The leader of the Ontario Liberals, W.E.N. Sinclair, an Oshawa lawyer, stood on the position he had earlier adopted – that it would be contrary to Liberal principles for the party to depart from the expressed will of the people as it had been made clear when a majority supported the OTA in the two recent plebiscites. The implication that party policy might change in response to future tests of public opinion was enough to keep Liberal 'wets' in the party, especially in view of the knowledge that the proportion of voters favouring the OTA had declined from 68 per cent in 1919 to 51 per cent in 1924. At the same time, the 'drys' would adhere to Sinclair's leadership as long as he supported the OTA.

As the campaign was beginning, three hundred Liberals from across the province gathered in the King Edward Hotel in Toronto at a banquet to honour their leader and to affirm their unity in the coming battle. In the main speech of the evening Sinclair declared the party's official commitment to the enforcement of the OTA and then went on to a discussion of policy on other matters. As the applause for Sinclair died down the chairman of the evening, Senator A.C. Hardy, introduced Rowell. At this point there were minor flurries in various sections of the audience as several men, including two at the head table, left the room. Unflustered, Rowell proceeded with a brief address endorsing Sinclair and his policies while the defectors fumed outside. The 'wet' dissidents had been well satisfied with Sinclair's statement, since they believed it was couched in terms they could sell to their followers, but Rowell's unexpected endorsation invited a different interpretation of Sinclair's meaning. Rowell's name had not been on the printed program for the evening, and they were entirely unprepared for this turn of events. The disaffected ones were already smarting under their belief that the previous leader, Wellington Hay, whom they had considered their man, had been 'done in' by the unwelcome support of the temperance elements in the party. Now 'Holy Wesley and the uplifters' had carried off a repeat performance with Sinclair. Since the 'wet' Liberals broadly overlapped the Murphy Catholic anti-Unionist elements in the party the emotional springs of their anger at yet another 'betrayal' were many and deep.[35] The day after the banquet, four Liberal members of the Legislature, all French Canadians, announced that they would run as independents since they could not accept the Liberal policy on liquor.[36] Although the majority of Liberals rallied to support the OTA and conducted a vigorous campaign, the liquor issue was once again a divisive force within Ontario Liberalism.

His brief address at the Sinclair banquet was Rowell's only direct contribution to the campaign, save for giving a legal opinion. A public controversy developed over whether government sale of liquor would make importation of liquor into Ontario legal. Ferguson, attempting to modify the picture painted by his opponents of a province swimming in booze, declared that importation would not be legal unless the government passed a specific measure making it so. In refutation, Rowell asserted that legalizing the sale of liquor would automatically legalize its importation, as was clear from a clause of the OTA itself. Furthermore, the province had no power to regulate interprovincial trade, a fact well established by several rulings of the Supreme Court of Canada.[37] Under government sale the sources of supply would be unlimited.

Apparently that was what the voters of Ontario wanted. The Ferguson government was returned in an overwhelming victory that gave it one more seat than before. Six months later the Liquor Control Board of Ontario was in business, and thousands of Ontarians were flocking to the new liquor stores to take out their permits. It was the end of an era in Ontario.

As chief counsel for the Royal Commission on Customs and Excise Rowell bore the primary responsibility for organizing the procedures followed in ferreting out the evidence to be placed before the commissioners. The parliamentary investigating committee had already required an audit of the operations of fifty-seven firms, mainly distilleries, and H.H. Stevens, minister of customs in the short-lived Meighen administration, had ordered the audit enlarged to include every distillery in the country. In preparation for the hearings of the commission, Rowell recommended that a sample selection of twenty breweries be added to the list. On the basis of the results of these audits the commission decided to include all seventy breweries operating in Canada. All told, two hundred and seven firms were subjected to audit and about half of these were brought before the commission for investigation.[38] Since the commission had been asked to make interim reports recommending immediate measures that could be taken by the courts and government agencies to prosecute violators of the law as they were unearthed by the commission, Rowell's work from the beginning involved much more than the securing of evidence. On more than one occasion he announced to witnesses before him in precise terms the penalties he would recommend to the commissioners. Pending the presentation of the final report, ten interim reports containing numerous specific recommendations were submitted to the government.

Opening its hearings on the west coast, the commission and the public were soon hearing the extraordinary tale of the vessel *Chris Moeller*. Possessing many of the qualities of an international spy story, it was a foretaste of similar revelations on both coasts and the Great Lakes. The *Chris Moeller* had sailed from Vancouver a week before the commencement of the hearings with a cargo of nearly eighteen thousand cases of liquor, originally purchased in Britain and now designated for a buyer in San Blas, Mexico. It had made many such voyages before. Under Rowell's relentless questioning of representatives of four firms connected with the transaction it emerged that San Blas was a small village with no port or harbour, that the shippers of the liquor had recently received payments in advance forwarded from banks in Los Angeles and San Francisco, and that no bond guaranteeing that the goods would actually be landed at the specified destination had been furnished and no duties paid as required by Canadian law. Any liquor openly billed to a US port would, of course, be seized, and several Vancouver interests had become highly skilled in the art of organizing shipments of liquor, ostensibly to ports in Mexico and Central America, but in fact always for delivery to a consignee in the United States.[39]

Of considerable dramatic interest was Rowell's questioning of George Reifel, president of a local distillery, who was forced to admit that his company's records were falsified and liquor marked for export had been delivered in Vancouver. Proceeding to bombard Reifel with further questions about irregularities in connection with a number of cancelled cheques, Rowell contended that they were for payment of forged American revenue stamps. Undeterred by the protests of Reifel's counsel, J.W. deB. Farris, a former Liberal attorney general of British Columbia, that the chief counsel's questions were unnecessarily vigorous, Rowell got what he wanted and ended by assuring Reifel that he would take personal responsibility for seeing that his company's licence was cancelled.[40] Later in the hearings, Reifel's brother, Henry, president of Vancouver Breweries, testified that $100,000 would cover the political contributions his firm had made in the past five or six years. But no favouritism had been shown and no strings attached, for the Conservatives, Liberals, and the anti-prohibitionist Moderation League had all been beneficiaries of the company's generosity.[41]

Before going to Vancouver Rowell had found it hard to believe the assertions of Dugald Donaghy, former Liberal member of Parliament for North Vancouver and a member of the Commons committee on the customs, that Vancouver would prove to be just as bad as Montreal when the facts were known. But what Rowell had heard on the west coast more than justified Donaghy's charge. He was encouraged by the press reaction to the evidence brought before the commission and the widespread demand in the province for a complete investigation and clean up. One editor, 'Benny' Nicolas of the *Victoria Times*, had told Rowell that 'unless the matter was thoroughly investigated at the present time he saw no hope for public life in British Columbia,' an opinion Rowell thought it worthwhile to pass on to Mackenzie King since he had 'no doubt there will be others who entertain quite different views conveying these views to Ottawa.'[42]

Alberta was given a relatively clean bill of health, as was Saskatchewan, although Rowell was astounded at the stories of rum-running carried on by sixty export houses in Saskatchewan before their suppression in 1922. Many of these businesses had been controlled by the Bronfman family of Ottawa and had displayed enormous ingenuity in devising methods of smuggling liquor into the United States, sometimes in the guise of alcohol for medicinal purposes and often as 'vinegar,' on which twenty-seven cents excise was paid instead of the nine dollars per drum levied on liquor. By these means vast fortunes had been made in a short time, on which little or no income tax seemed to have been paid. While these export houses flourished, 'practically a reign of terror prevailed along the American border,' and 'peaceful citizens were terrorized by thugs who came up from the United States and engaged in this contraband business and practically all of whom carried arms.' Had he not heard it from customs officials and Mounted Police and had the evidence confirmed by the Saskatchewan member of the commission, Chief Justice Brown, Rowell 'would not have believed it possible that such a state of affairs could have existed in Canada.'[43]

One of the first witnesses to appear before the commission in Toronto was W.T.

Kernahan, general manager of O'Keefe's Brewery. Asked to explain his company's failure to produce its books for the commission's auditors, Kernahan declared that they had disappeared mysteriously. Since he had failed in his efforts to persuade King to prevent the investigation of the breweries, Kernahan was apparently determined not to be a willing co-operator with the commission.[44] After waiting a week for the books to be found Rowell told the witness that since the company's conduct was a breach of the law the commissioners would recommend cancellation of O'Keefe's licence.[45] The cancellation was announced by the collector of customs the next day, while O'Keefe's posted a reward of $1000 for the return of the lost books.[46]

The records kept by the 'King of the Bootleggers,' Rocco Perri, also proved to be faulty. Called as a witness, the Hamilton bootlegger pleaded a poor memory as the source of his difficulties in recalling the details of his operations. Under Rowell's persistent pressure and leading questions, his memory began to show some improvement, enough to demonstrate that he had paid no income taxes on his large profits and was open to charges of perjury.[47] Later, a group of northern Ontario breweries admitted the confiscation of the books requested by the auditors. The Kuntz Brewery of Waterloo was shown to owe taxes of $123,000 and the Seagram Distillery $100,000. As was to be expected in the border city of Windsor, evidence appeared of incomplete or doctored books, bribery of customs officials, and tax evasion on a large scale.[48] With the holding of sessions in Quebec and the Maritimes, where much evidence had already been brought to light by the parliamentary committee, the commission's hearings were complete.

At the end of more than six months of extensive work with the commission he was ready for a quiet holiday in northern Quebec on the shores of Lake Temiskaming before going to Washington at the suggestion of the State Department for conferences with officials of the American customs service.[49] The members of the us Customs Commission were especially eager to answer Rowell's questions about their apparent failure to enforce their own laws, a failure that gave many Canadians the impression that the American government was not serious in its efforts. Rowell came away convinced that the executive branch of the us government was entirely sincere in its desire to enforce the law. The difficulties lay elsewhere; as he reminded King sometime later: 'The failure ... as in the case of many other laws, grows out of their administrative and judicial systems where politics are such an important factor, accentuated, no doubt, by the differences of opinion as to this particular law and the organized and systematic corruption, by the liquor interests, of Government enforcement officers.'[50]

At its conclusion Rowell was satisfied that the commission's work had been both thorough and impartial and that the government and country had been 'exceptionally fortunate in securing three such able, upright, conscientious and painstaking

Commissioners.' And King had been true to his promise to give him a free hand and to protect the commission from political interference.[51] There were few surprises for Rowell in the finished report when he read it just before it was tabled in the House of Commons early in 1928. In addition to their detailed account of commercial smuggling and a strong recommendation for the abolition of export houses, the commissioners made proposals for the complete reorganization of the Customs Department. Finally, and most controversially, it recommended that Canada accede to American requests for the denial of clearances to vessels or vehicles carrying liquor to the United States in violation of American law.

On one point in the report Rowell was both surprised and distressed. The commissioners had recommended that certain important appointments in the Customs Department be withdrawn from the jurisdiction of the Civil Service Commission and placed under the minister in charge of the department. Since counsel had submitted no evidence on this subject and had made no recommendation to the commissioners, Rowell felt bound to inform the prime minister of those facts and to register his disagreement. While fully agreeing that the department needed more competent personnel in many areas, he could not see how any improvement could result from bypassing the Civil Service Commission. Moreover, an important precedent would be set because the same principle could then be applied to other departments, thus jeopardizing the advances made in civil service reform in Canada.[52]

Responsibility for cleaning up the customs administration now rested with the government and Parliament.

25

The pinnacle of the legal profession

While Rowell was beginning the investigation of the customs in the autumn of 1926 Mackenzie King was in London for meetings of the Imperial Conference. Rowell hoped that these discussions would resolve the constitutional uncertainties that should have been tackled immediately after the war and had been approached only indirectly at the conference of 1923. He was not disappointed.

During two weeks of negotiations the conference sought a formula that would reconcile the demand of Premier Herzog of South Africa and the delegates of the Irish Free State for a declaration of the practical independence of the Dominions, the fears of the Australian and New Zealand delegates that they had already gone too far toward independence, and the British insistence on the unity of the Empire. In the search for a compromise Mackenzie King played a mediating role, although perhaps not a definitive one.[1]

The conference, presided over by the former British foreign secretary, A.J. Balfour, now the Earl of Balfour, embodied its wisdom in what was soon known as the Balfour Report. The position of the Dominions was asserted to be, in words soon to become famous, that of 'autonomous communities within the British Empire, equal in status, in no way subordinate one to another in any aspect of their domestic or external affairs, though united by a common allegiance to the Crown, and freely associated as members of the British Commonwealth of Nations.'[2] In an address to the Canadian Club of Winnipeg on his way home from the first round of customs hearings in Vancouver, Rowell admitted to one regret about the conference in a tone that implied at least slight criticism of the part played by King: 'It is that we were not able to make greater efforts to preserve Empire strength and unity, in the time at our disposal.' At the same time he declared it 'unthinkable that growing and expanding Canada would be served by continuing to occupy a subordinate position.'[3] Significantly, Rowell made no mention of consultation or a common foreign policy; he had not forgotten the lesson of Locarno. That lesson was now spelled out in the Balfour Report's statement that 'neither Great Britain nor the Dominions could be committed to the acceptance of active obligations except with the definite consent of their own governments.'[4]

Moving to comment on the specific recommendations in the report, Rowell found them all thoroughly acceptable. He fully recognized that they broke no new ground; they were simply clarifications of constitutional practices that had evolved gradually, but their formal elaboration was nevertheless an important landmark. Perhaps of greatest immediate interest to Canada, certainly to Mackenzie King, was the official recognition that the governor general was the representative solely of the crown and not of the British government. A corollary of this was the agreement that the governor general should no longer act as a channel of communication between London and the Dominions but henceforth the governments concerned should communicate directly with one another. Acceptance of the equality of status of the Dominions implied the right to sign treaties independently of Great Britain, and this was conceded under an obscure wording which appeared to maintain the symbolic unity of the Empire.

Of particular interest to Rowell was the conference's treatment of the question of appeals to the Judicial Committee of the Privy Council, a matter much discussed recently in Canada and one in which he had taken an active interest. Canada had abolished appeals in criminal cases in 1887, but early in 1926 their lordships of the Judicial Committee had considered whether they would hear the appeal of a Canadian criminal case, *Nadan* v *the King*. Although the decision had been not to entertain this particular appeal, the court had specifically declared invalid the section of the Canadian Criminal Code (Section 1025) abolishing appeals in criminal cases. In a letter to Mackenzie King the day after the decision, Rowell denounced the ruling as 'startling and reactionary' and urged an immediate protest to the British government.[5] Rowell was singularly well equipped to deal with this question. When arguing the Home Bank appeals to the Privy Council in 1924 he had prepared a defence of the validity of Section 1025, anticipating that he would need it, but the case had eventually been disposed of on other grounds. He remained no less convinced of the soundness of Canada's having full control of criminal justice: 'to hold that Canada has not this right' he told the minister of justice, Ernest Lapointe, 'restricts the legislative power of the Dominion to legislate fully and amply with respect to peace, order and good government of Canada, and it ignores the constitutional developments of the past twenty-five years.' Rowell acknowledged that the attorney general of Great Britain, to whom the Privy Council had granted permission to argue the validity of Section 1025, was the chief law officer of the crown: 'it is no doubt in that capacity that he appeared and argued the question, but he is also a Member of the Government of Great Britain, and ... the political significance of such a judgment should not have been ignored or overlooked by the British Government.'[6]

Now the Imperial Conference had conceded the right of the Dominions to abolish appeals if they wished. For Canada this was highly satisfactory, since it meant that Canada would still have final jurisdiction in criminal cases but could retain appeals in civil cases, as most Canadians, thanks to the complexities of Dominion-Provincial and English-French relations, still desired to do.

During the next year the Canadian presence in the world became more visible, at least to those eager to see it. The long-delayed appointment to Washington was made, with Vincent Massey as the first Canadian minister to the United States. Very shortly, Canadian legations were established in Paris and Tokyo. A further advance occurred at the sixth annual meeting of the Assembly of the League of Nations when Canada was elected to the League Council. 'If anything further were required to put an end to any controversy or discussion as to Canada's status within the Empire this should put an end to it,' Rowell told the prime minister. 'I am sure her voice on the Council will always be on the side of justice and peace. I congratulate you that this should have happened in the year in which we are celebrating the jubilee of Canadian Confederation.'[7] King was not convinced that congratulations were in order. It was all very well to rejoice in status, but he feared that Council membership might add to Canada's international obligations, and he had agreed that Canada should seek the seat only on the insistence of his chief Quebec lieutenant, Ernest Lapointe.[8]

The increasing acknowledgment of Canada's position in the world gave added impetus to a movement central to Rowell's interests since the war, the endeavour to foster more informed Canadian opinion on international affairs. A major figure in this endeavour was John Nelson, a former Vancouver newspaperman and recently appointed director of public relations for the Sun Life Assurance Company of Canada in Montreal, who had been the moving spirit in the organization of the Canadian delegation to the Honolulu conference of the Institute of Pacific Affairs, which Rowell had visited briefly on his way to Australia. Soon after Rowell's return to Toronto, Nelson invited him to become the chairman of a Canadian section of the IPR, then being organized. Pressure of his other work obliged Rowell to decline and also to reject the appeals of Nelson and J. Merle Davis, the American secretary of the IPR, that he become the first Canadian representative on the IPR Council. At the same time Rowell helped to set in motion events which were to have important results.[9]

In 1920, at the invitation of Lord Robert Cecil, who was then organizing the British Institute of International Affairs, Rowell had become one of the ten original members of the British Institute of International Affairs in Canada.[10] At that time he had been enthusiastic about the formation of a Canadian branch of the Institute,[11] but subsequently his energies had been diverted into efforts to promote the League of Nations Society in Canada. The two organizations differed in emphasis, since the League of Nations Society was directed at a large popular audience while the Institute was designed to promote more serious and detailed study of international relations among business and professional men. By 1925 there were some twenty-five Canadian members of the British, now the Royal, Institute of International Affairs, among whom there was continuing talk of establishing a Canadian branch. Like Rowell, some of these men were also interested in the IPR. As an alternative to the establishment of two overlapping organizations Rowell proposed that a Canadian branch of the Royal Institute be formed in association with the IPR through which, he hoped, influential members of the RIIA could be interested in the IPR.[12] In the autumn of 1926 Rowell encouraged and attended two meetings in Toronto when a group met first with Merle Davis of the IPR and later at the home of Sir Joseph Flavelle with Rowell's friend the British journalist H. Wilson Harris, representing the RIIA. As a result of these discussions it was agreed to form a Canadian organization affiliated with both the IPR and the RIIA, and before long local branches were being formed in Montreal, Toronto, Winnipeg, and Vancouver.[13] When Rowell was in Vancouver for the customs enquiry he addressed a gathering of business and university men interested in the new organization who agreed to form a Vancouver committee.[14] An indication of the growing interest was the strong twenty-seven-member delegation from Canada headed by Sir Arthur Currie that attended the IPR conference in Honolulu in the summer of 1927. Rowell's work with the customs enquiry prevented him from going, but he read the reports of the returning delegates attentively and welcomed the obvious impetus the meetings had given to the work of organizing in Canada. At the end of January 1928 the new organization, the Canadian Institute of International Affairs, was formally constituted at a meeting at the Ottawa home of Sir Robert Borden. Legal work kept Rowell in Toronto, but he gave his proxy for the meeting to Professor N.A.M. Mackenzie of the University of Toronto, the chief organizer and first secretary of the Toronto branch.[15] After approving a constitution, which included provisions for affiliation with both the RIIA and the IPR, the CIIA elected Sir Robert Borden as president and J.W. Dafoe as vice-president. Rowell was one of the twelve founding members and a member of the executive council.

At this time Rowell was involved in several legal cases of more than ordinary interest and importance.

Ever since women had received the franchise a variety of women's groups had been endeavouring to secure the appointment of a woman to the Senate of Canada.

They had been informed by successive prime ministers that the law officers of the crown advised that Section 24 of the BNA Act, providing for the appointment of qualified 'persons' to the Senate, referred only to men and women were therefore not eligible for appointment. A group of Alberta women, led by Judge Emily Murphy of Edmonton, the first woman police magistrate in the British Empire, decided to test the question in the courts. Under a provision of the Supreme Court Act any five citizens could seek from the Dominion government an order-in-council directing the Supreme Court of Canada to rule on any matter of interpretation of the BNA Act. The government issued the requested order-in-council and, in view of the significance of the question under debate, agreed to foot the bill for the appeal. As her co-appellants Judge Murphy chose Mrs Henrietta Muir Edwards, convenor of the legal committee of the National Council of Women, Hon. Irene Parlby, a former member of the Alberta cabinet, Mrs Louise C. McKinney, a leading figure in the WCTU and member of the Alberta Legislature, and Mrs Nellie McClung, also a former member of the Legislature of Alberta but better known as a popular novelist and public speaker on temperance, women's rights, and kindred subjects. The women wanted the best legal representation they could secure, and if their lawyer was personally committed to their cause so much the better. Rowell was, and his being a Liberal would make it harder for critics to say that the reference was a political manœuvre.[16] When Judge Murphy nominated Rowell to take the case the Dominion government agreed to appoint him, and subsequently he was empowered to act as well for the government of Alberta, which was supporting the women. The Canadian government was represented by Rowell's old antagonist of the war years, Lucien Cannon, now solicitor general in the King government, and was supported by the government of Quebec.

In mid-March 1928 at the Supreme Court hearings in Ottawa Rowell adopted a direct common sense argument, depending primarily on the contention that 'persons' should be interpreted in accord with contemporary social customs and not those of sixty years ago. The Canadian Election Act of 1920, which made women eligible for election to the House of Commons, used 'persons' to include females, and there was no reason to believe that the term should be interpreted in a more restricted sense in relation to the Senate. Moreover, Section 33 of the BNA Act gave the Senate power to judge the qualifications of its own members. In Rowell's view, if the governor general were to call a woman to the Senate there was nothing to prevent her from taking her seat immediately. In a survey of the position of women going back to Roman times, Rowell's opponents relied heavily on the fact that women did not have political rights anywhere in Canada in 1867 and asserted that it was therefore clearly not the intention of the Fathers of Confederation to include women in the Senate. Six weeks later the court delivered a unanimous judgment that women were not eligible for appointment.[17] On the same day the minister of justice assured Parliament that the government would proceed immediately to amend the BNA Act,[18] but the session ended without any action having been taken. There the matter rested.

As a result of his work with the customs investigation Rowell was heavily involved with a number of suits against breweries and distilleries for recovery of unpaid gallonage and sales taxes. As counsel for the commission he knew more than any lawyer in the country about the methods of tax evasion used by the companies, and the government was naturally eager to have the benefit of the unique combination of legal expertise and special knowledge he possessed. Rowell did not personally argue all the cases, but he conducted a number of appeals to the Exchequer Court in Ottawa himself and gave his advice on others. By mid-1929, judgments for over $4 million had been rendered against some twenty companies, while two major cases were still outstanding and under appeal.[19]

Rowell's success in adding so much to the public treasury was not universally appreciated. During the 1928 session of Parliament, members of the Conservative opposition had enquired about the remuneration Rowell had received for the customs investigation and now for the ensuing litigation. One critic warned the minister of customs against the continued use of Rowell's services, which he contended had already cost the taxpayers more than they were worth. As counsel to the customs investigation Rowell had been paid two hundred dollars a day, twenty dollars a day living allowance, and travel expenses, for a total of over fifty thousand dollars. The minister, W.D. Euler, defended the government and declared that as counsel for the commission and now in the tax cases Rowell was receiving less than he would have in his private practice, and was achieving excellent results for the government and taxpayers of Canada.[20]

Opposition attack did not bother Rowell, but he very much resented the remarks made later by a government supporter, C.G. Power. The member for Quebec South, never any friend of a policy that would make life difficult for brewers and distillers, suggested to the House that the sums paid to Rowell for the prosecution of the companies were out of all proportion to the amount collected, a charge that Euler again firmly rejected.[21] Since Rowell felt he had neglected his private practice to give priority to the commission work and later to the government taxation cases, he thought he deserved better than this kind of public sniping from the government side of the House.[22] But it was not in the government's power to control the utterances of its own backbenchers, especially those of the ebullient Power and a handful of other Laurier Liberals who from time to time felt compelled to fight again the battles of temperance and Union Government.

Since Rowell's good causes were rarely theirs, it is unlikely that such criticism would have been allayed had the critics known that Rowell was giving away at least half his income in these years.[23] Although he continued to live comfortably in his

Rosedale home and liked to entertain visitors well there or at the York Club, he was no more given to 'conspicuous consumption' than he had ever been. As always he was immaculately and conservatively dressed. He owned a car, chauffeur-driven because he had never learned to drive, but that was for convenience rather than for display. One of his great satisfactions in professional success lay in his ability to support generously the causes in which he believed, notably his church, especially its overseas missions, as well as needy individuals and local enterprises such as the Toronto Hospital for Sick Children.

Another major legal case involving Rowell concerned relations with the United States. For decades many Canadians and Americans in the Great Lakes region had dreamed of a deep water seaway that would permit ocean-going vessels to sail two thousand miles inland to the head of Lake Superior. Since the war a variety of American interests had been actively planning to realize this dream, and the American government was pressing Canada for an agreement on the matter. Canada was already engaged in the deepening of the Welland Ship Canal, a work to be completed in 1930. The major obstacles remaining were those presented by the series of rapids on the St Lawrence between Lake Ontario and Montreal. These lay in both Ontario and Quebec, and part of this section lay along the boundary between Canada and the United States where the waterway must be an international undertaking. Increasingly, the engineering problems in building the necessary canals appeared simple compared to the constitutional, financial, and diplomatic complexities involved.

Since coming to power, Mackenzie King had resisted American pressure for negotiations because there was no great support for the seaway from Canadian interests and even some hostility from Quebec, where Montreal feared the challenge to her pre-eminence as a port if ships were able to proceed past the city to the upper lakes. Premiers Ferguson of Ontario and Taschereau of Quebec both claimed provincial jurisdiction over the power resources lying within their provinces, and although Taschereau was in no hurry, the time was foreseen when Ontario would face a power shortage. Another obstacle arose from the differing traditions of power development in the two provinces, with Ontario committed to publicly developed and controlled hydro, and Quebec to private enterprise.

Early in 1928 King decided that he should at least appear to be moving on the seaway issue. He referred to the Supreme Court of Canada the question of the relative responsibilities of the Dominion and the provinces in power development on navigable streams. He also reactivated the National Advisory Committee on the seaway, appointed three years earlier, and asked it to report on the financing of the project. The committee recommended that the United States should finance the whole of the international section, a fair arrangement, it was argued, in view of all that Canada had already spent. The strictly Canadian section, which should be constructed by private corporations in return for the right to develop the water power thereby created, should be developed first. Only when Canadian industries were able to use all this power would the international section be built. These recommendations clearly reflected the priority Canada assigned to power development and flew in the face of the primary American interest in the seaway itself. There was also a minority report from two members of the committee opposed to the participation of private interests in St Lawrence power development. That these two men were connected with the Shawinigan Water and Power Company seems more than coincidental and suggests that their devotion to public ownership was based on something other than principle. A group of Montreal capitalists, the Beauharnois syndicate, was eager to secure the contract for the power development in Quebec, and the power they would then try to sell the city of Montreal might threaten the Shawinigan company.[24]

When it was made public Rowell studied the report carefully. On two important points he found himself in agreement with the authors of the minority report, although from at least partially different motives. He rejected the idea that the United States should construct and pay for the entire navigation and power installations in the international sector. Quoting the minority report to the prime minister, he argued that the sectors should not be separated in this way and Canada should retain a direct interest in the whole system from Lake Superior to Montreal. Although Canada had heavy financial burdens at present, in twenty years' time the saving effected by letting the Americans pay for all of it would appear slight indeed. Money was not the most important consideration: the proposal would 'affront Canadian national sentiment' and was politically inexpedient as well. Rowell was also strongly opposed to the participation of private enterprise in the development of the seaway and its power resources: 'In my view it is a great national undertaking, the increasing advantages of which will become more and more apparent as generation succeeds generation. I believe that national development should be undertaken and absolutely controlled by the Dominion Government.'[25]

It is not clear whether this letter had anything to do with giving the prime minister or the Department of Justice an idea about who might best argue the Dominion's position in the reference of the water power question to the Supreme Court. His professional competence might well have given Rowell the assignment. In any case, he was asked to represent the federal interest in the appeal and appeared before the Supreme Court in the autumn of 1928 against several formidable opponents representing various provinces, among whom were W.N. Tilley for the province of Ontario and Eugene Lafleur for Quebec. The core of Rowell's argument was that under Section 132 of the BNA Act the government of Canada had whatever powers it needed to give effect to its international treaty obligations, such as any that might be entered into for the development of the St Lawrence and its water resources. That power was superior to any property and civil rights vested in the provinces. In addition, Rowell contended that the Dominion's right under the BNA Act to declare works 'for the general advantage of Canada' was unlimited and could be used without restriction. Four months later the Supreme Court gave an indecisive judgment which left all parties uncertain about where they stood.[26] Rowell assumed there would be an appeal to the Judicial Committee of the Privy Council, but instead King decided to try to resolve his problems with Ontario and Quebec by discussions with their premiers. Among other advantages offered by this course was the opportunity it provided for delay and for postponing negotiations with the United States.

In the meantime the Beauharnois interests went ahead with their plans, and the Dominion government announced a public hearing before a committee of the cabinet. Again Rowell protested, this time to the minister of public works, J.C. Elliott. Although recognizing that the Beauharnois proposal was in line with the majority report of the advisory committee, Rowell still believed that to accept it would be 'not only a grave national blunder but also a serious political blunder from the standpoint at least of the Province of Ontario, and I believe, if the matter were fairly presented, from the standpoint of the whole of the Dominion of Canada.' He was not trying to promote the cause of public ownership in Quebec: 'If the Government owns and controls the work it can lease the power to private interests just as it is leasing the power today on the Welland, Soulanges and other canals ... I have no interest in the matter other than my interest in the country and in the Government. I am equally opposed to any other company acquiring rights such as the Beauharnois are asking.'[27]

Seeking to follow up his written protests with a personal interview, Rowell found his request to see King refused, the first time he had been denied access to the prime minister. King's attitude was dictated by his desire to prevent public discussion of the matter as far as possible and to avoid the appearance of responding to the variety of pressures being put upon him.[28] With modifications, the Beauharnois plan was accepted.

On another matter of public policy as well, Rowell's view seemed to be a losing one. Although he believed that the administration of the Customs Department had been improved, it was a great disappointment to him that after almost a year the King government had taken no action on the strong recommendation of the customs commission that Canada should refuse liquor clearances to vessels engaged in smuggling to the United States. As Rowell pointed out to King in a sixteen-page letter, the report had confirmed the recommendation of the earlier parliamentary committee on this point, and in the last election all parties had pledged themselves to act on that report, 'so that whether the Government feels under any obligation to carry out the report of the Royal Commission or not, I should think that the

Government assumed a direct obligation in the last election to carry out the report of the Parliamentary Committee in this respect.' Rowell's impressions of the lawlessness prevalent along the border, he explained, had been reinforced by what he had learned during his conduct of the current taxation cases. There was no doubt in his mind that the former manager of a Windsor dock operated by an Ontario brewery had been murdered at the behest of Canadian liquor exporters who did not want his testimony to be heard in court. 'The actual murderer has not been found and the real persons responsible for the crime can never be convicted. An occurrence like this would have roused the country a few years ago; today it is scarce a nine days' wonder. People shrug their shoulders and say "Oh it is just an incident of the business and we are getting the Americans' money." ' Not all incidences of law breaking were so dramatic, but their effects were serious: 'Canadians are being trained as law breakers and the public is being educated that law breaking is not a crime but is praiseworthy if it is breaking the laws of a neighbouring country rather than your own; you cannot educate the public along this line without having them apply the same principles to their own laws if it suits their purpose or they make money thereby.'

The international implications of continued granting of liquor clearances seemed especially crucial to Rowell since Canada's behaviour was the subject of considerable and, he thought, justified hostility among many Americans. While it was true that 'we may be literally conforming to the terms of the Treaty ... we are not trying to stop smuggling at all.' In practice, Canadian policy amounted to the provision of special facilities to enable acknowledged smugglers to carry on their business. Rowell was aware that King was faced by political considerations in handling this question, but, he told the prime minister, that was no excuse for 'failure to do that which appears to be right and in the national interests.' In any case the political considerations did not operate in one direction only; thousands of Canadians wanted the clearances ended: 'If the Government should fail to deal with the situation before the next election I am sure you will face political difficulties growing out of such a failure.'[29]

Six months later, when it seemed that the question of liquor clearances was about to come before Parliament, Rowell wrote to King again at length, this time dealing mainly with a newly discovered legal aspect of the issue. The Department of National Revenue had taken the position that under existing law it had no power to refuse clearances, a view Rowell had assumed until recently to be correct. Now, after studying the problem, he had concluded that this position was quite wrong and no new legislation would be necessary. Indeed, he now believed that in failing to abolish clearances the government was violating international law. Supporting his argument with citations from recent court decisions in both Britain and the United States, Rowell declared his strong conviction that Canada was in an unacceptable legal position: 'It is a well-settled principle of private international law, recognized by the courts of civilized countries, that a contract the performance of which involves the violation of the laws of a friendly foreign country is illegal. On this general rule there has been ingrafted an exception that a country is not bound to take cognizance of the revenue laws of a foreign country.' Many Canadians seemed to view the selling of liquor to be smuggled into the United States as being legal on the grounds that only a revenue law was being violated. In believing this, Rowell contended, they overlooked the fact that 'the law in question is not a revenue law of the United States, it is part of the fundamental law of the country, embodied in the Constitution and the National Prohibition Act, which is an Act to enforce the Constitutional Amendment. It is therefore in no sense a revenue law, and, in my opinion, does not come within the exception.'[30]

In theory, King was just as opposed to the liquor clearances as Rowell, but he was in office and subject to the political pressures Rowell had recognized. King transmitted Rowell's views to the cabinet, where Euler took the position that a refusal of clearances would lead to 'rum-running from all parts of the international boundary' and a situation even less amenable to control than the present one. Further, there was still in Canada a widely held belief that the Americans were lax in enforcing their own laws and a strong reluctance to do it for them. The Canadian government, King explained, had recently proposed that American authorities be permitted to have their own anti-smuggling officers on Canadian docks with the right to be advised of all clearances given, but the United States government had rejected this and was holding out for the abolition of clearances.[31]

Rowell was not in the least impressed with King's reaction. He had no doubt that the Americans could do more to enforce their own laws, but that was no excuse for Canadian complicity. From his detailed knowledge of how the smugglers operated, he was not surprised that the Americans had rejected the remedy recently proposed by Canada, since he believed it would be altogether ineffective. He completely dismissed Euler's contention that there was a degree of control under current conditions: 'The present system does not control smuggling; it facilitates it and dignifies it as legitimate because the Government participates in it.'[32] A week later a statement from Euler in the House did little more than put the onus on the Americans to enforce prohibition. While King again expressed his gratitude for the support Rowell had given him,[33] the possibilities that any decisive action would be taken seemed remote. The unfinished business remaining from the customs' investigation was still substantial.

But within two months King had done an about-face and was launched on a crusade against liquor clearances to which he expressed such commitment as to vow to leave office if it failed. Criticism such as Rowell's may have had some effect, but the main reason for the switch was not that King had been at last overwhelmed by the moral force of the arguments against clearances. Rather, he had suddenly decided that it would be expedient to try to win American gratitude, which might assist him in bargaining with the United States over threatened increases in the American tariff and, to a lesser extent, over the seaway. Once determined on this course, King mustered the considerable energy necessary to convince his cabinet and caucus, and legislation prohibiting clearances was passed in the spring of 1930.[34] With the ending of prohibition in the United States the following year the whole problem disappeared.

Rowell's growing eminence in his profession was recognized in his election as vice-president for Ontario of the Canadian Bar Association at its annual meeting in Regina early in September 1928. From that gathering he went to Winnipeg, where the fifty-four delegates to a conference of the Empire Parliamentary Association were spending a few days in the course of their tour across Canada. Staying in the Fort Garry Hotel with the visitors Rowell thoroughly enjoyed his many opportunities to renew acquaintances with parliamentarians from all the countries of the Commonwealth he had visited, and to meet new ones.[35] He remained in Winnipeg for the meetings of the third General Council of the United Church of Canada where his principal task was to present the report of a special committee he had chaired during the past year on 'Peace and War.' While the document was the work of many hands its spirit was identical with that of Rowell's pronouncements from numerous public platforms during the preceding decade. Declaring the fundamental mission of the church to be a crusade for peace, the council wholeheartedly endorsed the report and called on United church members to do all in their power to create an informed and Christian opinion on international issues and to support all efforts to eliminate the causes of war. The report noted with satisfaction that a General Council commission on cadet training in schools found that 'the evidence accumulated should allay the fear that the Cadet Corps as at present organized, foster militarism in Canadian youth.'[36]

Shortly after his return from the west the Board of Regents of Victoria University, on which Rowell had served now for twenty-seven years, elected him its chairman, the first layman to occupy the position. He assumed the chairmanship at an important stage in the life of the university. Recent expansion in the enrolment in arts at Victoria had put a strain on facilities in both arts and theology. For a time it was anticipated that the situation would be relieved when the United church acquired Knox College, the Presbyterian theological college, but in the settlement after church union the Ontario Legislature had awarded not only the college building but also the Knox charter and two-thirds of the endowment to the continuing Presbyterians. Thus, in 1928, the Victoria Board of Regents embarked on a campaign under the chairmanship of the Toronto textile manufacturer, Sir James

Woods, to raise funds for the building of new college residences and a theological college, Emmanuel, which opened in the autumn of 1931.[37]

Rowell was also deeply involved in another money-raising campaign at this time. During the winter of 1928 fire destroyed Metropolitan Church. The Gothic style building, erected in 1872, was demolished, leaving only the foundations and the massive tower with its carillon, installed six years earlier. The fire raised in acute form a question which the congregation of Metropolitan was already facing: What place, if any, did their church have in a changing downtown Toronto, where office buildings rose all around and the once prosperous residential area east of the church, now in decline, was suffering from the social problems common to the centres of big cities? Was it worthwhile to rebuild at all? With the northward expansion of the city, many former members of Metropolitan had already joined other congregations, notably Eaton Memorial on St Clair Avenue. Others left after the fire. Rowell and W.G. Watson, general manager of the Toronto General Trusts, were among the handful of men of substantial means who remained, and they were primarily responsible for the rebuilding on the old site.[38] The church was fully restored, with the addition of the chancel-style sanctuary then coming into vogue in the United church in a movement which critics decried as liturgical social-climbing, imitative of Anglicanism, a charge that did not trouble Rowell's ecumenical spirit. The decision to rebuild and the later addition of a centre for religious education and social work gave the church in the ensuing decades a continuing role in the centre of the city.

The five Alberta Women decided to carry the question whether women were 'persons' in the meaning of the BNA act to the Judicial Committee of the Privy Council. That they had lost their case in the Supreme Court they were sure was no fault of their counsel, and they remained convinced that no other lawyer in Canada was so well qualified to represent them again.[39] Early in the summer of 1929, therefore, Rowell went to England with his daughter Mary, who was secretary of the Student Christian Movement at the University of Toronto and was to spend the summer at student conferences in Britain and on the continent.

Just before their arrival in England, Ramsay MacDonald's second Labour government had come into office. As a consequence, the membership of the Judicial Committee of the Privy Council had changed, and there was speculation about what difference this might make to the character of the committee's judgments. Ever since the war the Judicial Committee had interpreted the BNA Act in a rigid fashion and on principles that had tended to enhance the powers of the provinces at the expense of the Dominion. Many observers believed the new members of the court were likely to take a broader approach that recognized the force of changing social patterns. If this proved to be true, Rowell's chances of winning his case were good.

One immediate consequence of the reorganization of the Judicial Committee, however, was a series of annoying postponements of Rowell's appeal. Thus he had more time than he had anticipated for discussions with members of the Royal Institute of International Affairs, notably Lord Hailsham and Lionel Curtis, on British and Canadian participation in the meetings of the Institute of Pacific Relations in Japan in the coming autumn.[40] He enjoyed his meetings with many old friends in politics and journalism. A frequent subject of discussion was the prospect for the new Labour government. A long talk on religion and politics with Arthur Henderson and his wife provided some interesting sidelights on the social aspects of labour's rise to power:

> Mrs Henderson as the wife of the Foreign Secy. had to make the presentations of the wives and daughters of the diplomats at the Court this year. She told me it was her first appearance herself as she had not been to Court before and naturally she was very nervous but it passed off all right and she thought she would not mind it in the future. How practical these English people are. The quiet little wife of a Labour member and Wesleyan local preacher ... playing a leading role in this most brilliant Court in Europe.[41]

There was also time for several visits to the theatre. With Mary he went to see *By Candle Light*, a highly popular but ephemeral feature of the London theatre season. 'It was brilliant but ultra modern. I said to Mary I did not wish any more ... sex and suggestive beyond words. And it is all the rage. Is considered very free and has been running longer than any other play. I am afraid I am not very up to date in my tastes, but I don't want to be, if this kind of play is up to date, though I imagine this much better than many.' On the other hand, that very day he had been glad to have been caught in the traffic jam created by the funeral of the founder of the Salvation Army, General William Booth. 'It was one of the most impressive sights I have seen in years. Just think all traffic stopped and the streets kept clear for nearly an hour in the very heart of London for the funeral of a Christian leader ... It shows London is essentially good at heart.'[42] He was deeply moved too by the service of thanksgiving he and Mary attended in Westminster Abbey for the recovery of the health of King George v after his recent serious illness, and as usual 'dearest Nell' was sent a full account of the political and diplomatic celebrities present.[43]

At Oxford for a day he was the guest of Philip Kerr, secretary of the Rhodes Trust, for the opening of Rhodes House and later attended a reception given by Lady Astor at Cliveden. 'Lady Astor certainly knows how to do things. The lion of the occasion was George Bernard Shaw. Wasn't it an idea to get him out for the Rhodes scholars. Wherever he went he was followed by a group who wanted to talk with him or rather to hear him talk.'[44]

The next day he spent in Cambridge with Professor J. Holland Rose, editor-in-chief of the *Cambridge History of the British Empire*, who expressed satisfaction with the chapter Rowell had just written on Canadian constitutional development for the volume of the history devoted to Canada, which was soon to be published. In contrast with the young people who appeared to dominate the scene in Oxford, the numerous Cambridge dons he met seemed aged. Nor did he see in Cambridge 'many good looking or attractive women & you know' he told Nell 'how they add to the beauty of the landscape. They must have made up in brains what they lacked in beauty.'[45]

Interesting also, although unsuccessful in its purpose, was his journey to Leeds to invite Rev. Leslie Weatherhead, one of Britain's leading Congregationalists, to come to Toronto for the opening services of the rebuilt Metropolitan Church. Weatherhead was already well advanced in the career of preaching and writing that made him for thirty years the idol of liberal Protestants throughout the English-speaking world. He declined the invitation to Toronto, but Rowell went back to London well pleased with a gift copy of Weatherhead's recently published book, *Psychology in the Service of the Soul*.[46]

During the weeks following his return to Toronto, Rowell was busy with preparations for the Kyoto conference of the IPR. As chairman of the Canadian delegation he was anxious that Canada should send a strong and representative group to Japan. He was well satisfied with the delegation of twenty-nine, plus staff and wives to the number of forty-three, who made the trip. In order to fulfil their long-standing desire to visit China, Rowell and Nell set out ahead of the rest of the Canadians and sailed from Vancouver in mid-September on the *President Cleveland*. They were accompanied by the secretary of the Canadian delegation, Alan Plaunt, a recent graduate of Toronto and Oxford for whom they both soon acquired a lasting affection. Reaching Yokohama after a far from pacific crossing they travelled across Japan via rail and proceeded to Shanghai.

It was an even more than usually interesting time to be in China. Shanghai, through which half of China's foreign trade passed, was in the process of adjusting to the new order inaugurated by the coming into effect six months earlier of the treaties giving China control at last of her own customs. Much of Rowell's two days in Shanghai was spent discussing the consequences of this development with businessmen, both Chinese and foreign, while Nell was shown the extensive work of the YWCA among Shanghai's youth and women industrial workers and met with several Canadian missionaries.[47] Even had time permitted, it would have been difficult to visit the West China Mission of the United church in Szechwan; for although the country was quieter than in earlier years, much of it was still threatened by civil war. To his regret Rowell was forced to remain an entirely 'absentee' member of the Board of Governors of West China Union University.

Arriving in Nanking, the capital of whatever central government China could be said to possess, on 10 October, the eighteenth anniversary of the founding of the Chinese Republic, they found the city in holiday mood and were immediately involved in a government reception for local dignitaries and foreign diplomats. Thus they were presented to General Chiang Kai-shek, who had assumed the leadership of the Nationalist government of China two years earlier, and to Madame Chiang and several other members of the government.[48] The next day there were visits to Ginling Christian College for Women and the University of Nanking, followed by a luncheon in their honour given by the British consul general in Nanking where the guests were other foreign consuls and some Chinese civil servants. In an interview with China's minister of finance, T.V. Soong, Rowell heard of the government's problems at first hand and was assured by Soong that in another ten years no nation would impose on China as foreign powers had done in the past.[49]

Pleasantly surprised by the comfort of the train journey from Nanking to Peking, they made the most of their journey to observe rural life. In Peking the Summer Palace, the Forbidden City, and other standard attractions were everything they had expected, although the city generally seemed no more prosperous than Nanking, and it was hard to think of either city as the past or present capital of a great nation.[50] Since Manchuria was the trouble spot of the Far East at the moment Rowell wanted to see something of it, and they therefore spent three days in Mukden, long enough to get the feeling of the international rivalries that made the future of the area so contentious and uncertain. While Nell visited another very active YWCA staffed by Britons, Rowell lunched with Wellington Koo, a former foreign minister in the national government who had recently been arrested by Chiang Kai-shek and was in Mukden to avoid being taken captive. There he also met the Australian journalist W.H. Donald, later known as 'Donald of China,' whose devotion to Chinese unity gave him an important place in Chinese affairs in the following decade.[51] Altogether, Rowell's brief visit to China dramatically enlarged his appreciation of the enormous undertaking on which the Chinese had embarked in their attempt to unify and modernize their country.

Returning to Japan they found a cable from Toronto announcing that the Judicial Committee of the Privy Council had decided that women were 'persons' and might therefore be appointed to the Senate. In celebration they allowed themselves the luxury of hiring a private car to drive from Tokyo to Nara for meetings of the executive committee of the IPR.[52] Later, at the conference itself in Kyoto, more than two hundred delegates focused their discussion on the impact of industrialization on the countries of the Pacific area. Speaking for the Canadian group in a series of opening addresses by the chairmen of the various delegations, Rowell noted the recent exchange of ministers by Canada and Japan and spoke warmly of China's aspirations and her growing independence. Discussing Canada's role in the world, he pointed out that her recent adherence to the Kellogg-Briand Pact denouncing war was Canada's first international act under the new autonomy agreed on by the Imperial Conference of 1926. Pursuing a theme long favoured by Canadian speakers, he cited the long peace between Canada and the United States across their common four thousand miles of unguarded frontier as a demonstration of the efficacy of disarmament. Later, he chaired the successive sessions of the round table on China's foreign relations when the main topics were extraterritoriality and Manchuria. During the conference Rowell was elected second vice-chairman of the IPR. The new president was Jerome D. Greene of the United States, with Dr Inazo Nitobe, chairman of the conference and president of the Japanese Council of the IPR, as first vice-chairman.[53]

The presence in both the Chinese and Japanese delegations of several men prominent in the government and business life of their countries meant that current tensions, notably over Manchuria, were discussed at Kyoto with some hope that any understanding reached might affect official policy. By the end of the meetings many personal friendships had developed between Chinese and Japanese who had earlier been cool toward one another. To many of them, and to Rowell and other observers, this seemed the most important achievement of the conference and one that made the whole gathering worthwhile even if nothing else resulted.[54]

After the conference followed another ten days in Tokyo in a round of receptions, garden parties, and dinners given by Japanese members and friends of the IPR, and an audience with the emperor, with whom they exchanged a few words on good relations between Canada and Japan.[55] Then came sightseeing and shopping, visits to several missionary schools and churches and the YWCA, and a dinner for all the United church missionaries in the area when Rowell spoke on the Kyoto conference.[56]

A cold but calm and bright crossing on the CPR's *Empress of Canada* brought them back to Vancouver, and they reached Toronto in good time for Christmas. At home, family interest was centred on Mary's forthcoming marriage in the spring to Henry Jackman, a Toronto lawyer whose strong Conservative affiliations seemed to present no barrier to his acceptance into the Rowell family.

During the weeks following his return from Kyoto Rowell gave several addresses in centres from Vancouver to Montreal on problems of the Far East. One of the more important was delivered before the Empire Club in Toronto on 'China and the Foreign Powers.' Partly historical and partly an account of the current form of government under the Kuomintang party, it presented a sympathetic interpretation of China's success in gaining control of her own tariffs and of her demands for an end to the 'unequal treaties' that conferred extraterritorial rights on foreigners and had allowed the growth of foreign concessions in Shanghai and elsewhere. Referring to the limitations of Chiang Kai-shek's Nationalist government, Rowell observed that the regime had come to power and was maintained there by military force and did many things that western democrats could not approve. But it was a government unique in the modern history of China since it had at least the nominal allegiance of the vast majority of the Chinese people; it should be supported as the only force in sight with any hope of leading China to the realization of her aspirations for independence and social reform.[57]

By the time of his return from the Orient, Rowell had been away from his law practice for almost six months, and there was no dearth of work awaiting him. He had agreed to act for the Consolidated Mining and Smelting Company of Trail, British Columbia, before the International Joint Commission and went to Washington early in 1930 for the hearings. In requesting the reference to the international body, the American government had asked for an examination of the damage done to vegetation and property in the State of Washington by fumes from the company's smelter at Trail and compensation for the destruction. It was impossible to make a good case for the company. The commission recommended that it pay $350,000 in compensation and made proposals that later led to the signing of a convention by Canada and the United States on the arbitration of subsequent claims. At the same time the Trail company began to improve its methods of disposing of waste gases.[58]

In the spring of 1930 he was at work preparing for as important a case as any he had ever argued before the Judicial Committee of the Privy Council. The Proprietary Articles Trade Association of Canada had been found to be violating the Combines Investigation Act and had challenged the constitutionality of the Act in the courts. Rowell had defended the measure for the federal government before the Supreme Court of Canada, and its validity had been upheld in a judgment that appeared to fly in the face of the 1922 decisions of the Judicial Committee of the Privy Council throwing out post-war legislation to regulate commerce and prices. The association was now carrying its appeal to the Judicial Committee supported by the provinces of Ontario and Quebec. If the Judicial Committee followed the main precedents of the twenties, the Supreme Court's judgment would likely be reversed. But there was one indication that the trend in the Judicial Committee's thinking might be changing and Rowell's chances of winning the case were good. In rendering judgment in 'the persons case' the new lord chancellor, Lord Sankey, had observed that 'the British North America Act planted in Canada a living tree capable of growth and expansion within its natural limits. The object of the Act was to grant a constitution to Canada.'[59] Although the applicability of this approach to constitutional interpretation was not obvious in the case in hand, it was different in spirit and direction from the main trend of the twenties and thus seemed to enhance the possibility of successfully defending the Combines Investigation Act.

Once more Rowell's antagonist was W.N. Tilley, and their five days in court was a 'classic' Tilley-Rowell encounter. As usual, Tilley seized on the two or three points he believed to be the weakest in his opponent's position and hammered them home. In this instance he made a great deal of the incompatibility between the Supreme Court's view of the Combines Investigation Act and the Judicial Committee's decisions of 1922. For his part, Rowell took a broader sweep, reviewing every aspect of the matter. While seeking to demonstrate that the Act had none of the provisions that had brought negative judgments against the post-war combines legislation, he also advanced a strong general argument for the authority of the federal government under the BNA Act to regulate all trade in Canada, except within one province. Rowell's argument illustrated well the thoroughness and breadth that made junior lawyers covet the chance to 'devil' for him. They soon learned there was little point in reporting to Rowell that they could find no earlier reference to a particular subject on which he had put them to work. He would always send them back to the law books with the assertion: 'There must be cases. There must be cases.'

In a judgment that noted the great importance of the case and the 'full and able argument' placed before them, their lordships upheld the earlier ruling of the Canadian Supreme Court.[60] It was a notable achievement for Rowell and one with implications which were highly satisfying; the verdict reaffirmed the power of the federal government in a manner that Rowell and many others believed to be in accord both with the intentions of the Fathers of Confederation and with the social and economic welfare of contemporary Canadians. Two years after this decision Rowell felt confident that the Judicial Committee of the Privy Council was on the right track permanently. Its decision in overturning a judgment of the Supreme Court and giving jurisdiction over aviation in Canada to the Dominion rather than to the provinces he believed marked 'definitely the "escape" of the Judicial Committee from the delusion that the determining provision in the BNA Act is that conferring control of property and civil rights upon the Provinces.'[61]

Within three months there was yet another proof that federal power was in the ascendancy when the Judicial Committee determined that control of radio communication belonged to the Dominion. Rowell was not associated with this case as a lawyer, but he had a personal and concerned interest in it. He had encouraged Alan Plaunt in organizing, with Graham Spry and others, the Canadian Radio League, whose object was to arouse public opinion in support of the establishment of a system of public broadcasting in Canada. Rowell worked with Plaunt in setting up the executive council and financing the organization and agreed to serve on the council and to contribute to its modest resources.[62] The League supported the Dominion government in its claim for jurisdiction over radio and participated in the appeal to the Judicial Committee. Failure in the case would have ended plans for a national public broadcasting system. After a favourable decision from the Judicial

Committee, the Radio League proved itself one of the most effective pressure groups in Canadian history and was the major force in directing Canadian national sentiment to the support of public broadcasting and the establishment of the Canadian Broadcasting Corporation.[63] In its early years Rowell followed the development of the CBC with close interest, convinced that it had an essential educational and unifying role to play in Canadian society.

26
A darkening world

In common with nearly all observers of 'the great crash' Rowell believed that the depression inaugurated by the world-wide financial collapse of October 1929 would be short-lived. Like most Liberals he failed to recognize that the depression had very quickly made an impact on the thinking of Canadian voters. Thus, he fully expected that Mackenzie King would be returned to office in the general election of 28 July 1930. Rowell made only one public statement during the campaign. He spoke in Sarnia in support of Ross Gray, the Liberal candidate in West Lambton. In a speech that received little publicity outside the constituency, perhaps because the campaign was almost over, Rowell emphasized, as all Liberal campaigners were doing, the economic and political merits of the recent Dunning budget, with its measures for diverting some of Canada's trade from the United States to Great Britain.[1] But, as Conservative leader R.B. Bennett had forced the Liberals to admit during the campaign, Canadians were also interested in the financing of unemployment relief, the effect of the importation of New Zealand butter on Canadian farmers, and Bennett's own dramatic promises to increase Canadian trade by using the tariff to 'blast' his way into the markets of the world. Bennett's answer to King's appeal to imperial sentiment was economic nationalism and the slogan 'Canada first, then the Empire.' Bennett's energy and enthusiasm won their way among an electorate increasingly apprehensive about the future, and the Conservatives triumphed with a comfortable majority, including twenty-five members from Quebec.

Rowell assured the defeated prime minister that 'the Government has gone down fighting for a great cause. Your Government made a very fine record during the past four years but trade and agricultural depression, unemployment and New Zealand butter apparently made a stronger appeal. You will lead a strong and homogeneous opposition in the House.'[2] Among other consequences of the Liberal defeat was that Rowell would no longer be asked to fulfil the enjoyable task of arguing cases on behalf of the Dominion government before the Judicial Committee of the Privy Council.

In the meantime he still had unfinished business before the highest court of appeal in the Commonwealth. At the end of 1930, with two other Toronto lawyers to assist him, Ivan Rand and Gordon Lindsay, he spent over a month in London, acting on behalf of the crown, first against the CPR, and then against the Carling Brewing and Malting Company, both represented by W.N. Tilley. The CPR was charged with trespassing on crown property by erecting telegraph poles along five hundred miles of the roadway of the Intercolonial Railway, part of the government-owned CNR in the Maritime provinces. The Supreme Court of Canada had in part dismissed the CPR's appeal and in part allowed the crown's case. From the outset it was a complicated case requiring many hours of work and five days of court hearings. On the third day Rowell observed that 'Tilley has succeeded in confusing the court on some points of importance and is still at it ... The difficulty is that Lord Dunedin who is presiding is disposed to think that he knows all that is necessary and will be impatient to get on.'[3] The Carling case, which had been before the courts ever since early in 1927, was even more difficult. At issue was $425,000 in taxes allegedly evaded by the company which the Supreme Court of Canada had ordered paid to the Canadian government. Rowell's endeavour to convince the Judicial Committee that this award should be confirmed was 'a very hard uphill fight ... and I do not know what will happen but I am going to get the facts before the Court in some form even if I have to fight every inch of the way.'[4]

Rowell's work in London overlapped the first Round Table conference on the granting of Dominion status to India. Although members of Gandhi's Congress party were notable by their absence, since they had chosen to boycott the meetings, a number of Indian princes and many Indian civil servants were present. At meetings of the Royal Institute at Chatham House and at several receptions for the conference delegates Rowell participated in discussions of the Indian question, finding it easy to sympathize with the desire of the Indians 'to be master in their house ... within the Commonwealth if that is possible. If not then outside, but masters.'[5] Also much discussed among the members of Chatham House were their plans for participation in the IPR conference in China in 1931, and Rowell spent a fascinating evening talking about China with Lionel Curtis and C. Mostyn Lloyd of the *New Statesman*. His old Quaker friends, Wilson Harris, secretary of the League of Nations Union, and Philip Noel-Baker, Labour member of Parliament, and his wife were the well informed and stimulating conversationalists he had always found them.[6] So too were Lady Astor and Philip Kerr, who had recently become Lord

Lothian. A quiet dinner with them ended when Lady Astor gave Rowell 'the opportunity of going to the theatre or going with her and Philip to the Christian Science prayer meeting. I chose the latter. I should think there were 700 or 800 present. Most interesting.' At a small dinner he met for the first time Professor Harold Laski of the London School of Economics who later displayed his brilliance in a lecture and discussion at Chatham House on communism as a world force.[7] London was still the Mecca of good talk.

By far the best of the several plays he attended was a performance of *Anthony and Cleopatra* at the Old Vic with a young actor, John Gielgud, as Antony: 'It was magnificent. There was not a dull or uninteresting moment in the more than 3 hours play.' The *Times* theatre critic, Rowell reported to Nell, had found 'that both Antony and Cleopatra were too coldly intellectual. There was nothing of the lustful gypsy in Cleopatra and a lack of ardour in Antony – This is probably why I liked it so much.'[8]

The two cases that had taken him to London were disposed of more quickly than he had come to expect of the Judicial Committee, the decisions being given only six weeks after his return to Canada. Among his most difficult cases, they were not his most successful. An extremely complex judgment in the CPR case reversed the decision of the Supreme Court of Canada and was generally favourable to the company.[9] More disappointing was the decision allowing the Carling appeal on 83 per cent of the amount claimed in taxes by the government and on part of the rest.[10] The Canadian treasury would unfortunately gain little by the decision.

As the depression deepened, the Liberal party had reason to be grateful that it was out of office. At the same time it had to plan for the future. The party agreed that a major factor in the defeat of 1930 was inadequate party organization across the country. Early in 1931, steps were taken to reorganize and to find new and steady sources of income. Mackenzie King invited Rowell to become one of a new group of financial supporters who would contribute one thousand dollars a year for a minimum of two years.[11] Rowell declined, claiming that he was not in 'that class of financial and business men' but adding that he might contribute something at a later date.[12]

Within a few months, party finance was front page news. Allegations were made in the House of Commons that profits of more than one hundred million dollars had been realized by the promoters of the Beauharnois project even before the canal was built; a Commons committee was appointed to investigate. The committee's report confirmed that exorbitant profits had indeed been made by the promoters of the enterprise. But that was not all. Two prominent Liberal senators, one of them a personal friend of Mackenzie King, the other a key figure in the party organization, were shown to have profited substantially from the Beauharnois project under circumstances implying they had been paid for their influence in the Liberal party. Senator W.L. McDougald, a member of the Montreal Harbour Commission and the National Advisory Committee on the St Lawrence Seaway, had been appointed to both these positions by the King government. In 1928 the Beauharnois syndicate had bought a worthless company that McDougald had incorporated four years earlier. It seemed such generosity could only be motivated by a desire to secure McDougald's influence in Ottawa on behalf of the Beauharnois application for a diversion of St Lawrence water. Subsequently, in 1929, McDougald became chairman of the Beauharnois Corporation. The second Liberal beneficiary of Beauharnois munificence was the law firm of Senator Andrew Haydon, which had been paid an annual retainer for legal services and a lump sum of fifty thousand dollars contingent on the passing of the order-in-council of 1929 permitting Beauharnois to divert water from the St Lawrence. Further, one of the leading promoters of Beauharnois, R.O. Sweezey, admitted to having contributed up to $700,000 to Liberal party funds in the election of 1930.[13]

While holidaying at Hammill's Point in Muskoka Rowell read the newspaper reports of the revelations made to the Commons committee. He was 'shocked at the large profits made by Senators closely associated with the Government and by the magnitude of the contributions to the Liberal party funds.' Rowell hastened to express to the Liberal leader his confidence that King knew nothing of this kind of fund raising and urged him to declare so, forcefully and publicly at the earliest possible moment, and to demand that the investigation be pursued until all the evidence was uncovered.[14]

Rowell put his views more strongly and at length to John Dafoe because, he explained, 'I feel so hot and indignant over the whole matter that I must speak or write to someone.' If King failed to dissociate himself entirely from the transactions revealed by the parliamentary committee 'he will deserve to forfeit the confidence of decent Liberals throughout Canada.' So great were the sums of money involved that 'compared to this the Pacific scandal and the Tea Pot Dome must pass into the shade.' Rowell was not satisfied that the examinations of witnesses had been 'as thorough and searching as they might have been' and supported the proposal of the Progressives in the Commons that a royal commission should be appointed to continue the investigation. In addition, he believed that the government should assure bona fide investors that their interests would be safeguarded, while cancelling the Beauharnois permit for water diversion and excluding the present promoters from any further participation in the enterprise. The Dominion government should complete its negotiations with the United States on the seaway and then proceed 'to build its own navigation works and develop the power incidental thereto.' He was not hopeful, however, that the government would have the courage to seize 'the chance to get this great national undertaking back into the hands of the people.' Failing that, Ottawa must at least exclude those guilty of graft from any connection with the development and ensure that 'all who have brought themselves within the range of the Criminal Law should be promptly and vigorously prosecuted. We think and we sometimes boast that we are better than our neighbours to the South in public and political morality. This case will be the test. In the Tea Pot Dome the US Government took steps to procure the cancellation of the oil leases and succeeded. They prosecuted and secured the conviction of the principal actors in the drama. Have we the courage to do the same?'[15]

King's statement to the House of Commons did not go far enough to satisfy Rowell. Declaring that he and his party were in 'the valley of humiliation' because 'individual members of the Liberal party may have done what they should not have done,' King disclaimed any knowledge of party finances and maintained that therefore he had not been corrupted.[16] In a personal letter to Rowell, King reaffirmed his innocence of financial matters; indeed, he had never written any financial appeals of any kind until recently, when he had sent out a number similar to the one Rowell had received a few months earlier.[17]

Rowell agreed that a party leader should not assume responsibility for either finance or organization. He had taken that position himself as leader of the Ontario Liberals, but he had also 'expressly stipulated to those responsible for raising funds that no contribution should be received, even if offered, from Mackenzie & Mann, or any others of similar position who were known to be seeking favours of Governments.' Although a leader must do his best for the party, 'if the support necessary to carry on a general election campaign is not forthcoming from legitimate channels, he should not seek it from illegitimate channels. It is not necessary that the party should win an election, but it is necessary, for the sake of the party and the Country, that it should maintain its standards of honour.' Rowell did not believe that King himself had sought support from 'illegitimate channels.' What bothered him was that King had not 'unreservedly condemned' the conduct of Senator McDougald, nor had he made 'clear and definite' his attitude on the party's acceptance of the huge contributions from Beauharnois. 'I quite agree with the statement you made in the house' he told King 'that the conduct of these senators as such is a matter for the Senate to deal with, but their conduct as members of the Liberal party comes under your jurisdiction as party leader.' Recognizing King's long and close association with both McDougald and Haydon, Rowell did not underestimate the difficulty facing King, 'but ... there are times when the honour of the Country and of the party compel the leader to put aside any personal feelings, and deal with such matters from the national point of view.' While it would have been better if King had taken this action when he made his first statement to the House, Rowell urged, it would still be worth something if he were to do it soon. Finally, Rowell regretted that the investigation had been terminated: 'the closing of the investigation has left a bad impression in the minds of the people. They feel that it was closed by some understanding between the parties which was not in the public interest.' Altogether, the sorry tale of Beauharnois confirmed the views he had earlier advocated for public development of the St Lawrence for both navigation and power. All he could do now was to assure King 'how deeply, as a friend, I sympathize with you in the present situation, and how glad I should be if I could be of any assistance.'[18]

In acknowledging Rowell's letter King made no promises regarding any future statements he might make but, stressing the importance of securing support from within the party, again invited a contribution.[19] Rowell forwarded his cheque for $250 to the party.[20] It was scarcely an overwhelming gesture of confidence.

The Beauharnois affair concluded, in Rowell's perspective, with few positive results. McDougald and Sweezey were ousted from the board of Beauharnois, and the company was reorganized. In the aftermath of the scandal the company found it impossible to borrow money and survived only by becoming a subsidiary of Sir Herbert Holt's Montreal power monopoly. Although King discussed the scandal before a gathering of London Liberals in the autumn of 1931, he went no further than before in denouncing the acceptance of campaign funds from large corporations. King initiated the establishment of a central party organization, not because it would change the sources of party funds, but partly because it would serve to make clear that the party leader had no direct responsibility for finances.[21] Neither the Liberal opposition nor the government proposed any new legislation regulating campaign contributions.

Although the Beauharnois affair did nothing to alter the habits of financiers or politicians, it reinforced views on electoral reform Rowell had held for many years. During the fourth annual meeting of the Canadian Political Science Association, Rowell, who was a member of the executive council of that organization, took an active part in a discussion of the party system initiated by a paper read by Professor F.H. Underhill of the University of Toronto at a session presided over by John W. Dafoe. Underhill, who was then engaged in plans for the founding of the CCF, contended that 'the fundamental defect of the two-party system ... is that it does not provide an effective means by which economic interests other than those of organized business can exercise a reasonable influence on the determination of national policy.' What was needed was a loosening of the control of the rigid party machinery of the two old parties and the growth of 'the independent groups who are the only truly democratic elements in our House of Commons since they are financed by their own voting supporters, and who are the only elements in the House that can give effective voice to those sections of the nation whose bargaining power has been largely nullified in the caucuses of the two old parties.' Unless it could be demonstrated that they could organize social and economic life adequately, parliamentary systems of government would not survive.[22]

Although there was much in Underhill's paper with which Rowell could agree, he believed that the party system was less rigid and permitted more co-operation in practice among the holders of variant views than was often realized. Moreover, he could see 'no hope of the early emergence of a nationwide party to give effective challenge to the two major political parties of our day.' Consequently the only practical course was to improve the existing system. The first step must be a more informed and sustained interest in politics on the part of increasing numbers of citizens. Beyond that, he favoured three reforms: compulsory voting to reduce the pressure for vast campaign funds and educate the voters in their civic duty, the publication of campaign contributions before election day, and the prohibition of contributions from corporations, since 'the average corporation does so because it believes it will receive corresponding favors.' Was there a hint in his concluding remarks that he really expected little change in the old parties? 'I have every sympathy with groups – radical if you like – organized for the propagation of ideas. I think they are all to the good for the body politic. Some forty years ago, I recall, we had most active Young Liberal and Conservative organizations. I remember too, that we were betimes considered quite radical. I think it rather a pity that we have not more counterparts of these inquiring and curious organizations to-day. Old men are expedient. The young men are right in their views of starting up new thought on these matters.'[23]

Not until early in 1931 did Rowell pay much attention publicly to the continuing depression. By then it was clear that the world-wide economic slump was not a passing phenomenon. Even so, Rowell was able to report to the annual meeting of the shareholders of the Toronto General Trusts that 1930 had been the most successful year in the company's nearly fifty-year history. Although he saw cause for concern in the partial crop failure on the prairies and the low price of wheat on world markets, no one need despair over the future of western Canada, whose resources and people were as sound as ever. He believed, and continued to believe as the depression persisted, that Canada had suffered less than almost any other country in the world and would recover more quickly. Among the causes of the depression he put first the war debts and reparations dictated by the Versailles Treaty, followed by the accumulation of the world's monetary and gold supply in Britain and the United States, overproduction of the world's principal commodities, and trade barriers erected by misguided devotees of economic nationalism.[24]

In Canada the effects of depression might, he thought, be beneficial to at least one institution – the church. To a gathering of United church laymen in Toronto Rowell declared that in the present period of depression people had a chance to consider 'the real things of life' in contrast to materialistic values. Each individual must consider with his Maker how best to build up his spiritual life and only on that basis would Christianity be effective. But he was not arguing simply for private piety; the church had an undoubted responsibility to manifest unity and brotherly love in the community. While disclaiming any desire to laud communism he asserted that the progress of communism in the world was due to the fact that it was helping the workingman. In Russia, communism was 'the expression of helping one another that in the Christian Church found expression through brotherly love.'[25]

Since the causes of the depression were international, so were the remedies – lower tariffs, reduction or cancellation of war debts and reparations, redistribution of the world's gold supply, and international limitation of armaments. In an address given under the auspices of the League of Nations Society and the teachers of Windsor, Ontario, Rowell told an audience of seven hundred, with many more listening over a national hook-up of forty radio stations of the CNR's broadcasting network, that above all 'there is no hope unless there is no more war.' There was much talk of lack of leadership in the world: 'Is it to be wondered at when ten million men, a whole generation, laid down their lives?' he asked in a voice that declared the emotion this subject continued to evoke in him. 'These are the men who would have been our leaders to-day. It is essential for economic restoration and for the maintenance of civilization that the peace of the world be restored.' He urged all his listeners to sign the disarmament petition currently being circulated in Canada and thus demonstrate to 'the men who make war,' before the world disarmament conference to be held early in 1932, that Canadians were part of a world public opinion that would no longer tolerate war.[26]

Later in that autumn of 1931 he and W.G. Watson, the general manager of the Toronto General Trusts, spent two weeks visiting the company's branches in western Canada, and in each of the six cities he visited, Rowell gave a public address. The large and appreciative audiences, the newspaper coverage, and the respectful editorial comment on his views were evidence of the place he occupied in the minds of many Canadians as a student of public affairs. Always he stressed the international origins of the depression, the baneful effects of the armaments race, and the harm done to world trade by economic nationalism. Although he stopped short of endorsing the 'keep smiling' campaign currently being promoted by many politicians and newspapers, he decried the purveyors of blue ruin and urged his listeners to remember that neither Canada's natural resources nor her people had been fundamentally changed by the depression.[27] To the Vancouver Canadian Club he noted the view of some that capitalism had failed: 'Well, I believe in capitalism. I am no Socialist, but I do say that if those who favour capitalism do not bring about changes in that system so that it more adequately meets the world's needs, people will do away with it and try something else.' Among the encouraging signs of the times he gave high place to the overwhelming mandate given two weeks earlier by

British voters to the National Government, headed by Ramsay MacDonald but in effect a Conservative administration. Rowell did not specify what changes in the operation of capitalism he expected from the dominant Conservative element in the British cabinet, which had campaigned on a platform of higher tariffs and other conservative measures as a means of balancing the budget. 'The British people' Rowell declared 'have set an example to the world. They sacrificed party to do it, and other countries must accept Britain's example.'[28] Whether Canada was one of these he did not say.

It was not easy in the autumn of 1931 to believe that world peace was secure. In mid-September the Japanese army provoked the Mukden incident and began a rapid march into Manchuria. When China appealed to the League of Nations, the League Council requested Japan to withdraw and agreed to Lord Robert Cecil's proposal to hold an enquiry. Three days later the inquiry was abandoned in the face of the advice of the American secretery of state, Henry L. Stimson, who, while supporting the League's appeal, was against holding an inquiry in the absence of Japanese consent. A renewed appeal for Japanese evacuation of Manchuria by 16 November produced no result. Two weeks later Rowell discussed the Manchurian crisis before a special meeting of the Men's Canadian Club of Toronto. Introduced by former prime minister Arthur Meighen as Canada's greatest authority on Far Eastern questions, Rowell outlined the origins of the dispute and endeavoured to show that in an issue so complex there was no clear case for either side. But the major issue was not the correctness of the Chinese or Japanese positions 'but whether nations which are members of the League can settle their disputes either by economic boycott or by military operation or whether it is not the duty of peaceful nations to bring these matters to impartial arbitrament or judicial determination or conciliation.' Those who condemned Japan for repudiating her obligations under the League Covenant were wrong. The League's appeal for Japanese withdrawal carried moral force only, since Article 11 of the Covenant, under which China had appealed, gave the League no power to act without the consent of both parties to the dispute. It was therefore premature, in Rowell's opinion, to talk of economic boycotts or withdrawal of diplomatic representation as some observers were doing. Rather, since Canada and the British Empire were the friends of both disputants, they should join wholeheartedly in the League's efforts to resolve the problem.[29]

Within two months Japan bombed part of Shanghai and mounted a land attack in retaliation for China's trade boycott of Japanese goods. Rowell was still the epitome of caution. In an interview with Augustus Bridle of the *Toronto Star* he declared that Chinese and Japanese actions were equally 'logical' to those responsible for them and explained the economic and political motivations operative on both sides. Only at the end was there the hint of a judgment. In discussing the difficulties facing the League in trying to take effective action, Rowell lamented the absence of Russia and the United States from the League. Were the Americans in the League they could bring the Japanese invasion to a halt by threatening to cut off their very large trade with Japan.[30]

On the day of Rowell's address the evening newspapers reported that China had invoked Articles 10 and 15 of the Covenant. If endorsed by the League, this would mean the application of sanctions against Japan by members of the League. Two days later, Britain and the United States, supported by France, Italy, and Germany, presented a formal request to both China and Japan to end hostilities, to establish Shanghai as a neutral zone, and to begin negotiations at once for a permanent settlement. The fate of Shanghai was a vital concern to powers with commercial interests in China and action became imperative once Shanghai was attacked.

As now became clear, Rowell was not as neutral in this dispute as his public statements suggested. His public neutrality was dictated by a desire to see conciliation through the League, an objective that did not necessitate a judgment about the rights and wrongs on either side. But in common with most League supporters and most Canadians, he sympathized increasingly with the Chinese, although understanding the extent to which the near anarchy in China had precipitated Japan's action on behalf of her economic interests in Manchuria. With the presentation of the British and American proposals for ending hostilities he concluded that rejection by Japan would 'clearly indicate that the military is absolutely dominant in Japan and that Japan intends to pursue a war of aggression in defiance of the public opinion of the world and in repudiation of her international obligations.' If Japan failed to accept the proposals, the world would face the gravest consequences: 'If Japan can do this with impunity, then the League of Nations and all other organizations for the peaceable settlement of international organization, receives a blow from which it may take a generation at least to recover.'[31]

Rowell was under no illusion that Canada could take any effective initiative in the dispute, although he urged upon the undersecretary of state, O.D. Skelton, the importance of Canadian support for whatever action the League might take.[32] His hope that Britain would give a firm lead to League policy was not sustained by his own observation of events nor by the opinion of the capacities of the British foreign secretary, Sir John Simon, expressed to Rowell by Philip Noel-Baker and by Wilson Harris, who was now the chief political commentator for the *Spectator*.[33] In co-operation with the United States, Britain did negotiate a truce in Shanghai for the withdrawal of Japanese troops from the city and supported the League in sending the Lytton commission of inquiry to Manchuria. But in the autumn of 1932 neither Britain nor any other major power strongly supported the commission's report with its condemnation of the Japanese invasion and its proposal for an autonomous Manchuria under Chinese sovereignty. In the meantime, Japan had established the puppet state of Manchukuo and was in effective control of Manchuria. The League took no action, and Japan withdrew from the international body. In dealing with the first major violation of the peace of the world since the end of the great war the machinery of the League of Nations and the force of world public opinion had showed itself ineffective in curbing aggression. Like other friends of the League, Rowell did not misunderstand the message.

In 1932 Rowell was in his sixty-fifth year. It was a year full of recognition, responsibility, and new experience. In the spring he was waited on by a delegation of clergy and laymen who wished to nominate him for the moderatorship of the United church. The initiators of the move were former Presbyterians strongly supported by several former Methodists. One of the latter giving strong encouragement to the proposal was Rowell's old friend, Dr R.P. Bowles, who had recently retired as president and chancellor of Victoria University. Bowles believed that 'the practical mystic' whom he had admired and valued as a friend ever since the days of the Jackson controversy and before, might now use his unique combination of knowledge of affairs and spiritual sensitivity in the greatest of his many services to his church.

There was 'a widespread fear' Bowles told his candidate, that in the present difficult times, the office of the moderator 'will not be filled by one who can thoroughly and satisfyingly represent our church in all its wide interests and in its unity and unqualified catholicity of spirit unless those who feel keenly the situation which is developing take positive action in the matter.' Although there was no precedent in Canadian Presbyterianism or Methodism or in the brief history of the United church for giving the highest office to a layman, there was no constitutional barrier preventing it. And as Bowles reminded Rowell, his old friends Robert E. Speer and Sir Andrew Fraser had served as moderators of American and Scottish Presbyterian bodies, while Professor T.R. Glover of Cambridge had been the presiding officer of English Baptists. If Rowell accepted the nomination, Bowles was certain that he would be elected almost unanimously, since 'in you the grace and dignity of this young, old church you had so much to do in bringing into existence would be perfectly represented.' But the eyes of those who wanted Rowell as moderator were not fixed on the past. It was well known that at the forthcoming General Council 'the church's relation to the present social and economic order will be the supreme question up for consideration ... Nothing could be happier than that a layman of your standing in our Dominion should be leader and guide in such deliberation by a great ecclesiastical body.'[34]

Bowles was contending, not for the victory of his own social views, but for the informed and judicious handling that he believed Rowell could provide in a potentially divisive situation. Bowles was a pacifist and a socialist of sorts and later became a supporter of the new socialist party, the CCF. From their many discussions of social issues over the years, Bowles thought that the logic of Rowell's emotional and intellectual commitments should have led him to a socialist position too, and he had difficulty in understanding why it had not.[35] But whatever Rowell's conclusions, Bowles believed that he understood the issues. Moreover, Rowell did not feel the hostility displayed by most businessmen in the church toward the exponents of Christian socialism, such as the members of the recently organized Fellowship for a Christian Social Order, a movement of ministers and laymen, mainly professors, formed to arouse interest within the United church in social and political questions. Throughout the depression years the members of the FCSO regarded Rowell with some confidence as one of the few prominent lay leaders in the church who treated them with respect and courtesy.[36] In Bowles's view no one else occupied such a position, and he therefore hoped that Rowell's leadership would assist the church in grappling with social issues with a minimum of acrimony and disunity.

None of the arguments of those who wished to see him in the moderator's chair in 1932 prevailed with Rowell. As the chairman of a committee of the General Council currently meeting to study the duties of the moderator he was fully aware of the work involved. His committee shortly presented a report recommending that the moderator should be expected to give his full time and energy to the office.[37] He was unable to persuade himself, even had he felt qualified for the position, that he could or should give up his current responsibilities for two years to serve as moderator.[38] His early decision for law and public service still stood.

When the General Council met, the debate on social policy was not as sharp as many anticipated, and a 'moderate,' Dr T. Albert Moore, general secretary of the Council, was elected moderator. The gathering endorsed a statement on war prepared by a committee under the scholarly and pacifist Welshman, Dr Richard Roberts of Sherbourne Street United Church. It was stronger than the pronouncement prepared by Rowell's committee four years earlier. Declaring war to be 'contrary to the mind of Christ' and suggesting no exceptions, it urged, as the only means of ending the arms race, the abolition of the private manufacture of armaments.[39] Another controversial report, from the Department of Evangelism and Social Service and approved by the Council, declared in a study of the church and industry that unemployment should not be understood simply as a result of the current depression but as 'a more or less inevitable feature of the present economic system.' One of the most immediate requirements of a juster social order, therefore, was the institution of unemployment insurance.[40]

Rowell took no major part in the discussion of these reports, but it seems safe to assume that he voted for them. During the meetings he agreed to chair a committee to study a report of the church's committee on economy, a group endeavouring to suggest belt-tightening measures for survival in a period of declining revenues. From this time, although continuing as a delegate to the General Council, Rowell no longer served as a member of its executive council and generally took a less active part in the official courts of the church than he had done before.

Toward the end of June 1932, Rowell set out for Europe with Nell and Frederick and his sister Mary. Leaving Nell and Frederick in London, Rowell and his sister travelled to Herrnhut near Dresden where Rowell attended the Continuation Committee of the International Missionary Council, while his sister participated in a conference of the World YWCA. As the site of the eighteenth-century estate of the Count von Zinzendorf, founder of the Moravian Church, now celebrating the two hundredth anniversary of its own remarkable missionary endeavours, Herrnhut itself was of great interest to Rowell. Even stronger than the sense of history was the awareness pervading the conference of the difficulties Germans were increasingly experiencing under the Nazi regime. As the discussions progressed, Rowell was distressed by what seemed to him the excessively conservative tone of the theological views of the German and Scandinavian delegates. Under their influence a week's deliberation produced a report on missions in the modern world that Rowell thought 'might almost have been written 50 years ago.' He felt constrained to point out the inadequacies of the report and secured its referral back to the committee, but another lengthy discussion brought few changes.[41] A second purpose of the visit to the continent was to see something of Russia as the guests of the Society for Cultivating Cultural Relations with Foreign Countries, a branch of which was the Russian body related to the Institute of Pacific Relations. One highlight of a week in Moscow was a reception in honour of Sydney and Beatrice Webb, enlarged at the last moment to include the two visiting Canadians as guests of honour. Rowell and his sister found themselves with the Webbs at the head table at a lavish banquet, Rowell noting with interested amusement that Sydney Webb, in deference to communist egalitarianism, had dropped his title as Lord Passfield during his Russian visit.[42]

As always in foreign countries, Rowell was well armed with letters of introduction to people who could facilitate his efforts to gain information about industrial production, salaries, standards of living, exports, and a host of other matters. He was taken to all the usual tourist sights, from Red Square and Lenin's tomb to new complexes of apartment blocks for workingmen. The latter he thought 'much superior to the living conditions of the workmen in the past though I cannot think it can take the place of the workman having his own little home and plot of ground.' Since he had long believed that for generations the Russian Orthodox church had oppressed the Russian people, he was less perturbed by the official attitude to religion than many western visitors of the time, although he noted that 'you see anti-religious propaganda everywhere and there is no question that the Communist movement as part of its creed is bitterly hostile to religion.'[43]

Most absorbing of all was the time he spent in a 'people's court,' where the judge and his two assistants, both women, were elected by the workers. He was impressed by the simplicity and directness of the court procedures he observed and by the ease with which appeals could be made to higher courts. After watching two trials, which he described in some detail for Nell's benefit, he concluded that 'these people were being tried by their peers and perhaps on the whole justice was as fairly and impartially administered as in our more elaborate procedure.' Lawyers, he noted, had less work to do in Russia than in capitalist societies since 'the elimination of controversy between private parties over the ownership of property or rights arising out of such ownership greatly reduces the amount of litigation.' As a consequence of this and of the fact that all lawyers belonged to a trade union and received the same wages whatever their work, the calibre of law students in the universities was deteriorating, according to some of his informants, because the best minds were turning to engineering, where the social and financial rewards were greater. On the whole, Rowell was favourably impressed with what he saw in Russia, finding the people generally 'cheerful and happy though not particularly merry, many young couples walking arm in arm and holding hands quite affectionately. Human nature has not been changed by the revolution and I imagine in Russia youth is demonstrative.'[44] In Moscow, and again in Leningrad where he spent a day with an informed and historically minded young woman guide provided by Intourist, he was happy to learn that the revolution had by no means destroyed the pride of Russians in their past.[45] The return journey to England via Berlin offered opportunities for discussions of international affairs with several diplomats and academics in the German capital.

As the recently elected president of the Canadian Institute of International Affairs he spent some time at Chatham House in consultations with its committee on British Commonwealth relations. Much to his satisfaction the committee accepted the invitation of the CIIA to hold a conference in Toronto on Commonwealth relations in the summer of 1933, just after the next IPR meetings to be held in Banff, Alberta. There were also two days of Shakespearean theatre at Stratford-on-Avon and numerous trips to places of scenic and historical interest in the south of England, including, for Frederick's benefit, Eton, whose setting and atmosphere provided an interesting comparison with the Canadian private school he attended, St Andrew's College in Aurora.[46]

Crossing to France they drove through Ypres, Arras, Vimy, and Amiens, to give Frederick his first view of the battlefields and cemeteries, and then on to Geneva where the sixty states attending the world's first disarmament conference had just adjourned their discussions after six months without any visible signs of progress.

The conflict between French demands for security and German insistence on equality had produced a deadlock that seemed absolute. Rowell's discussions with League officials and Geneva journalists were far from heartening, for there was growing fear that the failure of the conference to agree on any vital matter would feed the world's increasing scepticism about the efficacy of the League, especially in Germany, Italy, and Russia. And on yet another front – the attack on economic nationalism – little advance had been made, and Canada had played an inglorious role. From abroad, Rowell saw the Imperial Economic Conference being held in Ottawa that summer developing as he feared it would. 'I did hope' he told J.W. Dafoe 'that Bennett would rise above party considerations and obligations and make a real offer of reduced tariffs, substantially reduced tariffs, but possibly that was too much to expect.'[47] In the end, the Ottawa agreements, although modifying tariffs within the Commonwealth slightly, increased them against the rest of the world. It was scarcely a noteworthy contribution to the expansion of world trade or to the alleviation of the effects of the depression on those segments of the Canadian people, the primary producers, who were suffering the most.

Rowell returned to Canada with an honour he greatly prized – election as an honorary bencher of Lincoln's Inn. Rarely was a barrister from outside Britain admitted to honorary membership, and only one other Canadian, Prime Minister R.B. Bennett, had been so privileged. A few weeks later he was elected president of the Canadian Bar Association. Even while receiving this recognition Rowell was reluctantly forced to admit that his energies would not permit him to practice law as vigorously as before, especially in view of the various obligations he had assumed, notably the presidency of the Canadian Institute of International Affairs. He did not view that position as a nominal one, even after the Massey Foundation provided funds for the appointment of an executive secretary and a recent University of Toronto graduate, Escott Reid, was appointed to the position. He took an energetic part in the preparations for the forthcoming Commonwealth relations and IPR conferences, attended numerous planning sessions, and later read and commented on the drafts of papers proposed for presentation at these gatherings.

For the present, he decided to take no new legal cases. But there was one that had been before the courts for five years and had to be seen through to the end. Early in the spring of 1933 he was before the Judicial Committee of the Privy Council again with the last of the litigation arising from the customs investigation, once again opposed by W.N. Tilley. There were three separate cases involving alleged tax avoidance amounting to $600,000 by Consolidated Distillers in smuggling out of Vancouver. This visit to London was unlike those of former years; in nearly five weeks he was out to dinner with friends but rarely, and under Nell's anxious eye kept early hours and rested as much as possible. He did manage to go to the House of Commons to hear Winston Churchill arguing against any gesture of conciliation toward Indian nationalists: 'His speech was most disappointing. He is leading a forlorn hope of the Tory die hards and his only capacity at the present time seems a capacity for mischief.'[48]

Among his few evenings of discussion was one with Arthur Henderson, who had presided over the Geneva Disarmament Conference and who still entertained hope that some good would come of the talks but was increasingly apprehensive that if a convention agreeable to Germany could not be agreed upon soon, Germany would rearm herself speedily. England, Rowell found, was 'deeply stirred by the tragic developments in Germany. The ruthless persecution of the Jews and the blatant ... nationalism of the Nazi leaders is fast alienating British sympathy and no one can foretell the outcome.' Amid the growing dominance of 'the forces of disintegration' Rowell and his English friends saw at least one ground for optimism in 'Roosevelt's energetic dealing with the grave problems facing his Government' and the hope that he would 'display a similar energy and constructive power in dealing with international affairs.'[49] Everything he heard and read justified the fears he had entertained ever since the signing of the peace treaties: 'The tragedy of the situation is that the great powers, Great Britain and France and more particularly France refused to meet Germany's just demands on reparations, disarmament, war guilt etc. while Germany had a democratic Government in power and when much less than they are now prepared to concede might have been accepted. Their refusal gave the Hitlerites their appeal to the German people and now that democracy in Germany is overthrown they are disposed to yield for fear of worse consequences.'[50]

His work in London finished, Rowell spent two weeks of a glorious spring with Nell in Menton in the south of France, an experience blighted only briefly by news that the Judicial Committee of the Privy Council had rejected his argument against Consolidated Distilleries and had thereby deprived the Canadian taxpayers of the $600,000 Rowell believed belonged to them.[51] Soon after their return to Canada they went to Muskoka for two months. Playing golf two or three times a week, reading, and enjoying a visit from Mary and her husband and the first grandchild, Henry Newton Rowell Jackman, he endeavoured to conserve his energies for the international conferences at the end of the summer.[52]

For a time he thought he would be forced to forgo attendance at the IPR conference in Banff in late August, but in the end he went, although he carried no major responsibility during the meetings, the Canadian group being led by E.J. Tarr of Winnipeg and the presiding officer Sir Robert Falconer. Immediately afterwards he was in Ottawa for the annual meeting of the Canadian Bar Association and the delivery of his presidential address on the work of the Permanent Court of International Justice. The court's achievements in the past ten years confirmed his earlier view that this international body was the greatest achievement of the League of

Nations, and he urged the members of the Canadian bar to use their influence to create the public opinion essential to the court's continued success.[53]

Soon, as chairman and leader of the Canadian group, he was deeply involved in the deliberations of the Conference on Commonwealth Relations organized by the CIIA and the RIIA and held at Hart House in the University of Toronto. At a pre-conference meeting of the Canadians, some of the delegates argued that the Canadian delegation should state openly that Canada had some interests that were not the same as Britain's. While Rowell agreed that this was so, he was averse to any blunt assertion of this truth; he still found it satisfying to wrap his Canadian nationalism in the rhetoric of empire. Although no extremely radical views were expressed at the conference, the tension between the views of older delegates like Rowell, Sir Robert Borden, Sir Joseph Flavelle, and Sir Robert Falconer and those of some of the younger men was never far below the surface.[54]

His conference duties over, Rowell resigned as chairman of the CIIA, feeling that for the sake of his health and Nell's, they must both take a prolonged holiday. At the same time he retired from the chairmanship of the Board of Regents of Victoria and was subsequently informed that the regents had elected him to the more honorary position of vice-chancellor of the university. In late October 1933 he and Nell set out for the Caribbean, where they planned to spend most of a three-month vacation in Jamaica, Trinidad, and Barbados. Thanks to the sea voyage from New York, the tropical warmth, and the stimulation of new experiences in a part of the world they had not visited before, both travellers soon felt rested and relaxed. Typical of their life was their stay in Trinidad, with visits to government officials, the law courts, the Imperial College of Tropical Agriculture, a large missionary rally in the Anglican cathedral, and to the schools and teacher-training college conducted by the United church mission on the island. Rowell was as impressed as might have been predicted: 'What a remarkable aggregation of countries and people this British Empire is and wherever the flag floats law and order prevail, justice is honestly and impartially administered and the condition of the people is steadily improving. Every time I visit a new part of the Empire the marvel increases and I prize more and more my British citizenship.'[55]

After his return to Toronto early in 1934 he accepted only a limited amount of legal work. Spring found him in England again to argue two cases before the Judicial Committee. One, concerning a disputed estate, was disposed of quickly. Hearings in the second extended over a couple of weeks, as two distributors of natural gas in Ontario contended for the right to lay gas pipes in a section of Hamilton; Rowell's clients, the Dominion Natural Gas Company, emerged victorious.[56] Later, his legal colleagues bestowed on him the highest honour open to a member of the Ontario bar when they elected him Treasurer of the Law Society of Upper Canada, thus placing him in a long line of distinguished Canadians going back to William Warren Baldwin, Robert Baldwin, and Edward Blake. At the same time he resigned as president of the trust company, and to make it easier to get the rest he and Nell often needed he purchased a farm in pleasant, rolling country near Kleinburg just north of Toronto, and this soon became a cherished retreat.

He had more time now to study international affairs and to indulge his interest in political biographies and memoirs, especially those of some of Britain's wartime leaders, now beginning to appear. There was also time for a steady and detailed correspondence with Manley O. Hudson, professor of international law at Harvard University, and with Newton D. Baker, the Cleveland lawyer, politician, and internationalist, on several aspects of international affairs, notably the overcoming of obstacles to American membership in the Permanent Court of International Justice.

Rowell's information about the contemporary world was garnered from a variety of sources. The four Toronto daily newspapers and the *New York Times* came to his house regularly, as did the *Moscow News*, the *Tokyo Transpacific*, the London *Observer*, the weekly *Times*, the *Spectator*, and the *Manchester Guardian*. Through the *Winnipeg Free Press* he kept abreast of developments in western Canada and the editorial pronouncements of J.W. Dafoe. Toronto's *Saturday Night* brought the comment of its informed editor, B.K. Sandwell, while the *Canadian Forum* presented a sympathetic view of Canada's new socialist party, the CCF.

He continued to see Roosevelt's 'New Deal' as the hope of a depression-ridden world, an experiment that would 'work a real revolution in the economic and industrial life of that country.' No country, he predicted, would return to the economic patterns existing before 1930, and Canada could expect increasing government regulation of industry, trade, and finance. He did not fear this development but urged that 'the nature of such regulation and its limits' demanded the early attention of the nation's best minds.[57] A current example of government intervention in the economy was the marketing bill that the Bennett government had placed before Parliament and on which Mackenzie King solicited Rowell's opinion. While Rowell agreed with opposition criticism that the measure was too indefinite and the details of some of its clauses inadequately worked out, in principle he was strongly in favour of the legislation to establish a marketing scheme for agricultural products under government auspices and control.[58]

This theme was pursued in Rowell's address to the Canadian Bar Association at the beginning of his second term as president. 'Our Heritage in the Civil and Common Law' was in part an historical outline of the origins and development of civil and common law, their influence on one another, and their fruitful association in the Canadian legal tradition. Contemporary threats to personal liberty and to free parliamentary institutions, in his view, came not primarily from new theories such as fascism and communism but from 'economic conditions ... which none can justify, and all should endeavour to remedy.' In Canada, he believed, the maintenance of 'the real liberty of the subject and of the free action of our Parliamentary institutions' would require Parliament to go further than ever before 'in restricting or regulating the conduct of the strong, so that all industrious citizens will be enabled to live under conditions which will permit them to enjoy the rights and liberties secured to them by our law.'[59] When he addressed the voters of Oxford county in his only speech during the federal election campaign of 1935, this theme was again prominent. Arguing conventionally that the Liberals would reduce unemployment, balance the budget, promote peace and international trade, fight economic nationalism, and secure reciprocity with the United States, he also asserted that while all parties were now committed to new social legislation, the Liberals and their leader were by experience and tradition most likely to pass the kind of measures that would free many Canadians from the economic fears and limitations restricting their social and political liberty.[60]

27
The chief justice

At the end of the summer of 1935 Rowell was preparing for a trip to the west coast. He planned to attend the annual meeting of the Canadian Bar Association and see his property in the Okanagan Valley and had agreed to address the Canadian Clubs of Winnipeg and Vancouver. By the time he left Toronto there was no doubt about the subject on which he would speak. All summer he had watched with mounting apprehension Italy's increasing belligerence toward Abyssinia. To make good his claims to share in Europe's 'civilizing mission,' the fascist dictator Mussolini seemed determined to conquer the small but independent kingdom of Emperor Haile Selassie. Rowell was under no illusions about the consequences if Italy were allowed to realize her ambitions. 'If Italy goes to war,' he told Lester Pearson of the Department of External Affairs with whom he was personally well acquainted, 'there could be no more flagrant violation of the Covenant of the League, of the Kellogg-Briand Peace Pact and of Italy's own treaty with Abyssinia of 1928 than Italy would then present, and unless the sanctions of the League are applied, it seems to me the scheme of collective security must be admitted to be a complete failure.'[1]

In the west he endeavoured to impress on his audiences the seriousness of the threat and Canada's vital stake in taking all measures to ensure peace: for Canadians there could be no genuine recovery from the depression without a revival of world trade, and that would not occur without the establishment of economic and political stability in the world. He believed that war could be averted if all members of the League honoured their obligations under the League Covenant. The most cheering factor in the current situation was the apparent determination of the British public and British statesmen to prevent war by honouring their country's pledges to the League. He was sure that Canada would do no less. It was clear to

Rowell that if economic sanctions were applied to Italy at once, Mussolini would not be so mad as to continue his plans for conquest.[2]

Rowell's conviction that Britain would take the lead in maintaining collective security under the Covenant seemed to find confirmation in the pledge of support from the British foreign secretary, Sir Samuel Hoare, before the Assembly of the League on 11 September. Much less satisfactory, in Rowell's opinion, was the statement to the Assembly by the Canadian delegate, G. Howard Ferguson, who declared that if the Covenant were violated Canada would consult with other members of the League to see 'how by unanimous action peace can be maintained.'[3] If he were in any doubt about the character of the advice the Canadian delegation was getting from the Department of External Affairs in Ottawa, Rowell's correspondence with the chief architect of Canadian policy, Dr O.D. Skelton, soon made matters clear. To Rowell's protest that Canada should announce plainly her intention to honour her obligations to the League in full, Skelton argued that it was impossible to define those obligations without reference to repeated expressions over the past fifteen years of 'Canada's reluctance to guarantee the territorial status quo and to enforce sanctions' and without consideration of the implications on any attempt to impose sanctions of the absence of the United States from the League.[4]

To Rowell, Skelton's position was wholly unacceptable. Rowell believed that Canadian attempts to secure modification of Article 10 of the League Covenant to ensure consideration of geographical location in the definition of any country's responsibilities applied to military obligations only, not to financial and commercial sanctions, which were all that was being contemplated at the present time. Under Article 16, Canada was as bound as every other League member to enforce economic sanctions against an aggressor if the League agreed upon such a policy. While American absence from the League might limit the effectiveness of sanctions, Rowell had never before heard it suggested that this should inhibit Canada's willingness to act.[5]

A further exposition of post-war Canadian policy by Skelton left him unconvinced. According to Skelton the Canadian view, stated many times both inside and outside the country, was that 'if the League was to survive and to advance the cause of peace, it must be through its functions of publicity, its fulfillment of the pledges of disarmament contained in the Covenant, its provision of means of equitable settlement of all disputes, its emphasis, in brief, on prevention rather than punishment.' Over the years, Canada had become well known for her opposition to 'the whole sanctions doctrine.' Moreover, since sanctions might well be the first step to war, Skelton asked, 'can we disregard the repeated and emphatic declarations of the necessity of prior approval by the Parliament of Canada?' Such approval would be difficult to secure at the moment, for instance, since Parliament had been dissolved and the country was in the midst of an election campaign. However, Skelton conceded regretfully that if Britain applied sanctions, Canada would 'back up the Mother Country,' and if that failed and Britain decided to use force 'we would probably do the same thing, on the good old ground that when Britain is at war, Canada is at war.'[6]

It was painfully clear to Rowell that he and the undersecretary of state had 'quite different views' of the League. Although British policy was obviously of importance to Canada, Rowell told Skelton that 'Canada is of age, and she is responsible for her obligations and for the discharge of them ... I confess I am old-fashioned enough to believe that an obligation is an obligation and that there is no excuse for not discharging it, except by proven inability to do so. I think that applies both to the individual and the nation, and I do not see how international relations can be carried on and world peace and stability secured unless these obligations are recognized as binding on the parties who solemnly enter into them.'[7] He urged the same view in two letters to Dr W.A. Riddell, advisory officer to the Canadian delegation in Geneva.[8]

While carrying on his private debate with Skelton, Rowell was also publicly urging full support for the League in whatever economic sanctions were agreed upon.[9] At the same time he refuted, privately and publicly, the recent utterances of Escott Reid, secretary of the CIIA. In a public address to the alumni of Trinity College and later in an article, Reid charged that Rowell and his colleagues at the first Assembly of the League of Nations in 1920 had, in rejecting Italy's requests for League consideration of the redistribution of the world's raw materials, contributed to the development of economic conditions that lay behind Mussolini's expansionist policies.[10] Rowell totally rejected Reid's contention. He still believed, as he had in 1920, that the question of raw materials did not come within the terms of the League Covenant, and further that it would have been especially detrimental to prospects for American adherence to the League even to suggest, by willingness to discuss the matter, that it did. If Canada had been wrong in her stand, then the League should have corrected the error by taking up the issue later, but it had never done so. Moreover, Italy herself had never in the past fifteen years asked to have distribution of raw materials put on the League agenda. It did not seem to be a burning issue to Italy. How then could there be even 'a shadow of justification' for blaming Canada? But even if everything Reid said about the Canadian stand were true, why should Abyssinia be made to suffer or be denied the full protection of the Covenant?[11]

For Rowell, the events of the first few days of October made adoption of the right view of the League imperative. Italian troops invaded Abyssinia, and the League quickly declared Italy an aggressor, with Canada supporting the declaration. Further, Canada accepted membership on the 'Committee of Eighteen,' charged with formulating concrete proposals for the application of sanctions. Also to

Rowell's satisfaction, Ferguson spoke twice before the League, advocating absolute adherence to collective security under the terms of the Covenant. The position Canada was taking at Geneva was scarcely Skelton's, and that was gratifying.

The day after Ferguson's second address, Mackenzie King defeated R.B. Bennett overwhelmingly in the federal election. Two weeks later the new King government issued a statement of policy whose authorship seemed to be indicated by phrases precisely the same as those Skelton had used in his correspondence with Rowell. However, despite all it had to say about the limitations of the League, the statement concluded that the government intended to make 'participation in the League the cornerstone of its foreign policy' and would co-operate in making economic sanctions against Italy effective.[12] Meanwhile, from Geneva itself, Rowell was assured by Dr Riddell that 'the measure of unanimity has been striking and seems to augur well for the successful application of sanctions.'[13]

In the weeks following, Rowell read approvingly the news dispatches from Geneva reporting the active role played by Dr Riddell in the Committee of Eighteen and especially his initiative in proposing to enlarge the list of strategic materials denied to Italy to include iron, steel, coal, and oil and its derivatives. Before long, the press of Canada and the world were discussing 'the Canadian proposal,' while Italy made increasingly hostile pronouncements, especially about the threat to her oil supply. None of this publicity worried Rowell, but it created consternation in Ottawa. While the League debated the extension of sanctions and the Italian armies continued their march into Abyssinia, Ernest Lapointe, who was acting prime minister while Mackenzie King was holidaying with Dr Skelton in Georgia, took a step that Rowell found almost incredible. Lapointe issued a press release denying that the Canadian government had taken any initiative in proposing to extend the embargo against Italy and asserting that Dr Riddell's proposal was purely his own and did not represent the views of the Canadian government.[14] Rowell immediately sent a long and strongly worded telegram to Lapointe expressing his shock and disappointment at the government's action. If the government felt it had to repudiate Riddell it should have done so at the time. To do so six weeks later was 'to encourage the aggressor and weaken the forces working for peace and maintenance of collective security.' Prohibition of the export of oil and other key materials was the 'clear and inescapable duty' of all League members under Article 16. To his knowledge no Canadian government had ever suggested that it would fail to perform that duty, despite the reservations about Article 10.[15]

What had happened? Rowell was not satisfied by the references in Lapointe's statement to difficulties in communication between Geneva and Ottawa that had arisen during the transfer of power from the Bennett to the King administrations. 'Your friends in Canada' he told Riddell 'feel that you have been sacrificed in a measure to some political exigencies of which we have no knowledge.'[16] What exigencies? Opinion in French Canada, where there was a good deal of sympathy for Italy, had been almost unanimously opposed to sanctions. Had collective security and Canada's honour among the nations been sacrificed to 'national unity?' But not only French Canada was lukewarm or opposed to sanctions. Much of public opinion across Canada was isolationist and unwilling to see Canada take a strong international position, and the stance of the King government accurately reflected that opinion. Few newspapers and even fewer public figures expressed views similar to Rowell's. J.W. Dafoe, Sir Robert Falconer, and Rowell were among a small group calling for unequivocal support of the League. Rowell publicly regretted that Canada was not to have the credit for initiating an oil embargo against Italy. But that was not the main issue. The only thing that mattered, he urged, was that all the nations should support the embargo without further delay.[17]

Soon, Rowell's confidence in Britain's commitment to the League was shattered. On 9 December a stupefied world learned of the Hoare-Laval plan under which the war was to end if Abyssinia ceded two-thirds of her territory to Italy, provided, of course, that Mussolini agreed to accept less than the whole of the African state. So much for the leadership of British statesmen in defence of collective security! One of the few heartening aspects of the whole affair was the widespread and intense feeling in Britain that forced Sir Samuel Hoare's resignation and for a time seemed to threaten the life of Stanley Baldwin's government, re-elected less than a month before on a platform of support for the League. The strength of pro-League opinion in Britain, coupled with a similar public opinion in France, enhanced the tragedy for Rowell and other League enthusiasts: British and French statesmen had betrayed the best instincts and the hopes of their own peoples, as well as the League and Abyssinia. It was difficult to avoid asking the uncomfortable question whether Canada's actions had encouraged British weakness.

While the League continued to delay over oil sanctions, Mussolini completed the conquest of Abyssinia. In Canada Mackenzie King told Parliament that had his government failed to repudiate Dr Riddell's initiative 'the whole of Europe might have been aflame to-day.'[18] Early in March 1936, Hitler reoccupied the de-militarized zone of the Rhineland, in violation of the Treaties of Versailles and Locarno. That summer, civil war broke out in Spain, and before long Italian and German armaments were being provided to the fascist General Franco, further eroding the prospects for peace in Europe. At the same time, on the other side of the world, Japan was clearly not inhibited by any fear of action on the part of the League of Nations from expressing her continuing aggressive intentions against China. It was a trying time for those who had put their trust in collective security. Addressing the IPR meeting in Yosemite, California, that summer, Rowell saw one major sign of hope in Russia's adherence to the League of Nations, her non-aggression pacts with several European powers, and her willingness to arbitrate the

Russo-Japanese border dispute. He was confident that as Russia continued to emerge from isolation her military strength would be used to maintain peace.[19]

The meeting of the League of Nations Assembly in the autumn of 1936 would be, as Rowell fully understood, one of the most important international conferences since the war. At a special meeting in the early summer the Assembly had abandoned sanctions against Italy and had decided to embark on a reconsideration of the principles of the Covenant, in short, to ask the League members to revise the Covenant to conform to principles they were prepared to support in practice. When Mackenzie King announced that he would himself lead the Canadian delegation to the autumn meetings, Rowell wrote to express his gratification that Canada would be represented by 'one who is so sympathetic with League ideals.'[20] To King's request for any comments he might care to make about the work of the Assembly, Rowell responded readily with a full exposition of his view of the League:

It can never provide any real degree of security against aggression unless sanctions are maintained, and behind the obligation, there is the will to enforce the sanctions ... It is only by the due administration of justice, backed up by an adequate police force that the rule of law has been established and can be maintained in any country, and I believe it is only by a similar process, although necessarily under very different conditions, that the rule of law in international affairs can be gradually established and international crime and anarchy suppressed. I therefore always have been and still am in favour of sanctions – universal, so far as economic [sic] are concerned, necessarily regional as far as military operations are concerned, although recognizing the obligation of all to come to the defence of any member who is attacked by an aggressor state when carrying out a mandate of the League in imposing economic sanctions ... I look upon the use of force to restrain an aggressor, not as war, but as a purely police measure and as the best possible means of avoiding war, and personally, I am firmly convinced had the members of the League lived up to their obligations under Article 16, Italy would not now be the conqueror of Abyssinia and Germany would have hesitated long before she re-occupied the Rhineland. Successful aggression breeds new aggression.[21]

Had Rowell seen the sceptical queries and comments King wrote on the margins of his letter, probably for Skelton's eyes, he would quickly have abandoned any hope he still retained that Canada would take a strong line at Geneva. When King addressed the Assembly it was clear that Canada would no longer pay even lip service to the League as the keystone of her foreign policy. Drawing a sharp distinction between the politics and interests of North America and Europe, stressing the weakness of the League because of the lack of universal membership, emphasizing the recent failure of collective security, and urging conciliation rather than coercion, King presented a view of the League as little more than an international debating society.[22] In contrast with many Canadians, Rowell could find no reason to congratulate King on his Geneva speech. It seemed, as J.W. Dafoe later declared that 'the League of Nations, with assurances of the most distinguished consideration, was ushered out into the darkness by Mr Mackenzie King.'[23]

No one could fairly argue that the failure of the League was primarily Canada's responsibility, but she had contributed to its demise. Henceforth the League was of little importance, and Rowell no longer attempted to give advice to Mackenzie King on international affairs. However, early in 1937 when King made his first major speech on defence policy since taking office in 1935, Rowell did take favourable note of the address. In supporting substantial increases in defence expenditures, King emphasized that the modest expansion of Canada's almost negligible armed forces was necessary for the defence of Canada itself and not for the equipping of an overseas expeditionary force. Although unwilling to say that war was likely, King conceded that any addition to Canadian strength was of value to the Commonwealth and to the other democracies of the world were they to be threatened by an aggressor, but that was as far as he was prepared to go in acknowledging any international dimension to Canadian policy.[24] Rowell congratulated the prime minister 'for stating the position so clearly and so forcefully.'[25] With collective security dead there was nothing to do but to encourage every step, however small, to prepare for the worst.

Early in 1936, the King government, whose laissez faire philosophy made it unenthusiastic about implementing the Bennett 'New Deal,' decided that the most politically advantageous method of disposing of the legislation was to refer it to the courts for a judgment on its constitutionality, about which there had been so much debate.[26] When Rowell agreed to present the case for the legislation before the Supreme Court of Canada, with the assistance of Louis S. St-Laurent and C.P. Plaxton, he hardly needed the instructions of the minister of justice, Ernest Lapointe, advanced in deference to public opinion, to present the strongest possible defence of the measures.[27] Rowell did not share the Liberal government's hostility to the Bennett legislation. Given his long-standing views on social reform, views reinforced by the experience of a depression that had left so many Canadians completely exposed to the harsh vagaries of economic fortune, the task of arguing for unemployment insurance, minimum wages and hours, co-operative marketing procedures, expanded farm credit, and kindred legislation was one to which he could set himself with conviction as well as intense interest. R.B. Bennett was delighted with Rowell's acceptance of the assignment, believing that his legislative program could not have enjoyed more competent or sympathetic advocacy.[28]

For more than two years he had practised law less than half-time, and now the steady court work extending over five weeks of an Ottawa winter left him the easy victim of a severe cold from which he recovered only after a holiday at Sea Island, Georgia, in the company of Nell and Sir Robert and Lady Borden.[29] His body's response to the pressure of such concentrated work was a distressing reminder of the continuing limits of his physical strength. However, when the Supreme Court, in a series of complex decisions, declared the bulk of the Bennett legislation unconstitutional, he agreed to continue to act for the government of Canada in its appeal to the Judicial Committee of the Privy Council in the autumn of 1936.

That trip to England was never made. In mid-September the minister of justice, Ernest Lapointe, asked Rowell to accept appointment as chief justice of the Supreme Court of Ontario. To contemplate acceptance of such high office in his seventieth year and in his uncertain health was not easy. Yet it was difficult for him to refuse a position any lawyer would consider the apex of a legal career or to reject the opportunity to render service to his native province. During recent years Rowell's name had been more than once mentioned in the press as a likely chief justice, but there had been no vacancy. Ontario's 'Grand Old Man,' Sir William Mulock, appointed chief justice when he was seventy-nine, had only just now vacated the office at the age of ninety-two. Judging from the recent legal history of Ontario, Rowell need not see his age as a barrier to his acceptance of the appointment. Yet, as he told Lapointe, 'the proposal ... involves such a complete change in my plans for the next few years that I feel I must think through this aspect of the matter.'[30] Among other sacrifices, acceptance would mean giving up the hope of a lifetime to visit India, the one major part of the Empire he had not seen. The time to visit India was in the winter, and as chief justice he would not be able to get away then. It would also mean a very large cut in his income; the chief justice received a salary of $10,000, a sum which the *Toronto Star*, in a somewhat exaggerated calculation, estimated as $90,000 less than Rowell's usual annual income in recent years.[31] Most immediately, it would mean giving up the group of Privy Council cases in which he was already deeply involved.

After a long weekend of careful thought and thorough discussion with Nell, he informed Lapointe that he would accept. The official announcement of the appointment came while he was attending the General Council of the United church in Ottawa, and the Council delighted in honouring him, for no son of Ontario Methodism had served both church and state with such distinction. Shortly after receiving the congratulations of the Council, the new chief justice moved the adoption of a message of loyalty to King Edward VIII who had assumed the throne earlier in the year. Later that day, Rowell moved the nomination of a former minister of Metropolitan Church, Dr Peter Bryce, as moderator of the church, citing his long experience in the social work of the church and his influence on social

N.W. Rowell 1930

Being sworn in as chief justice of Ontario, with the lieutenant governor,
Dr H.A. Bruce, the former chief justice, Sir William Mulock,
and Nell Rowell looking on

legislation in Ontario, notably mothers' allowances and old age pensions, as a
adornment of which the United church should be proud. The delegates expressed
their agreement by electing Dr Bryce moderator.[32]

A week later, his legal business wound up, Rowell was sworn into office by the
lieutenant governor, Dr Herbert Bruce. Thanks to the illness of Premier Mitchell
Hepburn, the province of Ontario was represented at the ceremony by the acting
premier, Harry Nixon, an agreeable coincidence because Rowell was no admirer of
Hepburn, whose vulgar flamboyance and demagoguery he believed did no credit to
Liberalism. The best wishes of the bar of Ontario were fittingly extended by his
antagonist of many notable court cases, W.N. Tilley, who noted with satisfaction
that this was the first time in the history of the province that a lawyer had been
appointed directly to the chief justiceship without prior service on the bench.[33]

Later, the directors and members of Toronto's National Club held a dinner in his
honour where representatives of bench and bar, church, university, and business
heard an address from the new chief justice that ranged from comments on the
founding of the National Club in the 1870s by the Canada First party to the subject
currently on everyone's mind. Lauding the two fundamental principles of the
Canada Firsters, 'a sound Canadianism and the maintenance of the Imperial connection,' Rowell regretted the attrition of the former due to the growth of provincialism under depression conditions, but found that imperial unity was in good
health and had indeed been strengthened by recent events. That very day the
British Parliament had passed the Declaration of Abdication Bill, Edward VIII had
ceased to be king, and George VI had succeeded his brother. Earlier, the National
Club had sent a cable of support to Prime Minister Stanley Baldwin in his stand
against Edward's marriage to the twice-divorced American, Mrs Wallis Simpson.
Now Rowell's 'personal tribute to the genius, patience, the sympathy and wise
statesmanship of Stanley Baldwin,' won prolonged applause from the club members. Mackenzie King was to be congratulated as well for maintaining a dignified
silence in the face of all demands for a public statement. For most Canadians, at
least for those of the classes represented in the National Club, the brief crisis over
the abdication had seemed to threaten the whole established order of things,
although few would have been able to explain how this could be so. The general
sense of relief over perils surmounted found an eloquent spokesman in Rowell that
evening.[34]

Rowell assumed the office of chief justice at a time when there was much anxiety
in the Ontario business community about the solidity of contractual obligations,
occasioned largely by the Hepburn government's recent cancellation of a series of
hydro contracts. If there was a tendency in some quarters to see Rowell's appointment as an attempt to strengthen the Ontario judiciary to resistance against actions
such as Hepburn's, Rowell did not allow that interpretation to flourish. Addressing

e Ontario Bar Association in London, he emphasized the importance of the idea of the rule of law as the basis of democratic life. At the same time he stressed the sovereignty of Parliaments in the British system of government, and pointed out that under the British North America Act the provinces had the power to abrogate contracts and to take property without due compensation. He noted, without passing judgment, that this was in contrast to the American constitution where the courts had considerable powers to restrict the actions of legislatures.[35] Property might be under attack in Ontario but the courts must not be expected to do the impossible.

During what was to prove a short term of less than two years on the bench, Rowell wrote and delivered the judgment in thirty-nine cases and participated in the formulation of an additional thirty judgments.[36] Most of these cases were concerned with corporation law and excited little interest beyond the business circles involved. One of the more bizarre hearings over which he presided was the 'Millar baby derby case.' An eccentric Toronto lawyer, Charles Millar, had willed half a million dollars to the Toronto mother who gave birth to the largest number of children in the ten years after his death. Millar's relatives contested the bequest on the grounds that it was contrary to public policy. Rowell and his colleagues were unanimous in denying that any issue of public policy was involved and upheld the ruling of a lower court that the will was valid, provided that 'children' was interpreted to mean legitimate children.[37]

A case of great popular interest that clearly did involve public policy concerned the Hepburn government's amendments of 1934 to the provincial Assessment Act, which had allowed corporations to list their Roman Catholic shareholders as separate school supporters for the purposes of allotting school taxes; under the amended law, corporations were *required* to divide their school taxes on this basis. From the first the Act had been the object of vociferous attack, not only from Protestants who saw it as an unwarranted extension of Roman Catholic privileges, but also from more detached citizens who believed the legislation ill-conceived and too complex to be workable. In 1937, when a composite case involving twenty-three companies arrived at the Supreme Court of Ontario, Rowell and his fellow judges had the task of reconciling the amendments with Ontario's system of municipal taxation and were unanimous in admitting their inability to do so. In the face of this development and the outspoken hostility of the Conservative opposition, the government quickly repealed the legislation.[38]

Rowell had been on the bench less than a year when yet another difficult personal decision faced him. Mackenzie King wanted him to act as chairman of a royal commission that could well prove to be one of the most significant enquiries in the history of the Canadian confederation. For many months there had been much agitation across the country for an investigation of public finance in Canada, especially in view of the plight of the prairie provinces, which had failed to share in the degree of economic recovery enjoyed by the central provinces and British Columbia. In late February 1937, King had told Parliament that a commission would be appointed. Now, in July, he was ready to act and asked Rowell to serve as chairman of a 'Royal Commission to examine, among other things, the present allocation of public functions and powers of the federal and provincial governments, with a view to effecting a more balanced relationship than exists at present, and a more efficient, independent and economic discharge of governmental responsibilities in Canada.'[39]

Although he need not resign from the judiciary to serve as chairman of the commission, Rowell would clearly be unable to give much attention to his court. He was only too well aware that so far he had made little progress in one of his major objectives in taking the position of chief justice – the reorganization of the Supreme Court. He had already discussed the reorganization of the court with King and Lapointe, especially with a view to injecting some younger blood by proceeding with their promised legislation to require the retirement of judges at the age of seventy-five. As Rowell had pointed out, six of the present eight members of the Supreme Court of Ontario were over seventy and the oldest was eighty-six. Ill health frequently prevented their attendance at court, and his own absence with the commission would put the court even further behind in its work. He discussed this problem again with King and was assured that it would be dealt with.[40] That J.W. Dafoe was willing to serve on the commission and French Canada was to be represented by the able Justice Thibaudeau Rinfret of the Supreme Court of Canada were considerable inducements in Rowell's mind and made the prospects of constructive work seem excellent.[41] Rowell's feeling about Dafoe was reciprocated. Even before King approached him, Dafoe, speculating on the personnel of the commission, had easily concluded that 'Rowell has qualifications beyond those possessed by anyone else' for understanding 'the creaking of the federal system.'[42] Perhaps the biggest question in Rowell's own mind was his health. By taking care, he had been able to work reasonably well during the past year, but should he take on a year or more of fairly concentrated and demanding work involving a great deal of travelling? With some trepidation about his physical strength, he agreed to accept what he believed was 'the most important and difficult task' he had ever undertaken.[43]

In consultations in Ottawa with King and Dafoe, Rowell agreed that public acceptance of the commission demanded that it include representation from British Columbia and the Maritimes. In a few days Professor Henry Angus, an economist from the University of British Columbia, and Dr R.A. Mackay of the Department of Political Science at Dalhousie University had agreed to serve. The appointment of the Royal Commission on Dominion-Provincial Relations was publicly announced in mid-August 1937. It was an indication of public expectations that the members of the Rowell commission were soon being referred to as 'The Fathers of Re-Confederation.'

Rowell immediately launched a series of discussions, mainly with King, Lapointe, and Dafoe about the organization and procedures appropriate to the work of the commission. Shortly, Alex Skelton, the brilliant and imaginative son of O.D. Skelton and currently research officer with the Bank of Canada, was appointed secretary and began to recruit a research staff. At the outset, Rowell conceived of the enquiry as almost purely constitutional in character, although embracing the financial consequences of constitutional arrangements. Before long, perhaps reflecting Dafoe's influence, he began to see the enterprise in a much broader historical and economic setting.[44] That agreed, the range of research studies needed was broad indeed. As always with Rowell, the work had to be done thoroughly, and he was insistent on the provision of adequate staff and funds. Soon, many of the country's brightest historians and social scientists were at work on specialized studies for the commission in the fullest investigation of the functioning of a federal system ever conducted.

A subject of considerable discussion in the initial stages of organization was the appointment of legal counsel. Rowell was convinced that in order to avoid any possibility of misunderstanding by the provinces about the impartiality of the counsel, the commission rather than the Dominion government should choose and appoint its own counsel. The services of James Macgregor Stewart, a leading member of the Halifax bar, were secured, and when Justice Rinfret succeeded in interesting Louis S. St-Laurent the commissioners agreed readily to his appointment.[45] Not only was St-Laurent an eminent member of the Quebec bar, but as past president of the Canadian Bar Association he was well known across the country. R.M. Fowler, a young Montreal lawyer, leaped at the chance to serve as Rowell's legal secretary since he wanted the experience of working under the man whom he regarded as probably the best constitutional lawyer in the country.[46]

While the research studies got under way, the commission began to prepare its schedule of public hearings. With Alex Skelton, Rowell travelled first to the capitals of the four western provinces and then to Quebec and the Maritime capitals, mainly to confer with politicians and civil servants about the presentation of briefs from the provincial governments, which were to be the most important part of the public hearings of the commission.

Before its work had really begun, the commission suffered a blow in the illness and subsequent retirement of Rinfret. Rowell believed that Rinfret inspired great confidence in Quebec, notably in Premier Maurice Duplessis; failure to find the right replacement from Quebec might seriously jeopardize the whole enterprise. The chairmanship of the commission had already proved to be a much heavier burden than Rowell had anticipated and might become intolerable without strong representation from Quebec.[47] Several consultations with King, Lapointe, and Dafoe resulted in the appointment of Dr Joseph Sirois, a Quebec notary and professor of constitutional law at Laval University who was personally unknown to Rowell but highly recommended by members of the Quebec bar whose judgment he trusted. Very soon it was clear that the choice could not have been a happier one, for Sirois quickly won the confidence of the other commissioners, the staff, and the public.[48]

A lesser threat was met and quickly turned aside. From the outset Rowell had understood that when the whole commission started to travel, the government would place a private railway car at their disposal. On the eve of their first trip to western Canada Rowell was dismayed and then angered to learn that the government claimed to know nothing of such an arrangement. When the question was brought before the cabinet with the recommendation of the minister of finance, Charles Dunning, that no private car be provided, the cabinet concurred since it was already alarmed at the expenses incurred by the commission and apprehensive about questions that would be asked in Parliament.[49] Rowell told Dunning in 'vigorous language what I thought of them and that if I could honourably retire I would.'[50] To Mackenzie King he protested that surely this commission had as much status as the recent ones on banking and transportation, and contended that the facilities provided by a private car were absolutely essential for conferences while travelling long distances and for the general efficiency of the commission's work.[51] Within two days the issue was resolved satisfactorily and Rowell observed: 'So the coon has come down. It must have been Mr King.'[52]

Just as the prairie winter descended on the city at the end of November, the commission arrived in Winnipeg for the first of its public hearings. Whether by accident or design the royal commissioners disposed themselves at the first hearing in the pattern they subsequently maintained, seated so that those addressing the commission saw before them a reflection of the map of Canada – Angus of British Columbia on the far left, Dafoe, the prairie editor, next to him, the Ontario chairman in the middle, then Sirois of Quebec, and Mackay of Nova Scotia on the far right. The first week was devoted to hearing the government of Manitoba, which presented nine large volumes of printed evidence, accompanied by well argued presentations from Premier John Bracken, the provincial treasurer, Stuart Garson, and others. The commissioners clearly thought that the Manitoba presentation had set a high standard for other provinces to follow. Only the argument on monetary policy left Rowell unimpressed; 'he dismissed Manitoba's brief on that question as "the weakest part of the province's case" and hinted that he regarded theorizing about currency as a waste of time.' Apparently the monetary reformers who abounded in the west would not have an easy time of it with the chairman of the commission. He was willing to consider more seriously Manitoba's proposal that the federal government should assume responsibility for unemployment relief, although his questioning suggested that he found it hard to believe that extensive unemployment could be a permanent problem in a country rich with unoccupied lands. Stuart Garson endeavoured to show the chief justice that the days of the heroic frontier when hard work would yield a living to anyone were gone forever and that some degree of unemployment was here to stay.[53] This was only the first of many occasions when the commission heard the argument supporting the Dominion government's assumption of the costs of unemployment relief.

The Manitoba witnesses seemed to have exhausted the possibilities in tales of gloom, but they proved to be 'pollyannas by comparison with the Saskatchewan citizens' who told their story in Regina.[54] Despite Rowell's knowledge of the devastation wrought by the depression on the prairies, he was unprepared for the saga of personal tragedy, loss of morale in whole communities, and public bankruptcy at both provincial and municipal levels that unfolded before the commission and in his conversations with local residents. According to the provincial government's brief, nearly 50 per cent of the total population of Saskatchewan were already on relief, and with little economic improvement in sight more would be wholly dependent on welfare before the end of the winter. Without help on 'a large and generous scale' Rowell found it hard to see how organized social and political life could continue.[55]

After the Regina hearings there was a month's break until mid-January. Rowell was well satisfied with the commission so far and with the degree of public interest in the hearings. That owed much to the excellent news coverage given by some of the best newspapermen in the country,[56] including J.B. McGeachy of the *Winnipeg Free Press*, Wellington Jeffers, financial editor of the *Globe and Mail*, Norman White of the *Financial Post* and D.A. McGregor of the Vancouver *Province*. On no subject had they written more positively than of the chairman himself. Some of the reporters who had previously seen him only at a distance or knew of him merely by repute as an austere and aloof character, and worst of all a teetotaler, were pleasantly surprised by the mild-mannered, soft-spoken gentleman whose unfailing courtesy even enabled him to turn a blind eye, when occasion demanded, on the drinking habits of certain members of the commission staff or the press corps. All were unanimous in their admiration of the intellectual power that resided in his frail physique, the clarity of diction in his questions and comments, and the range of his knowledge from the details of farm life to the intricacies of banking, federal and provincial finance, and constitutional law.[57]

Rowell himself had enjoyed the two western hearings, and his health had stood up well, but only by rigid disciplining of his time and energy. He attended few evening social functions, and left early when he did. He consistently refused all speaking engagements, as well as opportunities to hear his fellow commissioners, even when it meant missing an address from Dafoe on collective security. Most days he ate lunch alone in his hotel room, quietly enjoying the daily letter from Nell that awaited him and taking a brief nap before the afternoon session of the commission.[58]

He resumed the same stern regimen when the hearings continued in Ottawa, where a host of national organizations presented their solutions to the nation's ills. The Canadian Manufacturers' Association had a simple answer – cut taxes and reduce public expenditures – but Rowell was visibly unimpressed when its spokesman could suggest no single concrete measure for achieving this objective.[59] More interesting, although not necessarily acceptable to Rowell, were the socialist remedies of the League for Social Reconstruction argued ably by Professor F.R. Scott of McGill University and the brief on Canada and the treaty-making power presented by Professor N.A.M. Mackenzie for the League of Nations Society.[60] Mackenzie's passionate appeal for the granting of full treaty powers to Canada moved Rowell to an outburst against the Judicial Committee of the Privy Council that astounded his hearers, who had not realized that Rowell had become a convert to the abolition of appeals.[61] The recent decision of the Judicial Committee in 'the Labour Relations Case,' upholding the Supreme Court's decision against most of the Bennett 'New Deal,' which he had read with great care because of his earlier and intimate connection with the case, was in Rowell's view 'an amazing decision,' and one proving conclusively that British judges were incapable of understanding the Canadian federal system. If Canada were to have a modern system of social legislation she would have to get rid of their misinformed influence.[62]

In Halifax and Charlottetown the commission met the deeply rooted provincialism of the Maritimes in lengthy accounts of all that Nova Scotia and Prince Edward Island had suffered since joining confederation. Rowell found it hard to understand 'the psychology of the Maritimers who are constantly talking about what they lost by Confederation as if they think that will make it easier to get the other provinces to recognize their present needs.' At one point he felt compelled to ask the witness before him whether he thought it would contribute to domestic peace if he were to keep telling his wife that he made a mistake when he married her. Rowell assumed that the ensuing laughter was simply proof that he had made his point and was amused to learn later that the man addressing the commission had recently been divorced.[63]

Since the New Brunswick brief was not ready, the commission adjourned for several weeks, giving Rowell a chance to take a holiday with Nell in Augusta, Georgia. Nine holes of golf, some reading, and a lot of rest was the pattern of their days.[64] Rowell's relaxation was marred by his anxiety over what was then happening in Europe. Since the demise of the League he had seen the best chance for peace in Anthony Eden's efforts to lead in the formation of an alliance of anti-Axis powers to call a halt to the appeasement of the fascist dictators. Since the League was dead, some form of collective security among the democracies seemed the only hope.[65] That hope now suffered a heavy blow in Eden's resignation from Neville Chamberlain's cabinet, apparently over Chamberlain's willingness to seek an accord with Mussolini without first assuring at least a modification of Italian support for General Franco in the Spanish civil war. To Rowell, Hitler's march into Austria only a month later was 'the strongest possible vindication for Anthony Eden's policy ... Neither Hitler nor Mussolini will stop until stopped by force or the fear of force.'[66]

In Victoria in mid-March the commission met the most extreme provincialism it had yet encountered. British Columbia was the first province to hand over the assertion of its position to a barrister, and soon Senator J.W. de B. Farris had turned his presentation of British Columbia's 'special claims' into a forensic show. Rowell had several times pointed out that he was not conducting a court of claims, and the turn of the enquiry in Victoria disturbed somewhat his otherwise affable demeanour. The Pacific province paid too much to the federal treasury, Farris contended, as evidenced by the fact that since 1917 the province had paid as much in income taxes as Alberta, Saskatchewan, and the three Maritime provinces combined. That only proved that British Columbians made more money than other Canadians, Rowell told him, but Farris refused to admit any truth in that view.[67] Rowell was cheered to see that the province was almost universally chastised in the British Columbia press for being 'extreme in its demands and ultra provincial' in its attitudes, and he believed the government would realize that it had made a mistake.[68] It was a relief to turn to the well prepared and nationally oriented briefs of the Provincial Council of Women and the Youth Council of British Columbia. For the latter, two serious young men ardently defended a highly unpopular cause on the west coast – civil rights for orientals – and urged that all Canadians be obliged to learn both French and English. Although far from convinced of the practicality of some of their views, Rowell congratulated the youth group on its public spirit and the clarity of its brief. Reviewing the British Columbia hearings Rowell observed: 'The most remarkable feature is that all the briefs presented by public organizations stress the national point of view and urge the strengthening of the central authority whereas the Provincial brief has stressed little but BC grievances. It would appear that the people who came before us are ahead of the government in national sentiment.[69]

Nobody but members of the press met the commission on its arrival in Edmonton. It seemed that in the strange land of Social Credit the government's attitude would be as chilly as the tag end of the Alberta winter. The next morning Rowell spent an hour with Premier William Aberhart and his cabinet. The premier professed eagerness to present a brief but said that the Legislature would not let him. 'By legislature he no doubt meant the SC caucus. It is dominated by Major C.H. Douglas & I am told that Douglas cabled them some time ago not to submit a brief. This is a new form of government in Canada. Instead of government from Downing Street as the cry was a century ago it is government from the Social Credit headquarters in London.'[70] There were other explanations. Some believed that the absence of the Alberta government was due to Aberhart's extreme reluctance, or perhaps inability, to answer detailed questions about his theories.[71]

While the Legislature continued a feeble debate on the submission of a brief, Rowell opened the hearings, expressing the commission's interest in Alberta but never mentioning the government. The people of Alberta, it seemed, were interested in the commission, for they turned out in larger numbers than in any centre to date, filling a dismal courtroom, the poorest accommodation provided by any province. The aloofness of the government had one advantage for Rowell. There were no official luncheons or dinners to attend, and he was still doing as little extra as possible. The government provided no hospitality whatever, and the lieutenant governor was scarcely in a position to give a party since he was currently being ejected from Government House in retaliation for his refusal to give assent to several Social Credit bills.

Although the government finally decided to boycott the commission, the views of Albertans were well presented by private groups. Rowell congratulated John M. Imrie, managing editor of the *Edmonton Journal*, appearing on behalf of the Chamber of Commerce, for one of the most logical and coherent presentations the commission had received.[72] Also of interest to Rowell were the briefs of the United Farmers of Alberta and the CCF, although 'extreme and impossible in their suggestions, especially the latter. It is however most interesting to note that both favour a strong central government. In fact all the briefs here which touched on the question were to that effect.'[73] As everywhere, Rowell asked the Albertans whether health insurance should be under federal or provincial jurisdiction.

When the commission moved to Toronto for the first of its hearings in central Canada, there was widespread speculation that the Hepburn government might be as unco-operative as Alberta had been. Rumour had it that the alliance formed by Hepburn and Premier Maurice Duplessis of Quebec to fight Mackenzie King and defend 'provincial rights' was determined to boycott the Rowell commission. But this proved unfounded. The government of Ontario put the legislative chamber at the disposal of the commission for its sittings and the attorney general, Gordon Conant, extended a brief and cautious welcome. After a week of receiving briefs from groups ranging from mortgage companies to the British Israel Federation, which thought the laws of Moses would solve all the problems of Canadian federalism, the commission heard Premier Hepburn, flanked by twenty administrative colleagues. Since the commissioners had read the Ontario brief beforehand, they were not taken by surprise when Hepburn launched into a ninety-minute political harangue of the kind that had got him elected. Failing to get the cheers and wisecracks usually forthcoming from his audiences, and finding his jokes falling 'like pancakes in a puddle,' Hepburn continued to read his speech at breakneck pace. In so far as a coherent argument could be extracted from Hepburn's performance, it was largely an attack on Manitoba's presentation to the commission, an uncompromising assertion that Ontario stood by the status quo and rejected western proposals for a redistribution of taxing and spending powers as 'an unashamed raid by the orphans of Confederation on the pockets of central Canada.' The commissioners listened in grim silence; they were not amused. By general consent among press and public the Ontario brief was 'full of half-baked economics, appeals to prejudice, jumbled logic, and parish politics.'[74]

Nobody was more disturbed by the whole shoddy performance and by the total absence of any national vision from Canada's banner province than the chief justice of Ontario. Earlier, the commissioners had agreed not to allow Hepburn to succeed in provoking them into the negative reaction he would undoubtedly have welcomed. Clearly he was now extremely anxious not to be forced to answer any questions. Rowell's brief comments, 'like honey or salve, his diction chaste and cultured,' brought a memorable and unhappy session to a speedy end.[75]

Later that week Hepburn entertained the commission and its staff lavishly in the King Edward Hotel. Rowell went for dinner, reluctantly, as a matter of duty, and left almost immediately the meal was over. Thereupon the party assumed the boisterous and bawdy character of any affair having Mitch Hepburn as its star.[76]

That was Rowell's last public appearance. Two days later, early on the morning of 7 May, he suffered a heart attack, from which he rallied only to have a paralysing stroke deprive him of the power of speech. When the nature of his affliction was made public after several days, not a few wondered whether his encounter with the brash and vulgar Hepburn had contributed to his illness.

The commission was forced to conduct its hearings in Quebec and Fredericton without Rowell, with Sirois acting as chairman. At the end of three months Rowell had improved slightly, and his doctors entertained some hope that he might regain his speech, at least in some degree. By the autumn of 1938 there was no longer any reason to believe that he could resume any of his duties. He was able to read a little and evidently understood what was said to him, but the realization that so fine a tongue was permanently silenced seemed incredible and unbearable to relatives and friends. In mid-October his resignations as chief justice and as chairman of the Royal Commission were forwarded to Ottawa.

His fellow commissioners were busy on their report, and from time to time they or members of the commission staff visited him briefly. From the beginning of their work, Rowell had discouraged any discussion of the evidence until after the completion of the hearings.[77] Would he have concurred in the directions they were taking in their report? There can be little doubt that he would have approved. The report's attempt to put the federal government in a position to guarantee minimum standards of education and social services for all Canadians across the country, while putting the provinces in a financial position enabling them to administer these services, was thoroughly in accord with his vision of Canada. Although he had been unable to complete the work, there was some satisfaction in knowing that his contribution to the development of the report was far from insignificant.

Rowell died on 22 November 1941, after more than four years of illness during which his condition changed but little, despite the best of medical attention and Nell's constant and loving care. The funeral service in Metropolitan Church, where he had worshipped for fifty years, was conducted by Dr Peter Bryce, assisted by three other former ministers, including his friend since the early years in Toronto, Dr R.P. Bowles. Sections of the church were designated for representatives of the judiciary, the bar, government, business, the church, and education. His son Frederick wore the uniform of the Royal Canadian Air Force, a reminder that once again thousands of Canadian sons were at war. As Rowell himself had requested, the service was a simple one, with no eulogy and no pallbearers.

The dominant tone of much of the public commentary on Rowell's death was reflected in B.K. Sandwell's editorial in *Saturday Night*, under the title 'What Canada Missed.' 'Few recent funerals have created so profound a sense of public tragedy.' It was an event that should give 'all serious Canadians occasion for much searching of heart.' Why had a man possessed of such abilities and such unselfish desire for public service not been permitted to play a larger part in the life of Canada, especially during the last twenty years of his life? His 'austerity' was not a sufficient explanation, nor was his break with his party on conscription. 'A mature democracy does not reject great men for either of these reasons.'[78] Some observers recalled that by espousing conscription in 1917 Rowell had destroyed his prospects of succeeding Sir Wilfrid Laurier as leader of the Liberal party; sometimes it was implied that this was an error in political judgment.

Such speculation and questioning were foreign to the man himself. Those close to Rowell knew that he was singularly free of feelings of regret about what might have been. The present always provided intellectual and moral challenges in full measure; happiness lay in doing one's best to meet them. The hour for making the right decision, the time to serve, was always *now*. The consequences were in the safe keeping of God's good time.

Notes

ONE / METHODISTS AND REFORMERS

1 Rowell Family Papers, Joseph Rowell to Nathan Wannop, Brampton, Cumberland, 5 Sept. 1842. Some of this chapter is based on a family chronicle prepared in 1949 by Mrs N.W. Rowell.
2 Ibid., John Routledge, on behalf of himself and Joseph Rowell, to Nathan Wannop, 10 July 1842
3 Ibid., Joseph Rowell to Nathan Wannop, 5 Sept. 1842
4 Fred Landon and Orlo Miller, *Up the Proof Line* London, Ontario, 1955, p. 44
5 *History of Middlesex County* Toronto, 1890, p. 841
6 Fred C. Hamil, *Lake Erie Baron* Toronto, 1956, *passim*; C.O. Ermatinger, *The Talbot Regime* St Thomas, 1904, p. 106
7 Fred Landon, 'London and Its Vicinity in 1837,' *Papers and Records of the Ontario Historical Association* 24, 1927, p. 415
8 Fred Landon, 'Rebellion Losses Claims in the London District in 1845,' Ibid., 27, 1931, p. 430
9 *Christian Guardian* 29 Feb. 1888, obituary of Joseph Rowell
10 Rowell Family Papers, Rowell to his mother, 19 Sept. 1879 (henceforth 'Rowell' will refer to N.W. Rowell); Mary Rowell (Rowell's half-sister) to Mrs Edward Green, 23 Dec. 1880; Edward Rowell to Mrs Edward Green, 20 May 1881; D.M. Hefferman to Rowell, 21 Sept. and 25 and 26 Oct. 1883
22 Ibid., Rowell to Mary Rowell (his sister), 8 Feb. 1885
12 The total program for these years is outlined in Arthur E. Bestor jr, *Chautauqua Publications: An Historical and Bibliographical Guide* Chautauqua, New York, 1934, pp. 30–4
13 *History of Middlesex County* p. 841
14 Rowell Family Papers, Rowell to Mrs Thomas Green, 13 Aug. 1886
15 Ibid., Rowell to his sisters, 11 Aug. 1887
16 W.B. Selbie, *The Life of Andrew Martin Fairbairn* London, 1914, p. 183
17 Rowell Family Papers, Rowell to his parents, 7 Aug. 1887

18 Ibid., Rowell to Edward Rowell, 18 and 27 Nov. 1889
19 *History of Middlesex County* p. 679
20 Rowell Family Papers, Rowell to his mother, 31 Aug. 1890
21 London *Advertiser* 12 Sept. 1890
22 Rowell Family Papers, Rowell to his mother, 14 Aug. 1890
23 Ibid., Rowell to his mother, 14 Sept. 1890
24 London *Advertiser* 9 Oct. 1890
25 Rowell Family Papers, Rowell to Mary Rowell, 5 Oct. 1890
26 Ibid., Rowell to his mother, 12 Oct. 1890
27 London *Advertiser* 9 Oct. 1890
28 Ibid., 21 Nov. 1890; 12 and 22 Jan. 1891
29 London *Advertiser* 22 Jan. 1891
30 Rowell Family Papers, Rowell to Mary Rowell, 8 Dec. 1890
31 Ibid., Rowell to F.G. Calvert, 24 Nov. 1890
32 Ibid., Rowell to his mother, 21 Dec. 1890
33 Ibid., Rowell to Edward Rowell, 30 Dec. 1890
34 Ibid., Rowell to his mother, 4 Jan. 1891
35 Ibid., Rowell to Edward Rowell[?], 21 Jan. 1891

TWO / THE YOUNG TORONTO LAWYER

1 Rowell Family Papers, Rowell to Mary Rowell, 20 April 1891; Rowell to his mother, 14 May 1891
2 Ibid., Rowell to Mary Rowell, 24 Nov. 1891; Rowell to his mother, 9 Sept. 1892
3 Despite Mr Justice Rose's assessment of the importance of the case it is not reported in any of the official law reports. This account is based on some unidentified newspaper clippings in the Rowell Papers and a report in the *Globe* 6 March 1893.
4 Rowell Family Papers, Rowell to Edward Rowell, 2 June 1891
5 *Globe* 8 and 21 Dec. 1891
6 Ibid., 18 Jan. 1892
7 Queen's University, Douglas Library, W.D. Gregory Papers, unpublished autobiography of Gregory, p. 112. Gregory does not date this meeting precisely, but a variety of evidence suggests that it occurred early in 1893.
8 *Official Report of the Liberal Convention* Toronto, 1893, pp. 125–8
9 Ibid., pp. 81, 57
10 Rowell Family Papers, Rowell to Mary Rowell, 24 Nov. 1891
11 Ibid., Rowell to his mother, 23 Nov. 1891
12 *Globe* 8 Feb. 1892
13 Ibid., 1 March 1893
14 Victoria University, United Church Archives, Carman Papers, Dr W.H. Withrow to Dr A.R. Carman, 5 April 1894; *Christian Guardian* 19 Sept. 1894
15 Carman Papers, C.S. Jones to A.R. Carman, 9 March 1895
16 *Proceedings of the Third Ecumenical Methodist Conference* New York, 1901, p. 320
17 *Journal of the Proceedings of the Fourth Methodist General Conference* Toronto, 1894, p. 300
18 James T. Watt, 'Anti-Catholicism in Ontario Politics: The Role of the Protestant Protective Association in the 1894 Election,' *Ontario History* 59, no. 2, 1967
19 *Globe* 14 June 1894

20 Rowell Family Papers, Rowell to his mother, 1 Jan. 1894
21 Ibid., Rowell to his family, 9 July 1895
22 *Times* 6 July 1895
23 Rowell Family Papers, Rowell to his family, 9 July 1895
24 Ibid.
25 *Globe* 22 June 1896
26 PAC, Rowell Papers, ms. of speech, July [?] 1896
27 *Globe* 10 and 24 June 1897
28 I am grateful to my colleague Charles Humphries for allowing me to read his unpublished paper, 'Politics in Southwestern Ontario at the Turn of the Century,' which deals with this change.
29 *Globe* 16 Feb. 1898
30 *Kingston Daily Whig* 28 Feb. 1898
31 *Globe* 16 Feb. 1898
32 Ibid., 14 Sept. 1898
33 Rowell Papers, ms. notes of plebiscite speeches, 1898. For a general discussion of the prohibition movement, see Graham Decarie, 'Something Old, Something New ...: Aspects of Prohibitionism in Ontario in the 1890s,' in Donald Swainson, ed., *Oliver Mowat's Ontario* Toronto, 1972, pp. 154–171
34 Ruth E. Spence, *Prohibition in Canada* Toronto, 1919, p. 248
35 Ibid., p. 227

THREE / LIBERALISM IN EAST YORK

1 Rowell Family Papers, Rowell to Nellie Langford, 27 Sept. 1900
2 PAC, Rowell Papers, Rowell to Willison, 29 Aug. 1900
3 PAC, Laurier Papers, Willison to Laurier, 5 Jan. 1900; Laurier to Willison, 8 Jan. 1900; Mulock to Laurier, 19 Feb. 1900
4 Ibid., Laurier to Rowell, 31 Aug. 1900
5 Ibid., W. O'Connor to Laurier, 2 Sept. 1900. Laurier did not acknowledge this appeal until the day of the nominating convention and then, characteristically, said that he made it a policy never to interfere in local matters. Ibid., Laurier to O'Connor, 7 Sept. 1900
6 Rowell Family Papers, Rowell to Nellie Langford, 14 Nov. 1900
7 Laurier Papers, Rowell to Laurier, 8 Sept. 1900
8 PAC, Willison Papers, G.G.S. Lindsey to Willison, 5 Sept. 1900
9 Hector Charlesworth, *More Candid Chronicles* Toronto, 1928, p. 145
10 *Globe* 8 Sept. 1900; *Mail and Empire* 8 Sept. 1900
11 Ross Harkness, *J.E. Atkinson of the Star* Toronto, 1963, p. 27; Hector Charlesworth, *Candid Chronicles* Toronto, 1925, pp. 128–9; Willison Papers, John Crerar to Willison, 17 Nov. 1900
12 Harkness, *J.E. Atkinson*, pp. 10, 40–1; *Globe* 11 Sept. 1900; *Toronto Star* 11 Sept. and 23 Oct. 1900
13 *Globe* 20 Sept. 1900
14 Rowell Papers, no. 16313, rough draft of speech
15 *Globe* 20 Sept. 1900
16 *Globe* 23 Oct. 1900
17 Ibid., 23 Oct. 1900
18 *World* 22 and 23 Oct. 1900

19 *Globe* 23 Oct. 1900
20 Ibid., 1 and 7 Nov. 1900
21 Ibid., 26 Oct. and 1 Nov. 1900
22 *World* 6 and 7 Nov. 1900; *Toronto Star* 6 Nov. 1900
23 Rowell Family Papers, Rowell to his mother, 4 Nov. 1900
24 *Globe* 8 Nov. 1900
25 Laurier Papers, Willison to Laurier 10 Nov. 1900
26 Rowell Family Papers, Rowell to Mary Rowell, 9 Nov. 1900. The Toronto *Saturday Night*, no lover of Liberals or prohibitionists, agreed that 'the whole force of the Licensed Victuallers' had been directed against Rowell. *Saturday Night* 17 Nov. 1900
27 Ibid., Rowell to Mary Rowell, 23 Nov. 1900
28 Ibid., Rowell to his mother, 4 Nov. 1900; Rowell to Mary Rowell, 23 Nov. 1900
29 Ibid., Nellie Langford to Rowell, Nov. [?] 1900
30 Ibid., Rowell to Nellie Langford, 14 Nov. 1900
31 Ibid., Rowell to Mary Rowell, 10 Jan. 1901
32 Rowell Family Papers, Nell Rowell's Diary, 1 Aug. – 10 Sept. 1901

FOUR / SHAPING CANADA'S CENTURY

1 *Proceedings of the Third Ecumenical Methodist Conference* New York, 1901, pp. 77–8
2 Ibid.
3 Cited in Maldwyn Edwards, *Methodism in England* London, 1943, p. 173
4 K.S. Inglis, *Churches and the Working Classes in Victorian England* Toronto, 1963, p. 289
5 Rowell Family Papers, Rowell to his mother, 20 April 1902
6 PAC, Laurier Papers, Laurier to Clergue, 14 Sept. 1900
7 *News* 3 Oct. 1905. For a discussion of the Clergue enterprises, see H.V. Nelles, *The Politics of Development: Forests, Mines and Hydro-Electric Power in Ontario, 1849–1941* Toronto, 1974, pp. 56–62, 132–8
8 PAC, Sifton Papers, copy, G.W. Ross to Rowell, 2 Jan. 1901
9 *Globe* 26 Feb. 1902
10 Ibid., Ruth E. Spence, *Prohibition in Canada* Toronto, 1919, pp. 290–1; *Globe* 6 March 1902
11 PAC, Rowell Papers, Box 35, Memos and notes re pulpwood and lumbering; *Globe* 10 May 1902, also 26 April and 19 May 1902. For the debate over timber policy at this time see Nelles, *The Politics of Development* pp. 110–116
12 Ibid., 26 Nov. 1902
13 *Canadian Annual Review, 1902* pp. 385–6
14 *News* 30 Dec. 1902
15 *Report of the Royal Commission re the Gamey Charges* Toronto, 1903; Charles W. Humphries, 'The Gamey Affair,' *Ontario History* 59, 1967, pp. 101–9
16 *Canadian Annual Review, 1904* p. 282
17 *Globe* 24 Nov. 1904
18 Spence, *Prohibition in Canada* p. 314
19 *Globe* 24 Nov. 1904
20 Provincial Archives of Ontario, Hearst Papers, Memorandum prepared by the Dominion Alliance in 1915 relating the history of the parties on the liquor issue
21 PAC, Willison Papers, Rowell to Willison, 4 Nov. 1911, commenting on his earlier relationships with the party
22 *Christian Guardian* 8 Feb. 1905

23 Rowell Family Papers, Nell Rowell to Mary Rowell, 2 Oct. 1904
24 *Christian Guardian* 17 Sept. 1902
25 Ibid., 26 Nov. 1902
26 *Globe* 16 Sept. 1902
27 Ibid., 10 Sept. 1902
28 Ibid., 18 Sept. 1902
29 Ibid., 26 Oct. 1904
30 Rowell Papers, Rowell to Laurier, 20 Feb. 1905
31 Ibid., Laurier to Rowell, 22 Feb. 1905
32 *House of Commons Debates* 21 Feb. 1905, pp. 1458–9
33 Ibid., 1 March 1905, p. 1857
34 Rowell Papers, Rowell to Laurier, 10 March 1905. Section 43 of the Quebec Resolutions gave the provinces power to legislate over education, 'saving the rights and privileges which the Protestant or Catholic minority in both Canadas may possess as to their Denominational Schools at the time when the Union goes into operation.' The equivalent statement in section 93 of the British North America Act reads: 'Nothing in any such Law [passed by a province] shall prejudicially affect any Right or Privilege with respect to Denominational Schools which any Class of Persons have by Law in the Province at the Union.'
35 Rowell Papers, Rowell to Laurier, 10 March 1905
36 Ibid., Laurier to Rowell, 13 March 1905
37 Ibid., Rowell to Laurier, 20 March 1905
38 Willison Papers, Willison to G. Frank Beer, 29 Nov. 1912; Toronto *News* 4 May 1905. Willison was mistaken in thinking that Laurier's earlier policy on the Manitoba schools was based on any doctrine of provincial rights. H. Blair Neatby, *Laurier and a Liberal Quebec* Toronto, 1973, p. 151. For a discussion of Willison's disenchantment with the Liberal party, see Richard T. Clippingdale, 'J.S. Willison, Political Journalist: From Liberalism to Independence, 1881–1905,' unpublished PH D thesis, University of Toronto, 1970, pp. 563–87.
39 *Globe* 15 June 1905; *Canadian Annual Review, 1905* pp. 113–14
40 Rowell Family Papers, Nell Rowell Diary, 8 April – 26 June 1905
41 *News*, 22 Sept. 1906
42 *Globe* 20 Sept. 1906
43 *World* 20 Sept. 1906
44 *Journal of the Proceedings of the Seventh General Conference of the Methodist Church* Toronto, 1906, p. 274
45 N.W. Rowell, *Foreign Missions: Our Privilege and Responsibility* [Toronto, 1907] copy in Victoria University, United Church Archives
46 Ibid.
47 Ibid.
48 N.W. Rowell, *The Church and Immigration* [Toronto, 1908] copy in United Church Archives
49 *Calgary Daily News* 19 Oct. 1908
50 Rowell Family Papers, Rowell to Mary Rowell, 22 Jan. and 1 March 1908
51 Keewatin Power Company v. Town of Kenora, and Hudson's Bay Company v. Town of Kenora [1907] OLR, 237; [1908] OLR, 184
52 R.S. Fairty, 'Reminiscences: An Address to the Lawyers' Club of Toronto, October 30, 1947,' copy in Osgoode Hall Library, Toronto
53 Duryea v. Kaufman [1912] 3 OWN, 651; 2 DLR, 468; Fairty, *Reminiscences*

54 This is not to imply that businessmen were united in the policies they advocated. For a discussion of the varieties of attitudes within the business community in this period and of support among businessmen for limitations on competition see Michael Bliss, *A Living Profit: Studies in the Social History of Canadian Business, 1883–1911* Toronto, 1974.
55 If the typology used by the author of a recent study of the social gospel is adopted, Rowell may be considered a progressive social gospeller or perhaps a 'conservative-progressive,' favouring 'a broad ameliorative programme of reform' and 'holding the tension between the two extremes' represented by conservative and radical social gospellers. Richard Allen, *The Social Passion: Religion and Social Reform in Canada, 1914–28* Toronto, 1971, p. 17
56 William H. Magney, 'The Methodist Church and the National Gospel, 1884–1914,' *The Bulletin*, United Church Archives, 1968

FIVE / HIGHER CRITICISM AND CANADA'S DESTINY

1 *Globe* 26 Feb. 1909
2 Ibid., 27 Feb. 1909
3 Ibid.
4 Ibid.; the members of the committee were J.W. Flavelle, H.H. Fudger, Senator G.A. Cox, Richard Brown, S.R. Parsons, and John D. Ivey.
5 Ibid., 1 March 1909
6 PAC, Rowell Papers, Rowell to Carman, 1 March 1909
7 Ibid., Carman to Rowell, 2 March 1909
8 Interview with Rev. Dr R.P. Bowles by the author, 20 April 1956; Augustus Bridle, *Sons of Canada* Toronto, 1916, pp. 149–55; J.W.L. Forster, *Under the Studio Light* Toronto, 1928, p. 205. For a fictional portrayal of Dr Carman (as 'Dr Carboy') see 'Family Prayer,' in Ethel Wilson *The Innocent Traveller* Toronto, 1949.
9 Victoria University, United Church Archives, Proceedings of the Court of Appeal, 1888–1910, 18 July 1907, 19 Dec. 1907, 8 Dec. 1908, pp. 308–12, 314–19, 322–7
10 H.H. Walsh, *The Christian Church in Canada* Toronto, 1956, pp. 290–1. For a full discussion of the theological aspects of both the Workman and Jackson controversies, see G.A. Boyle, 'Higher Criticism and the Struggle for Academic Freedom in Canadian Methodism,' unpublished D TH thesis, Victoria University, 1965.
11 *Globe* 17 Feb. 1909; *Toronto Star* 17 Feb. 1909. There is also a stenographic copy of the address in United Church Archives, Carman Papers.
12 Interview with Dr Bowles, 20 April 1956
13 Carman Papers, Mrs Gordon Wright to Carman, 22 Feb. 1906
14 Annie Jackson, *George Jackson* London, 1948, p. 26; Rowell Papers, Rowell to Carman, 1 March 1909
15 Quoted in Jackson, *George Jackson* p. 29
16 Ibid., p. 28
17 Statement of the Pulpit Supply Committee of Sherbourne Street Church, *Globe* 28 Feb. 1909; Rowell Papers, 2 July 1910
18 Interviews with Dr Bowles, 20 April 1956; Jackson, *George Jackson* p. 30
19 Report of the Board of Regents of Victoria College, *Journal of the Proceedings of the Eighth Annual Conference of the Methodist Church* Toronto, 1910, p. 209
20 Carman Papers, Rowell to Carman, 10 March 1909
21 Ibid., Carman to Rowell, 11 March 1909

22 *Globe* 12 March 1909
23 Rowell Papers, Rowell to Carman, 12 March 1909
24 Carman Papers, Rowell to Carman, 13 March 1909
25 Ibid., Rowell to Carman, 16 and 23 March 1909
26 Rowell Papers, Rowell to Jackson, 15 March 1909
27 *Globe* 22 March 1909
28 Carman Papers, Rowell to Carman, 24 March 1909
29 *Globe* 24 March 1909
30 Victoria University, Minutes of the Board of Regents, 23 March 1909; *Christian Guardian* 31 March 1909
31 Carman Papers, Rowell to Carman, 24 March 1909; Rowell Papers, Carman to Rowell, 24 March 1909
32 Rowell Papers, Flavelle to Rowell, 24 March 1909
33 *Christian Guardian* 24 March 1909
34 *Canada's Missionary Congress* Toronto, 1909, pp. v–vi. The officers of the committee which organized the congress were, in addition to Rowell, S.J. Moore, E.R. Wood, John Mackay, S. Casey Wood jr, Hon. A.B. Morine, H.K. Caskey, executive secretary.
35 *Globe* 1 April 1909
36 *Canada's Missionary Congress* p. 36
37 Ibid., pp. 39–47
38 Ibid., pp. 45, 302, 320
39 Copy in Carman Papers
40 Rowell Papers, Rowell to Ross, 3 June 1909
41 Ibid., Ross to Rowell, 11 June 1909
42 Ibid., Rowell to Ross, 14 June 1909
43 Carman Papers, Rowell to Carman, 29 June 1909; Ross to Carman, 2 July 1909; Carman to Rowell, 12 July 1909; Rowell Papers, Rowell to Carman, 15 July 1909
44 Carman Papers, Carman to Burwash, 25 Sept. and 2 Oct. 1909
45 Ibid., Burwash to Carman, 29 Sept. 1909
46 Copy in Carman Papers
47 Rowell Papers, Burwash to Rowell, 27 June 1910; Jackson to Rowell, 2 July 1910; *Globe* 15 June 1910
48 Rowell Papers, Fudger to Rowell, 27 June 1910
49 Ibid., Jackson to Rowell, 2 July 1910
50 Ibid., Rowell to R.E. Bull. 9 Aug. 1910
51 Interview with Dr Bowles, 20 April 1956
52 Rowell Papers, Chester Massey to Rowell, 2 Aug. 1910. Businessmen who made large gifts to the college in the decade before the first world war included H.H. Fudger, A.E. Ames, J.W. Flavelle, Senator G.A. Cox, as well as the Masseys. See C.B. Sissons, *A History of Victoria University* Toronto, 1952, chap. 10, *passim*
53 *Journal of the Proceedings of the Eighth General Conference of the Methodist Church in Canada* Toronto, 1910, appendix, pp. 4, 9–10. Judged by at least two criteria Sherbourne Street Church was the wealthiest Methodist congregation in Canada. It raised more money for all purposes than any other, and its minister received the largest salary, i.e. $3,000. Metropolitan Church was not far behind. *The Methodist Year Book, 1910*
54 Sissons, *A History of Victoria University* pp. 238–40
55 *Christian Guardian* 14 Sept. 1910
56 Interview with Dr Bowles, 20 April 1956

57 *The Journal of John Wesley* 8 vols, London 1909–16, 7, p. 389
58 Carman Papers, Dr A.R. Dafoe to Carman, 10 March 1909
59 *Memoirs and Writings: Harris Henry Fudger, 1852–1930* compiled by his daughter, printed for private circulation Toronto, 1931
60 *Globe* 6 March 1909
61 Ibid., 21 Jan. 1909
62 For a discussion of the Methodist attempt to 'win the west,' see G.N. Emery, 'Methodism on the Canadian Prairies, 1896–1914: The Dynamics of an Institution in a New Environment,' unpublished PH D thesis, University of British Columbia, 1970

SIX / A LIBERAL MOSES

1 PAC, Willison Papers, Rowell to Willison, 4 Nov. 1911
2 *Globe* 3 March 1906
3 *House of Commons Debates* 7 April 1910, p. 6543
4 PAC, Graham Papers, Rowell to Graham, 9 April 1910
5 Ibid., Rowell to Graham, 13 April 1910
6 *Statutes of Canada* 9–10 Edw. VII, c. 10
7 *House of Commons Debates* 15 April 1910, pp. 718–19
8 *Globe* 21 April 1910
9 Ibid., 2 April 1911
10 For their status as Liberals see Robert D. Cuff, 'The Toronto Eighteen and the Election of 1911,' *Ontario History* 57, 1965, pp. 169–80
11 Graham Papers, Graham to Rowell, 15 March 1911; Graham to F.G. Inwood, 15 March 1911
12 *Globe* 3 March 1911
13 Ibid.
14 PAC, King Papers, King to Rowell, 24 Sept. 1911
15 PAC, Rowell Papers, ms. of speech used several times during the campaign
16 PAC, Laurier Papers, Rowell to Laurier, 26 Jan. 1912
17 *Globe* 25 Aug. 1911
18 Ibid., 14 Sept. 1911
19 It has been suggested, but not entirely demonstrated, that the Conservatives, thanks to the efficiency of their organization and the weakness of Liberal party organization, could have won on almost any issue. See Robert D. Cuff, 'The Conservative Party Machine and the Election of 1911,' *Ontario History* 57, 1965, pp. 149–56. On the same point, and for a discussion of Laurier's relations with Ontario in this period, see Paul Stevens, 'Laurier, Aylesworth, and the Decline of the Liberal Party in Ontario,' *Canadian Historical Association, Annual Report, 1968* pp. 94–113.
20 King Papers, King to Violet Markham, 15 Dec. 1911
21 Rowell Family Papers, Nell Rowell to Mary Rowell, [2] Nov. 1911
22 Ibid.; PAC, Murphy Papers, G.P. Graham to Murphy, [n.d.]
23 Rowell Family Papers, Nell Rowell to Mary Rowell, [2] Nov. 1911
24 King Papers, King to Violet Markham, 15 Dec. 1911; Rowell Papers, A.G. Mackay to Rowell, 3 Nov. 1911; Cyril T. Young to Rowell, 2 Nov. 1911
25 Willison Papers, Rowell to Willison, 24 Dec. 1913
26 Rowell Papers, Rowell to Rev. W.W. Anglin, 6 Dec. 1911
27 Ibid., Cyril T. Young to Rowell, 2 Nov. 1911; see also W.E. Rundle to Rowell, 2 Nov. 1911

28 *Address to the Electors by N.W. Rowell* Ontario Reform Association, 1911
29 *Journals of the Legislative Assembly of Ontario* 21 March 1911, p. 260
30 *Address to the Electors by N.W. Rowell* Ontario Reform Association, 1911
31 *Canadian Annual Review 1911* p. 456
32 Rowell Papers, G.F. Mahon to C.M. Bowman, 9 Nov. 1911
33 *Globe* 13 Nov. 1911
34 Ibid., 15 Nov. 1911
35 Rowell Family Papers, Nell Rowell to Mary Rowell, 16 Nov. 1911
36 *Globe* 15 and 16 Nov 1911
37 Rowell Family Papers, Nell Rowell to Mary Rowell, 16 Nov. 1911
38 *Globe* 7 Nov. 1911, open letter, Rowell to Mrs Flora McD. Denison
39 King Papers, King to Violet Markham, 15 Dec. 1911
40 Ibid., Rowell to King, 30 June 1909 and 31 Dec. 1909
41 Ibid., Laurier to King, 13 Nov. 1911
42 Ibid., King to Violet Markham, 15 Dec. 1911
43 Rowell Papers, Stewart Lyon to Rowell, 3 Nov. 1911; *Stratford Daily Herald* 2 Nov. 1911. The same editorial, originally published in the *London Free Press*, was reprinted in several papers.
44 *Globe* 21 and 30 Nov. and 1 Dec. 1911
45 *Weekly Sun* 6 Dec. 1911
46 King Papers, King to Violet Markham, 15 Dec. 1911
47 Rowell Family Papers, Rowell to Mary Rowell, 17 Dec. 1911

SEVEN / LEADER OF THE OPPOSITION

1 *Globe* 9 Feb. 1912
2 Ibid.
3 Alexander Brady, 'The Ontario Hydro-Electric Power Commission,' *Canadian Journal of Economics and Political Science* 2, 1936, pp. 331–53; W.R. Plewman, *Adam Beck and the Ontario Hydro* Toronto, 1947, pp. 82–3; *Globe* 24 Feb. and 15 March 1912
4 *Globe* 3 April 1912
5 Plewman, *Adam Beck* appendix A, p. 475
6 *Globe* 9 Feb. 1912
7 Ibid., 13 Feb. 1912
8 Ibid., 13 April 1912
9 Provincial Archives of Ontario, Whitney Papers, Whitney to Frank Cochrane, 26 Jan. and 6 Feb. 1912
10 *Globe* 9 Feb. 1912
11 Ibid., 22 Feb. 1912
12 *Statutes of Canada* 2 Geo V. c. 32
13 *Globe* 7 March 1912
14 Ibid., 15 Feb., 4 and 28 March 1912
15 Ibid., 26 March 1912
16 Ibid., 3 April 1912
17 Ibid., 26 March 1912
18 Catherine Lyle Cleverdon, *The Woman Suffrage Movement in Canada* Toronto, 1950, p. 37; *Globe* 26 March 1912
19 *Globe* 19 March 1912
20 Ibid., 4 April 1912

21 Ibid.
22 Ibid.
23 Whitney Papers, R. Millichamp to Whitney, 1 April 1912; Albert Grigg to Whitney, 29 March 1912
24 *Globe* 4 April 1912
25 *Ontario Sessional Papers* 1912, No. 62
26 *Globe* 13, 20, and 30 March and 10 April 1912
27 Ibid., 15 April 1912
28 *The World* 15 April 1912
29 *Globe* 20 April 1912
30 *Toronto Star* 7 Jan. 1911
31 *Globe* 20 May 1912
32 Rowell Family Papers, Nell Rowell to Sazie and Mary Rowell, [22] May 1912
33 *Globe* 15 May 1912
34 PAC, King Papers, Vol. 96, File 159, Reports on the Ontario Ridings to 1 Dec. 1912
35 Ibid.
36 *Globe* 18 May 1912
37 *Mail and Empire* 10 June 1912
38 *Globe* 2 July 1912
39 King Papers, Rowell to King, 5 July 1912
40 Ibid.; *Globe* 1, 5, and 10 Aug. 1912
41 *Workmen's Compensation: Address to the Working Men of Woodstock, Delivered by Mr. N.W. Rowell, K.C., MPP, at the City Hall, Woodstock, on August 29th, 1912* Revised for Publication, Ontario Reform Association, 1912
42 Ibid.
43 Ibid.
44 Ibid.
45 *Ontario Sessional Papers* 1912, No. 65
46 *Workmen's Compensation: Address to the Working Men*
47 *Globe* 14 Sept. 1912
48 Ibid.
49 King Papers, Rowell to King, 28 Sept. 1912
50 *Globe* 14 Sept. 1912
51 *Christian Guardian* 19 June 1912
52 *Canadian Annual Review, 1912* p. 350
53 King Papers, Rowell to King, 12 and 16 Oct. 1912
54 Ibid., Rowell to King, 17 Oct. 1912
55 *Globe* 23 Oct. 1912
56 *Globe* 18 May 1912
57 PAC, Dafoe Papers (microfilm), Atkinson to Dafoe, 19 Aug. 1912
58 Ibid., Dafoe to Atkinson, 22 Aug. 1912
59 *Globe* 29 June 1912
60 Ibid., 24 Sept. 1912
61 Henry Borden, ed., *Robert Laird Borden: His Memoirs* 2 volumes, Toronto, 1938, I, p. 374; *Globe* 24 Sept. 1912
62 King Papers, Rowell to King, 11 Oct. 1912
63 *Globe* 5 Oct. 1912
64 King Papers, Rowell to King, 22 Oct. 1912

65 N.W. Rowell, *Liberals and the Empire: An Address Delivered to the Montreal Reform Club, November 11, 1912* Central Information Office of the Canadian Liberal Party, Ottawa, n.d., p. 23

66 PAC, Laurier Papers, Rowell to Laurier, 26 Jan. 1912

67 N.W. Rowell, *Liberals and the Empire* pp. 14–15

68 *Globe* 7 Dec. 1912

69 Ibid., 18 Dec. 1912

70 Ibid., 20 Dec. 1912

71 PAC, Rowell Papers, ms. of address presented at Owen Sound, 16 May 1913

72 Ibid.

EIGHT / ABOLISH-THE-BAR

1 Quoted in the *Globe* 13 and 15 Jan. 1913

2 Ibid., 13 Feb. 1913

3 Ibid., 20 Feb. 1913

4 *Ontario Sessional Papers* 1913, No. 85

5 *Globe* 23 March 1913

6 Provincial Archives of Ontario, Whitney Papers, Frederic Nicholls, president of the Canadian General Electric Company, to Whitney, 25 March 1913, and J.O. Thorn, managing director of the Metallic Roofing Company, to Whitney, 27 March 1913, are good examples.

7 *Globe* 13 April 1913

8 Ibid., 15 Feb. 1913

9 Ibid., 25 Feb. 1913

10 Ibid., 22 Feb. 1913

11 Ibid., 24 April 1913

12 PAC, Rowell Papers, Atkinson to Rowell, 6 March 1913

13 *Globe* 7 April 1913

14 Ibid., 21 Dec. 1912

15 The evidence submitted is in *Journals of the Legislative Assembly of Ontario, 1913* appendix 2; the majority report is published in full in the *Mail and Empire* 6 May 1913, and the minority report in the *Globe* 7 May 1913.

16 *Globe* 31 May 1913

17 Ibid., 13 Feb. 1913

18 Whitney Papers, Whitney to J.A. Jackson, 8 Nov. 1911

19 *Globe* 19 Feb. 1913

20 Rowell Family Papers, Rowell to Mary Rowell, 15 July 1913

21 Ibid., Rowell to Mary Rowell, 18 July 1913

22 Ibid., Rowell to Mary Rowell, 19 July 1913

23 This opinion was reported to Rowell later by his old friend Hamar Greenwood, now a Liberal member of the British Parliament, and relayed by an appreciative wife to his sister. Rowell Family Papers, Nell Rowell to Mary Rowell, 8 Feb. 1914

24 This account of the visit to England is based on Rowell Family Papers, Rowell to Mary Rowell, 10 Aug. 1913; Rowell to Sazie Wright, 13 Aug. 1913; *Globe* 8 Sept. 1913.

25 Rowell Family Papers, Rowell to Mary Rowell, 30 Nov. 1913

26 *Statutes of Ontario* 4 Geo. V, c. 25

27 Laurier Papers, Atkinson to Laurier, 8 March 1916

28 *Statutes of Ontario* 4 Geo. v, c. 6
29 Rowell Papers, copy, Evanturel to the Hotelkeepers Association, 4 Sept. 1913
30 *Globe* 25 Feb. 1914; Toronto Public Library, Main Johnson Papers, Johnson Diary, 24 and 25 Feb. 1914
31 *Globe* 27 Feb. 1914
32 Rowell Papers, Rowell to T.A. Senecal, 28 Feb. 1914; Main Johnson Papers, Johnson Diary, 7 March 1914
33 Rowell Papers, M.C. Cameron to Rowell, 28 Feb. 1914
34 *Globe* 28 April 1914
35 Main Johnson Papers, Johnson Diary, 5 March 1914; PAC, King Papers, C.W. Hartman to King, 14 July 1914
36 *Globe* 15 April 1914
37 Main Johnson Papers, Report of secretarial fund, 1912–13; A.E. Ames to Main Johnson, 17 Feb. 1914; King Papers, Memo for Hon. W.L. McKenzie [*sic*] King re 1914 election (author unknown); PAC, Flavelle Papers, Rowell to J.W. Flavelle, 26 Sept. 1919; Flavelle to Rowell, 25 Sept. 1919
38 PAC, Murphy Papers, P.C. Larkin to Charles Murphy, 3 March 1913
39 *Globe* 3 March 1914
40 Ibid., 9 June 1914
41 *Canadian Annual Review, 1914* pp. 442–3; Whitney Papers, Whitney to A.A. Colwill, 4 June 1914
42 *Globe* 9 April 1914
43 Ibid., 20 June 1914
44 Rowell Papers, Rowell to Graham, 23 April 1914
45 Ibid., Evanturel to Rowell, 3, 4, and 11 May 1914
46 *Globe* 24 June 1914
47 Rowell Family Papers, Nell Rowell to Mary Rowell, 21 June 1914
48 *Globe* 26 and 27 June 1914
49 Whitney Papers, Whitney to Bishop Edward J. Bidwell, Anglican bishop of the diocese of Ontario, 2 July 1914
50 Rowell Family Papers, Rowell to Mary Rowell, 23 July 1914
51 King Papers, King to J.D. Aitchison, 7 July 1914
52 Ibid., King to Rowell, 1 July 1914
53 *Globe* 5 Dec. 1914
54 Ibid., 2 April 1915; *Statutes of Ontario* 4 Geo. v, c.47
55 *Globe*, 25 Feb. 1915
56 Ibid., 16 March 1915
57 Rowell Papers, Rowell to Warburton, 24 Jan. and 21 Feb. 1917; Warburton to Rowell, 27 Jan. 1917. These letters review the history of the Committee of One Hundred.
58 Ibid., Warburton to Rowell, 27 Jan. 1917
59 Rowell Family Papers, Rowell to Mary Rowell, 2 Jan. 1916
60 *Globe* 1 March 1916
61 Ruth E. Spence, *Prohibition in Canada* Toronto, 1919, p. 402.
62 *Globe* 9 March 1916
63 *Canadian Annual Review, 1916* pp. 518–20
64 *Statutes of Ontario* 6 Geo. v, c. 50
65 *Globe* 5 April 1916

66 Rowell Papers, Rowell to Warburton, 24 Jan. 1917
67 Ibid., Rowell to Warburton, 24 Feb. 1917

NINE / ONTARIO AND QUEBEC AT WAR

1 *Globe* 8 Feb. and 4 March 1913
2 Ibid., 19 Sept. 1913
3 Ibid., 24 Oct. 1913
4 Ibid.
5 W.R. Plewman to the author, 10 Aug. 1961
6 *Globe* 22 June 1914
7 Ibid., 27 June 1914
8 *Le Droit* 22 June 1914
9 Robert Rumilly, *Histoire de la Province de Québec* 41 vols, Montreal, 1941–69 19, p. 104
10 *Globe* 9 Jan. 1915
11 Ibid., 15 Jan. 1915
12 *Mail and Empire* 14 Feb. 1915
13 *Globe* 26 March 1915
14 Ibid. 2 April 1915
15 *Mackell v. Ottawa Separate School Trustees* [1915] 34 OLR 335
16 Rumilly, *Histoire* Vol. 21, pp. 47–8
17 PAC, Laurier Papers, Rowell to Laurier, 29 Feb. 1916
18 Ibid., Laurier to Rowell, 1 March 1916
19 Ibid.
20 Ibid., Lyon to Laurier, 6 March 1916
21 *Globe* 15 April 1916
22 Laurier Papers, Lyon to Laurier, 6 March 1916
23 Ibid., Rowell to Laurier, 15 April 1916
24 Ibid., Laurier to Rowell, 18 April 1916
25 Ibid., Rowell to Laurier, 26 April 1916
26 PAC, Rowell Papers, Laurier to Rowell, 28 April 1916; Rowell to Laurier, 9 May 1916
27 *House of Commons Debates* 10 May 1916, p. 3676
28 Ibid., pp. 3697–709
29 Rowell Papers, Laurier to Rowell, 11 May 1916
30 O.D. Skelton, *Life and Letters of Sir Wilfrid Laurier* 2 vols, Toronto, 1921, Vol. 2, p. 484
31 Rowell Papers, Rowell to Laurier, 19 May 1916
32 Ibid.
33 Laurier Papers, Laurier to W.M. German, 27 May 1916
34 Ibid., Laurier to E.M. Macdonald, 27 May 1916
35 Ibid., P.C. Larkin to Laurier, 7 June 1916
36 *Globe* 27 Oct. 1916
37 Rumilly, *Histoire* Vol. 21, p. 188
38 *Ottawa Separate Schools Trustees v. The City of Ottawa* [1916] AC 76
39 *Ottawa Separate Schools Trustees v. Mackell* [1916] AC 62
40 *Canadian Annual Review, 1917* p. 476
41 *Globe* 6 Feb. 1917

42 Ibid., 15 March 1917
43 *Globe* 31 March 1917
44 Laurier Papers, Rowell to Laurier, 29 March 1917
45 *Globe* 31 March 1917
46 Ibid., 4 April 1917
47 Laurier Papers, Laurier to Rowell, 4 April 1917

TEN / DEMOCRACY VERSUS MILITARISM

1 Rowell Family Papers, Rowell to Mary Rowell, 9 Aug. 1914
2 PAC, Willison Papers, Stewart Lyon to Willison, 15 Aug. 1914; *Canadian Annual Review, 1914; Globe* 27 Aug. 1914. The best general account of the organization of the war effort and of the impact of the war on Canadian society is Robert Craig Brown and Ramsay Cook, *Canada 1896–1921: A Nation Transformed* Toronto, 1974, chaps. 11 and 12.
3 *Journal of Proceedings of the Ninth General Conference of the Methodist Church, September 23–October 7, 1914* Toronto, 1914, p. 286. For an excellent discussion of the development of Methodist attitudes during the war, see Michael Bliss, 'The Methodist Church and World War I,' *Canadian Historical Review* 49, 1968, pp. 213–33.
4 *Journal of Proceedings of the Ninth General Conference* pp. 402–4
5 *Globe* 24 Sept. 1914
6 Ibid., 30 Oct. 1914
7 Ibid., 18 Nov. and 5 Dec. 1914
8 PAC, Rowell Papers, ms of address to the Empire Club of Toronto, 30 April 1915
9 Rowell Family Papers, Rowell to Mary Rowell, 7 March 1915
10 PAC, Foster Papers, Diary, 7 Sept. 1915
11 *Globe* 15 Oct. 1915
12 Rowell Papers, ms. of address at Woodstock, 3 Dec. 1915
13 Willison Papers, Rowell to Willison, 29 Aug. 1914. Beveridge's book, *Unemployment: A Problem of Industry*, was first published in London in 1909.
14 Willison Papers, Rowell to Willison, 10 Nov. 1914
15 *Globe* 15 Jan. 1915
16 *Ontario Sessional Papers* 1916, No. 55
17 PAC, A.K. Cameron Papers, Rowell to Cameron, 25 June 1915; PAC, King Papers, Main Johnson to King, 3 July 1915
18 Cameron Papers, Cameron to Rowell, 26 June 1915
19 Ibid., McMaster to Cameron, 6 July 1915
20 *Globe* 31 July 1915
21 Cameron Papers, Cameron to Rowell, 15 Oct. 1915; copy McMaster to Laurier, 22 Oct. 1915
22 Ibid., Cameron to Alex Smith, 27 Nov. 1915; Alex Smith to Cameron, 7 Dec. 1915
23 Ibid., Cameron to Smith, 8 Dec. 1915
24 PAC, Laurier Papers, Atkinson to Laurier, 8 March 1916
25 *Globe* 3 Aug. 1915
26 *Canadian Annual Review, 1916* pp. 303–4
27 *Senate Debates* 14 March 1916, p. 406
28 *Canadian Annual Review, 1916* p. 344; speech of 13 Jan. 1916
29 Rowell Papers, Rowell to McMaster, 25 March 1916
30 *Journal of the Legislative Assembly of Ontario* 28 March 1916

31 Rowell Papers, Rowell to Hearst, 10 April 1916; Hearst to Rowell, 14 April and 19 May 1916
32 Ibid., Hearst to Rowell, 25 May 1916; Rowell to Hearst, 5 June 1916
33 Ibid., Rowell to Hearst, 26 June 1916
34 Laurier Papers, Laurier to J.M. Godfrey, 14 June 1916
35 Rowell Papers, ms. of address at St Catharines, 28 May 1916
36 Ibid., ms. of address to the National Laymen's Missionary Congress, Washington DC, 30 April 1916
37 PAC, Murphy Papers, George P. Graham to Charles Murphy, n.d. [1918?] Rowell Family Papers, Rowell to Nell Rowell, 29 June 1916
38 Ibid., Rowell to Nell Rowell, 7 July 1916
39 Ibid., 9 and 12 July 1916
40 Rowell Papers, Notes on trip to the front, July 1916
41 Rowell Family Papers, Rowell to Nell Rowell, 25 July 1916
42 Rowell Papers, Notes on trip to the front, July 1916
43 Rowell Family Papers, Rowell to Nell Rowell, 25 July 1916
44 Ibid., 29 July 1916
45 Ibid., n.d.
46 Ibid.
47 Ibid., Rowell to Nell Rowell, 6 Aug. 1916
48 Ibid., 18 Aug. 1916
49 Ibid., 20 Aug. 1916
50 Ibid., 3 Sept. 1916

ELEVEN / THE FULL CURRENT OF THE WORLD'S LIFE

1 PAC, Rowell Papers, Rowell to Borden, 18 Sept. 1916
2 Ibid., Borden to Rowell, 23 Sept. 1916
3 Ibid., mss of addresses to the Women's Liberal Association of Toronto, and the Women's Canadian Club, Hamilton, 6 and 16 Oct. 1916, are examples.
4 Ibid., ms of address to Victoria College Alumni, Toronto, 13 Oct. 1916
5 Ibid., ms of address to the Men's Canadian Club, Toronto, 25 Sept. 1916
6 *Globe* 5 Oct. 1916
7 PAC Laurier Papers, Lemieux to Laurier, 5 Oct. 1916; Laurier to Lemieux, 6 Oct. 1916
8 Ibid., Laurier to P.C. Larkin, 9 Oct. 1916
9 Rowell Papers, ms of address to the Ontario Federation of Liberal Clubs, 11 Oct. 1916
10 Laurier Papers, Laurier to Sir Frederick Borden, 14 Oct. 1916
11 Ibid., Laurier to Rowell, 17 Nov. 1916
12 *Globe* 23 Dec. 1916
13 Rowell Papers, Rowell to Laurier, 20 Jan. 1917
14 Ibid., Laurier to Rowell, 23 Jan. 1917
15 Ibid., Rowell to Laurier, 25 Jan. 1917
16 Laurier Papers, Laurier to Lyon, 12 Feb. 1917
17 Ibid., Laurier to J.A. Calder, 3 March 1917
18 *Globe* 30 June 1916
19 Rowell Papers, W.C. Rean to Rowell, 12 July 1916; G.A. Warburton to Rowell, 27 Jan. 1916
20 Ibid., W.C. Rean to Rowell, 12 July 1916
21 Ibid., Rowell to G.A. Warburton, 21 Feb. 1917

22 Laurier Papers, copy, A.H. Beaton to G.P. Graham, 23 June 1916
23 *Globe* 14 Aug. 1916
24 Rowell Papers, F.J. Uffen to Rowell, 19 Aug. 1916; King Papers, Dewart to King, 26 Aug. 1916
25 Laurier Papers, Atkinson to C.M. Goddard, 26 Aug. 1916
26 Ibid., Harry Anderson to Laurier, 14 Sept. 1916
27 Ibid., H.F. Gadsby to Laurier, 21 Aug. 1916
28 Ibid., Peter Ryan to Laurier, 2 Sept. 1916
29 Ibid., Laurier to Peter Ryan, 5 Sept. 1916
30 Ibid., Laurier to Gadsby, 24 Aug. 1916
31 Rowell Papers, Rowell to G.A. Warburton, 21 Feb. 1917
32 Ibid., Rowell to James G. Cane, 12 Jan. 1917
33 Ibid., Rowell to G.A. Warburton, 21 Feb. 1917
34 Ibid., Rowell to James G. Cane, 12 Jan. 1917
35 *Globe* 23 Jan. 1917
36 Rowell Papers, Rowell to Warburton, 24 Jan. 1917
37 Ibid., Warburton to Rowell, 27 Jan. 1917
38 Catherine Lyle Cleverdon, *The Woman Suffrage Movement in Canada* Toronto, 1950, pp. 40–3
39 *Globe* 27 Feb. 1917
40 Ibid., 8 March 1917
41 Ibid., 23 Feb. 1915
42 Ibid., 25 Nov. 1916
43 Ibid., 22 Feb. 1917
44 *Canadian Annual Review, 1917* pp. 659–60. For a discussion of the nickel issue see H.V. Nelles, *The Politics of Development: Forests, Mines and Hydro-Electric Power in Ontario, 1849–1941* Toronto, 1974, pp. 348–61
45 Rowell Papers, Rowell to Hearst, 9 Dec. 1916
46 Ibid., Rowell to Hearst, 27 Jan. 1917
47 Ibid., Hearst to Rowell, 30 Jan. 1917
48 Ibid., Rowell to Hearst, 1 Feb. 1917
49 Rowell Papers, Rowell to G.P. Graham, 16 June 1917
50 Ibid., ms. of speech at Thamesford, 12 Feb. 1917
51 Ibid., Rowell to Hearst, 14 April 1917
52 Ibid., ms of address to the American Newspaper Publishers' Association, New York, 26 April 1917
53 *Globe* 14 May 1917
54 Rowell Papers, ms. of address at North Bay, 16 May 1917
55 Ibid., Rowell to A.K. Maclean 18 May 1917
56 Ibid., Rowell to Lemieux, 21 May 1917
57 Ibid., Lemieux to Rowell, 22 May 1917. The italics are Lemieux's.
58 Ibid., Rowell to Lemieux, 26 May 1917
59 Rowell Family Papers, Rowell to Mary Rowell, 27 May 1917. On 25 May Mr Justice A.C. Galt, commissioner appointed to investigate charges of fraud and political corruption in connection with contracts for the construction of the Manitoba Agricultural College, had brought in an interim report which substantiated the charges and established Rogers' responsibility for permitting fraudulent overcharges in the letting of contracts in return for

contributions to the Conservative party. Rogers had been a member of the Conservative Roblin government before joining the Borden cabinet.

60 Rowell Papers, Rowell to Laurier, 29 May 1917
61 *House of Commons Debates* 28 May 1917, p. 1772
62 Rowell Papers, Rowell to Laurier, 29 May 1917
63 Ibid., Laurier to Rowell, 2 June 1917
64 Laurier Papers, Rowell to Laurier, 6 June 1917
65 Rowell Papers, Pardee to Rowell, 18 June 1917
66 Henry Borden, ed., *Robert Laird Borden: His Memoirs*, 2 vols, Toronto, 1938, 2, p. 723
67 *Globe* 8 June 1917

TWELVE / THE LARGER CITIZENSHIP

1 PAC, Borden Papers, Willison to Borden, 8 and 12 June 1917
2 PAC, Laurier Papers, Larkin to Laurier, 9 June 1917
3 *Globe* 12 June 1917
4 PAC, Rowell Papers, Rowell to Graham, 16 June 1917
5 Ibid., Rowell's confidential memorandum of discussion with Willison, 18 June 1917
6 Ibid., 19 June 1917
7 Borden Papers, Willison to Borden, 24 June 1917; Willison received his information from a Liberal who was present. The two dissenters were almost certainly A.B. Aylesworth and P.C. Larkin.
8 Rowell Papers, Rowell's confidential memorandum of discussion with Graham and Pardee, 23 June 1917
9 Ibid., Rowell's confidential memorandum of discussion with Willison, 24 June 1917
10 Rowell Papers, Borden to Rowell, 24 June 1917
11 Ibid., Rowell to Borden, 6 July 1917
12 Ibid., Rowell to Willison, 11 Aug. 1917
13 Ibid., Rowell to Willison, 16 Aug. 1917
14 Borden Papers, Borden to Willison, 23 Aug. 1917
15 Borden Diary, in possession of Mr Henry Borden, QC, Toronto, 26 June 1917; Rowell Papers, Rowell to Laurier, 30 June 1917
16 Rowell Papers, Rowell to Laurier, 20 July 1917; Henry Borden, ed., *Robert Laird Borden: His Memoirs* 2 vols, Toronto, 1938, 2, p. 733
17 Rowell Papers, Rowell to Laurier, 30 June 1917
18 Ibid., Laurier to Rowell, 4 July 1917
19 *Globe* 4 July 1917
20 Rowell Papers, Rowell to Willison, 11 Aug. 1917
21 Ibid., Rowell to Laurier, 11 July 1917
22 Ibid., Laurier to Rowell, 14 July 1917
23 Ibid., Rowell to Laurier, 20 July 1917
24 Ibid., Rowell to Graham, 11 July 1917
25 Ibid., Graham to Rowell, 13 July 1917
26 Ibid., Pardee to Rowell, 17 July 1917
27 *House of Commons Debates* 17 July 1917, pp. 3459–60
28 Ibid., p. 3485

29 Rowell Papers, Rowell to Graham, 21 July 1917
30 *Globe* 21 July 1917
31 Rowell Papers, Rowell to Graham, 21 July 1917
32 Ibid., Graham to Rowell, 21 July 1917
33 *House of Commons Debates* 24 July 1917, p. 3721
34 Rowell Papers, Rowell to Dafoe, 21 July 1917
35 PAC, Dafoe Papers (microfilm), Dafoe to Rowell, 25 July 1917
36 Rowell Papers, Laurier to Rowell, 23 July 1917
37 Ibid., Rowell to Laurier, 27 July 1917
38 Rowell Papers, Rowell to G.E. McCraney, 27 July 1917
39 Rumilly, *Histoire* Vol. 22, pp. 82–3
40 Dafoe Papers, Arthur Hawkes to Dafoe, Sept. [?] 1929. Dafoe did not concur in this view, although he agreed that there was a good deal of such feeling about Rowell. 'To me his conduct seemed singularly frank and straightforward.' Ibid., Dafoe to Hawkes, 25 Oct. 1929
41 Rowell Papers, ms. of address to the Win-the-War Convention, 2 Aug. 1917; *Globe* 3 and 4 Aug. 1917
42 Rowell Papers, Rowell to Pardee, 3 Aug. 1917; Rowell to Graham, 8 Aug. 1917
43 Toronto Public Library, Main Johnson Papers, Johnson to Rowell, 6 and 9 Aug. 1917
44 *Canadian Annual Review, 1917* pp. 572–6
45 Rowell Papers, Rowell to Dafoe, 17 Aug. 1917
46 Borden, *Memoirs* Vol. 2, pp. 740–1
47 Borden Papers, Willison to Borden, 14 Aug. and 7 Oct. 1917
48 *Canadian Annual Review, 1917* p. 577
49 Borden, *Memoirs* Vol. 2, pp. 742–7. The substance of these negotiations was reported in the press at the time.
50 Rowell Papers, Rowell to Maclean, 28 Aug. 1917
51 Ibid., Maclean to Rowell, 1 Sept. 1917
52 Ibid., Pardee to Rowell, 5 Sept. 1917
53 PAC, Murphy Papers, Murphy to W.D. Gregory, 30 July 1917
54 Toronto *Telegram*, 30 Aug. 1917
55 Borden Diary, 6 Sept. 1917
56 *Statutes of Canada* 7–8 George V, c. 39; Roger Graham, *Arthur Meighen*, 3 Vols, 1960, 1963, 1965 Toronto, 1960, 1, pp. 163–9
57 Rowell Papers, Rowell to H.C. Brewster, 7 Sept. 1917
58 Ibid., Rowell to A.K. Maclean, 7 Sept. 1917
59 Ibid., Rowell to Brewster, 7 Sept. 1917
60 Ibid., Rowell to Pardee, 19 Sept. 1917
61 Rowell Family Papers, Rowell to Nell Rowell, 27 Sept. 1917
62 Rowell Papers, Pardee to Rowell, 6 Oct. 1917; O.D. Skelton, *Life and Letters of Sir Wilfrid Laurier* 2 vols, Toronto, 1921, 2, p. 530
63 Rowell Papers, Rowell to Laurier, 17 Oct. 1917
64 Rowell Family Papers, Rowell to Nell Rowell, 9 Oct. 1917
65 Borden Papers, Howard Ferguson to Borden, October 10, 1917
66 Borden Diary, 9 and 10 Oct. 1917
67 Rowell Family Papers, Rowell to Nell Rowell, 10 Oct. 1917
68 Toronto Public Library, Main Johnson Papers, Johnson Diary, 12 Oct. 1917
69 Ibid.

70 *Globe* 19 Oct. 1917; Laurier Papers, R.T. Harding to Laurier, 19 Oct. 1917
71 Rowell Papers, Rowell to Laurier, 17 Oct. 1917
72 Ibid., Laurier to Rowell, 23 Oct. 1917
73 Rowell Family Papers, Nell Rowell to Mary Rowell, [22] Oct. 1917
74 Borden Papers, G. Howard Ferguson to Borden, 3 July 1917
75 Rowell Papers, G.P. Graham to Rowell, 14 July 1917; G.N. Gordon to Rowell, 24 July 1917. Dafoe Papers, Arthur Hawkes to Dafoe, September [?] 1929
76 University of Toronto Library, Sir Edmund Walker Papers, Willison to Walker, 13 May 1917
77 King Papers, Diary, 9 Oct. 1917
78 Carl Berger, *The Sense of Power: Studies in the Ideas of Canadian Imperialism 1867–1914*, Toronto, 1970

THIRTEEN / SAVING CIVILIZATION AT THE POLLS

1 PAC, Borden Papers, Rowell to Borden, 17 Oct. 1917
2 *Canadian Annual Review, 1917* pp. 587–8
3 Borden Papers, Borden to Rowell, 24 Oct. 1917; Rowell to Borden, 26 Oct. 1917
4 PAC, Rowell Papers, Rundle to Rowell, 17 Oct. 1917
5 *Toronto Star* 13 Oct. 1917; *Globe* 17 Oct. 1917
6 *Sessional Papers of Canada* 1917, No. 210a
7 *Globe* 22 Oct. 1917
8 Rowell Papers, Flavelle to Rowell, 8 Nov. 1917
9 *Globe* 12 Nov. 1917
10 Ibid., 19 Nov. 1917
11 Rowell Papers, Rowell to Flavelle, 19 Nov. 1917
12 Ibid., Rowell to Borden, 7 Nov. 1917
13 The manifesto is printed in full in the *Canadian Annual Review, 1917* p. 589
14 Rowell Papers, Rowell to Borden, 17 Oct. 1917
15 *Labour Gazette* Oct. 1917, pp. 846–7, 850–1
16 Rowell Papers, Rowell to Borden, 17 Oct. 1917
17 Borden Diary, in possession of Mr Henry Borden, QC, Toronto, 20 Oct. 1917; Borden Papers, Reid to Borden, 19 Oct. 1917; J.M. Godfrey to Borden, 30 Oct. 1917; PAC, Laurier Papers, King to Laurier, 17 Oct. 1917; Rowell Papers, Rowell to John R. Shaw, 16 Nov. and 17 Dec. 1917; Toronto Public Library, Main Johnson Papers, Johnson Diary, 1–19 Nov. 1917
18 Borden Papers, Reid to Borden, 24 Oct. 1917
19 *Globe* 27 Oct. 1917
20 PAC, Sir George Foster Papers, Foster Diary, 2 Nov. 1917
21 Rowell Papers, Rowell to John R. Shaw, 16 Nov. 1917
22 Sir George Foster Papers, Foster Diary, 30 Oct. 1917
23 Borden Papers, Borden to J.M. Godfrey, 31 Oct. 1917; Rowell Papers, Rowell to E.C. Drury, 23 Nov. 1917; Rowell to John R. Shaw, 17 Dec. 1917
24 Mrs Rowell to the author, 11 Jan. 1957
25 Sir George Foster Papers, Foster Diary, 10 Nov. 1917
26 PAC, Laurier Papers, P.C. Larkin to Laurier, 23 Oct. 1917
27 Rowell Papers, Donald Sutherland to Rowell, 23 Oct. 1917; Main Johnson Papers, Johnson Diary, 1–19 Nov. 1917; Borden Papers, Senator J.H. Fisher to Borden,

17 Nov. 1917; Laurier Papers, King to Laurier, 7 Nov. 1917, Gregory to Laurier,
10 Nov. 1917

28 Main Johnson Papers, Johnson Diary, 1–19 Nov. 1917

29 Ibid.

30 *Globe* 7 Nov. 1917

31 Ibid., 3 Nov. 1917

32 Rowell Papers, transcripts of shorthand notes taken by a reporter of the Hamilton *Herald*
2 Nov. 1917

33 Queen's University, Douglas Library, Flavelle Papers, J.H. Gundy to Flavelle, 14 March
1917; Rowell Papers, Warburton to Rowell, 26 Dec. 1917

34 *Globe* 22 Nov. 1917

35 Borden Diary, 30 Nov. and 2 Dec. 1917; Main Johnson Papers, Johnson Diary, 1–3 Dec.
1917

36 Ibid. On the position of the farmers in the economy and their attitude to the war see W.R.
Young, 'Conscription, Rural Depopulation, and the Farmers of Ontario, 1917–1919,'
Canadian Historical Review 53, 1972, pp. 289–320

37 *Weekly Sun* 5 and 12 Dec. 1917

38 Rowell Papers, Rowell to J.W. Taylor, 4 Dec. 1917

39 *Globe* 11 Dec. 1917; *Christian Guardian* 12 Dec. 1917

40 Rowell Papers, Rowell to C.F. Paul, 4 Dec. 1917

41 *Globe* 11 Dec. 1917

42 Rowell Papers, ms. of a speech at Midland, 4 Dec. 1917

43 Ibid.

44 Ibid., F.L. Hutchinson to Rowell, 3 Dec. 1917

45 Borden Diary, 26 Nov. 1917

46 Rowell Papers, ms. of address presented at North Bay, 6 Dec. 1917

47 *News* 5 Dec. 1917

48 *Globe* 11, 12 and 15 Dec. 1917

49 Laurier Papers, R.T. Harding to Laurier, 16 Nov. 1917; Main Johnson Papers, Johnson
Diary, 1–19 Nov. 1917

50 Laurier Papers, R.R. Cromarty to Laurier, 30 Nov. 1917

51 Main Johnson Papers, Johnson Diary, 1–19 Nov. 1917

52 Ibid., 17 Dec. 1917

53 The following account of election day is based on a lengthy entry in ibid., 17 Dec. 1917

54 Rowell Papers, Rowell to Hearst, 20 Dec. 1917

55 *Globe* 18 Dec. 1917

FOURTEEN / THE ORGANIZATION OF VICTORY

1 Toronto Public Library, Main Johnson Papers, Johnson Diary, 18 Dec. 1917

2 PAC, Borden Papers, Borden to Rowell, 22 Dec. 1917

3 Borden Papers, memorandum on the conference prepared by a secretary in the Department of Labour; leaflet issued by the TLC, explaining its stand to the membership of the
Congress; *Sessional Papers of Canada* 1918, No. 78

4 *Globe* 15 Feb. 1918

5 Ibid., 18 Feb. 1918

6 PC 404, 23 Feb. 1918

7 PAC, Rowell Papers, Atkinson to Rowell, 2 March 1918

8 Borden Papers, copy, G.M. Murray, secretary of CMA, to Rowell, 9 Jan. 1918; Report on the 'National War Organization ... for Dealing with Industrial, Commercial and Labour Problems,' prepared by the government delegation to Washington

9 PC 337, 8 Feb. 1918

10 Main Johnson Papers, Johnson Diary, 17 Feb. 1918

11 Ibid.

12 Ibid.

13 Ibid.

14 PC 580, 9 March 1918

15 Borden Papers, Rowell to Borden, 8 March 1918; Memorandum re Women's War Conference

16 Rowell Family Papers, Nell Rowell to Mary Rowell, 5 Feb. 1918

17 Borden Papers, Memorandum Reid to Borden, n.d. (apparently around the end of February 1918)

18 Rowell Family Papers, Rowell to Mary Rowell, 24 March 1918

19 Borden Diary, 16 March 1918

20 Main Johnson Papers, Johnson Diary, 19 March 1918

21 *House of Commons Debates* 19 March 1918, pp. 35–45

22 Main Johnson Papers, Johnson Diary, 20 March 1918

23 Borden Diary, in possession of Mr Henry Borden, QC, of Toronto, 19 and 20 March 1918

24 Main Johnson Papers, Johnson Diary, March 20, 1918

25 PAC, Laurier Papers, H.H. Dewart to Laurier, 16 Jan. and 24 Feb. 1918

26 Rowell Family Papers, Rowell to Mary Rowell, 24 March 1918

27 PAC, Murphy Papers, Murphy to A.G. Mackay, 29 Dec. 1917; G.P. Graham to Murphy, n.d.; C.W. Kerr to Murphy, 5 March 1918; Murphy to H.H. Dewart, 14 Dec. 1918

28 Ibid., Andrew Haydon to Murphy, 22 March 1918; Lindsay Crawford to Murphy, 22 March 1918

29 PAC, Sir George Foster Papers, Foster Diary, 20 March 1918

30 Laurier Papers, Laurier to G.P. Graham, 22 Feb. 1918. O.D. Skelton appears to have believed that Laurier approved of Murphy's attack and to have assumed that Laurier did not want Rowell back in the party; see ibid., Skelton to Laurier, 23 March 1918. During the latter half of 1918 Laurier gave a dinner for a group of young Liberals in Quebec City; one of the guests, Louis S. St-Laurent, came away from the evening's discussion with the impression that perhaps Laurier's relaxed and tolerant attitude to Liberal-Unionists did not extend to Rowell. Mr St-Laurent to the author, 14 Nov. 1961

31 Laurier Papers, Laurier to Dewart, 25 Feb. 1918

32 Borden Papers, Rowell to Borden, 30 March 1918

33 PC 834, 4 April 1918

34 *House of Commons Debates* 5 April, pp. 390–6

35 Ibid., p. 398

36 Main Johnson Papers, Johnson Diary, 7 April 1918

37 Cited as translated in Ibid., 14 April 14 1918

38 Ibid.

39 Ibid.

40 Ibid.

41 Ibid.

42 Borden Diary, 16 April 1918

43 Main Johnson Papers, Johnson Diary, 16 April 1918

44 Borden Papers, Borden to Sir George Perley, 12 April 1918
45 *House of Commons Debates* 18 April 1918, p. 891
46 Ibid., p. 898
47 Ibid., 19 April 1918, pp. 933–40
48 Ibid., pp. 940–6; Borden Diary, 19 April 1918
49 *House of Commons Debates* 19 April, pp. 946–54
50 Borden Diary, 19 April 1918
51 Rowell Family Papers, Rowell to Mary Rowell, 21 April 1918
52 Borden Papers, Rowell to Borden, 8 May 1918; copy, Rowell to Mewburn, 4 May 1918
53 Henry Borden, ed., *Robert Laird Borden: His Memoirs* 2 vols, Toronto, 1938, 2, p. 802
54 Rowell Papers, Rowell to J.H. Gundy, 14 May 1918
55 Ibid., M.E. Nichols to Rowell, 16 May 1918
56 Ibid., Rowell to T.A. Crerar, 20 May 1918
57 Ibid., Rowell to Nichols, 20 May 1918; Borden to Rowell, 11 June 1918
58 Borden Papers, Memorandum, Borden to the English press of Canada, May 2, 1918
59 *House of Commons Debates* 12 April 1918, p. 702
60 Ibid., 8 April 1919, pp. 500–2
61 Rowell Papers, Rowell to A.K. Maclean, 24 April 1918
62 *House of Commons Debates* 30 April 1918, p. 1261
63 Ibid., 23 May 1918 pp. 2480–91, 2550

FIFTEEN / THE CORONATION OF DEMOCRACY

1 PAC, Borden Papers, notes re formation of the Union Government
2 Ibid., memorandum, Christie to Borden, 9 April 1918
3 Borden Diary, in possession of Mr Henry Borden, QC, Toronto, 7 May 1918
4 Ibid., 6 May 1918
5 PAC, Sir George Foster Papers, Foster Diary, 10 May 1918
6 Ibid., 20 May 1918
7 Borden Diary, 9 June 1918
8 Rowell Family Papers, Rowell to Nell Rowell, 9 June 1918. The origins and structure of the Imperial War Cabinet and its relation to the Imperial War Conference are discussed in Richard A. Preston, *Canada and "Imperial Defense"* Durham, NC, 1967, pp. 514–21
9 PAC, Rowell Papers, Rowell to Borden, 8 June 1918
10 University of Toronto Library, G.M. Wrong Papers, Rowell to Wrong, 8 April 1918
11 Toronto Public Library, Main Johnson Papers, Johnson Diary, 12 and 14 June 1918
12 Henry Borden ed., *Robert Laird Borden: His Memoirs* 2 vols, Toronto, 1938, 2, p. 813
13 Ibid., p. 810
14 Borden Diary, 3 June 1918
15 Borden Papers, minutes of the Imperial War Cabinet, 13 June 1918
16 Ibid.
17 Rowell Family Papers, Rowell to Nell Rowell, 13 June 1918
18 Borden Papers, Rowell to Borden, 15 June 1918
19 Ibid., Rowell to Crerar, Ames, and Maclean, 28 June 1918
20 Rowell Family Papers, Rowell to Nell Rowell, 7 July 1918
21 Maurice Ollivier, ed., *The Colonial and Imperial Conferences from 1887 to 1937* 3 vols, Ottawa, 1954, 2, pp. 306–7

22 Rowell Papers, Rowell to Borden, 23 July 1918; Rowell Memorandum, 25 July 1918, on earlier discussions with Borden, L.S. Amery, and Philip Kerr
23 Ibid.
24 Borden, *Memoirs* 2, p. 828
25 Rowell Papers, memorandum on discussion with Borden, 26 July 1918
26 Borden, *Memoirs* 2, p. 839
27 Ollivier, *The Colonial and Imperial Conferences* p. 335
28 Ibid., pp. 361–2
29 Rowell Papers, memorandum on discussion with Borden, 26 July 1918; Ballantyne to Rowell, 22 Oct. 1918
30 Borden *Memoirs*, 2, p. 842–3
31 Rowell Papers, Rowell to Borden, 26 July 1918
32 Main Johnson Papers, Johnson Diary, 9–23 July 1918
33 Rowell Papers, Rowell to Amery, 23 July 1918
34 Rowell Family Papers, Rowell to Nell Rowell, 14 July 1918
35 PAC, Laurier Papers, copy, Martin Burrell to H.S. Beland, 13 Aug. 1918
36 Rowell Papers, ms. of speech presented at Newcastle, 14 Aug. 1918
37 *Globe* 17 Aug. 1918
38 Rowell Papers, ms. of speech presented at Millbrook, 24 Aug. 1918
39 Norman Ward, ed., *A Party Politician: The Memoirs of Chubby Power* Toronto, 1966, pp. 69–70
40 Rowell Papers, Cannon and Power to Rowell, 16 Aug. 1918
41 Ibid., Rowell to Cannon and Power, 22 Aug. 1918
42 Ibid., Cannon to Rowell, 27 Aug. 1918
43 Ibid., Rowell to Cannon, 5 Sept. 1918
44 Ibid., Rowell to Borden, 2 Sept. 1918; Borden to Rowell, 4 Sept. 1918
45 Ibid., Rowell to Borden, 5 Sept. 1918
46 Ibid., Rowell to Borden, 18 Sept. 1918
47 Ibid., 5 Sept. 1918
48 Ibid., 7 Sept. 1918
49 Borden Papers, Rowell to Borden, 19 Sept. 1918
50 Ibid., copy of Cahan Report, received 14 Sept. 1918
51 PC 2384, 24 Sept. 1918
52 *Globe* 3 Oct. 1918
53 Rowell Papers, Rowell to Doherty, 18 Oct. 1918
54 Borden Papers, copy, commissioner of Police to Doherty, 16 June 1918
55 Ibid., Cahan to Doherty, 22 Oct. 1918
56 Rowell Papers, Rowell to Borden, 29 Oct. 1918
57 Borden Papers, memorandum by Crerar for the cabinet, 1 Nov. 1918
58 PC 2525, 11 Oct. 1918
59 *Globe* 13 Oct. 1918
60 Rowell Papers, Rowell to Robertson, 19 Oct. 1918
61 Ibid., ms. of address, 11 Nov. 1918

SIXTEEN / THE NEW ORDER

1 *Globe* 23 Nov. 1918
2 PAC, Rowell Papers, ms. of address presented in Metropolitan Church, 24 Nov. 1918. For a

522 N.W. Rowell: Ontario Nationalist

discussion of the general spirit of post-war Methodism, see Michael Bliss, 'The Methodist Church and World War I,' *Canadian Historical Review* 49, 1968, pp. 228–33

3 *Journal of the Proceedings of the Tenth General Conference of the Methodist Church* Toronto, 1918, p. 341
4 Rowell Papers, ms. of address ... 24 Nov. 1918
5 PAC, Borden Papers, Rowell to Borden, 28 Oct. 1918
6 Rowell Papers, Rowell to Borden, 24 April 1918
7 Provincial Archives of Ontario, Hearst Papers, Hearst to Willison, 17 July 1918
8 PAC, Willison Papers, White to Willison, 9 Nov. 1918
9 Rowell Papers, Rowell to Borden, 28 Oct. 1918
10 Borden Diary, in possession of Mr Henry Borden, QC, Toronto, 31 Oct. and 2 Nov. 1918
11 Ibid., 2 and 5 Nov. 1918
12 PAC, Laurier Papers, Laurier to A.R. McMaster, 17 Aug. 1918
13 Borden Diary, 4 and 5 Nov. 1918
14 Laurier Papers, Laurier to Larkin, 7 Nov. 1918
15 Ibid., Laurier to Larkin, 11 Nov. 1918
16 Ibid., Larkin to Laurier, 14 Nov. 1918
17 Ibid.
18 PAC, Murphy Papers, C.W. Kerr to Murphy, 18 Dec. 1918
19 Laurier Papers, copy, Murphy to Fred Hogg, 12 April 1918; Murphy Papers, W.C. Kennedy to Murphy, 17 and 19 June 1918, Murphy to Kennedy, 18 Oct. 1918
20 Murphy Papers, Murphy to C.W. Kerr, 17 Jan. 1918; Murphy to W.H. Adams, 2 Oct. 1918; Laurier Papers, Murphy to Laurier, 13 Feb. 1918
21 Murphy Papers, Murphy to H.H. Dewart, 19 Nov. 1918; Murphy to W.C. Kennedy, 20 Dec. 1918
22 Henry Borden, ed., *Robert Laird Borden: His Memoirs* 2 vols, Toronto, 1938, 2, p. 969
23 Roger Graham, *Arthur Meighen, Vol. I: The Door of Opportunity* Toronto, 1960, pp. 213–20
24 N.W. Rowell, *One Year of Union Government* n.d., n.p.
25 Rowell Family Papers, Rowell to Mary Rowell, 22 Dec. 1918
26 Rowell Papers, Rowell to Borden, 7 Nov. 1918
27 Borden Papers, Rowell to Borden, 19 Nov. 1918
28 Rowell Papers, Rowell to Wrong, 16 Nov. 1918
29 Ibid., Wrong to Rowell, 18 Nov. 1918
30 Ibid., Rowell to Wrong, 27 Nov. 1918
31 Ibid., Rowell to Borden, 7 Dec. 1918
32 Ibid., copy, memorandum by Christie for Borden, 1 Oct. 1918
33 Ibid., Borden to Rowell, 1 Jan. 1919
34 Borden Papers, Borden to Rowell and White, 26 Nov. 1918
35 Ibid., Rowell to Borden, 28 Nov. 1918; Willison Papers, Arthur Ford to Willison, 27 Nov. 1918
36 Borden Papers, White to Borden, 4 Dec. 1918
37 Rowell Papers, Rowell to Borden, 23 Dec. 1918
38 Borden Papers, Rowell to Borden, 26 Dec. 1918
39 Ibid., White to Borden, 21 Dec. 1918
40 Rowell Papers, Rowell to Borden, 24 Dec. 1918
41 Borden Papers, Rowell to Borden, 26 Dec. 1918
42 Rowell Papers, Rowell to Borden, 15 Feb. 1919

43 Ibid., Borden to Rowell, 25 Jan. 1919; Rowell to Borden, 15 Feb. 1919
44 Ibid., Rowell to Borden, 6 Feb. 1919
45 Ibid., Rowell to Borden, 14 March 1919
46 Borden Papers, Rowell to Borden, 29 April 1919 and 1 May 1919
47 Gaddis Smith, 'Canada and the Siberian Expedition,' *American Historical Review* 64, 1959, 868
48 Rowell Papers, General P.deB. Radcliffe to Rowell, 9 July 1918
49 Toronto Public Library, Main Johnson Papers, Johnson Diary, 11 July 1918; Rowell to General Radcliffe, 11 July 1918
50 Borden Papers, H.T. Meldrum to Borden, 26 Aug. 1918; Borden to Foster, 27 Aug. 1918
51 Ibid., Rowell to Borden, 9 Aug. 1918
52 Ibid., Mewburn to Borden, 13 Aug. 1918
53 Ibid., Borden to Mewburn, 13 Aug. 1918; Smith, 'Canada and the Siberian Expedition,' p. 872
54 Rowell Papers, ms. of speech at Millbrook, 24 Aug. 1918
55 *Addresses Delivered before the Canadian Club of Toronto, 1918–19*, Toronto, 1920, p. 80
56 Ibid., White to A.E. Kemp, 14 Nov. 1918
57 Ibid., Borden to White, 20 Nov. 1918
58 Rowell Papers, White to Borden, 26 Nov. 1918; Rowell to White, 21 Nov. 1918; T.A. Crerar to the author, 21 June 1958
59 Borden Papers, Borden to White, 24 Nov. 1918; Crerar to White, 22 and 28 Nov. 1918; Reid to Borden, 28 Nov. 1918; White to Borden, 28 Nov. 1918
60 Ibid., Rowell to Borden, 28 Nov. 1918
61 Ibid., Rowell to Borden, 28 Nov. 1918; Borden to Rowell, 2 Dec. 1918
62 Rowell Papers, copy, chief of General Staff to governor general, 12 Dec. 1918
63 Ibid., Rowell to Borden, 23 Dec. 1918
64 James Eayrs, *In Defence of Canada: From the Great War to the Great Depression*, Toronto 1964, p. 33
65 Ibid., pp. 34–9
66 Rowell Papers, copy, chief of General Staff to governor general, 13 Jan. 1919
67 Borden Papers, minutes of the Imperial War Cabinet, 30 Dec. 1918
68 Ibid., Borden to White, 17 Feb. 1919
69 Ibid.

SEVENTEEN / RECRIMINATION AND REFORM

1 Rowell Family Papers, Rowell to Mary Rowell, 24 Feb. 1919
2 *House of Commons Debates* 25 Feb. 1919, p. 27
3 Ibid., 6 March 1919, p. 244
4 Ibid., 11 March 1919, pp. 364–6
5 Ibid., pp. 367–9
6 Ibid., 10 March 1919, p. 355
7 Ibid., 1 April 1919, p. 1062
8 Ibid., p. 1065
9 Ibid., p. 1066
10 Ibid., p. 1067
11 Ibid., 10 June 1919, p. 3298
12 Ibid., 4 April 1919, p. 1164

13 Ibid., 10 April 1919, p. 1366
14 Ibid., 4 April, pp. 1165–6
15 Ibid., pp. 1168, 1185–1206
16 Ibid., 4 April, p. 1206
17 *Statutes of Canada* 9–10 Geo. v, c. 24
18 Provincial Archives of Ontario, Hearst Papers, Sir Thomas White to Hearst, 4 Dec. 1918
19 Ibid., Hearst-Rowell correspondence during January 1919; *House of Commons Debates*
      16 May 1919, pp. 2534–7, 2845–6
20 Ibid., p. 2546
21 Ibid., 25 June 1919, pp. 4208 and 4275
22 Ibid., pp. 4287, 4289
23 PAC, Rowell Papers, Rowell to Stewart Lyon, 16 June 1919
24 *House of Commons Debates* 12 June 1919, pp. 3407–8
25 Rowell Papers, Rowell to Stewart Lyon, 16 June 1919
26 *House of Commons Debates* 12 June 1919, pp. 3401–2
27 Ibid., 6 June 1919, pp. 3197 and 3217–27
28 Henry Borden, ed., *Robert Laird Borden: His Memoirs* 2 vols, Toronto, 1938, 2,
      pp. 977–8
29 PAC, Borden Papers, Borden to White, 1 Jan. 1919
30 Ibid., Cahan to Borden, 28 May 1919
31 *House of Commons Debates* 23 June 1919, pp. 3843–5. The details of these instructions
      were given to Parliament in 1926. Ibid., 2 June 1926, pp. 4004–5
32 Ibid., 16 May 1919, p. 2508
33 Ibid., 12 June 1919, pp. 3409–10
34 Ibid., pp. 3411–13
35 Ibid., pp. 3418–19
36 Ibid., 2 June 1919, p. 3055
37 Ibid., 23 June 1919, pp. 3844–5
38 The non-revolutionary intent of the strike is well established by D.C. Masters, *The
      Winnipeg General Strike* Toronto, 1950, K.W. McNaught, *A Prophet in Politics: A
      Biography of J.S. Woodsworth* Toronto, 1959, chap. 8, and David J. Bercuson, 'The
      Winnipeg General Strike, Collective Bargaining, and the One Big Union Issue,' *Canadian
      Historical Review* 51, 1970, pp. 164–76
39 The report was printed as a supplement to the *Labour Gazette* July 1919
40 Rowell Papers, Rowell to Borden, 4 July 1919
41 Supplement to the *Labour Gazette* July 1919
42 Rowell Papers, Rowell to J.F. Mackay, 2 April 1919
43 *Globe* 13 June 1919
44 Rowell Papers, Rowell to Lyon, 16 June 1919
45 Ibid., Lyon to Rowell, 17 June 1919
46 Rowell Papers, Rowell to Lyon, 23 June 1919
47 Borden, *Memoirs*, Vol. 2, pp. 980–2
48 Rowell Papers, Rowell to Calder, 17 July 1919
49 Ibid., Atkinson to Rowell, 1 July 1919
50 Ibid., Rowell to Borden, 4 July 1919
51 Michael Bliss, 'A Canadian Businessman and War: the Case of Joseph Flavelle,' in J.L.
      Granatstein and R.D. Cuff, *War and Society in North America* Toronto, 1971, pp. 20–36

EIGHTEEN / NO LIGHT IN THE WINDOW

1 PAC, Rowell Papers, Rowell to Proudfoot, 2 July 1919
2 Ibid., Rowell to Scott Davidson, 7 July 1919
3 Ibid., Rowell to Proudfoot, 2 July 1919
4 Ibid., Rowell to C.M. Bowman, 2 July 1919
5 Ibid., T. Scott Davidson to Rowell, 27 June 1919
6 Ibid., Atkinson to Rowell, 1 July 1919
7 Ibid., Rowell to Proudfoot, 10 July 1919
8 Rowell to W.J.B. Davison, 11 July 1919, printed in the *Globe* and the *Toronto Star* 14 July 1919
9 Rowell Papers, Rowell to Calder, 17 July 1919
10 *Globe* 15 July 1919
11 Ibid., 16 July 1919
12 Rowell Papers, Rowell to William Wallace, 18 July 1919. Wallace had recently returned from overseas. He was appointed Rowell's secretary after Main Johnson resumed his career in journalism with the *Toronto Star*.
13 *Toronto Star* 22 July 1919
14 Rowell Papers, M.A. James to Rowell, 14 July 1919
15 *Globe* 26 July 1919 and continued 28 July 1919
16 *Mail and Empire* 25 July 1919
17 *Globe* 26 July 1919
18 Ibid., 28 July 1919
19 *Toronto Star* 28 July 1919
20 PAC, Borden Papers, Rowell to Borden, 29 July 1919; Borden to Rowell, 1 Aug. 1919
21 Borden Diary, in possession of Mr Henry Borden, QC, Toronto, 8 July 1919
22 Rowell Papers, Borden to Rowell, 28 July 1919
23 Ibid., Rowell to Borden, 1 Aug. 1919
24 Ibid., Rowell to M.A. James, 15 Aug. 1919
25 Ibid., Rowell to Maclean, 18 Aug. 1919
26 *The National Liberal Convention: The Story of the Convention and the Report of the Proceedings* Ottawa, 1919; Also, R.M. Dawson, p. 298–303
27 PAC, King Papers, Rowell to King, 13 Aug. 1919
28 Rowell Family Papers, Rowell to Nell Rowell, 28 Aug. 1919
29 F.A. McGregor, *The Fall and Rise of Mackenzie King, 1911–1919* Toronto, 1962, p. 322
30 Rowell Family Papers, Rowell to Nell Rowell, 24 Aug. 1919
31 Rowell Papers, Moore to Rowell, 22 Aug. 1919
32 Ibid., copy, Ames to Moore, 27 Aug. 1919
33 Ibid., Rowell to Ames, 29 Aug. 1919
34 Borden Diary, 4 Sept. 1919
35 King Papers, King to Rowell, 6 Sept. 1919; Rowell to King, 19 Sept. 1916
36 PAC, Willison Papers, Willison to Rowell, 23 Sept. 1919
37 Rowell Papers, Rowell to Borden, 15 Aug. 1919
38 Ibid., Rowell to Borden, 6 Sept. 1919
39 Ibid., and Rowell to Borden, 1 Oct. 1919
40 Borden Diary, 17 and 18 Sept. 1919
41 *House of Commons Debates* 9 Sept. 1919, pp. 118–28

42 Ibid., pp. 12–30
43 Ibid., pp. 131–2
44 Ibid., 10 Sept. 1919, pp. 154–66; 11 Sept. 1919, p. 223
45 Ibid., 17 Sept. 1919, p. 374
46 Willison Papers, Rowell to Willison, 21 June 1919; Rowell Papers, Rowell to Coyne, 26 Aug. 1919
47 *House of Commons Debates* 17 Sept. 1919, p. 391
48 Ibid., pp. 392–400
49 Ibid., p. 401
50 PAC, Dafoe Papers (microfilm), J.A. Stevenson to Dafoe, 12 Dec. 1919; also, T.A. Crerar to the author, 23 June 1958
51 *House of Commons Debates* 17 Oct. 1919, pp. 1188–200
52 Ibid., 3 Oct. 1919, pp. 825–40
53 Ibid., 18 Sept. 1919, pp. 412–13
54 For Borden's views on railway policy see J.A. Eagle, 'Sir Robert Borden and the Railway Problem in Canadian Politics, 1911–1920,' unpublished PH D thesis, University of Toronto, 1972.
55 Ibid., 21 Oct. 1919, pp. 1205–9
56 PAC, Sir George Foster Papers, Foster Diary, 25 Oct. 1919
57 Borden Papers, Foster to Borden, 31 Oct. 1919
58 H.A. Logan, *Trade Unions in Canada* Toronto, 1948, pp. 510–13; *Canadian Annual Review, 1919*, pp. 509–13; *Globe* 19 and 22 Sept. 1919
59 *Report of the First Annual Meeting of the International Labour Conference, October 29–November 29, 1919* Washington, 1920, pp. 79–81, 208–13
60 Ibid., p. 58
61 Ibid., pp. 73–5
62 Ibid., pp. 116–17
63 Rowell Papers, ms. of address to the Canadian Club of Toronto, 15 Dec. 1919

NINETEEN / AN HONOURABLE DISCHARGE

1 PAC, Borden Papers, Reid to Borden, 27 Oct. 1919
2 PAC, Sir George Foster Papers, Foster Diary, 11 Dec. 1919
3 Henry Borden, ed., *Robert Laird Borden: His Memoirs* 2 vols, Toronto, 1938, 2, pp. 1017–18; PAC, Willison Papers, Arthur Ford to Willison, 4 Dec. 1919 and 5 Jan. 1920
4 Willison Papers, Arthur Ford to Willison, 10 Jan. 1920; PAC, Dafoe Papers (microfilm), J.A. Stevenson to Dafoe, 21 Dec. 1919
5 Borden Papers, Rowell to Borden, 4 Dec. 1919
6 PAC, Rowell Papers, Dafoe to Rowell, 13 Dec. 1919
7 Ibid., Rowell to Borden, 23 Dec. 1919
8 Ibid., Rowell to Reid, 5 Jan. 1920
9 Ibid., Rowell to Dafoe, 29 Jan. 1920
10 Ibid., Rowell to Foster, 20 Feb. 1920
11 Borden, *Memoirs* 2, p. 1025
12 Rowell Papers, Rowell to Borden, 25 Feb. 1920
13 Borden Papers, Rowell to Borden, 4 March 1920
14 *House of Commons Debates* 9 March 1920, pp. 231–54
15 Sir George Foster Papers, Foster Diary, 13 March 1920

16 *House of Commons Debates* 9 March 1920, pp. 254–64
17 Sir George Foster Papers, Foster Diary, 13 March 1920
18 Borden Papers, C.W. Yates to Borden, 29 March 1920
19 Rowell Papers, Willison to Rowell, 11 March 1920; Rowell to Willison, 13 March 1920
20 University of Toronto Library, G.M. Wrong Papers, Taft to Wrong, 14 Jan. 1920
21 Rowell Papers, Rowell to Wrong, 4 Feb. 1920
20 University of Toronto Library, G.M. Wrong Papers, Taft to Wrong, 14 Jan. 1920
21 Rowell Papers, Rowell to Wrong, 4 Feb. 1920
22 Ibid., Rowell to Wrong, 12 Feb. 1920
23 Ibid., Rowell to Aikins, 23 Feb. 1920
24 Wrong Papers, Taft to Wrong, 24 Feb. 1920
25 Ibid., Rowell to Wrong, 1 March 1920
26 *House of Commons Debates* 5 May 1919, pp. 2075–91; 8 May 1919, pp. 2201–2
27 Borden, *Memoirs* 2, pp. 1002–7
28 A.G. Dewey, *The Dominions and Diplomacy: The Canadian Contribution* 2 vols, London, 1929, 2, p. 109, quoting Lord Curzon, foreign secretary at the time. *Documents on Canadian External Relations, Vol. 3, 1919–1925* Ottawa, 1970, pp. 2–28
29 Rowell Papers, Rowell to Borden, April 22, 1920; Borden, *Memoirs* 2, pp. 1006–7
30 R.M. Dawson, *William Lyon Mackenzie King, 1874–1923* Toronto, 1958, p. 334
31 *House of Commons Debates* 10 May 1920, pp. 2444–49 and 30 June 1920, p. 4537
32 Borden Papers, Rowell to Borden, 16 May 1920
33 *House of Commons Debates* 1 June 1920, p. 2974
34 Rowell Family Papers, Rowell to Nell Rowell, 2 June 1920
35 *House of Commons Debates* 1 June 1920, pp. 2997–3012
36 Rowell Family Papers, Rowell to Nell Rowell, 2 and 3 June 1920
37 Rowell Papers, Rowell to Atkinson, 27 April 1920
38 *House of Commons Debates* 1 June 1920, p. 3012
39 Ibid., 10 May 1920, p. 221
40 Borden Papers, Rowell to Borden, 28 April 1920
41 Rowell Family Papers, Rowell to Nell Rowell, 1 July 1920
42 Rowell Papers, J.B. Coyne to Rowell, 7 July 1920; Rowell to Coyne, 9 July 1920
43 Borden Papers, Rowell to Borden, 7 July 1920; Borden to Rowell, 8 July 1920
44 Borden, *Memoirs* 2, pp. 1039–40
45 PAC, Meighen Papers, Rowell To Meighen, 8 July 1920
46 Rowell Family Papers, Rowell to Nell Rowell, 7 July 1920
47 Ibid.
48 Meighen Papers, Meighen and Rowell, 28 July 1920
49 Rowell Papers, Borden to Rowell, 8 July 1920
50 PAC, Sir Joseph Pope Papers, Pope Diary, 9 July 1920

TWENTY / CANADA IN THE LEAGUE OF NATIONS

1 Rowell Family Papers, Nell Rowell to Mrs A.L. Langford, July [?] 1920
2 Ibid., Rowell to his daughter, Mary, 2 Aug. 1920; Rowell to Langford Rowell, 12 Aug. 1920; Rowell to Mary Rowell, 13 and 17 Aug. 1920
3 Ibid., Nell Rowell to Mrs A.L. Langford, 22 and 27 Aug. 1920
4 Ibid., Rowell's memo of interview with Chief Khama, 24 Aug. 1920
5 Ibid., Nell Rowell to Mrs A.L. Langford, 29 Aug. 1940

6 Ibid., 1 Sept. 1920
7 Ibid., Rowell to his daughter Mary, 5 Sept. 1920
8 Ibid., Rowell to Langford Rowell, 12 Sept. 1920
9 Ibid., Nell Rowell to Mrs A.L. Langford, 17 Sept. 1920
10 Ibid., Rowell to Mary Rowell, 20 Sept. 1920
11 Ibid., Rowell to his daughter Mary, 26 Sept. 1920
12 Ibid., Nell Rowell to Mrs A.L. Langford, 22 and 26 Sept. 1920
13 Ibid., Nell Rowell to Mrs A.L. Langford, 28 Sept. and 2 Oct. 1920; Rowell to Frederick Rowell, 3 Oct. 1920
14 Ibid., Rowell to Langford Rowell, 7 Oct. 1920; Nell Rowell to Mrs A.L. Langford, 10 Oct. 1920
15 Ibid., Nell Rowell to Mary Rowell, 16 Oct. 1920
16 Ibid., Rowell to Langford Rowell, 17 Oct. 1920
17 Ibid., Nell Rowell to Mrs A.L. Langford, 23 Oct. 1920
18 Ibid., Rowell to Mary Rowell, 31 Oct. 1920
19 Ibid., Rowell to Nell Rowell, 17 Nov. 1920
20 Ibid., PAC, Loring Christie Papers, copy, minutes of the meetings of the British Empire Delegation, 5, 8, and 9 Nov. 1920
21 PAC, Rowell Papers, Rowell to Lloyd George, 8 Nov. 1920
22 Ibid., Borden to Rowell, 2 Oct. 1920
23 Rowell Family Papers, Rowell to Nell Rowell, 13 and 14 Nov. 1920
24 Ibid., Rowell to Nell Rowell, 20 Nov. 1920
25 Ibid.
26 Christie Papers, copy, minutes of British Empire Delegation, 17 Nov. 1920
27 Rowell Family Papers, Rowell to Nell Rowell, 19 Nov. 1920
28 Rowell Papers, Rowell to Meighen, 2 March, 1920
29 *Records of the First Assembly of the League of Nations, 1920* Eighth Plenary Meeting, 20 Nov. 1920, pp. 169–71
30 Ibid., p. 172
31 Ibid., p. 177
32 Rowell Papers, copy of Viviani's draft with Rowell's comments
33 Rowell Family Papers, Rowell to Nell Rowell, 28 Nov. 1920
34 Ibid., 30 Nov. 1920; Rowell Papers, Rowell to Viviani, 27 Nov. 1920
35 *Records of the First Assembly* Fourteenth Plenary Meeting, 6 Dec. 1920, pp. 282–5, 290, 303
36 Ibid.
37 Rowell Papers, Rowell to Meighen, 10 Jan. 1921
38 John MacCormac in *Mail and Empire* 8 Dec. 1920
39 Associated Press dispatch, *Globe* 8 Dec. 1920
40 *Records of the First Assembly* Sixteenth Plenary Meeting, 8 Dec. 1920, p. 328
41 Ibid., p. 330
42 Ibid., p. 333
43 Ibid., p. 335
44 Rowell Family Papers, Rowell to Nell Rowell, 10 Dec. 1920
45 Ibid.
46 Borden Papers, Christie to Borden, 12 Dec. 1920
47 Rowell Family Papers, Rowell to Nell Rowell, 5 Dec. 1920

48 *Records of the First Assembly* Meetings of the Committees, 2, Fifth Committee, 4 Dec. 1920, p. 187
49 Ibid., Twenty-Eighth Plenary Meeting, 17 Dec. 1920, p. 647; Rowell Family Papers, Rowell to Nell Rowell, 17 Dec. 1920
50 Ibid., Rowell to his daughter Mary 20 Dec. 1920
51 Rowell Family Papers, Rowell to Nell Rowell, 4 Dec. 1920
52 Ibid., Rowell to his daughter Mary, 20 Dec. 1920
53 Ibid., Rowell to Nell Rowell, 22 Dec. 1920
54 Wilson Harris, *What They Did at Geneva* London, 1921, p. 5; *The Guardian* 21 Dec. 1920
55 *The Nation* 24 Dec. 1920; *Daily Telegraph* 30 Dec. 1920
56 Rowell Family Papers, Rowell to Nell Rowell, 30 Nov. 1920
57 Borden Papers, Loring Christie to Borden, 12 Dec. 1920
58 Rowell Family Papers, Rowell to Nell Rowell, 10 Dec. 1920
59 Ibid., Rowell to his daughter Mary and Langford Rowell, 20 Dec. 1920
60 Ibid.
61 Ibid., Rowell to Nell Rowell, 22 Dec. 1920
62 Ibid., Rowell to his daughter Mary, 25 Dec. 1920
63 Ibid.
64 Ibid., Rowell to Nell Rowell, 30 Dec. 1920

TWENTY-ONE / CANADA, THE EMPIRE, AND THE NEW INTERNATIONALISM

1 PAC, Meighen Papers, Rowell to Meighen, 21 Jan. 1921; copy, Rowell to Arthur Vance, secretary, Conservative Association, riding of Durham, 5 Feb. 1921; Meighen to Rowell, 9 Feb. 1921
2 *New Statesman* 5 Feb. 1921
3 *Globe* 10 Feb. 1921
4 Ibid., 11 Feb. 1921
5 PAC, Rowell Papers, Rowell to Meighen, 2 March 1921
6 Ibid., Rowell to Milner, 24 Dec. 1920
7 Ibid., Rowell to Meighen, 2 March 1921
8 Ibid., 9 Feb. 1921
9 Ibid., 2 March 1921
10 Ibid., Meighen to Rowell, 8 March 1921
11 Ibid., Rowell to Meighen, 9 Feb. 1921
12 *House of Commons Debates* 18 Feb. 1921, pp. 118–19
13 Interview given to *New York Evening Post* 24 Jan. 1921
14 *House of Commons Debates* 18 Feb. 1921, pp. 110–19
15 Rowell Papers, Meighen to Rowell, 19 Feb. 1921
16 *House of Commons Debates* 28 April 1921, pp. 2722–8
17 Ibid., 21 April 1921, pp. 2394–5
18 Meighen Papers, Rowell to Meighen, 3 March, 1921
19 *House of Commons Debates* 27 April 1921, pp. 2647–58
20 Ibid., p. 2653
21 PAC, Loring Christie Papers, Rowell to Christie, 11, 14, and 26 March 1921; Christie to Rowell, 12, 24, and 30 March 1921

22 Rowell Papers, Rowell to Meighen, 11 March 1921
23 *House of Commons Debates* 27 April 1921, p. 2653
24 Rowell Papers, Rowell to Meighen, 9 Feb. 1921. See also Michael G. Fry, 'The North Atlantic Triangle and the Abrogation of the Anglo-Japanese Alliance,' *Journal of Modern History* 39, 1967, p. 53; Roger Graham, *Arthur Meighen, II: And Fortune Fled* Toronto, 1963, pp. 66–70
25 Rowell Papers, copy of address, 8 April 1921; *Globe* 9 April 1921
26 *House of Commons Debates* 27 April 1921, p. 2657
27 Saskatoon *Daily Star* 25 Feb. 1921; Halifax *Herald* 6 May 1921
28 I am indebted to Mr Donald M. Page of the University of Saskatchewan for sharing with me the results of his research on the organization of the League of Nations Society.
29 Graham, *Arthur Meighen, Vol II: And Fortune Fled* pp. 84–103
30 Ibid., pp. 104–5
31 Christie Papers, Rowell to Christie, 5 Nov. 1921
32 N.W. Rowell, *The British Empire and World Peace* London and Toronto, 1922, p. 69
33 Ibid., pp. 2–3
34 Ibid., p. 4
35 Ibid., pp. 146–7
36 Ibid., pp. 225–6
37 Ibid., pp. 220–1
38 Ibid., pp. 152–3
39 Ibid., p. 175
40 Ibid., p. 181
41 Ibid., p. 209
42 Ibid., p. 207
43 Rowell Family Papers, Nell's diary, June 1922
44 Ibid., Rowell Diary, July and August 1922; Rowell to Langford Rowell, 6 Aug. 1922
45 Cited in G.M. Gathorne-Hardy, *A Short History of International Affairs, 1920–1939* London, 3d ed., 1942, p. 39
46 Queen's University, Douglas Library, microfilm of Edward Grigg Papers, Rowell to Grigg, 9 Aug. 1922
47 Rowell Papers, Rowell to H. Wilson Harris, 21 Nov. 1922

TWENTY-TWO / AN OBSERVER OF KING LIBERALISM

1 *Ottawa Journal* 4 June 1921
2 See Margaret Prang, 'Mackenzie King Woos Ontario, 1919–1921,' *Ontario History* 58, 1966, pp. 16–17
3 Most of this account of the campaign is based on the *Canadian Annual Review 1921*, pp. 550–7; see also Gerald A. Hallowell, *Prohibition in Ontario, 1919–1923* Ontario Historical Society, 1972, chap. 4.
4 *Globe* 14 April 1921
5 Prang, 'Mackenzie King Woos Ontario,' pp. 18–19
6 R.M. MacIver, *Labor in the Changing World* New York & Toronto, 1919
7 N.W. Rowell, *The British Empire and World Peace* pp. 234–5
8 Ibid., pp. 244–8
9 Ibid., pp. 248–9
10 Ibid., pp. 253–4

11 Ibid., p. 255
12 See Ramsay Cook, *The Politics of John W. Dafoe and the Free Press* Toronto, 1963, chap. 7
13 PAC, King Papers, Rowell to King, 17 March 1923
14 Ibid., King to Rowell, 6 April 1923
15 *Globe* 23 June 1923
16 King Papers, Rowell to King, 12 May 1923
17 Ibid., King to Rowell, 14 May 1923
18 PAC, Willison Papers, Rowell to Willison, 6 June 1923
19 *Financial Post* 19 Jan. 1923
20 *Guelph Mercury* 27 Jan. 1923
21 Queen's University, Douglas Library, Edward Grigg Papers, Rowell to Sir Edward Grigg, 10 Feb. 1923
22 King Papers, Rowell to King, 9 Aug. 1923
23 *St Catharines Standard* 20 Oct. 1923
24 For an account of King's role in the conference, see R. MacGregor Dawson, *William Lyon Mackenzie King: A Political Biography* Vol. I, 1874–1923, Toronto, 1958, pp. 453–80
25 *St Catharines Standard* 20 Oct. 1923
26 Cited in Dawson, *William Lyon Mackenzie King* I, p. 465
27 King Papers, Rowell to King, 7 Aug. 1923
28 Dawson, *William Lyon Mackenzie King* I, pp. 471–2
29 Ibid., pp. 422–3
30 H. Blair Neatby, *William Lyon Mackenzie King, Vol. II, 1924–1932: The Lonely Heights* Toronto, 1963, pp. 33–4
31 King Papers, Rowell to King, 23 April 1924
32 Ibid., King to Rowell, 9 May and 30 July 1924
33 Neatby, *William Lyon Mackenzie King* 2, p. 39
34 King Papers, Rowell to King, 10 Sept. 1924

TWENTY-THREE / A NEW CHURCH AND A NEW
COMMONWEALTH

1 Victoria University, United Church Archives, Church Union Papers, Committee on Law and Legislation, Rowell Correspondence, gives some indication of the work of the committee.
2 The main outlines of the legal problems involved and of the process of securing passage of the legislation are discussed in Gershom W. Mason, *The Legislative Struggle for Church Union* Toronto, 1956. Other sources from which the general background of church union have been drawn include, *House of Commons Debates, 1924 and 1925*, *Canadian Annual Review, 1921–5*, the *Toronto Star* and the *Globe* 1922–5, John Webster Grant, *George Pidgeon* Toronto, 1962, and Allan Farris, 'The Fathers of 1925,' in *Enkindled by the Word: Essays on Presbyterianism in Canada* Toronto, 1966.
3 *Globe* 27 Nov. 1923
4 Church Union Papers, Wilson Correspondence, Rev. R.J. Wilson to J.E. Atkinson, 24 June 1925
5 Mason, *The Legislative Struggle* pp. 84–90
6 Ibid., pp. 90, 98, 102
7 PAC, King Papers, Rowell to King, 21 May 1924

8 Church Union Papers, Rowell Correspondence, Rowell to Rev. S.D. Chown, 23 May 1924
9 Re Toronto Railway Co. and City of Toronto [1925] AC 177
10 *Canadian Annual Review, 1924–5* pp. 582–7
11 Lord's Day Alliance of Canada v. Manitoba and Canada, [1925] AC 384
12 King Papers, Rowell to King, 13 June 1924
13 Ibid., King to Rowell, 30 July 1924
14 R. MacGregor Dawson, *William Lyon Mackenzie King: A Political Biography, Vol 1, 1874–1923* Toronto, 1958, p. 454; James Eayrs, *In Defence of Canada: From the Great War to the Great Depression* Toronto, 1965, p. 23
15 Cited in W.E. Armstrong, *Canada and the League of Nations* Geneva, 1930, pp. 140–2
16 Eayrs, *In Defence of Canada: From the Great War to the Great Depression* p. 11
17 *Toronto Star* 11 Oct. 1924
18 Cited in H. Blair Neatby, *William Lyon Mackenzie King, Vol. II, 1924–1932: The Lonely Heights* Toronto, 1963, p. 40
19 *Attorney-General for Ontario* v. *Attorney-General for Canada* [1925] AC 750
20 King Papers, Rowell to King, 27 March 1925
21 Gwendolen Carter, *The British Commonwealth and International Security: The Role of the Dominions 1919–1939* Toronto, 1947, pp. 120–3
22 *Toronto Star* 26 March 1925
23 Neatby, *William Lyon Mackenzie King* 2, pp. 40–4
24 PAC, Rowell Papers, ms. of address, 2 Dec. 1925
25 Church Union Papers, Rowell Correspondence, Perks to Rowell, 27 May 1925
26 Ibid., copy of resolution, 18 June 1925
27 Rowell Family Papers, Rowell to Nell Rowell, 22 June 1925
28 Ibid., Rowell to Nell Rowell, 30 June 1925
29 Ibid., Rowell to Nell Rowell, 14 July 1925
30 Ibid., Mary Rowell to her mother, 27 July 1925
31 Christchurch, New Zealand, *The Press* 30 July 1925; also, Rowell Family Papers, Rowell to Nell Rowell, 1 Aug. 1925
32 Rowell Family Papers, Rowell to Nell Rowell, 26 July 1925
33 Ibid., Rowell to Nell Rowell, 1 Aug. 1925
34 PAC, Murphy Papers, Murphy to W.R.P. Parker, 27 Nov. 1926
35 PAC, Dafoe Papers, Sir Robert Borden to Dafoe, 2 Jan. 1926, reporting Rowell's observation
36 Rowell Family Papers, Rowell to Nell Rowell, 29 Aug. 1925
37 *Toronto Star* and Toronto *Telegram* 26 Oct. 1925; see also King Papers, Rowell to King, 30 Nov. 1925
38 King Papers, Rowell to King, 13 Nov. 1925
39 Ibid., King to Rowell, 23 Nov. 1925
40 Ibid., Rowell to King, 30 Nov. 1925
41 Ibid.
42 King Papers, King to Rowell, 7 Dec. 1925; Neatby, *William Lyon Mackenzie King* 2, pp. 40–3
43 Ibid., Rowell to King, 31 Dec. 1925
44 James Eayrs, *The Art of the Possible: Government and Foreign Policy in Canada* Toronto, 1961, p. 46; King Papers, King Diary, 1 Dec. 1925
45 King Papers, King to Rowell, 7 Dec. 1925

TWENTY-FOUR / CLEANING UP THE LIBERALS

1 H. Blair Neatby, *William Lyon Mackenzie King, Vol. II, 1924–1932: The Lonely Heights* Toronto, 1963, pp. 64–7
2 PAC, King Papers, Rowell to King, 1 Nov. 1925
3 Ibid.
4 Queen's University, Douglas Library, Dunning Papers, Rowell to Dunning, 22 Dec. 1925
5 Rundle Papers, Rundle to J.M. Macdonell, 6 Jan. 1925, kindly loaned to the author by the late J.M. Macdonell and the National Trust Company
6 King Papers, King Diary, 9 Dec. 1925; PAC, Dafoe Papers, Dafoe to Arthur Hawkes, 25 Oct. 1929
7 King Papers, Rowell to King, 11 Jan. 1926; Dafoe Papers, Rowell to Dafoe, 11 Jan. 1926. King was so impressed by Rowell's 'very sane statement of the present position' that he read it to the Cabinet where it was well received. King Papers, King Diary, 12 Jan. 1926
8 Neatby, *William Lyon Mackenzie King* 2, pp. 110–11
9 Dafoe Papers, Sifton to Dafoe, 18 Feb. 1926
10 *Globe* 27 March 1926
11 Roger Graham, *Arthur Meighen, II: and Fortune Fled* Toronto 1963, pp. 393–5, gives a good account of the committee's findings.
12 King Papers, King to Rowell, 6 July 1926
13 Ibid., Rowell to King, 9 July 1926
14 PAC, Rowell Papers, Rowell to Ward Wright, 30 July 1926
15 Ibid., Robb to Rowell, 6 July 1926
16 Ibid., Rowell to Ward Wright, 30 July 1926
17 Ibid., Rowell to Robb, 23 July 1926, printed in the *Globe* 7 Aug. 1926
18 Ibid.
19 Rowell Papers, Rowell to William Houston, 14 Aug. 1926
20 Ibid., Rowell to Robb, 23 July 1926
21 Ibid., ms. of West Lambton address 11 Sept. 1926; *Globe* 13 Sept. 1926
22 See especially Eugene A. Forsey, *The Royal Power of Dissolution of Parliament in the British Commonwealth* Toronto, 1943; reprinted with revision, 1968, and Graham, *Arthur Meighen* Vol. 2, chaps 15 and 16. See also Neatby, *William Lyon Mackenzie King* 2, chaps 8 and 9.
23 Neatby, *William Lyon Mackenzie King* 2, pp. 144–8
24 Rowell Papers, ms. of West Lambton address, 11 Sept. 1926
25 King Papers, Rowell to King, 16 Sept. 1926
26 Ibid., King to Rowell, 18 Sept. 1926; King Diary, 25 Feb. 1926
27 Ibid., King Diary, 20 Sept. 1926
28 Ibid., 22 Sept. 1926
29 Ibid., 20 Sept. 1926
30 Ibid., 22 Sept. 1926; King Papers, Rowell to King, 24 Sept. 1926
31 For the background of this issue, see Richard N. Kottman, 'Volstead Violated: Prohibition as a Factor in Canadian-American Relations,' *Canadian Historical Review* 43, 1962, pp. 106–26
32 King Papers, Rowell to King, 24 Sept. 1926
33 Ibid., King to Rowell, 8 Oct. 1926
34 PAC, Murphy Papers, Murphy to S.B. Lynde, 23 Sept. 1926; Murphy to L.V. O'Connor, 5 Oct. 1926

35 *Globe* 28 Oct. 1926; Murphy Papers, numerous letters including Frank G.J. McDonagh to Murphy, 28 Oct. 1926; Bishop M.F. Fallon to A.C. Hardy, 11 Nov. 1926; Murphy to Rev. John E. Burke, 3 Dec. 1926
36 *Globe* 29 Oct 1926
37 Ibid., 6 Nov. 1926
38 King Papers, Rowell to King, 23 Dec. 1926 and 2 Nov. 1927
39 *Royal Commission on Customs and Excise* Ottawa, 1928, Interim Reports Nos 1 and 2, 3 and 17 Dec. 1926
40 Vancouver *Province* 15 Dec. 1926
41 Ibid., 25 Jan. 1927
42 King Papers, Rowell to King, 23 Dec. 1926
43 Ibid., Rowell to King, 5 March 1927
44 *Globe* 23 March 1927; Murphy Papers, W.T. Kernahan to Murphy, 11 March 1927
45 *Globe* 30 March 1927
46 Ibid., 1 April 1927
47 Ibid., 5 April 1927
48 Ibid., 27, 28 and 29 April 1927
49 King Papers, Rowell to King, 24 July 1927 and 1 Sept. 1927
50 Ibid., Rowell to King, 17 May 1929
51 Ibid., Rowell to King, 2 Nov. 1927
52 Ibid., Rowell to King, 6 Jan. 1928

TWENTY-FIVE / THE PINNACLE OF THE LEGAL PROFESSION

1 H. Blair Neatby, *William Lyon Mackenzie King, Vol. II, 1924–1932: The Lonely Heights* Toronto, 1963, pp. 177–91
2 C.P. Stacey, ed., *Historical Documents of Canada, Vol. V: The Arts of War and Peace, 1914–1945* Toronto, 1972, p. 457
3 *Manitoba Free Press* 21 Dec. 1926
4 Stacey, *The Arts of War and Peace* p. 464
5 PAC, King Papers, Rowell to King, 11 March 1926
6 Ibid., copy, Rowell to Lapointe, 11 March 1926
7 Ibid., Rowell to King, 7 Sept. 1927
8 Neatby, *William Lyon Mackenzie King* 2, pp. 194–5
9 Toronto, Canadian Institute of International Affairs Archives, (CIIA), ms. on 'CIIA Origins.' See also Edward D. Greathed, 'Antecedents and Origins of the Canadian Institute of International Affairs,' in H. Peter Krosby and Harvey L. Dyck, eds, *Empire and Nations: Essays in Honour of Frederic H. Soward* Toronto, 1969
10 The others were O.M. Biggar, Sir Robert Borden, Loring Christie, Sir George Foster, A.J. Glazebrook, Vincent Massey, Professor W.S. Milner, Sir Joseph Pope, and Professor G.M. Wrong.
11 PAC, Rowell Papers, Rowell to Lord Robert Cecil, 13 April 1920
12 CIIA, Nelson Papers, Rowell to Nelson, 21 Nov. 1925
13 Greathed, 'Antecedents and Origins,' p. 105
14 CIIA, Nelson Papers, Stanley Brent to Nelson, 11 Dec. 1926
15 Greathed, 'Antecedents and Origins,' p. 112

16 Provincial Archives of British Columbia, Nellie McClung Papers, Emily Murphy to Nellie McClung, 2 Dec. 1927
17 Henrietta Muir Edwards and others *and* Attorney-General for Canada and others [1928] SCR 276
18 *House of Commons Debates* 24 April 1928, p. 2311
19 King Papers, Rowell to W.D. Euler, 11 June 1929
20 *House of Commons Debates* 23 May 1928, p. 3295; 30 May 1928, p. 3572
21 Ibid., 10 June 1929, pp. 3524–5
22 King Papers, Rowell to Euler, 11 June 1929
23 H.R. Jackman to the author, May 1966
24 Neatby, *William Lyon Mackenzie King* 2, pp. 260–1
25 King Papers, Rowell to King, 14 June 1928
26 Reference *re* Water and Water Powers, SCR 200 [1929]; 2 DLR 481 [1929]
27 King Papers, Rowell to J.C. Elliott, 12 Jan. 1929
28 Neatby, *William Lyon Mackenzie King* 2, p. 274
29 King Papers, Rowell to King, 29 Nov. 1928
30 Ibid., Rowell to King, 10 May 1929
31 Ibid., King to Rowell, 13 May 1929
32 Ibid., Rowell to King, 17 May 1929
33 Ibid., King to Rowell, 23 May 1929
34 Neatby, *William Lyon Mackenzie King* 2, pp. 313–15
35 Rowell Family Papers, Rowell to Nell Rowell, 9 Sept. 1928
36 *Record of Proceedings of the Third General Council of the United Church of Canada, Winnipeg, September 1928* Toronto, 1929, pp. 134–6
37 C.B. Sissons, *A History of Victoria University* Toronto, 1952, pp. 285–6
38 Roy Courtice and H.R. Jackman to the author, May 1966
39 Nellie McClung Papers, Emily Murphy to Nellie McClung, 2 May 1928
40 Rowell Family Papers, Rowell to Nell Rowell, 28 June and 11 July 1929
41 Ibid., 14 July 1929
42 Ibid.
43 Ibid., 7 July 1929
44 Ibid., 11 July 1929
45 Ibid., 14 July 1929
46 Ibid., 20 July 1929
47 Ibid., Nell Rowell Diary, 8 and 9 Oct. 1929
48 Ibid., 10 Oct. 1929
49 Ibid., 11 Oct. 1929
50 Ibid., Nell Rowell to her daughter Mary, 19 Oct. 1929; Nell Rowell Diary, 13–15 Oct. 1929
51 Ibid., Rowell entry in Nell Rowell Diary, 18 Oct. 1929
52 Ibid., Nell Rowell Diary, 23 Oct. 1929
53 *Pacific Affairs* 3, 1930, pp. 27–33
54 Rowell Family Papers, Nell Rowell Diary, 28 Oct. – 9 Nov. 1929; Rowell Papers, Rowell to Sir Robert Borden, 27 Nov. 1929
55 Rowell Family Papers, Nell Rowell Diary, 9 Nov. 1929
56 Ibid., 22 Nov. 1929
57 Empire Club of Canada, *Addresses Delivered ... During 1930* Toronto, 1931, 'China and the Foreign Powers,' pp. 1–15

58 L.M. Bloomfield and Gerald F. Fitzgerald, *Boundary Waters Problems of Canada and the United States: The International Joint Commission, 1912–1958* Toronto, 1958, pp. 137–8
59 Henrietta Muir Edwards and Others *and* Attorney-General for Canada and others [1930] AC 124
60 *Proprietary Trade Association* v. *attorney general for Canada* [1931] AC 310
61 PAC, Dafoe Papers (microfilm), Dafoe to Brooke Claxton, 2 Dec. 1931
62 University of British Columbia Library, Plaunt Papers, Alan Plaunt to F.N. Southam, 30 Oct. 1930
63 See Margaret Prang, 'The Origins of Public Broadcasting in Canada,' *Canadian Historical Review* 46, 1965, pp. 1–31

TWENTY-SIX / A DARKENING WORLD

1 Sarnia *Canadian Observer* 26 July 1930
2 PAC, King Papers, Rowell to King, 29 July 1930
3 Rowell Family Papers, Rowell to Nell Rowell, 7 Dec. 1930
4 Ibid., 15 Dec. 1930
5 Ibid., 28 Nov. 1930
6 Ibid., 30 Nov. 1930
7 Ibid., 4 Dec. 1930
8 Ibid., 30 Nov. 1930
9 *Canadian Pacific Railway Company* v. *The King* [1931] AC 414
10 *Carling Export Brewery and Malting Company* v. *The King* [1931] AC 435
11 King Papers, King to Rowell, 21 Jan. 1931
12 Ibid., Rowell to King, 31 Jan. 1931. Shortly after this Rowell contributed $20,000 toward the reduction of the mortgage on Metropolitan Church.
13 For an excellent account of the Beauharnois scandal, see H. Blair Neatby, *William Lyon Mackenzie King, Vol. II; 1924–1932: The Lonely Heights* Toronto, 1963, chap. 18
14 King Papers, Rowell to King, 18 July 1931
15 PAC, Dafoe Papers (microfilm), Rowell to Dafoe, 21 July 1931
16 *House of Commons Debates* 30 July 1931, p. 4709
17 King Papers, King to Rowell, 8 Aug. 1931
18 Ibid., Rowell to King, 10 Sept. 1931
19 Ibid., King to Rowell, 16 Sept. 1931
20 Ibid., Rowell to King, 19 Sept. 1931
21 Neatby, *William Lyon Mackenzie King* 2, p. 385
22 *Papers and Proceedings of the Fourth Annual Meeting of the Canadian Political Science Association* Toronto, 1932, pp. 201–12
23 *Globe* 25 May 1932
24 Presidential Address, Toronto General Trusts Corporation, *Toronto Daily Star*, 4 Feb. 1931. See also, Presidential Address, 1932, ibid., 3 Feb. 1932
25 *Globe* 5 June 1931
26 *Border Cities Star* 6 Oct. 1931
27 *Winnipeg Free Press* 3 Nov. 1931; Saskatoon *Star-Phoenix* 5 and 6 Nov. 1931; Regina *Leader-Post* 6 Nov. 1931
28 Vancouver *Sun* 11 Nov. 1931
29 *Globe* 1 Dec. 1931
30 *Toronto Star* 30 Jan. 1932

31 PAC, Rowell Papers, Rowell to Wilson Harris, 3 Feb. 1932
32 Ibid., 19 Feb. 1932
33 Ibid., Wilson Harris to Rowell 7 March 1932
34 Rowell Family Papers, R.P. Bowles to Rowell, 29 April 1932
35 Bowles to the author. Also R.P. Bowles, *Socialism, Pacifism, Mysticism* Three lectures delivered to the Alumni of Emmanuel College, Victoria University, Toronto, 1934
36 The late Professor John Line of Emmanuel College to the author, June 1961
37 *Proceedings of the Fifth General Council of the United Church of Canada* Toronto, 1932, p. 406
38 Rowell Family Papers, Rowell to Dr Richard Roberts, 1 May 1932; Rowell to Dr R.P. Bowles, 6 May 1932. The first layman to serve as moderator was Dr Robert B. McClure, elected in 1969.
39 *Proceedings of the Fifth General Council* pp. 105–6
40 Ibid., pp. 289–90
41 Rowell Family Papers, Rowell to Nell Rowell, 2 July 1932; also *International Review of Missions* 21, 1932, pp. 488–97
42 Ibid., 5 July 1932
43 Ibid., 6 July 1932
44 Ibid.
45 Ibid., 10 July 1932
46 Ibid., Rowell to his sister Mary, 31 July 1932
47 Dafoe Papers, Rowell to Dafoe, 9 Aug. 1932
48 Rundle Papers, Rowell to W.E. Rundle, 9 April 1933, kindly loaned to the author by the late J.M. Macdonell and the National Trust Company
49 Ibid.
50 Rowell Family Papers, Rowell to his daughter Mary, 14 April 1933
51 *Consolidated Distilleries Limited* v. *The King* [1933] AC 508
52 Rundle Papers, Rowell to W.E. Rundle, 9 July 1933
53 *Canadian Bar Review* 11, 1933, pp. 435–53
54 F.H. Underhill to the author, 28 June 1960; 'The British Commonwealth Relations Conference,' *The Round Table* 93, 1933, pp. 195–202
55 Rowell Family Papers, Rowell to Mary Rowell, 30 Nov. 1933
56 *United Gas and Fuel Co.* v. *Dominion Natural Gas Co.* [1934] AC 435
57 Presidential Address, Toronto General Trusts Corporation, *Toronto Daily Star* 8 Feb. 1934
58 King Papers, Rowell to King, 11 May 1934
59 *Canadian Bar Review* 12, 1934, pp. 393–405
60 *Toronto Daily Star* 11 Oct. 1935

TWENTY-SEVEN / THE CHIEF JUSTICE

1 PAC, Rowell Papers, Rowell to L.B. Pearson, 19 Aug. 1935
2 Vancouver *Province* and Vancouver *Sun* 6 Sept. 1935
3 James Eayrs, *In Defence of Canada: Vol. II. Appeasement and Rearmament* Toronto, 1965, p. 11
4 Rowell Papers, O.D. Skelton to Rowell, 21 Sept. 1935
5 Ibid., Rowell to Skelton, 24 Sept. 1935
6 Ibid., Skelton to Rowell, 2 Oct. 1935

7 Ibid., Rowell to Skelton, 12 Oct. 1935
8 W.A. Riddell, *World Security by Conference* Toronto, 1947, pp. 135–6
9 *Globe* and *Toronto Star* 16 Oct. 1935; *Canadian Congress Journal* 14, 1935, pp. 14–18
10 *Saturday Night* 28 Sept. 1935. Arnold Toynbee also believed that some fault lay with 'the contemporary Canadians whose gentle spokesman had inflicted at Geneva in 1930, a diplomatic defeat upon the Italians' timid spokesman, Signor Tittoni.' *Survey of International Affairs, 1935* London, 1936, Vol. 2, p. 3
11 Rowell Papers, Rowell to Escott Reid, 26 Sept. 1935; Rowell to Donald Gordon, 11 Nov. 1935
12 Eayrs, *In Defence of Canada* 2, pp. 18–19
13 York University Archives, Toronto, Riddell Papers, Riddell to Rowell, 22 Oct. 1935, cited in Robert Bothwell and John English, 'Dirty Work at the Crossroads: New Perspectives on the Riddell Incident,' *Canadian Historical Association, Historical Papers, 1972* p. 275
14 *Globe* 2 Dec. 1935
15 Rowell Papers, Rowell to Lapointe, 2 Dec. 1935
16 Ibid., Rowell to Riddell, 3 Dec. 1935
17 *Toronto Star* 2 Dec. 1935
18 *House of Commons Debates* 11 Feb. 1936, p. 98
19 *Toronto Star* 24 Aug. 1936
20 PAC, King Papers, Rowell to King, 26 June 1936
21 Ibid., 9 July 1936
22 Eayrs, *In Defence of Canada* 2, pp. 37–40
23 *Proceedings, Conference on Canadian-American Affairs, 1937* Montreal, 1937, p. 225
24 *House of Commons Debates* 19 Feb. 1937, pp. 1045–52
25 King Papers, Rowell to King, 26 Feb. 1937
26 W.H. McConnell, 'The Judicial Review of Prime Minister Bennett's "New Deal" Legislative Programme,' University of Toronto, PH D thesis, 1968, pp. 139–70
27 Louis S. St-Laurent to the author, 14 Nov. 1961; McConnell, 'The Judicial Review,' p. 175
28 Ibid., p. 199
29 Rowell Papers, Rowell to Wilson Harris, 20 Feb. 1936; Rundle Papers, Rowell to W.E. Rundle, 7 March 1936, kindly loaned to the author by the late J.M. Macdonell and the National Trust Company
30 Rowell Papers, Rowell to Lapointe, 18 Sept. 1936
31 *Toronto Star* 26 Sept. 1936
32 Ibid., 24 Sept. 1936
33 Ibid., 30 Sept. 1936
34 'The Club and the Empire,' An Address by the Honourable Newton Wesley Rowell, LL.D., Chief Justice of Ontario ... 11 Dec. 1936, Toronto [1936]
35 'The Place and Functions of the Judiciary in our Canadian Constitution,' *Canadian Bar Review* 15, 1937, pp. 57–67
36 H.W. Silverman, 'Chief Justice Rowell,' unpublished manuscript submitted in the Prize Essay Competition of the Wallace Nesbitt Trust, 1953, Osgoode Hall Library, Toronto
37 *Toronto Star* 23 Feb. 1937
38 Neil McKenty, *Mitch Hepburn* Toronto, 1967, pp. 76–81, 96–9; *Canadian Annual Review, 1935–6*, p. 202; C.B. Sissons, *Church and State in Canadian Education* Toronto, 1959, p. 106
39 King Papers, King to Rowell, 23 July 1937
40 Ibid., Rowell to King, 16 April 1938

41 Rowell Papers, Rowell to King, 28 Oct. 1937
42 PAC, Dafoe Papers, (microfilm), Dafoe to King, 24 July 1937
43 Rowell Family Papers, Rowell to his sister Mary, 1 Aug. 1937
44 Interviews with R.M. Fowler, 8 June 1961 and Rt Hon. Louis St-Laurent, 14 Nov. 1961; R.A. Mackay, unpublished memorandum, 'Some Personal Reminiscences of the Rowell-Sirois Commission' [1964?]
45 King Papers, Rowell to King, 7 and 13 Sept. 1937
46 Interview with R.M. Fowler, 8 June 1961
47 King Papers, Rowell to King, 28 Oct. 1937
48 Rowell Papers, Rowell to R.A. Mackay, 5 Nov. 1937; Rowell to Dafoe, 19 and 23 Nov. 1937
49 King Papers, King to Rowell, 23 Nov. 1937 (not sent)
50 Rowell Family Papers, Rowell to Nell, 25 Nov. 1937
51 King Papers, Rowell to King, 23 Nov. 1937
52 Rowell Family Papers, Rowell to Nell, 25 Nov. 1937
53 'JBM' [J.B. McGeachy], *Winnipeg Free Press* 3 Dec. 1937
54 Ibid., 10 Dec. 1937
55 Rowell Family Papers, Rowell to Nell, 10 and 14 Dec. 1937
56 Ibid., 5 Dec. 1937
57 Wilfrid Eggleston, *While I Still Remember* Toronto, 1968, pp. 236–7; interview with R.M. Fowler, 8 June 1961; 'JBM,' *Winnipeg Free Press* 8 Dec. 1937; Wellington Jeffers, *Globe and Mail* 24 Nov. 1941
58 Rowell Family Papers, Rowell to Nell, 5 and 8 Dec. 1937
59 'JBM,' *Winnipeg Free Press* 18 Jan. 1938
60 Rowell Family Papers, Rowell to Nell, 20 Jan. 1938
61 Dafoe Papers, Dafoe to George V. Ferguson, 23 Jan. 1938
62 'JBM,' *Winnipeg Free Press* 21 Jan. 1938; interview with R.M. Fowler, 8 June 1961
63 Rowell Family Papers, Rowell to Nell, 13 Feb. 1938
64 Ibid., Rowell to Frederick Rowell, 27 Feb. 1937
65 Ibid., 23 Feb. 1937
66 Ibid., 14 March 1937
67 'JBM,' *Winnipeg Free Press* 18 March 1938
68 Rowell Family Papers, Rowell to Nell, 22 March 1938
69 Ibid., 23 March 1938
70 Ibid., Rowell to Frederick Rowell, 29 March 1939
71 'JBM,' *Winnipeg Free Press* 31 March 1938
72 Ibid., 29 March 1938
73 Rowell Family Papers, Rowell to Nell, 1 April 1938
74 'JBM,' *Winnipeg Free Press* 2 May 1938. See also Richard M.H. Alway, 'Hepburn, King, and the Rowell-Sirois Commission,' *Canadian Historical Review* 48, 1967, pp. 118–21
75 Eggleston, *While I Still Remember*, p. 236
76 Ibid., p. 237; 'JBM,' *Winnipeg Free Press* 5 May 1938
77 H.F. Angus, 'An Echo of the Past: The Rowell Sirois Commission,' *Canadian Tax Journal* 1, 1953, p. 439
78 *Saturday Night* 29 Nov. 1941

Index

Canada in 1891 10–16; as Toronto
lawyer 17–20; early Liberalism 20–2,
25–6, 29–32; as Methodist layman 22–7;
in England in 1895 27–9; and Dominion
plebiscite, 1898 32–4; runs in East York,
1900 35–45; marriage 45–6; and British
Methodism 47–8; legal activities 49–50,
55–6, 67–8; and Ross government
49–55; and Methodist church 56–8, 63–9
passim; and Laymen's Missionary
Movement 64–7, 79–81; and 'autonomy
issue' 59–62; trip to Middle East 62–3;
elected bencher, Law Society of Upper
Canada 68; and 'the Jackson
controversy' 70–9, 81–8

Laurier Liberalism and moral issues
91–4; and reciprocity, 1911 94–9; elected
Liberal leader 99–100; and election of
1911 100–5; character of Liberal caucus
106–7; maiden speech 107–9; and tax
reform 109, 126–7; and labour 110,
117–19, 127–9, 165; and prohibition
111–12, 115–16, 130–1, 133–5, 137–9,
141–4, 179–83; and bilingual schools
112–14, 145–57; and vice-regal visit
114–15; and party organization 115, 136,
164–5 and northern Ontario 108–9, 116;
and workmen's compensation 117–18,
127, 134; on party's effectiveness
119–20; and naval defence 120–4,
260–1; and the 'Proudfoot charges'
129–30; in England, 1913 131–3; election
of 1914 136–140; disagrees with Laurier
over bilingual schools 150–7; and response to war 158–60; criticizes
Borden's leadership 160, 166, 187, 189;
and recruiting 159–62, 175–7, 186; and
Unemployment Commission 162–3; tour
of west in 1915 164; and provincial Organization of Resources Committee
167–8, 185–6; and war aims 160, 168,
270–3; trip to England and France, 1916
169–75; urges Laurier to join coalition
177–9, 189–90, 193–6; on Quebec and
war 166, 187, 188, 199–200, 223–4, 227,
231–3, 244–6; and women's suffrage
183–4; and nickel production 185; public
call for coalition government 187; sup-

ports conscription 188–90; urges Graham
and Pardee to join coalition 191–3, 197;
declines Borden's invitation to join
coalition 193–203; urges meeting of Ontario Liberals 196–7; decries results
therefrom 198–9; urges meeting of provincial Liberal leaders 199, 203–4; and
'Win-the-War' movement 201–2; con-
tinues efforts to promote coalition 203–6;
joins Union Government 207–10; as
chairman of War Committee. 211–14,
233–8, 261; and packing-house profits
213–4, 236–9; and election of 1917
214–27; runs in Durham 218, 225; election
victory 226–7, 239

Relations with business community
234–8; responsibility for Department of
Public Information 234, 242, 245–7, 250,
265–6, 288; and opening of Parliament
239–40; attacked by Charles Murphy
240–2; and enforcement of Military Service Act 243–50, 262–4; and wartime
taxation 251, 296–7, 305, 319; and soldiers' pension 251, 296, 325–6; attends
Imperial War Cabinet and Conference
253–7, 258–62; visits France 257–8;
criticizes British leadership 261–2; attacked by Power and Cannon 264–5; and
subversive activities 266–8; and strikes
268; and armistice 269; and post-war
policies 270–5; and post-war political
alignments 275–7, 290; replies to
Murphy 277; and Canada at Peace
Conference 279–83; and Siberian
expedition 283–8, 291–4; and post-war
imperial relations 290–1; and Department of Health 294–5; and housing
295–6; and civil service 297–8; and
post-war prohibition 298, 327–8; on
Winnipeg strike 298–303; and continuation of Union Government 303–7, 313;
disaffection of *Globe* 304–7, 313–15; and
primacy of 'industrial question' 307–9;
attacks Laurier Liberals 310–12, 314;
and Liberal convention 316–17; recon-
siders position in government 317–19;
and government policies 319–20; outlines nature of new Commonwealth